Trams, Buses, and Rails

Trams, Buses, and Rails

The History of Urban Transport in Bangkok, 1886-2010

ICHIRO KAKIZAKI

Silkworm Books

ISBN: 978-616-215-080-7

First published in 2014 by
Silkworm Books
6 Sukkasem Road, T. Suthep
Chiang Mai 50200 Thailand
info@silkwormbooks.com
www.silkwormbooks.com

Typeset in Minion Pro 10.5 pt. by Silk Type

Printed and bound in Thailand by O.S. Printing House, Bangkok

5 4 3 2 1

Contents

List of Tables and Figures vii
Acknowledgments xi
Acronyms xiii

Introduction 1
- Trends in the Debate on Urban Transport 3
- Studies on Urban Transport in Bangkok 7
- Objectives and Scope 10
- The Sources 11
- Components of the Study 15

1. Introduction of Rail Transport, 1880s–1900s 19
- The Introduction of Tramways by Foreign Companies 19
- Competition of Thais for the Tramway Business 27
- Formation of Suburban Railways 33
- Merger of the Tramway Business by a Foreign Company 40
- Government Tramway Policy 46

2. Emergence of Competition, 1910s–1930s 51
- Revival and Expansion of Tramways 51
- Suburban Railways' Efforts to Become Urban Railways 62
- Emergence of Buses 73
- Unfavorable Winds against Tramways 82
- Limitation of Urban Transport Business by Foreign Enterprises 87

3. Expansion of Bus Networks, 1940s–1950s 97
- Urban Transport during the War Years 97
- Stagnating Rail Transport 106
- Emergence of a Bus Nationalization Plan 116
- Regulation by the Ministry of Communications 125
- From Rail Transport to Buses 136

4. Unification of Buses, 1960s–1970s 147
Disappearance of Rail Transport 147
Emergence of the Bus Unification Plan 160
The Problem of Fare Hikes 174
Realization of the Bus Unification Plan 188
Limitations of Buses in Urban Transport 195

5. Revival of Rail Transport, 1970s–1990s 207
Emergence of the Urban Railway Plan 207
Bus Operation after Unification 215
Three Urban Railway Plans 227
Struggle to Increase the Efficiency of Bus Operations 243
Stagnation of Urban Transport 253

6. A Confused Urban Transport Policy, 2000s 263
Urban Railway Policy of Thaksin Government 263
Confusion and Confrontation 270
Fight for Leadership over Bus Operations 283
Confrontation Continues 295
Limits on the "Dream-Selling Policy" 311

7. Regulation and Politicization of Urban Transport in Bangkok 331
Transition in Means of Transport 331
Strengthening of Regulation 339
Politicization of Urban Transport 345

Conclusion 353
Summary 353
Suggested Further Research and Measures 358

Notes 363
Bibliography 413
Index 425

Tables and Figures

Tables

1.1. Conditions of Tramway Concessions 20
1.2. Opening of Tramways, 1888–1910 21
1.3. Gross Receipts of Tramway Companies, 1889–1910 23
1.4. Dividend Rates for Tramway Companies, 1889–1910 24
1.5. Financial Situation of Suburban Railway Companies, 1893–1910 38
1.6. Gross Receipts of Suburban Railways, 1893–1910 40
2.1. Net Profit of Tramway Companies, 1911–1941 53
2.2. Dividend Rates for Tramway Companies, 1911–1941 55
2.3. Population Growth in Bangkok, 1912–1930 56
2.4. Opening of Tramways, 1911–1941 62
2.5. Frequency of Suburban Railways, 1893–1931 64
2.6. Electrification of Suburban Railways, 1912–1931 64
2.7. Gross Receipts of Suburban Railways, 1911–1941 65
2.8. Bus Routes in Bangkok, 1925 73
2.9. Bus Routes in Bangkok, 1939 78
2.10. Financial Situation of Suburban Railway Companies, 1911–1941 90
3.1. Tramway Operations, 1942–1950 98
3.2. New Bus Routes in Bangkok, 1940–1943 103
3.3. Suburban Railway Operations after Nationalization, 1946–1960 112
3.4. Bus Routes in Bangkok, September 1953 118
3.5. Bus Routes in Bangkok, June 1955 128
3.6. New Bus Routes in Bangkok, 1956 134
3.7. Number of Buses Operating on Each Route, June 1957 141
4.1. Maeklong Line Operations, 1961–1975 150

4.2. Receipts of Tramway Lines, 1958–1966 ... 155
4.3. Abolition of Tramways ... 157
4.4. Financial Situation of the MEA Tramways, 1958–1968 ... 159
4.5. Bus Routes in Bangkok, October 1960 ... 163
4.6. Bus Routes in Bangkok, October 1965 ... 175
4.7. Changes in Bus Fares, 1953–1976 ... 179
4.8. Bus Routes in Bangkok, November 1970 ... 183
4.9. Number of Printed Tickets for Tramway Lines, 1960–1966 ... 197
4.10. Population of Bangkok, 1912–1970 ... 198
4.11. Number of Buses Operating on Each Route, January 1965 ... 202
5.1. Bus Routes in Bangkok, 1977 ... 217
5.2. Financial Situation of BMTA, 1977–2000 ... 224
5.3. Changes in Bus Fares, 1976–2000 ... 225
5.4. Bus Routes in Bangkok, 1988 ... 228
5.5. Number of Buses in Bangkok, 1986–2000 ... 244
5.6. Number of Bus Routes in Bangkok, 1986–2000 ... 245
5.7. Number of Daily Bus Passengers, 1990–2000 ... 248
5.8. Urban Railway Plans of ETA and MRTA ... 254
5.9. Population and Registered Number of Automobiles in Bangkok, 1970–2000 ... 259
6.1. Urban Railway Plans during the Thaksin Administration ... 272
6.2. Proposed Urban Railway Lines in Three Transportation Plans ... 274
6.3. Number of Buses in Bangkok, 2001–2010 ... 291
6.4. Number of Bus Routes in Bangkok, 2001–2010 ... 292
6.5. Changes in Bus Fares, 2001–2010 ... 293
6.6. Mass Rapid Transit Master Plan in Bangkok Metropolitan Region, 2010 ... 299
6.7. Opening of Urban Railways, 1999–2010 ... 302
6.8. Bus Routes in Bangkok, 2008 ... 319
6.9. Number of Daily Urban Railway Passengers, 2000–2010 ... 327
6.10. Number of Daily Bus Passengers, 2001–2010 ... 329

Figures

1.1. Tramway Network in Bangkok, 1900s ... 30
1.2. Railway Network in Suburban Bangkok, 1930 ... 34
2.1. Tramway Network in Bangkok, 1930 ... 58

2.2. Bus Network in Bangkok, 1925 75
2.3. Bus Network in Bangkok, 1939 81
3.1. Bus Network in Bangkok, 1943 104
3.2. Tramway Network in Bangkok, 1955 109
3.3. Bus Network in Bangkok, 1953 120
3.4. Bus Network in Bangkok, 1955–1956 131
4.1. Maeklong Line Modernization Plan, 1960s 152
4.2. Abandoned Tramways in Bangkok, 1960–1968 158
4.3. Bus Network in Bangkok, 1960 165
4.4. Bus Network in Bangkok, 1965 177
4.5. Bus Network in Bangkok, 1970 187
5.1. Urban Railway Development Plan in Bangkok, 1982 209
5.2. Bus Network in Bangkok, 1977 219
5.3. Bus Network in Bangkok, 1988 232
5.4. Urban Railway Network in Bangkok, 2000 234
6.1. Urban Railway Network in Bangkok, 2005 268
6.2. Bus Rapid Transit (BRT) Plan by the BMA, 2004 288
6.3. Price of Diesel Oil, 1998–2010 293
6.4. Urban Railway Network in Bangkok, 2010 301
6.5. Bus Network in Bangkok, 2008 326

Acknowledgments

This book is based on my study of the history of urban transport in Bangkok, which I have been keenly pursuing since 2006. This is my third academic book, following *Laying the Tracks: The Thai Economy and Its Railways 1885–1935* (Kyoto University Press, 2005) and *The Political Economy of Railways and Highways: Transport Policy and Commodity Flow in Thailand 1935–1975* (Kyoto University Press, 2009, in Japanese), and my second research theme since gaining a position at Yokohama City University fifteen years ago.

I could not have realized this book without the support and cooperation of many people. I would like to express my great appreciation to my three teachers: Professor Akira Suehiro at the University of Tokyo, Honorary Professor Teruko Saito at Tokyo University of Foreign Studies, and Honorary Professor Setsuho Ikehata at the same university. In particular, I obtained newspaper articles, such as those from *Bangkok Times Weekly Mail*, in microfilm from the Institute of Social Science at the University of Tokyo when I worked there as an assistant to Professor Suehiro. Although I originally collected this material for him, I must admit that I have utilized it much more intensively than he did.

In Bangkok, I am indebted to the National Archives of Thailand. I am a regular "customer" at this institution and still search for archival materials over a period of about two months during my visits twice a year. This continuous survey became possible with the help of my colleagues and students at Yokohama City University and my family. Although I cannot acknowledge all the other people to whom I am indebted, I would like to thank all of them.

This study was supported by a grant for 2008 Strategic Research Projects (No. W20018) of Yokohama City University and the Japan Society for the Promotion of Science (JSPS) called the Grant-in-Aid for Scientific Research (*Kakenhi*, No. 21730276) from 2009 to 2011. The publication of this book was supported by the JSPS's Grant-in-Aid for Publication of Scientific Research Results (No. 265279).

Finally, my special thanks go to Mr. Alan Feinstein, and also to Ms. Susan Offner at Silkworm Books, both of whom edited my manuscript, and to Ms. Trasvin Jittidecharak, the director of Silkworm, who gave me the chance to publish this book.

It is my great pleasure if my study, while arising from personal interest, is able to contribute to Thai studies and transport studies.

Ichiro Kakizaki
August 2014

Acronyms

AS	*Asahi Shimbun*
BMA	Bangkok Metropolitan Administration (under Ministry of Interior, 1972–)
BMCL	Bangkok Metro Public Company, Ltd. (operator of subway, 1998–)
BMTA	Bangkok Mass Transit Authority (jurisdiction over buses in Bangkok, 1976–)
BMTIP	Bangkok Mass Transit Implementation Plan
BOT	Build-Operate-Transfer, type of concession
BP	*Bangkok Post*
BPWR	*Bangkok Post Weekly Review*
BPYEER	*Bangkok Post Year-End Economic Review*
BRT	bus rapid transit (bus system using dedicated bus lanes on roads)
BT	*Bangkok Times*
BTS	Bangkok Mass Transit System (elevated urban railway, 1999–)
BTSC	Bangkok Mass Transit System Company, Ltd. (operator of BTS, 1992–)
BTSG	BTS Group Holdings Public Company, Ltd.
BTWM	*Bangkok Times Weekly Mail*
CBTC	communication-based train control
DBI	DB International GmbH
DCR	Diplomatic and Consular Reports on Trade and Finance, Siam

DN	*Deli Nius*
ETA	Expressway and Rapid Transit Authority of Thailand (jurisdiction over expressways and urban railway, 1972–, under Ministry of Interior, then Ministry of Transport)
ETO	Express Transportation Organization (earlier government authority managing rail freight transport; then operator of provincial buses, lorries and ships; later operator of buses in Bangkok, 1947–2006)
FN	*Kan Faifa Nakhon Luang*
IN	*Ikhon Nius*
JBIC	Japan Bank for International Cooperation
JICA	Japan International Cooperation Agency
KK	Krasuang Khamanakhom,
KS	Borisat Khonsong Chamkat
KSMK	Ongkan Khonsong Muanchon Krungthep
KT	*Krungthep Thurakit*
KTB	Krom Kan Khonsong Thang Bok
KTM	Krungthep Mahanakhon
LRT	light rail transit
MEA	Metropolitan Electricity Authority (jurisdiction over tramways, 1958–)
MRC	Maeklong Railway Company (merger of Thachin Railway Company and old Maeklong Railway Company; 1907–1945)
MRTA	Metropolitan Rapid Transit Authority (controlled urban railway plans after ETA, 1992–2000; under Prime Minister's Office, later Mass Rapid Transit Authority, 2000–, then Ministry of Transport)
MTS	mass rapid transit system
N	*The Nation*
NA	National Archives of Thailand
NEDB	National Economic Development Board, later NESDB
NESDB	National Economic and Social Development Board
NGV	natural gas-fueled vehicles

NKS	*Nihon Keizai Shimbun*
OCMLT	Office of the Commission for the Management of Land Traffic (under Prime Minister's Office, 1992–2002; later OTP)
OE	Online Edition
OECF	Overseas Economic Cooperation Fund of Japan (later JBIC, then JICA)
OTP	Office of Transport and Traffic Policy and Planning (under Ministry of Transport)
PCC	*Prachachat*
PCK	*Phuchatkan*
PCT	*Prachachat Thurakit*
PRC	Paknam Railway Company, Ltd. (established to promote the construction of a railway line between Bangkok and Paknam, 1891–1936)
PSO	public service obligation
PTT	PTT Public Company, Ltd.
RFM	Ongkan Rotfaifa Mahanakhon
RFMT	Kan Rotfaifa Khonsong Muanchon haeng Prathet Thai
RFT	Kan Rotfai haeng Prathet Thai
RKMK	Borisat Rabop Khonsong Muanchon Krungthep Chamkat
RGI	*Railway Gazette International*
RKB	Ratchakitchanubeksa
RSP	Ongkan Rapsong Sinkha lae Phatsaduphan
RSRS	Royal State Railways of Siam
SC	*Sathiti Charachon*
SEC	Siam Electric Company, Ltd. (Siam Electric Corporation, Ltd., 1927–; TEC, Thai Electric Corporation, Ltd., 1940–; operator of tramways)
SK	*Si Krung*
SN	*Sayam Nikon*
SNK	Samnakngan Nayobai lae Phaen Kan Khonsong lae Charachon
SNR	Samnak Nayok Ratthamontri
SR	*Sayam Rat*

SRT	State Railways of Thailand (operator of suburban railways after nationalization, under Ministry of Transport, 1951–)
SRSW	*Sayam Rat Sapda Wichan*
SRWR	*Siam Rat Weekly Review*
SWPT	Sathaban Wichai Phuea Kan Phatthana Prathet Thai
SYB	*Statistical Yearbook of Thailand*
TIC	Thai Information Center
TM	*Thai Mai*
TPT	Kan Thang Phiset Haeng Prathet Thai
TS	*Transport Statistics*
TSK	*Than Setthakit*
URMAP	Urban Rail Transportation Master Plan
UTDC	Urban Transportation Development Corporation (Canadian-developed LRT system)

Introduction

Since the early 2000s, the convenience of urban transport[1] in Bangkok, the capital of Thailand, has improved rapidly, reaching a level comparable to megacities[2] in other semi-developed countries. Travelers who arrive at the Suvarnabhumi Airport, the aerial gateway to Bangkok that opened in 2006, can reach the inner city in about thirty minutes by using the Airport Rail Link that opened in August 2010. The Link's terminal station, Phayathai, is directly linked to the elevated urban railway, the Bangkok Mass Transit System (BTS),[3] which opened at the end of 1999. This can take passengers to destinations such as Silom Road, the business center, the shopping centers near the Siam station, and the residential districts along Sukhumvit Road, where many foreigners live. There is also now a subway line. By the end of 2010, the total length of urban railways in Bangkok, including the Airport Rail Link, was 74.2 kilometers.[4] The number of weekday users of the urban railways averaged about 700,000 people per day in 2010.[5] The use of urban railways has grown steadily in Bangkok.

Before the urban railways were opened, Bangkok was completely dependent on road transport, with the exception of some water transport. I first arrived in Bangkok in 1983 and lived there for three years. At the time, the city's traffic congestion was considered the worst in the world (Pendakur 1984, 34). Although as a junior high school student I had few opportunities to take public transport, I sometimes used the blue buses showing their route numbers or the converted trucks, *songthaeo*, operating with the same route numbers and colors as the buses.[6]

When I returned for a year in 1991, the city's transport situation was still the same—dependent mainly on buses. Although the blue buses were still in the majority, there were now new red buses with higher fares and there were more air-conditioned buses. *Songthaeo* had been removed from the main roads, and minibuses that had been converted from *songthaeo* were running alongside the large buses. Traffic congestion had worsened even further: it took more than one hour to get to a university campus only seven to eight kilometers away. By my third stay in 1997, the situation had still not improved. This time I used suburban trains of the existing railways operated by the State Railways of Thailand (SRT, *Kan rotfai haeng prathet thai*) in order to avoid traffic congestion on the roads.

I had begun questioning why there were no urban railways in Bangkok since I was in junior high school. In the mid-1980s, there was a rumor that there was a plan to construct a monorail, and such news was also reported in newspapers. But nothing seemed to come of it. During my stay in Bangkok in 1991, the Hopewell plan[7] was presented. It aimed to construct elevated railways and urban railways by using the right-of-ways of the existing SRT railway. Finally, the first urban railway was expected to appear in Bangkok. But the plan suffered a setback, and only a few pillars were completed after all. In 1997, the Hopewell plan came to a complete stop, while construction work on the elevated BTS tracks reached a climax. Therefore, although traffic congestion continued to worsen, the hope for an urban railway was realized at last.

I wondered why the development of urban railways progressed so slowly, even though the opening of the BTS in 1999 was a turning point for the city's urban transport. The urban railway, with the punctuality that was missing from road-dependent transport, had steadily increasing numbers of users despite relatively high fares. The subway, whose construction started in the latter half of the 1990s, was officially opened in 2004, and the total length of the urban railways then exceeded forty kilometers. However, subsequent development remained very slow. At that time, the Thaksin Shinawatra government, which came to power in 2001, stated that the "dream" of completing an urban railway network of three hundred kilometers by 2010 was "sold"; the term "dream-selling policy" (*nayobai khai fan*) began to appear.[8] Once again, however, concrete progress was barely seen, and only seventy-four kilometers of urban railways was completed by the end of 2010.

While Bangkok's mass transit rail system did not exist until the end of 1999, tramways and suburban railways had existed in earlier years. I learned this while studying Thai history as a junior high school student.

Surprisingly, the remaining tramway rails are still visible on Charoen Krung Road where the Bang Kholaem line existed, as I will explain later. Some books say that the first railway between Bangkok and Paknam opened in 1893, while others say that the first railway between Bangkok and Ayutthaya opened in 1897. It puzzled me that this former suburban railway parallel to congested Sukhumvit Road had been abandoned. It was also puzzling that sources of information about the early rail systems hardly existed.

Thus, my study began with many simple questions regarding urban transport in Bangkok that I had begun pondering over my many years of stay there.

Trends in the Debate on Urban Transport

Studies of urban transport can be conducted within the context of various disciplines, such as transport geography, transport economics, transport engineering, history, and politics. Here I intend to analyze trends in the debates on the historical deployment of urban transport and changes in transport policy based on my interest in transport geography, history, and politics.[9]

A major element in research on urban transport involves studying how transport types have changed. My study of the history of urban transport will try to show what types of transport appeared at particular times, and how the relative position of each type may have shifted. Such changes differ between developed countries and developing (including middle-income) countries.[10] In developed countries, the changes in rail transport were fairly stable: from tramways to suburban railways to urban railways (subways). In developing countries, on the other hand, rail transport disappeared for a while in many cases; hence, the transition was instead from tramways to buses to urban railways.[11] For example, Howard Dick and Peter J. Rimmer in their study of transport in the cities of Southeast Asia (2003) outline the history of urban transport in seven major cities such as Singapore, Bangkok, and Manila. Their work shows that transport had evolved from tramways to buses to urban railways in many cases; sometimes, the earlier form was completely replaced by the newer one. Josef Barat (1990), using the example of São Paulo, Brazil, explains the transition process of transport from the development of tramways and urban railways before World War II to the introduction of subways through the development of bus service in the postwar period.

A study such as this must necessarily include transport types not seen in developed countries, so-called "paratransit" types, which are often essential to urban transport in developing countries. Paratransit is an intermediate form of transport that bridges the gap between private transport and traditional types of public transport. According to Thomas R. Leinbach and Chia Lin Sien (1989, 202–4),[12] these can be classified into three types: minibus, hybrid, and taxi. A minibus type operates on the same routes as regular buses but uses smaller vehicles with a capacity for fewer than sixteen persons. Vans and *songthaeo* would fall into this category. A hybrid type uses the same vehicles as the minibus type, but the operation route is not fixed; it is rather similar to a shared taxi. The taxi type is a leased vehicle that has evolved from rickshaw to tricycle to motorized tricycle; its form is diverse. Motorbike taxis are also found in recent years. Paratransit modes are basically operated by private, small-scale operators and have not obtained formal operating permission in many cases. The regulation of the operators is always loose, except for the fare level (Armstrong-Wright 1993, 25–29). Although the term *paratransit* is commonly used, other terms such as *intermediate public transport, secondary urban transport,* and *informal transport* may also appear in the literature (Hilling 1996; Pendakur 1984; Vasconcellos 2001).

Because the paratransit mode does not exist in developed countries, it has generally been eliminated from the concept of "traditional" public transport, and consultants from developed countries and the government bureaucrats in developing countries tend to neglect its role (Leinbach and Chia 1989, 221–26). However, the World Bank's proposal to operate minibuses as regular buses in Kuala Lumpur and the success of the four hundred minibuses on seventeen routes used there in the 1970s shattered the myth that public transport should only be supplied by large-sized vehicles under public management (Pendakur 1984, 31–32).[13] Thus, the role of paratransits should be further emphasized in developing countries. For example, the operation of private minibuses was permitted after deregulation in 1988 by the government of Harare, Zimbabwe. Minibuses absorbed the demand that conventional bus service could not fulfill, thereby resulting in a rapid increase in minibus users (Simon 1996, 112–14). In Manila, a paratransit called the jeepney still serves as a major means of local transport, while bus service in Surabaya and Bandung, Indonesia, disappeared because of competition from paratransits (Leinbach and Chia 1989, 201).

Although the importance of paratransits has been emphasized, there are also opposing arguments. It is true that the traditional means of transport are generally operated by the public sector, and most of them are operated at a loss because of inefficient management, low fares, and they often receive subsidies (Armstrong-Wright 1993, 17–19). On the other hand, a paratransit is typically operated under private management; a loss-incurring operation would not be continued if it led to loss of income for the operator. Both the low level of personnel expenses and the low cost of maintenance of a small vehicle contribute to paratransits' profitability (ibid, 13–15). However, others argue that the operation of paratransits based on a market mechanism will cause free competition and create a monopoly, which will result in the deterioration of bus service because of the deteriorating conditions of buses or the reduction in passengers. For example, Eduardo A. Vasconcellos (2001, 144) presupposes that the entry of informal transport in Curtiba, Brazil, should not be permitted because prohibiting these "illegal" buses from operating as paratransits would lead to an improvement in bus service.[14] On the other hand, David Hilling (1996, 222–24) accepts the predominance of paratransit services but points out that the intermediate point between the two extremes—paratransit complementing traditional transit—would be the best option. Thus, Hilling says, there exists a formal/informal debate regarding paratransits.

Urban railways, which are regarded as the last option in the traditional transport policy in developed countries, may also be negatively evaluated in developing countries. For example, in the comparative study of urban railways in twenty-one cities in developing countries by J. M. Thomson et al. (1990), low-cost solutions are recommended, such as a bus lane and light-rail transit (LRT), since urban railways need huge investment. On the other hand, they conclude that urban railways may not be financially viable but are economically respectable, noting that the introduction of urban railways would be inevitable for large megacities. In addition, David Banister recommends that the traditional view of giving bus service lower priority than rail transport should be revised with the realization that bus rapid transport (BRT) can be cheap and flexible as public transport. He cites the immense capital and operational costs required for rail compared with the development of BRT in South American cities such as Curitiba and Bogota (2005, 201–4).[15]

Thus, the arguments regarding urban transport in developing countries tend to oppose the "common sense" about urban transport in developed countries, or the so-called "traditional" transport policy. That is, paratransit and BRT are promoted as the leading urban transport types in developing countries. However, their adaptability needs to be carefully examined for each city. In particular, it is interesting to consider whether these arguments can be applied to a megacity such as Bangkok.

Current studies focusing on the problems of transport policy in developing countries are unexpectedly scarce. As a concrete example, the study regarding the urban transport policy of Hong Kong by C. K. Leung (1993) is typical; it classifies the transport policy shifts into four periods, from the establishment of jurisdictional agencies to the formulation of urban transport plans. Moreover, a study of Saõ Paulo (Barat 1990) also considers the transition of transport policy focusing on the establishment of jurisdictional agencies and reveals the details of installing and later abolishing the comprehensive jurisdictional agency.

Arguing more generally, Vasconcellos's study of the supply cycle in public transport is laden with terms of regulation (2001, 133–39). He deals with the public transport supply cycle presented by J. Gómez-Ibáñez and J. Meyer and shows three modified circles: the "savage" public transport supply circle in which the competition in a market economy is considerably severe, the "corporate" public transport supply circle starting with the establishment of a public corporation, and the "irresponsible" public transport supply circle, pointing to examples in Brazil.[16] Each cycle reflects the transition of urban transport policy by interrelating the strength of governmental regulations and the differences in management—public or private—using examples from South America. In short, two opposite trends are explained: the public-owned types that result from strengthening the regulation of private corporations and the privately owned types that result from a decrease in the efficiency of the public corporation.

Very few studies concretely deal with the relationship between urban transport policy and politics. For example, Rikkie Yeung's study (2008) of urban transport in Hong Kong reveals that the government gave the power to decide fare levels to the operating corporation to prevent the intervention of politicians; they were expected to insist on a low fare system by emphasizing profitability less. Politicians were excluded so that the subway would not be used as a "political toy" during its development in the 1970s. Yeung also points out that the subways in Hong Kong are operated on a commercial basis without a subsidy as provided in other developing countries. Although it is an example focused on a developed country, the study by Daijiro Kitagawa (2001) regarding the subway (metro) construction in Paris also reveals the relationship between urban transport development and politics, including the fight for control between the central government, provinces, and cities. Hong Kong avoided political intervention. However, in fact, political intervention would have affected urban transport policies and brought certain disadvantages in many cities in developing countries. Nevertheless, very few studies directly focus on the relationship between politics and urban transport.

Thus, among studies on urban transport in developing countries, many question the traditional transport policy in developed countries, and there are more and more studies emphasizing the roles of paratransit and BRT. However, very few studies reveal the reason for the introduction of each transport type and how political pressure is applied in those cases. Although many studies examine the development of urban transport from a macroscopic viewpoint, there are no studies that pursue the background and concrete reasons in detail from a microscopic viewpoint.

Studies on Urban Transport in Bangkok

Studies on urban transport in Bangkok follow this general trend: some studies use a macroscopic viewpoint, but there is to date no empirical study from a microscopic viewpoint. Studies that concentrate on a specific era and transport types are limited because of a lack of source materials.

In the case of tramways, all existing studies concentrate on its inception. Among them, Kueakun Yuenyong-anan's study (1977) regarding land transport in the reign of King Rama V deals mostly with the tramways but limits the discussion to the period of 1900. Porphant Ouyyanont's study (1994) regarding the primary city of Bangkok includes only two pages on tramways and refers only to the extension of the network up to the 1920s. Wipharat Di-ong's study (1991) focusing on the then Siam Electricity Company, Ltd. (SEC), the operator of the tramways, also refers to the tramway business only briefly. Although the introduction of tramways is certainly mentioned in books of general interest on Bangkok, they focus on the age of inception and the information is limited, as in Kueakun's study. For example, Sa-nguan Ankhong's book, a representative example, refers to tramways in the age of inception but does not deal with tramways other than those operated by Siam Electric Company. Moreover, he seldom mentions the situation after the 1910s.[17] The period from the tramways' nationalization to their elimination is completely ignored.

In the case of suburban railways, no study focuses on them in terms of urban transport. Although both David Frederich Holm (1977) and Somchai Phairotthirarat (1974), the pioneers in studies of railway history in Thailand, refer to the opening of two urban railways, they do not mention the transition to urban railways by electrification. My own study of railway construction and its economic integration in Thailand (Kakizaki 2005) also refers to the opening of these railways, but does not mention the situation after that stage. All studies focus only on the opening of suburban railways and tramways, and none refers to the subsequent situation except for another study I published in 2012.[18]

As previously pointed out, many studies of urban railways consider the topic from a macroscopic viewpoint. Studies on the development of urban railways by Nara Khamanamun (2004) and Khamroplak Suratsawadi (2000) refer to the history of urban transport in Bangkok. Phongphan Chan-ngoen (1999) considers the access railroad to the new airport, while Witthaya Aphin-yanon (2001) deals with the revival of the Hopewell plan, which suffered a setback, as will be mentioned later. Danny Unger (1998), who studied the development of social capital in Thailand, refers to the three urban railway plans, and points out three reasons for the delay in urban railway development: corruption, ambiguous plans, and lack of cooperation among the plans. He also suggests that the frequent changes in political leadership and policy contribute to the problems. Walden Bello et al. (1998), who deal with the impact of urban railway development on the environment, focus on the promotion of the underground transport system under pressure from citizens who recognize the environmental problems.

A study on the change to the urban railway plan under the Thaksin government in 2001 would be indispensable for the study of urban railway policy, since both Kriangsak Charoensak (2007) and Samat Ratchaphalasit (2007) criticize it. Kriangsak criticizes the urban railway plan as the "Mega Project" and points out the problems of the "Thailand: Partnership for Development" plan and urban railway development by the barter method, as will be mentioned later. On the other hand, Samat refers to the problem of the BTS extension lines from his experience as the vice-governor of the BMA and mentions that the delay originated in the attitude of the Thaksin government. Although neither are academic studies, they are useful books that concretely mention the urban transport policy in Bangkok.

There are very few studies regarding buses. Similar to tramways and suburban railways, several descriptions about the beginning of bus services are available, such as Sa-nguan's book, but no academic studies have been reported. One pertinent example is Charuni Khongkun's study (2006), which deals with the period of 1976, immediately after the establishment of the Bangkok Mass Transit Authority (BMTA, *Ongkan khonsong muanchon krungthep*).[19] However, from the 1930s to the formation of the public authority, very little information can be found, even in the general literature. Therefore, the development of bus operations over time and the government's policy shifts concerning them are not considered.

Thus, studies on urban transport in Bangkok are insufficient. Those dealing with the beginning of transport types from the end of the nineteenth century, in the early twentieth century, and after the 1970s exist, but studies that cover the gaps between these periods are scarce. Even the studies outlining urban transport history, such as those of Nara and Khamroplak, mention few activities during these periods. Although there has been research on the topic of rail transport, few studies include buses. Therefore, it is necessary to resolve the historical development of urban transport in Bangkok as a prerequisite for the analysis, and this is one of the purposes of this study.

Most studies do not include the answer to my question as to why the development of urban transport in Bangkok was so slow. Although Unger refers to the factors causing delays in urban railway development, he does not mention how the three factors contributed to the delay in plans. Even Kriangsak and Samat, who criticize the policy of the Thaksin government, do not thoroughly explain the urban railway policy and background. I maintain that not only formulating minimally feasible plans but also elucidating reasons for formulating such plans are important for finding an answer to the main question.

Objectives and Scope

Based on my awareness of the issues and on a survey of the literature published about them, I aim in this study to assemble the complete history of urban transport in Bangkok and to analyze the policies that have been adopted. I will cover the period from the latter half of the 1880s, during which the first tramway was opened, to 2010. My analysis of urban transport in Thailand includes two perspectives: regulation and politicization.

The main task in dealing with regulation is to reveal the transition of the urban transport policy and its background. In line with Vasconcellos's public transport supply cycle, Thailand's urban transport operations also began as private enterprises, most of which became public operations through the strengthening of government regulation. However, the problem behind the strengthening of regulation is important to understand. According to this model, competition by private enterprises strengthens regulation by the government, which results in the reduction of profitability and the deterioration of service, and so they are finally nationalized or publicly owned (Vasconcellos 2001, 133–34). It is then essential to analyze the reasons for the strengthening or weakening of regulation in Bangkok, or the reasons for public management.

As for politicization, the main task is to reveal the possibility that the transitions of urban transport policy were carried out with political intentions. As with the example of Hong Kong, a measure was adopted to prohibit the urban railway development from being misused as a "political toy," although there is a possibility for the same to occur since urban transport is often a crucial issue for city dwellers, especially those who do not own private cars. In such a case, the maintenance of a low fare level for urban transport, even though it lowers profitability, becomes a concrete measure that is seen as a populist policy.[20] In fact, urban transport had already become a "toy" for politicians, and this had greatly influenced the delay in urban transport development and the subsequent worsening of the urban transport problem. Therefore, another objective of the study is to analyze the reasons that urban transport was politicized and how this influenced urban transport policy.

The modes of urban transport included in this study involve only public transport, and I exclude private transport such as privately owned cars. Furthermore, although public transport typically includes leased vehicles such as taxis, this study targets only regular public transport that operates on a regulated route: namely, tramways, suburban railways, buses (including some paratransits), and urban railways. The regular ferry and boat service, which functions as urban transport in Bangkok, is also excluded here since the available general sources and related studies are extremely limited.[21]

The Sources

Limited sources are the main reason for the insufficient research regarding urban transport in Bangkok. Although sources such as newspapers can be used for information on current urban transport systems, sources for the past are limited to archives, annual reports, and newspapers. However, not many archives are related to urban transport, and the information obtained from annual reports is also minimal, particularly when the urban transport businesses were managed by private enterprises. Since the students of history do not look for sources other than archives, especially in Thailand, previous studies have concentrated on certain periods and certain means of transport.[22]

The main archival resources are the Department of Royal Secretary records (*Ekkasan krom ratchalekhathikan*) and the Ministry of Communications records (*Ekkasan krasuang khamanakhom*, or Kho Kho.) at the National Archives of Thailand (NA, *Ho chotmaihet haeng chat*). The Department of Royal Secretary records are divided into files for each ministry; the archives regarding tramways and buses are in the file for the Ministry of Local Government (*Krasuang nakhonban*, Ro. 5 No.) and those related to suburban railways are in the file for the Ministry of Public Works (*Krasuang yothathikan*, Ro. 5 Yo Tho.). Since the Ministry of Local Government was unified with the Ministry of Interior (*Krasuang mahatthai*) in 1922, the archives related to tramways and buses shifted to the Ministry of Interior file (Ro. 7 Mo.) during the reign of King Rama VII.[23] Since the Ministry of Public Works changed to the Ministry of Communications in 1912, the Ministry of Public Works file moved to the Ministry of Communications file (Ro. 6 Kho Kho.) during the reign of King Rama VI. Then, in the reign of King Rama VII (1926), the Ministry of Communications merged with the Ministry of Commerce and became the Ministry of Commerce and Communications (*Krasuang phanit lae khamanakhom*, Ro. 7 Pho.). However, very few of these archives pertain to buses, and the archives regarding tramways are also few, except during the reign of King Rama V. Moreover, the archives related to suburban railways are abundant only during the reign of King Rama V because that was when they began, and they decreased after this. In addition, the archives of the 1930s and 1940s exist in the Secretariat of the Cabinet records (*Ekkasan samnak lekhathikan khana ratthamontri*, [2] So Ro. and [3] So Ro.), which were inherited by the Department of the Royal Secretary.

The Ministry of Communication records include the archives from the latter half of the 1940s to the early half of the 1960s, and is divided into a file for each subordinate agency. The archives related to urban transport can be found in the following: Office of the Under-Secretary of State (*Samnakngan palat krasuang*, Kho Kho. 0202. 2), the Department of Transport (*Krom kan khonsong*, Kho Kho. 0202. 3), the Royal Railway Department (*Krom rotfai*) or the SRT (Kho Kho. 0202. 9), the Express Transportation Organization (ETO, *Ongkan rapsong sinkha lae phattsaduphan*, Kho Kho. 0202. 11), and the Transport Company (*Borisat khonsong chamkat*, Kho Kho. 0202. 13). With the exception of the archives related to suburban railways that are located in the Railway Department file, all archives are related to bus operations. Although many archives related to buses exist during this period, no related study has been present until now. It appears that few students are interested in bus operations, and hence the archives are rarely used.[24] In addition, since the jurisdiction of the tramways during this period was under the Ministry of Interior, the archives related to tramways are not included.[25]

In addition to these, the archives regarding international cooperation dating from the latter half of the 1960s to 1970s are contained in the Fiscal Policy Office records (*Ekkasan samnakngan setthakit kan khlang*, [1] Ko Kho. and [2] Ko Kho.) of the Ministry of Finance. Among these are the sources regarding the urban railway plan and the bus improvement plan. Moreover, although small, the archives on the bus unification plan put forward by the Bangkok Municipality in the early 1960s exists in the Bangkok Metropolitan Administration (BMA, *Krungthep mahanakhon*, Ko Tho Mo.).

Nevertheless, since archival sources do not cover the period after the 1970s and very few or no sources are available during other specific periods, it is quite difficult to clarify the historical development of urban transport by using only archival sources.

Annual reports and newspapers were also used to compensate for the deficiencies of the archival sources. The operation of urban transport was mainly started by private enterprises, but not many of these reports can be used to support an urban transport study.[26] The main agencies to be reviewed for this study are as follows: the Metropolitan Electricity Authority (MEA, *Kan faifa nakhon luang*), which had jurisdiction over the tramways; the SRT, which operated the suburban railways after nationalization; the ETO and the Transport Co., which engaged in bus operations; the BMTA; the Expressway and Rapid Transit Authority of Thailand (ETA, *Kan thang phiset haeng prathet thai*), which controlled the urban railway plans in early days; and the Metropolitan Rapid Transit Authority (MRTA, *Ongkan rotfaifa mahanakhon*) that inherited them.[27] However, the existing reports are limited except for the SRT, and the amount of information acquired from the annual reports for the postwar period is less than those for the prewar period.[28] Therefore, compared with the study on railways, it must be said that these annual reports are not very useful for my study's purposes.

Although there are annual reports issued by private companies operating the tramways and suburban railways, they are even less informative compared with the annual reports of the public agencies, since they are merely financial statements presented at general meetings of shareholders. While some annual reports are maintained in the

National Archives of Thailand, not all are available there. However, whenever the general meetings of shareholders were held in those days, the contents of the annual reports and the arguments at the meetings were always reported by the newspapers. Therefore, data such as net profits and dividend rates can be found over a remarkable period even though the original reports no longer exist. Since the information that can otherwise be obtained is limited, the tramways and suburban railways during the age of private management will be analyzed from the management side.

As for newspapers, articles relating to urban transport were mainly collected from the *Bangkok Times Weekly Mail* (*BTWM*) in the prewar period and the *Sayam Nikhon* (*SN*) and *Sayam Rat Sapda Wichan* (*SRSW*) in the postwar period. Various online newspapers were used for the latter half of the 1990s and the 2000s. Information from newspapers became the sole source when neither the archival sources nor the annual reports could be used, and this information was quite important. However, few studies have utilized it because the search time is considerably high.

Finally, here is an assessent of the existing statistical data. When studying urban transport, data such as the number of vehicles, number of routes, length of lines, and number of users, as well as figures showing the financial condition of the operators are useful. However, these data are usually not available for the era of private operation; they are available after public management was established.[29] For example, the number of tramway users cannot be obtained except for a certain period in the 1940s, and after the formation of the MEA in 1958. Although statistics about the number of buses registered in Bangkok can be obtained after the 1930s, the number of regular buses operated in Bangkok is available only after the establishment of the BMTA in 1976. Since few annual reports of the BMTA are available before the 1990s, the actual statistics can only been found for the period after the 1990s. The statistics regarding the number of bus users encounter a similar roadblock; the number before 1988 cannot be found in the present sources.[30] On the other hand, the statistics for urban transport, including urban railways and water transport, are covered in the Traffic Statistics (*Sathiti charachon*, *SC*) that the BMA has been publishing since 2003; these statistics were easily obtained. Therefore, fragmentary descriptions have to be used during the periods when statistics were not available.

Components of the Study

This study is divided into seven chapters. The first six deal with the historical development of urban transport, and the seventh will summarize changes of urban transport policy from the 1880s to 2000s.

In chapter 1, "Introduction of the Rail Transport System, 1880s to 1900s," the aim is to analyze the progress of the tramway and suburban railway plans that appeared in the 1880s and to review the correspondence of the government during the reign of King Rama V. Although few studies about tramways have been published, even basic facts such as the year of opening for each line have not been fully established. As for the suburban railways, the movement toward urban railways is not seen at this time, but the management of the inter-urban railways should be interlinked with the subsequent movement toward urban railways.

Chapter 2, "Emergence of Competition, 1910s to 1930s," deals with the period from the reign of King Rama VI to the era of the People's Party government after the Constitutional Revolution, and through the reign of King Rama VII. The main points of this discussion include the emergence of buses, the movement of the suburban railways toward urban railways, and the competition between tramways and buses. The buses that appeared around 1910 rapidly expanded their network, and their competition with tramways began at the end of the 1920s. Moreover, the suburban railways sought entry into urban transport to acquire new customers, but their movements were affected by the government's policy toward the concessions. Both the government and the operators were forced to contend with the competition between tramways and buses.

Chapter 3, "Expansion of Bus Networks, 1940s to 1950s," deals with the period from the beginning of the war in 1941 to the end of the second Plaek Phibunsongkhram government in 1957. This era focuses on the process of urban transport's transition from rail to buses. The transport capacity of buses decreased greatly because of the shortage of fuel and parts during the war, and the roles of the tramways and suburban railways temporarily increased. While bus service rapidly expanded after the war, rail transport stagnated completely during that time. Therefore, the main objective of this chapter is to explore the stagnation of rail transport and to reveal the government's policy toward bus operation and changes in that policy.

Chapter 4, "Unification of Buses, 1960s to 1970s," describes the situation of urban transport and the changes in urban transport policy during the age of "development," and the age of "democratization": from 1957 to 1976. During the period of "development," which began under Sarit Thanarat, part of the suburban railway system disappeared from inner Bangkok, while all tramways and rail transport vanished from the city. On the other hand, the unification of buses, which had been surfacing for some time, finally materialized during the period of "democratization." Since the politicization of urban transport surfaced during this period, it becomes the main point of the argument in this chapter—how the changes in urban transport policy were related to the problem of politicization.

Chapter 5, "Revival of Rail Transit, 1970s to 1990s," deals with the period from the latter half of the 1970s to the opening of the first urban railway at the end of 1999. This chapter reveals changes in urban transport policy by focusing on the problem of bus operation after the unification and emergence of the urban railway plans. Although bus operation was unified as a public authority in 1976, many problems accumulated even after unification, and the authority was forced into running a loss-incurring operation. On the other hand, the urban railway plan surfaced in the 1970s to resolve the intensified transport problem. However, the progress of the plans was slow and took about thirty years to be realized. Therefore, this chapter strives to answer such questions as why the unification of buses did not bring an improvement in bus service and why the realization of the urban railway plans was so long in coming.

Chapter 6, "A Confused Urban Transport Policy, 2000s," analyzes changes of urban transport policy and the background to them after the organization of the Thaksin government in 2001–10. The period from the first urban railway plan to its realization was extremely long, as was the subsequent expansion of the urban railway network, as mentioned above. While it is certain that frequent policy changes took place in the background, it is important to show clearly why. Moreover, various plans surfaced for bus operation, but the realization of these was also slowed by political confrontations. The problem of politicization of urban transport is definitely at the bottom of such problems, too. Therefore, the main argument of this chapter is that the influence of politics on urban transport was crucial to its development.

Finally, chapter 7, "Historical Deployment of Urban Transport in Bangkok—Strengthening of Regulation and Politicization," summarizes the historical development of urban transport and the transitions in urban transport policies in Bangkok from two perspectives. Since it is the premise of the analysis that the overall history of urban transport in Bangkok would be revealed, the changes in the means of transport are summarized, comparing them with other cities. Moreover, the importance of the role of paratransits and BRT, which was emphasized in studies on urban transport in developing countries, is reexamined. Subsequently, the history of urban transport policy in Bangkok is analyzed from the two perspectives of regulation by the government and politicization. The main themes of this chapter are the two major beginning questions: why did the government strengthen the regulation of urban transport, and why did urban transport follow the way of politicization. My original questions will finally be answered.

1
The Introduction of Rail Transport, 1880s–1900s

The Introduction of Tramways by Foreign Companies

The First Tramway

The tramway business in Bangkok started as part of a foreigner's economic activity. A railway, a modern means of transportation, had been discussed by the government in the 1870s, and a plan to construct a Moulmein-to-Yunnan line emerged in the 1880s.[1] However, there was no mention of a tramway in these plans. As far as I can ascertain, the subject of a tramway was first introduced to the government when Axel Johnson, Siam's honorary consul in Stockholm, informed Phra Darunrak, the chargé d'affaires in Paris, of his intention to cooperate in the rumored tramway construction in Bangkok. This was then reported to Prince Thewawong (Krommamuen Thewawong Waropakan), the Thai minister of foreign affairs.[2]

One year later, on May 5, 1887, a British navigator hired by the Thai government, Alfred John Loftus, and a Danish deputy superintendent of the Thai Royal Navy, Commodore de Richelieu, gained the concession to construct seven tram lines in Bangkok.[3] The agreement stated that the concessionaire had to start construction of the first line within three years and complete it within five years, as shown in table 1.1. The first line to be built would run from Bang Kholaem to Tha Tian, near the Royal Palace, via Charoen Krung Road (New Road).[4] In this concession, the tramway was specified as a single track, as were all tramways built later.

Table 1.1. Conditions of Tramway Concessions

Company	Line	Date of Grant	Concession Term	Track Rent	Deadline for Start	Deadline for Completion	Purchase of Business	Remarks
Loftus & de Richelieu	7 tramlines	5 May 1887	50 years		Within 3 years (for the first line)	Within 5 years for the first line (within 7 years for other lines)	20 years after grant	
Siam Electric Railway	Samsen line	25 Jul 1900	40 years	2.5–4% of gross receipt	Within 6 months	Within 2 years	12 years after grant	
Siamese Tramway	4 tramlines	1 Apr 1904	End of 1949	1,200–5,000 baht per mile	Within 6 months	Within 18 months	At any time	Deposit of 10,000 baht per mile required.
Pakkret Tramway			End of 1949	400–1,200 baht per mile	Within 6 months	Within 30 months	12 years after grant	Based on concession draft.
Menam Motor Boat	Paklat Tramway	7 May 1907	End of 1949	600–1,000 baht per mile	Within 6 months	Within 18 months	After 1920	
Siam Electricity	Atsadang, Ratchawong, and Samsen extension lines	1907	End of 1949	3,000 baht per mile	N.A.	N.A.	N.A.	Water sprinklers along the tramways and fire protection within 300 feet of tramways required.

NOTE: Here, and in subsequent tables, N.A. means not available.
SOURCES: NA Ro. 5 No. 21/2; NA Ro. 5 No. 21/25; NA Ro. 5 No. 21/40; NA Ro. 5 No. 21/78; NA Ko To. 5/53; *BTWM*, 2 Sep 1907.

Although the reason these two persons were able to gain the tramway concession is unknown, it seems that they enjoyed considerable popularity since both were foreign employees of the government. De Richelieu had also obtained the concession for the Paknam Railway the previous year. However, the next month, the concession was transferred by these two men to a British man, Henry Sigg, and it was he who established the Bangkok Tramway Company to build it (*BTWM*, 24 September 1902).[5] The transfer would have already been decided before these two men gained the concession, since they also participated in the newly established company as directors. The company started construction of the first 5-kilometer section from Lak Mueang, the adjusted starting point at the east side of Sanam Luang, to the Bangkok dock near Wat Yannawa, and this opened on September 22, 1888 (see table 1.2) (*BTWM*, 19 April 1909).[6] By 1890, this tramway line had been completed up to Bang Kholaem.[7]

Table 1.2. Opening of Tramways, 1888–1910

Company	Line	Section	Length (km)	Opening Date	Remarks	Sources
Siam Electricity	Bang Kholaem	Lak Mueang–Bangkok Dock	*5.0*	22 Sep 1888	Electrified in 1894	*BTWM*, 19 Apr 1909
		Bangkok Dock–Bang Kholaem	*4.0*	1890	Electrifiied in May 1893	*BT*, 2 Dec 1891
	Samsen	Hua Lamphong–Bang Krabue	8.6	24 Nov 1901		*BTWM*, 23 Nov 1901
		Saphan Lueang–Hua Lamphong	0.5	20 Oct 1910		*BTWM*, 21 Oct 1910
	Atsadang		0.5	1907		NA [2] So Ro. 0201. 63. 2/8
	Ratchawong		0.8	1907		NA [2] So Ro. 0201. 63. 2/8
Siamese Tramway	Hua Lamphong	Hua Lamphong–Phra Sumen	4.4	1 Oct 1905		*BTWM*, 2 Oct 1905
	City Wall		7.2	1 Oct 1905		*BTWM*, 2 Oct 1905
	Dusit	Chakkraphet–Power Plant	4.8	1 Oct 1905		*BTWM*, 2 Oct 1905
	Dusit Extension	Khosua–Mouth of Samsen Canal	2.4	1 Oct 1905	Abandoned 1.6-km section in 1910	*BTWM*, 2 Oct 1905
Total			38.2			

NOTE: Italicized numbers are approximate numbers.

This first tramway was horse-drawn. Such horse-drawn tramways had already been introduced in several cities in Southeast Asia, first in Batavia (Jakarta) in 1869 and then in Manila in 1881 (Dick and Rimmer 2003, 68). The horse-drawn tramway of Bangkok was towed by eight horses, and these had to be changed along the way (Sa-nguan 1986, 81). Unlike in Europe or the United States, fatigue in horses was a large problem in Southeast Asia due to the hot weather and high humidity, and therefore the efficiency of the horse-drawn tramway was not high. Nevertheless, the daily number of trams in June 1891 was as high as 129 trips on the old section and fifty-six trips on the new section (*BTWM*, 15 August 1891). As shown in table 1.3, the gross receipts for the same year were about 120,000 baht, and the dividend rate to the stockholders reached as high as 10 percent per year in 1892, as shown in table 1.4.

Electrification of the Tramway

In order to raise the efficiency of the tramway, another source of power needed to be introduced to replace the horse. The first substitution was a steam tram that consisted of a small steam locomotive with one or two coaches and was used in various cities in Southeast Asia, though not in Bangkok. The first steam tramway in Southeast Asia emerged in Batavia in 1882, followed by Rangoon, Singapore, and Surabaya in the 1880s (Dick and Rimmer 2003, 68). Although the steam tramway could have been an option for Bangkok, newer technology would be introduced here. In 1887, the electric tramway had just been put into practical use in the United States.[8]

It was Aage Westenholz, a Danish engineer and the de facto founder of the tramway business in Bangkok, who played an important role in introducing the electric tramway in Thailand. He reached Bangkok at the end of 1885, after studying civil engineering in Copenhagen, and began working on the construction of the Bangkok Tramway (*BTWM*, 19 April 1909). He visited the United States in 1891 to study the electric tramway technology in use there, and after his return to Bangkok, he proposed electrification at a general meeting of shareholders (*BT*, 17 February 1892). He explained that electrification was indispensable for the reinforcement of transport capacity, and that it would cost 30,000 to 40,000 baht to electrify the newly opened section as a trial project. He had already negotiated with a contractor for the delivery of electrification equipment from the United States.

Although his electrification plan was approved by the general meeting of shareholders, the initial approved budget of 50,000 baht was increased to 80,000 to include an improvement for capacity at the power plant (*BT*, 17 September 1892). The electrification plan was implemented, and the first electric tram began operating on February 21, 1893 (*BTWM*, 19 April 1909). In May of the same year, the operation of the electric tram on the whole electrified section started, which meant that about half of the Bangkok Tramway line became an electric tramway.[9] This was the first electric tramway, not only in Southeast Asia, but also in all of Asia, including Japan.[10]

Table 1.3. Gross Receipts of Tramway Companies, 1889–1910 (THB)

Year	Bangkok Tramway			Siam Electricity			Siamese Tramway		
	First Half	Latter Half	Total	Bang Kholaem Line	Samsen Line	Total	First Half	Latter Half	Total
1888	N.A.	N.A.	N.A.						
1889	29,186	38,968	68,154						
1890	N.A.	N.A.	N.A.						
1891	59,779	59,367	119,146						
1892	58,752	57,866	116,618						
1893	N.A.	65,412	N.A.						
1894	66,469	N.A.	N.A.						
1895	73,020	69,806	142,826						
1896	74,527	75,578	150,105						
1897	83,953	86,547	170,500						
1898	96,671	88,901	185,572						
1899	101,475	N.A.	N.A.	190,057		190,057			
1900	114,975	133,008	247,983	247,983		247,983			
1901	130,958			275,268		275,268			
1902				305,786	256,054	561,840			
1903				404,051	303,013	707,064			
1904				449,312	315,431	764,743			
1905				513,256	337,155	850,411		197,556	197,556
1906				581,586	324,870	906,456	243,688	248,072	491,760
1907				568,036	322,996	891,032	207,028	207,771	414,799
1908				572,692	354,207	926,899	318,651		318,651
1909				529,144	308,887	838,031	207,460	204,244	411,704
1910				N.A.	N.A.	N.A.	208,410	173,444	381,854

NOTE 1: Figures of Siam Electricity include only gross receipts of the tramway business.
NOTE 2: Until 1907, the fiscal year of the Siamese Tramway corresponded to the traditional Thai year, April to March. In 1908, the fiscal year ran from April to December and subsequently corresponded to the Western calendar year, January to December.
SOURCES: *BT* 1889–97 (selected issues); *BTWM* 1898–1901, 1907–11 (selected issues); Wright (1994, 191); NA Ro. 5 No. 21/74.

Table 1.4. Dividend Rates for Tramway Companies, 1889–1910 (%)

Year	Bangkok Tramway			Siam Electricity			Siamese Tramway		
	First Half	Latter Half	Total	First Half	Latter Half	Total	First Half	Latter Half	Total
1888	N.A.	N.A.	N.A.						
1889	8.00	N.A.	N.A.						
1890	N.A.	N.A.	N.A.						
1891	7.50	0.00	7.50						
1892	7.00	3.00	10.00						
1893	8.50	8.50	17.00						
1894	6.00	N.A.	N.A.						
1895	7.50	0.00	7.50						
1896	6.00	6.00	12.00						
1897	8.50	6.00	14.50						
1898	6.00	6.00	12.00						
1899	6.00	6.00	12.00						
1900	10.00	9.50	19.50	4.00	4.00	8.00			
1901	10.00			N.A.	4.00	4.00			
1902				N.A.	N.A.	N.A.			
1903				5.00	6.00	11.00			
1904				6.00	9.00	15.00			
1905				6.00	6.00+B11.5	12.00+B11.5		0.00	0.00
1906				6.00+B5	6.00+B14	12.00+B19	2.00	2.00	4.00
1907				6.00	6.00+B12.5	12.00+B12.5	2.00	0.00	2.00
1908				6.00	6.00+B4	12.00+B4	0.00		0.00
1909				6.00	6.00+B4	12.00+B4	0.00	0.00	0.00
1910				6.00	6.00+B6	12.00+B6	0.00	0.00	0.00

NOTE 1: The dividend rate includes bonuses.

NOTE 2: Since the bonus for the pound-based shares of Siam Electricity was paid in baht, it is shown in real numbers. Here, and in subsequent tables, B = baht.

NOTE 3: Until 1907, the fiscal year of the Siamese Tramway corresponded to the traditional Thai year, April to March. In 1908, the fiscal year ran from April to December and subsequently corresponded to the Western calendar year, January to December.

SOURCES: Same as table 1.3; *BTWM* 1900–1911 (selected issues).

The merits of electrification were quite clear. In 1893, the first year of electrification, the monthly operating expenses for the electric tram were only 926 baht, compared to the expenses of the horse-run system of 1,390 baht. Revenue share on the electrified section increased from 42 to 49 percent after electrification (*BT*, 31 May 1893). Since electrification was so successful, the company continued to electrify the remaining sections so that electric tram operation on the whole line started during the first half of 1894.[11] The financial condition of the Bangkok Tramway continued to improve after the completion of electrification, with gross receipts in 1900 doubling to 240,000 baht, compared to that in 1891, as shown in table 1.3.

Electrification of the tramway might be seen as evidence of Thailand's positive stance for introducing modern technology. In fact, however, the Thai government was not involved in this electrification plan. As far as I know, no historical records show the government's involvement with or support for the electrification plan during this period, apart from those relating to the transfer of the company's registration from Britain to Siam in 1892.[12] Although the concession for the Bangkok Tramway indicated the use of locomotives that would run on a certain source of power, electrification had not yet been assumed. Electrification was the achievement of Westenholz, whose long-term thinking materialized it.

Construction of the Samsen Line

Although the Bang Kholaem line was developed by electrification, the extension of the tramway network following this line did not materialize easily. The 1887 concession for constructing seven tram lines called for the completion of all lines within seven years of the concession announcement, so there was no prospect for further construction. In December 1893, De Richelieu requested that the government extend the deadline for completion of the other lines, but the government did not approve this request.[13] Therefore, an application for a new concession was needed in order to extend the tramway system.

Westenholz applied to the government in 1895 for construction of a tramway from Hua Lamphong to Samsen via Yaowarat Road, which was then under construction.[14] The construction of Yaowarat Road started in 1892, but Prince Phitthayalap (Krommamuen Phitthayalap), the minister of public works, who received the application, held that the tramway should not be constructed on this new road.[15] So there was no further progress until another report appeared in January 1900 regarding negotiations between Westenholz and Prince Naret, the minister of local government, about the concession for the Samsen line.[16] Westenholz had also applied for the construction of the City Wall line that would run along the city wall of Bangkok in addition to the Samsen line, but Prince Naret asked Westenholz to exclude the City Wall line in the negotiations, and the latter consented. Moreover, Prince Naret asked that the government receive part of the tramway income as track rent, noting that the first concession was disadvantageous to the government.[17] It can be assumed that the delay of progress was based on the delay in the construction of Yaowarat Road.[18]

The concession for the Samsen line was finally given to the Siam Electric Railway on July 25, 1900. Although this concession was the second one for tramways in Bangkok, the conditions were more stringent than the first one. The major change was that the concessionaire had to pay track rent to the government every year, and the term of the concession was shortened to forty years. The deadlines for start and completion were also shortened to six months and two years respectively. By this agreement, the government would also receive 2.5 to 4 percent of gross receipts from the concessionaire every year.[19] It is supposed that such a concession provision was modeled on the tramway concession in India.[20]

The construction of the Samsen line was immediately started after acquiring the concession, and it opened for traffic on November 24, 1901. This tramway was an 8.6-kilometer line connecting Bang Krabue in Samsen and Hua Lamphong, the Bangkok terminus for the Paknam Railway. It was constructed as an electric tramway from the beginning. The terminal at Bang Krabue was a pier on the Chaophraya River, so that it functioned as the connecting point with water transport. As shown in table 1.3, gross receipts were increasing regularly until 1906, when the influence of the new Siamese Tramway would appear. Although its gross receipts were smaller than those for the Bang Kholaem line, the financial condition was favorable. This tramway did not have an independent power plant but received its electric power supply from the Siam Electric Company (SEC).

Westenholz's intention was to unify the tramway business in Bangkok within his SEC. Although Westenholz retired from the management of Bangkok Tramway in 1895 and was engaged in the construction of locks on the Rangsit Canal as well as the railroad construction between Bangkok and Phetchaburi, he was also inaugurated as the representative director of the SEC. This company was established in 1898 to succeed the failed power distribution business of the Thais (*BTWM*, 19 April 1909).[21] Although he gained the concession of the Samsen line in the name of Siam Electric Railway, he intended to maintain the SEC as the sole enterprise to manage both the power distribution business and the tramway business in Bangkok by unifying two tramway companies: the Bangkok Tramway and Siam Electric Railway. His other intention was to support the faltering power distribution business with the successful tramway business.[22]

He applied to the government for the merger of these companies in November 1901 and received approval for the stabilization of the power distribution business. However, the government had to adjust the conditions of these three different concessions since their terms and profit distribution rates differed. Eventually, the company made a new contract with the government on November 9, 1901, to unify all the concession terms by the end of 1949 (*BTWM*, 14 September 1902). By this time, the unification of Bangkok's tramway business with the SEC was achieved, and further prosperity must have been expected.

Competition of Thais for the Tramway Business

Formation of the Siamese Tramway

Both the Bang Kholaem and Samsen lines were tramway businesses developed by foreigners, and the SEC, the company that unified both lines, was also a foreign company registered in Denmark. However, as the tramway business developed and earned favorable profits, Thais also wanted entry into the tramway business. Thus entered the Siamese Tramway project developed by Prince Narathip (Krommaphra Narathip Praphanphong) and others.

Prince Narathip was the younger half-brother of King Rama V, and he was inaugurated as the deputy minister of finance at the time of the restructuring government ministries and agencies in 1892. However, having been guilty of misconduct for abusing his status, he had to resign the post, and he then participated in such businesses as rice-milling, exploitation of paddy fields, and forestry (Thawisin 1983, 58–67).[23] Furthermore, the prince also inherited the concession of the railway between Bangkok and Phetchaburi, which Westenholz had failed to garner in 1896, but he had to sell out the next year due to his own failure. Then, in 1901, he gained another concession for the Phrabat Tramway.[24]

In April 1903, Prince Narathip, together with Prince Sanphasat (Krommaluang Sanphasat) and others, applied for a tramway construction program in Bangkok.[25] This tramway plan consisted of a 14.6-kilometer route starting from Hua Lamphong via Bamrung Mueang Road to the City Wall, then taking almost one round along the wall before heading northward to the terminus at the Dusit Palace, which was then under construction. This line was almost identical to the City Wall line for which Westenholz had applied along with the Samsen line application. Moreover, the SEC had already applied for the construction of the City Wall line, Hua Lamphong line, and the Worachak line in January 1903.[26] Since these routes were exactly the same as those of the prince's plan with the exception of one line to Dusit, it can be said that the prince and others competitively applied later.

Prince Narathip and his group tried to emphasize that their company was registered in Thailand, so the foreign-owned companies raised the amount of track rent paid to the government to influence the government's decision.[27] Although the concession of the Samsen line set its track rent at 2.5 to 4 percent of annual gross receipts, Westenholz proposed a fixed track rent of 1,000 baht per mile, whereas Prince Naret, the minister of local government, had asked for a fixed amount system.[28] Then the competition of track rent heated up when Prince Narathip's group proposed 1,200 baht and Westenholz countered with 2,000 baht. Finally, when the track rent reached 5,500 baht from Prince Narathip's side, the bidding ceased.

In fact, Prince Narathip asked for an agreement at 5,000 baht, a bid that Westenholz had already met, but the total amount of track rent to be paid by the SEC would have been higher since the prince changed part of its route. However, after examination by the minister at a meeting on July 7, 1903, both Prince Thewawong, the minister of foreign affairs, and Prince Damrong (Kromphraya Damrong Rachanuphap), the minister of interior, agreed to accept Prince Narathip's plan, and decided to issue a concession to his Siamese Tramway Company (*Rot rang thai thun chamkat*).[29] The concession was announced on April 1, 1904, after taking considerable time to determine its contents.[30]

The conditions of the concession to the Siamese Tramway were stricter than those of the Samsen line, as shown in table 1.1. Track rent was set at the fixed amount of 5,000 baht per mile on the public road and 1,200 baht per mile on the company's newly built road in the Dusit area. Furthermore, the deadline for completion was shortened to eighteen months, and a deposit of 10,000 baht per mile would also be levied as security for the deadline. The routes were also changed as shown in figure 1.1. The lines were divided into four sections: the Hua Lamphong line, the City Wall line, the Dusit line, and the newly added Dusit Extension line, now totaling 18.8 kilometers in length. The power plant would be constructed at Wat Thewarat Kunchon at the mouth of the Padung Krungkasem Canal. Though the construction started just after the announcement of the concession, it was delayed due to a conflict with the contractor. However, the company completed the construction within the deadline and finally started operation on October 1, 1905 (*BTWM*, 2 October 1905).

The Tramway Project in Thonburi

Although all tramway projects in Bangkok up to this time had been built on the eastern side of the Chaophraya River, the first tramway project in Thonburi, on the western side of the river, was now being planned. In 1898, newspapers reported that several Thai officials such as Phraya Ruetthiwong planned a tramway construction project along the Bangkok Yai Canal and had already gained a sanction from the king (*BTWM*, 18 August 1898). At that time, no evidence was offered showing their official application for the concession. Then, in 1902, Phraya Ruetthiwong and Phraya Nonthaburi applied for the construction of two light railways: a 3.6-kilometer line from Talat Phlu to the Chaophraya River (the residence of Chaophraya Rattanabodin) and a 1.7-kilometer branch line to the mouth of Bangkok Yai Canal (Wat Kanlayanamit).[31]

Their application seemed to have been approved, but they could not start construction due to the opposition of the Thachin Railway, as their tramway would be close to the latter's line.[32] Therefore, they invited Prince Narathip to join them with the hope that he would smooth negotiations with the government. They established the Talat Phlu Tramway Company and submitted a new plan that extended the total length to ten kilometers with two lines: one from Talat Phlu to

Fig. 1.1. Tramway Network in Bangkok, 1900s

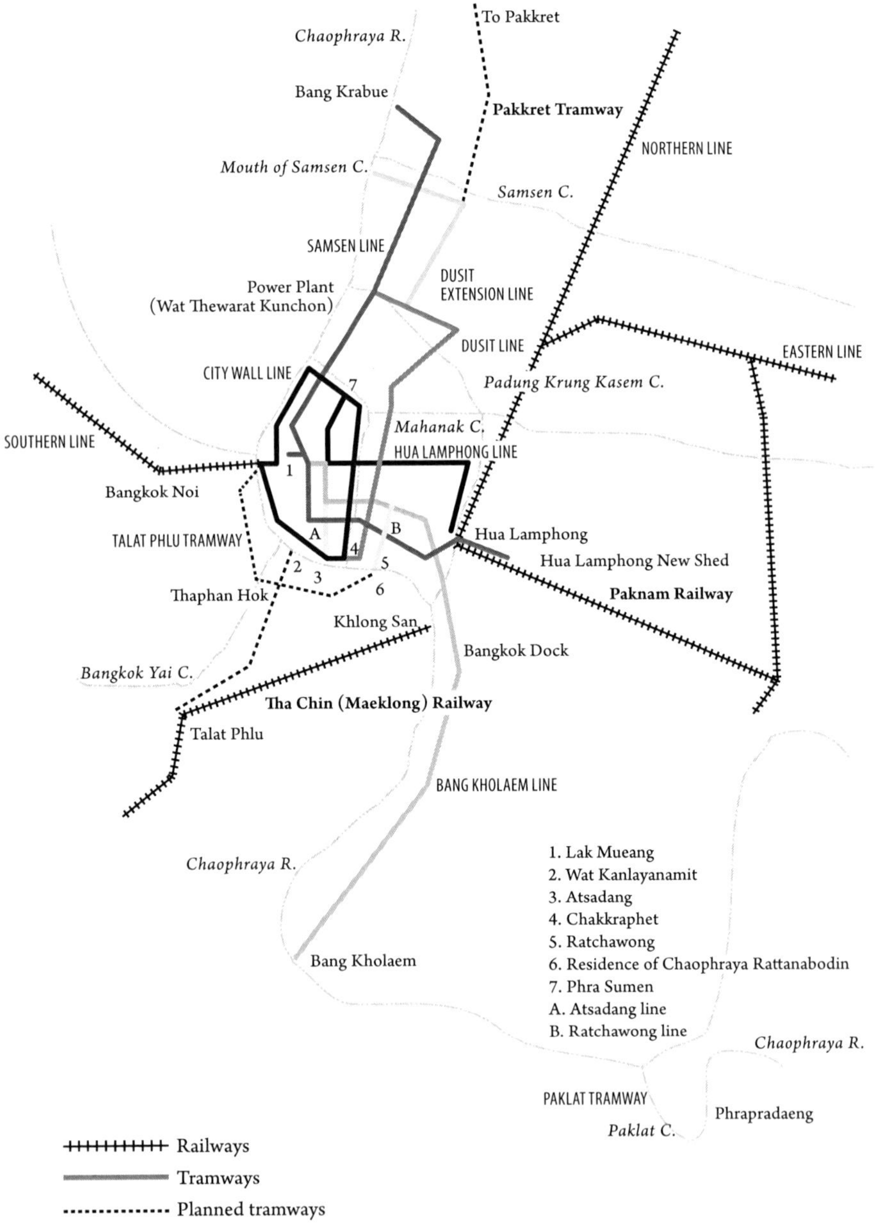

the residence of Chaophraya Rattanabodin, and another from Wat Kanlayanamit to Bangkok Noi station. They also changed their steam-hauled light railway to an electric tramway.[33] At the meeting with the ministers in May 1904, the king approved their application. However, the meeting reached the conclusion that they should reapply to establish their company since their plan had changed considerably.

Prince Narathip planned to merge the Talat Phlu Tramway into the Siamese Tramway Company and suggested a capital increase to construct three new lines— the Dusit Extension line, the Talat Phlu line, and the Pakkret line—at the shareholders meeting of the Siamese Tramway Company in September 1904 (*BTWM*, 10 September 1904). Though questions were raised about the profitability of the Talat Phlu line, the meeting approved all the extension plans. However, at a shareholders meeting in February 1905, the board of directors suggested beginning the construction of the Dusit Extension line, which had already been approved by the government, and the postponement of the other two lines (*BTWM*, 24 February 1905). They explained that some founders of the Talat Phlu Tramway had been opposed to the amalgamation plan, but the main reason actually was that they did not have enough time and capital to construct the other new lines when it became difficult to complete the original lines of the Siamese Tramway by the completion deadline.

Since Prince Narathip later concentrated on the construction of the Pakkret line, the Talat Phlu line project deadlocked. Phraya Ruetthiwong was worried about the situation and tried to move the project forward by inviting Chaophraya Surasakmontri, former minister of agriculture, who, like Prince Narathip, engaged in private business, to join them. In June 1907, Surasakmontri applied for the establishment of a company to construct the Talat Phlu line.[34] At a meeting with the minister, Prince Damrong insisted that the government should approve the tramway construction only after the road improvement was complete, since road construction in Thonburi had not yet progressed sufficiently. His opinion was finally accepted.[35] Hence, the tramway project in Thonburi was indefinitely suspended.

Competition for the Pakkret Tramway

Although Prince Narathip participated later in the Talat Phlu Tramway, the prince conceived of the Pakkret Tramway from the beginning, and fought for it over SEC's Westenholz, just as in the case of the Siamese Tramway. In May 1904, just after the concession for the Siamese Tramway was announced, Prince Narathip introduced the construction plan for the Pakkret Tramway.[36] The route for this tramway, which was about twenty kilometers long, went northward along the eastern side of the Chaophraya River to Pakkret from the Dusit Extension line of the Siamese Tramway. It was scheduled to be built as a steam tramway. Although the construction of this Pakkret line, as well as the abovementioned Talat Phlu line, was considered by the general meeting of shareholders of the Siamese Tramway in February 1905, it was postponed because the government's permission had not yet been obtained (*BTWM*, 24 February 1905).

When the Siamese Tramway started operation in October 1905, Prince Narathip pressed the government for a reply regarding the propriety of the concession for the Pakkret line. The king ordered an examination to determine if the project would interfere with the concession of the Samsen line. The concession for the Samsen line stated that the government would approve tram-line construction when Samsen Road was extended northward. The question was whether it would cause competition with the Northern line of the State Railways.[37] Prince Naret asked Edward H. Strobel, the general advisor, to consider the matter, and he concluded that the government had to make a decision with the SEC regarding the concession, but denied the possibility of competition with the State Railways.[38]

Although Prince Narathip insisted that he had already cleared the concession problem with Westenholz, the SEC applied for the tramway extension to Pakkret with the same conditions as the prince's. Prince Naret asked Prince Narathip to construct a road along the tram line, but Westenholz informed them that he would support road improvement expenses of 40,000 baht per mile, then 200,000 baht for the whole road, and would change the company's registration from Danish to Thai.[39] Westenholz recognized that this was one of the reasons the SEC had failed to gain the concession when competing with Prince Narathip.

Since a bidding competition seemed likely, Prince Naret tried to mediate by asking Prince Narathip to shift his route eastward, but this failed. When the arbitration proposal was decided, the Siamese Tramway was told to transfer part of the Dusit Extension line to the SEC, while the SEC's northward extension from Bang Krabue would not be approved unless the Siamese Tramway could complete the Pakkret extension within five years.[40] It is unclear whether Westenholz agreed with this since it was advantageous to Prince Narathip.

Prince Naret made a draft of the concession, as shown in table 1.1, and there was a rumor of its announcement in the near future. But the rumor never came true. According to the newspapers, the survey and construction started, and construction materials had been delivered since mid-1906, but should have been stopped, since the concession had not yet been awarded (*BTWM*, 20 July 1906).[41] In October 1906, Prince Narathip again pressed for the concession. This was his last attempt as far as I was able to determine.[42] The main reason for the disappearance of the Pakkret Tramway plan was that the prince could not raise enough funds due to the poor returns of the Siamese Tramway. Although the road paralleling this tramway would have become the first road extended from Bangkok, such a road would not be built until the 1930s.[43]

Formation of Suburban Railways

Opening of the Paknam Railway

The Paknam Railway was the first private railway in Thailand as well as the first Thai railway. This line connected Bangkok with the southern city of Paknam and would become the shortcut to the mouth (*paknam*) of the Chaophraya River. On September 13, 1886, a concession for this railway was granted to Loftus and De Richelieu, the concessionaires of the first tramway in Bangkok, and the rail line was opened on April 11, 1893. Originally it was explained that the reason it took almost seven years to complete this small railway was the difficulty of raising funds for the construction; this led to the king's investment.[44]

However, the real reason for the delay was that they put the construction of another line before this line. Both persons applied for three railway and tramway projects at the same time—the railway between Bangkok and Ban Mai (Chachoengsao), another railway between Bangkok and Paknam, and the Bangkok tramway program with seven lines.[45] The drafts of these three projects were drawn simultaneously, and the concession for the Bangkok–Ban Mai line was granted on the same day as the Paknam line, while the one for the tramway was granted later, on May 5, 1887.[46]

Fig. 1.2. Railway Network in Suburban Bangkok, 1930

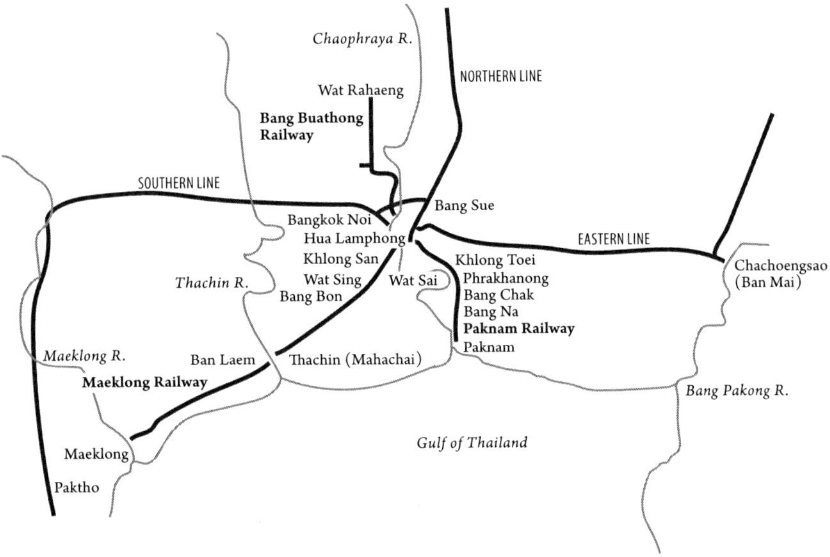

Although there was no reaction after gaining the concession, a meeting was held in September 1889 to establish a company to construct both railways that included government high officials such as Prince Thewawong and Prince Damrong, together with the original concessionaires. They decided the name of the company would be the Burapha Railway (*BT*, 21 September 1889).[47] In November, they decided to construct the Bangkok–Ban Mai line first, since their choice of standard-gauge railway would cost more than the original scheme of a meter-gauge line (see figure 1.2).[48] At this stage, the Burapha Railway made its priority the section between Bangkok and Ban Mai. The reason for converting the gauge was due to an expected increase in transport volume in the future; they did not want to repeat the mistakes made by Japan or Burma in this regard. That is, they changed to the standard-gauge rails as this line would play an important role if it could become a trunk line extending eastward to Battambang, Siemreap, and Ubon in the northeast (DCR 1890, 42–44).

Although the company announced the construction prospectus publicly in September 1890, and the sale of stocks then began, it was not easy to procure the capital of 1,360,000 baht since the government established the Railway Department (*Krom rotfai*) at the same time. The government then began to promote the construction of the state railway between Bangkok and Khorat. Therefore, Loftus and De Richelieu established another company for the Paknam line, the Paknam Railway Company, Ltd. (PRC) to try to promote construction of a line between Bangkok and Paknam (*BT*, 2 May 1891). They returned to the meter-gauge railway as in the original scheme, to the regret of Burapha Railway, and cut construction expenses by applying a style of tramway on the road that was partly constructed when the telegraph line was laid.[49] As a result, the initial capital was reduced to 400,000 baht, one third of the Burapha Railway, but still it was not until the king invested half of the funds that the procurement was finally achieved. After the success of the capital procurement, the PRC started construction in July 1893, and the first trial run was held at the Paknam side on January 14, 1893 (*BTWM*, 19 January 1929). They held an opening ceremony on April 11 with the king in attendance. Though the initial train service was limited to three trips per day, this railway became economically profitable, creating significant profit during its first year of operation. Therefore, De Richelieu tried to revive a railway plan to Ban Mai by reapplying for a new concession, as the original one had expired. After a competition with another applicant for the same route, the government decided to construct it as a state railway.[50] There were also several applications for the extension of the Paknam line, but none was approved.

Opening of the Thachin and Maeklong Railways

Stimulated by the success of the PRC, another railway project emerged in October 1896 for the western side of Bangkok, running between Bangkok and Krokkrak (Thachin). The applicant was L. M. Xavier, the Portuguese vice consul, and others. Krokkrak[51] lies on the eastern bank of the Thachin River and was famous for its fishing port. The king expressed his negative opinion about this application, since there were many applications for railway construction submitted to the government. Both favorable and unfavorable opinions were voiced at the ministers' meeting.[52]

This plan, together with other applications, was examined at the ministers' meeting in June 1899. It was decided that the government would order the applicants to report the feasibility of their raising capital to ensure that it did not interfere with the government's state railway–oriented policy (Kakizaki 2000, 129). Since Xavier reported that they could procure enough capital, the government finally granted their concession on May 17, 1901.[53] However, the conditions of the concession became stricter than those of the PRC due to the government's higher level of caution toward private railways in the time since the PRC had gained its concession. Unlike before, the draft of the concession was drawn up by the Railway Department, which had not yet been established when the PRC first gained its concession, and the government modified some clauses.

After being granted the concession, Xavier and others established the Thachin Railway Company at the end of 1902 and started construction on the Krokkak line (*BTWM*, 12 February 1903). This 33-kilometer line was one and a half times longer than the Paknam line, and the embankment for tracks had to be constructed all along the way as there was no road available to lay tracks. The PRC had not had to purchase right-of-way by using the existing roadside, even in the Bangkok urban area, but the Thachin Railway had to purchase it along the complete line, which made the negotiation time considerably longer. At first the company aimed to open in November 1904, but it had to postpone the opening due to the delay in land acquisition (*BTWM*, 29 August 1904). Finally, the opening ceremony was held on January 4, 1905, and many royals were invited to see the emergence of another suburban railway in Bangkok (*BTWM*, 4 January 1905). The initial capital of the company was 1 million baht, while the construction expenses were as high as 1.1 million baht, which made it much more expensive than the PRC.[54] The train made three trips per day, the same as the PRC.

During the construction of the Thachin Railway, a scheme to extend it as the Thachin–Maeklong line had emerged. This line, which would connect Thachin with Maeklong, was applied for by Phraya Waiyayutthiwiset in August 1904.[55] The starting point at Thachin was on the western side of the Thachin River so that ferry service would connect with the Thachin Railway terminus. At that time, the government's policy of state railway construction became stricter so that the approval for private railways was now restricted to the feeder light railway or rural tramway (Kakizaki 2000, 130–31). However, as this line was regarded as the extension of an existing line and not a trunk line, the government did not find any problems with it. As for the issue that this company might merge with the Thachin Railway Company since its applicants were board members of that company, the king was unconcerned, so the application was approved at the ministers' meeting in April 1905.[56]

The concession was granted on June 10, 1905, to the Maeklong Railway Company and construction started in the same year.[57] No road was available for the rail bed, but the construction proceeded smoothly since no land acquisition was necessary within the city limits. On July 12, 1907, the 34-kilometer line from Ban Laem (the west bank of the Thachin) to Maeklong was opened for traffic (*BTWM*, 13 March 1908). Daily train service consisted of two trips, which were connected with the Thachin line's trains by ferry. Meanwhile, the Thachin Railway Company and the old Maeklong Railway Company were merged into the new Maeklong Railway Company (MRC) on the same day. Although the merger had been anticipated by the government, it was approved ex post facto since the application for the merger was submitted after the actual amalgamation took place.[58] Contrary to the case of the SEC, their concessions were not unified. Therefore, the termination date of their two concessions remained different, which would become a problem later.

Operations after Opening

Although both the PRC and the MRC had limited train service and functioned as inter-city railways, their results were favorable. The construction prospectus for the PRC projected daily passenger demand at 180 persons one-way, and estimated that it could achieve a 10 percent annual dividend rate.[59] The third-class fare between Bangkok (Hua Lamphong) and Paknam seems to have been 0.5 baht, and the average daily receipts from passenger traffic during the first three months of operation were about 237 baht, so it can be estimated that the daily number of passengers was 474 persons, or seventy-nine passengers per train (*BT*, 19 August 1893).[60] In fact, the PRC achieved an annual dividend rate of 7–9 percent during the 1890s and more than 10 percent from 1901 onward, as shown in table 1.5.

Table 1.5. Financial Situation of Suburban Railway Companies, 1893–1910

Year	Net Profit (THB)		Dividend Rate (%)	
	Paknam	Maeklong	Paknam	Maeklong
1893	23,144		4.50	
1894	29,261		11.25	
1895	32,953		8.50	
1896	N.A.		9.00	
1897	N.A.		8.00	
1898	34,224		7.50	
1899	40,172		8.00	
1900	N.A.		9.00	
1901	43,911		10.00	
1902	47,397		11.00	
1903	64,917		13.00	
1904	57,950		13.00	
1905	59,488	38,671	13.00	3.50
1906	N.A.	77,978	14.00	5.50
1907	76,797	116,292	14.00	7.75
1908	56,650	123,233	8.00	5.00
1909	83,429	127,596	22.00	5.00
1910	88,065	137,254	15.00	5.00

Note: Figures for the Maeklong Railway up to mid-1907 are for the Thachin Railways.
Sources: *BT* 1893–97 (selected issues); *BTWM* 1898–1911 (selected issues).

The PRC also expected some demand for freight transport. As Paknam was situated at the mouth of the Chaophraya River and many fishing boats to Bangkok passed by there, they expected that fishery transport to Bangkok would be shifted to railway. According to the prospectus, they expected that 177 tons of fish would be shipped to Bangkok daily by railway; the revenue from this would be the same as the passenger revenue, assuming that the tariff of daily fish transport was one baht per ton.[61] However, the demand for freight transport was so low that the main source of income was the passenger transport. In the first half of 1895, the receipts from freight transport were only 870 baht against 26,479 baht for passenger transport (*BT*, 20 February 1896). Though the share of freight transport increased slightly later on, it did not exceed 10 percent of the total gross receipts; for example, the first half of 1922 showed that passenger receipts and freight receipts were 127,397 baht and 13,452 baht respectively.[62]

The situation of the MRC was basically the same. Assuming that the third-class fare between Bangkok (Khlong San) and Thachin was 0.75 baht, as this line was 1.5 times longer than the Paknam line, the daily number of passengers during its first year of operation can be calculated at around 300, based on the annual receipts from passenger traffic of 82,338 baht, or 225 baht per day.[63] According to the construction prospectus, the gross income was estimated to be double that of the Paknam line, but the actual number of passengers was lower than the Paknam line.[64] Table 1.6 shows that the gross receipts of the PRC and the MRC around 1910 were about 150,000 baht and 300,000 baht respectively, which means that the expectation on the prospectus had been finally achieved after the extension to Maeklong. Nevertheless, the profitability of the MRC was far lower than the PRC, as its dividend rate was only 5 percent after opening, as shown in table 1.5.

However, the importance of freight transport on the MRC was greater. Thachin was the largest fishing port around Bangkok and many fish were transported to Bangkok via canals. Therefore, the demand for fish transport here was far higher than for the PRC. In the first year of operation in 1905, the revenue from freight transport was 26,867 baht, about one-third of the passenger transport receipts, and in 1921, the income from freight transport of 95,504 baht accounted for about 40 percent of the passenger transport income of 194,799 baht.[65] The volume of fish transported differed according to the season, with the high period being the dry season, between November and April.[66]

Both railways enjoyed favorable results from their operations and their main source of revenue was passenger transport, though the MRC relied more on freight transport. Therefore, when the time came when they could not expect further development of inter-city passenger transport, they began to seek ways to increase the number of short-distance passengers by participating in intra-urban transport.

Table 1.6. Gross Receipts of Suburban Railways, 1893–1910 (THB)

Year	Paknam	Maeklong
1893	45,128	
1894	58,616	
1895	N.A.	
1896	N.A.	
1897	N.A.	
1898	81,890	
1899	100,777	
1900	N.A.	
1901	106,512	
1902	116,563	
1903	136,028	
1904	141,014	
1905	142,399	109,739
1906	N.A.	150,221
1907	173,886	224,169
1908	174,145	311,935
1909	169,562	314,308
1910	165,809	310,761

NOTE: Figures for the Maeklong Railway until mid-1907 are for the Thachin Railways.
SOURCES: Same as table 1.5.

Merger of the Tramway Business by a Foreign Company

Purchase of the Siamese Tramway

The SEC monopolized the tramway business in Bangkok until the emergence of the Siamese Tramway Company of Prince Narathip, which brought competition. The most affected line was the Samsen line whose route was proximate to the new Siamese Tramway lines. The gross receipts of the Samsen line fell after the opening of the Siamese Tramway, as table 1.3 shows. Westenholz estimated in the beginning of 1906 that the annual gross revenue of the Samsen line would decrease by about 30,000 to 50,000 baht.[67] Although the actual reduction was not that serious, the favorable situation of the SEC's operation was affected by the competition with the Siamese Tramway.

Westenholz tried to escape fruitless competition by interrupting the creation of the Siamese Tramway Company, but he then came to consider the future purchase of the Siamese Tramway after he realized that the creation of the new company would be unavoidable. At the general meeting of the SEC shareholders in February 1904, he expressed his opinion that the right of track-laying would be transferred to the company if the Siamese Tramway failed to procure enough capital. Even if it could achieve the opening of the new lines, it would be easy to find a cooperative situation if it went well, or he would be able to purchase their business if the business deteriorated. He estimated that 1908 would be good timing to do so, when the SEC would be able to issue more debentures (*BTWM*, 1 March 1904).

Westenholz's estimate turned out to be prescient. The outcome of the Siamese Tramway was not positive, and Prince Narathip fell into a difficult situation. As shown in table 1.3, though the gross revenue of the Siamese Tramway reached 490,000 baht in 1906, it decreased to 410,000 baht the next year. The situation in 1909, after changing the fiscal year from April–March to January–December, was almost the same. These losses were partly due to the low profitability of the lines, as their gross receipts per kilometer in 1907 were only 22,064 baht, compared to the Bang Kholaem line at 63,115 baht and the Samsen line at 37,578 baht. Furthermore, since the Siamese Tramway had to pay high track rent to the government, its net profit fell quite low to only 20,952 baht in 1906 (*BTWM*, 15 January 1908; *BTWM*, 6 May 1908).[68] Therefore, the dividend rate of the Siamese Tramway was also low, as shown in table 1.4. It maintained a 2 percent dividend rate per half year until the first half of 1907, then ceased paying dividends after that.

The deterioration of profitability for the Siamese Tramway finally forced Prince Narathip to sell off part of his shares. In August 1907, the prince asked the government to approve the disposal of 3,400 shares to W. T. Jacobsen, the vice manager of the SEC and the only person who offered to purchase them, at the rate of 170 baht per share.[69] At the next ministers' meeting, his application was regarded as the takeover of the Siamese Tramway by the SEC. It was finally confirmed that the government would approve the disposal of the shares, but the merger of the two tramway companies would not be accepted unless the SEC would change its nationality to Thai registry.[70] By this disposal, the SEC gained more than half of the 6,250 shares of the Siamese Tramway, so that the former could acquire the management rights of the latter.[71] Prince Damrong had once predicted the possibility of the bankruptcy of the Siamese Tramway or the purchase by Westenholz, and his prediction eventually came true.[72]

After the merger, the SEC began to reorganize the management of the Siamese Tramway. Westenholz, who became the general manager of the Siamese Tramway, tried to reduce expenditures by buying power from the power plant of the SEC and amalgamating the function of head office. He also raised the fares for the Dusit line and the Samsen line to a normal level, since they had previously been reduced by the heavy competition (*BTWM*, 15 January 1908; *BTWM*, 22 August 1907). However, the Siamese Tramway suffered for a certain period due to an economic depression and the abandonment of part of the Dusit Extension line in 1910.[73] As for the nationality of the SEC, Westenholz tried to persuade shareholders in Denmark to change to Thai registry, but they rejected his request.[74] Therefore, the Siamese Tramway itself continued and rights to its management were taken over by the SEC.

Expansion of Tramway Networks

After the SEC took control of the Siamese Tramway as its subsidiary, it continued to expand tramway networks to compensate for the loss of other interests in the power distribution business. Although the SEC had the right to distribute power in all areas of Bangkok, the government began to plan construction of its own power plant in 1906. Since the demand for electricity in the newly developing Dusit Palace and Dusit Garden was increasing, the government planned to construct their new plant at Dusit. The SEC expressed its disagreement over the plan, however, since the palace was also a big customer for the company.[75] According to the company, it could afford to continue its business owing to the large consumption of the palace, but this loss would reduce its annual revenue by 30,000 to 40,000 baht. So Westenholz proposed that the government should approve the extension of two tramways if he would return the right of power distribution in the area north of the Bang Lamphu and Mahanak Canals.[76]

The government then asked the company to separate the return of its power distribution right and the extension of the tramways, which was agreed by the company. It was decided in May 1906 that the SEC would return its right of power distribution in the designated area six months after the government's notice if it would construct its own power plant (*BTWM*, 28 February 1907). In 1907 the company gained approval for the extension of tramways and the addition of passing places for tram cars arriving from different directions. The approval included the construction of piers and tramways at Ratchawong and Atsadang roads, the construction of a pier at Bang Kholaem, the extension of a four-hundred-meter tram line at Hua Lamphong, and the addition of passing places on the Bang Kholaem line and Samsen line (*BTWM*, 2 September 1907).

Both tramways on Ratchawong and Atsadang roads were short branch lines to connect the existing lines with the piers at the end. The extension at Hua Lamphong had been applied for in 1905, and this involved extending the Samsen line eastward from the present terminus at the western bank of the Padung Krungkasem Canal to the newly planned shed via the Hua Lamphong station of the PRC.[77] The two branches on Ratchawong and Atsadang roads were opened in 1907, and the Hua Lamphong extension was completed in October 1910.

However, the SEC had new burdens apart from the return of the right to distribute electrical power. They included the installation of water sprinkling along all tram-line-laid roads and fire protection within three hundred feet of its tramways. As not all roads were yet paved, water sprinkling was needed to avoid dust, mostly caused by the increasing numbers of rickshaws and carriages. As for fire protection, the concession of the Bang Kholaem line had already stipulated that the company had to help convey the fire brigade. Since the company had its own fire brigade for use at its power plant, it had to expand its service to general fire-fighting along its tramways. The water sprinkling and fire protection were originally proposed by the company in exchange for the reduction of track rent when competing with Prince Narathip over the concession of the City Wall line and were stipulated for the first time in the concession granted in 1907 (*BTWM*, 2 July 1903). In return, the track rent for the extension lines was reduced to 3,000 baht per mile, which was lower than the Siamese Tramway.

The reason for constructing branch lines to the piers was the SEC's endeavor to increase the number of passengers on trams by connecting with navigation on the Chaophraya River and canals. In 1906 Westenholz established the Menam Motor Boat Company and opened navigation lines connecting with the SEC's tramways (Wright and Breakspear 1994, 192). It opened lines to Pakkret from Bang Krabue, the northern terminus of the Samsen line, and to Paklat (Phrapradaeng) from Bang Kholaem, the southern terminus of the Bang Kholaem line.[78] Then, in April 1909, it purchased another line on the Bangkok Yai Canal from the Transport Company "Motor", Limited and opened new lines to Talat Phlu from the termini of the Ratchawong and Atsadang Branches (*BTWM*, 29 April 1909).[79] These navigation lines played the role of feeders for the tramways.

Furthermore, Westenholz applied for a new tramway construction permit connecting with a feeder navigation line. In August 1906, he asked Prince Naret for the approval of tramway construction along the Paklat Canal.[80] This was a 1.9-kilometer tramway between the northern mouth of the Paklat Canal and Phrapradaeng, needed to improve traffic between Bangkok and Phrapradaeng by connecting with the navigation line from Bang Kholaem.[81] As he proposed to pay 8,000 baht for road improvement and an annual track rent of 600 to 1,000 baht, the government decided to grant a concession to the Thai-registered Menam Motor Boat Company.[82] The concession was announced in May 1907, construction work started the following month, and the line opened to traffic on May 16, 1908.[83] This was the first introduction of the gasoline-powered motor tramcar, as well as the first tramway outside Bangkok.[84]

Reinforcement of Transport Capacity

As the number of passengers increased, it became necessary to increase transport capacity on the existing lines. As all tramways in Bangkok were single-track lines, the addition of passing places, where tramcars arriving from different directions could cross, was indispensable to increase trips. At the Bang Kholaem line, the interval of trams was fifteen minutes at first, and then additional passing places were constructed in 1898 to improve the interval to seven and a half minutes (*BTWM*, 28 July 1898). Then, as passengers continued to increase, the SEC began to use double-car traffic on part of the Bang Kholaem line by running two tramcars continuously (*BTWM*, 1 August 1905). Although initially double-car traffic was adopted for every other trip, it was easy to see that transport capacity would double if all trips became double-car.

However, L. R. de La Mahotière, the civil engineer of the Local Sanitary Department (*Krom sukhaphiban*) and a supervisor of tramways, opposed double-car traffic, saying it was dangerous for carriages and people on the roads. He recommended the use of trailers connected to motor trams for the increase of transport capacity.[85] Through trial and error, however, it was found that the trailer system had a problem in terms of brakes, so Westenholz then requested approval for double-car traffic or the addition of passing places.[86] Therefore, the continuation of double-car traffic was approved at the ministers' meeting in February 1906.[87]

As La Mahotière had twice warned Prince Naret to stop double-car traffic, the government then changed its mind and approved an increase in the number of passing places from thirty to thirty-eight.[88] This was approved along with the concession for the Ratchawong and Atsadang extensions. The SEC then added passing places that would suspend double-car traffic in principle. Nevertheless, the double-car for beef transport from Bang Kholaem was permitted as an exception and the company also continued double-car traffic when exiting and entering the shed.[89] The government, however, ordered the company to abolish all double-car traffic after it learned that the company had used double-car traffic on the Chinese New Year holidays in February 1908 to cope with heavy demand.[90]

Westenholz then insisted that the government show evidence to warrant banning double-car traffic since there was no condition prohibiting it in the concession.[91] He asserted that the number of double-car trams was limited to only six cars a day and there had been no serious problems regarding double-car traffic on crowded roads during those twenty months. He vowed to fight to reconfirm the right given by the concession if the government continued to ban double-car traffic (*BTWM*, 1 March 1908). He appealed to Prince Damrong, his old friend, stating that the SEC was experiencing a difficult period by losing the rights to power distribution and hardships from the new burdens of providing water sprinkling and fire protection. Although most felt that the company had been enjoying prosperity due to the favorable assistance of the government, he warned that it would be difficult to do new business with the government if its regulation of the company would be further strengthened.[92]

Eventually, Westenholz escaped a confrontation with the government by legal means and coped with the situation by introducing a trailer system. Although it is unknown whether there was any change as a result of the trial, the SEC introduced the trailer again in September 1908, and these were eventually increased to every other trip, just as with the double-car system (*BTWM*, 2 September 1908). This brought an end to the confrontation with La Mahotière, and an increase in transport capacity was also achieved. The tramway traffic of two cars, one motor car, and one trailer on a single track became the fundamental system for Bangkok tramways until its elimination.

Government Tramway Policy

Rise of Requests for Profit Allotment

When the two types of rail transport, tramways and suburban railways, emerged in Bangkok after the end of the nineteenth century, the former was virtually the only means of urban transport, as the latter was merely for inter-urban use. Though tramways were public and a means of mass transport, when they emerged in Bangkok for the first time, the government's initial recognition of them was insufficient. The concession conditions were quite loose at first, and there was almost no supervisory system to monitor them, but the government changed its loose attitude as the tramway business proved economically viable and the number of passengers increased. The policies changed toward strengthening regulation and increasing profit allotment.

The increase of the profit allotment appeared as the levy of track rent and its increases, as shown in table 1.1. Since the concession of the Bang Kholaem line did not include track rent so that the company could lay tracks on roads rent-free, the concession for the Samsen line introduced a profit allotment system by levying track rent at 2.5 to 4 percent of the annual gross revenue. Then track rent changed to a fixed system with the concession of the Siamese Tramway; the rent was as high as 5,000 baht per mile at its maximum and later reduced to 3,000 baht for the Atsadang and Ratchawong lines.

Most likely the jump in track rent was due to the bidding competition between the SEC and Siamese Tramway, or between Westenholz and Prince Narathip, as well as due to the government's own intention. Though at first Westenholz offered only 1,000 baht per mile as track rent, it rose to 5,000 baht, thus five times as much. Calculating from table 1.3, the track rent for the Samsen line in 1907 was about 8,000 baht, corresponding to 1,480 baht per mile. This means that track rent rose more than three times within a few years, and the government could gain more profit than expected. The Siamese Tramway had to pay 50,000 baht annually to the government for track rent and registration fees for trams; this was equivalent to paying an 8 percent dividend of the total capital of the company.[93] As the dividend to original shareholders was only about 4 percent, the profit allotted to the government was a burden for the management.

This bidding competition was the result of the competition principle, assuming that the government would grant a concession to the more advantageous side, which was quite similar to the bid process for a tax farming system in the past. However, as the track rent became too high, Prince Narathip, who won the competition, fell into hardship and was eventually rescued by Westenholz. Through this situation, the SEC came to monopolize the tramway business once more, so it became more difficult for the government to request further profit allotments on the basis of the competition principle. Nevertheless, it still requested high track rents, though track rent was reduced to 3,000 baht per mile, since the SEC had to bear the cost of water sprinkling and fire protection along its line. Therefore, from the economic viewpoint, the profit from the tramway business in Bangkok could not be expected to compare with its initial stage, which can be deduced from the huge differences in the dividend rates between the pioneer, Bangkok Tramway, and the SEC and the latecomer, the Siamese Tramway (table 1.4).

Strengthening of Regulation

At first there was little government supervision of tramways, but a regulatory system was gradually established and strengthened when the government came to recognize the economic importance of the tramway business. The conditions of concessions in table 1.1 suggest that the deadlines for starting and completing construction were reduced to within six months and eighteen to thirty months respectively. This was quite different from the first concession, which fixed them at within three years and five years respectively. As for the purchase of a tramway business by the government, the first concession regulated that it could purchase the business after twenty years of the original grant, but later reduced that to twelve years in principle. The increase of track rent was also an example of restrictive regulation, as was the requirement of bridge-building when laying new tramways. The conditions of concessions for private railways were also strengthened, as will be mentioned later.

The registration of trams was also introduced so that they had to pay an annual registration fee to the government. The first concession for the Bang Kholaem line regulated that trams would be levied fees as much as two times that for ordinary carriages, which began when the Hackney Law was enforced in June 1905.[94] The tramway companies had another burden as the registration fee for trams was fixed at twenty-four baht, twice as much as the first category and the highest fee for carriages.[95] After the trailer system was introduced in 1908, Westenholz asked the Ministry of Local Government to reduce the registration fee for trailers because they would not be used year-round. The ministry rejected his request but instead agreed to change the number of trams registered in each half-year period.[96]

Regulation of the tramway operations was also strengthened by foreign engineers. Though the first concession required that the concessionaire submit drawings for tramway construction to the government's engineer to gain permission, it was unclear who was in charge of this task. Then regulations relating to technical issues attracted interest, as there was an article in the newspaper in 1899 reporting that C. Allegri, the civil engineer at the Public Works Department (*Krom yothathikan*) and supervisor of tramways, had ordered maintenance on some parts of the Bang Kholaem line (*BTWM*, 13 May 1899). Later, La Mahotière, who frequently intervened in the maintenance and operation of tramways, played an important role in regulation. As far I can gather, he began to participate in tramway regulation in 1905, and Prince Naret came to order him to examine applications whenever the tramway companies applied for an extension of lines or for the addition of passing places.

No supervisory system existed for private railways at the beginning, but after the Railway Department was established in 1890 to construct state railways, it became the supervisor for private railways. As most of the tramways were laid on existing public roads, their regulation was left to the Local Sanitary Department within the Ministry of Local Government, which supervised public roads. Since La Mahotière's job was to extend to all civil engineering works within Bangkok, he was not a specialist on tramways, so he sometimes became involved in confrontations with tramway companies, such as in the case of double-car traffic. Nevertheless, the government had to rely on a foreign advisor to reflect the government's tramway policy on technical matters. The strengthening of regulation, as well as the profit allotment, reduced the profitable performance of the tramway businesses.

Tramway Business as Economic Activity

Although the government came to request profit allotments and strengthened the regulation of the tramway business, it regarded the tramway business as one of many private economic activities. That is, the government had no intention of itself participating in the tramway business but only intended to strengthen its regulation. This was fundamentally different from the case of the railway, where the government established the Railway Department to construct state railways and adopted a state-railway-oriented policy that eventually put an end to private railways.[97]

The government adopted a state railway policy because it saw an invasion of its sovereignty through the foreign acquisition of interests in railways. Especially because the reign of King Rama V was an era of foreign imperialism, it was quite worrisome that the unofficial railway imperialism might harm Thailand's independence.[98] Therefore, only local short-distance private railways such as the Paknam and Maeklong Railways gained approval at that time, and all trunk lines connecting Bangkok with the provinces were constructed as state railways.

However, the government never adopted a state-oriented policy toward tramways in Bangkok. The first Bang Kholaem line might have been recognized as a local railway similar to the PRC, but the government continued to grant concessions to private companies for trams.[99] The government did not fear that tramways would threaten its independence, since their rights were limited locally, even though foreign capital was involved. Private railway plans were apt to accompany a request for rights of land use or forest or mineral exploitation, or the government's guarantee of an interest rate it disapproved, while the tramway concessions did not involve such disadvantageous conditions but would bring profit in the form of track rent.[100]

There was also no possibility of adopting a nationalization policy from the point of public transport. The average daily number of people passing through Charoen Krung Road in front of Bank Lane (near Bang Rak) in October 1900 was 9,081, among whom the number of tram passengers was 2,742, far fewer than the number of pedestrians (4,266) but more than rickshaw (1,323) and carriage passengers (427) (*BTWM*, 4 January 1901). As the share of tram passengers increased more in suburban areas, the importance of tramways as a means of mass transport should have been obvious. Nevertheless, the government worried about the inconvenience of other cars passing along roads more than the public or private nature of tramways. Even if trams were the "golden goose" bringing profit to the government, almost no recognition was given to them as a means of public mass transport.

Therefore, the government did not participate in the tramway business and allowed private operation, even if foreign capital was involved, and rather relied upon the economic profit it created. It is true that the operation of a Thai company was preferable, such as the Siamese Tramway of Prince Narathip. But the government finally nipped this in the bud by its excessive requests for profit-sharing. The tramway business at that time was regarded as one of the many economic activities of foreigners, rather than a means of mass transport with high public responsibility.

2

Emergence of Competition, 1910s–1930s

Revival and Expansion of Tramways

Recovery of Tramway Companies

The competition between the SEC (Siam Electric Company) and the Siamese Tramway over the acquisition of concessions in the 1900s resulted in high expenditures for track rent, which reduced the profitability of the tramway businesses. Although the competition between companies ceased after the purchase of the Siamese Tramway, the profit allocation and strengthening of regulation continued. The future of the SEC did not look hopeful, as it could not be predicted that there would be a rapid increase in passengers after the opening of the Siamese Tramway, and the agreement on relinquishing power distribution rights was also a negative factor. In fact, the gross revenues from the tramway in 1910 were the lowest recorded since 1904 (*BTWM*, 25 February 1911), and the number of passengers also dropped in 1912 due to the poor harvest of the previous year, which caused the sluggish economic situation to continue. Furthermore, in 1911 the Local Sanitary Department began construction of a new power plant by order of King Rama VI, so the SEC would have to relinquish its power distribution rights in the near future.[1]

A newspaper reported in September 1912 that Belgian financers were contributing to the SEC (*BTWM*, 2 September 1912). A Belgian syndicate had succeeded in negotiating the purchase of ten thousand shares of the SEC. Since at that time the company had only issued twenty-five thousand shares, if the Belgian syndicate procured a majority of shares, they would have the advantage and even be able to change the company's registry to Belgian nationality. The Belgian group sent a specialist from a tramway company in Brussels to investigate the situation of tramways in Bangkok. According to this specialist, the main problem with Bangkok's tramways was their single-track system, so the first task to be accomplished after acquiring managerial control was to measure for double-tracking (*BTWM*, 11 October 1912).

The participation of Belgian financers was due to Westenholz's worry about the SEC's future. The Belgians were able to become the majority shareholders since they were able to negotiate directly with Westenholz. He gave two reasons why he was willing to sell his shares: the unfeasible prospects for the company's future and the government's construction of a power plant (*BTWM*, 5 December 1912). He was particularly anxious about the new power plant, fearing that the government might not honor their agreement of not presenting any competition with his company's business, since the agreement was only an oral promise. Apparently his distrust toward the government had reached its peak.

Eventually Westenholz's sold his shares, and the Belgians gained a majority of shares in 1913 (*BTWM*, 1 March 1913). Although there was no major change in management, the double-tracking plan prioritized by the Belgians never materialized. Nevertheless, the gross revenue from the tramway business began to rise in 1913. The gross profits rose from 405,880 baht in 1913 to 446,494 baht in 1915 (*BTWM*, 18 March 1916). The loss of the right to distribute electrical power due to the new power plant did not seriously affect the company. As the net profit of the SEC shows (table 2.1), profits increased steadily after 1912 when they reached a low of 638,008 baht, and did not drop when the government's new power plant started operations in 1914. As a result of the favorable growth in demand for electricity and the company's efforts to reduce expenses through installing new equipment for the plant, the company did not suffer as seriously as Westenholz had feared, but rather improved quite rapidly.

On the other hand, it was the Siamese Tramway that fell into a severe depression. Its income had been dropping since 1906, when it had reached a peak of 491,760 baht and then slowly decreased to 306,333 baht in 1912, almost 60 percent of its maximum income (*BTWM*, 22 March 1913). As a result, its net profit also dropped dramatically to only

3,176 baht in 1912. The company could not allocate dividends from 1908 onward, except in 1911 when a 3 percent dividend was declared.[2]

One of the reasons for this deterioration was the abolishment of part of the Dusit Extension line in 1910. The government requested the removal of part of the line in order to expand the Dusit Garden and construct a new wall, so that the section north of Baiphon (Uthong Nai) Road would be abandoned. Instead the company constructed a substitute route to the Samsen line via Baiphon Road, which resulted in a fall in the number of passengers due to the loss of the previous route.

Table 2.1. Net Profit of Tramway Companies, 1911–1941 (THB)

Year	Siam Electricity	Siamese Tramway
1911	824,954	28,376
1912	638,008	3,176
1913	822,588	11,643
1914	952,291	35,858
1915	1,186,441	48,395
1916	1,249,785	80,893
1917	1,581,401	89,920
1918	1,459,537	114,187
1919	1,720,771	182,668
1920	1,806,856	183,576
1921	2,109,373	206,351
1922	2,097,744	201,057
1923	2,144,363	174,448
1924	2,125,156	163,882
1925	2,274,244	161,282
1926	2,449,380	178,532

Year	Siam Electric
1927	2,832,768
1928	2,903,170
1929	2,743,901
1930	2,666,901
1931	2,323,062
1932	1,968,190
1933	1,702,359
1934	1,580,070
1935	1,509,253
1936	1,358,511
1937	1,424,920
1938	1,483,663
1939	1,388,835
1940	1,739,833
1941	1,934,395

NOTE: Siam Electricity Company changed its name to Siam Electric Company in 1927.

SOURCES: NA Ro. 7 Pho. 12. 1/7; *BTWM* 1912–41; *BT* 1942 (selected issues).

Furthermore, the fundamental problem still was the high track rent to be paid to the government. The annual track rent of the Siamese Tramway was fixed at 5,000 baht per mile on existing roads and 1,200 baht per mile on newly constructed roads in the Dusit area. This amount was as high as 46,906.8 baht in 1913.[3] As the SEC enjoyed a cheaper track rent of 3,000 baht per mile for the new line, which was approved in 1907, the Siamese Tramway's track rent was comparatively high. Therefore, as the high track rent had to be subtracted from the decreasing gross receipts every year, its net profit was very low.

The company eventually applied to the government for a lower track rent. In 1913, Prince Narathip asked the king to change the track rent from the fixed rate of 5,000 baht per mile to a proportional rate of 5–7.5 percent of its gross receipts.[4] The reasons he gave were a decrease in demand due to the poor harvest and the competition with rickshaws. He insisted that the proportional rate was common in Europe. If approved, the track rent in 1906, when the company's gross receipts was the highest, would have been 24,588 baht at the rate of 5 percent and 36,882 baht at the 7.5 percent rate, which would be significantly lower than the fixed rent.

In April 1914, the Siamese Tramway was able to change its track rent to 7.5 percent of its gross receipts, as agreed by King Rama VI (*BTWM*, 17 February 1920). In exchange, the company had to accept some minor conditions, such as repairing bridges that its tram lines crossed, but the reduction of track rent greatly contributed to the improvement of its income. As table 2.1 shows, the net profit of the company increased rapidly after 1914, reaching 100,000 baht in 1918, and 200,000 baht in 1921. The dividend rate also increased dramatically (refer to table 2.2), reaching 20 percent in 1919 plus a bonus. The increase of passengers also contributed to the improvement of operations, apart from the reduction of track rent, so that the gross receipts that had dropped to about 300,000 baht in 1912 revived to 556,707 baht in 1919.[5] The increase in gross receipts also brought an increase in the track rent paid to the government, reaching 41,553 baht in 1919, which was about 5,000 baht less than the fixed rate (ibid.).

Expansion of Tramway Networks

After the opening of the Samsen line's extension between Hua Lamphong and Saphan Lueang, the expansion of tramway networks in Bangkok was suspended for a while. However, the expansion of the Bangkok urban area had been continuing apace. With the exception of the Bang Kholaem and Samsen lines that were laid beyond the urban boundaries toward the south and north respectively, the tramway networks were limited to the urban area. In 1910, the range of Bangkok's inner district (*amphoe chan nai*) was limited as far as the Samsen Canal in the north, the Northern line and Maenam branch line in the east, the Paknam Railway, Sathon Road and Bang Kholaem in the south, and the Chaophraya River and the area around Talat Phlu in the west. Dusit in the north and Pathumwan (Sa Pathum) in the east were the areas experiencing the most development.

Table 2.2. Dividend Rates for Tramway Companies, 1911–1941 (%)

Year	Siam Electricity	Siamese Tramway	Year	Siam Electric
1911	12.00+B8.5	3.00	1927	10.00
1912	12.00+B6	0.00	1928	10.00
1913	12.00+B11	0.00	1929	9.00
1914	12.00+B13	3.50	1930	9.00
1915	12.00+B17	5.00	1931	7.50
1916	12.00+B19	9.00	1932	7.00
1917	15.00+B5	10.00	1933	6.00
1918	10.00+B6	14.00	1934	5.50
1919	9.00+B8	20.00	1935	B5.50
1920	12.00+B11	24.00	1936	B5.25
1921	15.00+B10	25.00	1937	B5.00
1922	15.00	25.00	1938	B5.00
1923	15.00+B12	24.00	1939	B5.50
1924	15.00+B12	23.00	1940	B6.00
1925	15.00+B12	21.00	1941	B4.50
1926	15.00+B12	21.00		

Note 1: The dividend rate for the Siamese Tramway includes bonuses.
Note 2: Since the bonus for pound-based shares of Siam Electricity was paid in baht, it is shown in real numbers. Dividends were paid in baht since 1935.
Note 3: The bonus amount for Siam Electicity in 1922 is not known.
Sources: Same as table 2.1.

Table 2.3 shows the comparison of the populations living within the inner districts of Bangkok in 1912 and 1930. The population in 1912 was concentrated in the districts within the old city or within three canals, so that the population beyond the three canal districts of Bang Rak, Dusit, Pathumwan, and Ban Thawai was 58,266 persons, or 30 percent of the total population of Phra Nakhon.[6] Among these outer districts, Bang Rak and Ban Thawai had been developing their urban areas to some extent due to the existence of Charoen Krung Road with the Bang Kholaem tram line, but the other two districts were still new frontiers.

Table 2.3. Population Growth in Bangkok, 1912–1930

Province	District	1912	1930	Increase (%)
Phra Nakhon	Phra Nakhon	55,098	80,834	47
	Samphanthawong	38,996	67,669	74
	Bang Rak	20,414	59,712	193
	Pom Prap	29,847	58,454	96
	Nangloeng	13,557	28,692	112
	Dusit	10,703	33,004	208
	Pathumwan	10,773	46,206	329
	Ban Thawai	16,376	44,639	173
	Total	195,764	419,210	114
Thonburi	Bangkok Noi	13,328	20,647	55
	Bangkok Yai	9,910	13,542	37
	Bang Phlat	8,147	15,128	86
	Bang Yiruea	3,881	15,776	306
	Khlong San	23,520	24,221	3
	Bukkhalo	5,981	10,270	72
	Total	64,767	99,584	54
Grand Total		260,531	518,794	99

NOTE 1: The range of districts is based on the situation in 1930, and only inner districts (eight in Phra Nakhon and six in Thonburi) are included.
NOTE 2: In 1912, there were 104,961 more persons living on boats whose actual addresses were not known.
SOURCES: NA Ro. 6 No. 27/3; Porphant (1994, 335).

The urban area of Bangkok expanded after 1910, especially toward the north and east. As a result, the population of these four districts increased to 183,561 persons, representing 44 percent of Phra Nakhon province. The Pathumwan area in Phra Nakhon province, east of the old city, had the highest rise in population, followed by Dusit in the north, Bang Rak along Charoen Krung Road, and Ban Thawai in the south. There was also contributing population growth in Thonburi and Bang Yiruea, where the Talat Phlu locale had the highest increase.

Furthermore, such districts as Bang Sue and Phrakhanong, which were regarded as the outer districts (*amphoe chan nok*), also experienced high population growth, with populations in 1930 of 35,838 and 27,846 respectively (Porphant 1994, 335).[7] Although most areas in these districts were paddy fields, urban areas were developing along Samsen and Rama V Road in Bang Sue, and along the Paknam Railway in Phrakhanong. In Bang Sue, a new labor market was formed when Siam Cement Company built its cement factory and started operations. Bangkok's urban area was steadily expanding beyond the range of its inner districts.

To cope with such expansion of urban areas, the SEC and Siamese Tramway applied for the construction of new lines in 1925. At first, the SEC applied for an extension of the Samsen line from Saphan Lueang to Witthayu, and the Siamese Tramway applied for three lines: Bang Rak to Pratunam, Yotse to Ratchaprasong, and Dusit to Bang Sue station.[8] Among them, the extension of the Samsen line and the first two lines of the Siamese Tramway would extend eastward from the original network and the line to Bang Sue station would extend north. This plan, therefore, aimed to expand the tramway network to Pathumwan, Dusit, and Bang Sue and corresponded to the directions of the urban expansions.

All lines were approved with the exception of the Dusit–Bang Sue line of the Siamese Tramway. The reason it was rejected was that the area along it was still insufficiently developed (*BTWM*, 3 September 1925). Since the Bang Sue extension was rejected, the SEC applied for another line, from Bang Krabue to Bang Sue station, an alternative to the northern extension of the Siamese Tramway.[9] When this new application gained approval, four tramways were then constructed, as shown in figure 2.1. Part of the Silom line between Bang Rak and Sala Daeng on Silom Road seems to have started operation at the end of 1925, with the eastern extension of the Samsen line, the remaining Silom line, and the Bang Sue line following soon thereafter, as shown in table 2.4. Once the Pathumwan line opened in February 1929, all four lines were then complete. The reason for the delay on the Pathumwan line construction was that the Kasatsuek Bridge on Rama I Road was under construction, so the opening of the line had to wait for its completion. This bridge was the first two-level crossing between a railway and a road in Bangkok.

Fig. 2.1. Tramway Network in Bangkok, 1930

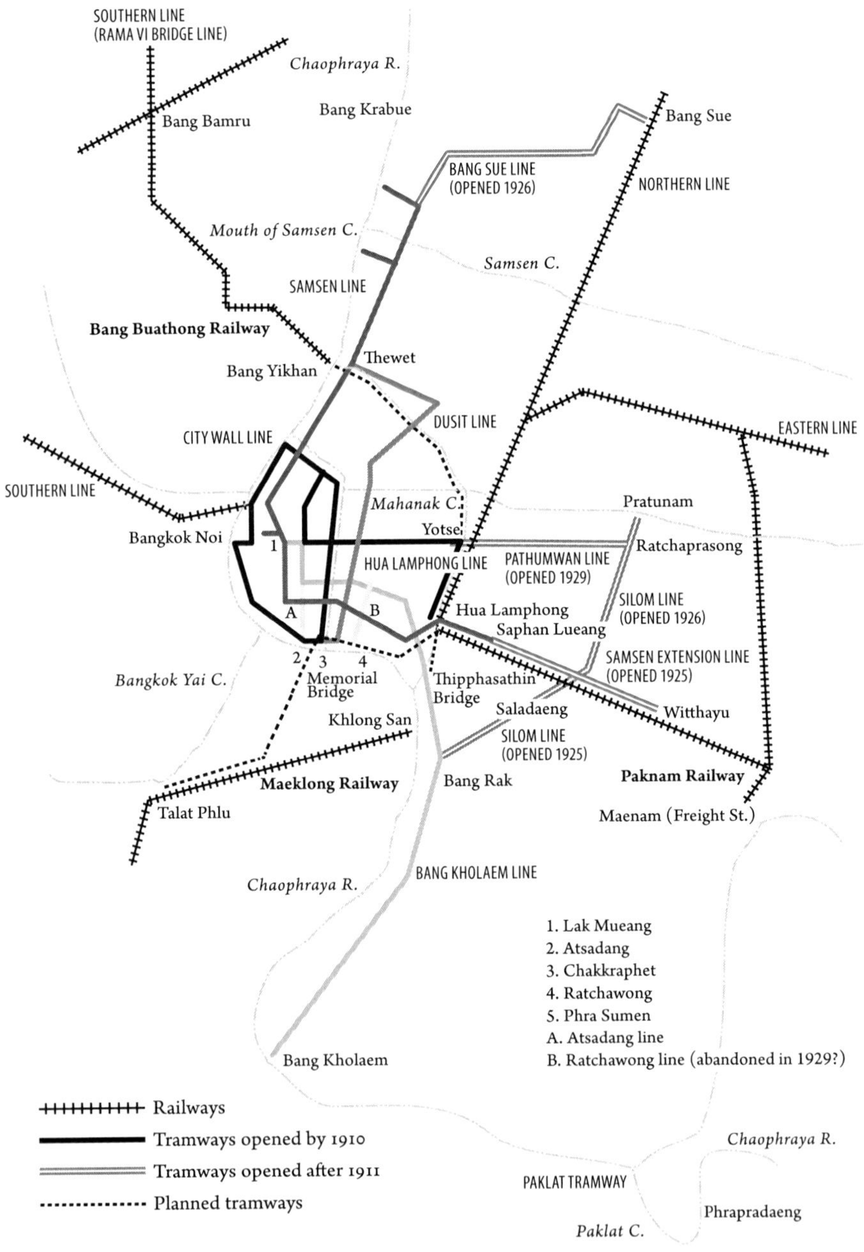

Table 2.4. Opening of Tramways, 1911–1941

Company	Line	Section	Length (km)	Opening Date	Remarks	Source
Siam Electricity	Samsen	Witthayu–Saphan Lueang	2.5	1 Jan 1926		*BTWM*, 3 Sep 1925
	Bang Sue	Bang Krabue–Bang Sue	4.0	1927		*BTWM*, 4 May 1927
Siamese Tramway	Silom	Bang Rak–Sala Daeng	2.3	end of 1925		*BTWM*, 12 Mar 1927
		Sala Daeng–Pratunam	2.2	31 Mar 1926	1.7-km section abandoned in 1940	*BTWM*, 3 Mar 1926
	Pathumwan	Yotse–Ratchaprasong	2.5	Feb 1929		*BTWM*, 8 Mar 1929
Total			13.5			

One of the reasons for extending tramways was to cope with the competition from buses, which had been gradually increasing in operation. As will be mentioned later, bus networks had been gradually expanding since the start of the first bus service in 1907, and twelve bus routes were in operation by 1925.[10] Although there was no competitive bus route that completely paralleled a tramway, buses were connecting the urban area with the suburban areas where tramways had not yet reached, so this deprived the tramways of passengers. Therefore, the tramway companies dared to construct new lines with the same conditions of previous concessions, even though their concession terms were only for twenty-five years.[11] However, since bus operations already existed along all of the new tramway lines, the extension of tramways led to direct competition with the buses.

The extension of the Samsen line to Witthayu had to gain consent from the PRC. The concession of the PRC regulated that the government would not approve any construction of railways or tramways that competed with its service. Therefore, when the SEC applied for an extension of the Samsen line to Khlong Toei along Rama IV Road in 1906, the government rejected the application, saying that the line was too near the Paknam line.[12] The extension of the Samsen line from Hua Lamphong to Saphan Lueang in 1910 was also opposed by the PRC.

Although it was quite difficult to extend the tramway along Rama IV Road paralleling Paknam Railway, the electrification plan of the whole Paknam line became the turning point. As will be mentioned later, the PRC started their electric tram operation in one section in the 1910s and planned for the electrification of the whole line in the 1920s. However, it hesitated to invest in the huge cost of electrification since the government did not approve the extension of the term of their concession. The SEC then offered to sublease the Paknam line by covering the costs for electrification. In exchange, it would extend the tramway to Witthayu, while the original electric tram service between Hua Lamphong and Khlong Toei would be shortened between Witthayu and Khlong Toei. Since the PRC approved the offer, the SEC could then monopolize tram operations between Hua Lamphong and Witthayu by extending the Samsen line to Witthayu.

Merger of Tramway Companies and Further Expansion Plans

When the SEC purchased shares of the Siamese Tramway in 1907, it had planned to merge with the latter. However, the merger could not take place due to the opposition of shareholders in Denmark. They opposed the change of its registration from Danish to Thai, although it was preferable to become a Thai-registered company since the Siamese Tramway was a Thai company. In 1913 when the Belgian financers became the major shareholders, it became possible to register in Belgium, but this never came to pass.

Then the SEC informed the government of its intention to register as a Thai company in 1919; this was approved by the government (Wipharat 1992, 198–99). Prince Ratchaburi, the minister of agriculture, explained that the company could then escape taxation in Denmark, and it would alter the company's disadvantageous situation concerning the new power plant at Samsen. However, the company could not change its nationality at this time, even with government approval, because the majority of shareholders in Belgium opposed the move.

Prince Kamphaengphet, the minister of commerce and communication, announced at the ministers' meeting on January 1927 that the SEC was planning to register in Thailand and to merge with Siamese Tramway.[13] The prince said that there was no problem regarding the merger and change of nationality, and suggested the ministers approve the plan without changing the concession terms. He explained that the reason for the change of nationality was to escape high taxation rates in Belgium.[14]

Through this merger, the tramway businesses in Bangkok were unified under the operation of the SEC. In fact, the former SEC transformed into a new company after the merger by changing its name to the Siam Electric Corporation, Ltd. (SEC). The merger was also financially successful as the gross revenue from the tramway business in 1927 was 2,396,651 baht and net profits in 1927 and 1928 exceeded the sum of the two companies before the merger, as shown in table 2.1. Since then the red tramcars of the Siamese Tramway disappeared and appeared as yellow SEC tramcars (Tho Phuthao 1989, 86).[15]

The SEC then planned further tramway extensions. In April 1928, it applied for the construction of two tramway lines, one from the Thipphayasathian Bridge on the Bang Kholaem line to Hua Lamphong via Maha Phruettharam Road, which was under construction, and from Yotse on the Hua Lamphong line to Thewet pier along Krung Kasem Road (*BTWM*, 23 May 1928). Both sections ran along the Phadung Krung Kasem Canal and would produce a line surrounding old Bangkok from east to north by connecting with the existing section between Hua Lamphong and Yotse.[16]

In 1930, the company applied for another tramway construction permit from Hua Lamphong to Talat Phlu on the Thonburi side via Songwat Road and the Memorial Bridge, which was just being built.[17] The line would go west as far as the Memorial Bridge and then head to Talat Phlu along the newly constructed Prachathipok Road, and it would be the first tramway to reach Thonburi, on the west bank of the Chaophraya River. The Memorial Bridge, constructed to commemorate 150 years since Bangkok's founding, was the first bridge connecting the east and west sides of the Chaophraya; construction began in spring 1930 and it was opened to traffic in 1932.[18] In 1929, double tramway tracks were expected to be laid in the center of the bridge (*BTWM*, 13 September 1929).

However, the company did not persist in constructing these lines as tramways and accepted the introduction of a trolley bus. In March 1930, the Department of Local Government (*krom nakharathon*) requested that the tramway on Charoen Krung Road should be removed or substituted with a trolley bus to ease traffic congestion. The company replied that it was difficult under the current conditions of its concession but new lines, including the two lines applied for in 1928, could be constructed as trolley bus routes.[19] Trolley buses could share the road with other vehicles as did ordinary buses, but they also used electricity as their source of power as did tramcars. Therefore, as the traffic on the road increased, the substitution of trolley buses for a tramway was suggested in order to use the tramway lane for traffic.

However, these extension plans did not materialize. The main reason for the failure remains unknown; furthermore, bus operators who already operated bus services along the proposed tramways opposed the proposal for the two lines (*BTWM*, 23 May 1928). Since there was no previous evidence of opposition by bus operators when four lines were approved in 1925, even though these lines also competed with existing buses, this seems to be the first case of opposition by bus operators. On the contrary, the abolishment of tramways started when the Dusit Extension line was slightly shortened due to the removal of the tracks in 1928, and the Ratchawong branch line was replaced by buses in 1929.[20] The expansion of Bangkok's tramway network ceased after the completion of 13.5 km of lines that were approved in 1925, and began to decrease after that.

Suburban Railways' Efforts to Become Urban Railways

Introduction of an Electric Tram on Paknam Railway

The suburban railways, which started as inter-city railways, tried to participate in urban transport to exploit the new demand. The Paknam Railway Company (PRC) led the way. Its effort to become an urban railway started with an increase in train services within the urban area by the introduction of motor railcars. At the general meeting of shareholders in 1903, a suggestion was made to electrify a three-kilometer section within the urban area to run electric trams. However, at the following meeting, the plan was postponed due to the need for new debentures of about 45,000 to 50,000 baht (*BTWM*, 7 August 1903; *BTWM*, 1 February 1904). Then at the 1907 general meeting of shareholders, another suggestion was made to run a motor railcar between Hua Lamphong and Sala Daeng (*BTWM*, 26 February 1907). The motor railcar should have arrived and started operation around the middle of 1908, since the PRC ordered a motor railcar in March 1908, but another report in September mentioned that this motor railcar experienced an accident at the crossing.[21]

The motor railcar had two axles with a capacity of forty passengers and could run for a maximum of forty-minute intervals, taking twenty minutes on the five-kilometer section between Hua Lamphong and Khlong Toei.[22] As table 2.5 shows, the trains between Bangkok and Paknam took three trips per day at first and then increased to four trips in 1903, which was too few for urban needs. The Paknam line came to function as an urban railway after the introduction of frequent train services by the motor railcar. However, the motorized railcar had a serious problem; the Railway Department concluded that it was not suitable to use for passenger transport after it derailed in January 1909 and engineers of the department investigated the accident.[23]

Therefore, the company decided to introduce an electric tram. In 1911, a newspaper reported that the company was planning to electrify the section between Hua Lamphong and Khlong Toei and to run two electric trams using the same system as the SEC's tramway (*BTWM*, 29 September 1911). The construction of the electric infrastructure was contracted by the SEC and the power was also provided by them. The total cost of electrification was 17,500 baht, far cheaper than the estimate in 1903 (*BTWM*, 22 January 1912). The construction proceeded smoothly and the trams started on May 1, 1912, as noted in table 2.6. Since two trams crossed each other at the middle point, the frequency of trains was reduced to every fifteen to twenty minutes (table 2.5).

Electrification was successful for the company. The monthly gross receipts from the electric tram in the latter half of 1912 increased from 900 baht before electrification to 1,800 baht, while expenses only increased from 40 to 50 baht per month (*BTWM*, 15 February 1913). In January 1913, the company reduced fares from sixteen satang (0.16 baht) to twelve satang between Hua Lamphong and Khlong Toei, and from eight satang to six satang between Hua Lamphong and Sala Daeng. A further reduction was also considered since the previous reductions brought additional income. The PRC strengthened its function as an urban railway by increasing the frequency of its service with electric trams.

Table 2.5. Frequency of Suburban Railways, 1893–1931

Company	Date	Frequency of Trains	
		Whole Line	Partial Section
Paknam Railway	11 Apr 1893	3 round trips	
	1903	4 round trips	
	1909	4 round trips	40-minute intervals, Hua Lamphong–Khlong Toei
	1 May 1912	4 round trips	15- to 20-minute intervals, Hua Lamphong–Khlong Toei
	1917	4 round trips	15- to 20-minute intervals, Hua Lamphong–Khlong Toei, 60-minute intervals, Hua Lamphong–Bang Na
	1 Jan 1926	4 round trips	10-minute intervals, Witthayu–Khlong Toei, 60-minute intervals, Hua Lamphong–Bang Na
	193?	60-minute intervals	10-minute intervals, Witthayu–Khlong Toei
Maeklong (Thachin) Railway	4 Jan 1905	3 round trips	
	1 Jan 1914	4 round trips	
	13 Feb 1926	4 round trips	30-minute intervals, Khlong San–Wat Sai
	1928	4 round trips	30-minute intervals, Khlong San–Wat Sing
	1931	4 round trips	30-minute intervals, Khlong San–Bang Bon

NOTE: Trains made two round trips daily on the Ban Laem–Maeklong segment of the Maekong line.
SOURCES: *BTWM* 1903–28 (selected issues); *BT*, 30 Dec 1925; *SK*, 2 Jan 1937.

Table 2.6. Electrification of Suburban Railways

Company	Section	Length (km)	Date
Paknam Railway	Hua Lamphong–Khlong Toei	6.0	1 May 1912
	Khlong Toei–Bang Na	5.0	1917
	Bang Na–Paknam	10.0	1 Jan 1926
Maeklong Railway	Khlong San–Wat Sai	7.6	13 Feb 1926
	Wat Sai–Wat Sing	1.0	1928
	Wat Sing–Bang Bon	2.6	1931?

SOURCES: *BTWM* 1912, 1918, 1926, 1928 (selected issues); *BT*, 30 Dec 1925.

The electrification could also be justified from the management perspective. Table 2.7 shows the gross income of private railways. Although the available figures for the PRC were limited, the gross receipts in 1914 exceeded 180,000 baht. Therefore, it expanded the electrified tram service to Bang Na in 1917, as noted in table 2.6. Although the number of trams in the extended section was limited to sixty-minute intervals (table 2.5), this was a convenience in the suburban area since only four trips by steam train had existed before. The extension of electrification also succeeded, as the gross receipts in the late 1920s increased to 200,000 baht. Passenger receipts in 1917 increased to 15,000 baht, and the electric tram contributed 12,000 baht (*BTWM*, 16 February 1918). The half-electrified PRC now planned electrification of the whole line.

Table 2.7. Gross Receipts of Suburban Railways, 1911–1941 (THB)

Year	Paknam Railway	Maeklong Railway	Year	Paknam Railway	Maeklong Railway
1911	151,630	333,281	1927	N.A.	377,526
1912	150,293	292,557	1928	N.A.	375,491
1913	N.A.	300,356	1929	N.A.	N.A.
1914	186,509	306,340	1930	N.A.	298,405
1915	N.A.	284,961	1931	N.A.	267,920
1916	N.A.	247,284	1932	N.A.	243,690
1917	N.A.	213,476	1933	N.A.	231,690
1918	N.A.	242,357	1934	N.A.	204,690
1919	N.A.	288,875	1935	N.A.	197,226
1920	265,465	303,526	1936	N.A.	203,458
1921	N.A.	294,246	1937		200,337
1922	265,654	304,686	1938		N.A.
1923	280,902	305,290	1939		N.A.
1924	N.A.	327,608	1940		N.A.
1925	N.A.	348,948	1941		300,460
1926	N.A.	N.A.			

SOURCES: *BTWM* 1911–42 (selected issues); *BT*, 26 Mar 1942.

Problems with Electrification on the Paknam Railway

As the electrification to Bang Na was successful, the company planned to electrify the remaining sections. They came up against a major obstacle, however—the termination of their concession. Since the term was fifty years and would terminate in 1936, it became more difficult to recover the investment for electrification. Therefore the company asked the government to extend the concession term so they could electrify all the lines. In July 1921, the company first asked the government for new terms, and the government Board of Railway Commissioners considered the matter.[24] After examination, the board decided not to approve the concession term extension as the company's assets had been depreciating as it neared the termination date in 1936. According to the balance sheet for the latter half of 1921, it had deposits and shares amounting to 180,000 baht, which would cover the total cost of the electrification of 170,000 baht.[25] At the same time, the board concluded that the government should purchase the railway for nationalization after the expiry of the concession.

Since the company hesitated to make a new investment without the extension of its concession, the electrification plan was deadlocked. In February 1925, however, the company reapplied to the government to electrify all lines by means of a sublease through SEC.[26] This meant that the SEC would pay for all electrification equipment, including electric trains, and operate the train service by paying rent to the PRC. The rent was fixed at 170,000 baht for the first year and would be increased by 2,500 baht per year thereafter. This was quite a favorable offer for the PRC since they could complete electrification without investing their own funds and would be able to receive a fixed rent every year. The government did not oppose the plan, provided the concession terms were not violated, and it finally approved the plan under the conditions of a sublease contract.[27]

As a result, the construction of the electrified rail system started in the middle of 1925, and the electric train service and sublease began in January 1926. Although initially the number of trains between Bangkok and Paknam did not increase, as table 2.5 shows, the number of trains to Paknam increased to sixty-minute intervals by extending the former sixty-minute service to Bang Na in the 1930s.[28] On the other hand, the electric tram service was reduced to the section between Witthayu and Khlong Toei and, although the service in the remaining section increased to ten-minute intervals, the number of trains between Hua Lamphong and Witthayu was dramatically reduced to only sixty-minute intervals with the Bang Na or Paknam trains.

The reason for the sublease by the SEC was connected to the problem of the tramway expansion on Rama IV Road, as mentioned above. The SEC offered advantageous conditions since it would bear all the costs of electrification as well as pay a fixed rent in exchange for the extension of the tramway and the abolishment of the tram service on the competing section of the PRC.[29] As the electric trams between Witthayu and Khlong Toei connected with trams on the Samsen line, tram service was virtually extended to Khlong Toei, although a transfer was needed. The SEC might have aimed to direct tram services to Khlong Toei when it applied for the construction of the connecting rail line between the Samsen and Paknam lines at Hua Lamphong and Witthayu.[30]

The electrification of the whole PRC ironically reduced its function as an urban railway. The original electrification plan in 1921 aimed to introduce a higher frequency of train service—ten-minute intervals between Hua Lamphong and Khlong Toei, thirty-minute intervals between Hua Lamphong and Bang Chak, and sixty-minute intervals between Hua Lamphong and Paknam—which would enhance its function as an urban railway.[31] But the virtual substitution of the tramway in some sections and the increase of train frequency beyond Khlong Toei never occurred. Therefore, its function as an urban railway reached its peak in the era of partial electrification between 1912 and 1926, and would gradually decrease after that.

Partial Electrification of the Maeklong Railway

The MRC, on the other hand, had planned for the electrification of a certain section since its founding, but it finally happened in the 1920s. The prospectus of the Thachin Railway mentioned that a four-mile section in Bangkok would be electrified to run an electric tram car, and the construction and procurement would be contracted out to the SEC.[32] Although the urban area of Thonburi on the west bank of the Chaophraya River was smaller than the east bank, there was enough population between the Bangkok terminus and Talat Phlu for the company to consider the feasibility of running electric trams between them.[33] There was another plan for a Talat Phlu Tramway whose proximity to the Thachin Railway became a problem, as mentioned above. However, neither the Thachin Railway electric tram nor the Talat Phlu Tramway ever materialized.

The Thachin Railway tried to introduce the motor railcar instead of electrification as the PRC had. The board announced at a general meeting of shareholders during the first half of 1905 that it was considering a motor railcar service between Khlong San and Wat Sing (*BTWM*, 3

August 1905). Two motor trolleys arrived in 1906, which should have been the first motorized railcars in Thailand (*BTWM*, 18 April 1906). However, they could not serve as general passenger transport since their capacities were limited to three or four passengers.

The electrification of the MRC was finally started in the 1920s. In 1925 the company applied for an electrification plan for a 7.6-kilometer section between Khlong San and Wat Sai.[34] It planned to contract the SEC to procure and construct the electric facilities, and the total cost was estimated at 60,000 baht. Three electric trams, which were the same as the PRC, would be introduced to run at thirty-minute intervals. As the Board of Railway Commissioners approved, the operation of the electric trams started in February 1926 (*BTWM*, 12 February 1926). The MRC, therefore, came to function as an urban railway. It was also justified from the management perspective as its gross receipts rose to 370,000 baht after electrification, as seen in table 2.7.

Since the introduction of the electric tram brought an increase in revenues, the company soon applied to extend electrification. In April 1927, it applied for a 1-kilometer extension to Wat Sing, which was approved by the Board of Railway Commissioners.[35] The electric tram operation in this extended section should have started in 1928. In 1931, it applied for another 2.6-kilometer extension of electrification to Bang Bon, which would have been completed within the same year that they gained approval from the Board of Railway Commissioners.[36] Although the total distance of the electrified sections increased to 11 kilometers, the company's financial situation did not improve; its gross receipts fell after the worldwide Great Depression in 1929, as table 2.7 shows. The main factors for the decrease were the reduction of fish transport and competition with motor boats (*BTWM*, 7 March 1934).

Nationalization of Suburban Railways

When the electrification plan of the entire PRC was considered, it was confirmed that the government would not approve the extension of the concession term. Nevertheless, the company started negotiations with the government regarding the termination of the concession from one year before the deadline. However, the government had not yet officially denied the extension. After an examination by the Board of Railway Commissioners, it was suggested that the government would not approve the extension of the concession but would instead purchase the railway or lease it back to the company in case of a budget shortage.[37]

The government then established a Committee for the Examination of the PRC Concession (*Khana kammakan phicharana rueang sampathan borisat rotfai paknam chamkat*). On examining the company's financial results and discovering that it was generating an annual net profit of about 100,000 baht, the committee concluded that the government should lease the railway back to the company for eight years at a rent of 60,000 baht per year, as its estimated net profit would not be lower than 60,000 baht, even after the opening of the new road between Bangkok and Paknam.[38] However, the cabinet meeting in January 1936 decided to confirm whether the government had a duty to buy the railway or not. As it would not approve the renewal of the concession, the argument would then shift to the interpretation of the concession.[39]

After the examination of the concession, it was confirmed that the government did not have to purchase the railway, so the committee then suggested that the government start negotiations with the company about the price of their assets. They realized that passengers of the railway would be in trouble if the railway was abolished before the completion of the road in 1937 or 1938.[40] The cabinet, at their meeting in March 1936, decided to negotiate with the company and also ordered the Ministry of Interior to complete the road between Bangkok and Paknam before the termination of the concession in case the negotiations failed.[41] This meant that the government might have purchased the railway under more advantageous conditions and it also showed that the railway would definitely be replaced by the road, even if it would not purchase the line.

The negotiations, therefore, became quite disadvantageous for the PRC. The government suggested that the value of its assets, including those for the SEC, was 570,000 baht at first, but then reduced this to 500,000 baht (*BTWM*, 8 September 1936). On the other hand, the government decided that the maximum price would be 350,000 baht but would not make the purchase if the negotiations fell through.[42] The government hastily prepared to introduce a bus service between Bangkok and Paknam and approved the Aerial Transport Company, the government's company under the Ministry of Economic Affairs, to operate the bus service.[43] The company then hurried to procure buses and finally started a bus service on September 12, the termination date of the PRC's concession (*BTWM*, 28 August 1936). The road between Bangkok and Paknam was also developed to a level that made automobile traffic possible, although some bridges had not yet been completed.

Under this situation, the PRC was forced to acknowledge the government's request. At an extraordinary meeting of shareholders on September 7, just before the termination of the concession, the chairman explained the process of negotiation with the government and asked for consent to accept its purchase offer of 350,000 baht since there was no alternative (*BTWM*, 8 September 1936). The proposal was approved at the meeting, and the company told the government that they would accept the purchase offer, thus finally deciding the nationalization of the PRC. As time was extremely limited, the company ceased its operations of all train services on September 12, and the Railway Department continued operations the following day using all existing labor (*BTWM*, 14 September 1936). This was the first nationalization of a private railway in Thailand, the PRC, after a concession term of fifty years.

Following the PRC, the MRC faced the termination of its two concessions. The termination date of the concession for the old Thachin Railway between Khlong San and Thachin would be May 1941, and that for the newly opened section between Ban Laem and Maeklong, August 1945. The company suggested a plan to sell both lines to the government in 1943, the mid-point between the two concession deadlines, to avoid the loss during the last four years after the termination of the concession for the profitable first section (*BTWM*, 12 March 1940). After an examination, the Board of Railway Commissioners recommended an extension of these concessions for eight years and twelve years respectively and the government would then decide their future within the extended period.[44] The estimated value of the assets differed according to the company's and the government's reckoning, as in the case of the PRC: the company claimed a value of 1,030,000 baht and the examination committee of the Railway Department evaluated it at 400,000 baht.[45]

Therefore, a committee to reexamine the concession of the MRC was established to confirm the government's necessity for purchasing the railways. The concession stipulated that the government might take possession of the railway (*thang rotfai*), so the committee concluded that the government would have to purchase only the company's rolling stock and buildings.[46] Although the company opposed this interpretation, the Council of State reaffirmed this interpretation, so the conflict deepened. It became quite difficult to conclude the matter before the termination date of the concession, so the committee reexamined the starting date of the concession at their meeting in April 1941. They interpreted the duration of the concession as forty years from November 23, 1902, the date it was sanctioned by the king, so the concession would then expire in 1942.[47] The company was informed of this change.

Although this would extend the deadline of the negotiation with the company for one year, the termination date in 1942 eventually came without any consent regarding the future of the railway. The company insisted on resolving the problem with an arbitrator, and this was agreed.[48] To avoid the suspension of train service, the Railway Department took over the service and assets of the railway, and the operation of the section between Khlong San and Thachin was transferred to the Railway Department on November 24, 1942.[49]

In July 1945, when the termination of the remaining section approached without a fundamental resolution, the government proposed the purchase of both lines for 1,020,000 baht, a value that was previously presented by the company.[50] However, the company requested 2 million baht, halving the 4 million baht that shareholders were demanding. The Railway Department ended up taking over the operation between Ban Laem and Maeklong since the termination day, August 13, 1945, arrived before the agreement. In May 1946, they reached an agreement on a purchase price of 2 million baht and the cabinet meeting approved the purchase of the railway at that price (RFT 1970, 352–53).[51]

With the government purchase of the MRC, all the private railways that had ever existed in Thailand were now gone. While both PRC and MRC had operated until the termination of their concessions and were now nationalized by the government, the other two light railways of the Phrabat Tramway and the Bang Buathong Railway ceased before their concessions ended during the Second World War.[52] The SEC, the tramway company in Bangkok, would be nationalized later when its concession terminated at the end of 1949. Therefore, all railway and tramway businesses that emerged before the war were nationalized when their concessions ended.

Emergence of Buses

Beginning of the Bus Business

The first automobile in Thailand is said to have arrived between 1899 and 1902. According to Sa-nguan (1986, 62), Chaophraya Surasakmontri received an automobile from a foreigner during this period and this is considered the first automobile in Thailand, although there are several other rival claims. In 1904, Prince Ratchaburi went to Europe for medical treatment and bought a Daimler-Benz in France as a present for King Rama V (Castrol [Thailand] 1994, 15–16). After that, the import of automobiles increased for the royals, the rich, and foreigners. The number of automobiles registered in Bangkok in 1909 reached 401 cars (ibid., 29–30).

The first bus operation is generally ascribed to Phra (later Phraya) Phakdinoraset, or Loet Setthabut, as the pioneer. According to Sa-nguan (1986, 67), the first bus in Thailand started to operate between Yotse (later the Kasatsuek Bridge) and Pratunam in 1907. At first, this bus service was horse-drawn but was adapted to Ford motor omnibuses the next year. On the other hand, Chali (1981, 111–13) explains that the first scheduled carriage service was started on Charoen Krung Road in 1885 but was abolished by the introduction of the tramway two years later. A second scheduled carriage service was started by Phra Phakdinoraset in 1909 between Yotse and Pratunam. He made the change to omnibuses in 1913, five years later than Sa-nguan's assertion. Therefore, it may be true that the first bus service in Thailand was started by Phra Phakdinoraset around 1910, although the exact year of its start cannot be determined. He then established the Nai Loet Company (*Borisat Nai Loet Chamkat*), using his own name, and this would become the largest private bus company in Bangkok.[53]

The first Thai bus service business, however, was preceded by applications from foreigners. Historical materials at the National Archives of Thailand note that it was the SEC that planned the first bus operation in Bangkok. In November 1905, Westenholz applied for five bus routes as feeders for its tramways.[54] During the same period, C. L. Groundwater, a British engineer, applied for a bus operation with ten-minute intervals between Bang Rak and the royal palace.[55] Westenholz also applied for a tramway extension, aiming to fill gaps between tramways and navigation routes, but this eventually fizzled. The Groundwater bus plan paralleled the Bang Kholaem tram line, so Prince Naret told him that the bus operation was not suitable as the roads were too narrow.[56] Therefore, since neither of the foreigners' bus plans materialized, Phra Phakdinoraset became the first bus operator in Bangkok.

Although plans to expand bus routes are not traceable after the first bus operation started, a catalogue of bus routes was available in 1925, as shown in table 2.8. According to the table, twelve bus routes operated in 1925; Phraya Chongrak Norasin operated five routes, followed by Phra Phakdinoraset's four routes, and three operators with one route each. It is notable that there was no Chinese operator according to the source, although the Chinese were said to dominate economic activities in Thailand at that time.

Table 2.8. Bus Routes in Bangkok, 1925

Operator	Number of Buses	Line	Fare	Route
Khun Sirayut Koson	3–6	Nangloeng Market–Bang Sue District Office	5–20 satang	Rama V Road
Phra Phakdinoraset	5	Yotse–Pratunam	5–10 satang	Rama I, Ratchadamri Road
Phra Phakdinoraset	4	Yotse–Thewakam Bridge	3–6 satang	Krungkasem Road
Phra Phakdinoraset	3	Bang Rak–Pratunam	5–20 satang	Silom, Ratchadamri Road
Phraya Chongrak Norasin	8	Raphiphatthanaphak Bridge–Witthayu	5–25 satang	Luan, Rama IV Road
Phraya Chongrak Norasin	4	Chakkrawat–Trok Siangkhong	5–10 satang	Songwat Road
Phraya Chongrak Norasin	4	Si Phraya–Si Ayutthaya	3–26 satang	Si Phraya, Phayathai Road
Phraya Chongrak Norasin	4	Surawong–Sanam Ma	5–20 satang	Surawong, Sanam Ma Road
Fak Samankaeo	2	Khiao Khaika–Bang Sue	5–20 satang	Samsen, Thahan, Techawanit Road
Phra Phakdinoraset	3	Lanluang–Makkasan	5–20 satang	Lanluang, Phetchaburi, Ratchaprarop Road
Sam-ang Anuchitsongkhram	2	Norarat Bridge–Khiao Khaika	5–25 satang	Samsen Road

Operator	Number of Buses	Line	Fare	Route
Phraya Chongrak Norasin	4	Sathon–Phloenchit	5–20 satang	Sathon, Witthayu Road

SOURCE: Data from NA Ro. 6 No. 8. 4/11.

The main routes were the suburban routes toward the north and east rather than those within the inner old city, or within three canals. Most routes were concentrated in the eastern area surrounded by the Bang Kholaem tram line and the Eastern and the Maenam rail lines, as shown in figure 2.2. This area experienced rapid population growth, as mentioned previously, and tramways had not yet reached here. The bus routes at that time served as access to suburban areas without tramway lines.

At first bus operation ran without regulation, and special permission (*bai anuyat phiset*) was granted to the operators according to the Motor Vehicles Act of 1930.[57] Although a concession (*sampathan*) was granted to railways or tramways, scheduled bus service on public roads was conducted under special permission and a concession was granted only when the bus service was exclusively operated on a concession road. The terms of the special permission had to be renewed every year, unlike the tramway concessions with terms of several decades.[58] The special permission was granted by the Department of Public and Municipal Affairs (*krom yotha thetsaban*) and its Committee for Examining the Applications of Bus Operations (*kammakan phicharana rueangrao lae kham kho doen rotyon satharana pracham thang*).[59]

Expansion of Bus Networks

Although bus routes were extended to the east and the north as the urban area expanded, they were limited by the range of the road networks in Bangkok. Bangkok's road network was isolated without a connection to the outer road networks, and only railways and navigation could connect Bangkok with the outer regions. Therefore, bus routes in Bangkok could not extend beyond the city, and the emergence of inter-province bus service had to wait until such road networks were constructed. Furthermore, the first bus service in Thonburi only started in the 1930s when the road development was finally completed.

Fig. 2.2. Bus Network in Bangkok, 1925

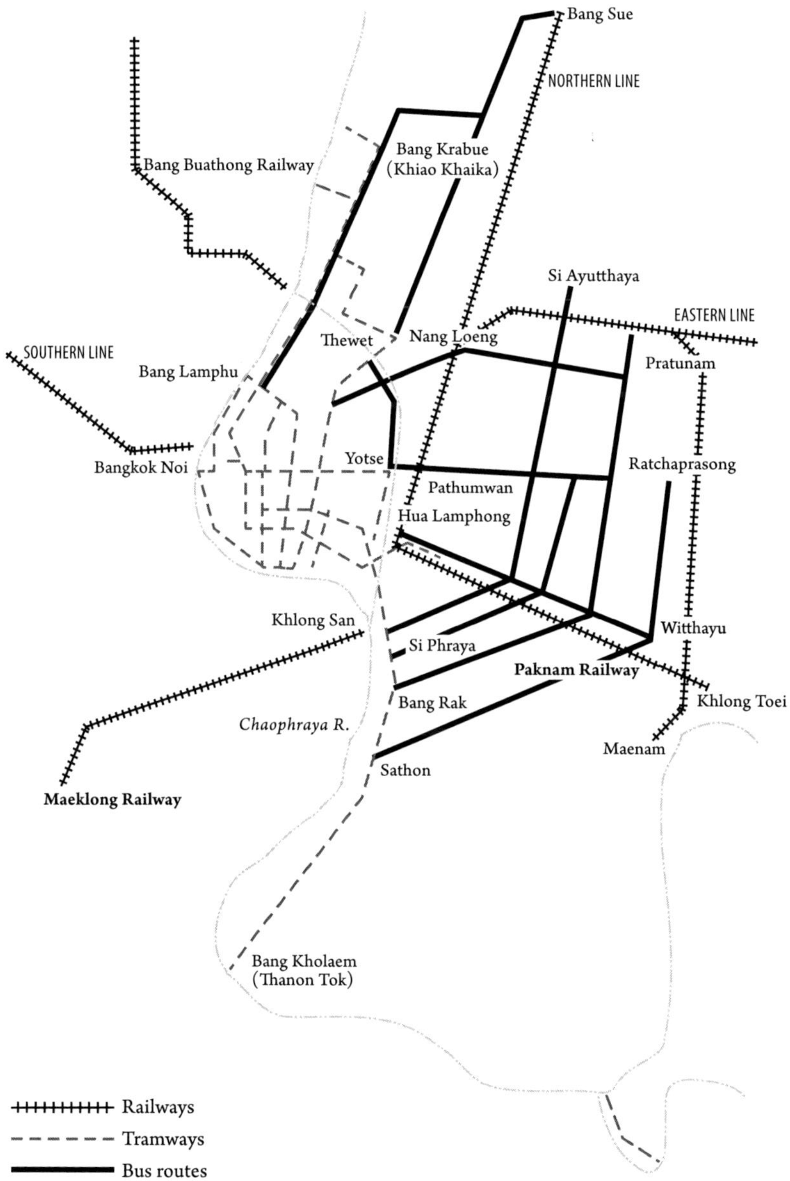

The first inter-province bus was one to Paknam. This bus operation was hastily decided to assure a means of transport in case the government did not purchase PRC before its concession terminated. The unit operating this, the Aerial Transport, was a state enterprise established in 1931 to operate domestic air routes. They applied for permissions to operate a bus service between Bangkok and Don Mueang and between Bangkok and Paknam, in order to improve their profits. In fact, it did not expect the government to approve the bus operation to Paknam since, as was explained at the general meeting of shareholders in August 1936, the bus service permission would be given to the Bangkok Municipality.[60]

Paknam was the center of Samut Prakan province, south of Bangkok, a suburb only about twenty kilometers from the city center. The PRC had already reached there and electric train service had also started in 1926, although the frequency of service was still low. However, the frequency of bus service was significantly higher as the company started fifteen-minute intervals of service (PCC 1936/09/11).[61] Therefore, it functioned as both a suburban bus of Bangkok and the first inter-province bus.

Bus service to Don Mueang, although not an inter-province bus, should have started in 1936. The construction of Don Mueang Road, a part of the trunk road northward, started after the rebellion of Prince Boworadet in 1933.[62] Since the Bangkok airport was at Don Mueang, the railway had been the only method of transportation before the completion of this road. The Aerial Transport applied for bus operation to Don Mueang, but permission was instead granted to the Air Force Club (*Samoson thahan akat*). This club entrusted the bus operation to Siam Automobile, which was succeeded by the Aerial Transport in November 1938.[63] As the trains to and from Don Mueang were limited, this bus service significantly enhanced the convenience of travel between Bangkok and Don Mueang and became another suburban bus in Bangkok.

Another inter-province bus provided service to Nonthaburi. The road to Nonthaburi was as unimportant as the road to Paknam since it was situated on the east bank of the Chaophraya River, which was navigable, and on the west bank of the river was the Bang Buathong Railway. However, in 1930, construction plans were presented for a new jail and new provincial offices at Bang Khwang (east bank of the Chaophraya River), and so was a plan for road construction from Bangkok.[64] A royal decree for the construction of the highway between

Bangkok and Nonthaburi was issued the next year, but construction did not begin due to the 1932 revolution. This construction was eventually included in the first five-year program of highway construction in 1936, although the highways to Paknam and Don Mueang held greater priority. Finally the road to Nonthaburi opened in November 1939 (*BTWM* 2 November 1939).[65] The bus operation between Bangkok and Nonthaburi then started, with Route 29 granted to the Nonthaburi Municipality, as noted in table 2.9. Since Nonthaburi was twenty kilometers away from Bangkok, this bus service was also a suburban bus. Therefore, as the construction of the roads toward outlying regions started during the 1930s, the suburban buses began operating to three destinations: Paknam, Don Mueang, and Nonthaburi.

The start of bus service in Thonburi was linked to the opening of the Memorial Bridge in 1932. Road development in Thonburi was so slow that there were almost no roads for automobiles. Therefore, the construction of ten roads, including a road from the bridge to Daokhanong, was planned in conjunction with the construction of the Memorial Bridge (Kanokwali 2001, 157). The big round-about (Wongwian Yai) where the statue of King Taksin stands was also constructed at that time.[66] According to table 2.9, the first bus route in Thonburi was Route 12, approved in 1934, and the bus connecting the east and west banks of the Chaophraya via the Memorial Bridge did not exist until 1939 when Route 25 was approved. However, the bus service should have started earlier since, as Sa-nguan explains (1981, 68), the Chinese Nakhon Thon Company started a bus service between Bang Lamphu and Wongwian Yai in 1933.[67] The completion of the bridge and roads was the real opening for bus services in Thonburi, as well as other inter-province services.

Municipal Participation in the Bus Service

The expansion of bus routes also progressed in urban and suburban areas. There were twenty-two bus routes at the end of the 1930s, as shown in table 2.9, and the network also became more dense (see figure 2.3). While competition between buses and trams was quite limited in 1925, the increase in routes increased the competition, since the buses and trams mostly ran on the same roads. In many cases, the competition occurred due to bus operations on existing tramway routes, but a few cases were exactly the opposite, with new tramways built on the existing bus routes. The SEC came to an agreement with the government to prevent bus competition in Bangkok, but the agreement was eventually canceled for reasons that will be mentioned below. By comparing figures 2.2 and 2.3, it can be seen that the competition between the tramway and buses emerged in almost all areas in Bangkok through the rapid expansion of the bus network over a fifteen-year period.

Table 2.9. Bus Routes in Bangkok, 1939

Route No.	Line	Operator	Route	Date of Approval	Remarks
1	Kasatsuek Bridge–Phrakhanong	Loet Setthabut	Rama I, Paknam Road	18 Mar 1933	
2	Bang Lamphu–Makkasan	Loet Setthabut	Lanluang, Phetchaburi, Ratchaprarop Road	28 Apr 1932	
3	Kasatsuek Bridge–Pratunam	Loet Setthabut	Rama I, Ratchadamri Road	28 Apr 1932	
4	Si Phraya–Victory Monument	Loet Setthabut	Si Phraya, Phayathai Road	28 Apr 1932	
5	Pratunam–Silom	Loet Setthabut	Ratchadamri, Silom Road	28 Apr 1932	
7	Siyan–Sala Daeng	Sanong Yuwabun	Nakhon Chaisi, Rama VI, Ratchawithi, Ratchaprarop Road	30 Dec 1932	
8	Rama V Statue–Memorial Bridge	Loet Setthabut	Ratchadamnoen, Na Phralan Road	1 Oct 1932	
10	Bang Khunphrom–Samyaek	Si Nakhon	Wisut Kasat, Nakhon Sawan, Luang Road	28 Jul 1934	
12	Wongwian Lek–Wongwian Yai	Thonburi Municipality	Somdet Chaophraya, Latya Road	21 Apr 1934	Transferred from Nakhon Thon Co. on 17 May 1939
14	Hua Lamphong–Bangkok Port	Thai Automobile	Rama IV, Sunthon Kosa Road	12 Apr 1932	
15	Memorial Bridge–Bang Sue	Thai Automobile	Chakkraphet, Chakkraphong, Samsen, Luksuea, Rama V Road	13 Apr 1932	
17	Thewet–Phitthaya Sathian Bridge	Thai Automobile	Krungkasem, Maha Phruettharam Road	13 Apr 1932	
20	Hua Lamphong–Paknam	Aerial Transport	Rama IV, Rama VI, Rama I, Paknam Road	10 Jul 1936	Suburban bus

Route No.	Line	Operator	Route	Date of Approval	Remarks
21	Bang Sue–Wang Burapha	Si Nakhon	Rama V, Nakhon Sawan, Mahachai Road	9 May 1932	
22	Trok Chan–Bang Phong-phang	Prik Sathu	Chan, Sathu Pradit Road	13 May 1934	
23	Victory Monument/Saphan Daeng–Don Mueang	Air Force Club	Don Mueang Road	18 Sep 1936	Suburban bus
24	Tha Tian–Thanon Tok	Bangkok Municipality	Charoen Krung Road	May 1938	
25	Daokhanong–Bang Lamphu	Thonburi Municipality	Taksin, Tithong Road	17 May 1939	
26	Talat Phlu–Thaphrachan	Thonburi Municipality	Thoetthai, Prachathipok, Ban Mo Road	17 May 1939	
27	Kasatsuek Bridge–Bangkok Noi station	Thonburi Municipality	Bamrung Mueang, Mahachai, Prachathipok, Itsaraphap Road	21 Jan 1938	
28	Trok Phayamai–Sirirat	Thonburi Municipality	Thetsaban 2 Road	17 May 1939	
29	Khiao Khaika–Nonthaburi	Nonthaburi Municipality	Bang Krabue Road	12 Sep 1939	Suburban bus

Source: Data from NA [2] So Ro. 0201. 66. 3/7.

The number of bus operators also increased as the bus routes increased. Several companies, such as the Si Nakhon Company (*Borisat hang hun suan chamkat si nakhon*) and the Thai Automobile Company (*Borisat rot yon thai*) were organized, but long-time operator Loet Setthabut (Phra Phakdinoraset) was also present. Apart from private operators, the government's enterprises, such as the Aerial Transport, also participated in the bus business, along with the Bangkok and Nonthaburi municipalities. Therefore, the number of bus operators expanded with the inclusion of new participating companies or organizations.

The government at first did not restrict the bus business and granted special permissions in order of application. However, after the revolution of 1932, the government presented a policy to unify the bus business under the jurisdiction of each municipality (*thetsaban*). It was this trend toward municipal rule that prevented Aerial Transport from gaining permission to establish the Paknam route. Municipality status was established in thirty-five cities in 1935 by upgrading existing sanitation facilities (*sukhaphiban*) according to the Municipality Act in

1933 (Nagai 2003, 278–79). The tasks of the municipality included the supply of numerous public services, including transportation, similar to the municipalities in Japan. The Ministry of Interior, which supervised municipalities, assumed that transport management, that is, bus operations, should now be regulated by municipalities; therefore, bus service in Bangkok would eventually be operated by the municipality. This affected the extension of the agreement with the SEC to restrict bus competition. The government tried to extend it until the Bangkok Municipality would be able to manage bus service by itself.

When the Bangkok Municipality (*Thetsaban nakhon krungthep*) was established in April 1937, it became the municipal administration of Bangkok (Uthai 1980, 175). In 1939, the municipality began managing bus operations by starting a bus service on Charoen Krung Road. As table 2.9 shows, each municipality participated in bus operations after the special permission of Route 24 was granted to the Bangkok Municipality in 1938, while the Thonburi and Nonthaburi municipalities gained permissions in 1939. As can be seen from the table, the government limited new bus operations only to municipalities after the establishment of Bangkok Municipality; no new bus routes were granted to previous commercial operators. Therefore, it can be said that the government's policy of leaving bus management to each municipality was fixed for the time being.

The number of bus operators in Bangkok had been increasing with the new participation of state organizations and municipalities. Then the policy of municipalization in bus service seems to have been fixed after the participation of the Bangkok Municipality. There was also an example of transferring private bus operations to the municipalities after the private operator ceased service, as in the case of Route 12. Given this trend, bus operation in Bangkok should have been unified under the municipality. However, private and state companies would eventually return to the bus business due to the municipality's lack of capacity, and this would later produce a situation of competition from too many operators.

Fig. 2.3. Bus Network in Bangkok, 1939

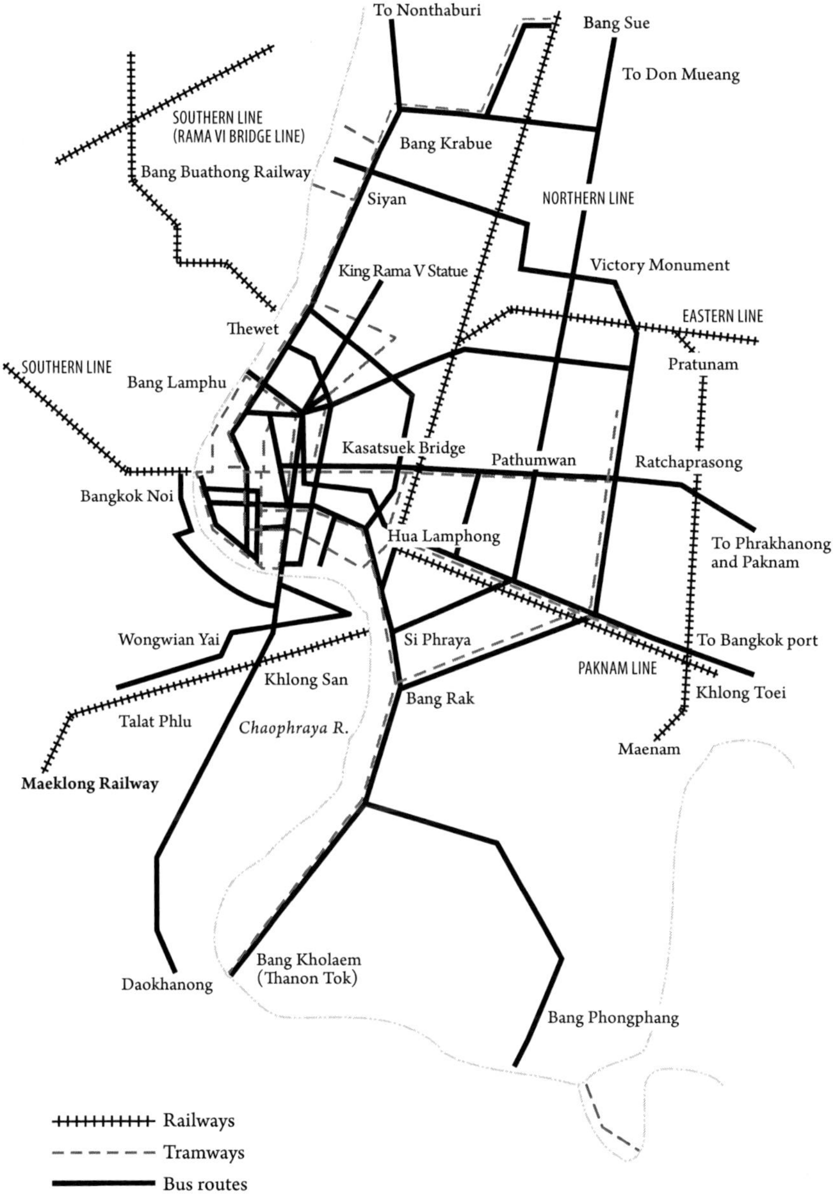

Unfavorable Winds against Tramways

Competition with Buses

Although the tramway business was sluggish for a short while, it revived in the latter half of the 1910s due to an increase in passengers and a reduction in track rent. This allowed for extension of the network in the latter half of the 1920s, although the Great Depression brought reduction in passenger numbers and thus profits to the tramway business. Furthermore, the competition with buses became so serious that the SEC had to negotiate with the government to restrict competitive bus operations. The competition with buses had started on the newly extended lines in the latter half of the 1920s. As these new lines were laid on roads where bus services already existed, competition for passengers between the tramway and the bus resulted. In 1927, the fare for the tram on the newly extended Samsen line was reduced from four satang to three satang to cope with the bus fares that had just been reduced to the same levels (*BTWM*, 6 August 1927).[68]

In 1931, as the competition on the existing lines also emerged, the SEC proposed that the government not approve new bus routes paralleling its tramways in return for an increase in track rent.[69] The proposal specified that the government would not approve new bus routes along certain sections of the Bang Kholaem, Samsen, and Hua Lamphong lines and the company would change its track rent for certain lines from 3,000 baht per mile to 7.5 percent of its gross receipts. It also suggested a reduction of the power charge for official use from two baht per unit to one baht. The company essentially asked the government not to approve competitive bus routes in return for an increase in revenue and a decrease in expenditure for the government.

The government accepted the offer since it would bring more profit and ease traffic congestion by preventing an increase of bus operators. Although the special permissions for bus operations had been renewed every year, the government gained no revenue from these permits. Moreover, the tramway was more profitable than the bus since the government would earn track rent. When an extension to the tramways was requested in 1925, Chaophraya Yommarat, the minister of local government, asked the king to sanction it because the government would gain more revenue from track rent, even though these routes were already served by buses.[70] In fact, the additional profit to the government was about 75,000 baht after the track rent increased to 122,000 baht from 70,000 baht and the power charge was reduced to 23,923 baht in 1933.[71]

The agreement between the government and the SEC was condemned by the Thai bus operators. For example, in July 1932, Phraya Thepphahatsadin and others applied for three bus routes that competed with the tramways. They brought their complaints to the newly inaugurated prime minister, Phraya Manopakon, and explained that the rejection of this application was due to possible competition with tramways, which resulted in a monopoly by the SEC on public roads in Bangkok and the lack of opportunities for Thais.[72] They pointed out that the agreement, which was made by the royal government before the revolution in 1932, was not appropriate for the new government since their philosophy was to increase opportunities for Thais and limit the influence of foreigners.

Nevertheless, the agreement of the newly formed People's Party government was successfully secured. The term of the original agreement was two years, but this was examined for renewal in 1935 after the previous renewal in 1933. The result was that the government decided to extend it for one more year since the Ministry of Interior claimed that it was premature to operate buses through cooperating organizations. The agreement was renewed for another year in 1936, and another half year in 1937 since the bus operation plan by the Bangkok Municipality had made no progress.[73] The SEC first proposed the termination of the agreement, and it was finally abolished in March 1937.[74] Though the company argued that the competition with tricycle rickshaws (*sam lo*) had become severe, the main reason was actually noted at the general meeting of shareholders: the illegal "mosquito buses" (*songthaeo*) had started operation and were competing with the tramway (*BTWM*, 19 March 1937; *BTWM*, 23 March 1937).[75]

The restriction of bus routes as agreed by the government could not improve the difficult financial situation of the company. The net profit of the company dropped after 1928, its peak year, and remained at only 1,360,000 baht in 1936, almost half of that peak, as table 2.1 shows. As the profitability of the company declined, so did the dividend rate, to 5.5 percent in 1934 (see table 2.2). The company, therefore, aimed to increase revenues and reduce expenditures by increasing the power charge to the government and reducing track rent to its original level. It also tried to cope with the hardship by reducing tramway fares in the sections where competition with buses became severe.

Problems on Charoen Krung Road

Since Charoen Krung Road, where the Bang Kholaem line ran, was the most heavily congested road in Bangkok, traffic congestion became more problematic with an increase in automobiles. The Department of Public and Municipal Affairs therefore asked the SEC to remove the tramway track or substitute it with a trolley bus system. The company instead suggested establishing a joint company to replace the tramway business due to the heavy investment that it would need.[76] Since the government was opposed to it, solving the problem of the trolley bus did not proceed right away.

In January 1936, the government again requested the substitution of trolley buses on the congested roads, so the company submitted a plan in June that followed this suggestion (*BTWM*, 17 March 1937). The government once again did not agree with the plan, though its details remain unknown. The company might have asked the government to share some of their cost of investment, since it already asked the government in 1930 to extend the term of concession or to purchase assets after the termination of concession. The company had reserved 2 million baht of depreciation as the capital for introducing the trolley bus, but it decided to return this to the shareholders since the government did not agree with the planned bus service.[77] A newspaper article noted that the company had decided to substitute the trolley bus in 1939, but there are no facts to back this up.[78]

Although the trolley bus plan was now blocked, the company had to cope with the new bus operation plan of the Bangkok Municipality on Charoen Krung Road. The Bangkok Municipality, established in April 1937, had been considering bus operations and decided in August 1938 that it would start the first bus service between Bang Kholaem and Tha Chang (*BTWM*, 30 August 1938). Since the route would be completely parallel to the Bang Kholaem tram line, the company asked the municipality to suspend this bus plan. The company offered three options instead: free lighting of all roads at night, an increase of track rent to 25,000 baht, or a decrease of 25,000 baht for the lighting charge. In return, the municipality promised that it would not operate bus services that ran parallel to the Bang Kholaem and Hua Lamphong lines, as well as parts of the Samsen and Dusit lines. In addition, it would search for the purchaser of buses that the municipality had already ordered (*BTWM*, 6 February 1939). Although this agreement was similar to the one offered to the government, the financial burden of the company was reduced to 25,000 baht per year, compared to 75,000 baht for the previous agreement. However, the restriction of buses did not completely resolve the situation since competition with other means of transport was also severe, including the increase in the ten thousand tricycle rickshaws.

In fact, there was much opposition to the bus operation proposed by the municipality since it would worsen the congestion on Charoen Krung Road.[79] However, the municipality proceeded with the plan by refusing the company's offer and started bus operations in June 1939. The SEC had to discount fares on the Bang Kholaem line to cope with the competition (PCC, 2 June 1939). Nevertheless, the competition on the entire Bang Kholaem line, the most profitable tramway, had badly damaged its profitability and caused a further reduction in gross receipts. The competition with the bus, starting in the latter half of the 1920s, came to seriously affect the tramway business after the participation of the Bangkok Municipality, although the damage could be mitigated for a while by the agreement with the government.

Labor Dispute with Tramway Companies

The competition with buses was not the only factor reducing the profitability of the tramway business; demands to improve the treatment of workers became another significant factor. The history of the labor disputes date back to problems such as the closure of shops, disturbances by the Chinese, who were opposed to the levy of the poll tax in 1910, and the strike of rickshaw workers opposing the increase in car rents in 1916.[80] The tramway companies also had to cope with strikes when their employees participated.

The first strike by tramway employees was against the Siamese Tramway in 1921. On the morning of February 10, 1921, seventy-eight employees, including drivers, gathered at Wat Saket temple, went on strike, and were arrested by police for their illegal gathering (*BTWM*, 10 February 1921).[81] They complained that their average monthly salary was only 55 baht and appealed for help to improve the situation. They noted that the company levied fines so steep that their salary had to be reduced by 2.5 baht per month. The police attempted to persuade them to return to work by asking the company to examine their claims and make improvements. The problem was resolved within one day.

Then the employees of the SEC suddenly went on strike again on December 31, 1922. More than one hundred employees of both the Bang Kholaem and Samsen lines gathered in front of the Ministry of Local Government to forward seven requests, such as an increase in their bonuses.[82] Since arbitration by the police failed, they requested six further conditions on the following day. The strike ended on January 2, and the company replied to their request on January 10 (*BTWM*, 15 January 1923). Even though the company accepted several of the requests, such as an increase in the allocation for bonuses to 27,000 baht per year, 350 employees from both the SEC and the Siamese Tramway went on strike again on January 13.[83] The Ministry of Interior tried to resolve the problem by establishing a reconciliation committee comprised of representatives from the government, company, and employees, but the workers refused to return to work. The company reacted to the matter by dismissing employees who refused to return to work (*BTWM*, 18 January 1923). Normal service resumed by the end of January, but the company's expenses were inevitably increased by the incident.

After the revolution of 1932, many strikes occurred one after another due to the rapid rise in awareness of workers' rights. In August 1932, about six thousand rickshaw workers went on strike to request a reduction in car rentals (Phanni 1999, 108). This led to a strike at the SEC in November (Thompson 1967, 615–16). That strike was sparked by the dismissal of several employees and was resolved when some of the employees were reinstated. The situation did force the company to review its working regulations and new ones were enacted in April 1933. These regulations improved the treatment of employees by increasing the salary by one baht every year and paying a normal salary in the case of sick leave (*BTWM*, 11 April 1933). The labor movement organized the establishment of a labor union for tramway workers in October 1932, just before this strike.[84]

The labor disputes were another unfavorable factor affecting the tramway business. They caused an increase in expenditure to improve the treatment of workers as well as a decrease in gross receipts due to the suspension of service due to strikes. The labor movement that originated during the Constitutional Revolution spread to other industries, and the tramway labor union members assisted the strikers at the rice mills in Bangkok and the Railway Department in 1934. Though the strikes of tramway laborers ended, the company still had to improve the treatment of workers to avoid further explosions of employee complaints.

Limitation of Urban Transport Business by Foreign Enterprises

Failure of Suburban Railways to Become Urban Railways

The private railways in Bangkok could not develop into urban railways for two reasons: the government's caution toward private railways and the passive attitude of the private railways caused by the government's attitude. Thailand entered into the era of railway construction in the 1880s and its fundamental policy was a state-owned railway. Although private railways proposed many plans, since most of them were led by foreigners the government was wary of acquisition by foreign interests.[85] The government had become wary from observing similar cases in countries such as China, and it came to regard private railways as a means for foreigners to acquire major financial power. Therefore, its attitude toward private railways, though somewhat tolerant at first, became more strict and finally reached the point where it prohibited private railways altogether.[86] Although it initially permitted a private railway plan that would not affect national security, it later prohibited in 1899 the trunk lines that it felt should be constructed as state railways since it felt that such lines in private hands would cause political disadvantage. Furthermore, in 1901, then Minister of the Interior Prince Damrong insisted that the government should not approve private railways with the exception of a branch tramway from the national trunk lines. He strengthened his opinion in 1906 by saying that all private railways should be opposed, and this opinion became the policy of the government. At this point, the possibility of constructing new private railways in Thailand completely disappeared.

The PRC was virtually the first private railway that was granted a concession and also the first private railway to open in Thailand. On the other hand, the first section of the MRC, or the old Thachin Railway, was approved according to the principle in 1899, and the second section was approved as an exception to the new policy since it was an extension of the existing line. Therefore, the conditions of the PRC and MRC concessions were different, and this could be seen when the concession term for the MRC ended. The PRC concession required that the government purchase all assets of the railway, but the MRC concession allowed the government to acquire the railway free of charge. The government changed the conditions to increase its interest when it drafted the concession of the MRC, since it recognized that the concession of the PRC was too advantageous for the company.[87]

Such caution toward private railways brought results in the period of stark imperialism between the end of the nineteenth and beginning of the twentieth centuries. However, the government did not change its attitude later and continued to refuse all private railway plans as well as rejecting accommodations toward the existing railways, such as the extension of concession terms. When the PRC applied for an extension of its concession term to electrify the entire line in the 1920s, the government rejected it, insisting that the company would be able to redeem the cost of its investment by its net profit. Rather, it maneuvered to eliminate the possibility of extending the concession term by using a sublease contract. The government came to question the economic profit made by private companies in providing public services, and it decided that such services should be supplied by the government.

Furthermore, after the 1932 revolution, economic nationalism rose, and the "recovery" of economic activities for Thais became important.[88] Although the main target was the Chinese, unfavorable winds were also blowing against Western foreign companies such as the SEC.[89] Given this situation, the concession term of the PRC would terminate, so it became more hopeless to seek an extension. Since the termination of the PRC's concession in 1936, all foreign companies that engaged in public services, including navigation, railways, and tramways, were nationalized up to the termination of the SEC's concession at the end of 1949.[90]

The extreme caution of the government toward private railways brought about passive attitudes by the railway owners. At first, they could invest aggressively and expect more profit, but they gradually became more careful during the middle stage. Finally, all new investments were frozen except potentially profitable ones. Furthermore, as the concessions secured the government's right to decide the purchase of assets even if the value of purchase was agreed by both sides, the company had no choice but to sell its assets as scrap if the government decided against the purchase. It was common that a company hesitated to make new investments when the remaining concession term was limited, as in the case of the PRC's electrification. Therefore, from the management perspective, maintaining the original situation with considerable profit would be preferable to risking a new investment that was aimed at urban railways.

Table 2.10 shows the management situation of the PRC and MRC. Both railways should never have fallen into deficit, since they always seemed to show a profit. The net profit of the PRC was less than 100,000 baht up to the 1900s, and then it exceeded 100,000 baht in 1913; this would have been the result of partial electrification the previous year. Then it had a profit of around 170,000 baht until the termination of concession, although the availability of actual figures is limited.

On the other hand, the net profit of the MRC reached 100,000 baht after the opening of all their lines in 1907, which was higher than the PRC's profit. A similar level was maintained during the 1920s, and then the results of electrification also can be observed. However, profits were largely reduced after the Great Depression in 1929 and dropped to less than 100,000 baht in 1933. Although it finally recovered to the level of the 1920s, the effect of the Depression during the 1930s was significant, and this was quite different from the case of the PRC, which maintained the same levels.

Large gaps between the PRC's and MRC's dividend rates were evident, as shown in table 2.10. The PRC achieved around a 10 percent rate at its beginning and maintained around 30 percent during the 1920s. The MRC recorded its lowest rate of 2.5 percent in the 1930s and reached its highest in the latter half of the 1920s at 10 percent. These gaps were due to the difference in their capital, or construction, costs, as well as to the difference in demand. In summary, the PRC's more favorable concession conditions brought higher profitability.[91]

Table 2.10. Financial Situation of Suburban Railway Companies, 1911–1941

Year	Net Profits (THB)		Dividends (%)	
	Paknam	Maeklong	Paknam	Maeklong
1911	84,899	143,152	14.00	5.00
1912	85,048	118,574	13.50	5.00
1913	116,146	132,578	18.50	5.00
1914	111,495	134,600	17.50	5.00
1915	N.A.	137,706	18.00	5.00
1916	N.A.	81,386	N.A.	3.00
1917	N.A.	N.A.	N.A.	4.00
1918	N.A.	108,461	N.A.	5.00
1919	N.A.	138,471	N.A.	7.00
1920	164,708	154,889	27.00	7.50
1921	N.A.	142,971	28.00	7.00
1922	183,469	172,624	28.00	8.00
1923	179,990	177,146	29.00	8.50
1924	N.A.	187,227	N.A.	9.00
1925	N.A.	224,887	28.50	10.00
1926	172,057	198,125	32.00	10.50
1927	182,385	214,478	33.00	10.00
1928	177,692	208,817	33.50	10.00
1929	N.A.	192,779	34.00	10.00
1930	N.A.	162,294	N.A.	8.00
1931	N.A.	157,934	34.00	6.50
1932	N.A.	158,007	N.A.	7.50
1933	160,631	96,933	31.00	4.50
1934	N.A.	80,974	28.00	3.00
1935	172,501	77,680	28.00	3.00
1936	89,466	80,344	17.00	2.50
1937		80,379		2.50
1938		75,765		2.50
1939		77,497		2.50
1940		167,383		2.50
1941		197,433		2.50

NOTE: Figures for the Paknam Railway in 1936 are those until the concession was terminated.

SOURCES: *BTWM* 1911–41 (selected issues); *BT*, 26 Mar 1942.

The PRC's sublease to the SEC allowed it to remain unaffected by the Great Depression. Since the SEC had to pay a minimum of 170,000 baht annually as rent, only the SEC suffered damage from the Depression. As the net profit of the PRC remained around 170,000 baht since 1926, as far as can be determined, the rent from the SEC became its net profit. Therefore, the PRC maintained a high dividend rate despite the Depression.[92]

The PRC's management methods were well justified. As a cooperating company, its most important task was ensuring return of profits to its shareholders. However, the sublease was the first step in its decline as an urban railway. On the other hand, the MRC began further investments in the latter half of the 1920s, but it suffered deterioration after the Depression and faced the termination of its concession by securing the least net profit without any further investment. Therefore, as the concession terms of private companies were strictly fixed and the government had no intention of extending them, the railways' incentives for new investment declined.

Criticism of Foreign Tramway Businesses

The tramway business in Bangkok started as a foreign economic activity in the 1880s, and it was merged under the SEC, a foreign company, in 1927 after the establishment of a Thai company in the 1900s. Therefore, the tramway business came to be recognized as a foreign business and was criticized as a foreign monopoly in public transportation. On the other hand, the bus business was regarded as a Thai business since its founder, Loet Setthabut, was a Thai, and subsequent operators were also mostly Thai. The image of a foreign tramway network and a Thai bus system was established.

Therefore, the agreement for preventing competition between bus services and tramways between the government and SEC was criticized by Thai bus operators. A principal agreement to secure occupations for all citizens was included in the six principles of the Revolution and this led to economic nationalism. Thais wanted to recover all economic activities dominated by foreigners. Due to this principle, Thai bus operators insisted on the "recovery" of the urban transport business for Thais by abolishing the previous agreements and approving new bus routes paralleling the tramways.

However, the agreement was not abolished immediately after the Revolution but remained in place until 1937. One of the reasons was the high "return" from the SEC; the government wanted to keep its annual profit of 75,000 baht. Another reason was the hope for the Bangkok Municipality's scheme to become involved in bus operations. The government considered that it was better to maintain the agreement until the municipality was able to manage the bus business by itself rather than allow the opening of new bus routes by numerous private operators until their termination dates. Therefore, it concluded that it was not the private operators but the Bangkok Municipality that would provide Thai jobs in the bus business.

The government also came to recognize that it would be necessary to substitute buses for tramways on main roads such as Charoen Krung Road since traffic congestion had become an increasingly serious issue. Thus it was not proposing the abolishment of the tramways as foreign businesses due to economic nationalism, but because tramways came to be regarded as an obstacle for road traffic. The government asked the SEC to substitute trolley buses for tramways because they could utilize electricity like tramways. Whether trolley buses or ordinary buses was of little concern if tramway track was eliminated from roads. Therefore, it was not only the effects of economic nationalism but also the trend from tramways to buses to resolve traffic congestion that acted as negative factors for the SEC's tramway business.

One solution appeared to resolve the traffic congestion of tramways: double-tracking in the center of roads. When the Belgian funders acquired the majority of shares in the 1910s, double-tracking was their top priority since several examples of double-tracking were seen on narrow roads in Europe (*BTWM*, 11 October 1912). At that time, tramway tracks in Bangkok were laid on one side of the road and double-tracked at passing points. As road traffic increased, vehicles concentrated in the remaining lanes to avoid tramway tracks, especially at the passing points. The pavement of tramway tracks enabled other vehicles to run on the track, but its usage was limited since the direction of tramcars would be in the direction opposite to that of road traffic on the single track system. The solution to this problem seemed to be double tracks in the center of roads in accordance with the direction of road traffic.

However, the SEC hesitated to make this new investment since the termination of its concession was approaching, just like electrification for the PRC. It dared to invest in a tramway extension although its remaining term was less than twenty-five years away, but it asked the government to extend the term or to coestablish a new company when the removal of tramways or the introduction of trolley buses was requested in 1930. It was the approaching termination of the concession term that caused a passive attitude in the company, although the improvement of the existing line was less profitable than the construction of a new line.

Since the company's proposal was not accepted by the government, the SEC decided to reduce its capital to minimize the risk at the end of the concession. In 1935, the company reduced the value of a share from 100 baht to 90 baht, which brought the reduction of capital from 22,560,000 baht to 20,310,000 baht.[93] Then the value per share was further reduced to 80 baht in 1937 and 60 baht in 1938 so that the total reduction rate was 40 percent from 1935.[94] From the example of the PRC, which was nationalized in 1936, it was clear that the government had no intention to extend the concession term and it would beat the price down when pursuing nationalization. The company also had no choice but to accept the value of its assets regarding electrification of the PRC as 130,000 baht, although the face value was 300,000 baht (*BTWM*, 8 September 1936). Therefore, the company decided that the way to redeem its value for shareholders was by reducing its capital. Capital reduction of more than 50 percent became impossible as the government rejected the company's plan to revise its articles of association regarding the rate of capital reduction from 50 percent to 25 percent.[95]

The company chose to prepare for the termination of its concession by restraining new investments and redeeming its capital to shareholders under the status quo, since it could not expect an extension of its concession term or the disposal of its assets at a reasonable price. The government had no intention of succeeding in the tramway business or of pursuing further development. The Bangkok Municipality, which was expected to manage urban transport in the future, was interested only in bus operation and did not consider the role of tramways in urban transport. Therefore, the tramway business completely stagnated in the

1930s and was heading for decline due to severe competition with buses and without further extensions or improvements of the network.

Regulation of the Bus Business and Its Limitation

Although both the suburban railways and tramways were foreign businesses, the bus operations were regarded as Thai businesses. Bus operators started as individual operators, but some operators, such as Loet Setthabut, came to be organized or to expand their businesses. Although the government's enterprises or organizations, such as the Aerial Transport and the Air Force Club, participated in the business, the majority of bus operators were Thais, with the exception of the Chinese company Nakhon Thon. Therefore, the economic policy after the 1932 revolution that supported nationalism should have been advantageous to them.

However, the government decided to grant permission only to municipalities, such as the Bangkok Municipality's bus operation on Charoen Krung Road in 1938. Although it was impossible to unify the senior private bus operators immediately because the municipalities were latecomers, the merger of bus operations within each municipality was the long-term objective. The municipalization of bus operation, therefore, had already emerged in that period.

It was understood that the apparent policy of the government toward bus operation had changed from private-oriented to municipality-oriented. However, the regulations it adopted were not severe. In 1925, all bus operators acquired permissions from the government, and the Motor Vehicle Act in 1930 regulated the special permissions for bus operators issued by the Department of Public and Municipal Affairs. Each permission was examined by considering the existence of bus routes or the agreement with the SEC.

However, some "illegal" bus operations existed apart from those that acquired special permissions. Unlike the railways or tramways, it was possible for anyone to operate buses if he had an automobile. Therefore, a considerable number of non-permitted buses were running on several roads in Bangkok. They were called "mosquito buses" (*songthaeo*), trucks with two parallel benches on their carriages.[96] These buses were mostly used to connect local towns with their nearest railway stations.

A considerable number of *songthaeo* seem to have been operating in Bangkok, and these were troublesome to the official buses. One of the reasons for terminating the agreement of the SEC in March, 1937 was the emergence of *songthaeo* on Charoen Krung Road.

The government eventually decided to regulate these *songthaeo* in Bangkok. When it considered the revision of the Motor Vehicle Act in 1937, the treatment of *songthaeo* became a problem. Although the revised draft prohibited their operation on scheduled bus routes where special permissions were granted, opposition for this limitation was voiced in the discussions of Parliament, stating that it would deprive the poor of income opportunities (PCC, 25 February 1937). Eventually it was decided that *songthaeo* would be allowed to operate apart from the scheduled bus routes until their retirement, as long as they were registered with the police (PCC, 10 April 1937). This shows that there had been a considerable number of *songthaeo* competing with ordinary buses and that they affected bus operators.

The government seems to have regulated *songthaeo* aggressively on the one hand, but protected them as small businesses on the other. When Aerial Transport applied for a twenty-five-year concession for bus operations between Paknam and Trat in 1938, the minister of interior expressed his caution to the prime minister about granting privileges to the company; he insisted that the government consider the occupations of existing small hired-car operators (*rot rapchang*) when considering the concession.[97] Two opposite opinions were expressed: the necessity of bus regulation for the sake of passengers' convenience, and the denial of jobs for the poor. As these small operators were Thais, it was not easy to regulate and ban their operations.

The government tried to regulate bus operation with a view to the future takeover by municipalities on the one hand, but eased its control for small *songthaeo* operators by recognizing their existence, on the other hand. As a result, these *songthaeo* were allowed to operate in Bangkok and would later play a role in the decline of municipal buses. Furthermore, the protection of "illegal" buses for the purpose of helping poor people secure their jobs had emerged in various forms up to this point and eventually led to conflict with the legal operators who had official permissions or concessions.

3
Expansion of Bus Networks, 1940s–1950s

Urban Transport during the War Years

Situation of Tramways

The tramway business of the Siam Electric Corporation (SEC) encountered considerable difficulty from the 1930s because of competition with buses. In particular, the start of a bus route on Charoen Krung Road by the Bangkok Municipality in 1939 cast a dark shadow over the future prospects of the tramway business. Furthermore, the company had to cope with the end of its concession term in late 1949; hence, it reduced its scale gradually through capital reduction, beginning in the latter half of the 1930s. In the process, it decided to get rid of its unprofitable sections; thus, a 1.6-kilometer section of the Silom line between Sala Daeng and Ratchaprasong was abolished in November 1940 (*BTWM*, 19 November 1940).[1] The Atsadang branch line was also abolished around this time, although the exact date is unknown.[2] In addition, because the name of the country changed from Siam to Thailand, the company similarly changed its name to the Thai Electric Corporation (TEC) in September 1939 (*BTWM*, 15 March 1940).

However, when Thailand entered World War II in December 1941, the competition with buses abated temporarily, and tramways again were preferred. This was due to the shortage of and rise in prices of fuel and repair parts due to the war; thus, buses, which relied heavily on imported items, from oil to consumables like tires, suffered more severely than tramways. So, the competitive power of buses diminished gradually once the war began, and tramways became more important. Although part of the Silom line was abolished in 1940, in fact, the number of tramway passengers had been increasing since 1939, and more remarkably so after the war began. Whereas the number of passengers in 1939 was set to 100, the index in 1940 was 130, and it increased greatly to 163 in 1942 and 238 in 1943 (until October) (*TM*, 23 November 1943). A rapid increase of passengers was also observed on railways.

Table 3.1 shows the operating condition of tramways from 1941 to 1950. Since there are almost no statistics available regarding the number of tramway passengers but only statistics on income and profit for the pre-1941 period, these are likely the first available figures. From the table we learn that the number of tramway passengers increased until 1943, when it reached 150 million, or 410,000 per day. Based on a previous index, the number of passengers in 1939 was about 67 million, so the number of passengers more than doubled from the prewar period. Although there are no figures for the period before the 1930s, it is likely that the passenger figure for 1943 was the highest on record.

Table 3.1. Tramway Operations, 1942–1950

Year	Number of Tram Cars	Number of Passengers	Receipts (THB)	Expenditures (THB)	Balance (THB)
1942	217	109,446,013	2,113,095	1,089,895	1,023,200
1943	217	156,408,042	3,131,893	1,625,823	1,506,070
1944	217	118,248,666	4,894,882	2,466,614	2,428,268
1945	201	70,913,752	7,306,459	3,815,528	3,490,931
1946	201	96,895,208	13,677,103	8,801,225	4,875,878
1947	201	133,603,685	12,176,848	9,728,119	2,448,729
1948	202	144,373,098	12,489,779	12,151,010	338,769
1949	202	135,347,174	11,447,858	11,136,035	311,823
1950	202	140,518,093	12,056,277	11,768,048	288,229

Source: Data from *SYB* for 1952.

The sharp increase in traffic volume reversed in 1944 and fell to about 70 million passengers in 1945, which was similar to the level in 1939. This was due to the damage to the lines and power stations from the bombing of Allied forces. The first bombing of Bangkok occurred immediately after the outbreak of war, and bombings became severe at the end of 1943 when the war worsened. Although there had been a sporadic influence on tramways, the most serious blow was the bombing of the TEC power station at Wat Liap on April 14, 1945, during which the newest power generation turbine was damaged.[3] It seems that this was the main factor in the reduced traffic volume in 1945 because it forced the stoppage of all tramway lines.[4]

In addition, in response to the rapid general price inflation, the TEC asked the government to allow a fare hike when its service was suspended due to the bombing. The minimum fare doubled from five to ten satang, but the company asserted that the cost was still lower than that of other means of transport.[5] Because the fare price hike was accepted, and even though passenger volume dropped drastically in 1945 compared with the previous year as shown in table 3.1, income from passenger fares increased dramatically. The fare rose about five times between 1942 and 1945 as the average income per passenger increased from two to ten satang during this period. Because these average revenue-per-passenger figures remained unchanged—around nine satang after reaching the highest point in 1946—the fare level in 1945 was maintained after that.

The traffic volume, once reduced by the bombing of the power station, also recovered to exceed 100 million passengers from 1947 until the end of the term of concession in 1949. As shown in table 3.1, the income it generated was about 12 million baht during the latter half of the 1940s, a sharp increase compared with the income from 1942. However, expenditures were also increasing more rapidly and the company's income and expenditures reached parity from 1948. As a result, its gross profit dropped from millions of baht to hundreds of thousands of baht, and the profitability of the tramway business dropped drastically. Probably the jump in labor costs was an important factor in the rapid increase of expenditures, although the exact reasons remain unknown. Passenger volume increased drastically during the war and the company revenues increased more as a result of the fare hike, but the rapid increase of expenditures reduced the overall profitability of the tramway business. As a result, the TEC's concession term was terminated, although its income and expenditures were mostly balanced.

"Revival" of Suburban Railways

The fall in bus transport capacity caused by the war led to a "revival" of not only tramways but also suburban railways, especially the Paknam line. The Paknam line, nationalized in September 1936, was exposed to competition with buses on the Bangkok–Paknam Road, and its income had also seen a slight increase. Although its monthly average income for three months (January to March) in 1937 immediately after nationalization was 5,951 baht from passengers and 845 baht from freight, these were reduced to 5,023 baht and 669 baht respectively during the same three-month period in 1940.[6] The number of trains between Bangkok and Paknam increased to one-hour intervals. However, the railway service was still inferior to the bus system. The Aerial Transport Company offered buses running at fifteen-minute intervals, and there were also a considerable number of illegal *songthaeo*.[7]

For this reason, the Paknam line faced the prospect of being abolished. Because a plan to construct a new Bangkok port at Khlong Toei emerged, an increase in traffic volume on the Rama IV Road, which connected the new port and inner Bangkok, was assumed. So the Ministry of Economic Affairs proposed to abolish part of the Paknam line between Hua Lamphong and Khlong Toei to expand the Rama IV Road (Kakizaki 2009, 48). The director of the Railway Department insisted that the department would oppose the plan unless it could have a monopoly on operation of alternative buses, but because there were several bus routes on the road that had already obtained special permission in the meantime, it was difficult to accept the Railway Department's request. Thus, the cabinet decided only to postpone the abolishment of the line in the future (ibid., 407). Although the abolition plan for the Paknam line also surfaced just before the end of the concession term, it resurfaced after nationalization. To cut down on the original construction costs, the section between Hua Lamphong and Khlong Toei adopted a type of tramway in which track was laid on only one side of the road (Rama IV Road). There were several discussions regarding abolition after that, and ultimately, the line was abolished for this reason.

Although conditions after nationalization were by no means favorable, when the war started and the competitive power of buses declined, the importance of the Paknam line increased, and its function as urban transport would be temporarily strengthened again. We do not know the situation immediately after the outbreak of war. We do know that operations on the Paknam line had to stop temporarily in 1942 due to record flooding. Train operation was restored on November 2, 1942, although there were only six trips a day between Bangkok and Paknam, and partial electric tram service between Witthayu and Khlong Toei had not resumed (*PCC*, 7 November 1942). It was announced that the operation of the Paknam line would return to normal with twelve trips between Bangkok and Paknam in the same month. This number, therefore, became the standard number of trains (*PCC*, 22 November 1942).

The operation of electric trams was expanded beginning in March 1943 to include ten-minute intervals between Hua Lamphong and Khlong Toei and ten trips a day between Hua Lamphong and Phrakhanong (*PCC*, 25 February 1943). This meant that the frequent operation of electric trams between Hua Lamphong and Khlong Toei, abolished since the whole-line electrification in 1926, was revived for the first time. It seemed that the expansion was carried out to compensate for the decrease in the transport capacity of buses and the TEC's tramways on the Rama IV Road. However, the Paknam line's function as an urban railway was temporarily revived as a result. The train intervals were almost the same as in the original plan for the whole-line electrification of the Paknam Railway as mentioned above. Thus, the plan from twenty years earlier was realized at last, although it was far behind.

Operation of the electric trams to Phrakhanong must have aimed to improve service for suburban passengers. When the number of trains increased to make about twenty trips a day, including train service to Paknam, the frequency of trains between Khlong Toei and Phrakhanong rose to its highest level. This was doubtless related to the evacuation of the population from Bangkok to suburban areas, which had been taking place since 1943. The improvement of bus service for commuters and students from suburban areas also became an important task as will be described below. Although the Paknam line was not in the proximity of the Bangkok–Paknam Road (Sukhumvit Road) at Phrakhanong, the reinforcement of its transport capacity responded to urbanization along the road as far as Phrakhanong.

On the other hand, the Maeklong Railway did not seem to experience the growth of its function as an urban railway during the war. As of January 1942, it scheduled three trips a day between Khlong San and

Mahachai (Thachin), the same as when the line started, and electric trams to Bang Bon made twenty-seven trips a day. However, the actual number of trains was reduced because of the small number of passengers, and the terminal for electric trams was shortened to Wat Sing.[8] Although the operation of this section was nationalized in November 1942, the enhancement of an urban railway like the Paknam line was uncalled for because there were no parallel bus routes or tramways.

Reinforcement of Buses

Bus networks in Bangkok were still being extended even during the war. Table 3.2 shows the establishment of new bus routes from 1940 to 1943. It can be seen that seven new routes were established during that time. The network of bus routes was also expanded further as shown in figure 3.1, and the length of the roads where buses passed was also increasing as compared with the situation shown in figure 2.3. The policy of municipalization, established at the end of the 1930s, was corrected to some extent, and as a result, private operators were also permitted. Among the seven routes in the table, two were permitted to have private operators, and Route 35 was granted to a private operator from the beginning. Permitting private operators was likely inevitable since they would be able to help meet the ever-increasing demand for transport due to the municipality's lack of capacity. The policy of municipalization of the bus service was not completely reversed, because the municipality's bus routes were new, but the policy was adjusted.

Moreover, there are two inter-provincial bus routes included in table 3.2: the routes to Singburi and Prachinburi. From the 1930s, new bus routes were established to provincial cities no less than one hundred kilometers away from Bangkok in response to the construction of trunk highways between the capital and the provinces. Both routes were operated by the Transport Company (*Borisat khonsong chamkat*), the former Aerial Transport Company, and were the first middle-distance, inter-provincial buses apart from suburban buses between Bangkok and neighboring provinces.[9] Although they also functioned as suburban transport to some extent because their routes in Bangkok were the same as the Don Mueang route run by the Transport Company, they primarily functioned as inter-provincial transport, since the number of buses was fewer than those to Don Mueang or Paknam.[10]

Table 3.2. New Bus Routes in Bangkok, 1940–1943

Route Number	Line	Operator	Route	Date of Approval	Remarks
9	Hua Lamphong–Singburi	Transport Co.	Rama IV, Rama VI, Rama I, Phayathai Road	17 Aug 1940	Inter-provincial bus
33	Chakkrawat–Pratunam	Phuak Yuwabun	Worachak, Nakhon Sawan, Phetchaburi, Rama VI, Ratchaprarop	3 Apr 1941	
19	Hua Lamphong–Prachinburi	Transport Co.	Rama IV, Rama VI, Rama I, Phayathai Road	22 Sep 1941	Inter-provincial bus
35	Wongwian Yai–Bukkhalo	Bangkok Municipality	Taksin, Mahaisawan Road	17 Aug 1942	Transferred from Nakhon Thon Co. on 23 Jul 1942
36	Victory Monument–Saphan Daeng	Loet Setthabut	Don Mueang, Patiphat Road	27 Nov 1942	
30	Bang Lamphu–Victory Monument	Bangkok Municipality	Nakhon Ratchasima, Ratchawithi Road	25 Oct 1943	
31	Ratchawong–Nangloeng	Bangkok Municipality	Sueapa, Luang, Krungkasem Road	25 Oct 1943	

Sources: Data from NA [2] So Ro. 0201. 66. 3/7.

When the war started, bus operators were forced to reduce transport capacity drastically in the face of shortage of commodities such as fuel and tires. For example, the number of buses between Bangkok and Paknam operated by the Transport Company dropped to eight cars in January 1942, compared to twelve to fourteen cars in the prewar period, and on the Don Mueang route it fell from seven to nine cars, to five.[11] This was due to the shortage of tires. As of March 1942, it was estimated that two hundred tires were immediately required to continue bus operation, and it was also necessary to continue to change eighty tires each month.[12] Moreover, the operation of some bus routes was suspended because of the shortage of commodities. For example, among the bus routes started in the 1930s, as shown in table 2.9, Routes 10 and 28 stopped their operation in 1943.[13] The shortage of bus transport capacity was an important factor in strengthening the role of tramways and suburban railways.

Because private automobiles were conscripted, and dependence on the public transport facility was still increasing, bus operators tried

Fig. 3.1. Bus Network in Bangkok, 1943

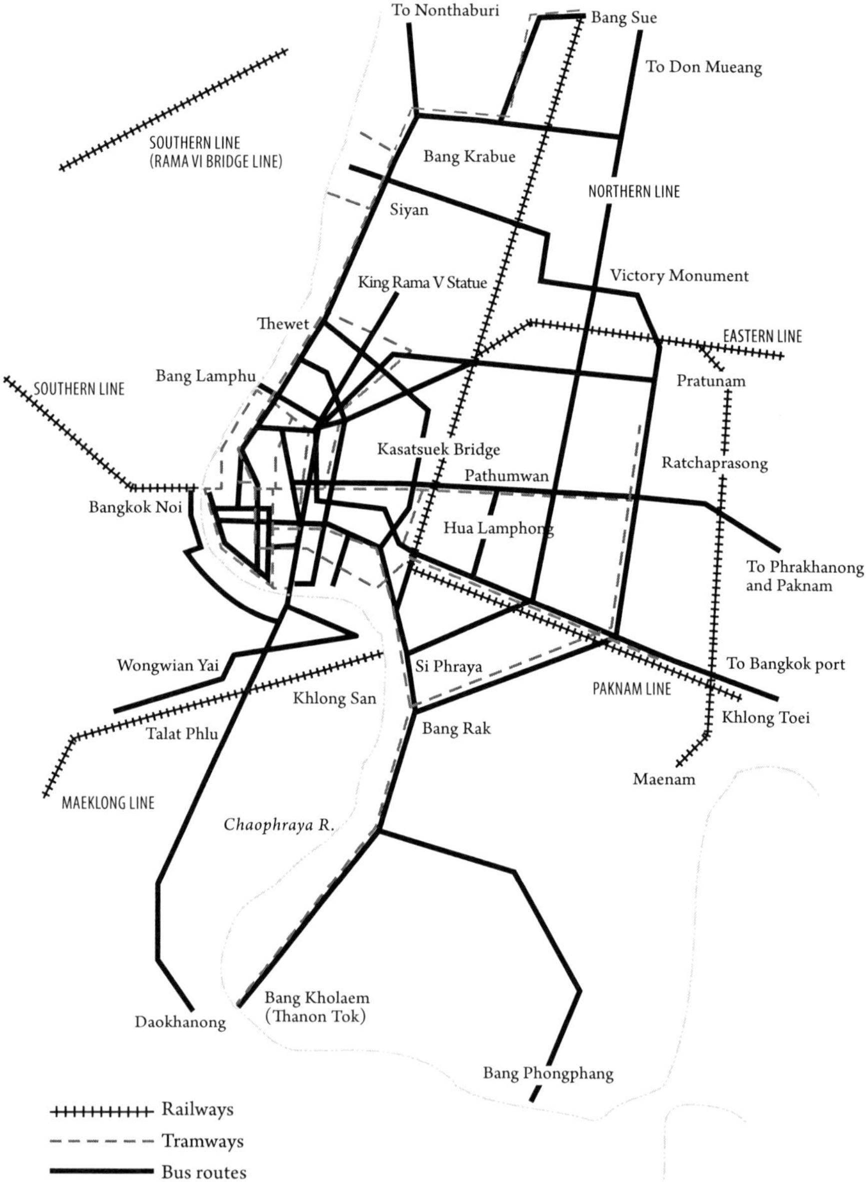

to expand their reach, which was something the government also recommended. Prime Minister Phibun stated in May 1943 that bus service in Bangkok should be expanded to meet the residents' needs and ordered the Ministry of Interior to consider the matter.[14] Then in August of the same year, he stressed the need to improve bus service asserting that bus service within each city should be owned by each municipality, and he ordered the Ministry of Interior to examine the situation.[15] Thus he tried to revive the principle of municipalization of the bus service, which was gradually being emasculated. The Ministry of Interior then ordered the Bangkok Municipality to consider starting four new bus lines and accepted applications from operators to start supplemental bus service on Route 24 between Tha Tian and Thanon Tok and Route 1 between Kasatsuek and Phrakhanong.[16] Two lines were established as Routes 30 and 31, shown in table 3.2, among the four lines that had to be considered by the Bangkok Municipality. However, in regard to the municipalization of the bus service, it was decided to continue the existing operation system because rapid municipalization would cause the municipality to suffer a deficit. It was also concluded that the Ministry of Interior would continue to supervise as usual until the municipality took over regulation, and even so, it should carry out municipalization, city by city.[17]

Both the establishment of new routes and an increase in the number of buses on existing routes were indispensable. The Ministry of Interior planned to increase to a total of twenty-six buses on ten routes such as Route 2, the Bang Lamphu–Makkasan route, and asked each operator to cooperate.[18] The operators then replied to the ministry that they could increase the number of buses if they could acquire spare parts for repairs and submitted the list of required materials to the Ministry of Interior. The most desired materials were tires, and there were more than a few companies that asked for batteries or fuel. Ultimately, it was decided that the Ministry of Interior would collect old tires and provide them to the Ministry of Defense to recycle them into new tires, and that the Ministry of Defense would procure fuel.[19]

To ease the shortage of buses, *songthaeo* would also be used. By the revision of the Motor Vehicles Act in 1937, the operation of *songthaeo* in Bangkok was exceptionally admitted on the regular bus routes under special permission until the cars were taken out of service. In 1944, there were forty-nine such *songthaeo* registered at the Police Department (*Krom tamruat*).[20] It was decided to reinforce the transport capacity for the main routes every morning and evening by using these *songthaeo*; twenty cars on the Hua Lamphong–Talat Phlu route, three on the Bangkok–Rangsit route, ten on the Bang Krabue–Nonthaburi route, and ten on the Kasatsuek–Phrakhanong route. However, because only twenty-nine owners came when the Police Department asked *songthaeo* owners to appear, the prearranged distribution was impossible.[21]

Furthermore, trucks were procured to operate as substitutes for buses in 1945. As the cabinet ordered the Ministry of Communications to conscript trucks to be operated as buses in April 1945, the ministry started to run trucks on the Lak Mueang–Bang Krabue route, Lak Mueang–Bang Kholaem route, and Thewet–Hua Lamphong under the regulation of the Department of Transport (*Krom kan khonsong*).[22] These trucks were mainly for military use and provided by the Ministry of Defense, and the existing bus operators on such routes took charge of actual operation.[23] As mentioned above, tramways were suspended because of the bombing of the power station, so these trucks seem to have played the role of substituting for tramways.

Thus, the shortage of materials or fuels for buses due to the war reduced the competitive power of bus transport and resulted in augmenting the use of tramways and suburban railways. Additionally, newly granted permission to use private operators to solve the problem of insufficient buses signaled the retreat of the municipalization policy that was being established, and the utilization of *songthaeo* would later come to infringe on the existing bus operators' interests.

Stagnating Rail Transport

Bangkok Electricity's Tramway Business

Reconstruction was swift after the war, but tramways suffered various kinds of damage. As shown in table 3.1, the number of passengers exceeded one hundred million in 1947. The term of concession of TEC would end at the end of 1949, when Thailand was still in the reconstruction period, and its business would be taken over by the government. Unlike the example of the Paknam or Maeklong Railways, there are no materials available to show the details of the process of nationalizing the TEC. Thus, although it is unknown how the company negotiated with the government, it seems that it did not experience an unfavorable situation because of the existence of the power station. There were two power stations in Bangkok: one at Wat Liap owned by the company and one at Samsen owned by the Department of Public and Municipal Affairs (formerly the Local Sanitary Department), but the latter was also damaged in the war and rebuilt in June 1949 (FN 1988, 22). The company power station had been functioning as Bangkok's only power station for a long time, so there was no choice of abolishing it without purchase.

Hence, the government purchased the TEC and transformed it into Bangkok Electricity (*Kan faifa krungthep*) under the Ministry of Interior. The final purchase amount was 11,281,600 baht.[24] This was the same amount as the TEC's final capital after capital reduction during the 1930s. For the Paknam and Maeklong Railways, the Railway Department could succeed in the businesses, but the government had to establish a new agency to supervise the business of power distribution and tramway operation because there was no existing agency with jurisdiction over them. The main business of the TEC was power distribution rather than tramway operation; thus, it was put under the jurisdiction of the Ministry of Interior, which supervised urban infrastructure.

Bangkok Electricity formulated a tramway improvement program after the succession of tramway operations. Apart from the expansion of the tramway network, the installation of trolley bus lines was also newly included in this plan. The tramway improvement plan, submitted to the Ministry of Interior in August 1951, included the construction of eight trolley bus lines totaling 48.6 kilometers in Bangkok.[25] Their total length was almost the same as that of existing tramway networks, and the network would reach destinations that tramways had not yet reached: for example, in the northeast, the Victory Monument or Saphan Khwai, and on the Thonburi side, Talat Phlu or Daokhanong. Ninety-two trolley buses needed to be purchased for this plan, and the total cost was estimated at 73.5 million baht.

The abolition of some lines, the construction of new lines, and the procurement of new trams were also included in the plan for the tramways. The 1.1-kilometer section between Yotse and Hua Lamphong on the Hua Lamphong line and the 1.9-kilometer section between Saphan Daeng and Bang Sue on the Bang Sue line were to be abolished. Instead, the 1.6-kilometer section between Sala Daeng and Ratchaprasong on the Silom line and the 1.1-kilometer section between Ratchaprasong and the level crossing with the Maenam branch line of the Phloenchit line would be constructed. Moreover, a plan to import 100 new tramcars was also included to replace the 202 prewar-era tramcars. The total cost for tramway improvement was 53,385,170 baht.[26] The trams of the Hua Lamphong line went through the Pathumwan line from 1940, and the operation between Yotse and Hua Lamphong was separated from the main line (*PCC*, 8 August 1940). The newly constructed section of the Silom line was the revival of the abolished section in 1940; it was not an entirely new line. The last Phloenchit line was the extension of the Pathumwan line to the east as shown in figure 3.2. Although the initial terminal was the level crossing of the Maenam branch line at the easternmost end of Phloenchit Road, it was planned to extend the line to Watthana or Phrakhanong along the Bangkok–Paknam Road (Sukhumvit Road) in the future.[27]

The extension plan to Phrakhanong would further expand the tramway network of Bangkok to the suburbs. Sukhumvit Road had been rapidly constructed to meet the end of the concession of the Paknam Railway, and only fifteen years had passed since its opening. Because it was one of the first roads extending beyond the Bangkok city limit, along with the road to Don Mueang, urbanization along the route was progressing. The evacuation plan during the war must have also accelerated the movement. Therefore, the numbers of students and commuters traveling to the inner city were increasing along the road, and the transport capacity of buses became insufficient. At that time, this road consisted of two lanes, and the tramway was to be constructed on the vacant right-of-way along the road. The plan asserted that it was possible to increase transport capacity by introducing a tramline without affecting existing road traffic.[28]

However, the Ministry of Finance showed resistance to the trolley bus plan. They claimed that because they had already fixed the budget for the fiscal year 1952, it would be difficult to procure such a large amount of funding. Although, in fact, Bangkok Electricity planned to borrow from the Ministry of Finance, the ministry recommended creating a

Fig. 3.2. Tramway Network in Bangkok, 1955

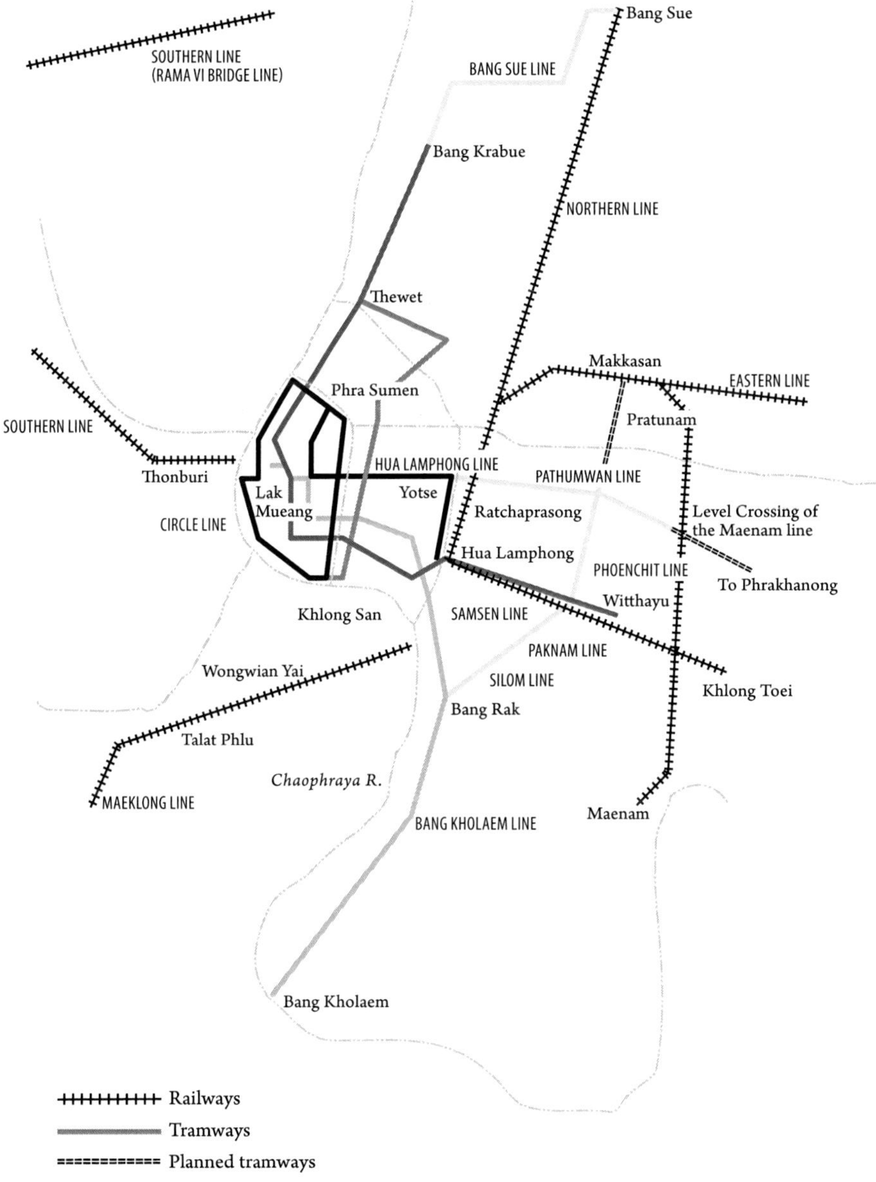

Source: NA [2] So Ro. 0201. 63. 2/20.

long-term plan. Moreover, at the cabinet meeting in November 1951, the prime minister had stated that it was unrealizable to introduce such heavy vehicles on Bangkok's narrow streets, where heavy maintenance was badly needed.[29] For this reason, the grand plan was not realized after all, and the trolley bus plan again did not materialize.[30]

To extend the tramways, the Silom line was revived and the Phloenchit line constructed. The former was the revival of the abolished section from the prewar period, and as such it should have been resumed within a short period. The latter was said to have started in 1951, but its operation cannot be confirmed.[31] The extension to Phrakhanong was not realized because of the opposition by the State Railways of Thailand (SRT) to construct a level crossing between the tramway and the Maenam branch line.[32] On the other hand, there is evidence that the newly built Ratchaprarop line, seven hundred meters of line from Pratunam to Makkasan, would start in 1957, but there was no sign of actual construction.[33]

Because the trolley bus plan did not materialize, the abolition of the partial section of the Hua Lamphong and Bang Sue lines was suspended. However, Bangkok Electricity had applied to abolish the two branch lines of the Samsen line in 1951: the 0.5-kilometer section between the Sukhothai Palace and the mouth of Samsen Canal and the 0.3-kilometer section between Bang Krabue and Bang Krabue Pier; these were permitted at the end of 1951.[34] The former was the terminal section of the Dusit Extension line of the old Siamese Tramway, and the latter was the connecting line between the Samsen line and water transport on the Chaophraya River. Because these two sections were the last tramways to connect with piers, all connection between water transport and tramways disappeared as a result of their abolition.

Although expansion of tramways in Bangkok was still not yet realized, Bangkok Electricity formulated a tramway plan for other cities. Lopburi was chosen as the first site, and a 5.5-kilometer line was started there in 1955 (*SRWR*, 4 March 1955). This plan aimed to reuse tramcars in Bangkok after the substitution with newly introduced trolley buses was carried out. If the first introduction would prove successful, then other cities such as Chiang Mai, Lampang, Khorat, and Songkhla would follow suit (*SN*, 23 January 1953). However, the Lopburi tramway, which connected the western old city and the eastern new town, suffered severe competition from buses. In the event, Bangkok Electricity's tramway plan for local cities was realized only in Lopburi.

Stagnation of the Paknam Line

The Paknam line revived its function temporarily as an urban railway during the war. However, it was exposed again to competition with tramways or buses and stagnated after the war. It is unknown how long the frequent tramcar service between Hua Lamphong and Khlong Toei, which began in 1943, would last, but it was probably temporarily suspended by the damage of the TEC power station in April 1945. There is no evidence of a partial tramway service between Hua Lamphong and Khlong Toei or between Witthayu and Khlong Toei after the war; it is likely that only the train service between Hua Lamphong and Paknam continued. For example, Takada (1952a, 40–41), who visited Bangkok in 1952, mentioned that the Paknam line had a two-hour interval service between 6:00 am and 6:00 pm and did not refer to the partial tramcar service.

The financial condition of the Paknam line did not improve in this situation. As table 3.3 shows, the income of the Paknam line increased until 1954, then decreased gradually. It still maintained an income of one million baht until 1958, but the problem was its deficit, which had resulted from a rapid increase of expenditures. The Paknam line had fallen into deficit in 1952, and the deficit was increasing every year. This was because the SRT owed additional expenditures, such as tax and living expense assistance for its employees, that the Ministry of Finance had expended before the Railway Department became the SRT in 1951. Then, the SRT raised employees' wages and established a welfare fund in 1952 (RFT for 1951, 10; RFT for 1952, 98). Thus, the financial condition of the Paknam line deteriorated in the 1950s, and its deficit exceeded 700,000 baht by the end of the decade.

Although the Paknam line operated at a loss in the 1950s, the SRT planned to modernize it. The number of trains on the Paknam line was lower than it had been in the prewar days because of the shortage of electric power. The electric power supply of the Paknam line was dependent on Bangkok Electricity's power station at Wat Liap. Increase in the number of trains had been barred because of the lack of electric power supply.[35] To solve the problem, the SRT planned to construct an independent power station in 1954 to secure sufficient power and increase

Table 3.3. Suburban Railway Operations after Nationalization, 1946–1960 (THB)

Year	Paknam Line					Maeklong Line				
	Receipts			Expenditures	Balance	Receipts			Expenditures	Balance
	Passengers	Freight	Total			Passengers	Freight	Total		
1946	896,855	40,917	944,443	274,591	669,852	N.A.	N.A.	N.A.	N.A.	N.A.
1947	769,307	47,349	834,140	234,149	599,991	N.A.	N.A.	N.A.	N.A.	N.A.
1950	669,652	48,464	739,573	475,374	264,199	N.A.	N.A.	N.A.	N.A.	N.A.
1951	1,028,765	72,671	1,120,323	838,152	282,171	3,241,433	421,304	3,795,640	2,834,993	960,647
1952	1,211,373	71,979	1,314,067	1,411,134	-97,067	3,277,838	391,599	3,815,098	3,430,236	384,862
1953	1,317,117	73,022	1,420,521	1,501,245	-80,724	3,501,119	398,075	4,059,042	3,610,970	448,072
1954	1,504,021	72,452	1,617,994	1,728,449	-110,455	3,661,374	533,232	4,431,495	3,730,133	701,362
1955	1,338,028	88,702	1,464,353	1,837,679	-373,326	3,843,761	453,809	4,500,524	4,441,865	58,659
1956	1,164,495	130,504	1,332,937	1,753,160	-420,223	4,489,366	378,719	5,301,362	5,078,146	223,216
1957	1,028,854	129,187	1,191,960	1,916,453	-724,493	4,712,715	335,572	5,286,894	5,899,477	-612,583
1958	943,667	130,643	1,112,675	1,817,793	-705,118	5,525,100	309,869	6,086,291	5,812,768	273,523
1959	716,195	85,495	838,115	1,577,165	-739,050	5,646,625	263,513	6,154,960	5,685,274	469,686
1960						7,021,059	255,599	7,551,959	6,425,933	1,126,026

SOURCES: RSRS for 1947, 12–13; RFT for 1951–60 (selected years).

train operation. Then, in the following year, there was a report that the SRT was planning to install a 500-kilowatt generator at its Makkasan workshop, but rolling stock was insufficient to run three trains.[36]

The SRT finally changed its plan to introduce diesel cars in place of electric trains to improve service on the Paknam line. The plan to introduce diesel cars on the Paknam line was included in the five-year plan of the SRT as of 1960 to increase the number of trains by dieselization instead of using old electric facilities.[37] The Maeklong line had also decided to introduce diesel cars instead of electric tramcars, as mentioned later, and the same measure was adopted by the Paknam line. We do not know how many trains were to be added by this dieselization, but the measure probably did not aim to increase frequency within the city or enhance the line's function as an urban railway even if its function as an inter-city railway would increase.

An extension plan was also made for the Paknam line. In April 1952, Prime Minister Phibun ordered the Ministry of Communications to consider the extension of railway from Paknam to Bang Pu.[38] Bang Pu was located about ten kilometers southeast of Paknam, where seashore recreation facilities had been constructed by the order of the prime minister in prewar days. Therefore, the prime minister ordered a plan to extend the railway as an access route to these recreation facilities. There was also an extension plan from Paknam to Chonburi, so the Paknam line faced the possibility of being part of the main line to the east. A news report in 1953 stated that the government had decided to construct a railway from Paknam to Chanthaburi through Chonburi and would start construction work the next year, completing it by 1959 (*SN*, 13 September 1953). Although these extension plans for the Paknam line were not formally included in the new line construction plan of the SRT, they did sometimes appear up until the middle 1950s.

However, neither the increase in frequency by electric or diesel cars nor the extension to Chonburi were realized in the end. Because the frequency of trains in the city section of the Paknam line did not increase, its function as an urban railway, temporarily revived during the war, was ultimately lost; the Paknam line came to serve only as an inter-urban railway. However, competition with automobiles became more serious than in the prewar days due to the revival of automobiles in the postwar period, and passengers on the Paknam line decreased steadily in number.

Development of the Maeklong Line

The nationalization of the former Maeklong Railway was completed in two stages: the Bangkok section between Khlong San and Mahachai was nationalized in 1942, and the remaining section between Ban Laem and Maeklong was nationalized in 1945. At first, the independent Maeklong Railway Authority (*Ongkan rotfai sai maeklong*) operated the line, and then regulation was transferred to the SRT after the latter was established in 1951. However, the SRT established the Maeklong Line Office (*Samnakngan rotfai sai maeklong*) in 1952 to avoid complications in case the agency was to be unified.[39] Jurisdiction of the Maeklong line was finally unified in 1955 by the merger of the office into SRT.

The business of the Maeklong line after nationalization was changing favorably. As table 3.3 shows, the income level of the Maeklong line was far more than that of the Paknam line in 1951; it had doubled by 1960. Considering that the incomes of both Paknam and Maeklong Railways were similar during the earlier half of the 1920s, it can now be seen that the income of the Paknam line only slightly increased in the meantime. The important factor in this lack of increase was the competition with roads. There had been no roads running parallel to the Maeklong line until 1952, when the first road between Bangkok and Samut Sakhon started. However, the new road was a detour route and its condition was poor.[40] Thus, unlike that of the Paknam line, the income of the Maeklong line increased consistently, and it earned a surplus almost every year. Nevertheless, operating costs still increased as in the case of the Paknam line after the merger in 1955, and its profit suffered.

Modernization of the Maeklong line, therefore, was generally more advanced than that of the Paknam line. Whole-line electrification between Khlong San and Mahachai (Thachin) was planned in 1950, but the plan to purchase new electric cars was instead replaced with one to purchase steam locomotives and passenger cars because of the difficulty in procurement of electrical power.[41] By using this new rolling stock, an express train using two steam locomotives and six passenger cars started operating between Khlong San and Mahachai in August 1953, and the number of trains in this section would increase henceforth (*SN*, 8 August 1953). Then, two diesel locomotives were also introduced in 1957, and two diesel locomotives and seven passenger cars for the main lines were transferred in the next year (RFT 1970, 355). As a result, by the end of 1957, the number of trains between Khlong San and Mahachai was increased to make seven trips: four trips on express trains and three trips on ordinary trains. The Ban Laem–Maeklong section also increased its service to three trips from the two trips it had provided since its opening (RFT for 1957, 79). Because the changes of rails and bridges were also carried out in accordance with the increase of rolling stock, the time distance between Khlong San and Mahachai was shortened from eighty minutes in its pre-nationalization days to just forty-five minutes (RFT 1970, 356).

On the other hand, unlike on the Paknam line, the operation of electric trams in the city section also continued. The frequency of electric trams in 1952 was one-hour intervals, which was the same as during the wartime period (Takada 1952b, 7). When the whole-line electrification plan was scrapped in 1950, the purchase of diesel cars was to substitute for electric cars, but this was probably never realized. However, after the cable under the Chaophraya River, which supplied power to the Maeklong line, broke down in 1955, the operation of electric trams became impossible.[42] Since then, the operation of electric trams was abolished; internal combustion railcars, formerly belonging to the Japanese army, were moved from the main line to replace them, and six new diesel trains were ordered.[43] The newly purchased diesel cars began operation in 1959, running at thirty-minute intervals between Khlong San and Wat Sing.[44]

The positive investment in the Maeklong line resulted in a favorable increase of passenger traffic revenue. Conditions such as competition with motor transport were different when compared to the Paknam line. However, it is clear that the positive investment in the Maeklong line generated new passenger demand. That is, if the number of trains was increased by introducing new rolling stock, and the speedup was realized by permanent improvements, not only an increase in passengers, but also an increase in the revenue exceeding new investment costs could be expected. There is no doubt that the strategy of investment in the Maeklong line was successful, as its surplus exceeded one million baht in 1960, although its balance worsened temporarily after it merged with the SRT in 1955.

The investment in the Maeklong line during this period provided the enhancement of its function as an inter-urban railway rather than an urban railway. Frequent service between Khlong San and Wat Sing only returned to the level of the prewar days, and the shortening of the train interval beyond it was not realized. Rather, the inter-urban transport between Khlong San and Mahachai, with only three trips per day by then, was drastically improved in terms of the number of trains and time distance. The Maeklong line experienced the most remarkable development among rail transport in Bangkok; however, its function as an urban railway decreased after the war under competition from buses.

Emergence of a Bus Nationalization Plan

Revival of Buses and Attendant Problems

The supply of buses in Bangkok was exhausted by the war, and this shortage continued after the war as well. Although there was a new supply of automobiles from the disposal of the Japanese army trucks, the number of buses had decreased because of their heavy use during the war, and they were insufficient to meet the increasing user demand.[45] To accommodate this shortage of buses, *songthaeo* and trucks were drawn into service as buses in Bangkok. The situation did not improve immediately after the war. None of the operators with special permits could offer enough buses, hence, the *songthaeo* and trucks compensated for the lack.

Since the demand for passenger transport in Bangkok increased, truck owners gained business opportunities. Those who purchased old army trucks converted them into *songthaeo* and began operating them as buses. Thus, the number of *songthaeo* increased remarkably in Bangkok, and legal buses, operated by existing operators, became a minority. For example, the buses on Charoen Krung Road, which the Bangkok Municipality operated under special permission, were overwhelmed by *songthaeo* after the war and disappeared completely at one time.[46] The number of *songthaeo* running on Charoen Krung Road in 1947 grew to over one hundred cars and became the main means of transport on the road (*SN*, 30 September 1947).

Although the increase of *songthaeo* served to supplement the deficiency in transport capacity, it brought with it the problem of deteriorating service. The number of *songthaeo* increased rapidly, but demand still exceeded supply in Bangkok's bus service. The operators of *songthaeo* were interested only in profit and neglected to improve their service.[47] Most operators were small entrepreneurs who owned only one or two *songthaeo*, so there was no coordination among *songthaeo*. In addition, passenger scrambles took place, and *songthaeo* often picked up as many passengers as possible, so it was common to see a crowded *songthaeo* with passengers hanging on the steps. To increase the number of trips, they ran at high speeds and often neglected traffic rules. Furthermore, the *songthaeo* were also in poor condition. There were less than fifty *songthaeo* among those operating on Charoen Krung Road that would have met the standards if they were inspected closely (*SN*, 30 September 1947).

Moreover the significant shortage of buses led to more operators participating in providing bus service. For example, the Phira Bus (*Borisat rotme phira chamkat*), the operator of the Thewet–Surawong route, had begun operating in 1947.[48] Similarly, the Bunphong Company (*Borisat bunphong chamkat*), the operator of the Silom–Bang Lamphu line, participated in the bus business after the war (*SN*, 13 May 1969). Table 3.4 shows that there were seventeen operators in 1953. There were ten operators in 1943, so many new operators had entered the bus business during this period. The Bangkok Municipality had already withdrawn from the bus service, and the Thonburi Municipality reduced its size to operate only two routes in cooperation with other private operators. That is, the municipalization policy of the bus service promulgated in the prewar days disappeared completely, and anyone capable of operating buses could get "special" permission.

As the road network expanded, bus routes were also extended. Figure 3.3 shows the network of bus routes in 1953. We can see from this map that suburban buses extended to the suburbs: to Pakkret in the north and Bang Khae in the west. Since in 1943 (see figure 3.1) Nonthaburi and Talat Phlu were the northernmost and westernmost terminals respectively, the bus network was further expanded toward the north and west in the following ten years. The extension corresponded to the extension of highways, as the highway from Nonthaburi to Pakkret (Route 306, or Tiwanon Road) was opened for traffic in 1941. Also, Bang Khae was located on the trunk highway toward the south (Route 4, or Phetkasem Road), and the section to Bang Khae was opened in 1949. In addition, the bus route to Paknam was still operating as it had in the prewar days, although it is not shown in figure 3.3.

Table 3.4. Bus Routes in Bangkok, September 1953

Route Number	Line	Operator	Route	Remarks
1	Outer Circle Line (right rotation)	Nai Loet	Phayathai, Rama IV, Yaowarat, Samsen, Patiphat, Phahonyothin Road	Originating at Victory Monument
2	Outer Circle Line (left rotation)	Si Nakhon	Phahonyothin, Patiphat, Samsen, Yaowarat, Rama IV, Phayathai Road	Originating at Victory Monument
3	Bang Sue–Wang Burapha	Si Nakhon	Rama V Road	
4	Phrakhanong–Pakkhlong Talat	Nai Loet	Sukhumvit, Phetchaburi Road	
5	Khlong Toei–Si Phraya	Former operators on Charoen Krung line	Rama IV Road	
6	Daokhanong–Saochingcha	Central Bus, Thonburi Municipality	Prachathipok Road, Memorial Bridge	
7	Talat Phlu–Saochingcha	Thonburi Municipality, former operators on Talat Phlu–Hua Lamphong line	Prachathipok Road, Memorial Bridge	
8	Wongwian Yai–Wongwian 7.22	Si Lueang	Prachathipok Road, Memorial Bridge	
9	Makkasan–Bang Lamphu	Yanyon Insurance	Si Ayutthaya, Ratchadamnoen Road	
10	Silom–Bang Lamphu	Bunphong	Silom, Rama I Road	
11	Surawong–Thewet	Phira Bus	Surawong, Phayathai, Phitasanulok Road	
12	Inner Circle Line (right rotation)	Thai Pradit	Phayathai, Rama IV, Krungkasem, Samsen, Ratchawithi	Originating at Victory Monument
13	Inner Circle Line (left rotation)	Red Bus	Ratchawithi, Samsen, Krungkasem, Rama IV, Phayathai	Originating at Victory Monument
14	Siyan–Tha Phrachan	Sinakhon	Nakhon Chaisi, Rama VI, Lanluang	
15	Bang Khae–Wongwian Lek	Bang Khae Transport	Bangkok–Nakhon Pathom Road	

Route Number	Line	Operator	Route	Remarks
16	Ratchawong–Phlapphlachai		Ratchawong, Bamrung Mueang Road	
17	Samyaek–Bang Khunphrom	Former operators on Khlong Toei–Hua Lamphong line	Wisut Kasat Road	
18	Bang Krabue–Wat Pho	Chawanaphan	Ratchasima Road	
19	Pakkhlong Talat–Rama V Statue	Nai Loet	Ratchadamnoen Road	
20	Tha Tian–Thanon Tok	ETO	Charoen Krung Road	No change
21	Hua Lamphong–Banthat Thong		Banthat Thong Road	
22	Tha Dindaeng–Don Mueang		Phahonyothin Road	
23	Sathon–Ratchaprasong		Sathon, Witthayu Road	
24	Tha Chang–Nonthaburi	Transport Co.	Samsen Road	No change
25	Sanam Luang–Nonthaburi	Nonthaburi Municipality	Samsen Road	No change
26	Sanam Luang–Pakkret	Transport Co.	Samsen Road	No change

NOTE: No change means the route remains the same as the original route.
SOURCE: Data from NA Kho Kho. 0202. 3. 5/1.

The bus network expanded considerably, but the increase of unauthorized *songthaeo* and entry of more operators called for bus regulation. The unification plan for bus service that had previously been suggested in the form of municipalization thus emerged again, although this time in a different form.

Bus Unification Plan under Government Management

The municipalization of the bus service started with the establishment of municipalities in the 1930s, and those such as the Bangkok Municipality and the Thonburi Municipality came to engage in bus operation. However, the war almost completely destroyed municipal bus operations. Thus, the bus unification plan that emerged after the war took the form of nationalization in order to establish a new government authority.

Fig 3.3. Bus Network in Bangkok, 1953

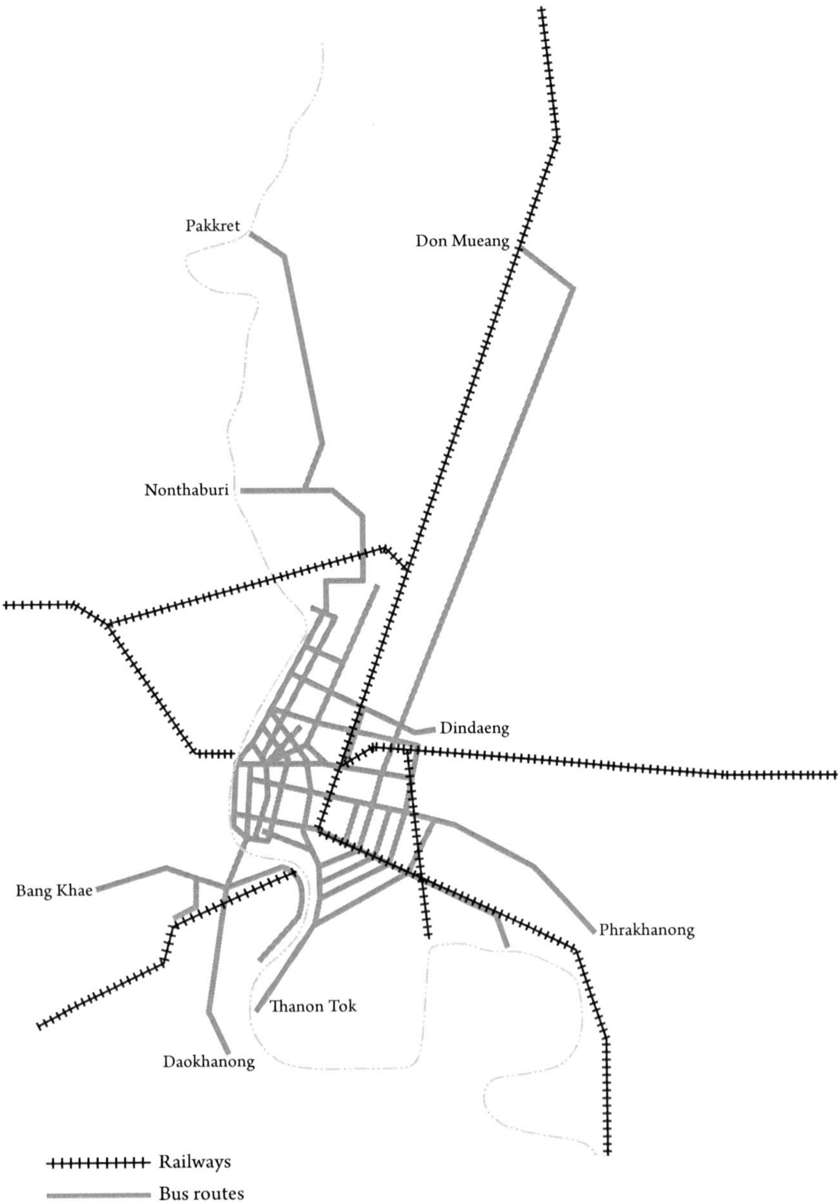

The minister of interior proposed the implementation of a Bus Operating Authority (*Ongkan borikan doen rot*) to the cabinet in March 1952.[49] The plan called for the authority to take charge of the bus service starting with important routes such as the one on Charoen Krung Road. The minister explained that many small private operators had entered the bus business because of the shortage of service offered by the municipalities, but the convenience and safety of passengers were being neglected because these operators pursued only profits. Fifty million baht would be borrowed from the Ministry of Finance as capital to establish the authority, and funds for annual capital expenditures would also be needed. The ministry drafted a bill for establishing the authority and submitted it at the cabinet meeting.

The cabinet ordered the Ministry of Communications to examine the plan. They did so and reported back at the cabinet meeting in August 1952.[50] They recommended that the Transport Company should take charge of the matter by asserting the principle that had been confirmed by the cabinet on May 6 of the same year that the Express Transportation Organization (ETO) and the Transport Company should manage freight and passenger transport respectively throughout the country. They proposed a plan under which the Transport Company would build eighty buses at an estimated cost of 15 million baht and operate them on Charoen Krung Road; existing *songthaeo* on the route would be purchased and transferred to other routes.

The ETO was a government authority established in February 1947. Its original business included the shipping and discharging of freight at railway station yards (RSP 1987, 19). Later, it started contract transport by arranging freight wagons, replacing the shippers in conveying freight, and transporting freight by truck. It then started operation of long-distance buses in the northeast in 1951.[51] It also entered the business of water transport on rivers and coastal lines. Thus, it was expanding its business rapidly, especially for government transport, as the sole public institution in charge of land and water transport (excepting rail transport). The Transport Company, on the other hand, was a state-owned company that began with air transport. It schemed to expand by entering the bus operation business and then expanded inter-provincial bus routes, starting with the buses to Paknam. The government separated the air transport business of the Transport Company after the war, but it merged with the Thai Navigation Company (*Borisat ruea thai chamkat*) instead. The main businesses of the Transport Company thus became bus operation and water transport.[52]

The reason behind the Ministry of Interior's plan to establish a new authority was to bring all agencies involved in the bus business under its control. Special permission for bus operations was issued by the Department of Public and Municipal Affairs under the Ministry of Interior, and municipalities that would regulate bus operations were also placed under it. For this reason, the Ministry of Interior proposed establishing the new authority for bus operations. On the other hand, because the Ministry of Communications already had two subordinate agencies, the ETO and the Transport Company, it proposed utilizing them by quoting the cabinet decision. It can be seen that there was competition between the two ministries to acquire new interests in the Bangkok bus business.

When the plan of the Ministry of Communications was approved at the cabinet meeting on September 10, it seemed that bus unification by the Transport Company had started. However, it was suddenly decided at the cabinet meeting on January 7, 1953, that the ETO and not the Transport Company would take charge of bus operations in Bangkok.[53] The real reason for this change is unknown because the stated one was only that the ETO had sufficient capital. The cabinet decision in May 1952 that the Ministry of Communications quoted was not implemented after all, and a new governmental agency, ETO, thus entered the bus business in Bangkok.

Although the background of this sudden change is unknown, the ETO was expanding its business quickly, while the Transport Company was losing money. In early 1947, debts in both its bus and ship sections amounted to more than one million baht each, and the company could operate only five to six buses per day.[54] The profitability of water transport in particular was quite low because of its old boats and severe competition with private boats, so the Transport Company operated at a loss through 1950.[55] Because it was decided by the cabinet in May 1952 that the government would operate the main bus lines, the Transport Company had to increase its buses for this purpose.[56] Thus, it may have been outside the company's ability to request permission for bus operations in Bangkok in addition to running long-distance buses.

In contrast, the ETO was expanding its business favorably and started long-distance bus service, which the Transport Company would later take charge of. Praman Adireksan, the then director of the ETO, seems to have been behind this. He had been the director since September 1948 and maintained the post until the Phibun government collapsed in the coup d'état of September 1957 (Praman 1997, 35–38). He also served as the deputy minister of communications from March 1952 to April 1955, and the ETO was under his jurisdiction. This may explain why the ETO acquired the bus business in Bangkok.

Entry of the ETO into the Bus Business

The ETO rapidly prepared to operate buses in Bangkok. It was decided to purchase one hundred new buses from Nissan and as many existing buses and *songthaeo* as possible.[57] Twenty-one buses were purchased from the Bangkok Municipality, for 30,000 baht per bus on average, but private *songthaeo* refused to sell because of the low purchase price that was offered, although four owners had negotiated.[58] As a result, more than one hundred *songthaeo* on Charoen Krung Road were transferred to operate on another route. They gained Route 5 on the Khlong Toei–Si Phraya line, as shown in table 3.4. Since almost all buses would arrive by the end of June, the ETO decided to start its operation on Charoen Krung Road in July. Probably these buses were the first box-type buses in Bangkok and were distinguished from truck-based buses with a homemade body on their frames. However, passengers complained that ventilation was bad near the backseats and that the buses were hot.[59]

The ETO proposed a new bus route between Khlong Toei and Talat Phlu, and the board approved it in May 1954.[60] In fact, the ETO's operation must have already been assumed as of 1953 given that *songthaeo* operators on the Talat Phlu–Hua Lamphong and Khlong Toei–Hua Lamphong routes, which overlapped with the ETO's new route, had gained Routes 7 and 17 respectively, as table 3.4 shows. The ETO gained this route at the next route rearrangement in 1955, and its routes totaled four after it gained another route between Tha Wasukri and Chakkrawat.[61]

Furthermore, the ETO also advanced the establishment of a joint company with private companies to aim at expanding the bus business. The ETO Automobile Operation Company (*Borisat ro so pho doen rot chamkat*), established in 1954, was the first such case, and it started an inter-provincial bus by collaborating with private companies operating between Bangkok and the provinces on the Southern line.[62] The next year, the Eastern ETO Automobile Operation Company (*Borisat ro so pho doen rot tawan-ok chamkat*) was established to start bus service from Bangkok toward the east.[63] Originally the operation of these inter-provincial buses was to be the task of the Transport Company; thus, the ETO was clearly infringing on the territory of the Transport Company. In Bangkok, the ETO established the ETO Nakhon Thon Company (*Borisat ro so pho nakhon thon chamkat*), upon the recommendation of the Department of Transport, to succeed in the bus operation of the Phranakhon Thonburi Transport Company (*Borisat phranakhon thonburi khonsong chamkat*), which was suffering from infighting.[64]

However, this ETO Nakhon Thon Company would put an end to the expansionist policy of the ETO. The reason the ETO participated in management was that the Phranakhon Thonburi Transport Company was a mishmash of small bus owners and its service was not satisfactory. The initial plan supposed that 70 percent of the share of ETO Nakhon Thon Company would be distributed among shareholders of the Phranakhon Thonburi Company.[65] However, most stockholders refused to participate in a joint corporation with the ETO when the negotiation of share prices failed. Ultimately, although concession was granted to the ETO Nakhon Thon Company, the buses of Phranakhon Thonburi Transport Company continued operation.

The Department of Transport permitted both to continue operation, but the Phranakhon Thonburi Transport Company asked the ETO to withdraw. The company asserted that it was the second case, besides the case of the Charoen Krung route, in which the ETO had disadvantaged the private sector. It further accused the ETO Nakhon Thon Company of merely borrowing the ETO's buses to operate.[66] Eventually Praman ordered the withdrawal of the ETO, and its operation ceased on June 18, 1956.[67] The withdrawal had sparked a political debate since opposition to the government for disadvantaging private business was increasingly reported in the press.[68]

The experiment of bus unification in Bangkok under the ETO was thus eventually suspended in response to criticisms of unfair competition with the private sector. To cope with this problem, the cabinet decided to halt expansion of the ETO's bus business in 1955.[69] The cabinet ordered the Ministry of Communications to stop expansion of the ETO's business for the sake of stabilizing the state because people were opposed to it. It approved both existing and new private operators to operate buses by asking the Ministry of Interior and the Ministry of Communications for positive support.[70] The Phibun government was at the time adopting a mitigation policy and promoting democratization by liberalizing political activities, so the people's criticism of the government, which had earlier been suppressed, arose (Kakizaki 2007b, 2011). Phibun reckoned that humbly accepting criticism would be advantageous for the upcoming general election.

The policy of nationalization, in which the governmental authority would unify the Bangkok bus business, therefore, came to a deadlock, and the bus policy returned once again to one of private orientation. The ETO's expansion policy was also suspended, and its regional bus business, including joint companies, would be completely abolished by the start of the 1960s, although its bus business in Bangkok would be maintained.

Regulation by the Ministry of Communications

Establishment of the Transport Regulation Committee

Although the Ministry of Interior had been regulating bus transport for a long time, the Ministry of Communications took charge in the 1950s. As noted in the previous chapter, special permits were to be issued by the Committee for Examining the Applications of Bus Operations under the Department of Public and Municipal Affairs, the Ministry of Interior, and it was the Motor Vehicles Act of 1930 that provided this authority.[71] Later this committee was unified under the Public Service Regulation Committee (*Khana kammakan khuapkhum satharanupaphok*), but there was no change in its jurisdiction under the Department of Public and Municipal Affairs. In 1948, the prime minister transferred authority of bus operation from the Department of Public and Municipal Affairs to the Police Department.[72]

The committee examined the situation of bus regulation under the Police Department and observed the following problems.[73] Although the existing bus operators used company names, they were, in fact, only assorted collections of automobile owners, and the companies played the role of brokers by taking part of the owners' earnings. This was the origin of competition among buses. Moreover, bus operators competed to extend their bus routes to reach the inner city as much as possible, but hesitated to extend them toward suburbs where few passengers were expected, and this prevented the development of the city area. To solve these problems, the committee came up with a few fixed principles: Special permits would only be given to operators that were true companies, and the duration of special permission would be five years. Also, operators would change all buses to meet the standard within a grace period of three years.[74]

This plan was supposed to start in accordance with the route rearrangement in September 1953. However, there was insufficient time to put it into place. Thus, existing operators were allowed to continue their business for a while, and special permits were to be granted later. However, the Ministry of Communications suggested to the cabinet in January 1954 that it suspend the bus regulation plan by the Ministry of Interior because the newly drafted Transport Act would be enforced, and this suggestion was approved.[75] The authority of bus regulation, therefore, was transferred from the Ministry of Interior to the Ministry of Communications, and the Department of Transport under the Ministry of Communications would perform this regulatory role. The regulation of bus business by the Department of Transport was in line with the cabinet decision on May 6, 1952, that the Department of Transport would exclusively regulate land transport.[76] This had also been the policy of Praman when he was the deputy minister of communications, and it was said to be the second phase of the competition between the Ministry of Communications and the Ministry of Interior for acquiring interests in the bus business.

Although the bus regulation plan of the Ministry of Interior was not realized, the Ministry of Communications was examining almost the same regulation plan. As for the regulation of land transport, the Department of Transport decided to regulate in the order of regular bus transport, taxi transport, transport operator, freight transport, and transport by a privately owned vehicle, and it placed priority on bus transport in Bangkok within the category of regular bus transport.[77]

Instead of the former Committee for Examining the Applications of Bus Operations, the Transport Regulation Committee (*Khana kammakan khuapkhum kan khonsong*) would consider the establishment and revision or abolition of bus routes, and the minister of transport would serve as the chairperson.[78] The content of the proposal was almost the same as that of the Ministry of Interior: concessions, that is, the former special permits, were to be granted only to a legitimate company, and not only operators but also vehicles and employees would come under the proposed regulation.[79]

Because the Transport Act was enforced in 1954, bus operators in Bangkok had to comply with the new law. The most serious task was to form legitimate companies. As mentioned above, some companies were only assorted collections of bus owners and some were unable to operate satisfactorily even within their own companies. For this reason, the new law forced all buses to be registered with company names. Although concessions were not obtained immediately, the operators asked each bus owner to change their names on the registration, as it could become a problem when the time came for the renewal of the concession.[80] If the owners refused, they would be unable to operate their buses. It seems that the bus owners were forced to change their buses' registration in that the majority obeyed the request to continue operation.

Since the requirement to change was advantageous to companies, some enhanced their roles as brokers and confronted the bus owners. For example, the bus owners on the Hua Lamphong–Rangsit route were not able to gain special permission in the bus route rearrangement in September 1953, shown in table 3.4, because they had not yet become a legitimate company.[81] Therefore, they used the name of an existing company, Mit Songsoem Trading Company (*Borisat mit songsoem kan kha chamkat*), and applied for a concession. In the bus route arrangement in 1955, as shown in table 3.5, this company gained a concession for Route 34, the Hua Lamphong–Rangsit route. However, the amount of collateral paid to the company rose from 2,100 baht per month in the beginning to 5,500 baht after gaining the concession. Exploitation by companies was also seen in other cases, and complaints from bus owners were voiced to the Department of Transport or the Transport Regulation Committee.

Table 3.5. Bus Routes in Bangkok, June 1955

Route Number	Line	Operator	Route	Remarks
1	Thanon Tok–Tha Tian	ETO		No change, former Route 20
2	Phrakhanong– Pakkhlong Talat	Nai Loet		No change, former Route 4
3	Mochit–Chakkrawat	Si Nakhon	Patiphat, Samsen Road, Memorial Bridge	
4	Talat Phlu–Wat Traimit	ETO	Prachathipok, Yaowarat Road, Memorial Bridge	
5	Bang Sue–Wang Burapha	Si Nakhon		No change, former Route 3
6	Bukkhalo–Sanam Luang	ETO Nakhon Thon		No change
7	Bang Khae–Sanam Luang	Bang Khae Transport		Former Route 15
8	Mochit–Memorial Bridge	Nai Loet	Phahonyothin, Si Ayutthaya, Lanluang Road	
9	Talat Phlu–Bang Lamphu	Thonburi Automobile		No change, former Route 7
10	Daokhanong–Sanam Luang	Thonnakhon Transport		No change, former Route 6
11	Makkasan–Hua Lamphong	Nai Loet	Pratunam Road, Pathumwan	
12	Tha Dindaeng–Ministry of Economic Affarirs	Chawanaphan		No change
13	Wat Thewarat– Wongwian 7.22	Sirimit		Former Route 17
14	Siyan–Khlong Toei	Si Nakhon	Victory Monument, Pratunam, Ratchaprasong,	
15	Silom–Bang Lamphu	Bunphong		No change, former Route 10
16	Thewet–Surawong	Phira Bus		No change, former Route 11
17	Sathon–Bang Lamphu	Yanyon Insurance		No change, former Route 9
18	Ratchawithi–Si Phraya	Thai Thawon	Victory Monument, Pathumwan	
19	Thonburi station–Saochingcha	Thonburi Union Transport		No change
20	Khlong Toei–Wat Traimit	ETO	Rama IV Road	

Route Number	Line	Operator	Route	Remarks
21	Wongwian Yai– Wongwian 7.22	Si Lueang		No change, former Route 8
22	Tha Wasukri–Chakkraphat	ETO	Ratchadamnoen Road, Memorial Bridge	
23	Thewet Circle Line (right rotation)	Red Bus	Krungkasem, Yaowarat Road, Tha Phrachan	
24	Thewet Circle Line (left rotation)	Thai Pradit	Tha Phrachan, Yaowarat, Krungkasem Road	
25	Charoen Phon Circle line	Thai Bamrung Transport		No change
26	Minburi–Saphan Khao	Minburi Transport		No change
27	Bang Kapi–Bang Krabue	Mueang Nonthaburi Automobile	Latphrao, Saphan Khwai	
28	Hua Lamphong–Paknam	Transport Co., Samut Prakan Transport, Sinthumit		No change
29	Hua Lamphong–Don Mueang	Transport Co.		No change

NOTE 1: No change means the route remains the same as the original route.
NOTE 2: Former route numbers are those at the time of table 3.4. These were identified by the author, although some routes might have been extended slightly.
SOURCE: Data from NA Kho Kho. 0202. 3/65.

Rearrangement of Bus Routes

In the initial stage of enforcing the Transport Act in 1954, the Transport Regulation Committee did not rearrange bus routes immediately, but announced that the rearrangement of bus routes was under consideration.[82] Then, in 1955, the committee presented a new bus route plan. There were a total of thirty-five routes, as shown in table 3.5, and most of them followed the existing routes. "No change" in the table means that those routes basically inherited former bus routes, shown in table 3.4. The routes that have no previous route numbers are those that were changed after the rearrangement in September 1953, shown in table 3.4, but were not further changed in the rearrangement in 1955. The former Routes 15 and 17 are basically the same routes, with only a slight change in their starting or ending points. Therefore, only eleven routes were substantially changed.

From figure 3.4, which shows the network of bus routes in the rearrangement, it can be seen that the rearrangement was accompanied by the further expansion of suburban buses. As compared with the routes in figure 3.3, new bus routes reached Pathumthani, Rangsit, Minburi, and Bang Kapi, and some new routes were also added in the city. These bus routes were established to replace illegal *songthaeo* that were operating; they did not correspond to new roads. For example, as mentioned above, the buses to Rangsit had operated before 1953. The roads to Minburi and Bang Kapi were also opened for traffic in 1946 and 1949 respectively, and the *songthaeo* had started operating then.

The bus operators opposed the plan, saying that they wished to maintain their existing routes insofar as possible. They made their own counter plan, which they submitted to the Transport Regulation Committee.[83] This plan was the manifestation of the operators' intentions regarding their favorable bus routes; it indicated the operator of each route as well as the route plan. The bus operators warned that they would go on strike if the plan was not accepted, and the Minister of Communications asked for the committee to respect their plan as much as possible. The committee revised the plan, respecting the operators' plan as much as possible, and posted it as a notice in the Royal Gazette in March 1955 (RKB vol. 72, no. 22, 693–706).[84] Although the operators had finally consented to the assignment, as shown in table 3.5, they continued to argue with each other over who would operate the newly established routes.

The number of verified operators in 1953 was seventeen; this number increased to twenty-six by 1955. The increase was also the result of establishing many new bus companies by unifying small bus owners as mentioned above, and bus routes such as the Hua Lamphong–Rangsit route had already been established. Moreover, by this rearrangement, the Thonburi Municipality withdrew from the bus business, and only the Nonthaburi Municipality continued its bus business. Although it was thought that the Thonburi Municipality was certain to gain the concession, since it did not own buses, the concession was granted to the original operators.[85] In fact, both Routes 6 and 7 had already been under the joint operation of the Thonburi Municipality and private operators at the time (see table 3.4), so private buses should have already acted as the center of operation. The bus operation of the Nonthaburi Municipality seems to have been a mishmash of private bus owners. When the municipality gained special permission for the bus route to Pakkret in 1954, it asked the ETO to operate it instead because a confrontation

Fig 3.4. Bus Network in Bangkok, 1955–1956

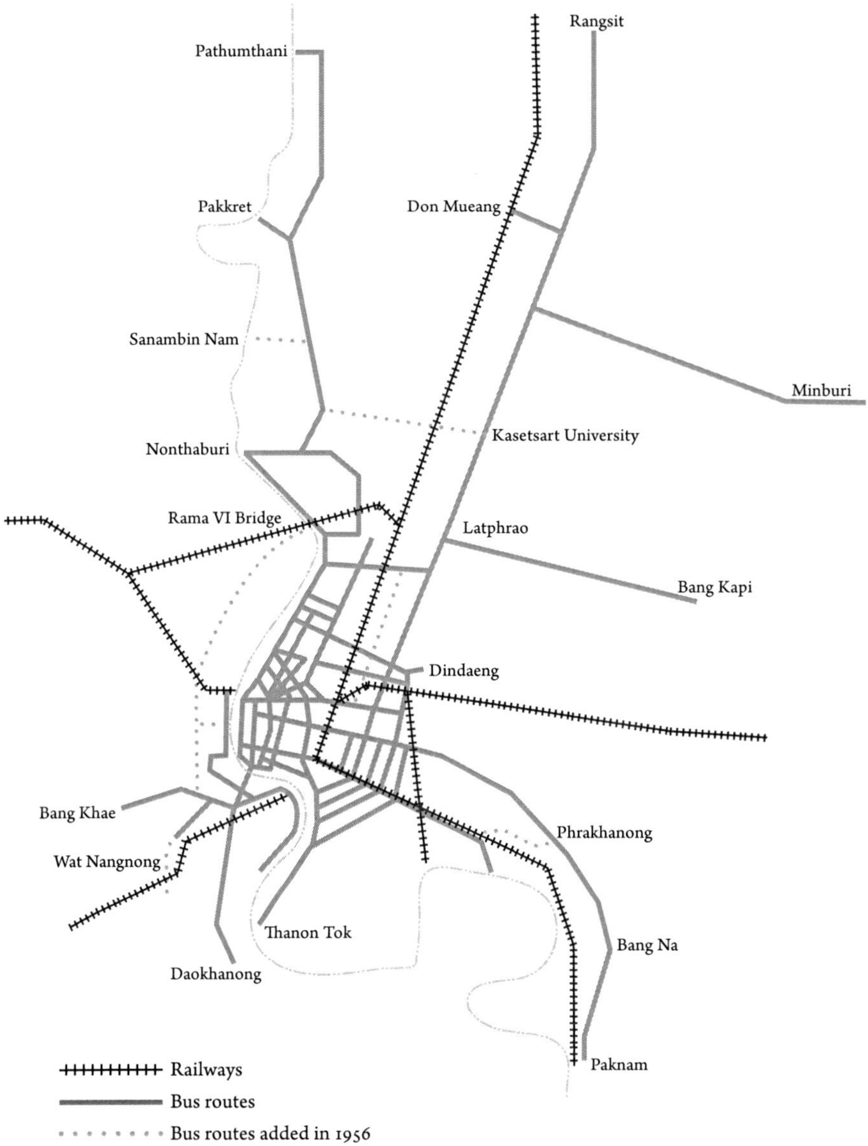

Sources: NA Kho Kho 0202. 3/65; NA Kho Kho 0202. 3. 4. 1/13; RKB vol. 72, no. 22, 693–70, and vol. 72, no. 94, 2912–16.

had occurred between the municipality and private bus owners.[86] As the Bangkok Municipality also withdrew from the bus business in 1953, municipality-run bus operations, which aimed at expansion in the beginning, basically disappeared.

In addition, although the number of bus routes changed drastically, a radical change of route numbers had not occurred until now. For example, buses on Route 1 between Thanon Tok and Tha Tian still ran on the same section, and Route 2 between Phrakhanong and Pak Khlong Talat was still maintained, with the extension of its starting point to Samrong. In the rearrangement, the bus route number would be shown on each bus, and those route numbers have generally come to be used ever since.[87] To avoid passenger confusion, the number of each bus route would not be changed in principle, and newly established routes would use the numbers of abolished routes. It can be said that the origin of the bus route numbers of present-day Bangkok is in the bus route rearrangement of 1955.

Frequent Changes to Bus Routes

The rearrangement of bus routes by the Ministry of Communications was carried out from June 24, 1955. However, because it had not satisfied all the bus operators' requests, the requests to change their routes needed to be considered in succession. Operator requests were divided into two categories: those seeking to establish a new route (by operators who had been unable to secure concessions) and those seeking to change an existing route (by operators who already had a concession).

As mentioned above, although the number of bus operators had grown to twenty-six in 1955, there were still some operators who were unable to obtain a concession. For example, the Samakkhitham Company (*Borisat samakkhi tham chamkat*), which operated buses between Bang Kapi and Latphrao, could not secure a bus route, so it asked to merge with the Mueang Nonthaburi Automobile Company (*Borisat rotyon mueang nonthaburi chamkat*), which operated Route 27, the partly overlapping route. However, when the latter asked for a change of registration and the expense of the registration fee, the former requested its own bus route.[88] The Makkasan Automobile Company (*Borisat rotyon makkasan chamkat*), also unable to obtain a concession, wished to have its own route, asserting that its income was low because it had to rent buses to other concessionaires.[89]

Some operators who were able to secure a concession also complained that their profitability worsened because of the competition with other operators, and they asked for changes to their bus routes. For example, the Thai Bamrung Transport Company (*Borisat thai bamrung khonsong chamkat*), which gained a concession for Route 25, complained that its route suffered competition with the buses run by the Nai Loet Company on Banthat Thong Road after the route rearrangement and asked for a substitute concession for the route between Wongwian July 22 (the "July 22" roundabout) and Watthana.[90] The Mueang Nonthaburi Automobile Company, which Samakkhitham Company had asked to merge with, also requested to change its terminal on Route 27 from Bang Krabue to Pratunam. It said that the number of passengers on Route 27 was low except during rush hours, and most passengers from Bang Kapi left its buses at Latphrao to transfer.[91] It was reported at the Transport Regulation Committee in the beginning of September 1955 that they had already received thirteen requests to change bus routes.[92] The high number of requests in the two months following the route rearrangement shows that there was high dissatisfaction among bus operators.

Because either governmental agencies or passengers requested the change or establishment of bus routes, the Transport Regulation Committee decided to establish new bus routes, which were announced in December 1955 in the Royal Gazette (RKB vol. 72, no. 94, 2912–16). There were fourteen newly established routes as shown in table 3.6; thus, the number of bus routes in Bangkok rose from thirty-five to forty-nine. The dotted routes in figure 3.4 are the roads where the new bus routes were established. Those such as Ngamwongwan Road, running westward from Kasetsart University, and Charansanitwong Road, starting from the Rama VI Bridge and going southward on the Thonburi side, gained new bus routes.[93] Both Ngamwongwan and Charansanitwong Roads had already been opened to traffic in 1941 and 1955 respectively, and *songthaeo* were already operating on them.

Table 3.6. New Bus Routes in Bangkok, 1956

Route Number	Line	Operator	Route
36	Bang Krabue–Wongwian 7.22	Sirimit	Samsen, Wisut Kasat Road
37	Wongwian Yai–Mahanak	Makkasan Automobile	Memorial Bridge
38	Soi Watthana–Wongwian 7.22	Thai Bamrung Transport	Sukhumvit, Rama I, Banthat Thong, Rama IV Road
39	Don Mueang–Sanam Luang	Sahaiyon	Phahonyothin, Phetchaburi Road
40	Rama VI Bridge–Wongwian Yai	Yatmit	Charansanitwong Road
41	Rama VI Bridge–Phrannok	Saha Watthanakit	Charansanitwong, Phrannok Road
42	Phrannok–Tha Phra	Si Borikan	Phrannok, Charansanitwong Road
43	Wat Nangnong–Pakkhlong San	Watchanakun	Wutthakat, Thoetthai Road
44	Patiphat–Sanam Luang	Si Nakhon	Rama VI, Lanluang Road
45	Kasetsart University–Saphan Khao	Samakkhitham	Ngamwongwan, Pracharat Road
46	Phrakhanong–Witthayu	Si Nakhon	Rama IV Road
47	Witthayu–Tha Chang	Yanyon Insurance	Rama IV, Phayathai, Rama I, Bamrung Mueang
48	Soi Sammit–Ministry of Agriculture	Nai Loet	Sukhumvit, Rama I, Bamrung Mueang Road
49	Tha Chang–Sanambin Nam	Transport Co.	Samsen Road

Source: Data from NA Kho Kho. 0202. 3. 4. 1/13.

According to the Department of Transport, the addition of these bus routes had been considered based on requests from members of parliament and governmental agencies, complaints from passengers, and contributions in newspapers. The decision was made by considering the operators who would take charge.[94] Furthermore, the requests from operators were taken seriously. For example, Route 38 between Watthana and Wongwian July 22 was the route claimed by the Thai Bamrung Transport Company instead of Route 25, and it did in fact receive the concession. Route 46 between Phrakhanong and Witthayu was in response to the claim of the Si Nakhon Company that its Route 14 should be extended from Khlong Toei to Phrakhanong, and a concession was given in the form of a new bus route rather than a route extension.[95] Also, Route 49 between Tha Chang and Sanambin Nam was the route requested by the Transport Company.

Moreover, new operators were also recognized to some extent by adding these bus routes. Among the operators who gained concessions (see table 3.6), six had newly entered the business. The abovementioned Samakkhitham Company and Makkasan Automobile Company were also included. As there were twenty-four operators hoping to enter the bus business, only a quarter had actually obtained concessions. Nevertheless, the number of operators engaged in the bus business in Bangkok rose to a total of thirty-two and was still increasing.

Furthermore, to avoid a fare hike as requested by the operators owing to the poor results of their businesses, the changes to bus routes they applied for were largely approved in 1957. In March 1957, the Transport Regulation Committee decided to approve the change of bus routes to rescue operators and increase convenience for passengers if there were reasonable grounds, and it approved seventeen applications to change bus routes.[96] Included among them was the change of the terminus of Route 26 from Bang Krabue to Witthayu, requested by the Mueang Nonthaburi Automobile Company. Furthermore, the change of another twenty bus routes was also accepted by the committee the following month, which resulted in the change of thirty-seven routes in total.[97] By these two changes of bus routes, two-thirds of all bus routes were changed from their original routes, indicating that the operators' requests were accepted automatically.

As the expansion of the bus business by the ETO was suspended in 1955, and the promotion of private bus operators was emphasized, a policy led by the private sector was adopted. However, as the bus problem would not be solved despite this policy, as will be mentioned below, opposition toward the government's private-operator-oriented policy began to surface. Moreover, because there were several operators that could not offer enough bus service, passenger complaints toward bus service also increased.

From Rail Transport to Buses

Decline of Rail Transport

It was in this period that the main actor of urban transport in Bangkok changed from rail transport (railways and tramways) to bus transport.

The role of railways in urban transport decreased as they became prominent as inter-urban railways, and tramways fundamentally maintained the status quo, although some lines were either newly established or abolished. On the other hand, the network of bus routes was further expanded both within the inner city and in the suburbs. Therefore, from the viewpoint of network expansion, buses saw a trend of expansion and rail transport maintained its status quo.

Even from examining the number of passengers, the decline of rail transport can be clearly seen. As shown in table 3.1, the number of passengers on tramways in 1942 and 1950 was 109 million and 140 million respectively. However, this number declined to 63 million persons in 1960.[98] The number of tramway users was halved, given that the length of the line, about fifty kilometers, had not changed during this period.[99] The daily number of passengers on the Paknam line just before its abolition was about 3,500, and that on the Maeklong line was about 8,000 per day in the beginning of the 1960s, as will be discussed in chapter 4. Thus, the number of passengers using rail transport was less than 200,000, including 170,000 on tramways. Although only the figure from 1960 is available, the number of bus passengers was about 200 million per year, or about 550,000 per day. As the number of buses registered in Bangkok rose from 451 cars in 1941 to 1,993 cars in 1960, the number of bus passengers should have increased at least four times during this period (*SYB* for 1940–44, 390; *SYB* for 1963, 224). Even from the perspective of the number of passengers, we can thus see a change in the roles of rail and bus transport.

This change also reflects the difference in investment in the two businesses. All rail transport was operated by the government: the SRT and Bangkok Electricity, after the nationalization of the Maeklong Railway in 1945, and the Thai Electric Corporation at the end of 1949. Although both SRT and Bangkok Electricity made investments to maintain existing networks and transport capacities, they could not invest in the reinforcement of transport capacities or the extension of networks, so the status quo continued. Only the Maeklong line enjoyed increased investment. However, it aimed at strengthening its function as inter-urban rather than intra-urban transport.

Government policy was the main factor restraining investment in rail transport. The government had no intention of further expanding the networks of both railways and tramways but instead considered that the expansion of urban transport could be achieved through improving roads and bus service. It did not consider the conversion of both the Paknam and Maeklong lines into urban railways, and both returned to being inter-urban railways, their original function. The expansion plan for trolley bus routes or tramways was formulated by Bangkok Electricity, but it was shelved due to lack of budget. The move of tramlines to the middle of roads or double-tracking was not considered, although their importance had been recognized in the 1930s. Therefore, the structural problem of tramways persisted without any improvement. The negative response to such rail transport made the competitive power of rail transport decline as a result, and would soon result in rail transport being abolished in Bangkok in the 1960s.

The passive measures of the government toward rail transport also stemmed from the fact that both suburban railways and tramways were not the main business of the agencies that regulated them. Even if the government was against rail transport, when the agencies that regulated rail transport were eager for development, new investment programs might have been realized. However, neither the SRT nor Bangkok Electricity regarded rail transport in Bangkok as their main business. For the SRT, the reinforcement of transport capacity on the main lines between Bangkok and the periphery was their highest priority. It had no intention of investing largely in the Paknam or Maeklong lines. The main parts of SRT were not intra-urban but inter-urban transport between cities, and their highest priority was to reinforce and expand inter-urban rail transport capacity. The main business of Bangkok Electricity was power distribution, and tramways were only a complementary business. Therefore, neither SRT nor Bangkok Electricity vigorously promoted investment plans for suburban railways or tramways, and these were to permanently decline even though at the time the decline seemed temporary.

Development of the Private-Sector-Led Bus Business

On the other hand, because the expansion of the bus business was fundamentally private-sector-led, the bus network expanded quickly corresponding to the expansion of demand. Although the policy of municipalization of the bus business was promulgated in the second half of the 1930s and new bus routes came to be restricted to municipal management in principle, the lack of buses and fuel caused by the outbreak of war made the principle of municipalization strictly nominal. As the existing operators' transport capacity declined while demand increased, private *songthaeo* filled the gap. Thus, the bus business was opened up again to the private sector as a result of the war.

The sluggish recovery of the existing buses resulted in a further increase of illegal *songthaeo*. *Songthaeo* not only operated on the existing bus routes, but also spread toward suburban areas using rapidly expanded highway networks after the 1940s. Municipality-run buses further isolated themselves from this process. The evacuation of population from the inner city to the suburbs during the war was probably also an important factor in activating these *songthaeo* in the suburbs. The *songthaeo* eventually asked for legal operation and petitioned the government to establish new bus routes. On the other hand, municipal buses isolated themselves, and eventually, the municipalities, except Nonthaburi, withdrew from the bus business.

As unauthorized *songthaeo* came to be more important in Bangkok, the government began to recognize that the bus business should be regulated. Because the bus businesses run by municipalities had rather failed, a plan to unify buses under government management emerged. After a competition between the Ministry of Interior and the Ministry of Communications, the latter gained jurisdiction over the bus business in Bangkok, and the national bus unification plan, initially put forward by the Ministry of Interior, was finally realized by the ETO under the Ministry of Communications. The ETO began bus operations on Charoen Krung Road, one of the main bus routes in Bangkok, and extended its operating routes. The authority to regulate the bus business was also transferred to the Ministry of Communications from the Ministry of Interior, and the Transport Regulation Committee, established under the Department of Transport, was responsible for dealing with the opening of bus routes and decisions on operators.

However, the ETO's expansion policy for Bangkok's bus business was rejected by Prime Minister Phibun and transformed into a policy of promoting private operators. That is, the policy of nationalization was converted to a private-sector-led policy. This was due to the complaints voiced by newspapers and the public that the expansion policy of bus business by the ETO represented unfair competition with the private sector. The prime minister wanted the sources of complaint to be removed as much as possible before the upcoming general election. As a result, from the latter half of 1955, the private operators' interests came to be reflected in government policy on buses, so the establishment of new routes and changes in the existing routes were advanced according to the demands of private operators.

Private operators took good advantage of the prime minister's intention and acquired and changed bus routes in their own interests. They made their demands directly to the prime minister with the aim of putting pressure on the Transport Regulation Committee under the prime minister's authority. For example, the Thai Bamrung Transport Company applied for a change in its bus route in July 1955 to the Transport Regulation Committee, and then sent the same petition to the prime minister. The result was that the Secretariat of the Prime Minister (*Samnakngan lekhathikan nayok ratthamontri*) ordered the Ministry of Communications to consider the petition.[100] The Makkasan Automobile Company also petitioned the prime minister directly, and as a result, the Transport Regulation Committee decided to grant the concession for Route 37 to this company, since during the installation of fourteen new lines in 1956, the Secretariat of the Prime Minister had asked the committee to consider the matter.[101] The strategy of direct petition to the prime minister was also used for highway development, and there were several cases in which the construction of new highways was seemingly ordered by the prime minister to the Department of Highways (*Krom thang luang*) (Kakizaki 2009, 71–74).

But Prime Minister Phibun's paternalistic policy ultimately turned out to cause trouble. The Thai Bamrung Transport Company gained Route 38 in 1956 as the result of its petition to the prime minister, but the business on both Route 25, the original route, and Route 38 was quite poor, as Route 38 had only one to two buses daily and no bus on Route 25 as of June 1957.[102] This was because of the desertion of the bus owners from the company after its creditors sued for bankruptcy. The Makkasan Automobile Company faced a similar situation; it was able to operate only five buses on Route 37 in September 1956, in contrast to the agreed-upon number of twenty-five.[103] When all buses on this route stopped operation, the Transport Regulation Committee ordered the company to resume service by December of the same year.[104] However, the procurement of buses failed finally, and the company was deprived of its concession.

Dissatisfaction with Bus Service

Prime Minister Phibun's policy change from nationalization to privatization increased the number of bus operators and made the regulation of the bus business even more difficult. The number of bus operators increased to thirty-two as of 1956, and small operators like the Thai Bamrung Transport Company, which were merely assorted collections of bus owners, also entered the bus business alongside large-scale operators like the Nai Loet Company and the Si Nakhon Company As a result, the gap between operators widened, and bus service steadily declined. The dissatisfaction of passengers toward bus operators turned on the government, therefore. Thus, Prime Minister Phibun's paternalism backfired in the end.

Amidst the general dissatisfaction over bus service, the most serious complaint was that of congestion in the buses. This was mostly caused by the shortage of bus trips, which in turn stemmed from the fact that the number of buses was lower than the number provided by the Transport Regulation Committee. For example, on Route 18 between Ratchawithi and Si Phraya, operated by the Thai Thawon Company, there was extreme congestion because the company operated only fifteen to twenty buses, even though there were no fewer than ten schools and governmental agencies on the route. In particular, it was quite difficult to ride the bus from the middle stops, so there were many complaints that passengers arrived at their destinations late every day.[105] Because there were many other complaints about the service on this route, the Department of Transport directed the company to increase the number of buses, and it increased slightly. Immediately following the route rearrangement in June 1955, the head of the Department of Transport said that he wanted a four-month extension to resume bus operation as it had mandated (*SN*, 28 June 1955).

However, the problem of the bus shortage had not been solved at all by 1957. Table 3.7 shows the mandated number of buses and the actually operated number according to the routes in June of the same year. From this table, it is understood that the total mandated number was 1,333 cars, but the actual number in operation was 981 cars, or only 74 percent. The lowest rate was 12 percent for Route 38 operated by the Thai Bamrung Transport Company, mentioned above; it ran only three buses against the mandated number of twenty-five. Subsequently, 14 percent for the Yatmit Company (*Borisat yatmit chamkat*) on Route 40 and 17 percent for the Samakkhitham Company on Route 17 followed. All three were new operators in 1956. The sufficiency rate of Route 18 by the Thai Thawon Company, the dissatisfactory route, was 50 percent; this means that the situation of bus shortages had returned after the temporary increase that had occurred following the orders of the Department of Transport.

Table 3.7. Number of Buses Operating on Each Route, June 1957

Operator	Route Number	Line	Length (km)	Number of Buses Provided	Actual Number of Buses Used	Sufficiency Rate (%)	Remarks
Bang Khae Khonsong	7	Bang Khae–Nopphawong	13.0	28	21	75	Route changed
Bang Buathong Transport	33	Pathumthani–Sanam Luang	47.2	16	20	125	
Bunphong	15	Ban Mai–Bang Lamphu	14.8	42	35	83	Route changed
Chong Nonsi Transport	35	Chong Nonsi–Witthayu	4.2	6	5	83	New route
ETO	1	Thanon Tok–Tha Tian	10.5	95	60	63	
	4	Talat Phlu–Wat Traimit	7.3	50	30	60	
	20	Khlong Toei–Wat Traimit	7.3	30	24	80	
	22	Kiakkai–Chakkrawat	10.2	12	5	42	Route changed
Total			35.3	187	119	64	
Khlong Toei Trading	13	Khlong Toei–Dindaeng	8.0	12	9	75	New route
Minburi Transport	26	Minburi–Saphan Khao	37.5	15	14	93	
Mit Songsoem Trading	34	Rangsit–Hua Lamphong	32.3	35	23	66	

Nai Loet	2	Phrakhanong–Pakkhlong Talat	17.8	50	41	82	Route changed
	8	Latphrao–Memorial Bridge	13.6	30	23	77	Route changed
	11	Makkasan–Wat Pho	10.6	30	18	60	Route changed
	48	Phrakhanong–Wat Pho	15.0	37	26	70	Route changed
Total			57.0	147	108	73	
Nonthaburi Municipality	32	Pakkret–Sanam Luang	25.5	30	30	100	
Phira Bus	16	Bang Krabue–Surawong	10.6	29	32	110	Route changed
Phra Nakhon Thonburi Transport	6	Bukkhalo–Tha Kasem	10.9	24	18	75	Route changed
Red Bus	12	Dindaeng–Phlapphlachai	15.8	28	24	86	Route changed
	23	Thewet Circle Line (right rotation)	12.0	25	24	96	
Total			27.8	53	48	91	
Samakkhitham	45	Kasetsart University–Saphan Khao	23.8	12	2	17	
Sahaiyon Transport	39	Don Mueang–Sanam Luang	32.0	20	20	100	
Saha Watthanakit	41	Bangkok Noi–Bang Lamphu	10.4	15	8	53	Route changed
Samut Prakan Transport	52	Samyaek–Paknam	28.0	30	20	67	
Si Nakhon	3	Wongwian Yai–Mochit	14.7	40	30	75	Route changed
	5	Bang Sue–Chakkrawat	9.8	36	30	83	Route changed
	14	Siyan–Khlong Toei	13.0	40	25	63	
	44	Mochit–Sanam Luang	12.0	22	13	59	Route changed
	46	Phrakhanong–Samyan	9.3	14	6	43	Route changed
Total			58.8	152	104	68	
Si Borikan	42	Phrannok–Wang Burapha	10.0	10	5	50	Route changed
Si Lueang	21	Samre–Chulalongkorn University	9.0	25	25	100	Route changed

Sirimit	36	Rama VI Bridge–Wat Pathum Khongkha	11.7	24	20	83	Route changed
Sinthumit	28	Hua Lamphong–Paknam	27.0	30	15	50	
Thai Thawon	18	Bang Krabue–Wat Saket	13.1	30	15	50	Route changed
Thai Bamrung Transport	25	Charoen Phon Circle line	5.2				Operation suspended
	38	Phibunwet–Wongwian 7.22	13.2	25	3	12	Route changed
Total			25.0	25	3	12	
Thai Pradit	24	Thewet Circle Line (left rotation)	12.0	25	28	112	
Thephaniramit	27	Bang Kapi–Witthayu	23.8	10	9	90	Route changed
Thonburi Automobile	9	Talat Phlu–Samsen	10.2	40	34	85	Route changed
Thonburi Union Transport	19	Thonburi Station–Thewet	9.3	30	33	110	Route changed
Thon Nakhon Transport	10	Wat Nangnong–Ratchadamnoen Stadium	11.6	30	22	73	Route changed
	50	Phra Chunlachomklao Fort–Wongwian Yai	29.5	12	10	83	
Total			41.1	42	32	76	
Transport Co.	29	Tha Chang–Don Mueang	35.0	28	12	43	Route changed
	30	Tha Chang–Nonthaburi	16.5	11	7	64	
	31	Tha Chang–Pakkret	30.5	9	6	67	
	49	Tha Chang–Sanambin Nam	23.0	10	7	70	
	51	Tha Chang–Paknam	31.5	24	12	50	
Total			136.5	82	44	54	
Yatmit	40	Rama VI Bridge–Wongwian Yai	15.0	14	2	14	
Yanyon Insurance & Trading	17	Wat Ratchasingkhon–Tha Chang	16.5	46	45	98	Route changed
	47	Saphan Dam–Land Department	11.8	25	19	76	Route changed
Total			28.3	71	64	90	

Watchanakun	43	Bang Khunthian–Saphan Mon	10.8	22	16	73	Route changed
	37	Wongwian Yai–Mahanak	6.0				Operator being selected
Grand Total			859.3	1,333	981	74	

NOTE 1: Route changed means that part of the route has been changed since 1955 or 1956, as shown in tables 3.5 or 3.6. New route means that a route has been completely changed.
NOTE 2: Routes 50 to 52 were added since table 3.6.
SOURCE: Data from NA Kho Kho. 0202. 3. 4. 1/25.

The overall trend was for small, new operators to have lower rates of compliance. Among six operators who had new routes in 1956 (see table 3.6), the highest rate was 73 percent for the Watchanakun Company (*Borisat hun suan watchanakun chamkat*), which operated Route 43, following which was 53 percent for the Saha Watthanakit Company (*Borisat saha watthanakit chamkat*), the operator of Route 41. However, the rates of large-scale operators such as the Nai Loet Company and Si Nakhon Company were not as high: the average rates of their bus routes were 68 percent and 73 percent respectively. The rates of the government agencies, the Transport Company and ETO, were also below average, with 54 percent and 64 percent respectively. Conversely, all operators whose rates exceeded 100 percent took charge of only one route, so there were some small operators who could fulfill the number of buses provided in their concessions. This shows that the size of the operator was not necessarily related to the level of service they provided.

Nevertheless, the fact that operators who had newly gained bus routes had low rates clearly shows that there was a problem in the selection of operators. At a meeting held to express their opinions on the matter (*kan aphiprai khwam khit-hen*), held at Sanam Luang in December 1955, criticism was voiced that bribes had been offered by the operators during the selection of the fourteen routes. Such criticism was unavoidable, as the results seemed to prove it.[106] Although it was not known for certain whether bribes were actually offered, it was undeniable that the operators had been selected arbitrarily, and protests by those who had failed to be selected were voiced.[107]

Furthermore, the extension of bus routes accepted in 1957 was also accelerating the shortage of buses. To avoid the necessity of a fare hike as demanded by the operators, the government accepted the change of bus routes mostly unconditionally, but the operators neglected to increase the number of buses. Therefore, the passengers' dissatisfaction grew due to the extended interval between bus trips on the extended routes. Although this occurred after the Phibun regime had collapsed, in the October 21, 1957, issue of the newspaper *Sayam Nikon*, a complaint about the bus problem during the term of Phibun's government was described as follows:

> Furthermore, after the government of the Manankhasila Party [of Phibun] won the general election in February by "black vote," the man who gained authority became the minister and approved the extension of bus routes operated by those operators that supported him during the election campaign, although the number of buses was not increased. As a result, the congestion and dissatisfaction of people kept on increasing. The number of buses was insufficient, and two buses were inclined to come together after waiting for a long time. The conditions of bus operation under the regulation of the Ministry of Communications were far from the public's interest and completely went against the conditions of their concessions. Because the bus operators could still undertake their businesses "according to their feelings," people still suspect that those who regulate buses may have a certain relation or other with bus operators. (*SN*, 21 October 1957)

Thus, the paternalism of the Phibun government toward bus operators had eventually raised commuters' ire further, and the result was the complete opposite of the original aim. First, to dodge criticism directed toward the government, Phibun had converted the policy of nationalization, criticized in those days, to privatization. As seen by the situation of the bus operation by the Transport Company or ETO, shown in table 3.7, it is clear that the government's bus business was never a secret measure for the improvement of bus service. However, although the government encouraged private-sector bus business, users could not be satisfied only by enacting a policy advantageous to the operators. The extension of bus routes aimed at the avoidance of a fare hike that would be opposed by bus users, but it resulted in the increase of their dissatisfaction when the service further deteriorated.

Aside from the fare hike from twenty satang per kilometer to thirty satang in 1953, there were no further fare hikes (*SN*, 7 October 1953).[108] Although the fare differed according to the routes—for example, the Charoen Krung line of the ETO adopted a flat fare of 50 satang—the government evaded the opposition of users. Thus, the problem of maintaining a low fare while improving bus service would turn into an even larger political issue.

4
Unification of Buses, 1960s–1970s

Disappearance of Rail Transport

Elimination of the Paknam Line

Although the Paknam and Maeklong lines were in contrasting situations in connection with the "fine sight" policy of Sarit, who gained political power in 1958, they both faced a crisis.[1] As mentioned previously, the abolition of the Paknam line between Hua Lamphong and Khlong Toei had already been considered in 1940 to make way for the expansion of the Rama IV Road as an access road to the new port at Khlong Toei (Kakizaki 2009, 48). Later, in 1954, the Bangkok Municipality planned the expansion of the same road and asked the State Railways of Thailand (SRT) to abolish the section between Hua Lamphong and Khlong Toei. However, the SRT opposed the plan and argued that Bangkok Electricity's Samsen tramway line, which paralleled the Paknam line on the road, should be eliminated to solve the problem of traffic congestion.[2] At that time, the balance of the Paknam line had not deteriorated much, and it was expected that an increase in train frequency enabled by reinforcing the power supply would result in an increase in passengers. A plan also existed for an extension to Bang Pu or Chonburi. Therefore, plans to eliminate the Paknam line were finally withdrawn in 1954.

However, when the Ministry of Interior asked the SRT to abolish the section between Hua Lamphong and Khlong Toei and move its terminus to Khlong Toei for the expansion of the Rama IV Road in March 1959, the situation had already changed.[3] As shown in table 3.3 in the previous chapter, the income generated by the Paknam line had been decreasing since 1955, and its deficit had exceeded 700,000 baht since 1957. Because of a reduction in passengers, the number of trains had been reduced; its daily service of ten trips was cut to eight in 1959.[4] The frequency of trains was supposed to have been increased by reinforcing the power supply through the installation of an independent power station, which had been planned after the abolition plan was rejected in 1954. But this had not been achieved. Thus, the number of passengers on the Paknam line steadily decreased in the absence of new investment. For this reason, the Accounting Department of the SRT proposed to abolish the entire line, noting that the number of passengers would decrease further after the terminus of the line moved to Khlong Toei.[5]

The SRT then informed the Ministry of Interior in May 1959 that it would divert the section between Hua Lamphong and Khlong Toei to a road and that it preferred the elimination of the entire line to the move of its terminus to Khlong Toei, but would follow the government's decision.[6] Because an industrial area was to be developed around Samrong along the Paknam line, the Ministry of Interior proposed to reuse the line beyond Khlong Toei as a freight railway by connecting it with the existing freight line at Khlong Toei. However, the SRT opposed the plan, noting that a change of tracks would be needed in order to run heavy freight trains on the line and a large amount of investment would also be required, for example, to establish a new station. It was suggested, instead, that a new industrial railway should be constructed after the abolition of the existing line.

As the SRT's approval of eliminating the entire line was in harmony with Sarit's policy of solving the problem of traffic congestion at level crossings by abolishing railways within the city for the recovery of "fine sight," the cabinet decided on the abolition of the line by the end of 1959 (Kakizaki 2009, 132).[7] In response, fifty buses were to be employed on the Paknam line, and, because the line served about 3,500 persons per day concentrated especially during the morning and evening rush hours, the station at Hua Lamphong was to be used as the terminal of the substitute buses for some time.[8] Among the rolling stock on the Paknam line, thirteen relatively new electric cars, built after the war, were brought to the Makkasan workshop to be assigned new tasks, but were finally scrapped because the Maeklong line was also faced with elimination, as will be mentioned below.[9]

Thus, the Paknam line, the first railway in Thailand, disappeared and all former right-of-ways were diverted to roads. The Rama IV Road was expanded between Hua Lamphong and Khlong Toei by using sections from not only the Paknam line right-of-way but also from the Hua Lamphong Canal in the south. The section between Khlong Toei and Samrong was diverted to a road called the Old Paknam Line Road (*Thanon thang rotfai kao sai paknam*), and the section beyond Samrong became the extended land of the parallel Sukhumvit Road. Following the abolition of the Paknam line, the possibility of its revival as a freight line to Samrong was discussed several times without ever being realized.[10]

Crisis of the Maeklong Line

On the other hand, Sarit's "fine sight" policy also affected the Maeklong line, which had developed as an inter-urban railway. Sarit decided at the cabinet meeting in February 1960 that the terminus of the line would be moved from Khlong San to Talat Phlu (Kakizaki 2009, 134). The plan aimed at the conversion of railways into roads, given the increasing urbanization and that the level crossing with Taksin Road near Wongwian Yai caused traffic congestion. This was the first plan for elimination of the Maeklong line, even though there had been several concerning the Paknam line since prewar days.

This was completely unexpected for the SRT, as was the cabinet's 1959 decision to abolish the main line between Hua Lamphong and Bang Sue. Unlike the Paknam line, positive investment had been provided to the main line, and its income was growing favorably, so the SRT needed a contingency plan. The Maeklong line was not connected with other lines; its rolling stock was carried from Khlong San to the Maenam freight station by ship in order to enter the Makkasan workshop. For this reason, the SRT proposed either constructing a new line to connect with the main line (the Southern line) or leaving tracks to Khlong San and moving its terminus to Wongwian Yai, where the transfer with buses would be more convenient (ibid.).[11] As the latter lower-cost plan was adopted, the service between Wongwian Yai and Khlong San was abolished at the end of 1960, and it was diverted to a road with tracks left in the middle to ensure that an occasional train ran at times to transport its rolling stock (RFT 1970, 356–59).[12]

The change of the Maeklong line's terminus from Talat Phlu to Wongwian Yai aimed to effect better transfer with buses, but the loss of Khlong San at the bank of the Chaophraya further reduced the function of the Maeklong line as an urban railway. Khlong San was connected to the ferryboats on the Chaophraya, and access to the city center, such as Charoen Krung Road, was convenient. However, it was a detour from Wongwian Yai to Charoen Krung Road via the Memorial Bridge, and the travel time would be drastically increased because of road congestion. Nevertheless, the number of passengers on the Maeklong line increased after the shortening to Wongwian Yai, and as shown in table 4.1, the income from passenger traffic increased favorably through 1972.

Table 4.1. Maeklong Line Operations, 1961–1975 (THB)

Fiscal Year	Receipts			Expenditures	Balance
	Passengers	Freight	Total		
1961	5,321,349	175,677	5,648,633	5,013,283	635,350
1962	7,430,781	244,919	7,942,364	7,396,564	545,800
1963	7,869,513	249,794	8,295,278	7,641,296	653,982
1964	8,553,382	222,548	9,031,967	8,383,196	648,771
1965	9,160,053	212,555	9,754,110	8,835,524	918,586
1966	9,995,618	228,744	10,686,823	10,329,789	357,034
1967	11,113,275	217,303	11,922,098	9,161,338	2,760,760
1968	11,935,544	237,630	12,579,878	10,666,991	1,912,887
1969	12,646,665	245,733	13,420,990	11,314,066	2,106,924
1970	13,525,754	264,898	14,289,781	12,017,461	2,272,320
1971	14,774,355	287,320	15,439,733	13,518,218	1,921,515
1972	16,896,488	227,841	17,580,115	14,531,258	3,048,857
1973	11,424,903	219,032	12,418,214	15,287,735	-2,869,521
1974	5,810,643	224,951	6,673,078	15,778,467	-9,105,389
1975	5,714,580	276,079	6,625,545	16,364,751	-9,739,206

NOTE: The fiscal year in 1961 was from January to September, and after 1961, from October to September.
SOURCE: Data from RFT for 1961–75.

Soon after the change of terminus to Wongwian Yai, the Maeklong line faced the crisis of being abolished. As people who lived along the line had supported its complete abolition to convert it into a road, in March 1961 the cabinet decided to take up the matter (Kakizaki 2009, 134). Unlike the Paknam line, the Maeklong line clearly turned a profit for the SRT and thus it was difficult to order its elimination. However, because the cabinet hesitated to refuse the request outright, it decided to accept the abolition on unrealizable conditions. That is, the SRT replied that it would accept the abolition if the service could be immediately replaced by buses, noting that otherwise passengers would be inconvenienced. However, because there was no road paralleling the line, it was impossible to realize these terms. Furthermore, the Samut Songkhram governor also opposed the abolition. In July 1963, the cabinet decided not to abolish the Maeklong line and instead to consider a plan for its modernization (RFT 1970, 359–61). In this way, the Maeklong line averted the crisis, although only by the partial abolition of a section.

The SRT hurriedly formulated a modernization plan for the Maeklong line. The plan included not only the transfer of rolling stock from the main line and the improvement of tracks (as well as those of the main line), but also the construction of a new line between Taling Chan and Wat Sing, the connection of two separate sections by a new bridge across the Thachin, and the construction of a new line between Maeklong and Ban Kluai on the Southern line (see figure 4.1).[13] The Maeklong line would connect with the main line in two places and would function as one of its branch lines. However, the National Economic Development Board (NEDB) asked for a reexamination, noting that sufficient profit could not be expected because of a planned highway construction between Thonburi and Paktho.[14]

Therefore, the SRT changed its plan to include two more functions: the bypass line to the south and the urban railway of Bangkok. It added the construction of new lines between Hua Lamphong and Khlong San and between Maeklong and Paktho instead of the line to Ban Kluai.[15] It also planned to construct elevated tracks from Hua Lamphong to the Maeklong line across the Chaophraya and extend the line from the present terminus at Maeklong to Paktho on the Southern line. This meant that the Maeklong line would not only enter the urban transport of Bangkok but would serve as a bypass line to the south, which would shorten the distance by approximately fifty kilometers.[16] The plan was ambitious in that it would change the conventional, local suburban railway into a full-scale urban railway and the main trunk line to the south.

Fig. 4.1. Maeklong Line Modernization Plan, 1960s

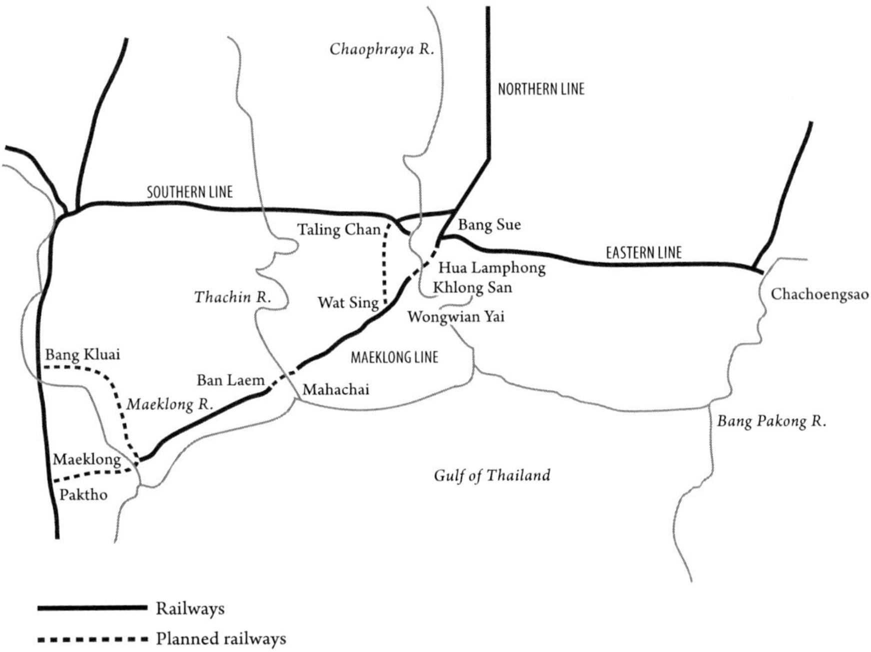

However, plans to build a highway between Thonburi and Paktho blocked the progress of the Maeklong line improvement plan. The final consultancy report that evaluated the feasibility of the road recommended to abolish the western section between Ban Laem and Maeklong, to maintain the eastern section between Wongwian Yai and Mahachai (as it might be utilized for a suburban Bangkok line in the future), and to suspend the extension plan to Paktho, which would not turn a profit.[17] The construction of this road started in 1970 with the help of a loan from the World Bank, and it opened for traffic in April 1973.[18] In the Maeklong line improvement plan, the bridges over the Thachin and Maeklong Rivers were to be used along with this road; independent bridges for the road had been previously constructed.

The opening of the Thonburi-Paktho Road (Route 35) not only buried the Maeklong line improvement plan but also had a great influence on the business of the Maeklong line. With a splendid and improved paved road paralleling the entire Maeklong line, the number of passengers on the Maeklong line decreased drastically. As shown in table 4.1, the income from passenger traffic suddenly decreased to one-third, that is, from approximately 17 million baht in 1972 to below 6 million baht in 1974. As a result, the balance of the Maeklong line fell into deficit beginning in 1973, and reached 9 million baht in 1974. The number of passengers in 1972 was 4,020,000, with an average of approximately 11,000 per day, but it was reduced to one-third in 1973, with 1.2 million per year, or an average of about 3,300 per day (RFT for 1972, 56; RFT for 1973, 49). In particular, there was a large reduction in the number of passengers from Maeklong, who used the ferry to cross the Thachin; the number decreased drastically from 2,220,000 to 130,000 persons in the same period.

The rapid reduction of passengers following the opening of a parallel road seems to have been far larger in scale than in the case of the Paknam line, and it is a remarkable example of how competition with automobiles caused a sharp decrease in the railway transport of Thai railways as well as a similar decrease in freight transport on the Northeastern line that accompanied the opening of Friendship Highway in 1958.[19] With the reduction of passengers, the transport capacity of the Maeklong line was greatly reduced; by 1976, the number of train trips between Khlong San and Mahachai had dropped from 21.5 to 17, and the trips between Ban Laem and Maeklong had dropped from 11 to 4, while the partial service to Wat Sing, which consisted of 17 trips daily, disappeared completely.[20] Thus, the Maeklong line's function as an urban railway disappeared, and its function as an inter-urban railway was also drastically reduced.

Disappearance of Tramways

Sarit's "fine sight" policy also influenced Bangkok Electricity's tramways. In August 1958, Bangkok Electricity and the Samsen Power Plant, under the jurisdiction of the Department of Public and Municipal Affairs, were merged as the Metropolitan Electricity Authority (MEA) (FN for 1958, 1). Although power distribution in Bangkok, divided between Bangkok Electricity (the former Thai Electric Corporation) and the Department of Public and Municipal Affairs (the former Sanitary Department) since the opening of the Samsen power station, was unified, for the MEA the financial importance of the power distribution business would increase further, whereas that of the tramway business would continue to wane.

Furthermore, the MEA lost many tramcars when its shed at Saphan Lueang caught fire in September of the same year (ibid., 22).[21] Fifty-three tramcars were damaged, which reduced the total number available by about a quarter: from 215 to 162 cars. The Bang Kholaem line was most affected by the fire; it is said that the number of tramcars in its operation was reduced to less than half (ibid.). Although it is difficult to tell for certain how much the fire affected revenues, the passenger receipts from the Bang Kholaem line clearly show a reduction. According to table 4.2, the revenue of the Bang Kholaem line in 1959 was 2,770,000 baht, which was lower than the revenue of not only the Samsen and Bang Sue lines but also of the Dusit line. There might have been other important factors other than the fire, but the total amount of income in 1959 dropped by 2 million baht compared with that in 1958.

In order to revive transport capacity, more tramcars were needed, but the opinion that the tramways should be removed to alleviate the increased volume of traffic in Bangkok had gradually gained strength. For this reason, the MEA attempted to revive a trolley bus plan that had suffered a setback long ago, instead of seeking to recover the tramways. Although the trolley bus plan, which had emerged immediately after the inauguration of Bangkok Electricity, was not realized, it appeared again in the press in 1955 (*SN*, 10 April 1955).[22] It was reported that companies in both Japan and France showed interest in the trolley bus plan, and the plan was estimated in 1958 to be implementable at a cost of approximately 200 million baht (FN for 1958, 23). As these companies seem to have aimed only to sell trolley buses, the MEA, which had sought joint investment, suspended the plan (FN for 1959, 5). There was a report that trolley buses would operate from Silom Road to the Victory Monument as a substitute for the to-be-abolished Silom line at the end of 1960, but this was not realized either (*SN*, 12 November 1960). Since then, the trolley bus plan of the MEA has completely disappeared.

Table 4.2. Receipts of Tramway Lines, 1958–1966 (THB)

Fiscal Year	Bangkok							Lopburi	Grand Total
	Bang Kholaem	Samsen & Bang Sue	Dusit	Hua Lamphong	Silom	Pathumwan	Total		
1958	N.A.	N.A.	N.A.	N.A.	N.A.	N.A.	18,053,235	710,696	18,763,931
1959	2,767,955	6,321,109	3,465,157	1,761,037	1,124,215	606,174	16,045,647	677,043	16,722,690
1960	3,340,544	6,738,913	3,319,568	1,737,687	1,085,136	596,591	16,818,439	622,892	17,441,331
1961	2,607,082	5,096,418	1,955,848	1,160,330		70,956	10,890,634	406,931	11,297,565
1962	4,015,191	5,692,340	2,412,823	1,480,906			13,601,260	475,557	14,076,817
1963	3,202,215	3,672,553	1,897,477	238,866			9,011,111	70,379	9,081,490
1964	398,483	2,550,559	873,494				3,822,536		3,822,536
1965			639,256				639,256		639,256
1966			513,410				513,410		513,410

NOTE: Until 1960, the fiscal year corresponded to the Western calendar year. In 1961, it ran from January to September and in subsequently, from October to September.
SOURCES: FN for 1959–66 (selected years).

Neither the introduction of trolley buses nor the restoration of tramways materialized; hence, the MEA tramway business would disappear. The first to be eliminated was the section between Yotse and the eastern side of the Kasatsuek Bridge on the Pathumwan line and the Silom line (FN for 1960, 9). The former aimed at relief of bottleneck traffic congestion on the Kasatsuek Bridge, and the latter was for the expansion of Silom Road. Both were eliminated in 1960, as shown in table 4.3. Then, the Bangkok Municipality asked for the abolition of a partial section of the Pathumwan line in order to improve the Ratchaprasong intersection. Accordingly, the Pathumwan line was abolished in February 1961 (FN for 1961, 1). As a result, all sections that the old Siamese Tramway had extended in the 1920s were abolished as well.

Although the abolition of tramways was ignited by the desire for road improvement, Sarit's "fine sight" policy would ultimately abolish all tramways. It was decided at the cabinet meeting on December 14, 1961 that all Bangkok tramways were to be abolished except for the Circle line, which would be "preserved" as a heritage for the future (FN for 1962, 1). For this reason, tramways would be abolished one by one from the next year through 1964. As shown in figure 4.2, the Bang Sue line and the east section of the Samsen line were abolished in 1962, so the two sections that the old Siam Electricity had extended in the 1920s also disappeared after the elimination of the extension section of the old Siamese Tramway; both were abolished to improve the roads. In 1963, the south of Maha Phruettharam Road on the Bang Kholaem line, the section between Thewet and Maensi on the Dusit line, and the entire Hua Lamphong line were abolished, reducing the total length of tramways to less than twenty kilometers. In 1964, the remaining section of the Samsen line between Bang Krabue and Sam Yaek was abolished in two stages, and the remaining section of the Bang Kholaem line was also eliminated. As a result, at the end of September 1964, the only remaining tramways in Bangkok were the 7.5 kilometers of the Dusit and Circle lines. At this time, all the lines of the old Siam Electricity had been abolished, and all that remained were those of the old Siamese Tramway. In addition, the tramway of Lopburi was also abolished at the end of November 1962, after having been in business for only seven years.

It was the Circle line that would be "preserved." However, annular operation was, in fact, already impossible. As shown in figure 4.2, the last tramlines were divided into two sections: those between Tha Chang and Samyot on the Circle line and those between the Enlistee Statue and Maensi on the Circle/Dusit line. This was because of a request by the Police Department to ease road traffic congestion. The sections between the Enlistee Statue and Tha Chang and between Samyot and Chakkraphet were abolished at the end of 1963 (FN for 1964, 3).[23] Although the former was only a 300-meter section, because the tramcars could no longer operate there, the convenience of the tram service was clearly curtailed. There were only eleven tramcars on the remaining sections.[24]

The MEA tramway business had been maintaining a surplus until the abolition started, but it started losing money in 1961. Table 4.4 shows that the MEA had maintained a favorable balance until 1960. However, its expenditures increased more than its income beginning in 1961, and it seems to have been in deficit since then, although there are a few years for which expenditure figures are not available. When only the preservation section of the Circle line remained, the deficit did not change, and there were no signs of business improvement.

Praphat Charusathian, the Minister of Interior, asserted that the Circle line should remain as a museum even though a loss of 10,000 baht per month was expected; however, the actual deficit exceeded this estimate (*SN*, 26 October 1963).

Table 4.3. Abolition of Tramways

Line	Section	Length (km)	Date Terminated	Sources
Bang Kholaem	Lak Mueang–Atsadang	0.3	15 Jun 1962	FN for 196)
	Maha Phruettharam–Bang Kholaem	5.3	31 July 1963	FN for 1963
	Atsadang–Maha Phruettharam	3.5	14 Jan 1964	FN for 1964
Samsen	Wang Sukhothai–Mouth of Samsen Canal	0.5	Dec 1951	NA [2] So Ro. 0201. 63. 2/19
	Bang Krabue–Bang Krabue Pier	0.3	Dec 1951	NA [2] So Ro. 0201. 63. 2/19
	Wat Traimit–Sathon	3.4	31 Jul 1962	FN for 1962
	Samyaek–Wat Traimit	0.3	12 May 1963	FN for 1963
	Bang Krabue–Bang Lamphu	7.4	14 Jan 1964	FN for 1964
	Bang Lamphu–Samyaek		30 Sep 1964	FN for 1964
Bang Sue	Bang Krabue–Bang Sue	4	30 Apr 1962	FN for 1962
Hua Lamphong	Hua Lamphong–Phra Sumen	4.4	30 Nov 1963	FN for 1963
Circle	Enlistee Statue–Tha Chang	0.3	22 Dec 1963	FN for 1964
	Samyot–Chakkraphet	*0.8*	30 Nov 1963	FN for 1964
	Chakkraphet–Enlistee Statue	*3.3*	30 Sep 1968	FN for 1968
	Tha Chang–Samyot	*2.8*	30 Sep 1968	FN for 1968
Dusit	Thewet–Saphan Dam	2.9	20 Jun 1963	FN for 1963
	Maensi–Chakkraphet	1.3	30 Sep 1968	FN for 1968
Silom	Bang Rak–Pratunam	4.5	15 Dec 1960	FN for 1960
Pathumwan	Yotse–East Kasatsuek Bridge	*0.3*	15 Oct 1960	FN for 1960
	East Kasatsuek Bridge–Ratchaprasong	*2.2*	28 Feb 1961	FN for 1961
Total		47.8		

NOTE 1: The length of the Samsen line between Bang Lamphu and Samyaek is included in the length between Bang Krabue and Bang Lamphu.

NOTE 2: The Phloenchit line is excluded due to the lack of sources regarding its abolition.

NOTE 3: Figures in italics are approximate.

Fig. 4.2. Abandoned Tramways in Bangkok, 1960–1968

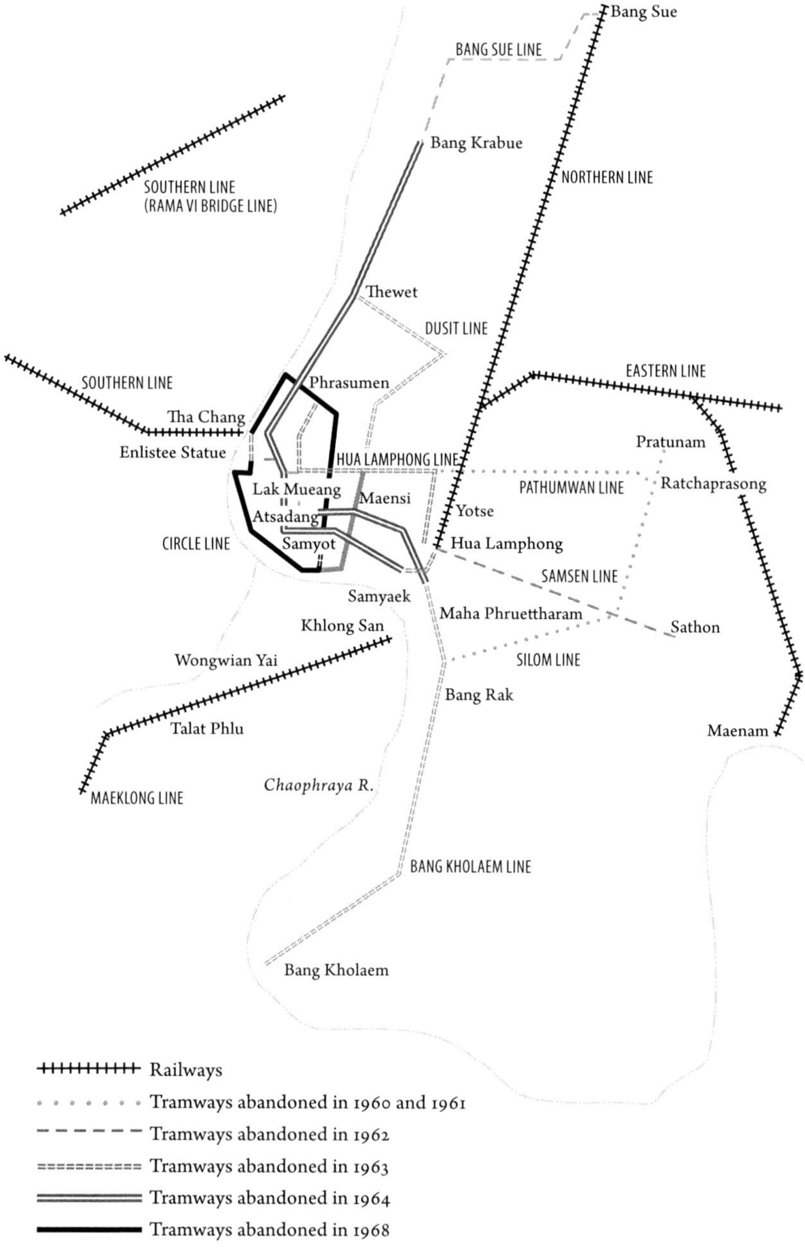

Table 4.4. Financial Situation of the MEA Tramways, 1958–1968 (THB)

Fiscal Year	Bangkok			Lopburi			Total		
	Receipts	Expenditures	Balance	Receipts	Expenditures	Balance	Receipts	Expenditures	Balance
1958	18,212,878	N.A.	N.A.	710,696	N.A.	N.A.	18,923,574	N.A.	N.A.
1959	16,689,424	16,272,175	417,249	677,142	809,988	-132,846	17,366,566	17,082,163	284,403
1960	17,685,076	16,910,978	774,098	622,892	848,191	-225,299	18,307,968	17,759,169	548,799
1961	11,566,454	N.A.	N.A.	406,931	N.A.	N.A.	11,973,385	17,083,948	-5,110,563
1962	14,588,993	N.A.	N.A.	475,557	N.A.	N.A.	15,064,550	19,443,714	-4,379,164
1963	9,159,896	N.A.	N.A.	70,379	N.A.	N.A.	9,230,275	N.A.	N.A.
1964	3,822,536	N.A.	N.A.				3,822,536	N.A.	N.A.
1965	639,256	N.A.	N.A.				639,256	N.A.	N.A.
1966	957,369	1,179,524	-222,155				957,369	1,179,524	-222,155
1967	952,999	1,260,211	-307,212				952,999	1,260,211	-307,212
1968	853,601	1,411,410	-557,809				853,601	1,411,410	-557,809

NOTE 1: Until 1960, the fiscal year corresponded to the Western calendar year. In 1961, it ran from January to September and subsequently, from October to September.

NOTE 2: Receipts between 1963 and 1965 include only receipts from fares and advertisement.

SOURCES: FN for 1959–68 (selected years).

The Circle line was "preserved" from 1964 for some time, but it would eventually disappear after all. The line was abolished at the end of September 1968, and with that all tramways disappeared from Bangkok. This meant that the tramway completed its role exactly eighty years after the first tramway was opened for traffic in September 1888. It seems that there was little regret concerning the elimination of the tramways, judging from contemporaneous newspaper articles.[25] The newspapers largely expressed approval, and opinions to the contrary were few.[26] Although the government had been prepared to enact a law obliging the "preservation" of the Circle line, newspapers voiced opposition (*SRWR*, 13 September 1962).[27] Thus, except for the suburban trains of the Maeklong line, rail transport disappeared from Bangkok, and urban transport became dependent solely on buses.

Emergence of the Bus Unification Plan

Strengthening of Bus Regulation

In 1955, Prime Minister Phibun changed the policy on buses from one based on nationalization to one based on his own political aims, and enacted measures that were paternalistic to bus operators. However, when the Phibun government collapsed after the coup d'état of September 1957, national regulation of the bus business was strengthened again. Thirty-one applications for the establishment or change of bus routes were submitted by bus operators to the Transport Regulation Committee in October of that year, immediately following the coup d'état.[28] The committee concluded that several problems had arisen after it began to approve the bus operators' applications almost automatically. Therefore, it decided to return to the original process of posting notices of the new routes in the Royal Gazette and then accepting applications from operators and establishing a subcommittee to examine all the applications. In doing so, the Transport Regulation Committee re-strengthened bus regulation, and the frequent changes in bus routes that had occurred under the Phibun government were put to an end.

The Transport Regulation Committee also coped with operators who did not follow the terms of their concessions, such as those who had an extreme shortage of bus trips, by imposing a severe policy of revoking the concession. At the Transport Regulation Committee meeting in October 1957, the Thai Bamrung Company's concessions for Routes 25 and 38, with the lowest number of buses in table 3.7, were revoked. The Yatmit Company's concession for Route 40 and the Samakkhitham Company's for Route 45, were also revoked, as their situations were even worse than Thai Bamrung's.[29] This confirmed the principle that concessions would be revoked if the agreed upon number of buses was not secured, as there were still eleven operators who had not yet fulfilled their concession terms. At the same time, it was decided to suspend subsidies for bus operators and tax reductions that had been introduced by the previous government, as there was no guarantee of using them effectively, and legal revisions were required for the tax reduction measure.

Then, after providing a grace period to increase the number of buses by the end of November 1957, the Transport Regulation Committee decided in December to cancel the concessions for Route 34 held by the Mit Songsoem Company and for Route 28 held by the Sinthumit Company (*Borisat sinthumit chamkat*) because they could not improve their businesses. It further decided to accept the applications of substitute operators before the cancelation in order not to interrupt service.[30] Subsequently, the cancelation of bus route concessions was again examined at the meeting in January 1958, and it was decided to revoke the concessions for Route 18 of the Thai Thawon Company and Route 42 of the Si Borikan Company (*Borisat si borikan chamkat*) as well as to announce that applications for substitute operators would be accepted.[31] At this meeting, Phong Punnakan, the minister of communications, expressed his opinion that the number of operators should be reduced more severely because having fewer operators would result in smoother regulation of the bus business.

Furthermore, a movement for nationalization also resurfaced. In May 1958, the Transport Regulation Committee decided to abolish concession-revoked routes if competing routes existed, as the increased competition would jeopardize the safety of passengers.[32] It also decided to leave bus operations to government agencies or companies in which the government held a share of not less than 50 percent if there were no substitute bus routes available. Given that only the ETO and the Transport Company could fulfill these terms, this policy aimed at the unification of bus business under government management. As a result, it was decided that the operation of four routes (22, 40, 45, and 49) that no operators wished to apply for and two parallel routes (28 and 38) would be eliminated, and Route 34, which had no parallel routes, would be left to the Transport Company.[33] The concession for Route 41 of the Saha Watthanakit Company (*Borisat saha watthanakit chamkat*) was also revoked at the end of June 1960, and its operation was transferred to the Transport Company.[34] The Saha Watthanakit Company insisted that this was unfair, noting that the concession was suddenly revoked after only twenty days, even though the Department of Transport had granted ninety days to improve bus operations (*SN*, 2 July 1960).[35]

The government also established a new state-owned firm to realize nationalization. The director of the Department of Transport stated at the shareholders' meeting of the Transport Company in May 1958 that the Ministry of Communications would purchase the bus operation section of both the Transport Company and the ETO to establish a new bus operating company.[36] Although the unification plan should have sought to unify the bus operators of Bangkok, it went beyond that, and the Transport Company would gain the concession of regional buses on a large scale, as will be discussed below. A plan to merge with the Transport Company was also suggested. However, a problem arose with the license renewal in 1960, so only a minimal conversion of routes took place with this route rearrangement.[37]

Table 4.5 summarizes the route rearrangement in 1960. The number of routes at this time was forty-nine; the abolished routes were not assigned route numbers, and four special routes were added. As can be seen by comparison with table 3.7, in 1957 the Transport Company increased the number of its operation routes from five to six, while the ETO decreased its number by one route.[38] Furthermore, because three routes between bus terminals were left to the Transport Company and one on Chan Road was left to the ETO, each new line reflected the policy of nationalization.[39] As a result, the number of bus routes operated by the ETO and the Transport Company rose to thirteen, or 27 percent of the total.

The network of bus routes in Bangkok was further widened. Figure 4.3 shows the bus network at the time of the route rearrangement in 1960. A comparison with figure 3.4 reveals that there were new bus routes that reached such destinations as Nongchok in the east, Khlong

Khwang and Bang Khunthian in the west, and Phrapradaeng and the Phra Chunlachomklao Fort in the south. The highway to the Phra Chunlachomklao Fort was opened for traffic in 1956, and the Thon Nakhon Transport Company (*Borisat thon nakhon khonsong chamkat*) had already started an unauthorized bus service. When the Nonthaburi Bridge built over the Chaophraya opened for traffic in 1959, buses could reach the city area of Pathumthani by changing a part of their former route. Several bridges across the Chaophraya in Bangkok opened during this period, including the Krung Thon Bridge in 1958 and the Bangkok Bridge in 1959. A bus route to the Krung Thon Bridge was also established. Additionally, a new bus route was established to Huai Khwang, where a residential estate had been constructed.

On the other hand, a bus route that had been newly established in 1956 was lost in the partial section of Ngamwongwan Road, or Charansanitwong Road. This was due to the lack of a new candidate after a badly managed concession was revoked; thus, we can conclude that there was not much demand for a regular bus route in these suburbs.[40]

Table 4.5. Bus Routes in Bangkok, October 1960

Route Number	Line	Operator
1	Thanon Tok–Tha Tian	ETO
2	Bang Na–Pakkhlong Talat	Nai Loet
3	Wongwian Yai–Mochit	Si Nakhon
4	Talat Phlu–Wat Traimit	ETO
5	Bang Sue–Chakkrawat	Si Nakhon
6	Bukkhalo–Bang Khunphrom	Phra Nakhon Thonburi Transport
7	Khlong Khwang–Nopphawong	Bang Khae Transport
8	Latphrao–Memorial Bridge	Nai Loet
9	Phasi Charoen–Samsen	Thonburi Automobile
10	Wat Nangnong–Ratchadamnoen Stadium	Thonnakhon Transport
11	Makkasan–Wat Pho	Nai Loet
12	Huai Khwang–Ministry of Economic Affairs	Red Bus
13	Khlong Toei–Dindaeng	Khlong Toei Trading
14	Siyan–Khlong Toei	Si Nakhon
15	Ban Mai–Bang Lamphu	Bunphong
16	Thewet–Surawong	Phira Bus

Route Number	Line	Operator
17	Wat Ratchasingkhon–Tha Chang	Yanyon Insurance
18	Bang Phlat–Si Phraya	Thai Thawon
19	Thonburi Station–Thewet	Thonburi Union Transport
20	Khlong Toei–Wat Traimit	ETO
21	Samre–Chulalongkorn University	Si Lueang
23	Thewet Circle Line (right rotation)	Red Bus
24	Thewet Circle Line (left rotation)	Thai Pradit
26	Nongchok–Saphan Khao	Minburi Transport
27	Bang Kapi–Khlong Toei	Thepphaniramit
29	Tha Chang–Don Mueang	Transport Co.
30	Tha Chang–Nonthaburi	Transport Co.
31	Tha Chang–Pakkret	Transport Co.
32	Pakkret–Sanam Luang	Nonthaburi Municipality
33	Pathumthani–Sanam Luang	Bang Buathong Transport
34	Rangsit–Hua Lamphong	Transport Co.
35	Chong Nonsi–Witthayu	Chong Nonsi Transport
36	Bang Son–Wat Pathum Khongkha	Sirimit
37	Wongwian Yai–Mahanak	Si Lueang
39	Don Mueang–Sanam Luang	Sahaiyon Transport
41	Krung Thon Bridge–Bang Lamphu	Transport Co.
42	Sirirat–Wang Burapha	Niyom Transport
43	Bang Khunthian–Sanam Luang	Watchanakun
44	Mochit–Sanam Luang	Si Nakhon
46	Phrakhanong–Samyan	Si Nakhon
47	Saphan Dam–Land Department	Yanyon Insurance
48	Phrakhanong–Wat Pho	Nai Loet
50	Phra Chunlachomklao Fort–Wongwian Yai	Thon Nakhon Transport
51	Tha Chang–Paknam	Transport Co.
52	Samyaek–Paknam	Samut Prakan Transport
Special 1	Trok Chan	
Special 2	Southern Line Bus Terminal–Eastern Line Bus Terminal	
Special 3	Southern Line Bus Terminal–Northern Line Bus Terminal	
Special 4	Northern Line Bus Terminal–Eastern Line Bus Terminal	

SOURCES: NA Kho Kho. 0202. 3. 4/7; NA Kho Kho. 0202. 3. 5/189.

Fig. 4.3. Bus Network in Bangkok, 1960

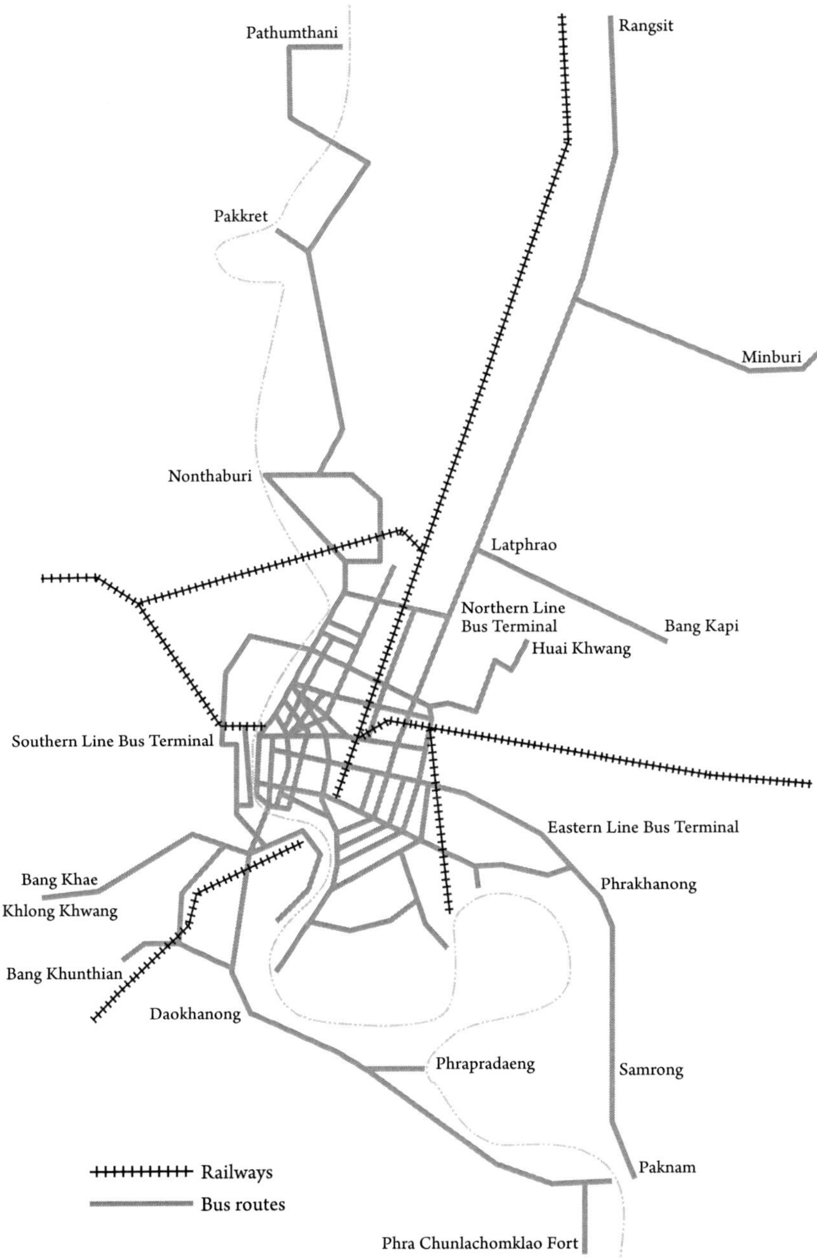

Unification of Regional Buses by the Transport Company

The policy of nationalizing bus operations affected not only the urban buses of Bangkok but also regional buses. There was no regulation on inter-provincial buses between Bangkok and provinces or for local buses in the provinces. Although the Transport Company had also begun providing inter-provincial bus service, many operators were in competition. In 1959, regional bus routes were as follows: sixteen routes by seventeen operators on the Northern line, eight routes by eighteen operators on the Northeastern and Central lines, sixteen routes by ten operators on the Southeastern line, and eighteen routes by eight operators on the Southern line.[41] There were eight operators who operated buses between Bangkok and Khorat, where road conditions had improved dramatically with the opening of the Friendship Highway in 1958. Since there were many operators for the number of routes, competition between operators was intense, and there were problems with respect to the convenience and safety of passengers, such as a scramble of passengers or excessive speed.

For this reason, the Department of Transport decided to regulate regional buses beyond Bangkok. In practice, the Transport Act, specifically enforced initially only in five provinces around Bangkok, was to be expanded to another twenty-five provinces to reach Nakhon Sawan, Khorat, Trat, and Chumphon, places that buses from Bangkok already reached.[42] The Department of Transport was planning to issue concessions to operators, giving it monopolistic control as in Bangkok. It was supposed to grant concession by initially unifying operators into five associations according to five lines.[43] Furthermore, the regulation would be expanded in three steps starting in 1959: inter-provincial buses originating in Bangkok in the first year, other inter-provincial buses in the second year, and the intra-provincial buses in the third year.

However, the Transport Company applied to gain concessions for all the routes within these twenty-five provinces.[44] The Transport Company proposed that it would regulate bus operations by allowing the existing private buses to continue operation, because it had already operated inter-provincial buses between Bangkok and other provinces over many years. In September 1959, the Transport Regulation Committee examined the proposal and decided that the concessions of all bus routes within twenty-five provinces would be granted to the Transport Company in accordance with its proposal.[45] The decision was made to leave regulation to the Transport Company rather than the Department of Transport because the Department of Transport had insufficient staff to regulate both regional and Bangkok buses. Moreover, most operators were collections of bus owners; few of them met the standard.

Because of this decision, the business of the Transport Company was to be extended considerably. The Transport Company had operated at a deficit since 1957, and its water transport business, which was the main reason for the deficit, was abandoned in 1958.[46] In December 1958, the number of buses was 113 on a total of eleven routes, including routes in Bangkok. The Transport Company owned 84 of these; all others were private buses.[47] However, the new decision would give the Transport Company jurisdiction over about eight hundred private buses; this meant that the number of buses under its regulation would increase sharply. Furthermore, the Transport Company gained concessions not only for the inter-provincial buses between Bangkok and the provinces or between province, but also for intra-provincial buses that connected province centers, districts, district centers, and *tambon*, or villages.[48] Therefore, even *songthaeo* connecting to villages were to be included in the concessions of the Transport Company when operating on the specified roads.

The Transport Company's acquisition of bus concessions in twenty-five provinces led to criticism not only from bus operators but also from passengers. Although the Transport Company got the concessions, it did not have the ability to operate the buses by itself and only allowed existing bus operators to operate under the Transport Company's concession. Thus, from the viewpoint of bus operators, they had to carry an additional burden of paying fees to the Transport Company. Also, a check of buses by the Department of Transport was added to the existing check by the Police Department, as the licenses issued by both the Department of Transport and the Police Department were needed.[49] The bus owner had to pay fees to the Transport Company at the rate of ten satang per kilometer of operation distance; thus, a bus owner in Phetchaburi province complained to Prime Minister Sarit that 300 to 400 baht per month out of 700 to 800 baht of their monthly income was being taken by the Transport Company as a fee.[50] So bus operators had to shoulder a new burden, and a portion of their profits was being taken by the Transport Company.

Criticisms of the Transport Company and government succeeded one another in newspapers. The following comment is a typical example:

> Just when regulation of the concession by the Transport Company started, they raised the fares. . . . While the Transport Company gets concessions free of charge, it established a provision for collecting royalties (*kha chai sampathan*) from bus owners who had been operating until then. And since it was so expensive that they could not continue their operations under the same fare and with the same number of passengers, they issued a complaint of appeal. However, ultimately, the complaint was rejected, and most owners decided to pay royalties under the concession terms of the Transport Company. This was because the newly defined fare was higher than the earlier fare and enough to secure a profit even after paying fees to the Transport Company, and their incomes were expected to be larger than before. . . . It is the passengers who have borne the brunt: they were forced to pay higher fares for the same distance, to ride the same buses, just only repainted, with the same drivers and owners. Did the passengers gain anything other than a fare hike? (*SN*, 18 November 1959)

Because there was no improvement of service and the fare hike weighed heavily on passengers, even though the Transport Company had the law behind it, public opinion was critical of the integration of regional buses by the Transport Company.[51] It was criticized as "a tiger lying down and eating (*suea non kin*)" and as a mere broker that took away profits from others.[52] For this reason, although unification by the Transport Company was temporarily considered on the occasion of bus concession renewals in Bangkok in 1960, it had already encountered difficulties in its implementation.

Unification Plan by the Bangkok Municipality

Since the bus unification plan of Bangkok under the Transport Company had become difficult to implement, the Bangkok Municipality appealed against its jurisdiction over bus business in Bangkok. In February 1961, it asked the Ministry of Interior to regulate the bus business by itself, and in the same month, the cabinet agreed that the municipality would form a plan for regulation.[53] The opinion of the Bangkok Municipality was as follows:[54] Because twenty or more operators were engaged in the Bangkok bus business, jurisdiction would be difficult. The municipality could not bear the entire responsibility for it, but would take on the burden of road repair. However, since all municipalities in foreign capitals were running bus businesses, or private companies were running them under the jurisdiction of municipalities, the Bangkok Municipality proposed to unify the bus business in Bangkok under a new company that would merge all existing bus operators. Although the reason the municipality applied to regulate the bus business at this time is unknown, it mentions the results of a transport survey by the United States Agency for International Development (USAID) in 1959 that pointed out that the largest problem in Bangkok was the need for unification of bus operators.[55]

Given that new concessions had just been granted to Bangkok bus operators in October of the previous year, the cabinet asked the Bangkok Municipality not to immediately unify the Bangkok bus business, but to formulate a plan. The municipality decided to investigate its bus business plan with assistance of the District of Columbia (DC) Transit System in the United States.[56] This was the bus operator in Washington, DC, that Chamnan Yuabun, the mayor of the Bangkok Municipality, asked for the assistance from when he attended an international conference in Washington, DC, in June 1961. Simultaneously, the municipality negotiated with the Export-Import Bank of the United States, expressing its wish to use a foreign loan in the amount of 320 million baht to promote the bus plan. The loan plan was approved at the cabinet meeting on July 25, 1961, and it was also accepted that specialists from DC Transit Company would come to investigate the Bangkok bus business situation.[57]

Experts from the United States investigated the situation of bus services in Bangkok and formulated a unification plan.[58] According to their plan, a new company called the Bangkok Municipal Bus System would be established. The Bangkok Municipality would contribute 25 percent of the shares, and the remainder would be distributed according to an asset evaluation of the bus operators. The new company would purchase the existing 1,867 buses. Those in good condition would continue to operate after being repaired, and the others would be sent to the provinces. Moreover, a total of 500 new model buses would be imported from the United States in a span of three years, and the DC Transit Company would dispatch personnel for five years to train Thai employees. To implement this plan, a suppliers' credit of 2,800,000 dollars and a foreign loan from the Export-Import Bank of 13,700,000 baht would be extended. Passenger fares would be hiked from fifty satang to one baht with the assumption that free transfers from one line to another would be allowed.

The Ministry of Communications and the bus operators, however, opposed this unification plan. At the cabinet meeting on December 19, 1961, under pressure from the Ministry of Communications, it was decided to establish a committee to consider bus unification, and the minister of communications was selected as the committee chair.[59] Then, at a meeting in January of the following year, it was decided that the bus operators would determine whether they would continue their bus operations until the expiration of their concessions or transfer their businesses to the Bangkok Municipality. Additionally, if they were able to unify their businesses independently within six months, the committee would ask them to formulate a bus unification plan. Thus, the Ministry of Communications was proposing unification not by the municipality, but voluntary unification by private operators. If the operators' unification plan was satisfactory, the ministry intended to scrap the municipality's plan, asserting that the improvement of the bus business would be possible without the need for such a large foreign loan.

The press also criticized the Bangkok Municipality's plan. Editorialists claimed that the municipality's bus business plan was the same "tiger lying down and eating" as in the case of the Transport Company and doubted its efficiency to operate buses in Bangkok.[60] There were also many criticisms that the new company to be established by the municipality would take the same form as the Transport Company, and the municipality would become a broker taking away profits from private operators. Moreover, some held that it was impossible for the municipality to add operating buses to its list of services since it was unable to even carry out its existing public services satisfactorily. There were also doubts whether the service would be worth the proposed fare of one baht. In fact, some critics misunderstood the municipality's unification plan, which differed from that of the Transport Company. But public opinion was critical of the plan because of the bad example of the latter company.

Finally, the Bangkok Municipality's plan was rejected. Based on the proposal of the Ministry of Finance, the cabinet decided on July 24, 1962, to suspend the foreign loan from DC Transit as unsuitable, and to establish a new committee headed by the deputy prime minister to consider the matter.[61] This was because the interest on the supplier's credit from DC Transit was higher than that of the Export-Import Bank, and it would cost more than international bidding by free competition.[62] The government had already asked the municipality to use only the foreign loan from the Export-Import Bank and to limit the support from DC Transit to technical support, but the municipality replied that it was difficult to do so.[63] Thus, the municipality's plan was finally dismissed over concerns that the problem of the foreign loan had not been solved.

A new committee, named the Public Service and Transport Problem Solution Committee (*Khana kammakan phicharana panha kiaokap kan prapprung kan satharanupaphok lae kan charachon*) was established, and its first meeting was held in August of the same year.[64] At this meeting, the committee concluded that bus business unification would be left to private operators in order to ease the budget burden and that it was desirable to propel unification towards the expiration of concessions in 1965. It was also pointed out that the addition of new work would be difficult to handle for the Bangkok Municipality, which had to undertake various other construction projects, and it was indicated that the municipality should concentrate on road improvement instead. The municipality's bus unification plan was completely called off, and private-sector-led unification was sought.

Promotion of Private-Sector-Led Integration

On the other hand, private bus operators also vigorously promoted the unification of the bus business. Since it was decided in January 1962 that the unification by private operators would be approved if they could formulate a unification plan within six months, the twenty-six operators jointly invested to establish the Nakhon Luang Transport Company (*Borisat nakhon luang khonsong chamkat*).[65] The company's initial aim was to take over the operation of Route 21, which had been suspended because of the internal trouble of the Si Lueang Company (*Borisat si lueang chamkat*), but it was considered as the sole operator after unifying the bus business.[66] The Public Service and Transport Problem Solution Committee accepted the integration plan of the Nakhon Luang Transport Company and asked it to formulate a concrete unification plan.

The Nakhon Luang Transport Company then formulated the Bangkok Bus Unification Plan in January 1963.[67] This plan aimed to unify bus business under the Nakhon Luang Transport Company by means of asset sales, lease, or trust operations, and it provided that the operation by the Nakhon Luang Transport Company would start in June and complete the change of jurisdiction by December after the investigation of each operator's intention. The fare would be kept at the existing rate of fifty satang, and one free transfer would be allowed. Existing buses would be improved, and at least fifty new buses would be put into service every year. The capital would be 200 million baht, and the estimated value of the buses would be 160 million baht. Although the company asked for an extension of the concession term from five to twenty-five years, the Transport Regulation Committee decided that it would be set at ten years.[68] The number of bus routes would be reduced from forty-eight to forty, and the suburban routes would terminate at Lumphini Park and Sanam Luang with the possibility to transfer to city routes (*SN*, 5 March 1963).

The Nakhon Luang Transport Company's unification plan was approved at the cabinet meeting in April 1963, and it was to be implemented by October 1, 1965.[69] As all bus operators in Bangkok were to be unified, the buses run by both the Transport Company and the ETO would also be unified. The ETO applied for the bus business improvement plan in Bangkok but could not gain funds for this plan. As a result, it decided to sell its assets to the Nakhon Luang Transport Company.[70] The Transport Company sought to secure the routes to the provinces as much as possible anticipating bus business in Bangkok becoming unified under the Nakhon Luang Transport Company.[71] There were only four operators who had not given their consent to unification as of November 1963: ETO, the Nonthaburi Municipality, the Thai Thawon Company, and the Si Lueang Company. Thus, it seemed that the integration plan was developing well (*SN*, 9 November 1963).

Nevertheless, the unification plan by the Nakhon Luang Transport Company was ultimately called off. On January 14, 1964, the cabinet decided to annul its previous decision to unify all bus businesses under the Nakhon Luang Transport Company. It confirmed that the company was one of the operators that would be able to renew their concession, and those operators with favorable operations would be allowed to continue their businesses.[72] The decision is attributed to the rise of passenger dissatisfaction toward the deteriorating bus service, which occurred as a result of bus operators' hesitancy to invest in the bus businesses after the decision to unify. As the end of the operators' concessions approached in 1965, the operators postponed new investment in order to secure their profits. The number of bus trips was reduced because of the decrepit state of buses due to inadequate investment.[73] In fact, the unification of this miscellaneous collection of bus operators did not go smoothly. Even the number of buses on Route 21, for which the Nakhon Luang Transport Company had obtained the concession, was less than half the agreed-upon number. Therefore, the Ministry of Communications asked the cabinet to reexamine its decision as incentive for operators' positive investment.

Thus, the plan for bus unification by the private sector was also called off, and the Bangkok bus business returned to a situation in which the twenty-eight operators took charge of their assigned routes. It seems that political speculation had also been present in the unification plan of the Nakhon Luang Transport Company because it emerged immediately after the formation of the Thanom government, accompanying Prime Minister Sarit's death in 1963. Although the strengthening of bus regulation after the collapse of the Phibun regime revived the Bangkok bus business unification plan and resulted in several unification plans that used the strategies of nationalization, municipalization, and privatization, all of them finally ended in failure. Despite the fact that the unification of bus operations had been realized as one of the expressions of Sarit's "fine sight" policy, together with the elimination of the railway in Bangkok and the removal of tramways, it fell apart with the death of Sarit, and the bus business returned to the status quo.

The Problem of Fare Hikes

Large-Scale Expansion of the Route Network

Following the cancelation of the bus unification plan of the Nakhon Luang Transport Company in January 1964, operators resumed new investments in the bus business, which had been temporarily put on hold. When it was decided to allow the continuation of bus operations for acceptable operators, the Department of Land Transport (formerly the Department of Transport) asked each operator to resume bus operations as agreed upon before the start of the new school term in May (*SN*, 2 February 1964).[74] Although the renewal of concessions, other than for the Nakhon Luang Transport Company, had been approved, since it was announced that the concession of operators whose services were deteriorating would be canceled and given over to favorably operated companies, the operators reacted positively to the department's request in order to prevent the cancelation of their concession. No fewer than four hundred buses were under construction in March, but it was estimated that only half of them would be put into service in time for the new school term (*SN*, 12 March 1964). Through such measures of stimulation of bus operators, bus service gradually improved.

Yet, according to the terms of the renewal of concessions in 1965, the rearrangement of bus routes was to be planned by the Ministry of Communications. Large reinforcement of bus routes was planned at this time, and initially the Ministry of Communications had announced that forty new routes would be added (*SN*, 20 February 1964). Since there were forty-five bus lines at the time, the announcement meant that this number would be effectively doubled. For this rearrangement, the Department of Land Transport distributed questionnaires to schools, governmental offices, and private enterprises in four provinces of Phranakhon, Thonburi, Samut Prakan, and Nonthaburi to better understand users' demands (*SN*, 9 May 1964). By June 1964, two hundred thousand copies of the questionnaires had been distributed. The rate of return of filled questionnaires at governmental offices was lower than that at schools. The Department of Land Transport, therefore, attempted to collect more samples by widening the scope of the survey (*SN*, 17 June 1964). It is unknown how the detailed investigation was conducted. The questionnaire represented the first trial to gauge the opinions of bus users on the route rearrangement.

As a result, a new network of bus routes to be applied from 1965 was formulated. As shown in table 4.6, the number of bus routes increased to 108; this was more than the original plan of an increase of 40 routes. According to the Transport Regulation Committee, the actual increase was not as high because many original routes were divided into two or more routes and some corresponded to the opening of new roads or the abolition of tramways.[75] Because according to the survey 32 percent of all users changed buses, it was expected that the number of users that had to transfer would decrease due to the large increase in bus routes. Moreover, an unprecedented characteristic of this rearrangement was the establishment of many circle routes. The provided number of buses would also increase from 2,200 to 2,799, and the added routes would be impartially distributed among the twenty-eight operators.

Table 4.6. Bus Routes in Bangkok, October 1965

Route Number	Line	Route Number	Line
1	Thanon Tok–Tha Tian	55	Bang Son Circle Line (left rotation)
2	Pakkhlong Talat–Samrong	56	Bang Son Circle Line (right rotation)
3	Mochit–Khlong San	57	Krung Thon Bridge Circle Line (left rotation)
4	Talat Phlu–Khlong Toei	58	Krung Thon Bridge Circle Line (right rotation)
5	Bang Sue–Chakkrawat	59	Thonburi Circle Line (left rotation)
6	Bukkhalo–Bang Lamphu	60	Thonburi Circle Line (right rotation)
7	Nopphawong–Khlong Khwang	61	Chong Nonsi Circle Line (left rotation)
8	Memorial Bridge–Latphrao	62	Chong Nonsi Circle Line (right rotation)
9	Siyan–Talat Phlu	63	Nonthaburi–Sanam Luang
10	Wat Nangnong–Nangloeng	64	Nonthaburi–Sanam Luang
11	Makkasan–Memorial Bridge	65	Bang Son–Sanam Luang
12	Huai Khwang–Ministry of Economic Affarirs	66	Bang Sue–Talat Phlu
13	Huai Khwang–Khlong Toei	67	Bang Sue–Thung Mahamek
14	Siyan–Customs Department	68	Siyan–Sala Daeng
15	Bang Lamphu–Bangkok Bridge	69	Bang Khen–Sanam Luang
16	Surawong–Tao Pun	70	Makkasan–Bang Kapi
17	Bangkok Bridge–Tha Chang	71	Khlong Chan–Wat Pho
18	Rama VI Brudge–Si Phraya	72	Kluai Namthai–Thewet

Route Number	Line
19	Thewet–Bangkok Noi
20	Tha Dindaeng–Phra Chunlachomklao Fort
21	Chulalongkorn University–Bang Pakok
22	Thanon Tok–Kluai Namthai
23	Thewet Circle Line (right rotation)
24	Thewet Circle Line (left rotation)
25	Tha Chang–Paknam
26	Saphan Khao–Minburi
27	Bang Kapi–Khlong Toei
28	Northern Line Bus Terminal–Southern Line Bus Terminal
29	Don Mueang–Hua Lamphong
30	Nonthaburi–Tha Chang
31	Pathumthani–Tha Chang
32	Pakkret–Sanam Luang
33	Pathumthani–Sanam Luang
34	Rangsit–Hua Lamphong
35	Suan Mali–Sathu Pradit
36	Phutthamonthon 4–Bang Khae
37	Daokhanong–Mahanak
38	Northern Line Bus Terminal–Ekkamai
39	Sanam Luang–Don Mueang
40	Ekkamai–Southern Line Bus Terminal
41	Sanam Luang–Setthakit Estate
42	Sirirat–Saochingcha
43	Bang Khunthian–Sanam Luang
44	Mochit–Tha Tian
45	Samyaek–Paknam
46	Bang Chak–Rong Mueang
47	Land Department–Customs Department
48	Bang Chak–Wat Pho
49	Bang Lamphu Circle Line (left rotation)
50	Bang Lamphu Circle Line (right rotation)
51	Sisao Circle Line (left rotation)
52	Sisao Circle Line (right rotation)
53	Huai Khwang Circle Line (left rotation)
54	Huai Khwang Circle Line (right rotation)

Route Number	Line
73	Dindaeng–Memorial Bridge
74	Huai Khwang–Khlong Toei
75	Daokhanong–Tha Tian
76	Sathon–Bang Lamphu
77	Silom–Pratunam
78	Sathon–Tha Chang
79	Khlong Toei–Wat Traimit
80	Bang Khae–Phahurat
81	Bang Wa–Sirirat
82	Phrapradaeng–Memorial Bridge
83	Phrapradaeng–Phra Samut Chedi
84	Thonburi Technical College–Saochingcha
85	Ratburana–Memorial Bridge
86	Phrapradaeng–Bang Lamphu
87	Nangloeng–Daokhanong
88	Talat Phlu–Wat Traimit
89	Wat Diduat–Thonburi Commercial College
90	Bang Phun–Sanam Luang
91	Pakkret–Tha Chang
92	Pakkret–Don Mueang
93	Bang Khen–Sanambin Nam
94	Nonthaburi–Sanambin Nam
95	Rangsit–Bang Phun
96	Minburi–Nongchok
97	Ekkamai–Tha Chang
98	Paknam–Bang Pu
99	Paknam–Hat Amara
100	Phrapradaeng–Samrong
101	Bangkok Noi -Taling Chan
102	Ratburana–Bang Mot
103	Samrong–Bang Phli
104	Minburi–Khlong Luangphaeng
105	Rama VI Bridge–Krung Thon Bridge
106	Victory Monument–Si Phraya
107	Huai Khwang–Bang Khunphrom
108	Nana–Tha Chang

SOURCE: Data from NA Kho Kho. 0202. 3. 4. 1/61.

Fig. 4.4. Bus Network in Bangkok, 1965

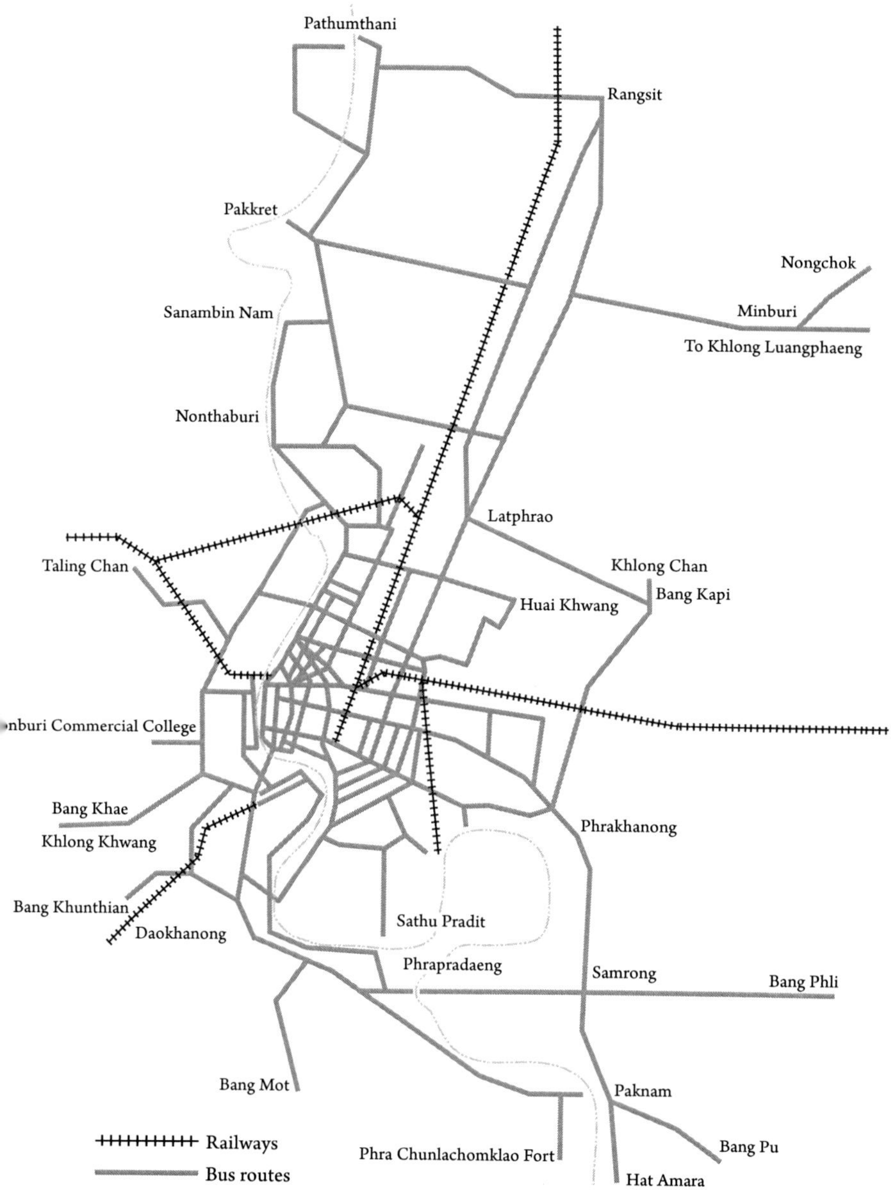

The number of routes as well as the range of the bus route network expanded drastically under the rearrangement, especially toward the suburbs, as shown in figure 4.4. Compared with the situation in 1960, as seen in figure 4.3, the difference is clear: many sections gained new bus routes. For example, the bus route from Phrakhanong to Bang Kapi was established for the first time under the new rearrangement. The bus route on Ngamwongwan Road was also recovered and a new route was established on Chaeng Watthana Road toward Pakkret. Additionally, there were new bus routes in accordance with the opening of new roads: one was established on the bypass going north along the railway from Latphrao (the present Wiphawadi Rangsit Road); it opened in 1965. Buses also began to operate on the eastern extension of Phetchaburi Road (New Phetchaburi Road), which opened in 1961.

Moreover, local bus routes were also established in Nonthaburi and Samut Prakan. For example, routes from Samrong to Bang Phli or Phrapradaeng or from Paknam to Hat Amara or Bang Pu were local, intra-province buses, not those connecting with inner Bangkok. These bus routes functioned with regional buses within each province rather than with the urban buses of Bangkok. This was because the rearrangement of bus routes was intended not only for Bangkok but for all municipalities, including the suburban provinces of Bangkok.[76] For this reason, the network of bus routes in Bangkok was greatly expanded; later, the local routes would be excluded from Bangkok's bus system, however.

The rearrangement went into force from October 1, 1965. In the beginning, there was some confusion as users, unfamiliar with the new routes, took the wrong buses (*SN*, 2 October 1965). Moreover, since the number of routes that each operator was in charge of increased, the number of buses on some routes decreased, and some routes suspended operations for lack of buses. Four months was allotted to the operators to acquire new buses. By February 1966, eleven routes had suspended bus operations because of a shortage of buses. The total number of buses in operation was 2,550.[77] On the whole, bus conditions had improved, and complaints from users were less frequent.

The Fare Hike and Its Revocation

In 1967, bus operators requested a fare hike. At the time, a flat fare of fifty satang in the city (within the zone) had been in place since 1959.

As shown in table 4.7, the fare had been raised ten satang in 1953 and twenty satang in 1959 before reaching fifty satang. The fare raise in 1959 also changed the fare system; the original fare of thirty satang for one kilometer changed to fifty satang for up to ten kilometers. Thus, it was higher for a short distance and lower for a longer distance. The zone system was put in place in 1960, and the fare within the city, or the zone, became uniform at fifty satang.[78] Thus, bus operators regarded the fare as having remained the same since 1953.

Table 4.7. Changes in Bus Fares, 1953–1976

Date	Fare System	Fare (THB)	Remarks	Sources
	Sectional	0.20 (up to 1 km)	Add 0.10 baht per km after 1 km	*SN*, 7 Oct 1953
1 Oct 1953	Sectional	0.30 (up to 1 km)	Add 0.10 baht per km after 1 km	*SN*, 7 Oct 1953
15 Feb 1959	Sectional	0.50 (up to 10 km)	1 baht for more than 10 km	NA Kho Kho. 0202. 3. 4. 1/39
10 Jan 1960	Zonal	0.50		NA Kho Kho. 0202. 3. 6/7
1 May 1968	Zonal	0.75		*SN*, 1 May 1968
19 Jul 1968	Zonal	0.50		*SN*, 19 Jul 1968
1973	Zonal	0.75		*SR*, 9 Mar 1978

The bus operators asked the Ministry of Communications for a fare hike, citing high price increases in fuel and repair parts. The government initially stated that it would support bus operators through measures other than a fare hike. Phong, the minister of communications, said in August 1967 that the government would first help operators procure fuel or bus parts before increasing the burden on users (*SN*, 17 August 1967). However, the operators persisted in their request for a fare hike, asserting that it would be difficult to further improve their services with the present fare, and that the continuation of their business would be barely feasible (*SN*, 29 October 1967). The operators proposed a fare hike with the return of a sectional fare system: the existing fare of fifty satang for four kilometers and one baht for up to ten kilometers (*SN*, 11 January 1968). Bus users opposed this plan because it would impose a 100 percent fare hike for those who rode four to ten kilometers, although the fare would be the same for short-distance users.

However, the Transport Regulation Committee accepted the opinion of the operators and decided to approve the fare hike. The operators had complained that each bus could only take in 300 to 400 baht in income per day, and the Transport Regulation Committee sympathized (*SN*, 2 May 1968), provided that the Ministry of Interior ask for the improvement of employee treatment in the form of a monthly salary of 300 to 400 baht and the shortening of work hours to fewer than ten hours a day (*SN*, 26 April 1968).[79] For the actual fare hike, the committee decided on a raise from 50 to 75 satang with the same zone system instead of the sectional system that the operators had proposed. The fare hike was put into effect on May 1, as shown in table 4.7; thus, the bus fare in Bangkok saw a 50 percent increase.[80]

Bus users exploded with criticism of the new fare increase, and articles on the topic were published every day in the newspapers. The Prime Minister's Office received complaints from users expressing directly to Prime Minister Thanom their opposition to the fare hike (*SN*, 2 May 1968). Although operators asserted that their businesses were facing a deficit due to the previously cheap fare, some people doubted these assertions, pointing out that the operators would not have competed for concessions in that case and that they would have already gone bankrupt if they were really operating at a loss. It was also argued that it was wrong that politicians or government officials who do not normally use the bus should decide the fare raise. The communications minister Phong, who approved the fare hike, explained that it was impossible to simultaneously achieve improvement of service and keep the same fare. He explained that the Ministry of Communications approved the fare hike despite the opposition of users, because the deterioration of service would result in difficulty for users, and opinions in favor of accepting a fare hike of twenty-five satang outweighed those that opposed the plan (*SN*, 19 May 1968).

Prime Minister Thanom was abroad at the time, but because the opposition to the fare raise was so strong, he decided to hold a public hearing for examining the problem immediately after his return on May 20 (*SN*, 22 May 1968). Moreover, a Committee for Investigating Bus Operators' Accounting (*Khana kammakan truat sop banchi borisat rot doisan pracham thang*) was established to reinvestigate whether the operators' claims of operating at a loss were true (*SN*, 31 May 1968).[81]

Meanwhile, the Ministry of Communications asked operators to introduce a discount for students in order to evade criticism and made an agreement with them that they would sell coupon tickets for students to secure twenty-five-satang rides for elementary and junior high school students and fifty-satang rides for senior high school students (*SN*, 30 May 1968). However, news reports continued which revealed the injustice of the operators and government. One such report stated that the operators had failed to improve treatment of their employees, and employee incomes had actually decreased after the fare raise; another accused the high officials of the Ministry of Communications of holding shares in bus operations in the names of their relatives.

Furthermore, immediately after the Permanent Constitution took effect on June 20, students demonstrated against the bus fare hike (*SN*, 29 June 1968). Following Sarit's "revolution" in October 1958, a new constitution was not promulgated for a long time; the Government Charter substituted for it in 1959. However, Thanom, who wanted to secure the post of prime minister under parliamentary democracy, came up with a Constitution in expectation of general elections. The bus fare hike problem developed into a political issue when students began demonstrating the day after the Constitution was put into effect. Meanwhile, the Committee for Investigating Bus Operators' Accounting investigated the accounting of the bus operators and asked the cabinet for its final decision after noting that there were both profit-making and loss-ridden operators (*SN*, 29 June 1968).

In response, the cabinet settled the matter of the bus fare hike at its meeting on July 3 with the decision that the fare would be reversed to fifty satang (*SN*, 5 July 1968). The enforcement date of the price reduction was July 18. This was important for Prime Minister Thanom, who had decided to enact a constitution and hold a general election in order to nip in the bud criticism of the government and to win the election. The government became sensitive to public opinion; it abolished the monopolistic system of pork supplies, which had become another point of criticism alongside the bus fare, and allowed pork to be imported from outside the city.[82] The government withdrew the bus fare hike to appease the public, hoping that this act would give them an advantage in the electoral campaign. Thus, the bus fare of 75 satang lasted only seventy-eight days.

Increased Operator Dissatisfaction

Reduction of the bus fare to fifty satang because of public opposition presented a grave problem for the operators. Earlier, along with the raise, they had been asked to improve the way their employees were treated and to increase the number of buses they operated. They had performed these measures one by one after the fare raise in May 1965, but had done so on the condition of a fare increase. When the fare hike ended after only two months, the operators' incomes returned to previous levels even though their expenditures to improve employee treatment were now higher (*SN*, 7 July 1968). Some operators had already ordered new buses, and this investment in service improvement brought a heavy burden.

Thus, the operators demanded bail-out packages from the government. When the government decided to cancel the fare hike, it ordered them to draft a request for the required bail-out packages (*SN*, 5 July 1968). The government decided to consider the request at the Committee of Fact-Finding for Conditions of Bus Operators' Management in Bangkok and Thonburi (*Khana kammakan sueksa kho thetching kiaokae kan damnoen ngan khong borisat rotyon doisan pracham thang nai changwat phra nakhon lae thonburi*), headed by the vice president of NEDB. The operators' requests consisted of fifteen measures, such as a reduction in fuel tax, reduction of the renewal fee for bus registration, introduction of cheap credit for operators, extension of concession terms to ten years, and a change in the opening and closing hours of schools and governmental offices. The committee concluded that twelve of these requests should be accepted.[83]

These measures aimed at a reduction of necessary expenses rather than an increase of revenue. Apart from the introduction of a sectional fare system for long-distance routes, there were no measures to increase revenue. Therefore, the operators asked the government for cost-cutting measures in the form of tax or fee reductions. The committee recognized the necessity of these and recommended that a great portion of their demands should be fundamentally accepted. On the other hand, requests for exemption from bus import duties, commercial tax, income tax, and bus examination fees were denied, as was the introduction of a government subsidy.[84]

However, these concrete measures were not enacted despite the recommendation of the committee. There was no concrete response from the government even in January 1969, and operators were being forced to bear severe burdens (*SN*, 31 January 1969). The shortage of buses became significant again, and the operators claimed that the reason for this was the shortage of drivers and repairmen. The operators asked the government to regulate illegal *songthaeo* running parallel to bus routes, another factor that was cutting into their incomes, but the government was still hesitant to do so, noting that it would affect the convenience of users (*SN*, 19 March 1969). After Thanom secured the post of prime minister in the general election in March 1969, Thawi Chunlasap was appointed as the new minister of communications, but the measures that the operators required were not included in his new improvement plan for bus business (*SN*, 11 May 1969). Although he announced policies such as introducing double-decker buses with an increased standing space and separate entrance and exit doors, approval was never obtained.

While radical measures were not taken after all, the season of the renewal of concessions came in 1970, and it was decided to renew the concessions with the fundamental status quo. As shown in table 4.8, there were ninety bus routes after this renewal, a decrease of eighteen compared with the route rearrangement of 1965 (see table 4.6). Important factors for this were the change of numbering on circle routes and the elimination of local bus routes in suburban provinces. Although the circle routes, most established in 1965, had had two independent numbers for anti-clockwise and clockwise directions, the system changed to use the same number, thereby halving the number of circle routes. The closure of local bus routes occurred in the network in 1970 (see figure 4.5). Many local bus routes in the south, north, and east disappeared, compared with the network in 1965 (see figure 4.4). This was because the local buses within the provinces in these areas were removed from Bangkok's bus network, and the actual bus routes continued as regional buses.[85]

Table 4.8. Bus Routes in Bangkok, November 1970

Route Number	Line	Length (km)	Number of Buses Provided	Operator
1	Thanon Tok–Tha Tian	12.0	55	ETO
2	Pakkhlong Talat–Samrong	24.0	80	Nai Loet

Route Number	Line	Length (km)	Number of Buses Provided	Operator
3	Mochit–Khlong San	16.0	60	Si Nakhon
4	Talat Phlu–Khlong Toei	15.0	90	ETO
5	Bang Sue–Chakkrawat	10.0	40	Si Nakhon
6	Bukkhalo–Bang Lamphu	8.0	25	Phra Nakhon Thonburi Transport
7	Nopphawong–Khlong Khwang	23.0	40	Bang Khae Transport
8	Memorial Bridge–Latphrao	16.3	60	Nai Loet
9	Siyan–Talat Phlu	14.0	55	Thonburi Automobile
10	Wat Nangnong–Nangloeng	12.6	20	Thon Nakhon Transport
11	Makkasan–Memorial Bridge	11.0	25	Nai Loet
12	Huai Khwang–Ministry of Economic Affarirs	13.0	45	Red Bus
13	Huai Khwang–Khlong Toei	13.4	45	Khlong Toei Bus
14	Siyan–Khlong Toei	12.0	35	Si Nakhon
15	Bang Lamphu–Bangkok Bridge	20.3	50	Bunphong
16	Surawong–Tao Pun	14.8	60	Phira Bus
17	Bangkok Bridge–Tha Chang	21.3	60	Yanyon Insurance & Trading
18	Rama VI Bridge–Si Phraya	17.0	50	Thaithawon Bus
19	Thewet–Bangkok Noi	10.0	50	Thonburi Union Transport
20	Tha Dindaeng–Phra Chunlachomklao Fort	29.0	15	Thon Nakhon Transport
21	Chulalongkorn University–Bang Pakok	14.0	60	Nakhon Luang Transport
22	Thanon Tok–Kluai Namthai	14.5	45	ETO
23	Sutthisan–Ministry of Economic Affairs	14.0	30	Red Bus
24	Makkasan–Hua Lamphong	13.0	15	Transport Co.
25	Tha Chang–Paknam	30.0	75	Transport Co.
26	Saphan Khao–Minburi	45.0	35	Minburi Transport
27	Bang Kapi–Khlong Toei	27.0	40	Thepphaniramit Transport
28	Northern Line Bus Terminal–Southern Line Bus Terminal	16.0	25	Transport Co.
29	Rangsit–Hua Lamphong	30.0	35	Transport Co.
30	Nonthaburi–Tha Chang	15.0	30	Transport Co.
31	Pathumthani–Tha Chang	47.5	15	Transport Co.
32	Pakkret–Sanam Luang	28.5	25	Nonthaburi Municipality
33	Pathumthani–Sanam Luang	47.0	15	Nai Loet

Route Number	Line	Length (km)	Number of Buses Provided	Operator
34	Rangsit–Hua Lamphong	33.0	35	Transport Co.
35	Saochingcha–Sathu Pradit	12.0	35	Transport Co.
36	Victory Monument–Si Phraya	6.0	10	Thai Thawon Bus
37	Daokhanong–Mahanak	10.0	50	Si Lueang
38	Northern Line Bus Terminal–Ekkamai	14.0	35	Transport Co.
39	Sanam Luang–Don Mueang	32.0	40	Sahaiyon
40	Ekkamai–Southern Line Bus Terminal	18.0	45	Transport Co.
41	Sanam Luang–Setthakit Estate	22.6	45	Bang Khae Transport
42	Sirirat–Saochingcha	10.0	40	Niyom Transport
43	Wat Sing–Sanam Luang	13.0	75	Watchanayon
44	Mochit–Tha Tian	13.0	50	Si Nakhon
45	Samyaek–Paknam	29.0	80	Samut Prakan Transport
46	Bang Chak–Rong Mueang	12.5	45	Yanyon Insurance & Trading
47	Land Department–Khlong Toei	12.0	50	Yanyon Insurance & Trading
48	Bang Chak–Wat Pho	16.0	50	Nai Loet
49	Bang Son–Sam Yaek	14.0	25	Sirimit
50	Bang Son–Samyan	15.3	25	Sirimit
51	Pakkret–Tha Chang	25.0	25	Transport Co.
52	Sisao Circle Line (left rotation)	9.8	10	Nai Loet
52	Sisao Circle Line (right rotation)	9.8	10	Nai Loet
53	Thewet Circle Line (left rotation)	12.0	35	Red Bus
53	Thewet Circle Line (right rotation)	12.0	35	Thai Pradit
54	Huai Khwang Circle Line (left rotation)	15.0	20	Red Bus
54	Huai Khwang Circle Line (right rotation)	15.0	20	Thepphaniramit Transport
55	Amnuai Songkhram Circle Line (left rotation)	20.0	25	Sirimit
55	Amnuai Songkhram Circle Line (right rotation)	20.0	25	Sirimit
56	Krung Thon Bridge Circle Line (left rotation)	18.7	45	Thai Pradit
56	Krung Thon Bridge Circle Line (right rotation)	18.7	45	Transport Co.
57	Thonburi Circle Line (left rotation)	15.2	20	Saha Transport
57	Thonburi Circle Line (right rotation)	15.2	20	Niyom Transport

Route Number	Line	Length (km)	Number of Buses Provided	Operator
58	Huamak–Tha Chang	18.0	25	Yanyon Insurance & Trading
59	Don Mueang–Sanam Luang	30.0	40	Sahaiyon
60	Huamak–Pakkhlong Talat	20.0	25	Nai Loet
61	Chong Nonsi–Witthayu	6.0	10	Chong Nonsi
62	Sathu Pradit–Witthayu	10.0	15	Chong Nonsi
63	Rama VI Bridge–Dindaeng Estate	11.5	15	Thai Thawon
64	Nonthaburi–Sanam Luang	12.0	60	Nai Loet, Nonthaburi Municipality
65	Bang Son–Sanam Luang	12.3	25	Sirimit
66	Bang Sue–Talat Phlu	23.0	55	Si Nakhon
67	Bang Sue–Thung Mahamek	14.0	50	Si Nakhon
68	Siyan–Sala Daeng	9.0	15	Si Nakhon
69	Bang Khen–Sanam Luang	13.0	20	Sahaiyon
70	Makkasan–Khlong Chan	20.5	30	Thepphaniramit Transport
71	Khlong Chan–Wat Pho	25.0	40	Nai Loet
72	Kluai Namthai–Thewet	15.0	50	Nai Loet
73	Dindaeng–Memorial Bridge	13.0	30	Nai Loet
74	Huai Khwang–Khlong Toei	13.0	40	Thepphaniramit Transport
75	Daokhanong–Tha Tian	13.5	65	ETO
76	Silom–Bang Lamphu	13.5	20	Bunphong
77	Silom–Victory Monument	6.5	15	Bunphong
78	Sathon–Tha Chang	15.5	25	Yanyon Insurance & Trading
79	Ekkamai–Tha Chang	14.0	50	Transport Co.
80	Bang Khae–Phahutrat	13.5	35	Bang Khae Transport
81	Bang Khae–Sirirat	10.0	20	Niyom Transport
82	Phrapradaeng–Memorial Bridge	19.5	20	Thon Nakhon Transport
83	Taling Chan–Bangkok Noi	4.7	10	Saha Thonburi Transport
84	Bang Mot–Saochingcha	17.6	40	Thon Nakhon Transport
85	Ratburana–Memorial Bridge	10.6	10	Thon Nakhon Transport
86	Phrapradaeng–Bang Lamphu	18.0	35	Phra Nakhon Thonburi Transport
87	Nangloeng–Daokhanong	11.6	35	Thon Nakhon Transport
88	Bang Mot–Khlong San	10.0	15	Phra Nakhon Thonburi Transport
89	Bang Waek–Sirirat	7.0	10	Niyom Transport
90	Bang Phun–Sanam Luang	48.0	15	Nai Loet
Total		921.3	2,115	

SOURCE: Data from NA [1] Ko Kho. 1. 4/53.

Fig. 4.5. Bus Network in Bangkok, 1970

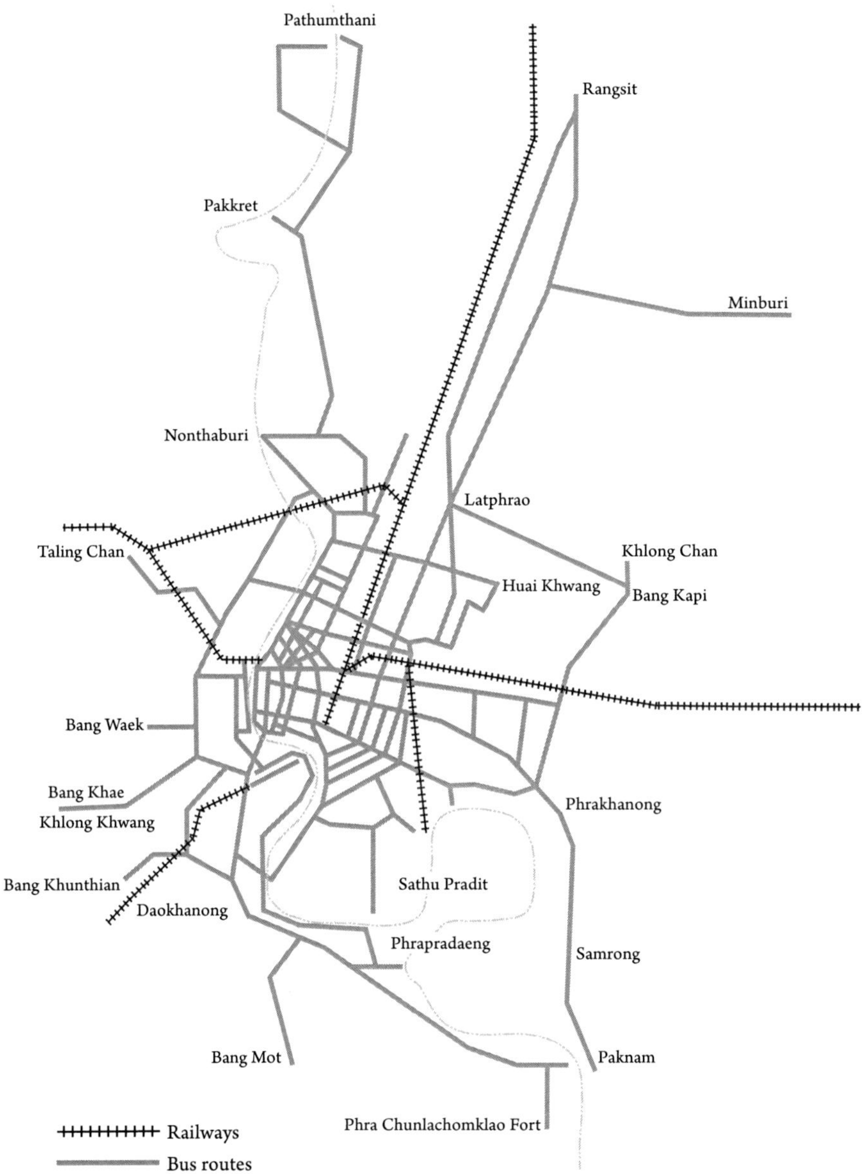

Sources: Data from table 4.8. and RKB vol. 87, no. 111, 3308–55.

Realization of the Bus Unification Plan

The Unification Plan Resurfaces

After the fare hike and its revocation in 1968, measures were considered to reduce operators' expenditures without raising fares, but the idea that finally surfaced was the promotion of unification of bus operators. The Working Group for Bus Business Improvement (*Khana thamngan prapprung kitchakan rot doisan*) was installed by the Ministry of Communications in July 1969 to consider the solution.[86] It concluded that the only way to improve service without a fare hike was to decrease operational expenditures, and two measures were needed to achieve this end: the expansion of operators' size and government support for operators.[87] To expand the operating companies, it provided that the operator's minimal capital should be 40 million baht, and that the company should possess a minimum of two hundred buses. The number of operators should be reduced by the existing large-scale operators' purchase of small operators or their merging with the Nakhon Luang Transport Company. For the latter, it proposed that the government would form a foundation to offer cheap credit to the operators and sell fuel and materials at a special price. Although this report was issued before the renewal of the concessions in 1970, recommendations in it were not immediately implemented due to inadequate time to prepare.

The bus operators then returned to the idea of unification as one operator—the idea once pursued by the Nakhon Luang Transport Company. An investigation of Bangkok's transportation problems, carried out by a specialist from West Germany in 1971, resulted in a proposal that the bus operators in Bangkok should be unified into a single operating company (*SRSW*, 21 October 1984). Having received this recommendation, the Bangkok/Thonburi Bus Examination Working Group (*Khana thamngan phuea phicharana kiaokap rotyon doisan pracham thang nai khet krungthep thonburi*) that had been set up by the Ministry of Communications in April 1972 concluded that the operators should be unified as a public company with 30 percent of its shares held by the government (ibid.). Prime Minister Thanom established a Bangkok Bus Improvement Examination Committee (*Khana kammakan phicharana prapprung borikan rot doisan pracham thang nai krungthep mahanakhon*) in January 1973 to reexamine the matter (*SRSW*, 12 April 1981). That committee proposed that the bus operators be unified as a single stock company, and the operations of those not participating in the unification would be allowed until the expiration of their concessions at the end of September 1975. The cabinet approved the proposal in September 1973 (ibid.). The plan to unify bus operators thus became formalized and was required to be completed by the agreed-upon deadline.

However, since the Thanom government collapsed shortly thereafter in the events of October 14, 1973, the unification plan did not proceed after all, given the extreme confusion of the political situation. The jump in the worldwide price of oil also directly hit the bus operators, so the Thanom government approved a fare hike from fifty to seventy-five satang before it collapsed. However, the operators asked for even higher fares (*SRSW*, 28 April 1974). The newly organized government of Sanya Thammasak did not approve the fare hike and announced that it would relieve operators that found it impossible to continue their bus business (*SRSW*, 29 September 1974). Operators suffered other, new problems such an attack on a bus. In response, the government decided at the cabinet meeting in August 1974 to establish the Bus Problem-Solving Committee (*Khana kammakan kaekhai panha rot pracham thang*) to consider support in response to the increase of fuel price and personnel expenses (ibid.).[88]

The unification plan did not progress quickly, even as the designated deadline of September 1975 approached. Therefore, the operators demanded that the government define a policy for a concrete unification plan. Loesak Sombatsiri, the president of the Nai Loet Company, the largest private operator in Bangkok, announced the sale of her bus business in August 1974, which surprised many in Bangkok. The company not only announced its intention to sell its bus business, but also asked how the government would push ahead with the unification plan, noting that it would be difficult to continue operating buses if governmental policy remained unsettled (*SRSW*, 29 September 1974). Loesak criticized the government by pointing out that although it was proposing the unification of operators, the number of operators in Bangkok continued to increase, with seventeen new operators in the newly established regional bus routes.[89] The previous Bus Problem-Solving Committee had been established in response to the appeal of the Nai Loet Company, so the impact on the government was considerable. Nevertheless, the Sanya government was a caretaker cabinet before a transition to civilian rule, and the matter of operator unification would, after all, have to be taken up by the new government without any substantial progress.

The Unification Plan Takes Shape

The time remaining before bus concessions lapsed at the end of September 1975 was less than one year, and in early 1975, the unification plan finally took shape. The government of Kukrit Pramoj was put in power in March 1975, after many twists and turns, after the parliamentary general election in January. The Kukrit government came up with various populist policies, including bus service in Bangkok. This included the free bus plan for poor people whose monthly income was less than 1,000 baht. This plan aimed to reduce the living expenses of the poor. The free ride would be possible with the use of free passes issued to those who were eligible. In the first phase, the government planned operation of free buses for students, and this was implemented from June 2 (*SR*, 19 May 1975). The exclusive buses were only for students who wore uniforms and showed their student identification card. It was the first case of free bus service for students, although support for students had previously been offered in the form of exclusive buses for students or the issue of student discount coupons.[90] The government was paying 780 baht per bus per day to the operators to run the free buses, and this drew criticism from some as being excessive (ibid.).

The government established the Bangkok Bus Operation Improvement Committee (*Khana kammakan prapprung rabop kan doen rotyon doisan pracham thang nai krungthep mahanakhon*) in April 1975 to start a concrete study on the potential unification of bus operators (*SRSW*, 21 October 1984). Bus operator representatives also participated on this committee, and a study was conducted on how to concretely proceed with unification. Since it had already been decided under the Thanom government that the unification should be done in the form of a stock company, the question at hand became how the existing operators would unify their businesses. Finally, two plans were formed, that of the Bus Operator Association (*Samakhom phu prakop kan khonsong*) and that of the Nai Loet Company; the former was adopted by a majority vote of the committee on August 25, 1975 (ibid.).[91]

The Nai Loet Company opposed the plan (*SR*, 25 August 1975). The Bus Operator Association's plan called for a new central company to be established with jurisdiction over bus operations and for each operator's employees to be transferred to this new company. However, the maintenance of buses and procurement of fuels and parts would be performed by each operator, and income from passenger fares would be distributed to each operator after deducting the costs to the new company. This was a loose unification that left flexibility to each operator, and it was advantageous to small and midsize operators. On the other hand, the Nai Loet Company had proposed to realize unification by establishing a public company that would distribute its shares to each operator based on its assets; this was similar to the unification plan of the Nakhon Luang Transport Company.[92]

The Nai Loet Company asserted that the Bus Operator Association plan was merely an apparent unification, not a true one, and claimed that the central company would be "a tiger lying down and eating" like the Transport Company (*SR*, 30 August 1975). On the other hand, according to the Nai Loet Company's own plan, the stockholding ratio of each operator would differ according to its assets, and the larger operators would have the advantage of a larger voice. That is why the Bus Operator Association, which consisted of small and midsize businesses, opposed the plan. When drawing their conclusion, government representatives did not hold a vote without the operator representatives' presence, noting that it respected each operator's intention (*SRSW*, 21 October 1984). In this way, the plan of the Bus Operator Association was adopted by the majority of the community. Although the Nai Loet Company objected to the result, it nevertheless accepted the plan on August 30, 1975, as its employees would suffer losses if they did not participate (*SR*, 30 August 1975).

The Bus Operator Association tried to establish the Bangkok Transport Company (*Borisat krungthep khonsong chamkat*) as a new central company to advance unification. But their hopes were not realized. Although both plans were deliberated in parliament, parliament rejected the Bus Operator Association plan, and instead resolved to adopt the plan of the Nai Loet Company, on September 11, 1975. Meanwhile, Prime Minister Kukrit decided on September 15 not to adopt either of the plans but instead to unify in the form of a newly established state-owned company (*SRSW*, 21 October 1984). His decision was based on the grounds that it would be easier for a state-owned company to proceed with the free bus project, which was the government's campaign pledge to the poor, and that there was a question of timing in that it would have to wait another five years if the concession lapse at the end of September were to be missed.

Thus, the government established a state-owned firm called the Mahanakhon Transport Company (*Borisat maha nakhon khonsong chamkat*) on September 29, 1975, and the unification of bus business was realized when all concessions were granted to it (ibid.). The government held the majority of the company's shares, and the remainder were distributed according to each operator's assets. Although the unification resembled the Nai Loet Company's proposal, it differed in terms of the role of the government in that the government grasped the majority of stocks to secure managerial rights, rather than leaving them to the private sector as the Nai Loet Company proposed. The bus business in Bangkok run by the private sector since the 1900s was unified as a state-owned firm, and bus operations would henceforth come under the authority of a state enterprise.

Formation of the Bangkok Mass Transport Authority

The unification under the Mahanakhon Transport Company was realized. However, it was, in fact, only a formal unification. Although the bus concessions that had expired at the end of September 1975 were renewed and granted solely to the Mahanakhon Transport Company, the company, having been established immediately prior, had nothing and was not able to perform bus operations on its own. Moreover, the period from its establishment to the start of bus business was quite short, the transfer of business from the existing operators was completely neglected, and even the procedure of succession had not yet been settled. Therefore, in order to continue bus operations, there was no choice but to allow the existing operators to continue their operations; they thus continued their operations in October. The long-desired operation of free buses for the poor also started, but their operation was entrusted to existing operators, just like the student buses.

As a state-owned firm, the Mahanakhon Transport Company needed to improve its treatment of employees. The salary at state-owned firms was higher, so employees would enjoy an increase in their incomes. However, since the Mahanakhon Transport Company asked the existing operators to pay the allowances for living expenses before it had completed the transfer of employees, some operators were willing to pay those expenses and others were not (*SR*, 12 November 1975). Therefore, the employees of the Nai Loet Company went on strike on November 10, 1975, to secure the provision of this allowance for living expenses. Since the Nai Loet Company was a large-scale operator with a long history in Bangkok and its relatively good service was acknowledged by users, the strike had a large impact.

The appraisal of the existing operators' assets started in November 1975. Depreciation was taken into consideration for the appraisal; the appraisal standards included 8 to 12 percent of the cost for a five-to seven-year-old bus. The appraisal was aimed to finish within three months (*SRSW*, 23 November 1975). Operators asked for a quick survey because the estimated amounts fell as time passed; they requested that the appraisal be completed by mid-December (*SR*, 28 November 1975). In fact, however, the appraisal was not performed smoothly, and the bus operations entrusted to the existing operators continued. The first change in operations occurred when the Mahanakhon Transport Company purchased 305 buses from the Si Nakhon Company and started operating on March 1, 1976; over half a year had already passed since it gained the concessions (*SRSW*, 14 March 1976). At the end of April, it had just finished the unification of six out of twenty-four operators. This meant that 5,000 employees and 1,300 buses out of 20,000 employees and 3,000 buses were integrated (Samrit n.d., vol. 1, 57).

However, the unification did not progress well because not only was asset appraisal overdue, but the operators opposed the estimated amounts that had been assessed. The operators tried to raise the sale amounts as much as possible in order to maximize their profits. The new minister of communications, Thawit Klinprathum, following the change of the prime minister from Kukrit to Seni Pramoj in the general election in April 1976, announced that the unification would be completed by the middle of July (ibid., 86). However, the operators were also strong, and in July, eleven small- and middle-size operators, such as the Thai Pradit Company, asked the prime minister to reexamine the method of asset appraisal (ibid., 104). The government took a hard-line stance by ordering that all buses that had not been purchased by July 20 be prohibited from operating. The asset appraisal was made to finish by the end of August, with the government forcibly realizing unification (*SRSW*, 2 April 1978).

In the meantime, the legal basis of the establishment of the Mahanakhon Transport Company became an issue. The operators insisted that the Mahanakhon Transport Company, to which the government contributed 100 percent, was illegal as a stock company, and the government had to admit that this was true (ibid.).[93] For this reason, it hurriedly established on August 18 a new agency by issuing the Royal Decree on the Establishment of the BMTA (Bangkok Mass Transit Authority). Under this plan, the Mahanakhon Transport Company would be taken over by the newly installed public corporation, and the BMTA would take over the business of operating buses as of October 1. The Bangkok bus business, now integrated in the form of a state-owned firm, was finally taken over by a public corporation under stronger government regulation.

The bus business of the Mahanakhon Transport Company ended within one year. However, it had caused two problems: sharp degradation in bus service and a huge deficit. In order to advance negotiations on the taking over of the bus business, the old operators went on strike to increase pressure on the government by eliciting more user complaints (*SRSW*, 16 May 1976). Moreover, although only the good buses should originally have been purchased, the Mahanakhon Transport Company had also accepted the purchase of old buses in order to realize unification within the provided time period (ibid.). Therefore, even if the change of jurisdiction over the buses was to be realized, there were few buses that could operate satisfactorily; only 65 percent of the purchased buses were usable. Furthermore, after the government forbade the operation of buses that had not yet been purchased in July 1976, the shortage of buses became even more serious. The unauthorized *songthaeo* flourished as alternatives, but their passenger capacities were insufficient, and users had to pay the high fares that they levied (ibid.).

Furthermore, the Mahanakhon Transport Company had racked up huge losses. The government had initially appropriated 100 million baht as capital for the company capital and then added 229,200,000 baht, bringing its total capital to 329,200,000 baht (*SRSW*, 21 October 1984).

However, the purchase of buses and parts cost a total of 286,900,000 baht, and the government had to return the expense for transferring management to the state-owned company of 83,100,000 baht to each operator, even though it had gone into debt for 40,800,000 baht at the beginning. Moreover, the operating balance showed a loss of 99,070,000 baht, as expenditures of 289,180,000 baht exceeded its revenue of 190,110,000 baht. These debts were all inherited by the BMTA, and it would start off in deficit.

In the end, it was the existing bus operators and their employees whose interests had been served by the unification. The bus operators earned money from selling more than the actual asset values, and they had made profits in the last stage of their withdrawal from the bus business. Employees had earned salaries and allowances more hospitable than before under the state-owned firm. Although personnel expenses represented 30 percent of total revenue in the private-sector period, this increased to 49 percent under the Mahanakhon Transport Company. This was the main factor of the deficit in operations (*SRSW*, 21 October 1984). In contrast, the government and bus users bore the brunt: the government had made huge fiscal expenditures, and users were negatively affected by the degraded state of the buses and service.

Limitations of Buses in Urban Transport

Low Appreciation for Rail Transport

The unfavorable winds blowing against suburban railways became stronger in the Sarit era: The whole Paknam line and part of the Maeklong line were eliminated, and the abolition of the remaining section of the Maeklong line was also considered. It was decided to abolish tramways, which had played an active part as the means of transport in Bangkok; they disappeared altogether by 1968. Although both actions were based on Sarit's "fine sight" policy, which aimed at alleviating road congestion in Bangkok, the low value put on rail transport was also a background factor.

First of all, the government's appreciation of the Paknam line had been low from the 1930s; it threatened to abolish the railway if the company rejected the purchase price the government offered. In the government's view there would be no problem if it replaced the Paknam line with buses by hastening the completion of a parallel road. That is, the role of the Paknam railway could just as well be carried out by buses, which were rapidly rising in influence at the time. The partial abolition of the Paknam line for the new port construction plan of Khlong Toei was also proposed in 1940.

The elimination of the Paknam line was again raised for discussion in the Sarit period to enable road expansion, and this time the idea was agreed to, since the the Paknam line was running at a loss. It operated only eight trips per day, but the number of daily users was still about 3,500 persons, and congestion on the parallel Rama IV Road had been growing worse.[94] Of course, when the railway was abolished to expand the road, conventional railway users became bus passengers. It was not understood that even after the road was expanded and congestion relieved temporarily, traffic congestion would soon return due to the increase in transport needs, and that a railway could help reinforce transport capacity.[95]

The situation was about the same with the partial elimination—and plans for the entire elimination—of the Maeklong line. There were about 3 million passengers per year, or 8,000 passengers per day, on that line (RFT 1970, 357), and even though access to buses at the Khlong San terminus was inconvenient, the eastern side of the Chaophraya, the commercial center, could easily be reached by ferry. Nevertheless, Sarit ordered the abolition of the most congested section of the line. Furthermore, the terminus was changed to Wongwian Yai to accommodate bus transfers. In the end, elimination of the entire line was avoided, but it was clear that Sarit saw removal of railways as crucial to achieving his "fine sight" of Bangkok; there was no appreciation of railways as means of mass transport.

Tramways had more users than suburban railways. Based on the number of printed tickets, as of 1960 they carried an average of 176,000 passengers per day (see table 4.9). Although the Samsen and Bang Sue lines had the largest numbers, the number of passengers on the Bang Kholaem line would probably have exceeded them but its capacity was reduced by the fire in 1958. With the reduction of the route network, the number of passengers gradually decreased to only 4,000 passengers in

1968. Most passengers shifted to using buses, so the closure of tramways directly aggravated the bus transit problem.

Table 4.9. Number of Printed Tickets for Tramway Lines, 1960–1966 (Thousands, Except Daily Average)

Fiscal Year	Bang Kholaem	Bang Sue & Samsen	Dusit & Hua Lamphong	Silom & Pathumwan	Total	Daily Average
1960	10,390	24,660	19,610	9,430	64,090	175,589
1961	8,510	18,380	11,400	250	38,540	141,172
1962	12,450	18,310	16,160		46,920	128,548
1963	9,140	8,190	5,550		22,880	62,685
1964	240	3,220	3,070		6,530	17,890
1965			1,820		1,820	4,986
1966			1,470		1,470	4,027

Note: Until 1960, the fiscal year corresponded to the Western calendar year. In 1961, it ran from January to September and subsequently, from October to September.
Sources: FN for 1961–66 (selected years).

It was difficult for tramways to survive without moving the tracks to the middle of road and using double-tracking. The Bangkok tramways occupied one side of the road with single track. As mentioned in the previous chapter, radical improvement of tramways was not carried out after nationalization, and they became the victims of Sarit's "fine sight" policy. Therefore the failure to transfer tramway tracks during road expansion or to use double-tracking marked an unavoidable point in the eventual elimination of tramways. If tramways had been appreciated as a means of mass transport, they might have been developed to extend their networks using the widened roads beyond the three canals and beyond the narrow roads of the old city.

Given the increasing rise in population, the use of rail transport as a means of mass transport should have been justified. Table 4.10 shows the rise in the population of Bangkok. In 1912, when the Paknam Railway introduced electric trams, the population was about 300,000; the population of Thonburi in 1930, just after the electrification of the Maeklong Railway, was about 100,000. Bangkok's population reached 1.7 million in 1960 and 2.5 million in 1970, including both Bangkok and

Thonburi. Although the transport volume on the Paknam line was lower than on the Maeklong line due to the progress of road improvement, it would have been easy to upgrade urban railways by increasing their frequency of trips. The section for which the introduction of a means of mass transport was first planned in the 1970s was, ironically, the section between Hua Lamphong and Khlong Toei on the Paknam line which Sarit regarded as an obstacle to his "fine sight" policy, as will be described below.

Table 4.10. Population of Bangkok, 1912–1970

Year	Phra Nakhon	Thonburi	Total
1912	300,725	64,767	365,492
1930	419,210	99,584	518,794
1947	604,538	177,132	781,670
1960	1,299,528	403,828	1,703,356
1970	1,867,297	628,015	2,495,312

NOTE 1: The figure in 1912 is the population of twenty-five inner districts, among which six districts are regarded as districts in Thonburi. The population of boat dwellers (about 105,000 persons) is included in Phra Nakhon.
NOTE 2: The figure in 1930 is the population of the inner districts (eight in Phra Nakhon and six in Thonburi), and the figures after 1947 are the population of the city (*thetsaban*).
SOURCES: NA Ro. 6 No. 27/3; Porphant 1994, 335; Wilson 1983, 38.

Thus, there was a failure to recognize that rail transports was a means of mass transport and that a means of transport itself was important. This failure prevented the evolution from suburban railways to urban railways and the utilization of tramways in Bangkok. By eliminating urban railways, Bangkok would have to depend only on road transport until the end of the 1990s, and urban transport problems would only grow more acute.

Politicization of the Bus Problem

In the 1950s, buses had gradually become a political issue, as the Ministry of Interior and the Ministry of Communications fought for leadership over a bus unification plan, and Prime Minister Phibun shifted the policy of nationalization in advance of the next general election. This trend only intensified during "the age of development" under Sarit and Thanom. Fights for leadership and sudden changes in bus policy for political reasons continued. These changes were very haphazard and often illogical.

Discord between the Ministry of Interior and the Ministry of Communications was rife during this period. Although the private-sector-oriented policy of the Phibun government was opposed and government regulation strengthened, the idea of nationalizing the bus business by unifying the bus businesses of the Transport Company and the ETO had resurfaced. This took the form of a proposal put forward by the Ministry of Communications, which controlled both of them, and a revival of a plan for the ETO to unify them, an idea that had for a time been floated during the Phibun period. But since the unification of provincial buses by the Transport Company at that time had elicited public criticism, the Ministry of Communications' unification plan ended in failure.

The Ministry of Interior aimed for a comeback with its plan to hammer out the municipalization of the bus business by pushing forward the Bangkok Municipality. When municipalities were established in the 1930s, the municipalization of bus business was promoted temporarily, but municipalities' bus businesses declined because of the Second World War. The Ministry of Interior then formulated a plan for bus unification under the national government instead of the municipality, but the Ministry of Communications took the lead and it declared the principle that each municipality should again have jurisdiction over transport business in each city. This plan suffered a setback over the issue of loans from the United States and opposition from the Ministry of Communications, which sought to win the existing operators over to its side.

The Ministry of Communications supported the unification plan by private operators, so unification by the Nakhon Luang Transport Company was advanced. However, this, too, failed. The deterioration in bus service caused by the operators' passive measures due to weaknesses in the unification plan was the backdrop of the failure. The government then tried to assuage dissatisfied bus users by suspending the unification plan. Although there was no conflict between the Ministry of Interior and the Ministry of Communications over the jurisdiction of bus business after that, the Ministry of Interior would take the leadership role in the plans for mass transport and expressways in the 1970s.

Moreover, the politicization of the bus problem in anticipation of general elections or to realize campaign pledges is noteworthy. Although Prime Minister Phibun tried to win over bus operators, he also tried to attract bus users, i.e., voters. The revocation of the fare raise in 1968 was a classic example of politicization: the Thanom government, facing a general election, ingratiated the voters, who were intensely resistant to the bus fare hike. Because the fare raise had been legitimately by the Transport Regulation Committee, it was unreasonable to revoke it temporarily, but that is precisely what the government did based on political considerations. Naturally this was opposed by the bus operators, but the government won them over by promising bail-out packages. The renewal of concessions in 1970 should also be considered a kind of bail-out package, too, to maintain the status quo.

Even when the "age of development" was over and the "age of democratization" had begun, buses continued to be a political issue. The Kukrit government had promised free buses for the poor as a campaign pledge, and in order to fulfill this promise, it leased buses from operators to run as free buses. When problems arose over the unification plans for bus businesses, the government, for political motives, ultimately adopted neither of the plans. The chosen unification plan, which called for a state-owned firm, was selected to make good on the government's campaign pledge and to favor the voters over the operators. However, the purchase of bus businesses by the Mahanakhon Transport Company did not progress smoothly, and operators questioned the legality of the Mahanakhon Transport Company

Thus, the politicization of the bus issue resulted in a populist bus policy and measures that would most be welcomed by users. Maintaining cheap fares and operating free buses are clearly populist policies that benefit low-income groups. But how these policies were really accepted by voters depended on improvements in bus service. Even with a cheap fare, users expected an appropriate level of bus service. Unless such a level was realized, these populist policies would not have much effect on the voters. Although Prime Minister Thanom revoked the fare raise in 1968, in the general election in February of the next year, his United Thai People's Party (*Phak saha pracha thai*) was beaten by the Democrat Party (*Phak prachathippat*) in Bangkok (*SN*, 11 May 1969).[96] Prime Minister Kukrit's free bus policy was also ineffective, so Seni Pramoj's Democrat

Party became the winning party in the general elections in April 1976.[97] Thus, these policies did not actually have the effect that the politicians had expected.

Limits to Bus Service Improvement

The reason that the populist policies were not effective on bus issues was user dissatisfaction with bus service. The shortage of buses had not been addressed, so users had to take crowded buses. The conditions of the buses were poor, as was the service attitude of employees. Although the fare remained low, service reflected the idea of "the cheaper, the better." Operators claimed that investment in the improvement in service was difficult to achieve with cheap fares, and the government promoted the unification of operators for cost reduction.

In fact, the number of buses was increasing steadily. Table 4.11 shows the number of buses by route in January 1965. Although the provided number of buses at the time was 1,586 in total, the actual number in operation was 1,666. The sufficiency rate was 105 percent, a steady improvement given that it was 74 percent in 1957 (see table 3.7). Because this was the period in which the unification plan by the Nakhon Luang Transport Company was rejected and concessions were renewed for approved operators, this may have been the result of securing the agreed-upon number of buses to secure renewal of concessions at the end of September 1965.

Nevertheless, there were still gaps in the sufficiency rates according to operators or routes; some routes had buses that were more than double the agreed upon numbers, but some had only one-third. In particular, those routes operated by the Transport Company had low sufficiency rates: 33 percent for Route 29, the lowest rate, and less than 50 percent for Routes 28 and 40. Among them, Route 29 was operated directly by the Transport Company, and Routes 28 and 40 accepted private buses. Therefore, neither directly operated nor privately operated routes could achieve the desired level of operations.[98] Since the sufficiency rate of Route 4, operated by ETO, was also as low as 68 percent, it is clear that the nationalization of the bus business was not the solution for the improvement of bus service.

Table 4.11. Number of Buses Operating on Each Route, January 1965

Operator	Route Number	Line	Number of Buses Provided	Actual Number of Buses Used	Sufficiency Rate (%)
Bang Khae Transport	7	Khlong Khwang–Nopphawong	36	51	141
Bang Buathong Transport	33	Pathumthani–Sanam Luang	17	28	164
Bunphong	15	Bangkok Bridge–Bang Lamphu	48	50	105
Chong Nonsi	35	Chong Nonsi–Witthayu	7	6	86
ETO	1	Thanon Tok–Tha Tian	84	70	83
	4	Talat Phlu–Khlong Toei	55	37	68
	22	Thanon Tok–Lumphini	10	12	122
	Total		149	119	80
Minburi Transport	26	Nongchok–Saphan Khao	23		
Nai Loet	2	Bang Na–Pakkhlong Talat	53	45	85
	8	Latphrao–Memorial Bridge	33	34	102
	11	Makkasan–Memorial Bridge	35	34	97
	48	Phrakhanong–Wat Pho	39	40	103
	Total		160	153	96
Nakhon Luang Transport	37	Samre–Mahanak	15	32	211
Niyom Transport	42	Phrannok–Saochingcha	20	30	150
Nonthaburi Municipality	32	Pakkret–Sanam Luang	32	28	88
Phira Bus	16	Bang Krabue–Surawong	38	36	96
Phra Nakhon Thonburi Transport	6	Bukkhalo–Bang Lamphu	30	40	132
Red Bus	12	Huai Khwang–Ministry of Economic Affarirs	40	42	105
	23	Thewet Circle Line (right rotation)	27	26	96
	Total		67	68	101
Khlong Toei Trading	13	Khlong Toei–Phromphan School	30	30	99
Sahaiyon Transport	39	Don Mueang–Sanam Luang	34	43	127

Operator	Route Number	Line	Number of Buses Provided	Actual Number of Buses Used	Sufficiency Rate (%)
Samut Prakan Transport	45	Paknam–Samyaek	42	63	150
Si Nakhon	3	Northern Line Bus Terminal–Latya	46	46	99
	5	Bang Sue–Chakkrawat	40	40	100
	14	Siyan–Customs Department	33	31	93
	44	Northern Line Bus Terminal–Sanam Luang	25	26	104
	46	Phrakhanong–Samyan	17	25	148
Total			161 ·	168	104
Si Lueang	21	Samre–Chulalongkorn University	50	37	73
Sirimit	36	Bang Son–Wat Pathim Khongkha	30	36	120
Thai Thawon	18	Rama VI Bridge–Si Phraya	40	48	120
Thai Pradit	24	Thewet Circle Line (left rotation)	27	29	107
Thepphaniramit	27	Bang Kapi–Khlong Toei	33	55	166
Thonburi Automobile	9	Phasi Charoen–Samsen	42	36	86
Thonburi Union Transport	19	Thonburi Station–Thewet	39	48	124
Thon Nakhon Transport	10	Wat Nangnong–Ratchadamnoen Stadium	33	47	141
	20	Tha Dindaeng–Phra Chunlachomklao Fort	20	42	208
Total			53	89	168
Transport Co.	25	Tha Chang–Paknam	39	56	144
	28	Northern Line Bus Terminal–Southern Line Bus Terminal	20	7	37
	29	Tha Chang–Don Mueang	30	10	33
	30	Tha Chang–Nonthaburi	14	23	166
	31	Tha Chang–Pathumthani	18	23	128
	34	Rangsit–Hua Lamphong	30	23	75
	38	Northern Line Bus Terminal–Ekkamai	20	18	88
	40	Ekkamai–Southern Line Bus Terminal	30	14	46
	41	Krung Thon Bridge–Bang Lamphu	34	36	105
Total			235	210	89

Operator	Route Number	Line	Number of Buses Provided	Actual Number of Buses Used	Sufficiency Rate (%)
Yanyon Insurance & Trading	17	Bangkok Bridge–Tha Chang	55	45	81
	47	Khlong Toei–Land Department	35	34	96
	Total		90	79	88
Watchanakun	43	Bang Khunthian–Sanam Luang	38	57	150
	Grand Total		1,586	1,666	105

SOURCE: Data from NA Kho Kho 0202. 3. 5/215.

Even if the number of buses increased, it would become more difficult to maintain the provided trips on congested roads. As table 4.10 shows, the population of Bangkok increased consistently after the war and amounted to a total of 2.5 million in 1970. The number of automobiles in Bangkok was also increasing steadily: from 26,170 in 1960 to 154,751 in 1975 (*SYB* for 1963, 224; *SYB* for 1976–80, 322). Given that the rate of increase for automobiles was far higher than the population growth rate, we can presume that the traffic volume on roads in Bangkok also increased sharply in the meantime.

However, the expansion of roads in Bangkok did not catch up with the rapid increase in automobiles. The length of paved roads in Bangkok around 1960 was about 245 kilometers, but this increased to 805 kilometers in 1973; the rate of increase was thus less than the rate of increase in automobiles.[99] The road area was 805 square kilometers as of 1973, which accounted for only 4 percent of the area of the Bangkok Municipality. It was internationally recognized that the percentage of road area should be at least 20 percent of a city's area, a standard that Bangkok clearly did not meet (*SN*, 17 May 1969). Even with the construction and extension of roads, such as the extension of Phetchaburi Road and the expansion of Silom and the Rama IV roads in the 1960s, the roads in Bangkok were still insufficient.

The rapid increase of automobiles and the delay in road improvement caused traffic congestion, which constrained the number of possible bus trips. Even if the operators arranged for the agreed-upon number of buses, the number of trips per bus would be low if roads were congested. Also, the time distance would be lengthened, and users would have to wait longer for buses. If the operation interval of buses increased, the number of passengers on each bus would also increase, and the congestion on each bus would also increase. Yet, even if the number of buses increased, the improvement of bus service could not be achieved unless the smooth operation of buses was also secured. The problem of users waiting a long time to ride crowded buses existed also in the 1950s, when the number of buses was insufficient. The problem would remain even if the numbers of buses increased because of the increasing road congestion.

The low level of bus service was related to the aggravation of road congestion. With the new middle class, including government officials, white-collar workers, and intellectuals, emerging in Bangkok, and an increase in those who had become comparatively rich, there was a rapid increase of automobiles in the "age of development" and this further aggravated the poor level of bus service. The buses, operating under the concept of "the cheaper, the better," by which cheap fares were maintained, were a means of transport for the poor, but were avoided by the new middle class. The latter purchased their own automobiles for commuting, and this brought about an increase of automobiles and trucks on roads. This problem continues up to today. A movement to shift modes of transport away from privately owned cars to public transport by opening urban railways is starting to be seen. However, private cars are still the fundamental and most important factor in Bangkok's transport problems.

In the end, any radical improvement of bus service with the cheap fares promoted by populist policies was impossible. The government therefore tried nationalizing the privately operated bus businesses. But this could not solve the problem of improving the bus service because it did not address the issue of traffic congestion. The government then planned to introduce a means of mass transport above the roads, or urban railways, as a new solution to the problem of urban transport.

5
Revival of Rail Transport, 1970s–1990s

Emergence of the Urban Railway Plan

Bangkok and the Urban Railway

By the 1960s, almost all rail transport in Bangkok had disappeared, except the Maeklong line as a suburban railway, part of which was also abandoned. However, a movement pushing for a new urban railway emerged in the mid-1960s. It was in 1967 that plans for a new urban railway first surfaced in Bangkok. The city's mayor decided to introduce plans for a monorail and to dispatch engineers to Germany in January to develop those plans (*SN*, 19 January 1967). Later in the same year, a French commission conducted a survey for the monorail and proposed the construction of three monorail lines (*SRSW*, 21 June 1970).[1] Although the Bangkok Municipality planned to introduce the urban railway first, slow government reaction made their plans impossible.

After the suspension of the transfer of the Hua Lamphong terminus to Bang Sue in 1964, the removal of the level crossings in Bangkok became a concern. Although initially the railways were scheduled to be elevated, the cheaper option of constructing road bridges soon became more realistic. In 1966, the State Railways of Thailand (SRT) and the Bangkok Municipality agreed to build bridges across fourteen level crossings (Kakizaki 2009, 131). However, while the municipality wanted to change the current level crossings into two-level ones, the SRT aimed to remove all level crossings. Therefore, no concrete progress was achieved. As mentioned previously, construction of the elevated track from Hua Lamphong to Wongwian Yai over the Chaophraya River, as part of the modernization plan for the Maeklong line, was planned to be developed as an urban railway.

The road traffic congestion in Bangkok continued to deteriorate. In 1966, the government established the Land Transport Problem and Planning Committee (*Khana kammakan phicharana samruat kaekhai het khatkhong lae wang phaen kan charachon*) to examine how to solve Bangkok's transportation problems (TPT 1982, 14). After examination, the committee proposed requesting assistance from West Germany and dispatching specialists to investigate the city's problems in order to develop a master plan (ibid.). Hence, the first full-scale investigation regarding the transport problem was to be conducted in Bangkok. From 1971 to 1974, West German railway specialists, in cooperation with Thai agencies, conducted a detailed survey and submitted a final report in July 1976 (*SRSW*, 28 June 1981).

The survey proposed three steps to solve Bangkok's transport problem. The master plan consisted of short-, mid-, and long-term plans. The introduction of an expressway and mass rapid transit system (MTS, *Rabop khonsong muanchon*) was incorporated into the mid-term plan, with a scheduled completion date set for 1980 (TPT 1982, 16). The 27-kilometer expressways consisted of three routes from the junction at Khlong Toei—northward to Dindaeng, eastward to Bang Na, and westward to Daokhanong—and were designed to connect with trunk highways toward the north, east, and south respectively. These roads were to act as bypasses for travelers passing through Bangkok's inner city (ibid., 14). The first stage of the MTS plan consisted of three routes: a 15-kilometer Phrakhanong line between Phrakhanong and Bang Sue; a 20-kilometer Sathon line between Wongwian Yai and Latphrao; and a 14-kilometer Memorial Bridge line between Wongwian Yai and Khlong Tan (TPT for 1974, 2). Furthermore, the long-term plan, targeted for completion by 1990, included construction of extension lines as shown in figure 5.1.[2]

This MTS plan became the first urban railway plan in Bangkok. At the beginning, the plan did not necessarily assume the need to introduce urban railways. Rather, it contained three options for MTS: bus, light rail transit (LRT), and heavy rail. However, it recommended introducing

Fig. 5.1. Urban Railway Development Plan in Bangkok, 1982

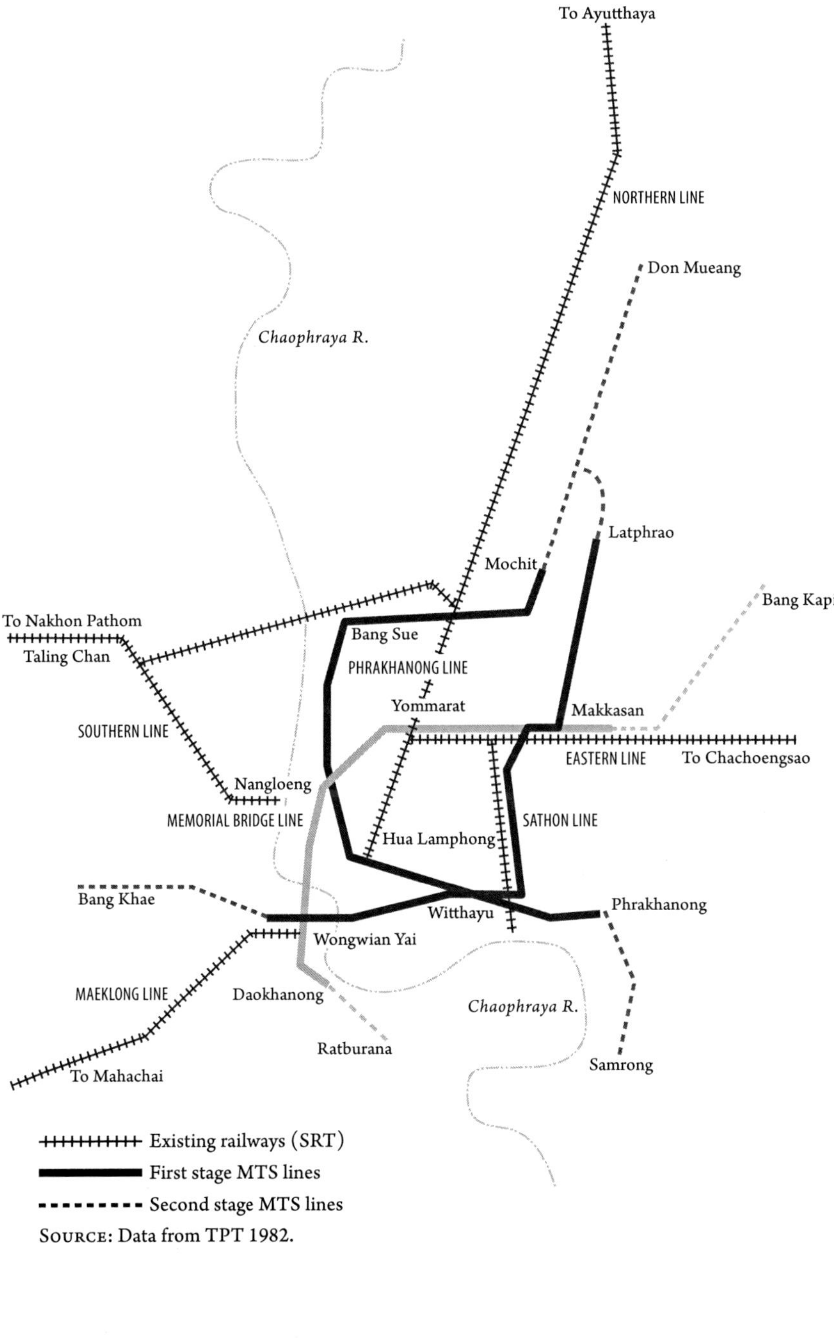

SOURCE: Data from TPT 1982.

bus service on an elevated structure first, and after an increase in the demand, substituting it by rail service, thus reducing the large initial cost for the introduction of the urban railway.[3] To reduce construction costs, most routes were established on roads, some sections of which ran parallel to existing railways. Although there were some changes, the MTS routes included in the plan were successful, and the plan's overall impact on forthcoming plans was rather significant.[4]

Progress of the Skytrain Plan

The government decided to establish a new agency to carry out the first stages of the expressway and the MTS programs contained within the mid-term plan of the West German transport survey. This decision was taken almost simultaneously with the start of the survey. In April 1971, the Land Transport Problem and Planning Committee formed a Subcommittee for Preparing the Establishment of a Toll-Collecting Agency (*Khana anukammakan triam chattang ongkan kep kha phan thang*) (TPT 1982, 14). Since the rapid development of the expressways depended on domestic or foreign loans, the method of collecting tolls, like in other developed countries, was necessary to repay the loan. Furthermore, establishing an independent agency was required to apply for a World Bank loan (ibid.).

This subcommittee was then promoted as the preparatory committee and eventually incorporated as the Expressway and Rapid Transit Authority of Thailand (ETA) in November 1972 (ibid., 15). The Thai name of this public corporation is very ambiguous: *Kan thang phiset haeng prathet thai*. The words "*thang phiset*" only mean "special way," which has no connation of an urban railway. However, the English name clearly specifies it as "rapid transit." The newly established agency was to have been the one that collected tolls, that is, the agency with jurisdiction over expressways at the beginning of their establishment in Bangkok. However, the actual agency had jurisdiction over not only expressways but also urban railways.

The ETA was established not under the jurisdiction of the Ministry of Communications but of the Ministry of Interior. The agencies with jurisdiction over national transport, such as the Department of Highways and the SRT, were parts of the Ministry of Communications, while the streets in Bangkok were under the jurisdiction of the Bangkok Metropolitan Administration (BMA), subordinate to the Ministry of Interior.[5] For this reason, it is not unusual that this agency with control of expressways and urban railways in Bangkok was placed under the Ministry of Interior. This resulted in further strengthening of the Ministry of Interior's status, which already enjoyed great authority, including power over the local administration and police. As mentioned previously, discord between the Ministries of Interior and Communications began in the 1950s, caused by a dispute about jurisdiction over bus operations with the result that the Ministry of Communications retained power over them. Thus the Ministry of Interior eventually reentered the sphere of urban transport. The assumption is that since a large budget was required for the ETA, Praphat, the then minister of interior, intentionally had it placed under his jurisdiction (*SRSW*, 28 June 1981).

The newly established ETA carried out the first stages of the expressway and MTS programs. In truth, however, only the expressway program proceeded. In March 1974, the Sanya cabinet approved the ETA's proposal for both programs (TPT 1982, 16). The expressway program proceeded smoothly by advancing its economic and engineering survey and design, and the cabinet ordered construction to begin in January 1977 (ibid., 7). The first expressway was opened in 1982, and the entire first stage of the expressway, consisting of twenty-seven kilometers, was completed before 1987.

For the MTS program, the introduction of bus service was assumed from the beginning based on the West German proposal. The World Bank also supported introducing bus service and constructing an elevated structure between Hua Lamphong and Khlong Toei on the Phrakhanong line.[6] This is the section on which the Paknam line once ran, and ironically it became the busiest section and the one in which the necessity for mass rapid transit increased the most in the fifteen years since the abolition of the original line. However, since almost no precedent existed in the world for bus operations on an elevated structure, dissenting opinions against the idea were deep-rooted. Therefore, it was decided to commission a consulting company to investigate and recommend the best system for mass rapid transit (TPT for 1978, 12–13). The consultants concluded that heavy rail was suitable, a conclusion with which the Kriangsak cabinet agreed and approved at a meeting in January 1979.[7] Thereby, the MTS program at last became an urban railway program.

In response, the ETA gave the detailed design for three lines to the same company and prepared the bid for construction, which was planned to start in 1981. A reexamination of the terminus resulted in the extension of the total length to fifty-nine kilometers, ten kilometers longer than the original plan. The ETA planned to construct these lines with loan funds and asked the government to allocate 40 percent of the total cost of construction, a total of 14,480 million baht, in its budget.[8] However, as the country's financial situation quickly worsened owing to the second global oil crisis, the government hesitated to bear the immense burden of urban railway construction. At the Prem Tinsulanonda cabinet meeting in June 1980, the government ordered the National Economic and Social Development Board (NESDB, formerly the NEDB), to reexamine the program in order to shift construction and operation to the private sector (*SRSW*, 28 June 1981). This was a sudden change of policy that, in fact, was influenced by Bunchu Rotchanasathian, the then deputy prime minister (ibid.).[9]

Although the survey and design of the first stage of the MTS was completed in October 1980, movement on the project stopped until an examination into the best method for private-sector handling of the project was completed. The government meanwhile decided to continue the construction of two road bridges across the Chaophraya. Since the Sathon and the Memorial Bridge lines passed across the Sathon Bridge and new Memorial Bridge respectively, contractors from the Department of Public Works (*krom yothathikan*), which had assumed charge of the construction of road bridges, were commissioned to construct the urban railway bridges.[10] The foundation of the Taksin (Sathon) Bridge on the Sathon line and the railway bridge at the Phra Pokklao Bridge (New Memorial Bridge) on the Memorial Bridge line were completed in 1982 and 1984 respectively.[11]

Finally, at the cabinet meeting in January 1982, the government consented to the construction and operation of the first stage of the MTS by issuing concessions to private sector contractors, as the NESDB had proposed. The concession conditions were released in July 1982 (*SRSW*, 30 October 1983). The concession was to be of the Build-Operate-Transfer

(BOT) type, which aims to develop social capital through the private sector. Under this system, a private enterprise would independently raise funds to construct the urban railway and would transfer the railway to the ETA after thirty years of operation.[12] The government would only pay for the expenses of bridge construction over the Chaophraya, survey and design, and land procurement. The total amount of capital, including the cost of rolling stock, was approximately 12,200 million baht, provided that construction could be finished in 1986 (TPT 1982, 45).[13]

Although fifteen companies were candidates, none accepted all the government's conditions (RFM for 1993, 63). Since the private company would have to bear every expense from construction to preparing for train operation, there arose the question of whether such a large amount of capital would be available. Moreover, it was doubtful whether the company would be able to make enough profits to recoup its invested capital within the thirty-year term. This question was extremely relevant to potential developers because, in the end, the construction program for the first stage of urban railway failed.

Grant and Cancelation of the Concession to Lavalin

The government recognized that the major reason that the first stage of the MTS program could not attract private interest was the large investment cost. Therefore, it began considering ways to reduce construction costs. Wira Muksikkaphong, the then deputy minister of interior, visited West Germany and learned that using the German-invented LRT with a linear motor rather than the conventional heavy rail would cut construction costs in Bangkok by a third. In 1983, Wira commissioned a German company to conduct a feasibility study (*SRSW*, 30 October 1983). Furthermore, after the reexamination of the first stage of the MTS program performed in 1985 with the Canadian government's help, it became apparent that the total length of the railway should be shortened from 59 kilometers to 38.5 kilometers, and that the Canadian-developed LRT system, known as the Urban Transportation Development Corporation (UTDC) system, should be used (RFM 1993, 6).[14] Because the UTDC-type LRT in Vancouver was called the "Skytrain," the ETA urban railway program was also called the "Skytrain Program."

The ETA reexamined the first stage of the MTS program and reported its findings to the government at the May 1986 cabinet meeting (KT 1997,

34). At that time, the government declared that it would change its policy and invest a maximum of 25 percent of the total cost in the program. Furthermore, the ETA reduced the scale of the first stage of the program and announced the changes in the concessions in September 1986 (ibid.). The first-stage Part I lines consisted of the entire Phrakhanong line as well as the section between Witthayu and Latphrao of the Sathon line, resulting in a total of thirty-four kilometers. Overall, the scale of the first stage of the program was reduced by about 40 percent.

Among the eighteen companies that bid, three were selected as final candidates: Lavalin International, Inc. and UTDC, Inc., both of Canada, Asia-Euro Consortium from Germany and Austria, and the Franco-Japanese Consortium (TPT for 1988, 42–43).[15] However, no company completely consented to the ETA's conditions (*SRSW*, 30 July 1989). Lavalin accepted the condition of 25 percent investment by the government but asked for a guarantee from the government for receiving a low-interest loan of 800 million dollars from the Canadian government. Asia-Euro also consented to the 25 percent investment; however, because the government would have to invest 100 percent to establish a rolling-stock leasing company that the contractor would use to operate the system, the government would also have to shoulder the foreign exchange risk. Franco-Japanese did not consent to the 25 percent investment terms but asked for the whole investment by the government.

The task of selecting a company was difficult. Initially, the ETA recommended Asia-Euro's plan as the most desirable because of its having the lowest construction costs and a short construction period. However, it began negotiating with Lavalin because the company had already obtained a loan offer (*SRSW*, 2 June 1990), but since Lavalin made no change in its demand that the government guarantee that loan, the ETA started negotiations with Asia-Euro in December 1989. Lavalin, however, soon learned that the Canadian government no longer insisted upon the Thai government's guarantee for the loan (ibid.), and therefore the ETA halted negotiations with Asia-Euro and reopened negotiations with Lavalin. Once the negotiations concluded, the cabinet approved the contract with Lavalin in September 1990 (Rangsan and Kanlata, 1993, 619). Many claim that political intervention was the cause of the delay, because political power had shifted from the Prem government to the Chatchai Choonhavan government (*SRSW*, 16 December 1989).

The Lavalin plan was the same as the UTDC plan proposed originally after investigation by the Canadian government. The ETA and Lavalin adjusted the conditions, and the concession created under the first Anan Panyarachun government was granted to Lavalin in February 1992 (RFM 1993, 6). Thereafter, plans for the first urban railway began to move forward. However, Lavalin was unable to obtain the participation of Bombardier Inc., which had purchased the rights to the UTDC system under the terms of the concession.[16] Therefore, the second Anan government, established after the Black May incident, revoked the concession in May 1992 because the concession terms had been broken (ibid.). In the end, the first-stage Part I of the plan also failed.

In addition, to improve a situation in which various agencies formulated expressway or urban railway plans without any coordination, the Office of the Commission for the Management of Land Traffic (OCMLT, *Samnakngan khana kammakan chat rabop kan charachon thang bok*) was established under the Prime Minister's Office in March 1992, immediately after the concession was issued to Lavalin (SNR 1992, 94).[17] The OCMLT played an important role not only in coordinating each agency but also in making master plans for expressways and urban railways.

The failure of the ETA's urban railway plan was probably due to the unattractive investment environment for the private sector caused by the ambiguous government attitude and its numerous policy changes. Lavalin's inability to secure Bombardier's participation should be attributed to the Black May incident, because it badly damaged Thailand's attraction in terms of investment. The government's insistence on the BOT method, given its high investment cost, was yet another reason why private involvement was discouraged.

Bus Operation after Unification

Improvement of the Bus Service

The BMTA (Bangkok Mass Transit Authority), established in October 1976, succeeded the Mahanakhon Transport Company and also inherited various problems at the time of unification. Mahanakhon Transport had purchased 2,703 buses from the private sector, of which no less than 1,000 were out of service and unusable (KSMK 1985, 5). As a result, the number of operating buses sharply decreased, resulting in a large influx of illegal buses, as will be mentioned later in this chapter.

Therefore, an urgent task for the BMTA was to increase the number of buses. The 1977 cabinet meeting approved the purchase of 2,500 buses, all of which were delivered by the end of the following year (KSMK 1985, 17–18). Because the minimum number of operating buses was fixed at 3,500 by the Department of Land Transport at that time, this number should have been met after the purchase of the new buses. But the operating rate of the old buses purchased from the private sector was so low that they were being decommissioned one after another (*SR*, 29 July 1977). Therefore, despite the introduction of 2,500 new buses, the bus shortage remained uncorrected.

The BMTA approved the purchase of 1,640 new buses in 1980 in an attempt to reinforce transport capacity (KSMK 1985, 18). At this time, because the consultancy firm employed with support from the World Bank proposed to increase the number of leased buses, the government did not purchase but instead leased the new buses. Although the government's goal was to ease the financial burden that bus operations put on its budget, leasing buses later came to be recognized as a factor that increased the BMTA's deficit. Nevertheless, since the BMTA supplied more than 4,000 buses, the problem of lack of buses was solved by the initial activities of the BMTA.

Moreover, air-conditioned buses also began operating after the establishment of BMTA. The operation of air-conditioned buses had been planned by private companies since approximately 1970, and Mahanakhon Transport Company began operations on two routes in July 1976 (Samrit n.d., vol. 1, 105).[18] After the merger, the BMTA expanded and increased the operation of air-conditioned buses. Of the 2,500 buses purchased by the 1977 approval, 200 were air-conditioned, and of the 1,640 new buses leased in 1980, 500 were air-conditioned.

These air-conditioned buses usually operated on different routes from those of ordinary buses. Table 5.1 shows the bus routes published by the Royal Gazette from the establishment of the BMTA in 1976 to 1977. Among these, ten were routes for air-conditioned buses, which were comparatively long-distance routes between city centers and suburbs, such as from Paknam, Bang Kapi, Don Mueang, Pakkret, Bang Khae, and Phrapradaeng to the central areas, as shown in figure 5.2. Except

Routes A9 and A10, all routes for air-conditioned buses connected suburban residential areas and the city center.[19]

Table 5.1. Bus Routes in Bangkok, 1977

Route Number	Line
1	Thanon Tok–Tha Tian
2	Pakkhlong Talat–Samrong
3	SRT Quarters (Ko Mo 11)–Khlong San
4	Phasi Charoen Pier–Khlong Toei Port
5	Bang Sue–Chakkrawat
6	Bukkhalo–Thewet
7	Nopphawong–Khlong Khwang
8	Memorial Bridge–Latphrao
9	Siyan–Phasi Charoen Pier
10	Wat Nangnong–Nangloeng
11	Dindaeng–Memorial Bridge
12	Huai Khwang–Ministry of Commerce
13	Huai Khwang–Khlong Toei Port
14	Siyan–Khlong Toei Port
15	Bang Lamphu–Bangkok Bridge
16	Surawong–Tao Pun
17	Bangkok Bridge–Bang Lamphu
18	Rama VI Bridge–Si Phraya
19	Thewet–Bangkok Noi
20	Tha Dindaeng–Phra Chunlachomklao Fort
21	Chulalongkorn University–Thonburirom Park
22	Thanon Tok–Ramkhamhaeng University
23	Onnut–Thewet
24	Prachaniwet 2 Estate–Victory Monument
25	Tha Chang–Paknam
26	Saphan Khao–Minburi
27	Khlong Kum–Khlong Toei Port
28	Northern Line Bus Terminal–Southern Line Bus Terminal
29	Rangsit–Hua Lamphong
30	Nonthaburi–Southern Line Bus terminal
56	Krung Thon Bridge Circle Line
57	Thonburi Circle Line
58	Ramkhamhaeng University–Bangkok Noi Station
59	Don Mueang–Sanam Luang
60	Khlong Chan–Pakkhlong Talat
61	Ramkhamhaeng University–Victory Monument
62	Sathu Pradit–Victory Monument
63	Nonthaburi–Victory Monument
64	Nonthaburi–Sanam Luang
65	Rama VI Bridge–Tha Tian
66	Prachaniwet 1 Estate–Phasi Charoen Pier
67	Prachaniwet 1 Estate–Bangkok Technical College
68	Bang Pakaeo–Bang Lamphu
69	Sanambin Nam–Northern Line Bus Terminal
70	Prachaniwet 2 Estate–Sanam Luang
71	Khlong Chan–Wat Pho
72	Khlong Toei Port–Thewet
73	Dindaeng–Memorial Bridge
74	Huai Khwang–Khlong Toei Port
75	Thonburirom Park–Tha Tian
76	Wat Lao–Lumphini Park
77	Silom–Victory Monument
78	Sathon–Bang Lamphu
79	Taling Chan–Saochingcha
80	Nongkhaem–Sanam Luang
81	Bang Khae–Sirirat
82	Phrapradaeng–Memorial Bridge
83	Taling Chan–Bangkok Noi Station
84	Omnoi–Khlong San
85	Wat Chaengron–Sanam Luang

Route Number	Line
31	Pathumthani–Tha Chang
32	Pakkret–Bang Pakok
33	Pathumthani–Sanam Luang
34	Rangsit–Hua Lamphong
35	Saochingcha–Sathu Pradit
36	Saphan Khwai–Si Phraya
37	Bang Pakok–Nangloeng
38	Northern Line Bus Terminal–Ekkamai
39	Sanam Luang–Don Mueang
40	Ekkamai–Southern Line Bus Terminal
41	Saochingcha–Setthakit Estate
42	Sirirat–Saochingcha Circle line
43	Wat Sing–Bang Lamphu
44	Mochit–Tha Tian
45	Bang Lamphu–Lumphini Park
46	Bang Na–Hua Lamphong
47	Land Department–Khlong Toei Port
48	Samrong–Wat Pho
49	Bang Son–Sam Yaek
50	Rama VI Bridge–Samyan
51	Pakkret–Sanam Luang
52	Pakkret–Victory Monument
53	Thewet Circle Line
54	Huai Khwang Circle Line
55	Amnuai Songkhram Circle Line
86	Phrapradaeng–Bang Lamphu
87	Nangloeng–Thonburirom Park
88	Wat Thungkhru–Khlong San
89	Sanam Luang–Bangkok Technical College
90	Bang Phun–Sanam Luang
91	Setthakit Estate–Sanam Luang
92	Ramkhamhaeng University–Victory Monument
93	Laem Thong Athlete Village–Si Phraya
94	Minburi–Sanam Luang
95	Don Mueang–Khlong Toei Port
96	Khlong Chan–Nangloeng
201	Victory Monument–Sanam Luang
202	Chulalongkorn University–Sanam Luang
203	Nonthaburi–Sanam Luang
A1	Khlong Chan–Pakkhlong Talat
A2	Khlong Chan–Silom
A3	Don Mueang–Phra Pinklao Bridge
A4	Don Mueang–Khlong Toei Port
A5	Pakkret–Lumphini Park
A6	Nonthaburi–Land Department
A7	Bang Khae–Thewet
A8	Paknam–Tha Rat
A9	Thewet Circle Line
A10	Phloenchit Circle Line

NOTE 1: "A" in route number means air-conditioned bus.
NOTE 2: These routes were announced in 1976 and 1977 in RKB, but some air-conditioned routes did not start operating until after 1977.
SOURCES: RKB, vol. 93, no. 51; vol. 93, no. 148; vol. 93, no. 157; vol. 94, no. 68.

Although the introduction of air-conditioned buses was primarily described as relief for insufficient bus services, it was also expected to attract commuters from the suburbs to the city who typically traveled by privately owned cars (*SR*, 30 November 1977). The air-conditioned buses applied a sectional fare system, and the fare for its first ride was as much as 5 baht, in contrast with 0.75 baht charged for ordinary, non-air-conditioned bus rides (Samrit n.d., vol. 1, 105). Nevertheless, the

Fig. 5.2. Bus Network in Bangkok, 1977

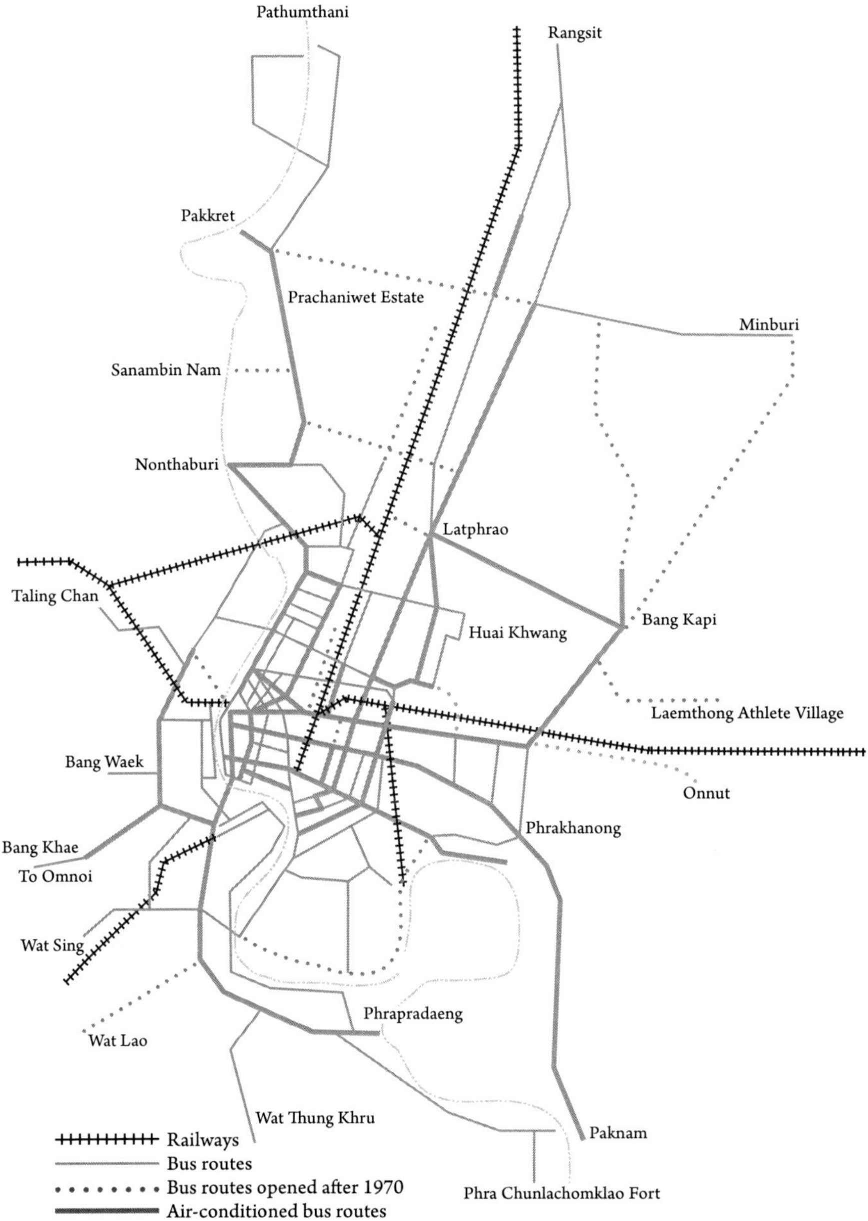

Note: Map excludes bus routes of category four (bus routes within the province).

air-conditioned buses provided a more comfortable space and better environment than the hot and crowded ordinary buses, and they cost less than operating a privately owned car. Therefore, the number of passengers on air-conditioned buses increased steadily, and some commuters began to use air-conditioned buses instead of their personal vehicles (*SR*, 30 November 1977).

While the number of buses increased, the operation of private buses continued in order to relieve the shortage of buses. As will be discussed below, to relieve the shortage of BMTA buses, the operation of illegal buses, *songthaeo*, continued. There were also legal private buses under the jurisdiction of BMTA. As of 1986, there were 734 private ordinary buses and 240 private air-conditioned buses in existence. These buses operated on the routes specified by the BMTA. The BMTA held ownership of the routes, and the private buses were only allowed to operate by paying commissions. That was the same type of operation system as the Express Transportation Organization (ETO) or the Transport Company, and in this regard the BMTA was similar to "a tiger lying down and eating."

Solution to the Illegal Bus Problem

When bus operations were integrated in 1976, the government prohibited the operation of private buses that were not yet transferred to Mahanakhon Transport. Consequently, the shortage of buses became more serious. Many illegal *songthaeo* flowed into Bangkok from rural areas and started operating. Furthermore, after the establishment of BMTA, illegal buses sprung up, including former fixed-route buses operated by private companies that refused to sell their businesses to the BMTA. The BMTA had to reinforce its transport capacity by increasing its number of buses as well as eliminating these illegal buses.

Songthaeo previously operated in Bangkok and competition with them was one factor that aggravated private companies' profitability. However, the number of *songthaeo* rapidly increased in 1976, when the Bangkok bus shortage became even more severe. It was not only *songthaeo* in Bangkok but also newcomers from the region who participated in the business. These *songthaeo* did not operate freely but paid commission to a broker (*nai na*) for each route, who in turn bribed the police to avoid exposure (*SRSW*, 2 October 1983). In Bangkok, the number of *songthaeo* and these illegal buses amounted to about 10,000 at the end of the 1970s (*SRWR*, 22 April 1979).

The increase of these illegal buses became a problem for users from the time of rapid increase in the number of illegal *songthaeo* during World War II until immediately after the war ended. The main reason for the increase was that the bus services supplied by the BMTA failed to satisfy passenger demand. Therefore, illegal buses were important for users. However, these buses operated poorly because they were not under the regulation of the Department of Land Transport. For example, illegally operated buses often did not leave the bus stop until they were full or a BMTA bus arrived; some collected three baht at night instead of the standard fare of one baht; and some suddenly stopped operation during the trip (*SR*, 20 March 1978). Therefore, users reluctantly used *songthaeo*, making authorities predict that the use of illegal buses would be curtailed if the number of BMTA buses increased.

However, despite the introduction of more than 4,000 buses, the problem of the shortage of buses in Bangkok was not resolved. One reason was the extension of the route network that accompanied the expansion of the city area. As shown in table 5.1, the number of bus routes increased from ninety in 1970 to 109 (ninety-nine ordinary and ten air-conditioned) in 1977. As shown in figure 5.2, new bus routes were created in the suburbs, such as those to Prachaniwet, Laem Thong Athlete Village, and Onnut. The newly introduced buses had to be put in service not only on existing routes but also on newly installed routes. Thus, the increase in the number of buses did not immediately guarantee sufficient service on all routes.

After all was said and done, however, the BMTA planned to unify these illegal buses in the same manner in which the private buses had been integrated. First, the Department of Land Transport and the BMTA decided to return *songthaeo* to small *soi* (lanes) where bus routes were not yet fixed, and large-sized buses were to be run on BMTA's routes as private buses (*SRSW*, 22 April 1979). It was recommended that *songthaeo*, return to the rural areas where they usually came from, and spontaneous withdrawal was expected as the number of buses increased and demand for illegal buses decreased. The Department of Land Transport advanced a plan for bus routes of category four (local buses) in Bangkok and gave concessions to the BMTA. The BMTA planned to unify *songthaeo* according to three areas—northern Bangkok, southern Bangkok, and Thonburi—and allow them to operate under concessions from the BMTA (*SRSW*, 22 January 1978).

However, because there were too many *songthaeo* to accommodate on the category four routes, and because the operation on the main streets with fixed bus routes would result in more income, some *songthaeo* were reluctant to operate in *soi*. Therefore, beginning in 1981, the BMTA decided to allow *songthaeo* to run on category one bus routes on the main streets as private BMTA buses, but only if they charged the same fare and improved the condition of their vehicles (Samrit n.d., vol. 2, 1048). Thereby, *songthaeo* began operating on the BMTA's routes using the same BMTA large bus route numbers and even the same bus colors of cream and blue. By September 1983, the number of buses registered was 2,412 and that of illegal buses decreased to about 1,000 (*SRSW*, 2 October 1983).

These *songthaeo* were to be further converted into minibuses. Because they were truck-based buses, their use on the main streets created safety problems. Therefore, in February 1986, the Ministry of Communications decided to change *songthaeo* that operated on main streets into box-type small buses while retaining their original chassis (*SRSW*, 22 April 1989). These new buses were painted green and were called "minibuses." *Songthaeo* were asked to renew their registration by the end of June 1987, and a total of 2,221 minibuses began operating in July (ibid.). The result of this was that *songthaeo* disappeared from category one bus routes on main streets and only legal *songthaeo* remained on category four bus routes in the *soi*.

Finally, minibuses were unified under one organization. In connection with the renewal of concessions for minibuses at the end of September 1989, the BMTA decided to grant concessions to companies instead of individual owners (Samrit n.d., vol. 3, 2193). Thereby, the minibus concessions were granted to the Bangkok Rattanakosin Automobile Company (*Borisat rattanakosin yanyon krungthep chamkat*), formalizing and completing the unification of minibus operators. However, because the operation of minibuses by original *songthaeo* owners posed numerous service problems, the BMTA wished to abolish them entirely by updating to large-sized buses (Somsi 1992, 10–11).[20]

Continuation of Loss-Making Operations

Although the BMTA improved bus service and eradicated illegal buses, its financial condition was rather poor. The BMTA had acquired Mahanakhon Transport's deficit, and it had a deficiency account from the beginning. Furthermore, as shown in table 5.2, the operating balance went into the red after 1977, indicating that the cumulative deficit was expanding. Therefore, the BMTA became one of the public corporations and agencies in debt, much like the SRT, which fell into debt in the 1970s.

The main reason for this deficit was that the BMTA had inherited Mahanakhon Transport's problems, such as the purchase of private buses at a high price and the increase in personnel expenses. The lease of buses and depots was also said to be a contributing factor. Although the lease of buses in 1980 enabled the agency initially to save expenses, the lease contracts were advantageous to lenders: the lease payment was fixed at 1.78 baht for a bus per one-kilometer journey and was required to be paid even if the bus could not actually operate (*SRSW*, 19 April 1981). Moreover, since the BMTA did not own independent bus depots, the burden of rents for the depots and offices became as much as 4 million baht per month. Therefore, high rents, including bus leases, forced the increase of unsustainable expenditures (ibid.). Other factors such as inefficient management and corruption also increased costs.

The low fare became the restraint on increasing income because the BMTA's source of income was virtually restricted to fares. As shown in table 5.3, the fare when the BMTA was established in 1976 was 0.75 baht, the same as after the fare hike from 0.5 baht in 1973. However, since the BMTA was afflicted by operational losses from the beginning, a fare hike was decided upon after it was established. As shown in the table, the fare in zones was increased from 0.75 baht to 1 baht in April 1978; bus fares were raised only one and a half years after the BMTA's establishment. The reason given for the fare hike was explained as sweeping away the loss-making operations of the BMTA, and the government asked people to understand that thanks to the fare hike, bus service would be dramatically improved within four months. At the time, there seems to have been no great resistance to the hike, and it materialized relatively smoothly (*SR*, 9 March 1978).

Table 5.2. Financial Situation of BMTA, 1977–2000 (Thousand THB)

Fiscal Year	Receipts	Expenditures	Balance
1977	622,923	870,633	-247,710
1978	1,058,229	1,438,311	-380,082
1979	1,421,256	1,898,256	-477,000
1980	1,777,383	2,523,348	-745,965
1981	2,524,497	3,344,300	-819,803
1982	2,965,012	3,939,781	-974,769
1983	3,137,775	4,214,242	-1,076,467
1984	3,064,176	4,303,742	-1,239,566
1985	3,458,237	4,558,071	-1,099,834
1986	3,142,717	4,368,748	-1,226,031
1987	3,216,900	4,129,800	-912,900
1988	3,397,739	4,164,840	-767,101
1989	3,839,862	4,723,434	-883,572
1990	4,069,886	5,039,161	-969,275
1991	5,029,460	5,254,223	-224,763
1992	6,402,827	6,341,237	61,590
1993	6,363,202	6,962,823	-599,621
1994	6,198,353	7,097,117	-898,764
1995	6,395,298	8,222,111	-1,826,813
1996	6,473,178	8,599,889	-2,126,711
1997	6,682,385	9,153,212	-2,470,827
1998	6,816,858	9,548,676	-2,731,818
1999	7,103,040	9,795,586	-2,692,546
2000	7,054,938	9,944,113	-2,889,175

Source: Data from KSMK 2005.

However, BMTA's financial situation failed to improve after the hike. Although its income in 1978, immediately after the hike, increased by more than 400 million baht (table 5.2), its deficit expanded because its expenditures also increased. Therefore, talk of another fare hike, this time to 1.5 baht, surfaced in 1979 (*SRSW*, 1 July 1979). Since a second fare hike would have received criticism from passengers, a fare hike without changing the minimum fare level was adopted. As shown in table 5.3, the zone system was changed into a sectional fare system in August 1980. The fare for traveling up to ten kilometers remained at 1 baht, but users traveling more than ten kilometers had to bear a higher fare of 2 baht. The return to a sectional fare system had been requested by private companies since the latter half of the 1960s, and it was finally used after management shifted to the BMTA.

Table 5.3. Changes in Bus Fares, 1976–2000

Date	Fare System	Fare (THB)	Remarks	Sources
1976 (1 Oct)	Zonal	0.75	1.25 baht for two zones	KSMK 1986
1978 (1 Apr)	Zonal	1.00	1.50 baht for two zones	KSMK 1986
1980 (1 Aug)	Sectional	1.00	2 baht for more than 10 km	KSMK 1986
1981 (1 Mar)	Sectional	2.00	3 baht for more than 10 km	KSMK 1986
1981 (20 Mar)	Sectional	1.50	2.5 baht for more than 10 km	KSMK 1986
1982 (6 Nov)	Sectional	2.00	3 baht for more than 10 km	KSMK 1986
1982 (25 Nov)	Sectional	1.50	2.5 baht for more than 10 km	KSMK 1986
1985 (15 Feb)	Flat	2.00		KSMK 1986
1988 (Feb)	Flat	2.00, 3.00	Red buses introduced	KSMK 2002
1992 (1 Sep)	Flat	2.50, 3.50		*SRSW*, 9 Aug 1992
1997	Flat	3.50, 5.00	White buses introduced, blue buses abandoned	KSMK for 1997

NOTE 1: Fares are for ordinary, non air-conditioned buses.
NOTE 2: Since 1988, fares vary according to the type of bus.

Although this fare hike, too, did not elicit much reaction, bus users reacted harshly when the BMTA planned a third fare hike in 1981. Amendments to the bus fares were proposed at the February 1981 cabinet meeting, and a fare of 1.5 baht for traveling up to ten kilometers was approved (*SRSW*, 22 February 1981). However, during the cabinet meeting, the right of the Ministry of Communications to make a final decision on the issue was recognized. The ministry opted for a hike of 2 baht to be enforced from March 1 (*SRSW*, 8 March 1981). Since this hike doubled the fare, users significantly resisted the change. Students and workers both held meetings on March 3 and requested a repeal of the fare hike (*SRSW*, 15 March 1981). Since the immediate previous hike was to 1.5 baht, they did not ask to return to the original 1 baht fare but rather requested adopting the 1.5 baht fare. This differed from passenger opposition in 1968, when users demanded the withdrawal of the entire fare hike.

Eventually, the bus fare was reduced by a political judgment. On March 20, as shown in table 5.3, the fare was reduced to 1.5 baht for up to ten kilometers, in accord with user demands. Minister of Communications Amon Sirikaya explained that the fare hike to 2 baht would create a financial surplus for the BMTA, while the 1.5 baht fare would create a deficit of 2 million baht per day, and urged that the fare hike should aim to sweep away the BMTA's losses (ibid.). However, since the 100 percent fare hike received intense resistance, the government had no choice but to accept a compromise 50 percent hike. It is doubtful whether the fare hike to 2 baht would have converted the agency's finances into black. In any case, the opportunity for obtaining a large revenue increase for the BMTA was lost. Although it was not the same as when the Kukrit government had announced a free bus policy, the bus service was still recognized to be a populist policy and the government was expected to accept the users' views on issues related to it.

As shown in table 5.3, although the BMTA obtained a fare hike to 2 baht in the next year, it was immediately reduced to the original fare level for the same reason that had previously influenced its reduction: user resistance. The deficit of the BMTA continued, and by 1983 it exceeded 1 billion baht. A fare hike to 2 baht was finally obtained in 1985, breaking through the 2-baht fare wall that had existed since 1981. In this fare hike, the conventional sectional fare system was changed to a flat fare system. Therefore, in some cases, fares were reduced for long-distance travels.[21] Although there seemed to be a goal of reducing costs, the reduction in the costs of certain types of tickets and the number of inspectors indicates that the government was inclined to avoid user resistance. Furthermore, in 1988 the BMTA adopted a new fare for the newly introduced buses, which was 1 baht higher than that of ordinary buses. The new buses had automatic doors, an increased number of seats, and also electric fans. These improvements were used as reasons for levying higher fares. Unlike the conventional cream-and-blue buses, these buses were painted cream and red, making the distinction clear. By 1997, the fare hike was introduced and all cream-and-blue buses were replaced by the new red-and-cream buses (see table 5.3). In addition, a 0.5 baht fare hike was imposed in 1992.

As a result of these measures, the BMTA's deficit started to decrease. As shown in table 5.2, the deficit decreased after 1987, and again significantly declined in 1991. In 1991, the BMTA had a deficit of only 2,200 million baht. In 1992, it finally went into the black for the first time. The main reason was the Anan government's subsidy for fuel costs from 1991 to 1992, but several measures of the BMTA to eliminate loss-producing practices were also significant (KSMK 2005, 12).[22]

Table 5.4 shows that the network of bus routes was also expanded. The number of routes sharply increased compared to the number in 1988, and now included 148 ordinary and 19 air-conditioned bus routes. The expressway bus service started in 1982, and certain ordinary bus routes introduced all-night bus service in 1985. The bus service was also diversified to include the suburbs (see figure 5.3). The expansion of the network was particularly remarkable toward the east and north. Although routes were also opened on existing roads, such as the section between Bang Na and Bang Phli, most new bus routes were fixed to accord with newly opened roads, such as in the Bang Buathong area and Ratchadaphisek Road. Moreover, the number of expressway bus routes increased to thirteen, and the number of all-night bus routes to ten in 1988. Since the number of passengers reached its peak in 1992, as mentioned below, it was between the end of the 1980s and the beginning of the 1990s that the BMTA's bus operations finally got off the ground and entered a golden age.

Three Urban Railway Plans

Emergence of a New Urban Railway Plan

While the first-stage Part I of the ETA's plan did not progress, two urban railway plans by other agencies emerged. These were the Bangkok Elevated Road and Train System Program Plan (Hopewell plan), made by the SRT, and the Elevated Railway Plan, created by the BMA. Since these plans were formed without any help from the ETA, several sections overlapped with ETA's urban railway routes. Therefore, the ETA had to reexamine its routes for the first-stage lines.

Table 5.4. Bus Routes in Bangkok, 1988

Route Number	Line	Remarks
1	Thanon Tok–Tha Tian	
2	Pakkhlong Talat–Samrong	N, E
3	SRT Quarters (Ko Mo 11)–Khlong San	
4	Phasi Charoen Pier–Khlong Toei Port	N
5	Bamrat Naradun Hospital–Chakkrawat	
6	Bukkhalo–Bang Khunphrom	
7	Nopphawong–Khlong Khwang	
7/1	Bang Khae–Phahurat	
8	Memorial Bridge–Happy Land Market	
9	Siyan–Phasi Charoen Pier	
10	Phasi Charoen Pier–Nangloeng	
11	Makkasan–Memorial Bridge	
11K	Makkasan–Phasuk Estate	
12	Huai Khwang–Ministry of Commerce	
13	Huai Khwang–Khlong Toei Port	
14	Siyan–Khlong Toei Port	
15	Bang Lamphu–Tha Phra	
16	Surawong–Tao Pun	
17	Tha Phra–Bang Lamphu	
18	Rama VI Bridge–Si Phraya	
19	Bangkok Noi–Bang Lamphu Circle Line	
20	Tha Dindaeng–Phra Chunlachomklao Fort	
21	Chulalongkorn University–Thonburirom Park	
22	Thanon Tok–Ramkhamhaeng University	
23	Samrong–Thewet	E
24	Prachaniwet 3 Estate–Victory Monument	

Route Number	Line	Remarks
25	Tha Chang–Paknam	
26	Victory Monument–Minburi	
27	Minburi–Victory Monument	N
28	Ratchadaphisek–Tha Phra	
29	Rangsit–Hua Lamphong	
30	Nonthaburi–Tha Phra	
32	Pakkret–Sanam Luang	
33	Pathumthani–Sanam Luang	
34	Rangsit–Hua Lamphong	N
35	Saochingcha–Sathu Pradit	
36	Saphan Khwai–Si Phraya	
37	Bang Pakok–Mahanak	
38	Chankasem Educational College–Ekkamai	
39	Sanam Luang–Thammasat University Rangsit Campus	
40	Ekkamai–Wat Chaoam	
42	Tha Phra–Saochingcha Circle line	
43	Pinthong Market–Bang Lamphu	
44	Happy Land Market–Tha Tian	
45	Samrong–Phra Pinklao Bridge	E
46	Ramkhamhaeng University Bang Na Campus–Rong Mueang	
47	Land Department–Customs Department	
48	Ramkhamhaeng University Bang Na Campus–Wat Pho	
49	Bang Son–Sam Yaek	
50	Rama VI Bridge–Sathon	
51	Pakkret–Wat Pho	
52	Pakkret–Bang Sue Station	
53	Thewet Circle Line	

Route Number	Line	Remarks
54	Huai Khwang Circle Line	N
55	Amnuai Songkhram Circle Line	
56	Krung Thon Bridge Circle Line	
57	Thonburi Circle Line	
58	Minburi–Ptratunam	
58	Happy Land Market–Bangkok Noi Station	
59	Rangsit–Sanam Luang	
60	Patwikon Estate–Pakkhlong Talat	N
61	Ramkhamhaeng University–Victory Monument	
62	Sathu Pradit–Victory Monument	
63	Nonthaburi–Victory Monument	
64	Nonthaburi–Sanam Luang	N
65	Wat Paknam–Tha Tian	
66	Prachaniwet 2 Estate–Phasi Charoen Pier	
67	Prachaniwet 1 Estate–Chong Nonsi	
68	Bang Pakaeo–Bang Lamphu	
69	Sanambin Nam–Victory Monument	
70	Prachaniwet 3 Estate–Sanam Luang	
71	Chorakhe Bua–Wat Thatthong	
72	Kluai Namthai–Thewet	
73	Mass Communication Organization of Thailand–Memorial Bridge	
74	Huai Khwang–Khlong Toei Port	E
75	Wat Phutthabucha–Tha Tian	
76	Thonburi Estate–Lumphini Park	
77	Silom–Phahonyothin Yard	
79	Taling Chan–Ratchaprasong	
80	Nongkhaem–Sanam Luang	
81	Bang Khae–Sirirat	

Route Number	Line	Remarks
82	Phrapradaeng–Memorial Bridge	N
82K	Bang Pakok–Sanam Luang	
83	Taling Chan Circle Line	
84	Omyai–Khlong San	
85	Wat Chaengron–Phahurat	
86	Phrapradaeng–Bang Lamphu	
88	Wat Thungkhru–Wongwian Yai	
89	Saochingcha–Bangkok Technical College	
90	Bang Phun–Phahonyothin Yard	
91	Setthakit Estate–Sanam Luang	N
92	Khlong Tan–Priest Hospital	
93	Laem Thong Athlete Village–Si Phraya	
95	Minburi–Sanam Luang	
95	Happy Land Market–Khlong Toei Port	
96	Khlong Chan–Nangloeng	
97	Nonthaburi–Priest Hospital	
98	Huai Khwang–Kluai Namthai	
99	Ramkhamhaeng University–Thewet	
101	Wat Mueang–Phothong Market	
102	Paknam–Chong Nonsi	E
103	Talat Phlu–Nonthaburi	N
104	Pakkret–Victory Monument	
105	Samaedam–Charoen Nakhon Market	
106	Latya–Lumphini Park	
107	Bang Khen–Khlong Toei	E
108	Bang Khae–Nonthaburi	
109	Ramkhamhaeng University–Hua Lamphong	
110	Rama VI Bridge–Thewet	
111	Talat Phlu–Bukkhalo Circle Line	
112	Si Narong–Si Phraya	

Route Number	Line	Remarks
113	Minburi–Hua Lamphong	
114	Nonthaburi–Lam Lukka Junction	
115	Khlong Chan–Silom	
116	Samrong–Sathon	
117	Wat Mai–Huai Khwang	
119	Paknam–Samyaek	
120	Pinthong Market–Khlong San	
121	Sathon–Taling Chan	
122	Ramkhamhaeng University–Phahonyothin Yard	
124	Mahidon University Salaya Campus–Arun Amarin Bridge	
125	Mahidon University Salaya Campus–Krung Thon Bridge	
126	Khaelai–Ramkhamhaeng University	
127	Arun Amarin Bridge–Bang Buathong	
128	Krung Thon Bridge–Bang Yai	
129	Kasetsart University–Samrong	E
130	Happy Land Market–Minburi	
131	Minburi–Nongchok	
132	Bang Chak–Bang Phli Estate	
133	Khlong Tan–Bang Phli Estate	
134	Phahonyothin Yard–Bang Buathong	
136	Chatuchak Park–Customs Department	
137	Ramkhamhaeng–Ratchadaphisek Circle Line	
138	Chatuchak Park– Phrapradaeng	E
140	Victory Monument–Thonburi Estate	E
141	Bang Kradi–Chulalongkorn University	E
142	Wat Lao–Paknam	E
145	Chatuchak Park–Paknam	

Route Number	Line	Remarks
146	Bang Khae–Outer Ring Road Circle Line	
148	Bang Sue Station–Lumphini Park	
149	Bangkok Noi Station–Khlong Toei	
150	Pakkret–Ramkhamhaeng University	
201	Victory Monument–Sanam Luang	
203	Nonthaburi–Sanam Luang	
204	Huai Khwang–Ratchawong Pier	
205	Wat Lao–Khlong Toei	
206	Kasetsart University–Phrakhanong	
207	Ramkhamhaeng University–Ramkhamhaeng University Bang Na Campus	
A1	Happy Land Market–Pakkhlong Talat	
A2	Happy Land Market–Silom	
A3	Rangsit–Phra Pinklao Bridge	
A4	Rangsit–Thonburirom Park	
A5	Pakkret–Wongwian Yai	
A6	Pakkret–Phrapradaeng	
A7	Samrong–Tha Phra	
A8	Paknam–Tha Rat	
A9	Nonthaburi–Bang Khae	
A10	Rangsit–Bang Pakaeo	
A11	Paknam–Phra Pinklao Bridge	E
A12	Phahonyothin Yard–Pakkhlong Talat	
A13	Rangsit–Puchao Samingphrai	E
A14	Ramkhamhaeng University–Victory Monument	
A29	Rangsit–Hua Lamphong	
A39	Thammasat University Rangsit Campus–Sanam Luang	

Route Number	Line	Remarks
A44	Happy Land Market–Tha Tian	
A126	Nonthaburi–Samrong	
A138	Chatuchak Park–Phrapradaeng	E

NOTE: "E" in remarks means expressway bus service and "N" means all-night bus service.
SOURCE: Bangkok Guide 1988.

The Bangkok Elevated Road and Train System Plan, proposed by the Hopewell Corporation in Hong Kong, emerged first. This plan consisted of building a three-layer elevated structure along SRT's existing lines. The first layer was for local road and commercial stores, the second for the existing railway and newly introduced urban railway, and the third for an expressway. The plan also included redeveloping the SRT's lot of 633 *rai* (about one square kilometer) to earn profits from real estate. The plan adopted the BOT method for a thirty-year period, and the total cost of construction was estimated at the immense amount of 80 billion baht. However, it was a convenient plan for the SRT, which would have to do nothing except offer land and would be able to remove all level crossings in Bangkok to reinforce transport capacity, which had been a pending issue for some time. Furthermore, the agency would obtain an annual concession fee of 300 million baht (KT 1997, 35; RFT for 1994, 41).[23]

The Hopewell plan consisted of two trunk lines: one running from north to south and another from east to west, both through inner Bangkok. The 34-kilometer north-south trunk line ran from Rangsit to Phonimit through Hua Lamphong, and the 23-kilometer east-west trunk line ran from Huamak to Taling Chan with an interchange at Yommarat. By adding the 3.3-kilometer branch to Khlong Toei port, the total length of the lines became about 60 kilometers. Among them, the sections between Rangsit and Yommarat, and Yommarat and Huamak, were planned to be constructed first and partially completed in 1994 (SR 1992, 46).

In November 1990, Minister of Communications Montri Hongphanit issued the concession to Hopewell (KT 1997, 35). However, when granted, the concession only consisted of four pages and contained no details (ibid.). Since it adopted the design-and-build method, a detailed survey and design were to be conducted only after receiving the concession.

Fig. 5.3. Bus Network in Bangkok, 1988

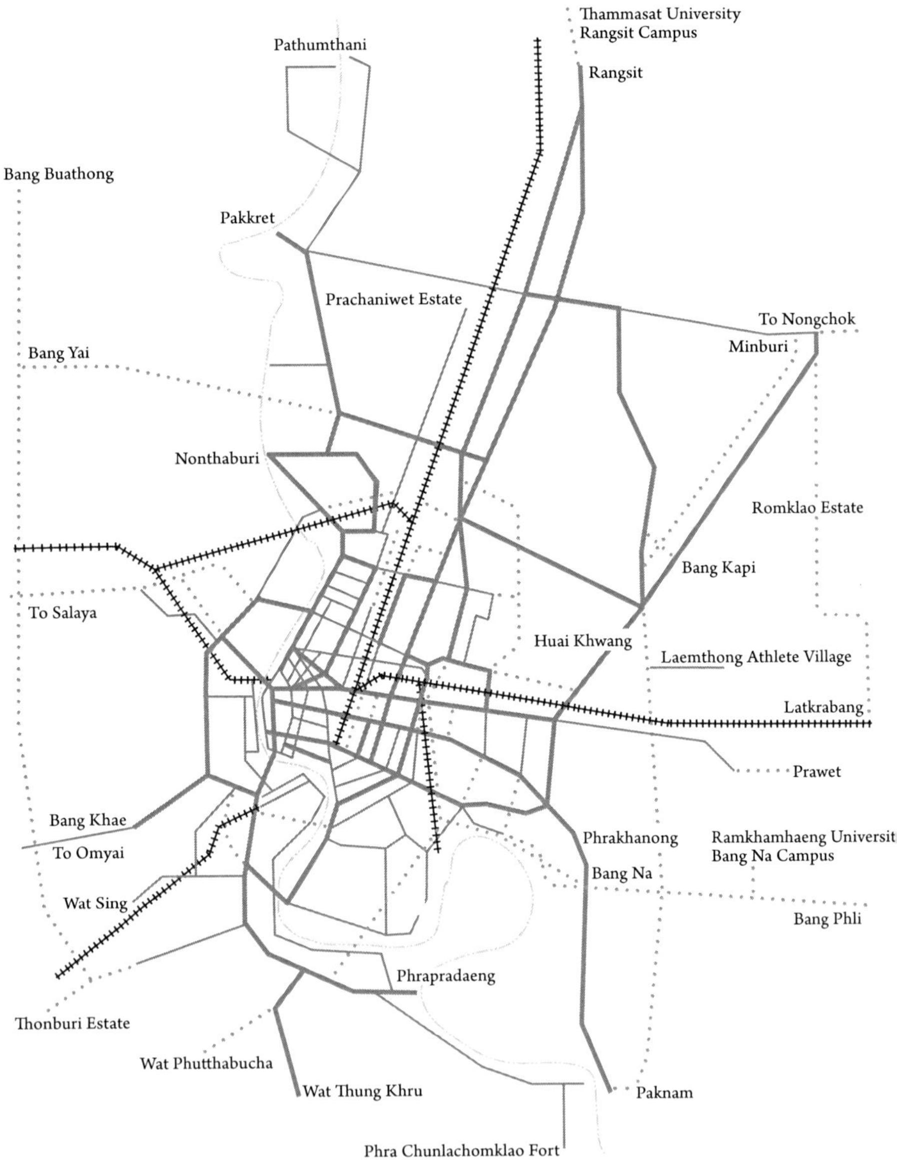

Railways
Bus routes
Bus routes opened after 1977
Air-conditioned bus routes

NOTE: Map excludes bus routes of category four (bus routes within the province).

It was thus quite an ambiguous plan. After adjusting the plan according to the information gathered from other urban railway and expressway plans, it was not until May 1993 that the construction actually started (Samrit n.d., vol. 4, 2756).

Subsequently, the BMA's Elevated Railway Plan surfaced. This plan focused on constructing, under the BMA's jurisdiction, an elevated railway over the road, and was proposed to then BMA governor Chamlong Srimuang as the solution to Bangkok's transport problem. The routes planned at the beginning were the 6-kilometer Sukhumvit line between Phrakhanong and Siam and the 8.5-kilometer Victory Monument line between Surasak and Victory Monument. The total length of the lines was 14.5 kilometers (SR 1992, 42). Unlike the Hopewell plan, these routes lay completely within the city area and assumed the LRT-type rolling stock. The construction method was also the same: the BOT method for a thirty-year period. The estimated construction cost was 17.7 billion baht.

The BMA released the concession conditions in April 1991 and searched for interested private enterprises (*KT* [OE], 23 November 1999). Although a large number of companies showed interest, the Bangkok Mass Transit System Company, Ltd. (BTSC, *Borisat rabop khonsong muanchon krungthep*), a subsidiary of the real estate company Thanayong Company, Ltd., received the concession.[24] In April 1992, BTSC gained the concession from the BMA for construction and operation of the elevated railway (KT 1997, 35). Since this plan also adopted the design-and-build method, details of the line were not decided when the concession was granted. Therefore, it took further time before the construction started.

The ETA plan should be examined here. When the government revoked Lavalin's concession, it decided to abandon the ETA's idea of the construction of an urban railway and establish a new agency that only had jurisdiction over urban railways. This agency was called the Metropolitan Rapid Transit Authority (MRTA, *Ongkan rotfaifa mahanakhon*) and was established in August 1992 (IN 1993, 48). It seems that MRTA was established under the Prime Minister's Office to prevent political intervention in the urban railway plans by releasing it from the strong authority of the Ministry of Interior. Since the BMA was under the jurisdiction of the Ministry of Interior, even though the Ministry of

Fig. 5.4. Urban Railway Network in Bangkok, 2000

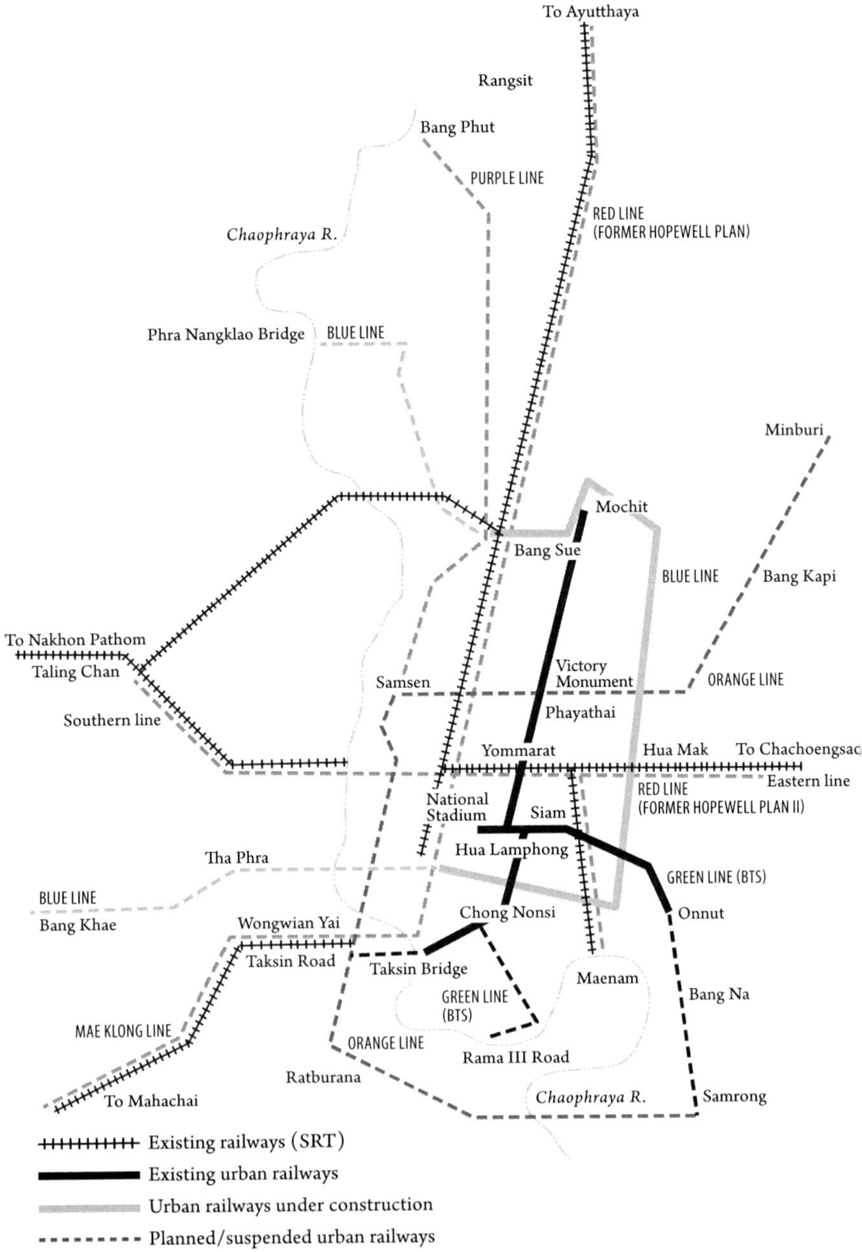

Interior acquired jurisdiction over a new urban railway, it lost authority over the ETA's urban railway plan.

Initially, the MRTA tended to promote an urban railway plan with a 100 percent investment by the government. However, since a part of the 34-kilometer first-stage Part I line overlapped with or became closed off by the new routes being established by Hopewell and BTS, the agency was forced to change the route. Subsequently, the 20-kilometer route from Hua Lamphong to Bang Sue was chosen as the first-stage line of the MRTA, as shown in figure 5.4. This new route was understood to have connected two former lines: part of the Phrakhanong line and part of the Sathon line.

However, after Chuan Leekpai's first government was inaugurated in September 1992, then Deputy Prime Minister Amnuai Wirawan re-proposed the involvement of the private sector. In January 1993, the government established a committee headed by Amnuai to consider how to involve the private sector in the urban railway plan (IN 1993, 48). This was the same situation as in 1980, when the ETA began to consider involving the private sector. Although the Lavalin plan failed, the government once again hoped to leave the MRTA plan to the private sector without providing financial support because the two BOT plans, the Hopewell and BTS, were progressing with 100 percent private investment.

After reexamination, the agency decided to construct the first-stage line of the MRTA using the BOT method. Muang Thong Mass Transit Company, Ltd., a subsidiary of the real estate firm Bangkok Land Company, Ltd., gained the concession in February 1994 (RFM for 1994, 14–15). In addition, although about a 600-meter-long section near Hua Lamphong was to be an underground line, the company accepted this condition (IN 1993, 49). Compared to the case of Lavalin, the time taken to determine the plans, methods, and finance was considerably shortened, and it seemed that the MRTA's urban railway construction would be swiftly up and running.

Impact of Placing Lines Underground

After the concessions of the MRTA urban railway plan were approved, all three urban railway plans in Bangkok were to be built using the BOT method. The Hopewell plan finally began construction in May

1993. Although the BTS and MRTA were also to start construction work immediately, citizen opposition to the depot construction and fears that the elevated structures might have a harmful environmental impact obliged the agencies to change their plans.

In July 1993, an environmental community development organization, "Magic Eye" (*Ta wiset*), headed by Chotchoi Sophonphanit, revealed that BTS's depot would be constructed on a part of Lumphini Park (Bello et al. 1998, 101–2).[25] In general, the details of an urban railway plan were not exhibited until the beginning of its construction, and hence the public did not know that the park would be used for the depot. Lumphini Park is constructed on land presented by King Rama VII at the beginning of the twentieth century to commemorate the birth of the Buddha and is the largest park in Bangkok. The BTS track was scheduled to pass through the park's west side and to use a part of the west side as a depot.[26]

Public opinion was against this idea, and anti-depot meetings were held at Lumphini Park. Although Chamlong, the former BMT governor and a founder of the BTS plan, attended the July 22 meeting and tried to resolve the issue, the plan failed (McCargo 1997, 285). The BTSC and BMA abandoned the idea of using Lumphini Park and looked for new land. However, a suitable alternative lot was not found along the routes because they would need to pass through the city. One month later, the plan surfaced to use the Northern Bus Terminal at Mochit, located about five kilometers north of the original terminus at Victory Monument.

This land, however, was owned by the Treasury Department (*Krom thanarak*), which planned to redevelop it for its effective use using private sector companies. In 1996, although the department agreed to lease the land to the BTSC, it permitted the redevelopment of all the lots including the depot by Sun Estate Company, Ltd. A confrontation between BTSC and Sun Estate over the position of the depot took a long time to settle (*BPYEER* 1996).[27] In the end, the construction according to the BTS plan started in March 1994 after Mochit was finalized as the site of the depot (Samrit n.d., vol. 2, 783–84).

Chotchoi demanded that all planned elevated railways be sited underground instead. On October 21, 1993, she published an advertisement in all the major newspapers asking citizens to request the change of elevated railway plans into underground ones. She requested the laying underground of the MRTA's first-stage line, for which no concession had yet been granted (Chotchoi et al. 1995, 6). Along with academic experts and intellectuals, she asked the government and the BMA for an official announcement of the details of the elevated railway plans and for a public hearing.[28] Since a flyover had already been constructed on Rama IV Road and the BTS's elevated track would cross above it on the southwestern corner of Lumphini Park, the planned MRTA track had to cross over the BTS. This meant that three elevated structures had to cross each other at a single point. Therefore, citizens responding to Chotchoi's announcement requested that the section of the Rama IV Road on MRTA's line should be placed underground to avoid the deterioration of the environment surrounding the park (SWPT 1994, 7–8).

Although the concession for the MRTA's first-stage line was granted to Muang Thong in February 1994 on the basis of the original plan for elevated tracks, the OCMLT in April 1994 altered these plans to include the placing underground of urban railways within 25 square kilometers of the center of Bangkok; this was accepted by the government (Unger 1998, 161). With this decision to place railways underground, a half of MRTA's line, including the section in front of the park, would have to go underground, and Hopewell and BTS would also face the need to place some lines underground, even though construction had already begun. Since some sections were within this 25-square-kilometer area, both plans had to be partially altered for placement of lines underground. This would require the plans to be redesigned, resulting in an unavoidable rise in construction costs and delays in completion. In addition, since both companies had already gained their concessions before the requirement to place lines underground and both had started construction, they hinted at their inclination to sue the government for these additional costs (ibid.). In the end, the government approved the construction of the elevated tracks as originally planned, and it also allowed continuation of the BTS's construction work that had been suspended during August of that year (Chotchoi et al. 1995, 8).

As for the MRTA, although Muang Thong consented to placing half of the line underground, it asked the government for compensation for the increased expenses incurred by the change (KT 1997, 35). Unless this issue was settled, construction of the MRTA line would be even further postponed. Therefore, in May 1995, the government revoked the concession for Muang Thong and decided to construct the line itself (Samrit n.d., vol. 4, 3132). Since cabinet members expressed a desire for laying the whole line underground, the government decided to do just that in September of the same year (*BPWR*, 22 September 1995).The government established a two-tiered system in which it would perform the civil engineering work and the private sector would provide the supplies and operate the trains using the BOT method (RFM 1998, 2). With this system, the government would fund about 80 percent of the whole endeavor, and the private burden would became much less than in the conventional BOT method based on 100 percent private investment.

A loan from the Overseas Economic Cooperation Fund of Japan (OECF, presently the Japan International Cooperation Agency, or JICA) would cover 60 percent of the entire expenditures the MRTA had to bear. The concession term was fixed at twenty-five years (ibid, 4). Bids for the civil engineering work were invited, and the construction work started in December 1996 (RFM for 1996, 15). The Skytrain plan, which had restarted twice without any progress, once under Lavalin and once under Muang Thong, finally began to be actualized with these plans for an underground system.[29]

In addition to delays and changes in plans, the urban railway faced opposition from many parties. In March 1995, Chotchoi and others sued the BMA and its governor for the release of the details of the BTS plan and the measures taken to protect the environment (Chotchoi et.al. 1995, 12).[30] In the following year, both BTSC and MRTA confronted opposition from residents (*BPYEER* 1996). The BTSC faced opposition from the teachers and parents of the Mater Dei School on Phloenchit Road, who argued that the construction of the Chitlom station in front of the school would damage the school's environment. The MRTA was opposed by the Dusit Thani Hotel on Rama IV Road, which claimed that the construction work of the Silom station would interfere with its business.[31] Nevertheless, the urban railway plans began to look quite solid, as construction on all three plans had already begun.

From Economic Crisis to the Opening of the BTS

The transfer to a floating exchange rate system for the Thai baht in July 1997 and the consequent currency and economic crisis in Thailand influenced the urban railway plans, which until then had shown progress. The government had to control its fiscal expenditure according to the advice of the International Monetary Fund (IMF), and private enterprises were also affected by the deterioration of capital procurement and the expansion of debt by the weakened baht. Moreover, when the construction costs of the urban railways, which depended on imports, soared under the influence of the weakened baht, the amount of investment initially exceeded the amount anticipated.

The most affected was the Hopewell plan. This plan took three years after the grant of concession until construction began, and the subsequent progress was extremely slow. Since the groundbreaking had been late, the planned completion date was naturally impossible to meet. The government decided that the section between Rangsit and Huamak via Yommarat, the first section of the plan, should be completed by December 1998 (*N* [OE], 26 March 1997). This was the time when the Thirteenth Asian Games were to be held in Bangkok. The government hoped to utilize the line as the means of passenger transport for the Asian Games.

Difficulty in obtaining financing was the most serious cause of the delay in the Hopewell plan. Apart from the large amount of 80 billion baht that was needed, profit from the development of the SRT's land shrunk following the collapse of the economy. Nevertheless, to eliminate distrust, the company signed a contract to purchase 172 EMUs from Germany and Britain in October 1996, and exhibited one sample car in front of the Hua Lamphong station (RFT for 1996, 39).

However, after July 1997 when the currency crisis occurred, all construction work was interrupted. Of the whole plan, only about 14 or 19 percent for the first section had progressed. This first section should have been completed within the remaining year and a half of the deadline (RFT for 1997, 35). Therefore, the government opted to revoke the concession on September 30. Seven years after the concession was granted, the plan reached a deadlock. The construction of a local road proceeded before the opening of the Asian Games. However, the argument about how to utilize the ruins of the Hopewell plan continued.[32]

The MRTA was similarly affected. In September 1994, the government approved the Mass Transit Master Plan, upon which the OCMLT relied. In this plan, two lines were proposed under MRTA's jurisdiction: the Blue line containing the first-stage line and its extension (Hua

Lamphong–Bang Khae section and Bang Sue–Phra Nangklao Bridge section), and the Orange line between Minburi and Samrong (see figure 5.4) (RFM for 1996, 27).[33] Among them, in April 1995 the government approved the MRTA to proceed with the construction of two sections: the extension of the Blue line and the first stage of the Orange line (Bang Kapi–Ratburana section) (RFM 1998, 11). According to the master plan, both sections were to be constructed by 2001.

Since a total of 200 billion baht was needed to proceed with these plans, both lines became the target of budget freezing after the reduction of fiscal expenditures became indispensable to resolve the economic crisis. The NESDB released the frozen funds for the transport development plans in October 1997, which included funds for three new sections of the MRTA (*N*, 10 October 1997). Therefore, the MRTA delayed the opening schedule for these three sections, originally set for 2003–5: to 2006–10 for the western extension of the Blue line, to 2012 for the northern extension, and to 2015–17 for the first stage of the Orange line (RFM for 1999–2000, 23).

Work on sections under construction also faced potential discontinuation. The NESDB advised the MRTA to suspend construction in early 1998. Deputy Prime Minister Phichai Rattakun negotiated with the OECF to ease loan conditions, resulting in an interest rate decrease to 0.75 percent per annum and an extension of the return period from twenty-five to forty years (*BPYEER* 1998). In addition to the 35 billion baht loan it acquired at the beginning of the project, the MRTA tried to borrow an additional 20 billion from the OECF because domestic procurement had become more difficult. Although the government first asked to reduce the amount requested by 8 billion baht, the MRTA obtained the additional loan of 20 billion baht in September 1999 (*BPYEER* 1999). The opening schedule of the southern section was delayed by one year owing to the problem of the Dusit Thani Hotel, as mentioned previously. However, it became feasible that the northern section would be opened by the end of 2002, and the whole section would be completed by the middle of 2003.[34]

It was the BTS plan that was least affected by the economic crisis. Following the devaluation of the baht, the total cost increased from 43,500 million to 55,200 million baht; additionally, the BTS was forced to postpone the first public stock offering, which had been planned for

1997 (*BPYEER* 1998). Nevertheless, the company steadily progressed on construction by using a new loan. Although the opening schedule was delayed by three years, it was finally decided to open the system on December 5, 1999, the king's birthday. The BTS plan was not much affected by the economic crisis because: (1) the loans had been secured before the crisis; (2) about 60 percent of the loans were baht loans, which were not influenced by the devaluation; and (3) it succeeded in acquiring a loan from the United Nation's International Finance Corporation (IFC) (*N* [OE], 1 March 1999).

The construction of the BTS proceeded smoothly, and the train test runs started in October 1998 (*N* [OE], 23 October 1998). The final obstacles were the problem of fare amounts and stock sale. The original concession in 1992 provided for a flat fare of fifteen baht, but at the time of opening, a fare hike was permitted according to the price increase (*KT* [OE], 23 November 1999). Then, although a flat fare of twenty-four baht was seemingly accepted when it was decided to extend the route, the company asked the BMA to raise it to thirty baht in 1997. Furthermore, it was announced at the end of April 1999, half a year before the opening, that a sectional fare system would be adopted, ranging from ten to sixty baht according to distance (*N* [OE], 29 April 1999).

Opposition then arose from the Metropolitan Assembly, which argued that the fare would be too high and requested reinstatement of the flat fare of fifteen baht [*BP* [OE], 1 May 1999). The company insisted that the sectional fare system would be convenient for short-distance users because a flat fare would need to be as high as thirty baht. Although the BMA governor had the authority to decide, the conclusion was not easily reached because of the assembly's opposition. Finally, the company's claim was accepted after a judgment was sought from the Supreme Prosecutor's Office (*KT* [OE], 20 October 1999). One month before opening, the sectional fare system was established, charging between ten and forty baht. It should be noted that during the dispute over the fare, criticism arose that the concession given to the BTSC was deficient and disadvantageous to the BMA (*KT* [OE], 23 November 1999).

The problem of stock sales was that Thanayong would lose management rights over the BTSC. It could possibly fail to maintain its majority holding, which would violate a condition of the concession that a Thai company had to possess the majority of stock. The BTSC mainly used the loan from Siam Commercial Bank and its own stock as security. But, since Thanayong's payment was overdue, the bank transferred the stocks in security to cover the bad debt. The bank that inherited them auctioned 265 million shares of those stocks in November 1997, which were awarded to Credit Suisse-First Boston (CSFB) of Hong Kong (*KT* [OE], 6 November 1999). By accepting the stock transfer in this auction, Thanayong's share would fall from 51 percent to 28 percent.

CSFB independently held 250 million shares of BTSC stock and decided to auction them on December 7, immediately after the BTS's opening. Because the BTSC's management rights would be acquired by the CSFB, Thanayong insisted in court that the transfer was invalid. The company also tried to procure enough capital to buy back the stocks before the auction, and finally succeeded in doing so just four days before the opening (*N* [OE], 2 December 1999). Thanayong thereby maintained the majority of stock, including those auctioned in November, the sale of which had not yet been approved for transfer. The conditions to open the railway line were thus finally fixed.

Bangkok's first urban railway finally began operating on December 5, 1999. It is claimed that the BTS was not only the first urban railway in Bangkok but also the first in the world that was completed with 100 percent private investment (*TSK* [OE], 5–8 December 1999). The number of users immediately after the opening was only about 150,000–200,000, far less than the target of 600,000 persons per day. This was because the route was restricted within the city area, and the development of park-and-ride facilities or feeder bus services were delayed. However, the BTS had supplied a new means of transport in Bangkok, which had previously been heavily dependent on road transport.[35]

Struggle to Increase the Efficiency of Bus Operations

Promotion of Privatization

The BMTA was forced to accept loss-making operations after its establishment, and the amount of deficit continued to increase every year until the middle of the 1980s, despite various measures to curb those losses. Therefore, the government decided to expand privatization of bus operations to control the agency's deficit.

As described previously, privatization began immediately after the BMTA's establishment. However, the transfer of bus operations from the BMTA to the private sector only began to be seriously considered in the 1980s. Samak Sundaravej, the minister of communications in the Prem government, suggested privatizing bus operations as a means of solving the BMTA's deficit problem. The Land Transport Problem-Solving Committee (*Khana kammakan kaekhai panha khonsong thang bok*), which Samak established, proposed that private buses should gather at one of the BMTA's eleven Bus Operation Divisions (*Khet doen rot*) and at the Twelfth Bus Operation Division newly established in 1984 (*SRSW*, 4 December 1983).[36] Since the BMTA's labor union and the NESDB opposed this plan, privatization of the existing divisions never took place (*SRSW*, 29 January 1984). However, the Twelfth Division was built and entrusted to operations by a private sector company, the Bangkok Transport Company, Ltd. (*Borisat krungthep mahanakhon khonsong chamkat*).

Privatization advanced in two ways: the transfer of existing routes and the establishment of new routes. For example, in fiscal year 1988, seven routes were transferred from the BMTA's direct operation to private operation, and all four of the newly established routes were entrusted to private operators (KSMK for 1988, 35). By promoting privatization, it was possible for the BMTA not only to obtain commissions (*kha phonprayot*) from private contractors, but also to save on operational costs. For example, from the seven routes transferred to private operators, the BMTA anticipated earning 30.66 million baht in commissions over four years, and the privatization brought a total of 81 million baht to the BMTA, including 50.4 million for disposal of 168 buses, and 84,000 baht in bus registration fees (ibid.). Through these savings, the BMTA could eliminate the deficit it had generated through bus operations and was able to secure new income, such as commissions for privatization. The decrease in the deficit during the latter half of the 1980s was the result of privatization, which brought about a decrease in expenditures and an increase in revenues.

However, these commissions, which could be said to be "a tiger lying down and eating," were also the target of criticism from private operators. When the BMTA raised the commission for minibuses from 40 baht to 140–190 baht per day and charged 10 percent of fare incomes in April 1989, minibus operators protested (*SRSW*, 22 April 1989). The commission came to be seen as a form of pressure on private operators, and hence the BMTA had to postpone the fare hike by reducing commissions whenever private buses requested an increase in the fare. Thus, the easy income source of commissions had not radically improved BMTA's loss-making operations.

The number of private buses steadily increased. Table 5.5 shows the changes in the number of buses under the BMTA's jurisdiction. The highest number of BMTA buses was in 1991 when the agency operated 5,287 buses, but that number gradually decreased. On the other hand, the number of private buses more than doubled from 974 in 1986 to 2,467 in 2000. The increase had two peaks: one during the latter half of the 1980s and another at the end of the 1990s. In addition, the number of minibuses converted from *songthaeo* decreased by half of their highest number in 2000 to about 1,100. *Songthaeo* in category four routes also gradually decreased.

Table 5.5. Number of Buses in Bangkok, 1986–2000

Fiscal Year	BMTA Buses			Private Buses			Minibuses	Songthaeo	Total
	Ordinary	Air-conditioned	Total	Ordinary	Air-conditioned	Total			
1986	3,765	218	3,983	734	240	974	N.A.	N.A.	4,957
1988	3,990	444	4,434	1,093	239	1,332	2,151	3,514	11,431
1990	4,368	464	4,832	1,313	239	1,552	2,113	2,701	11,198
1991	4,831	456	5,287	1,326	249	1,575	2,056	2,414	11,332
1992	3,939	486	4,425	1,460	269	1,729	2,043	2,603	10,800
1993	3,925	900	4,825	1,460	269	1,729	2,016	2,551	11,121
1994	3,914	922	4,836	1,471	269	1,740	1,838	2,516	10,930
1995	3,588	1,164	4,752	1,474	319	1,793	1,770	2,497	10,812
1996	3,460	1,164	4,624	1,474	349	1,823	1,703	2,454	10,604
1997	3,041	1,194	4,235	1,506	359	1,865	1,622	2,448	10,170
1998	2,563	1,535	4,098	1,537	436	1,973	1,518	2,376	9,965
1999	2,279	1,988	4,267	1,655	535	2,190	1,390	2,202	10,049
2000	1,808	1,988	3,796	1,864	603	2,467	1,117	2,239	9,619

Note 1: Figures are from the end of the fiscal year (end of September).
Note 2: Figures exclude microbuses.
Sources: KSMK for 1986–2000 (selected years).

Table 5.6 shows the expansion of the number of routes operated by private buses. Although in 1986 the numbers of BMTA-operated routes and privately operated routes were 121 and 28 respectively, resulting in a ratio of about 4:1, the ratio in 2000 became 3:2. The increase in the number of private bus routes is also remarkable during the latter half of the 1980s and the end of the 1990s. Judging from the changes in the number of BMTA-operated routes, the privatization of newly established routes was common during the latter half of the 1980s and the transfer of existing routes to private operators during the end of the 1990s. As for the latter, the phenomenon corresponded to the BMTA's downsizing plan, as will be discussed later.

Table 5.6. Number of Bus Routes in Bangkok, 1986–2000

Fiscal Year	BMTA Buses			Private Buses			Minibuses	Songthaeo	Total
	Ordinary	Air-conditioned	Total	Ordinary	Air-conditioned	Total			
1986	111	10	121	21	7	28	N.A.	N.A.	149
1988	112	11	123	29	8	37	N.A.	N.A.	160
1990	109	11	120	35	8	43	58	174	395
1991	111	11	122	46	10	56	71	128	377
1992	109	9	118	37	8	45	58	123	344
1993	109	25	134	37	8	45	57	124	360
1994	109	26	135	37	8	45	59	118	357
1995	121	30	151	37	11	48	59	116	374
1996	122	33	155	37	12	49	58	111	373
1997	114	23	137	36	8	44	58	113	352
1998	N.A.	N.A.	139	N.A.	N.A.	44	N.A.	N.A.	183
1999	N.A.	N.A.	130	N.A.	N.A.	60	N.A.	N.A.	190
2000	N.A.	N.A.	113	N.A.	N.A.	76	N.A.	N.A.	189

NOTE 1: Figures are from the end of the fiscal year (end of September).
NOTE 2: Figures exclude microbuses.
SOURCES: Same as table 5.5.

Although privatization was important to eliminate the BMTA's loss-making operations, it had a negative impact on users. Because private operators tended to use old BMTA buses, the condition of private buses was worse than those under public operation. Moreover, incomes of private operators' employees were also lower than those of BMTA employees. In addition, the attitude and behavior of the private bus employees were also inferior to those of the BMTA bus employees. According to an investigation the BMTA conducted in 1999, user satisfaction with BMTA buses was higher than with private buses (KSMK for 1999, 27–28). Therefore, the more the BMTA expanded privatization, the more user dissatisfaction toward the BMTA grew. The BMTA needed to identify how to maintain a high service level while promoting privatization to eliminate its debt.

Emergence of Microbus and Van Services

Privatization to help correct the BMTA's loss-making operations strengthened in the latter half of the 1980s. In 1991, the cabinet decided that the number of BMTA buses should be limited to a maximum of four thousand and the share of private buses should be increased (KSMK for 1996, 39). Thereafter, the BMTA tried to provide new bus services by working with the private sector. This resulted in the microbus plan, which surfaced in 1991.

The plan was to operate small, air-conditioned buses in the business district by a cooperative investment with the private sector. A new company with a capital of 200 million baht would be established by the BMTA, with 20 percent of its stock held by the BMTA and 70 percent by the private sector. Around 350 to 400 air-conditioned microbuses would operate on ten routes throughout Bangkok (Somsi 1992, 9–10). The buses would have less than twenty seats, would allow no standing passengers, and would be aimed at higher-level passengers than those who typically rode conventional buses. The private company would distribute 5 percent of its income, or at least 20 million baht, to the BMTA during the concession term of ten years, in addition to paying a commission. These bus routes were to be separate from the conventional bus routes, and the buses were to be called "special air-conditioned buses (*rot doisan prap akat chanit phiset*)."[37]

Three companies were candidates for this plan. Eventually, the Bangkok Microbus Company, Ltd. (*Borisat bangkok microbus chamkat*) was founded under joint management with the Bangkok Motor Equipment Company, Ltd. (*Borisat bangkok motor equipment chamkat*), which began operations in April 1993 (KSMK for 1993, 25). Although it initially consisted of only one route, by 1997 this had been extended to a total of thirty-five routes, and the number of buses increased to 1,200 (KSMK for 1997, 57). The routes ran mainly to and from the suburbs via the city center; middle-class passengers who used to commute by private car were the main customers. Moreover, except for *songthaeo*, these were the first buses being operated by one person: there was no conductor to collect fares, but rather a fare box was placed beside the driver. Although the fare was fixed at a flat rate of twenty baht, which was higher than the conventional air-conditioned bus fare, since all passengers could sit, the operator's reputation was high, resulting in an increase in users.

However, vans appeared as a new means of public transport, and were used to transport microbus passengers. This was a kind of omnibus taxi that used a light van and could transport a maximum of fourteen passengers. They normally ran on routes between the city and suburbs, where bus service had become inconvenient since the middle of the 1990s. This service gradually gained favor. However, these vans were also illegal buses and operated the same way as did the illegal *songthaeo*: the brokers bribed the police to allow them to operate. The vans were fully air-conditioned and usually provided non-stop service with no standing allowed.[38] Therefore, since they were able to reduce the time distance and were as comfortable as microbuses, many microbus customers shifted to vans.

The appearance of these new illegal buses forced the BMTA to take action to regulate them. In 1997, the BMTA had agreed with the BMA to establish the van operation association, and it now changed the plan to unify the van operators so that they, too, would operate under the BMTA (KSMK for 1997, 30). The vans would be legalized by putting them under the jurisdiction of the BMTA; this was also true for the illegal *songthaeo*. The BMTA investigated the situation of van operation and registered 3,605 vans, which, by the beginning of the 1999 fiscal year, were operating on 90 routes (KSMK for 1999, 26). Following this, a total of 120 new van routes were specified from 1999 to 2000, and van operation under the jurisdiction of the BMTA began in 2000.[39] There were 5,337 legalized vans in fiscal year 2001; vans had quickly become the new means of transport for Bangkokians.

At the same time, the microbuses, which lost their customers to the vans, were pressed for changes in their management. The company operated at a loss until 1996, and although a chance of moving into the black arose during the first half of 1997, their financial condition worsened owing to the currency crisis (*BPYEER* 1997). The reduction in users was remarkable: only sixteen of the thirty-eight routes in the concessions were in operation by January 1998 (*N* [OE], 31 January 1998). The opening of the BTS at the end of 1999 also had an adverse affect on the microbus company by forcing it to either allow standing passengers for a reduced fare or to contract with the BTSC for feeder bus operations using its surplus buses (*BP* [OE], 22 July 2001].[40] Both the microbuses and vans focused on the demands of commuting and traveling to schools coming from the middle class by using small, air-conditioned vehicles. However, it was ironic that the formally approved microbuses were overwhelmed by the informal vans as a form of para-transit. The number of users of conventional large buses gradually decreased because of the emergence of this new bus service.

Table 5.7. Number of Daily Bus Passengers, 1990–2000

Fiscal Year	BMTA Buses			Private Buses			Total		
	Ordinary	Air-conditioned	Total	Ordinary	Air-conditioned	Total	Ordinary	Air-conditioned	Total
1990	3,735,058	209,283	3,944,341	1,122,741	107,799	1,230,539	4,857,799	317,082	5,174,880
1991	3,847,064	207,220	4,054,284	1,055,932	113,153	1,169,085	4,902,996	320,373	5,223,369
1992	3,820,278	253,605	4,073,883	1,415,995	140,370	1,556,365	5,236,273	393,975	5,630,248
1993	3,360,663	426,440	3,787,103	1,250,081	127,458	1,377,539	4,610,744	553,898	5,164,642
1994	3,022,395	483,860	3,506,255	1,135,908	141,170	1,277,077	4,158,303	625,030	4,783,332
1995	2,831,131	548,453	3,379,584	1,163,068	150,306	1,313,374	3,994,199	698,759	4,692,958
1996	2,743,496	581,856	3,325,352	1,168,761	174,457	1,343,218	3,912,257	756,313	4,668,570
1997	2,664,412	688,142	3,352,554	1,319,502	206,904	1,526,405	3,983,914	895,046	4,878,959
1998	2,366,444	814,182	3,180,626	1,419,128	231,260	1,650,387	3,785,572	1,045,442	4,831,013
1999	1,805,892	1,123,083	2,928,975	1,311,431	302,238	1,613,669	3,117,323	1,425,321	4,542,644
2000	1,596,357	1,215,083	2,811,440	1,645,802	368,559	2,014,361	3,242,159	1,583,642	4,825,801

NOTE: The number of private bus users is estimated by using the ratio of BMTA buses to private buses.
SOURCES: KSMK for 1993; *SC* for 2010.

Table 5.7 shows the average number of daily users of BMTA buses and private buses. Since statistics for the number of users on private buses are unobtainable, the number allocated to them was estimated using the ratio of BMTA buses to private buses on the basis of the number of users of BMTA buses. The table shows that the total number of users gradually decreased but peaked at 5,630,000 in fiscal year 1992. The reduction of BMTA bus users is particularly remarkable; this number decreased from 4,070,000 in 1992 to 2,810,000 in 2000. With the influence of urban railways, the number of bus users decreased even further after 2000.

BMTA's Downsizing Plan

Although the BMTA finally stopped operating at a loss in 1992, it went into the red once again the following year (see table 5.2). The deficit reached its largest amount at 1,800 million baht in 1995. Therefore, the necessity for improving operations again impressed itself on the BMTA. The government would have to push for the transfer and downsizing of the agency.

Transfer of the BMTA to the BMA had already been considered since the 1980s. The talk of transfer to the BMA surfaced for the first time in 1981 under the Prem government, immediately after the fare hike controversy in March. Prime Minister Prem requested the transfer of the BMTA to Chaowarat Sutlapha, the BMA governor, because stopping BMTA's losses after the fare hike became difficult (*SRSW*, 22 March 1981). However, since BMTA employees, fearing mistreatment, opposed the plan and because the BMA's financial situation was not healthy enough to support BMTA's deficit, this transfer never occurred. In 1983, Samak, the then minister of communications, again proposed the transfer plan idea, but no action was taken on the proposal (*SRSW*, 29 May 1983).

Then, in 1991, it was accepted that the problem could be managed by expanding privatization, as mentioned above, and the Anan government considered radical dissolution measures to handle the BMTA's deficit. The government made the following decisions in May 1991: the payment of 1,796 million baht, which the BMTA borrowed from the Ministry of Finance, would be exempted; the Ministry of Finance would repay any unpaid fuel costs and the interest of 2,763 million baht to the Petroleum Authority of Thailand (*Kan pitroliam haeng prathet thai*); and the government would assist with paying fuel costs by providing

6.1 million baht per month (Somsi 1992, 3–4).[41] Through these measures, payment of the interest accompanying the unpaid debt of the BMTA was eliminated, and the first operating profit occurred in fiscal year 1992 (see table 5.2). However, since this assistance ended in June 1992, the BMTA again fell into deficit after fiscal year 1993.[42]

Therefore, the plan to transfer the BMTA to the BMA resurfaced in the latter half of the 1990s. The transfer was approved at then Prime Minister Banharn Silapa-acha's cabinet meeting in February 1996 (KSMK 1998a, 1). The following Chavalit Yongchaiyut government consented to the restructuring plan of the government corporation, which the NESDB had proposed at the cabinet meeting in April 1997 (KSMK 1998b, 1). Furthermore, it was suggested that the BMTA should be transferred to the BMA urgently since its services could be managed by a private sector company and the government had to reduce its role in the agency's operations. Phichit Rattakun, the governor of the BMA, welcomed the transfer, but asked for the eradication of BMTA's accumulated debt and an exemption from taxes on fuel and vehicle parts as preconditions (*N*, 14 March 1997).

However, it was difficult to simply cancel the cumulative deficit of 20 billion baht; the transfer to the BMA did not progress smoothly. Therefore, at the cabinet meeting in February 1998, the government ordered the BMTA to make short- and long-term plans for downsizing and for increasing the private sector's role rather than accepting the loan of 1,665 million baht for unpaid bus repair charges (KSMK 1998b, 1–2).[43] Moreover, the Budget Department (*Krom banchi klang*) asked the BMTA to formulate a plan within the month to reduce the ratio of BMTA buses to private buses to 2:8 over a five-year period (KSMK 1998a, 1). The BMTA formulated both plans and submitted them to the government. In addition, it was decided that a reexamination of the cabinet decision opting for the transfer to the BMA was possible, depending on the contents of the restructuring plans. After this, the transfer plan to the BMA was temporarily put on hold.

As for the downsizing plan, to achieve the reduced ratios requested by the cabinet, BMTA buses were to be reduced to 20 percent before 2002, and private operation buses to be increased, instead of scrapping BMTA's old buses. The BMTA established a maximum lifespan of ten years for buses, and in 1991 and 1992 purchased a total of 2,840 vehicles

(2,040 ordinary and 800 air-conditioned buses) to replace its old buses (KSMK for 1992, 6). Therefore, since these buses would have to be taken out of service in 2001–2, the BMTA planned to supply 860 ordinary buses, with the remainder to be supplied by private companies (KSMK 1998a, 5). As table 5.5 shows, the number of BMTA buses in 1998 was about 4,000, and their ratio to the total number of buses under BMTA's jurisdiction, including minibuses and *songthaeo*, was about 40 percent. When 2,840 buses were taken out of service and 860 were added, the number of ordinary BMTA buses became about 2,000, making the ratio exactly 20 percent.

The plan for increasing private companies' role in public transportation included an increase in the ratio of private buses and the lease of public BMTA buses. Although the lease of 1,640 buses was approved for the first time in 1980, the procurement of buses was changed to purchases instead of leases, after expensive leases had become a problem. However, the increase of leased buses was reconsidered in order to encourage the role of private companies: the BMTA planned to lease 797 air-conditioned buses to replace 895 old buses, which would reach their ten years of use in 1997 or 1998, and to lease 860 ordinary buses, as mentioned previously (KSMK 1998b, 34). Maintenance of these leased buses was also privatized, and fare boxes were to be leased from the private sector to be installed on 797 air-conditioned buses. When the number of public BMTA buses decreased to 2,000 by the end of 2002, more than 60 percent of them were set to become leased buses.

These plans were carried out one by one. As mentioned previously, the remarkable reduction in the number of BMTA buses and their routes in the latter half of the 1990s and the rapid increase in the number of private buses were the result of these two plans. The introduction of 797 air-conditioned buses by lease was also completed by 1999. Since these air-conditioned buses were substitutes for ordinary buses, the number of directly operated, ordinary buses began to significantly decrease after this, and air-conditioned buses began operating on ordinary bus routes. However, fare boxes, which were tentatively installed in 1997 in eighty ordinary and thirty air-conditioned buses, were eliminated in 1999 because of poor results (KSMK for 1999, 47). The planned lease of 860 ordinary buses never occurred. Ordinary red buses that were introduced early in the 1990s had to be used for longer than ten years, therefore.

The transfer plan to the BMA would emerge again under the following Thaksin government.

Stagnation of Urban Transport

Although the three decades from the 1970s to the 1990s were a time in which plans surfaced for urban railways to become the new means of urban transport and in which bus operations were integrated, the urban railway plans were largely delayed and the situation of bus operations remained poor.

The delay in urban railway construction was caused by three factors: the duplication of plans, frequent changes in policy, and immense construction costs.

Duplication of Urban Railway Plans

In many cases, the agencies did not consider the duplication or coordination of plans in the process of drawing urban railway or expressway plans. As a result, it became a situation of "first come, first served," and a latecomer was forced to change its plans. This problem was caused by the lack of a coordinating system that would adjust the plans of each agency. To address this problem the OCMLT was established in 1992.

For example, in the 1970s, the West German investigation and report identified three routes for the first stage of the MTS, parts of which were to be constructed in the SRT's right-of-way. About half of the Memorial Bridge line overlapped with the SRT's Eastern line. However, while the ETA's plans progressed slowly, the Hopewell plan surfaced. Since the plan included the construction of urban railways that were parallel to existing SRT lines, a section that overlapped with the ETA's urban railways appeared. The first-stage lines of the ETA, which had been overtaken by the Hopewell plan, required route adjustments in the MRTA plan: the Orange line, the successor to the Memorial Bridge line, shifted to the north in the section overlapping the Eastern line, and the Blue line changed its route in the section overlapping the SRT's Maenam freight line.

The BTS plan was also similarly affected. The ETA's first-stage Part I line was the northern half of the Sathon line and the whole Phrakhanong line from the West German study. However, since the BTS plan included the route to Phrakhanong via Sukhumvit Road, the eastern half of the Phrakhanong line was omitted after being succeeded by the MRTA. The southern half of the Sathon line was also suspended because of its proximity to the BTS Silom line. In the end, the Blue line route between Hua Lamphong and Bang Sue was formed by combining the central section of the Phrakhanong line and the northern part of the Sathon line.[44] With the principle of "first come, first served," the ETA/MRTA's plan with its longest history and slow progress was obliged to conduct multiple route changes, resulting in further delay.

Duplication was also seen in the Hopewell expressway plan. For example, the expressway ran completely parallel to the Don Mueang Tollway, which was under the jurisdiction of the Department of Highways, and the eight-kilometer section between Bang Sue and Hua Lamphong was close to the north-south route of the ETA's second-stage expressway plan. Since both plans had already emerged when the concession was given to Hopewell, the duplication could have been avoided.[45] The Hopewell plan was the latecomer in terms of expressway plans. Therefore, the revision of the former Hopewell plan excluded the expressways and only included the SRT's urban railways and existing elevated lines (*BP* [OE], 17 July 2000).[46]

Duplication of plans occurred not only when the agencies with jurisdiction belonged to different ministries, but even when they belonged to the same ministry. Both the ETA and BMA are agencies within the Ministry of Interior, and, similarly, the SRT of the Hopewell plan and the Department of Highways of the Don Mueang Tollway belonged to the Ministry of Communications. This means that no adjustments were made to avoid duplication, even though the agencies belonged to the same ministry. The OCMLT, established in 1992, was expected to improve situations like these.

Frequent Policy Changes

Frequent policy changes were also an important factor in the delays in implementing urban railway plans, as Unger has pointed out. Although there were many policy flip-flops, they can be summarized as relating to two main issues: construction methods and railway structure. The plans of the ETA/MRTA suffered the most from these frequent policy changes.

Problems with construction methods centered on who would cover the costs of building the railways, that is, whether the government or private companies would be the sole investor. A review of the ETA/MRTA's urban railway plans shows that the government changed its policy no less than five times (see table 5.8). Although the government planned to invest in the MTS plan by itself at the beginning, it changed the policy to 100 percent private investment in 1980. In 1986, because the bid for first-stage lines failed after the change, the government again changed the policy to 25 percent of investment, and granted the concession to Lavalin. Then, after Lavalin failed and the plan was returned to the MRTA in 1992, the government changed the policy and agreed to bear 100 percent of the cost by itself. This policy was again reversed in 1993 with a return to 100 percent private investment and the granting of the concession to Muang Thong. Finally, with the decision to lay lines underground in 1995, the policy returned to two-tiered, public-private operation.

Table 5.8. Urban Railway Plans of ETA and MRTA

Agency	Date	Plan	Number of Lines	Length (km)	Construction Method	Operation Method	Remarks	Sources
ETA	5 Mar 1974	First Stage MTS Plan	3	49	Detail design (public operation)	Not yet decided		TPT for 1974
	26 Jan 1982	First Stage MTS Plan	3	59	BOT	Concession		TPT 1982
	27 May 1986	First Stage Part I MTS Plan	2	34	BOT	Concession	25% investment by the government	TPT n.d.
MRTA	8 Sep 1992	MRTA First Stage Plan	1	20	Detail design (public operation)	Under consideration		RFM for 1994
	14 Sep 1993	MRTA First Stage Plan	1	20	BOT	Concession		RFM for 1994
	12 Sep 1995	MRTA First Stage Plan	1	20	Design & build (two-tiered operation)	Concession	Whole-line underground	RFM for 1996

Thus, the government repeated the same changes twice. That is, the cycle of policy changes—public investment, private investment, and joint investment—occurred twice. The changes from the public to private investment might have been influenced by the economic depression caused by the second oil crisis, and the progress of the Hopewell and the BTS plans by 100 percent private investment.[47] The failure of exclusively private investment resulted in a joint investment policy. However, it differed in that the first joint investment was led by the private sector, while the second was led by the government. In the end, the first case failed.

Reexaminations of the plan in accordance with policy changes resulted in further delay. When the government decided for 100 percent private investment in 1980, it ordered the NESDB to reexamine the plan. Even after the bid in the first-stage plan failed in 1982, the ETA reconsidered the plan, and the reduced plan, called the first-stage Part I plan, was approved. Such reexamination was routinely performed whenever a policy was changed, which wasted time and increased survey and design expenses.

The policy of placing railways underground was the biggest challenge for the railway structure. Since the Hopewell and the BTS plans acquired concessions before the decision to put things underground, and because construction had already started, the requirement was eventually avoided. However, construction was interrupted until the final decision was made. The MRTA negotiated for putting underground half of a line, but those negotiations failed. Then, the plan shifted to laying the entire line underground, and the two-tiered operation adopted by revoking the original concession, which was the second change to the joint investment.

The below-ground policy reflected the citizens' opinions, who viewed above-ground railways as an environmental problem, which was not unique to Bangkok if global trends are considered. However, it is at least true that the sudden opting for underground solutions caused delays for the urban railway plans. Both Hopewell and the BTSC opposed underground railways, and Muang Thong requested compensation for the increased cost of the change to laying the lines underground. When the total cost of construction was compared, the construction costs of the first-stage line of the MRTA, the completely underground railway line became twice that of the construction cost of the BTS, the completely elevated railway line.[48] Therefore, the government's below-ground policy decision meant an increased financial burden.

Immense Construction Costs

The government had not decided the degree to which it would participate in these building projects because of the immense construction costs of the urban railway. Since the construction costs were so high, the government aimed for the construction to be funded and performed by private sector companies. The process of achieving this aim continued until the two-tiered operation of the first-stage line of the MRTA was finally decided upon.

The construction of expressways preceded the urban railway not only because, as generally argued, the government prioritized road development over railways, but also because the government could not simultaneously afford both plans. Although the total construction cost of the first-stage expressways was about 8,500 million baht, the total construction cost of the first-stage MTS was estimated at 12,200 million baht, and that was just at the beginning.[49] Comparing these estimated costs in 1993, the second-stage expressway would cost 687 million baht per kilometer, while the BTS plan would cost 1,180 million baht per kilometer (SWPT 1993, 7). Eventually, the BTS plan cost as much as 2,300 million baht by the time its operations actually started.

The construction costs for the urban railway plans were so high because of the large amounts necessary not only for the construction of tracks, but also for the supply of rolling stock, operations equipment, and signal systems. In the case of the BTS, about 650 million dollars (approximately 25 billion baht) had to be spent both on the civil engineering work and train operation equipment (*BPYEER* 1999).[50] Since they tended to use modern technologies developed in advanced nations, the cost of operational equipment became higher. Moreover, the high dependence upon imports from foreign countries resulted in an increase in construction costs when the baht was devalued in 1997. The opening of the BTS brought numerous firsts to Thailand, such as ticket vending machines and automatic ticket gates. However, these firsts also increased initial investment expenses.

Even though the immense construction costs were inevitable, the urban railway plans could not expect to immediately earn income.

Since urban railways are a means of mass transport, they must provide services at the cheapest fare possible. This creates rather small profits for businesses and forces the central or local government to cover the deficit. The SRT and the BMTA continue to operate at a deficit because of low fares. The government's failure in receiving bids with the condition of 100 percent private investment at the time of the ETA was also due to the hesitation of private sector companies, who feared that their profits would be comparatively low despite the requisite large investment. The number of BTS users after the opening was far less than expected owing to its relatively high fare price, and as a result, the BTS fell into a situation that raised doubts over whether it could pay the interest on its debt.[51]

The immense construction costs and low profits made the entry of the private sector into the urban railway business difficult. The government's insistence on private involvement resulted in the delay in plans. From this perspective, it must be said that the second policy change from public to private investment was a failure. Since it will probably be difficult to build an urban railway with 100 percent private investment, even if an elevated structure is adopted, as the case of the BTS shows, the development of urban railways in Bangkok seems centered on the same two-tiered operation system as that of the MRTA.[52]

Since the government had to bear most of the construction costs even in a two-tiered operation, its financial situation would greatly influence the execution of the plans. Therefore, low-cost construction was necessary to develop many routes. To achieve cheaper construction costs, it was necessary to reexamine the below-ground policy. Although placing lines underground is unavoidable in certain areas where roads are narrow, such as the city center, the use of as many elevated structures as possible can save construction costs, but only if the road is wide enough. Although there are several reports that the air pollution of the road under the BTS station has worsened, it is better for rapid expansion of the urban railway network to solve the problem by changing the station's structure and using elevated structures.[53] The below-ground policy could lead to further increases in the huge construction costs of urban railways.[54]

Thus, another factor in the delay in the urban railway plans was the high construction cost that forced the government to hesitate in making a policy decision, which, in turn, discouraged entry of private companies.

It was these immense construction costs that made the government try to establish a policy to reduce the investment as much as possible, which resulted in frequent policy changes, as laid out above. The delay in the ETA's first-stage plans was also one of the reasons for the duplication of the plans, which further factored into the immense construction costs. In summary, the delay in the urban railway plans in Bangkok was due to the immense construction costs and the government's negative reactions. The delay of the urban railway plans prolonged the situation in which urban transport in Bangkok was dependent solely on buses, and it caused the stagnation of urban transport development by aggravating traffic congestion.

Failure of the Bus Unification Plan

Although the urban railway plans surfaced in the 1970s, because those plans had to wait until the end of the 1990s to be acted upon, buses were the only means of urban transport during that period. Since the old earnest wish of unifying bus operations was achieved by the establishment of the Mahanakhon Transport Company in 1975 and its transfer to the BMTA in the following year, the realization of two opposite propositions—the improvement in bus service and the maintenance of low fares—was expected.

However, it is hard to say that the BMTA fully achieved both. The improvement in service was accomplished to a certain degree because of the increase in the number of buses and introduction of air-conditioned buses. It was impossible for private operators to supply a thousand or more new buses at once, and the state of the buses purchased or leased from major makers in large quantities was far better than the casual buses that private operators built themselves.[55] The air-conditioned buses were also a new service that aimed to shift the use of privately owned cars by middle-class users and had the potential to wipe away the image of buses as only for low-income people. Moreover, the network was also expanded in terms of the increased number of buses, and new services such as expressway and all-night buses were also started. The dependence on illegal *songthaeo* gradually decreased, and eventually they were swept away from the main road bus routes, being converted to minibuses.

However, these measures were insufficient for Bangkok, which continues to grow. As seen in table 5.9, Bangkok's population increased from about 3 million in 1970 to 6,350,000 in 2000; the city's area also expanded significantly. The increase in automobiles surpassed the population growth, growing as much as almost seventeen times from 260,000 cars in 1970 to 4,500,000 in 2000. Although the rate of increase of two-wheelers (motorbikes) is a remarkable thirty-three times, the rate of increase of sedans, which the middle class uses for commuting, was about ten times. In particular, the number of automobiles increased rapidly in the latter half of the 1980s and mid-1990s, when Thailand enjoyed prosperity. The rate of increase from 1980 to 1990 was the highest. Thus, the fact that the number of automobiles increased faster than the population meant a significant increase in the number of commuters who used privately owned cars. As seen in table 5.7, the decrease of bus users, after reaching its peak in 1992, showed that the transition to privately owned cars was progressing.

Table 5.9. Population and Registered Number of Automobiles in Bangkok, 1970–2000

Year	Population (thousands)	Number of Automobiles (thousands)			
		Sedans	Motorcycles	Other	Total
1970	3,077	128	59	73	260
1980	4,697	220	172	148	540
1990	5,882	598	645	719	1,962
2000	6,355	1,241	1,965	1,290	4,496

Note 1: Population includes that of former Thonburi province. The population in 1970 is larger than the figure shown in table 4.10 since it includes the population of rural areas (outside the *thetsaban*).

Note 2: Sedan refers to a four-wheel, privately owned car for fewer than seven passengers.

Sources: *SYB* for 1972–73; for 1981–84; for 1991; for 2002; for 2010.

Against such a rapid increase in the number of automobiles, road development in Bangkok naturally could not catch up. As shown in the previous chapter, the length of roads in Bangkok in 1973 was only 805 kilometers, and the road area only 11.3 square kilometers. However, both increased about five times in 2003, reaching 4,149 kilometers of road length and 58 square kilometers of road area (SC for 2003, 81).[56]

Many expressways built by the ETA also opened for traffic from 1980, amounting to 171 kilometers in 2000 (TS for 2000). Nevertheless, such road development could not compete with the increase in automobiles, and traffic congestion has worsened. Since buses have to share the roads with privately owned cars, traffic congestion has caused degradation in bus service, decreasing the attraction of bus transport. Although this degradation had already begun before the formation of the BMTA, it has worsened. As a result, the improvement in bus service after the establishment of the BMTA has been offset by increased traffic congestion.

Additionally, maintaining a low fare was also difficult. When the BMTA was inaugurated in 1976, the minimum fare of the ordinary bus was 0.75 baht, but this was raised as high as 3.5 baht in 1997 (see table 5.3).[57] Although fare hikes were sometimes suspended for political reasons, the fare increased to 4.7 times the original fare. On the other hand, from 1976 to 1996 the consumer price index of Bangkok only increased to 3.3 times the original rate (Suehiro 1998, 225); the increase in the bus fare far exceeded that of the consumer price index. Although the fare level before the establishment of the BMTA was also too low, even if bus operations were unified by nationalization, maintaining a low fare would continue to be difficult.

Because the BMTA could not raise the fare to a level high enough to rid itself of loss-making operations, bus service should have been a prominent political issue during this period. However, this issue became less significant after the Kukrit administration, which introduced a free bus service. The fare hike was a compromise between maintenance of the low fare as a populist policy and the improvement of the BMTA's deficit. Therefore, in spite of the fare hike, the BMTA was mostly forced to continue its loss-making operations. It is true that the introduction of new buses, which were not obtained during private operation, was achieved, but in fact it resulted in a burden on BMTA's cumulative deficit. Although the government occasionally managed the debt, the deficit situation of the BMTA did not change after all.

Therefore, as a result of all these changes, the downsizing of the BMTA to decrease its deficit and the encouraging of privatization will continue. Private operators tried to reduce costs to secure profits, and as a result, could only provide a low level of service in comparison to BMTA buses. Although bus operations were nationalized once, they were later privatized; they returned to the original situation before amalgamating with the BMTA. Eventually, the bus unification plan failed.

6
A Confused Urban Transport Policy, 2000s

Urban Railway Policy of Thaksin Government

When we explore the history of the urban railway policy of the Thaksin Shinawatra government, we see a clear tendency for each term of the three ministers who took charge of the Ministry of Transport: the passive term of Wan Muhammad Noor Matha; the aggressive term of Suriya Chungrungruangkit; and what can only be called the confused term of Phongsak Raktaphongpaisan. Therefore, we will survey the changes in the urban transport policy of the Thaksin government according to these three periods.

The Passive Term (February 2001–October 2002)

In February 2001, when the Thaksin government was organized, the 23.5-kilometer Bangkok Mass Transit System (BTS) was operating, and the 20-kilometer Blue line between Hua Lamphong and Bang Sue—which was under the jurisdiction of the MRTA and had changed its name to the Mass Rapid Transit Authority of Thailand (MRTA, *Kan rotfaifa khonsong muanchon haeng prathet thai*)—was under construction.[1] The number of users immediately after the opening of the BTS remained low, forcing it to face a hard fight. The actual number of users capped at about 150,000 persons per day, but its target was 600,000 persons. On the other hand, the MRTA's Blue line was a subway line under construction with a two-tiered operation, the Bangkok Metro Company, Ltd. (BMCL) having the concession in August 2000 through competitive bidding (*KT* [OE]*)*, 2 August 2000).

The first minister of transport under Thaksin had negative opinions about the development of urban railways. The extension plan for the BTS was promoted by the Bangkok Metropolitan Administration (BMA), as will be discussed below, but the government did not support its efforts. As for the extension of the MRTA, the Land Transport Management Committee decided that priority should be given to the extension of the Blue line between Hua Lamphong and Bang Wa (RFM for 1999–2000, 16). However, in August 2001, the Ministry of Finance requested a reexamination of this decision, noting its low rate of return (*BP* [OE], 14 August 2001). The ministry's doubts about the extension became stronger due to the smaller than expected number of BTS users and because of an expected delay in the opening of the MRTA's first line due to a delay in the procurement of rolling stock.[2] In July 2002, the ministry insisted that the construction of the new section should only begin after checking the number of passengers at the opening of the first section (*DN* [OE], 4 July 2002).

Thaksin himself rejected the plan for the revival of the State Railways of Thailand's (SRT) Hopewell plan, which had been interrupted in 1997, noting that the expense was too high. The SRT employed a consultancy firm to conduct a feasibility study for reviving the plan in November 1999, and the development plan excluding expressways was proposed in July 2000 (RFT for 2000, 53; *BP* [OE], 17 July 2000). Then, when a plan based on this proposal was submitted by the Office of the Commission for the Management of Land Traffic (OCMLT) in September 2001, Thaksin rejected it because the total cost of 40 billion baht was too high, and he suggested an alternative plan to construct a four-track line between Bang Sue and Don Mueang by removing the pillars constructed by Hopewell (*BP* [OE], 28 September 2001). This led to criticisms such as "it is a waste of resources to discard one thousand pillars." Therefore, he adapted the policy with the idea of constructing an elevated line using those existing pillars and ordered the OCMLT to reinvestigate the plan (*DN* [OE], 25 October 2001; *BP* [OE], 3 November 2001).

Construction of an access railway to the new airport also surfaced during this time, just as the construction of the Suvarnabhumi Airport, the new airport of Bangkok, began. Initially, though, Thaksin denied there was need for an access railway. The origin of the airport access railway plan was a decision taken at the cabinet meeting in May 2000 to construct a connecting line to the airport in accordance with the double-tracking plan of the Eastern line (RFT 2003, 65). Since the section within the city center overlapped with the route of the suspended Hopewell plan, this represented the revival of the Hopewell plan. However, when Thaksin dismissed the Hopewell reexamination plan in September 2001, he claimed that the connection to the new airport would be provided only by road for the time being (*PCT* [OE], 1 October 2001). Then, when the construction of the new airport was well underway, the SRT proposed the construction of an underground station for future use while the airport terminal building was being built, a proposal that was approved at the cabinet meeting in September 2002 (KK for 2002, 134). In summary, although the construction of the underground station was started, the access railway to the airport was not. Thus, during this passive term, urban railway development did not show much progress except for the decisions regarding the MRTA subway construction.

The Aggressive Term (October 2002–August 2005)

After a large-scale restructuring of government ministries and agencies in October 2002, the MRTA and the Office of Transport and Traffic Policy and Planning (OTP, *Samnakngan nayobai lae phaen kan khonsong lae charachon*), the former OCMLT—which had previously been under the jurisdiction of the Prime Minister's Office—were put under the jurisdiction of the Ministry of Transport, the former Ministry of Communications (KK for 2002, 54–71).[3] Therefore, all agencies pertaining to the urban railway, except for the BMA, were put under the jurisdiction of the Ministry of Transport. Suriya Chungrungruangkit became the minister of transport and began to take action on urban railways.

At first, Suriya began to work for an earlier opening of the MRTA subway, which was liable to be delayed. In the original plan, a part of the line would be opened by the end of 2002, and the whole line would be completed by the end of the following year (RFM for 1998, 8). However, since the concession grant to the BMCL, the operator, was delayed until August 2000 and the contract for the rolling stock procurement made in December 2001 was behind schedule, the scheduled opening dates were no longer feasible.[4] Therefore, Suriya negotiated with Siemens AG for the rolling stock and asked the BMCL to ensure that the delivery would be moved up from August to May 2004 by paying additional charges (*DN* [OE], 25 December 2002). In the end, the opening of the subway took place in July 2004, although the first stage of the partial section had not yet been opened.

Suriya later became interested in the airport access railway; the SRT hired a consultancy firm to investigate the plan in September 2003 (KK for 2003, 113; *BP* [OE] 16 April 2003).[5] Then, since Thaksin asked that the airport access railway be completed by the time of the Suvarnabhumi Airport opening, scheduled for the end of 2005, the construction of the railway was approved at the cabinet meeting in June 2004 (KK for 2004, 117; *DN* [OE], 19 May 2004). This airport access railway plan, which came to be called the "Airport Rail Link," progressed rapidly, and the contract for a turnkey project involving a six-company consortium led by Sino-Thai Engineering and Construction Company, Ltd. was signed in January 2005 (KK for 2005, 148). Construction work was started with the target of a November 2007 opening. Although the turnkey method enabled its completion in a short period by leaving the line's financing to the private sector, the rough-and-ready plans caused many problems, as will be described below.[6]

The Thaksin government's first urban railway development plan was announced at this time. Suriya announced a plan to develop a 100-kilometer urban railway over ten years, beginning in May 2003, while Thaksin ordered the urgent development of a 130-kilometer urban railway to be managed by the Land Transport Management Committee (*BP* [OE], 16 May 2003; *BP* [OE], 5 July 2003). The plan was to start constructing the 130-kilometer urban railway within a year. These railways were the result of a change in attitude towards expanding the urban railway network, which had been viewed indifferently until then. It was the first time that the turnkey method—as adopted by the Airport Rail Link—surfaced, which would subsequently emerge several times later during the Thaksin era, because it enabled rapid construction by postponing the funding issue.

The plan was then expanded just as the reexamination of the urban railway master plan began, as will be described in detail below. In September 2003, Thaksin announced that the construction of a 213-km urban railway would occur over six years (*PCT* [OE], 15 September 2003). Next, the cabinet approved the Bangkok Mass Transit Implementation Plan (BMTIP) in February 2004 (SNK 2005, 19). This plan served as the basis of the Thaksin government's urban railway plan and aimed at the construction of a total of 292 kilometers of railway consisting of seven lines over six years. The urban railway development plan became one of the five important components in the concept of a "Four-Year Investment for the Future," which was announced as the government's next policy vision after the election to be held in 2005 (*PCK* [OE], 8 September 2004).[7]

The urban railway plan was expanded even further. In addition to the 292-kilometer network, 62 kilometers—consisting of two lines—were added in December 2004; the result was a total of 354 kilometers consisting of nine lines (*PCT* [OE], 20 December 2004). When the Thai Rak Thai Party easily won the next general election and the second Thaksin government was organized, Suriya once again served as the minister of transport. The so-called Mega Project, with a total investment of 1,700 billion baht, was approved, in principle, at the June 2005 cabinet meeting as a means of implementing the campaign pledges made during the election (*N* [OE], 14 June 2005). Although education, public health, housing supply, and road development were included in this project, the investment in urban railway development had the largest share of all the developments, comprising 25 percent of the total proposed investment.

While the urban railway plan was expanded, the implementation of the plan also progressed. The Airport Rail Link and the section of the Purple line between Bang Sue and Bang Yai proceeded first (see figure 6.1). Although the section of the Blue line between Hua Lamphong and Bang Khae was prioritized during the previous passive term, the section between Bang Sue and Bang Yai became the priority after early 2004.[8] It was assumed that the Purple line would be constructed first, in conjunction with the Airport Rail Link, according to the "Four-Year Investment for the Future." The Land Condemnation Decree for this section was made official in June 2005, and the MRTA performed bid notification and started the registration for screening on August 19 (KK for 2005, 170; *DN* [OE], 16 June 2005; *PCT* [OE], 29 August 2005). Thus, urban railway development seemed to shift to a stage of action from its previous position of being in a purely planning stage.

Fig. 6.1. Urban Railway Network in Bangkok, 2005

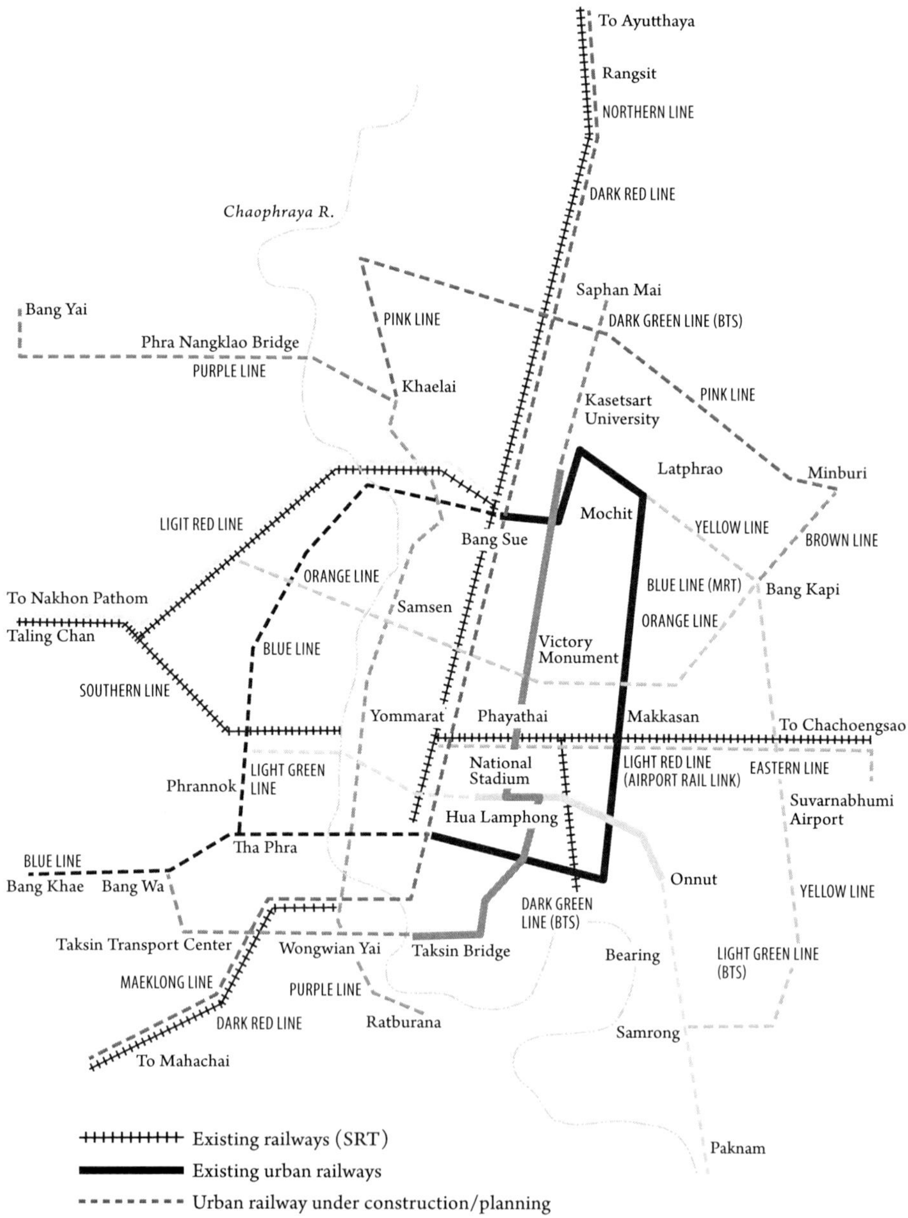

Term of Confusion (August 2005–September 2006)

However, when Suriya was replaced after a corruption scandal involving baggage-screening equipment supply at the Suvarnabhumi Airport, and Phongsak assumed the minister's post, the favorable response to the plan shifted, and the urban railway policy became convoluted.

On August 25, 2005, Thaksin announced that four of the seven lines included in the urban railway plan had to be reviewed because of their low investment return. The bidding for the Purple line was also suddenly stopped (*BP* [OE], 27 August 2005). Phongsak declared that the section of the Purple line between Bang Sue and Bang Yai would be substituted with a bus rapid transit (BRT) system by changing a route, and that the other unprofitable line would receive similar treatment. The residents and developers who had already begun real estate development along the line were perplexed and opposed the sudden change.

Therefore, Phongsak examined ways to reduce as much as possible the budget required for developing urban railways. These included reducing the number of tracks on the Red line, which was the same as the revived Hopewell plan, or reducing and downsizing urban railway stations.[9] Since reexaminations and route revisions were being reported daily, the public came to eventually distrust the project. Although the development of the four lines was first agreed as the first stage of Thaksin's plan, the BMA announced that it would start construction of the BTS's extension line by itself. This was a big blow to the government, for whom plans for urban railway development were still in confusion.

In November, Thaksin radically changed the funding model for the Mega Project, announcing that international bids for a turnkey project would be solicited (*PCK* [OE], 17 October 2005; *PCK* [OE], 30 November 2005). This plan was announced on a grand scale as the "Thailand: Partnership for Development" plan, and diplomats from various foreign countries were invited to participate at an announcement ceremony on December 14. Thaksin declared that potential construction plans, from the source of capital to the construction method, would be sought from all over the world to develop the 361 kilometers of the ten urban railway lines within a budget of 550 billion baht, as originally planned (*PCK* [OE], 15 December 2005). The entrepreneur who presented Thailand with the most advantageous—that is, cheapest—proposal would be selected to develop the Mega Project since the substantial funds necessary for funding urban railway development had not yet been procured.

Although bidding was scheduled to be held in April 2006, the anti-Thaksin movement, which expanded rapidly after early 2006, set that back. The parliament was dissolved on February 24, the Thaksin government became a caretaker, interim government, with its term of office extended in advance of a general election. Since it became difficult to promote the Mega Project under an interim government, the government decided to progress with part of the urban railway plan. The cabinet on June 6 consented to the development of seventy kilometers of the three lines by separating it from the Mega Project (*PCK* [OE], 6 June 2006). Although the SRT and MRTA, which had jurisdiction over these lines, were due to invite bids in July, they had not yet started negotiations with the Japan Bank for International Cooperation (JBIC, the former OECF, and now the Japan International Cooperation Agency, JICA) to reexamine the construction methods. Thus, the bid notification, which had already been delayed till the end of August, was further postponed, and progress was no longer expected until the conclusion of negotiations with JBIC. Finally, there was a military coup d'état on the night of September 19 and the Thaksin interim government collapsed, thus ending the Thaksin era after a little less than six years.

Confusion and Confrontation

From URMAP to BMTIP

Frequent changes were the most prominent feature of urban railway policy in the the Thaksin era. Table 6.1 shows that at least ten plans were set forth from 2003, ranging from a small-scale reexamination to a large-scale change. Although the basis of these plans was the Bangkok Mass Transit Implementation Plan (BMTIP), which had been approved in February 2004, since reexaminations occurred so frequently, consistency of policy was lost, causing confusion. This raises the question of how the BMTIP itself was decided upon.

The Mass Transit Master Plan, decided by the OCMLT in September 1994, was the origin of the master plan for the urban railways in Bangkok. It was a concept for developing a total 261.5-kilometer urban railway network by fixing the Hopewell lines as the Red lines, the BTS lines as the Green lines, and the first section of the MRTA line between Hua Lamphong and Bang Sue as the Blue line; it would also add an extension of each line as well as new Orange and Purple lines (see table 6.2).[10] However, since economic conditions worsened rapidly because of the 1997 economic crisis and the Hopewell plan suffered a complete setback, the OCMLT decided to begin working on the Urban Rail Transportation Master Plan (URMAP). The work of creating the URMAP was started in 2000, and a report was submitted at the end of 2001. In this report, although the previous master plan was used as a starting point, the routes are changed (see table 6.2): the report called for the Red, Green, Blue, Orange, and Yellow lines, no Purple line, and a circle section was added to the Blue line.

The URMAP was the basis for the BMTIP, on which the Thaksin government's urban railway policy was based, but further changes were made to it. These changes included a route network and a shortening of the development period. The route network change is shown in table 6.2: the total length was reduced from 361.1 kilometers in the URMAP to 292 kilometers in the BMTIP. The largest change was the restoration of the Purple line and change in routes for the Blue and Orange lines. The Purple line was rearranged for a north–south route, the Orange line for an east–west route, and to the Blue line was added a circle line.[11]

Projected opening dates for each section were moved up significantly. Although the URMAP assumed a three-stage development every ten years—in 2011, 2021, and post-2022—the BMTIP proposed completing the entire network by 2009.[12] The BMTIP omitted some routes such as the Yellow line. The opening dates for some sections were moved up, such as the section between Bang Yai and the Phra Nangklao Bridge, whose original opening date was fixed for post-2022 in the URMAP, but advanced to as early as 2009 in the BMTIP.

In the end, the draft proposal for the urban railway policy of the Thaksin government was the OCMLT's master plan, used for policy purposes only. What was new in the BMTIP was the shortening of the development period, which we can see as having populist intentions. Whereas in the URMAP the gradual development over a period of twenty or more years was assumed for the section nearest to the city center and the radiating routes from the city center, the BMTIP aimed for

Table 6.1. Urban Railway Plans during the Thaksin Administration

Date	Plan	Number of Lines	Lines										Length (km)	Cost (billion THB)	Duration	Construction Method	Operation Method	Fare	Remarks	Sources
			Dark Red	Light Red	Dark Green	Light Green	Blue	Purple	Orange	Yellow	Pink	Brown								
4 Jul 2003	Development of 130-km urban railways	5			○	○	○	○	○				130	300.0	Start construction within 1 year	Turnkey	Concession		Purple line (as far as the Phra Nangklao Bridge) and Orange line (Rama IV Road–Minburi). The government subsidize fares.	*BP* (OE), 5 Jul 2003
23 Feb 2004	Bangkok Mass Transit Implementation Plan (BMTIP)	7	○	○	○	○	○	○	○				292	446.7	6 years (2004–9)	Detail design	Public operation	Sectional System	Master plan of OTP. Included purchase of BTSC and BMCL.	OTP 2004
7 Sep 2004	Four-Year Investment for the Future	7	○	○	○	○	○	○	○				292	480.0	6 years (to 2009)	Detail design	Public operation		Priority is put on Light Red line (Makkasan–Suvarnabhumi Airport; Airport Rail Link) and Purple line (Bang Sue–Bang Yai).	*PCK* (OE), 8 Sep 2004
22 Dec 2004	Addition of two urban railways	9	○	○	○	○	○	○	○	○	○		354	545.0	6 years (to 2009)	Detail design	Public operation	Flat Fare		*PCT* (OE), 20 Dec 2004
14 Jun 2005	The Mega Project	7	○	○	○	○	○	○	○				293	555.7	5 years (to 2009)	Detail design	Public operation			*N* (OE), 14 Jun 2005
17 Oct 2005	First-Stage Urban Railway Development Plan	4	○	○			○	○					94	120.0	3 years (2006–8)	Turnkey	Jurisdiction by MTA	Flat Fare	Dark Red line (Bang Sue–Rangsit), Light Red line (Phayathai–Taling Chan), and Purple line (Bang Sue–Bang Yai). Barter method is required.	*PCK* (OE), 18 Oct 2005

Date	Plan	Number of Lines	Lines										Length (km)	Cost (billion THB)	Duration	Construction Method	Operation Method	Fare	Remarks	Sources
			Dark Red	Light Red	Dark Green	Light Green	Blue	Purple	Orange	Yellow	Pink	Brown								
14 Dec 2005	Thailand: Partnership for Development	10	○	○	○	○	○	○	○	○	○	○	361	550.0	3 years (2006–8)	Turnkey	Jurisdiction by MTA	Flat fare		*KT* (OE), 13 Dec 2005
6 Jun 2006	Three Urban Railways Development Plan	3	○				○	○					70	193.0		Turnkey	Jurisdiction by MTA	Flat fare	Dark Red line (Bang Sue–Rangsit) and Purple line (Bang Sue–Bang Yai).	*PCK* (OE), 6 Jun 2006
1 Aug 2006	Three Urban Railways Development Plan (Revised)	3	○				○	○					70	145.4		Design & build	Jurisdiction by MTA	Flat fare	Dark Red line (Bang Sue–Rangsit) and Purple line (Bang Sue–Bang Yai). Barter method is one of the options.	*KT* (OE), 1 Aug 2006
29 Aug 2006	Ten Urban Railways Development Plan	10	○	○	○	○	○	○	○	○	○	○	333	570.0		Design & build	Jurisdiction by MTA	Flat fare	Barter method is one of the options.	*PCK* (OE), 30 Aug 2006

Table 6.2. Proposed Urban Railway Lines in Three Transporation Plans

Mass Transit Master Plan, 1994

Line	Section	Length (km)
Dark Red	Rangsit–Hua Lamphong (under construction)	27.8
	Hua Lamphong–Bang Khunthian	12.5
	Total	40.3
Light Red	Taling Chan–Yommarat	14.0
	Yommarat–Huamak (under construction)	16.7
	Makkasan–Maenam	4.0
	Huamak–New Airport	12.3
	Total	47.0
Dark Green	Ratchayothin–Mochit	3.1
	Mochit–Taksin Bridge (under construction)	14.3
	Taksin Bridge–Wongwian Yai	2.3
	Total	19.7
Light Green	National Stadium–Onnut (under construction)	9.4
	Onnut–New Airport	19.3
	Total	28.7
Blue	Phra Nangklao Bridge–Bang Sue	11.0
	Bang Sue–Hua Lamphong (under construction)	20.8
	Hua Lamphong–Bang Khae	13.0
	Total	44.8

Urban Rail Transportation Master Plan (URMAP), 2001

Line	Section	Length (km)	Opening Year
Dark Red	Rangsit–Bang Sue	22.7	2011
	Bang Sue–Hua Lamphong	7.5	2011
	Hua Lamphong–Taksin Transport Center	6.5	2017
	Taksin Transport Center–Mahachai	28.3	2021
	Total	65.0	
Light Red	Taling Chan–Bang Sue	14.9	2018
	Bang Sue–Phayathai	6.1	2006
	Phayathai–Suvarnabhumi Airport	28.5	2005
	Total	49.5	
Dark Green	Lam Lukka–Don Mueang	14.0	After 2022
	Don Mueang–Ratchayothin	7.8	2014
	Ratchayothin–Mochit	2.9	2005
	Mochit–Taksin Bridge	14.3	Opened
	Taksin Bridge–Taksin Transport Center	6.8	2008
	Total	45.8	
Light Green	Pinklao–National Stadium	4.6	2021
	National Stadium–Onnut	9.4	Opened
	Onnut–Samrong	9.0	2011
	Samrong–Paknam	7.9	2014
	Total	30.9	

Bangkok Mass Transit Implementation Plan (BMTIP), 2004

Line	Section	Length (km)	Opening Year
Dark Red	Rangsit–Bang Sue	22.7	2009
	Bang Sue–Hua Lamphong	7.5	2008
	Hua Lamphong–Taksin Transport Center	6.5	2009
	Taksin Transport Center–Mahachai	28.3	2009
	Total	65.0	
Light Red	Taling Chan–Bang Sue	14.9	2008
	Bang Sue–Phayathai	6.1	2008
	Phayathai–Suvarnabhumi Airport	28.7	2008
	Total	49.7	
Dark Green	Saphan Mai–Mochit	12.0	2009
	Mochit–Taksin Bridge	14.3	Opened
	Taksin Bridge–Taksin Road	2.2	2005
	Taksin Road–Bang Wa	4.5	2007
	Total	33.0	
Light Green	Phrannok–National Stadium	6.8	2010
	National Stadium–Onnut	9.4	Opened
	Onnut–Samrong	8.9	2007
	Samrong–Paknam	7.9	2009
	Total	33.0	

Mass Transit Master Plan, 1994 (*cont.*)

Line	Section	Length (km)
Purple	Bang Phut–Bang Sue	15.6
	Bang Sue–Samsen	4.5
	Total	20.1
Orange	Bang Na–Ratburana	17.3
	Ratburana–Bang Kapi	31.7
	Bang Kapi–Minburi	11.9
	Total	60.9
Grand Total		261.5

Urban Rail Transportation Master Plan (URMAP), 2001 (*cont.*)

Line	Section	Length (km)	Opening Year
Blue	*Bang Sue–Hua Lamphong	20.8	Constructed
	Hua Lamphong–Bang Wa	9.1	2009
	Bang Wa–Bang Khae	4.7	2012
	*Bang Sue–Tha Phra	13.1	2016
	*Tha Phra–Khlong Toei	17.5	2022
	Bang Yai–Phra Nangklao Bridge	8.1	After 2022
	Phra Nangklao Bridge–Bang Sue	11.6	2020
	Total	84.9	
Orange	Samrong–Wang Burapha	21.5	After 2022
	Wang Burapha–Huai Khwang Depot	11.9	2019
	Huai Khwang Depot–Minburi	19.9	2014
	Total	53.3	
Yellow	Latphrao–Bang Kapi	10.7	After 2022
	Bang Kapi–Samrong	21.0	After 2022
	Total	31.7	
Grand Total		361.1	

Bangkok Mass Transit Implementation Plan (BMTIP) 2004 (*cont.*)

Line	Section	Length (km)	Opening Year
Blue	*Bang Sue–Hua Lamphong	20.8	Opened
	*Hua Lamphong–Tha Phra	6.5	2009
	Tha Phra–Bang Khae	7.6	2008
	*Bang Sue–Tha Phra	13.1	2009
	Total	48.0	
Purple	Bang Yai–Phra Nangklao Bridge	8.1	2009
	Phra Nangklao Bridge–Bang Sue	11.6	2009
	Bang Sue–Samsen	5.0	2010
	Samsen–Ratburana	14.8	2009
	Total	39.5	
Orange	Bang Bamru–Samsen	4.0	2010
	Samsen–Bang Kapi	19.8	2009
	Total	23.8	
Grand Total		292.0	

NOTE: Asterisks in the Blue line denote circular sections.

SOURCES: Khamroplak 2000; OCMLT 2001; OTP 2004.

completing about 300 kilometers of the route within the short period of only six years. This was what led, in fact, to the delay of urban transport development in the Thaksin era.

Hypertrophy and Contraction of Plans

Although the urban railway plan expanded after the formation of the BMTIP, the main factor for its expansion was power politics—the formulation of populist policies. Four plans approved after the cabinet approval of the BMTIP in February 2004 show the role and impact of politics on transport policy.

The plan referred to as the "Four-Year Investment for the Future," announced in September 2004, contained urban railway development as part of its concept. This five-measure plan was a campaign pledge during the general election, as mentioned previously, and there were no changes in it in terms of the urban railway policy when compared to the BMTIP's policy of February 2004. In fact, though, the plan was presented as a response to the victory of Aphirak Kosayothin of the opposition Democrat Party in the election for BMA governor. Thus, it was nothing than a scheme to recover power for Thaksin's Thai Rak Thai Party in Bangkok. Thaksin presented it on the day following Aphirak's inauguration as governor and put urban railway development to the fore; this caused much concern among Bangkokians (*PCK* [OE], 8 September 2004).[13]

The two-line addition to the urban railway plan made in late 2004 was put forward to garner election support in Bangkok. It added the thirty-two kilometer Yellow line between Latphrao and Samrong and the thirty-kilometer Pink line between Pakkret and Minburi. This was regarded as a measure to attract votes in election, as was the simultaneous three-month lowering of fees on the Don Mueang Tollway (*PCT* [OE], 20 December 2004).[14] The Mega Project was also promoted to implement various campaign pledges made during the election.

In December 2005, the "Thailand: Partnership for Development" plan was set forth as a means of regaining popular support for the project, which had waned due to the reexamination of the plan when Phongsak headed the Ministry of Transport. Although the announcement ceremony, to which diplomats from eighty nations were invited, was set for December, the announcement of the idea came on November 30.

This seems to have been a countermeasure to the groundbreaking of the BTS extension line on December 1, after Bangkok governor Aphirak decided the city would construct the line by itself after being frustrated by the government's lack of cooperation. Since the government was criticized for lack of motivation in yet again reexamining the plans and because support for the project had fallen after the expansion of the urban railway network by the BMA, Thaksin came back with another populist policy. The 9.5-kilometer Brown line between Bang Kapi and Minburi was added to the plan, making it a total of ten lines and the largest-scale plan so far.

This latest development plan for ten urban railway lines in August 2006 was also a vote-getting measure before the election. Since the makeup general election in November 2006 was approaching, the Democrat Party set forth the "Democrat Railway Plan" on August 27 (*BP* [OE], 28 August 2006). This was a plan for developing a 139-kilometer network. The Thai Rak Thai Party responded with its urban railway policy announcement two days later. This plan aimed to develop 333 kilometers consisting of ten lines with a flat fare of fifteen baht (*PCK* [OE], 29 August 2006). Although current negotiations with the JBIC had only proposed to develop three lines, the necessity of selling a "dream" became essential after the Democrat Party's plan was released.

While the plan was enlarged because of the election, actual implementation of the plan became more difficult. Therefore, two reductions to the plan were made during what we are calling the "term of confusion."

The first reduction was the narrowing of the plan in October 2005 to 94 kilometers consisting of four routes during the First Stage Urban Railway Development Plan. This was a response to the confusion stemming from the sudden demand for a reexamination of the urban railway plan announced on August 25. The plan had to be reexamined because it was projected that four of the seven planned lines would not turn a profit even after thirty years, even the Purple line, for which a construction bid had already been announced (*BP* [OE], 27 August 2005).[15] Moreover, after completing the detailed design in July, the construction cost had to be raised from 46 billion baht to 50.8 million baht, which also spurred public demands for reexamination (*PCT* [OE], 14 July 2005).

There was another factor: the demand by residents along the Purple line to place part of that line underground. This demand had become more pronounced since June. The residents asked for the section between Bang Sue and Khaelai, where the road below the railway was narrow, to go underground (*PCT* [OE], 23 June 2005). Khamroplak, the director of the OTP, said that doing so would cost an additional 8 billion baht and would prolong the construction time by three years, but that the final decision should be left to the prime minister (*PCT* [OE], 18 July 2005). Although not related to the Purple line, there was opposition from residents about the construction of the planned Taksin Transport Center in Thonburi in August, which also dampened enthusiasm for the urban railway plan (*N* [OE], 8 August 2005).[16]

Therefore, the sudden suspension of construction on the Purple line and the reexamination of its route were identified as retaliatory measures taken against the residents voicing opposition. In particular, because the revised plan changed the route that connected the planned Red line at Bang Khen instead of Bang Sue, the section between Bang Sue and Khaelai, which the residents requested to be placed underground, would be abandoned not only by the urban railway but also the alternative BRT (ibid.).[17] Phongsak's nonsensical utterance about the reexamination of the route and the changes in the plan resulted in a rapid decline of support for the government's urban railway policy. The result of this popular reaction of disapproval was the First-Stage Urban Railway Development Plan. This plan did not aim for complete suspension of the Mega Project, but rather the conversion to a practical-line policy of prioritizing construction of the lines. However, this plan, although more realistic, also suffered a setback when the populist policy, "Thailand: Partnership for Development" was released to the public.

Further reduction to the plan came with the 2006 development plan for three urban railway lines. This reduced the plan in order to realize a "dream." Although the international bid for the Mega Project was launched on a grand scale, fulfillment of the Mega Project as it was scheduled became difficult because of the ensuing political turmoil. However, since it was impossible to suspend all plans given the possibility of Thaksin's reelection, and because it would lead the opposition to support any plans created by the interim government, the government decided to proceed with the development of the first three lines. This reduction of the plan was more or less realistic.

Thus, the urban railway policy of the Thaksin government continuously had the tendency to expand and contract, even though it was based on the BMTIP. But the plan got out of control and attempts to implement it were actually few. Since it was a rather unfeasible plan designed with populist political motives in mind, it can be said that its failure was inevitable.

Confrontation with the BMA

As table 6.1 shows, several lines were omitted from the plans after they were downsized. Not only the Orange line, which had not yet begun, but also the Dark Green and Light Green lines were omitted, despite the fact that these were BTS lines and their extensions were to be developed at an early stage. Nevertheless, the government was very negative about the extension plan for the BTS, over which the BMA had jurisdiction, and this was obvious from the beginning.

As for the extension of the BTS, the cabinet meeting in February 2000, during the era of the Chuan government, approved the construction of three extension lines by 100 percent private investment: the Taksin Bridge–Wongwian Yai (Taksin Road) line, the Onnut–Samrong line, and the Chong Nonsi–Rama III Road line (*DN* [OE], 2 March 2000).[18] Then, when Samak was elected as the new BMA governor in July, he stated that the BTS would be extended by about twenty kilometers in three directions: to Lam Lukka to the north, Mahachai to the west, and Thepharak to the south (*PCT* [OE], 14 August 2000). By so doing, he showed the BMA's positive stance on urban railway development. This stance was further supported by his discussion of the idea of constructing an eighty-kilometer circle railway in the suburbs of Bangkok, scheduled to begin in April 2001 (*PCK* [OE], 4 April 2001).

The BMA started construction of the elevated line from the Taksin Bridge station to the Phasi Charoen Canal in 2000. Although there was a tramway plan along the canals, which was former Governor Phichit's campaign pledge and which would be temporarily used by automobiles, the BMA decided in February 2001 to use this elevated line for the extension route of the BTS (*BP* [OE], 7 February 2001).[19]

The BMA then tried to sell the construction rights for the BTS extension lines by 100 percent private investment. However, since there was no private company interested in it, the BMA appealed to the BTSC (*BP* [OE], 25 May 2001; *DN* [OE], 6 June 2001). The BTSC replied that it was interested in the extension to Wongwian Yai and Samrong, but that it preferred to leave the construction of infrastructure to the BMA (*BP* [OE], 14 August 2001). Thus constructing the extension by 100 percent private investment became impossible.

Next, the BMA aimed at funding construction by the two-tiered method and asked the government to withdraw the 2000 cabinet decision. However, the Thaksin government took a non-cooperative attitude to this request and criticized numerous details. In January 2002, the BTSC expressed its intention to construct three extension lines by changing the Rama III line into a northern extension to Ratchayothin. The Mass Rapid Transit Examination Subcommittee (*Khana anukammakan chat rabop khonsong khanat yai*) consented to this (*BP* [OE], 4 January 2002; *BP* [OE], 17 January 2002). The BMA came up with a terms of reference for the construction of the Taksin line and the Samrong line, and preparations were made to start the bidding process once the cabinet's consent had been secured. But the government did not accept the plan. Finally, an annoyed Samak made available the bidding terms of reference on July 18, 2003, and bidders submitted their documents on October 3 (*BP* [OE], 18 July 2003).

Thaksin opposed the BMA's plan by bringing up the restructuring problem of the BTSC and ordered the BMA to refrain from granting a concession to the BTSC for the extension lines until it obtained a guarantee of financing (*BP* [OE], 11 September 2003).[20] Although the BMA set the day for inviting bids as November 3, the cabinet's consent was still not forthcoming. The bidding, therefore, had to be repeatedly postponed. Since the BTSC had been negotiating with creditors and they had accepted its restructuring plan, it claimed that the obstacles had been overcome. However, the government did not accept this argument, noting that the final decision had not yet been made. Nevertheless, the elevated Phasi Charoen line was connected with the elevated track of the BTS at the Taksin Bridge station in September of the same year, and the civil engineering work on the Taksin line was completed except for the construction of stations (*KT* [OE], 23 September 2003).[21] In the end,

Samak completed his four-year term as BMA governor without being able to start on the extension of the BTS.

Radicalization of Confrontation

Since the inauguration of Aphirak, a member of the opposition Democrat Party, as the new BMA governor in September 2004, Thaksin's attitude against the BTS extension increasingly hardened, and he tried to resist it entirely. Although Samak had entreated Aphirak to realize the BTS extension plan, the greatest difficulty was the change in the cabinet decision. As will be discussed below, because the BMTIP included the purchase of the BTSC, the government postponed the reexamination of the cabinet decision by adding the problem of the buyout to the restructuring problem. The buyout problem was not resolved, and as an election tactic Thaksin softened his policy, asserting that the buyout would not be required if the financial situation of the BTSC could be fixed, and stating that he would not oppose the extension plan after making a decision about the restructuring plan. However, the situation did not change after the election (*PCK* [OE], 26 January 2005).

Aphirak then decided to officially announce on April 27, 2005, the opening of bids for the construction of two extension lines that had been stalled for about a year and a half (*BP* [OE], 30 April 2005).[22] The government then changed its policy from favoring a buyout to the establishment of a holding company and warned the BTSC that alternative routes would be added to the master plan instead of the BTS extension lines, unless it was willing to come under the jurisdiction of a holding company. The OTP summarized the plan to construct twenty-eight kilometers of the two alternative lines with a total of 40 billion baht in August (*DN* [OE], 22 July 2005).[23] It was the government's secret desire to force the company to admit that developing the lines in competition with the BTS extension lines would reduce the feasibility of the latter. Since both the company and the BMA distrusted the government's intentions, the confrontation intensified.

Aphirak finally decided to have the BMA extend the Taksin line by itself, amidst the confusion of the urban railway plan, from the end of August 2005. He decided on the day following the cabinet meeting to invest 100 percent to construct a 2.2-kilometer section to the Taksin Road with the budget of 2,200 million baht. He had already asked the cabinet to change its decision five times since taking over from Samak, and the sixth request had not even been discussed at the cabinet meeting on October 18 (*PCT* [OE], 22 October 2005). Although the BMA hitherto had wished for development by joint investment with the private sector and had asked for the support of the government for 65 percent of the civil engineering costs, it reasoned that the BMA could sidestep the need for a revision in the cabinet's decision by itself investing 100 percent of the costs.

The government was severely critical. Thaksin claimed that Aphirak's move should have been decided after talking with the government, noting that "the BMA is not an autonomous country" (*BP* [OE], 22 October 2005). The government insisted that the construction of a few kilometers of railway would not generate surplus income, and noted that an environmental impact assessment had not yet been submitted.[24] However, since the Metropolitan Assembly, including the members of Thai Rak Thai Party, unanimously agreed to the plan, and the support of Bangkokians was stronger than anticipated, the government had no choice but to give in to the plan (*PCK* [OE], 26 October 2005; *BP* [OE], 5 November 2005). Aphirak promised Bangkokians that construction would be completed within a year, and the civil engineering work started on December 1 (*PCK* [OE], 5 December 2005).

Furthermore, when Thaksin's Mega Project suffered a setback in 2006, Aphirak decided in April that the BMA should undertake the extension of the remaining sections. He decided to construct three sections—the Mochit–Kasetsart University line, the Onnut–Bearing line, and the Taksin Road–Bang Wa line—by 100 percent BMA investment, which was approved by the Metropolitan Assembly in May (*PCK* [OE], 25 April 2006; *KT* [OE], 25 May 2006). Since the Onnut–Bearing line was a partial section of the Samrong line, which lay within the limits of the BMA, it was easy to obtain the consent of the Metropolitan Assembly.[25] The development that started from this line had already been offered by bid. Although the Italian-Thai Development Company, Ltd. was reluctant to agree to contract for the price tendered three years before, it finally signed the contract in July (*PCK* [OE], 20 July 2006). Since it was necessary to build a 5.2-kilometer elevated line, unlike the Taksin line, the time required to complete the project was set at three years, and construction started on August 26, aiming for an opening in April 2009 (*PCK* [OE], 21 August 2006).

Thus, since the government was uncooperative on the extension of the BTS, the BMA finally started construction of two lines without obtaining government permission. The government opposed the extension plan by bringing up concerns about the BTSC's financial condition and a high fare. The extension of the BTS was easy compared with building a new line from scratch, since it only consisted of extending currently operating routes, and there was a section for which civil engineering work had been mostly completed. Although the BTSC's restructuring plan was also overdue because it had declared that the investment in the equipment for the operation was possible for the Taksin line, the cabinet should have agreed to revise its decision in order to promote construction using a two-tiered operation.

The BMA, which decided to construct the extension lines by itself, had to bear more of the investment than it would have in a two-tiered operation. And since the BMA would undertake operation of the extension lines, complicated issues such as the burden of sharing operation costs and the distribution of fare revenues would intensify. Therefore, from a management viewpoint, it was not the best policy for the BMA to directly operate a short-distance railway, as Thaksin had claimed. Given the situation, however, the BMA could not avoid such a decision just because the government's urban railway plan had not progressed. Bangkokians were fully supportive, and the Metropolitan Assembly unanimously approved the governor's decision. Bangkokians desired a solution to the immediate transport problem, and the extension of the BTS was just that; they supported the BMA's drive rather than the government's populist politics. The government's uncooperative posture only increased Bangkokians' distrust.

Fight for Leadership over Bus Operations

Progress in Transferring Bus Operations

A similar discord between the BMA and the Thaksin government also characterized the policy on buses; populist policies again became an important factor. In the first stage, bus policies consisted of passive measures, just as in the case of urban railways, and the transfer of bus operations to the BMA as part of the downsizing plan that had surfaced in the late 1990s was the center of these passive plans. However, when the BRT plan emerged after Aphirak became the BMA governor, the government worked to interrupt the plan just as it had done for the BTS extension lines. This resulted in a significant confrontation with the BMA. Finally, the government tried to improve bus service as a populist measure through the radical reform of the loss-ridden BMTA (Bangkok Mass Transit Authority) by introducing air-conditioned buses with a low fare.

Although the problem of transferring bus operations to the BMA was resolved by promoting the BMTA's downsizing plan, which included reducing its share in bus operations to 20 percent, the transfer issue resurfaced after Samak was inaugurated as the BMA governor in July 2000. Immediately after being inaugurated as governor, Samak supported the transfer of BMTA's bus operations and made clear that the fare of the ordinary bus should be raised from 3.5 baht to 5 baht, and that the government should take over the BMTA's cumulative deficit, which was up to 20 billion baht (*N* [OE], 24 July 2000).[26] As mentioned above, Samak also vigorously promoted the extension of the BTS, and he hoped to change bus routes so that they would serve as feeders for the BTS. Thus, the BMA intended to strengthen the participation in urban transport by having jurisdiction over both urban railway and bus service.

The BMTA opposed the transfer plan, claiming that it should continue as the operator of air-conditioned buses by maintaining an appropriate fare level so that it could operate without losses, and that the operation of the ordinary buses could be left to its newly established subsidiary with a governmental subsidy (*BP* [OE], 24 October 2000). There was no clear government response to this, and the transfer problem persisted because of the deficit issue. The BMA began to take action at the beginning of 2003, aiming at the transfer of ordinary buses only. Since the BMTA's opposition was deep-rooted, the BMA was inclined to operate only ordinary buses and to abandon the operation of air-conditioned buses. The BMA employed a private consulting company and Thammasat University to investigate the bus operation transfer plan and decided to come up with a policy based on the results (*DN* [OE], 18 February 2003).

The investigation results were submitted in July 2003; the conclusion was that the air-conditioned buses should be left to the BMTA, and only ordinary buses should be transferred, as planned by the BMA (*BP* [OE],

3 July 2003). The recommendations did not include the abolition of the BMTA because the operation of the air-conditioned bus was slated to be left to the BMTA to avoid opposition by its employees. In addition, it was assumed that the BMA's jurisdiction should be restricted to only ordinary buses for the purpose of offering fundamental transport services to Bangkokians. The operation methods of the buses were fundamentally based on privatization, and two methods were suggested: 85 or 100 percent privatization. If the fare was four baht, the the BMA's operation of ordinary buses was expected to result in a 453 million baht surplus per year, and that was presumed to be a satisfactory level of profitability (ibid.).

In response, Samak told the Ministry of Transport and the Ministry of Finance that he accepted the transfer of the ordinary buses. Although the operation conditions of the buses was in accord with the consultancy recommendations, because the actual operation cost was six baht per passenger the BMA asked that the government compensate it for the one-baht gap between the operation cost and the fare of five baht, which was one baht more than that suggested by the consultants (*DN* [OE], 3 February 2004). Although the investigation results anticipated a profit, Samak foresaw that the BMA would not gain a big profit, noting that the actual operation might not work out as estimated. However, there was no reaction from the government's side to Samak's proposal, and the bus operation transfer plan was not realized during his era, just as had been the case with the BTS extension.

Meanwhile, the BMTA also conducted an investigation into improvements in bus operations. It gained the approval of the cabinet in October 2001 to conduct investigations into cost reduction options and employed Chulalongkorn University to do the study (*PCK* [OE], 8 March 2002). The study results showed that the cost for operation of the ordinary buses was 6.33 baht per passenger, but swelled to 6.77 baht if the repayment of the accumulated debt was included (ibid.). Since the present fare was 3.5 baht, it was proposed that the government should assist with operation costs in the amount of 18 billion per year for ordinary bus operation, as a type of public service obligation (PSO) (*BP* [OE], 9 May 2002).[27] Therefore, the BMTA asked the government to either raise the fare or provide a subsidy of 1.5 baht per person if a fare hike could not be approved. However, since the investigation also noted user dissatisfaction with the bus service, things did not pan out according to the BMTA's expectations.

The BMTA had also explored ways to improve its financial situation. To increase revenue, it started sales of advance tickets, such as a whole-day ticket, in February 2002 to earn secure fare revenue in advance as well as to fund the facilities available to users (KSMK for 2002, 35).[28] For example, the whole-day ticket for ordinary buses was set at ten baht, and by riding an ordinary bus, which had a three-and-a-half-baht fare, three times, the users recovered their cost. Therefore, for users who changed buses two or more times, their fare was cheaper, resulting in an increase in the number of advance ticket sales. However, the increased advance ticket sales resulted in a reduction in the sales of ordinary tickets, and the fare revenue decreased by no less than 500 million baht from the previous fiscal year in 2003 (KSMK 2005, 12).[29] Contrary to the original intentions, advance tickets worsened the financial situation of the BMTA, and the option was finally abolished in March 2004 (KSMK for 2004, 49).

In addition, since the operation of the air-conditioned buses on ordinary bus routes was increasing, and some ordinary bus routes were only run with air-conditioned buses, the number of air-conditioned bus routes was changed. In September 2001, a new route numbering was set by adding "500" to the former route number of air-conditioned buses, such as Route 501 for former Route 1 of the air-conditioned bus A1 (KSMK for 2001, 22).[30] Thus, the gap between air-conditioned and ordinary buses became even smaller, and future unification of ordinary buses to air-conditioned buses was attained. The raison d'être for the ordinary buses as PSO was still great, and the BMTA also continued maintaining operation of ordinary buses.

The BRT Plan Surfaces

The BRT plan surfaced in Bangkok in 2004, but did not actually begin until September 2004, when Aphirak was inaugurated as the BMA governor. The BRT operated its buses by securing dedicated lanes in the center of roads, such as tramways, and was an intermediate means of transport between buses and tramways. Although similar to the urban railway in terms of having a station equipped with a ticket gate and a dedicated right-of-way, the construction costs were lower and the time required for completion was shorter than for the urban railway.

However, it caused other problems such as reducing the number of lanes for general vehicles, and the buses still had to pass through signals at crossings. Although the exclusive bus lanes were installed in the middle of Latphrao Road and Narathiwat Road, which were similar to the BRT, neither lasted long.[31]

Specialists from Bogotá, Colombia, where a BRT had already been introduced, visited Thailand in January 2004 and attended a conference on the introduction of a BRT in Bangkok (*PCT* [OE], 26 January 2004). The conference was held at the initiative of the Ministry of Transport to introduce the BRT plan by the OTP and BMTA. According to that plan, a total of 198 kilometers of BRT routes would be constructed in Bangkok by 2009 with a total cost of construction estimated at 2 billion baht (*BP* [OE], 2 February 2004). At that time, the BMTA was supposed to have jurisdiction over the operation of the BRT as one of the remedies for the BMTA's bus operation.

However, when Aphirak used the introduction of the BRT as a campaign pledge and announced the introductory plan of the BRT immediately after being inaugurated as the BMA governor, the BMA came to play the role of promoting the BRT plan (*BP* [OE], 9 September 2004). He announced the plan to introduce a total of ten BRT routes, (see figure 6.2), and the first two lines—the 14-kilometer Mochit–Nawamin line and the 13-kilometer Chong Nonsi–Bangkok Bridge line—would be completed within a year (*DN* [OE], 14 September 2004). Both were feeder routes to the BTS, and because the section between Kasetsart University to Nawamin Road in the former and the section between Chong Nonsi and the Rama III Road in the latter followed newly opened roads, the road was sufficiently wide for their establishment.

Nikon Chamnong, the deputy minister of transport, denied that the road width was not sufficient between Mochit and Kasetsart University, and hoped to construct the BTS extension line from Mochit to Kasetsart University, which would be the starting point of the BRT (*PCT* [OE], 14 September 2004). From Mochit to Kasetsart University, the BRT would follow the six-lane Phahonyothin Road, and it was a concern that the traffic congestion on this road would worsen by giving two lanes over for the BRT. Moreover, the road between Kasetsart University and Nawamin Road was under the jurisdiction of the Department of Highways, and the pillars for the ETA's future expressway had already been partially built

Fig. 6.2. Bus Rapid Transit (BRT) Plan by the BMA, 2004

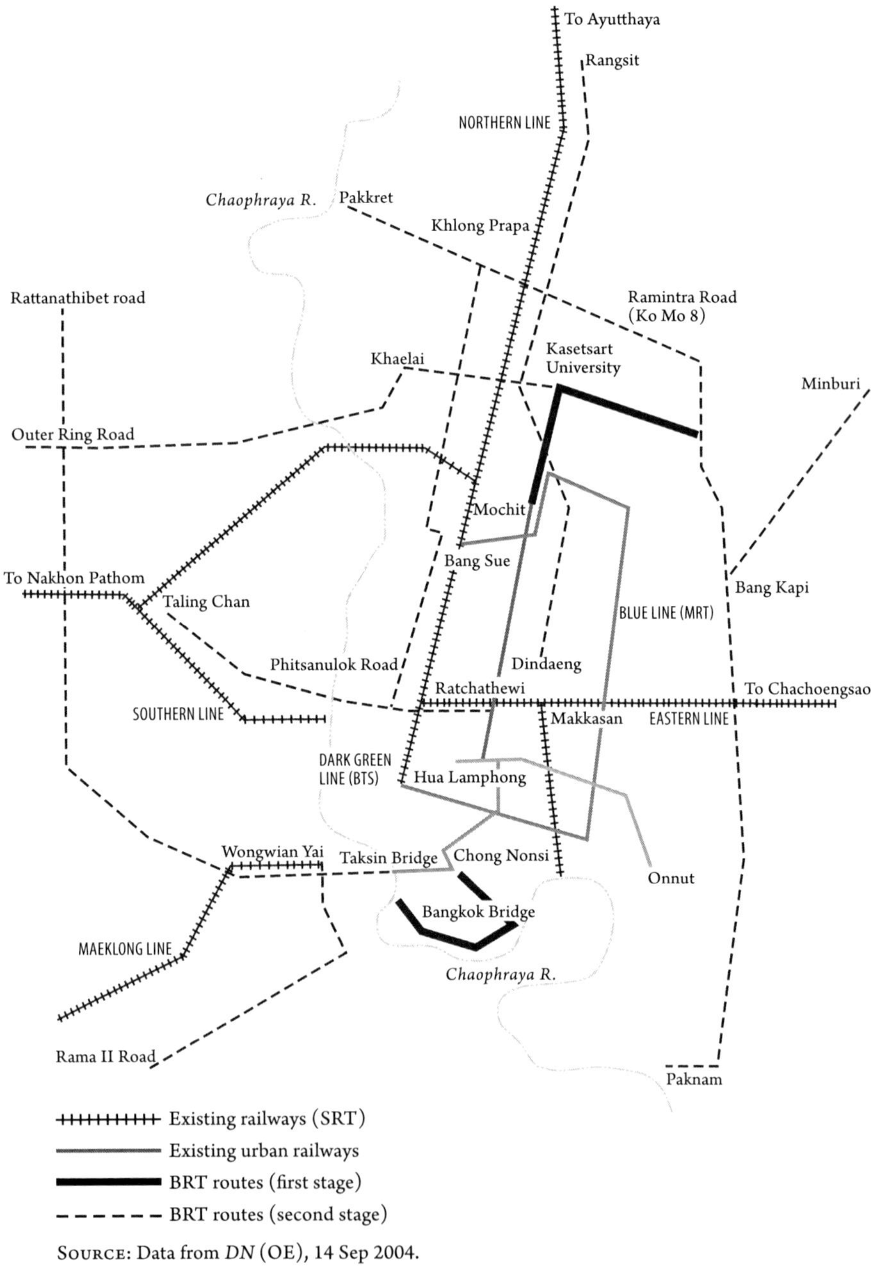

Source: Data from *DN* (OE), 14 Sep 2004.

in the middle of the road. Therefore, it was expected that negotiations with these agencies would be difficult. On the other hand, the Chong Nonsi–Bangkok Bridge line was extended to Ratchaphruek Road in Thonburi by crossing the newly constructed Rama III Bridge parallel to the Bangkok Bridge to solve the problem of the space needed for buses to make a U-turn at the Bangkok Bridge (*BP* [OE], 5 January 2005).[32]

The Thaksin government tried to block the BMA's plan for a BRT as well as the BTS extension lines. Since it was decided in the 1983 cabinet meeting that the BMTA was the sole bus operator in Bangkok and its suburbs, it was necessary to gain cabinet approval for the BMA to operate the BRT as an exception to this rule. Therefore, the BMA asked the Ministry of Interior for an exemption in September 2005, but the Ministry of Interior evaded with countermeasures so that this request was not submitted to the cabinet (*PCT* [OE], 13 October 2005). This was the same reaction as had occurred in the case of the BTS when the BMA asked for a reexamination of the cabinet decision that regulated the construction of the BTS extension lines by 100 percent private investment, and the Thaksin government had been uncooperative.

The BMA announced the terms of reference for bidding in September 2005, aiming at the commencement of business in mid-2006 (*DN* [OE], 4 October 2005). The bidding was postponed because there was no progress on the reexamination of the cabinet decision. The BMA then opened the bidding in November after deciding to construct the BTS extension line by itself (*PCK* [OE], 15 November 2005). However, since the government did not show an inclination to cooperate, a contract with a successful bidder could not be signed, thus indefinitely delaying groundbreaking. In the meantime, the BMA temporarily suspended construction of the controversial Mochit–Nawamin Road (Ko Mo 8) line to obtain the government's permission (*DN* [OE], 9 May 2006).[33] Furthermore, the BMA changed its strategy of asking through the Ministry of Interior for a reexamination of the cabinet decision to asking the BMTA for permission, in order to avoid the hurdle of a cabinet decision (ibid.). Despite these efforts, by the time the Thaksin government was overthrown, it had yet to give approval to the BRT plan, and the plan was shelved.

Rehabilitation of the BMTA

To oppose the BMA's BRT plan, the government turned to the populist policy of providing cheap air-conditioned bus service by rehabilitating the BMTA. Although the ratio of private buses had been raised according to the BMTA's downsizing plan made at the end of the 1990s, private buses were not necessarily able to gain user support. According to a user survey conducted in September 2002, only 40 percent of respondents supported private buses, and another survey conducted at the same time showed that 78 percent of respondents wanted the government to offer public transport services (*BP* [OE], 12 October 2002). Private buses, which were built using the old chassis of BMTA buses, were in bad condition—often emitting noxious black smoke, for instance—and employee attitudes were quite poor. Therefore, whenever private bus accidents occurred, support for public BMTA buses rose and the positive image of private buses fell.

Promotion of privatization, which had progressed from the end of the 1990s, stagnated in the 2000s. Table 6.3 shows the change in the number of buses since 2001. The number of BMTA buses had been around 3,500. The number of private buses gradually increased, reaching 3,500 in 2006 and exceeding the number of BMTA buses in 2008. Since the number of vans also increased, the share of BMTA buses fell from 25 percent in 2001 to 20 percent in 2009. The increase in the number of private buses resulted in a fall in the share of BMTA buses because the latter fell to as low as 150 buses during the period, implying that the downsizing plan of reducing the share of BMTA buses to 20 percent, which had been fixed at the end of the 1990s, was finally realized. There had been about 110 BMTA bus routes (see table 6.4). This remained unchanged after the number of private bus routes gradually increased to the same level as the number of BMTA bus routes.

Therefore, the government changed the policy of rehabilitating and downsizing the BMTA because of user support for public buses, and began to utilize it as a symbol of populist policy for Bangkokians. The government permitted the business improvement plan that the BMTA proposed in December 2005 (*PCK* [OE], 15 December 2005). The main point was the purchase of 2,000 air-conditioned, natural gas–fueled vehicles (NGVs), eventually increasing this number to 4,000 buses, to renew the buses directly operated by the BMTA. Both a reduction of fuel

Table 6.3. Number of Buses in Bangkok, 2001–2010

Fiscal Year	BMTA Buses			Private Buses			Minibuses	Songthaeo	Vans	Total
	Ordinary	Air-conditioned	Total	Ordinary	Air-conditioned	Total				
2001	1,683	1,987	3,670	2,188	632	2,820	1,180	2,269	5,337	15,276
2002	1,674	1,981	3,655	2,348	662	3,010	1,179	2,208	4,610	14,662
2003	1,670	1,936	3,606	2,423	870	3,293	1,175	2,072	5,531	15,677
2004	1,673	1,905	3,578	2,428	932	3,360	1,157	2,060	5,570	15,725
2005	1,674	1,905	3,579	2,502	960	3,462	1,118	2,080	5,522	15,761
2006	1,674	1,905	3,579	2,556	944	3,500	1,078	2,215	6,217	16,589
2007	1,674	1,861	3,535	2,559	932	3,491	1,069	2,304	6,510	16,909
2008	1,665	1,861	3,526	2,554	981	3,535	1,067	2,325	6,919	17,372
2009	1,663	1,855	3,518	2,674	1,327	4,001	1,054	2,365	6,647	17,585
2010	1,659	1,874	3,533	2,706	1,376	4,082	594	2,323	5,816	16,321

Note 1: Figures are from the end of the fiscal year (end of September), except in 2005 (end of July).
Note 2: Figures exclude microbuses.
Sources: KSMK for 2001–10; KSMK 2005.

costs by using natural gas as fuel and a reduction in personnel expenses by installing a smart card (IC card) system and omitting a conductor were expected (*PCK* [OE], 6 January 2006). The fare would be a ten-baht flat rate, lower than the current fare for air-conditioned buses, and free transfers would also be possible.[34]

This plan emerged because of the rapid increase in oil prices and the frequent fare hikes for ordinary buses. As shown in figure 6.3, the retail price of diesel oil in Bangkok rose suddenly in 2005. The price of diesel oil was about fifteen baht per liter in 2004, but rose to twenty-five baht only six months later. Therefore, demands for a fare hike from private bus operators were constant, and the ordinary bus fare rose rapidly. According to table 6.5, the ordinary bus fare, which was at least four baht in 2004, was raised twice until leveling at six baht in 2005, and soaring to seven baht in 2006. This meant that the ordinary bus fare doubled within only two years. Furthermore, in 2008, a fare hike to nine baht, the highest ever, was made to account for the jump in oil prices after the Thaksin government.

Table 6.4. Number of Bus Routes in Bangkok, 2001–2010

Fiscal Year	BMTA Buses			Private Buses			Minibuses	Songthaeo	Vans	Total
	Ordinary	Air-conditioned	Total	Ordinary	Air-conditioned	Total				
2001	N.A.	N.A.	111	N.A.	N.A.	88	N.A.	N.A.	N.A.	199
2002	N.A.	N.A.	106	N.A.	N.A.	95	N.A.	N.A.	N.A.	201
2003	N.A.	N.A.	102	N.A.	N.A.	103	N.A.	N.A.	N.A.	205
2004	N.A.	N.A.	102	N.A.	N.A.	104	48	104	116	474
2005	82	20	102	79	28	107	47	102	116	474
2006	N.A.	N.A.	108	N.A.	N.A.	N.A.	N.A.	N.A.	N.A.	108
2007	N.A.	N.A.	108	N.A.	N.A.	N.A.	N.A.	N.A.	N.A.	108
2008	N.A.	N.A.	112	N.A.	N.A.	105	22	115	131	485
2009	N.A.	N.A.	108	N.A.	N.A.	101	N.A.	113	123	445
2010	N.A.	N.A.	108	N.A.	N.A.	103	21	110	128	470

Note 1: Figures are from the end of the fiscal year (end of September), except in 2005 (end of July).
Note 2: Figures exclude microbuses.
Sources: KSMK for 2001–7; *SC* for 2003, for 2008–10.

Table 6.5. Changes in Bus Fares, 2001–2010

Date	Fare System	Fare (THB)	Remarks	Sources
1 Feb 2004	Flat	4.00, 5.00		KSMK for 2004
2 May 2005	Flat	5.00, 6.00		KSMK for 2005
8 Jul 2005	Flat	6.00, 7.00		KSMK for 2005
14 Feb 2006	Flat	7.00, 8.00	BMTA buses from 19 Apr	KSMK for 2006
15 Oct 2007	Flat	7.50, 8.50	Private buses only	*PCK* (OE), 12 Oct 2007
25 May 2008	Flat	9.00, 10.00	Private buses only	*DN* (OE), 24 May 2008
28 May 2008	Flat	7.50, 8.50	Private buses only	*KT* (OE), 27 May 2008
2 Sep 2008	Flat	9.00, 10.00		KSMK for 2008
28 Oct 2008	Flat	7.50, 8.50		*BP* (OE), 22 Oct 2008
22 Dec 2008	Flat	7.00, 8.00		*DN* (OE), 18 Dec 2008

NOTE: Fares are for ordinary, non air-conditioned buses (red buses, white buses).

Fig. 6.3. Price of Diesel Oil, 1998–2010 (THB/Liter)

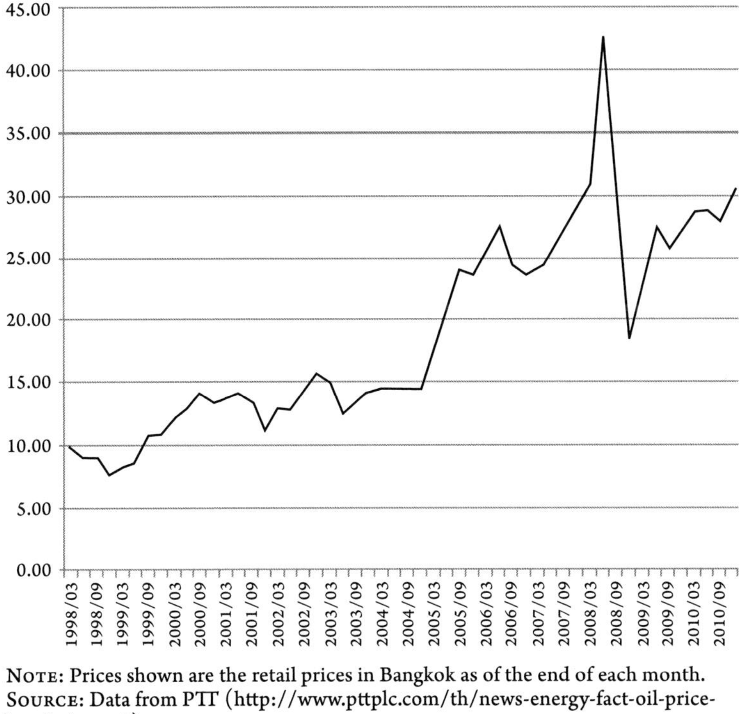

NOTE: Prices shown are the retail prices in Bangkok as of the end of each month.
SOURCE: Data from PTT (http://www.pttplc.com/th/news-energy-fact-oil-price-bangkok.aspx?).

The BMTA thus formed a plan to introduce NGV buses, with less fuel consumption, as a means of reducing fuel costs and proposed it to the government.[35] The government accepted the plan on the condition of a ten-baht flat rate (*PCK [OE]*, 15 December 2005). That is, it machinated to provide cheap air-conditioned bus service by making it into a populist policy using the BMTA business improvement plan. Since the ordinary bus fare rose to seven baht, even if the government abolished ordinary buses, it considered that the introduction of air-conditioned buses with a ten-baht flat fare would probably gain user support. Moreover, since personnel expenses would also be reduced by introducing the IC card, the operational costs of the NGV buses would fall sharply. The government thus estimated that the profitability of the BMTA would be secured if the ten baht fare could be adopted. Since the urban railway policy was confusing at that time and a new policy for "selling a dream" was required, this NGV bus introduction plan posed the chance for a comeback for the government.

If realized, the downsizing plan of the BMTA would mean that the agency would increase its role again. Since the newly introduced buses would be BMTA-operated buses, the share of BMTA buses would increase, even though some would be substitutes for old buses. In 2005, there were about 3,600 BMTA buses. Therefore, the number of newly introduced buses, which could be as many as 4,000, would exceed the existing number of BMTA buses. This plan meant the rehabilitation of the BMTA. It was not the private buses that repeatedly called for a raise in the fare, but the public BMTA buses that the government could utilize to carry out its populist policies.

The plan was agreed to at the cabinet meeting in February 2006, and the BMTA planned the operation to begin in the end of 2006 (*PCK* [OE] 2006/02/14). However, the BMTA delayed the bidding because of the growth of the anti-Thaksin movement and the parliament's eventual dismissal. Minister of transport Phongsak announced in August that a Chinese company proposed the sale of 8,000 NGV buses (*PCK* [OE], 1 August 2006).[36] Since the government did not need to work out the budget for bus purchase beforehand, it showed interest in this plan. Thaksin also utilized this plan in his "selling a dream" campaign for the next election, claiming that the twenty-baht difference in the fuel cost per liter by using these NGV buses would create an eight-baht surplus that could be used for further reduction in fares and salary increases for employees, even though twelve baht would be appropriated for paying for the purchase of the buses (*PCK* [OE], 5 August 2006).

This NGV bus plan suffered a setback with the fall of the Thaksin government and would be tackled by the following government, as would the BMA's BRT. Although a confrontation had arisen between the government and the BMA, and bus policy gradually turned into a vehicle for populist policy in the Thaksin period, there was no radical improvement in bus service.

Confrontation Continues

Creation of a New Master Plan

It seemed that the urban railway policy would be free from confrontation after the the Thaksin regime. However, when another pro-Thaksin government came to power through the 2007 general election, confrontation arose again, even though progress on the plan was overdue. Confrontation continued even under the anti-Thaksin government that came to rule at the end of 2008, and thus development of urban railways progressed slowly.

After the coup d'état in September 2006, Surayud Chulanont served as interim prime minister. He pursued the urban railway development plan that had suffered a setback during the Thaksin period. At the cabinet meeting in November 2006, the government agreed to construct five urban railway lines for a total of 118 kilometers (*PCK* [OE], 7 November 2006). These five lines included the 23-kilometer Purple line between Bang Sue and Bang Yai, the 27-kilometer Blue line between Bang Sue and Tha Phra and between Hua Lamphong and Bang Khae, the 41-kilometer Red line between Taling Chan and Rangsit via Bang Sue, the 13-kilometer Dark Green line between Mochit and Saphan Mai, and the 14-kilometer Light Green line between Bearing and Paknam (see figure 6.1). The construction method changed from the turnkey method to the detailed design method for the elevated section and the design-and-build method for the underground sections (ibid.).[37] Moreover, to acquire local residents' consent, the government decided to carry out an environmental impact assessment and a public hearing. Finally, it was decided that the construction work on the first line should be started by the end of 2007.

A feature of this plan was the inclusion of the Dark Green and Light Green lines, which were under the jurisdiction of the BMA. Although the Thaksin government resisted the extension of these two lines, the new government incorporated them in the plan, for which preparation for construction had already progressed. National budget funds would also be appropriated for the extension of both lines. Although it was an interim government (because the Surayud government was organized with the anti-military coup-makers and the anti-Thaksin group's support), it alleviated the previous discord with the BMA.

In fact, no construction on any line proceeded in 2007 because the search for funds for the Purple line, the most advanced line, was overdue, as will be discussed below. Then, after the pro-Thaksin political party came back to power in the general election in late 2007 with Samak, the former BMA governor, as prime minister, a new urban railway plan was formulated. He announced the new plan in February 2008, calling for construction of nine urban railway lines at a budget of 500 billion baht (*PCT* [OE], 11 February 2008). Although the old plan was fundamentally followed, the extension to the suburbs was thought important in this plan: the Dark Green line was to be extended to Lam Lukka, the Purple line to Sainoi, and the Light Green line to Bang Pu. Furthermore, while extending the Blue line from Tha Phra along the Chaophraya to build a 40-kilometer circle line by connecting it with the existing Hua Lamphong–Bang Sue line, another 100-kilometer circle line would be constructed by extending the original Yellow line toward the west; an urban network composed of nine radial lines and two circle lines would also be constructed (*PCK* [OE], 10 February 2008). Since the extension to the suburbs and the construction of the circle lines had already emerged when Samak was the BMA governor, this plan was completely based on his own ideas. The cabinet approved what was labeled a new plan in March (SNK 2010, 3–13).

The BTSC purchasing plan that surfaced during the Thaksin period was also contained within this plan. Although he had once promoted the construction of the BTS extension lines and placed importance on the extension of the Dark Green and Light Green lines, he stated that the government would operate the urban railways directly, including the existing BTS lines. Therefore, while the government tried to purchase the BTSC, it planned for the government to grant the concession instead of the BMA (*DN* [OE], 19 March 2008). The government would also pay for the construction costs of the two extension lines that the BMA was building itself and decided to leave the survey and design of the newly built sections to the OTP and MRTA (*DN* [OE], 10 March 2008). The government insisted that the extension lines of the Dark Green and Light Green lines should not be connected using the existing BTS lines if the negotiations about buying out the BTSC did not pan out. This put pressure on the BTSC by noting that the connecting point of the extended Dark Green line would be changed from Mochit to the Phahonyothin station of the Blue line, and the connection of the extended Light Green line at Bearing would also be changed from the BTS extension line to the Yellow line by changing the latter's route (*PCK* [OE], 14 March 2008). Thus, the urban railway plan began to follow a populist policy again, as during the Thaksin period, and the buyout problem of the BTSC, which was a prerequisite for the low fare policy, resurfaced.

Confrontation between the government and the BMA became obvious once again, although Samak's urban railway policy never proceeded since he lost his position in September 2008. His successor, Somchai Wongsawat of the pro-Thaksin group, also lost his position in December of the same year, so there was no big change in the urban railway policy. However, at a cabinet meeting on November 27 just before Somchai left office, it was decided that the construction of the Dark Green line between Mochit and Saphan Mai and the Light Green line between Bearing and Paknam would be left to the MRTA. The change in the cabinet decision became an indispensable condition for the BMA to promote the construction of the former line that had already been approved by the Metropolitan Assembly (*PCK* [OE], 24 February 2009).

This issue became moot when political power shifted to Abhisit Vejjajiva of the anti-Thaksin Democrat Party, who formed a government after Somchai's removal in December 2008. Both Aphirak, who had been reelected as BMA governor in October 2008, and Sukhumphan Boriphat of the Democrat Party, who replaced Aphirak as governor when the latter had to resign under accusations of corruption, promoted the development of the BTS extension lines.[38] However, the Bhumjaithai Party, a breakoff from the then banned Thai Rak Thai Party, lobbied successfully for the post of minister of transport. Bhumjaithai's Sophon Saram, the new minister, opposed the change in the cabinet decision (*DN* [OE], 27 February 2009).[39] Therefore, although the government was decidedly anti-Thaksin, discord between the BMA and the Ministry of Transport continued. The prime minister asked the Ministry of Transport and the BMA to settle their differences, and it was decided in August 2009 that jurisdiction over the operation would be decided later by consulting the BMA, but that for now the MRTA had jurisdiction over construction (*PCK* [OE], 24 August 2009). Then, although Sukhumphan once again appealed to Abhisit to return jurisdiction of the BTS extension lines to the BMA, the prime minister accepted that the Ministry of Transport, controlled by the coalition partner Bhumjaithai Party, had jurisdiction, as the cabinet had decided (*PCK* [OE], 22 January 2010). To maintain the coalition government, Abhisit had to respect the wishes of the Bhumjaithai Party.

The BMA also lost its plan for construction of the extension section of the Light Green line between the National Stadium and Phrannok. As a new master plan replaced the BMTIP, the period for which expired at the end of 2009, the OTP formulated a "Mass Rapid Transit Master Plan in the Bangkok Metropolitan Region" (SNK 2010, 1–11). This plan aimed at developing no less than a 500-kilometer urban railway network over twenty years (see table 6.6), with twelve lines, the most lines ever among all prior urban railway development plans. The table shows that the extension between the National Stadium and Phrannok of the Light Green line was omitted and instead only included a 1-kilometer extension to Yotse, the connecting station with the Red line.[40] A part of the Orange line changed directions to connect with the Thonburi side as an alternative line, as shown in figure 6.4.

The OTP stated that the reason for the change in the Light Green line route was that it was not suitable and that the original plan would remove two lanes on the Rama I Road (*DN* [OE], 3 August 2009).[41] However, when the OTP first announced the draft of this master plan in March 2009, the section between the National Stadium and Phrannok of the Light Green line was included (*DN* [OE], 30 March 2009). The change in the Light Green line was first reported in August, making it certain that the change in the plan was made during this period. Since Sukhumphan also promoted this extension line, I suspect that certain political considerations were at work to cause the change (*PCK* [OE], 3 April 2009). The BMA, whose BTS extension plans were obstructed, then concentrated on monorail development as feeder lines, and the two new monorail lines, the Gray line and the Sky Blue line, both under the jurisdiction of the BMA, were incorporated into the master plan, as shown in table 6.6.[42]

Table 6.6. Mass Rapid Transit Master Plan in Bangkok Metropolitan Region, 2010

Line	Section	Length (km)	Jurisdiction	Opening Year	Remarks
Dark Red	Thammasat University–Bang Sue	36.3	SRT	2014	Preparing for bidding
	Bang Sue–Hua Lamphong	6.5	SRT	2016	
	Hua Lamphong–Bang Bon	18.0	SRT	2016	
	Bang Bon–Mahachai	20.0	SRT	2020	
	Total	80.8			
Light Red	Salaya–Taling Chan	14.0	SRT	2016	
	Taling Chan–Bang Sue	15.0	SRT	2013	Under construction
	Bang Sue–Makkasan	9.0	SRT	2016	
	Bang Bamru–Makkasan	10.5	SRT	2025	Alternative underground line
	Makkasan–Huamak	10.0	SRT	2016	
	Total	58.5			
Airport Rail Link	Don Mueang–Phayathai	21.8	SRT	2016	
	Phayathai–Suvarnabhumi Airport	28.5	SRT	2010	Opened in Aug 2010
	Total	50.3			
Dark Green	Lam Lukka–Khukhot	6.5	MRTA, BMA	2024	
	Khukhot–Saphan Mai	7.0	MRTA, BMA	2015	
	Saphan Mai–Mochit	11.4	MRTA, BMA	2014	
	Mochit–Onnut	16.5	BMA	Opened	
	Onnut–Baering	5.3	BMA	2011	Under construction
	Bearing–Paknam	12.8	MRTA, BMA	2014	
	Paknam–Bang Pu	7.0	MRTA, BMA	2029	
	Total	66.5			
Light Green	Yotse–National Stadium	1.0	BMA	2015	
	National Stadium–Wongwian Yai	9.2	BMA	Opened	
	Wongwian Yai–Bang Wa	5.3	BMA	2011	Under construction
	Total	15.5			

Line	Section	Length (km)	Jurisdiction	Opening Year	Remarks
Blue	Bang Sue–Hua Lamphong	20.0	MRTA	Opened	Underground
	Hua Lamphong–Bang Khae	14.0	MRTA	2016	Bidding, partial underground
	Bang Khae–Phutthamonthon 4	8.0	MRTA	2021	
	Bang Sue–Tha Phra	13.0	MRTA	2016	Bidding
	Total	55.0			
Purple	Bang Yai–Bang Sue	23.0	MRTA	2014	Under construction
	Bang Sue–Ratburana	19.8	MRTA	2019	Partial underground
	Total	42.8			
Orange	Taling Chan–Thailand Cultural Center	17.5	MRTA	2017	Partial underground
	Thailand Cultural Center–Bang Kapi	9.0	MRTA	2017	Partial underground
	Bang Kapi–Minburi	11.0	MRTA	2017	
	Total	37.5			
Pink	Khaelai–Minburi	36.0	MRTA	2015	Monorail
Yellow	Latphrao–Phatthanakan	12.6	MRTA	2020	Monorail
	Phatthanakan–Samrong	17.8	MRTA	2024	Monorail
	Total	30.4			
Gray	Watcharaphon–Latphrao	8.0	BMA	2028	Monorail
	Latphrao–Rama IX Bridge	18.0	BMA	2026	Monorail
	Total	26.0			
Sky Blue	Dindaeng–Sathon	9.5	BMA	2023	Monorail
Grand total		508.8			

Source: Data from SNK 2010.

BMA's Slow Urban Railway Development

As long as the inter-agency conflict involving the urban railway continued, progress on the extension of the urban railway network was slow. The total distance of the urban railway open for traffic was 74.2 kilometers by 2010 (see table 6.7). Among these lines, since the Light Green line between the Taksin Bridge and Wongwian Yai and the Airport Rail Link opened in 2009 and 2010 respectively, very few lines were opened after the completion of the BTS lines and the Blue line of the MRTA, whose construction started during the 1990s. Moreover, the Airport Rail Link functioned as more of a suburban railway than an urban railway, as will be discussed below.

Fig. 6.4. Urban Railway Network in Bangkok, 2010

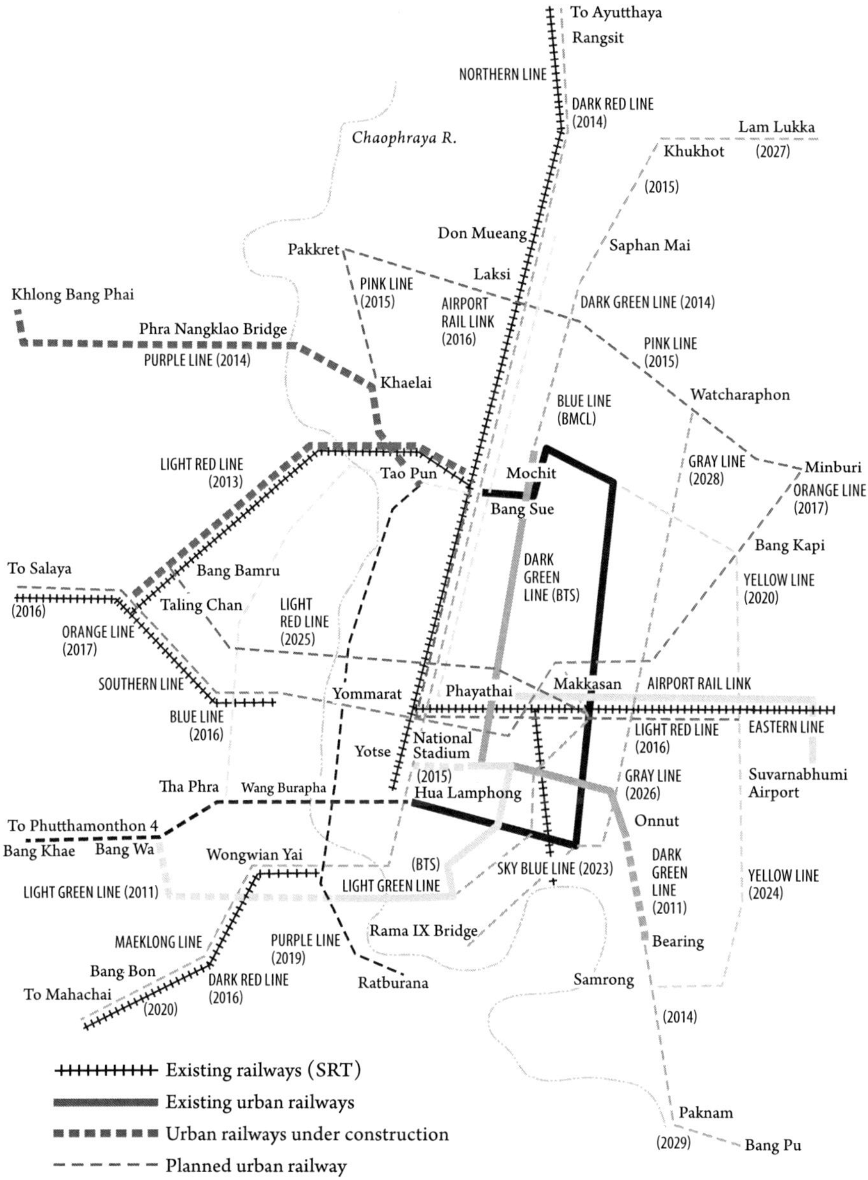

Note: Figures in parentheses are the estimated opening year, as of 2010.

Table 6.7. Opening of Urban Railways, 1999–2010

Jurisdiction	Line	Section	Length (km)	Opening Date	Remarks	Sources
BMA	Dark Green	Mochit–Onnut	17.0	5 Dec 1999		RKMK 2008
	Light Green	National Stadium–Taksin Bridge	6.5	5 Dec 1999		RKMK 2008
		Taksin Bridge–Wongwian Yai	2.2	15 May 2009	Formally opened on 23 Aug	KTM 2009
MRTA	Blue	Hua Lamphong–Bang Sue	20.0	3 Jul 2004		RFMT 2004
SRT	Aiport Rail Link	Phayathai–Suvarnabhumi Airport	28.5	23 Aug 2010		*PCK* (OE), 23 Aug 2010
Total			74.2			

NOTE: Names of lines are based on table 6.6.

The section between the Taksin Bridge and Wongwian Yai, which was a BTS extension line, was set by the BMA to be constructed during the confusion of the urban railway policy in the era of Thaksin. Then BMA governor Aphirak promised to complete it within one year after the groundbreaking at the end of 2005. Since the elevated structure was completed, the remaining work only included constructing stations, laying tracks, and installing power supply and signal equipment. The contractor for the stations and track construction was already identified, and the civil engineering work started immediately.

In fact, however, as table 6.7 shows, the opening was much delayed. The main reason was a problem with signal equipment. Although the BMA had initially negotiated for a private contract with Siemens to supply the BTS signal system, Siemens presented the BMA with a price of 1,800 million baht, while the BMA's estimate was 1,290 million baht (*DN* [OE], 22 March 2006). Therefore, a competitive bid was offered, and Siemens and Alcatel of France submitted bids in June 2006 (*DN* [OE], 16 June 2006). Although Alcatel's price was cheaper, it still exceeded the estimated price; further negotiations were necessary. At that point, the opening schedule was postponed by half a year, until mid-2007.

But it was necessary to revise the terms of reference in October 2006, because the BTSC wished to change its signal system from a track circuit system to a communication-based train control (CBTC) system (*PCT* [OE], 19 October 2006).[43] The BTSC planned to change the signal system and to introduce twelve new trains in preparation for the extension, a plan accepted by the bankruptcy court in December 2006 (*BP* [OE], 7 December 2006).[44] The BMA also entered into negotiations with Alcatel, which the BTSC was sure to agree to. However, since the BTSC decided to adopt the Bombardier system in March 2007, the BMA had to renegotiate with Bombardier (*PCT* [OE], 29 March 2007). The BMA's attitude to the contract with Bombardier changed several times, and it was finally decided that it would offer a bid by separating the signal equipment and other facilities, such as power equipment, from it. Finally, the contract with Bombardier was signed in February 2008, and the contract for other equipment was signed in April of the same year (KTM 2009, 116).

The railways started temporary operations on May 15, 2009, more than two years behind the original schedule, and they formally opened on August 23.[45] The BMA appointed its subsidiary, Krungthep Thanakhom Company, Ltd., to operate the extension line and Krungthep Thanakhom Company entrusted train operations to the BTSC (ibid.).[46] The BTSC purchased twelve new trains from China, which would be put into service on the Silom line, including the extension section. There were 42,682 passengers on September 1 after the official opening, less than the original target of 50,000, but this first urban railway to reach the Thonburi side was welcomed by the public. There were some troubles with the frequency of trains on the Silom line, which was low because of the single-track structure at the Taksin Bridge station, and the changeover to the new signal system took some time to iron out.[47]

Construction of the section between Onnut and Bearing, which started in the Thaksin period, went more smoothly than on the Wongwian Yai line. Although the line was scheduled to open in April 2009, the civil engineering work was only finished at the end of 2009 (*KT* [OE], 5 January 2010). After the bid for the signal system and electrical equipment was offered at the beginning of 2010, Italian-Thai Company, one of the three companies that passed screening, objected that one of the other companies was not qualified (*PCT* [OE], 22 March 2010). This problem was solved by the Italian-Thai Company's finally reducing its price, and construction started in July 2010 after it won the bid (*PCT*

[OE], 7 June 2010). Although the original opening scheduled for May 15, 2011 had to be extended to August 12, 2011, there were no more delays.

Since the section of the 4.5-kilometer elevated structure from Wongwian Yai to Bang Wa was already completed, the construction of station buildings and the remaining 800 meters of elevated structures remained. The construction of this section was to be performed after the construction of the Onnut–Bearing section, and it was due to be opened by 2009 (*PCT* [OE], 7 January 2008). Although there was no tangible movement during 2008, Sukhumphan announced during his electoral campaign for the BMA governorship that he aimed at its completion within two years (*DN* [OE], 17 December 2008). However, after his inauguration as governor, there was no immediate bidding. The opening schedule was postponed until the end of 2011 following the bidding for the equipment for the section between Onnut and Bearing (*KT* [OE], 5 January 2010). Although the terms of reference were announced in 2010, it became clear that the plan would not be adopted in May as part of the government's "Strong Thailand Plan" (*Khrongkan thai khemkhaeng*), as the BMA had hoped: government funds, which had been counted upon, were no longer there (*DN* [OE], 24 May 2010).[48] Therefore, the BMA hurriedly tried to generate funding for construction by using a bank loan to Krungthep Thanakhom Company (*PCT* [OE], 16 August 2010). Construction finally started in December 2010 and an opening at the end of 2012 was anticipated (*PCK* [OE], 29 December 2010).[49]

Movement toward New Construction

Apart from the BTS extension lines, the development of new urban railways was also slow. Among the five urban railways that the Surayud government selected to proceed in 2006, the Purple line and the Red line, for which preparations had already progressed, were the first to be developed. The MRTA had jurisdiction over the Purple line, and the plan was to extend the existing Blue line from Bang Sue to Tao Pun, and then head for Khlong Bangphai in the Bang Yai district, Nonthaburi province, on the west bank of the Chaophraya via existing roads. Since this was a line that the Thaksin government had offered up for bidding in 2005 but which was eventually suspended, construction work for it could be started immediately. However, the MRTA advanced cautiously by creating a detailed design and then holding a public hearing. Furthermore, the late approval of a loan from the JBIC also resulted in a delay.

Therefore, the government decided in October 2007 to construct the Purple line without specifying the source of funds and announced that a loan from China would also be investigated (*N* [OE], 3 October 2007). This playing of the "China card" led to a Japanese decision: it recognized the loan formally in December 2007 (*AS*, 5 December 2007). In response, preparations for the bids were made and offered in August 2008 (*KT* [OE], 14 August 2009). Successful bidders were chosen in August 2009, and the contract for the first section was signed in the same month (RFMT for 2009, 86). Construction started in November 2009, and is currently largely progressing as planned, with an opening date estimated in 2014 as of the end of 2010.[50] However, the total cost of construction soared from an initial 31 billion baht to 41 billion baht because of the 2008 jump in oil prices.[51]

A detailed design was also made for the SRT Red line. Construction of the Light Red line between Bang Sue and Taling Chan, for which design work was already finished, was approved at the cabinet meeting in May 2007 (*BP* [OE], 23 May 2007). Since the total cost of construction was 8.7 billion baht, which was lower than the Purple line, it was presumed that the SRT would itself supply the funds with guarantees from the Ministry of Finance; the bid was notified in October 2007 (*DN* [OE], 2 October 2007). However, since the SRT left it to the contractor to recover the right-of-way from residents in the SRT-owned property, major contractors such as Italian-Thai Company did not bid; only two companies tendered bids (*PCT* [OE], 15 May 2008). Because one company did not pass screening, the SRT negotiated with the remaining one. Since it took a long time to examine the rebidding and to hear the appeal of the dismissed company, it was not until December 2008 that the contract was finally signed (*PCT* [OE], 22 December 2008). Construction started in January 2009. The original schedule of groundbreaking in May 2008 and completion in June 2011 was delayed by half a year, and completion was anticipated at the end of 2011. However, since the electrification and supply of trains for this section were included in the building program for the section between Bang Sue and Rangsit, the SRT would use existing diesel cars for the time being.[52]

As for the section of the Dark Red line between Bang Sue and Rangsit, which was also under the jurisdiction of the SRT, negotiations proceeded with Japan for using a loan from JBIC because the total construction cost was as much as 59.9 billion baht, and the construction was approved at the cabinet meeting in December 2007 (*PCK* [OE], 16 October 2007).[53] At that point, the bid was to be offered in May 2008, and construction to be started in October. However, since the political conditions in Thailand were still unstable in early 2008, the JBIC's approval had to be postponed until Prime Minister Abhisit's visit to Japan in February 2009 (*PCK* [OE], 8 February 2009). Although the loan was signed in March, because the JBIC did not agree to the SRT's request that the contracts be increased from three to five, the bidding was much delayed (*PCT* [OE], 17 December 2009).[54] When the change in the number of contracts did not work, the Thai side, which wished to enhance the possibility for a successful bid from Thai companies, demanded that the ratio of a Thai company in a joint venture should be raised, which Japan agreed to (*PCT* [OE], 4 January 2010). In December 2010 the bidding was finally carried out (*DN* [OE], 2 December 2010).[55] It should be noted that a part of the Hopewell plan pillars were to be reused during the construction of this section.[56]

The Blue line plan also began to move toward groundbreaking following the Purple and Red lines. The Blue line was under the jurisdiction of the MRTA and was composed of two sections: the 13-kilometer section from Bang Sue to Tha Phra on the Thonburi side across the Chaophraya River, and the 14-kilometer section from Hua Lamphong to Bang Khae via Tha Phra.[57] The section from Hua Lamphong to Tha Phra was to go underground and the remainder elevated. Since there was an underground section, the total cost of construction in 2006 was estimated at 52.6 billion baht, which was considerably higher than that of the Purple line (*PCK* [OE], 17 November 2006).

Therefore, the JBIC loan was scheduled to be used at the beginning for the Blue line as well as the Purple and Red lines. When Santi Phromphat, the minister of transport in the Samak government, visited Japan in July 2008, the JBIC agreed for the loan to be used for the Red and Blue lines (*KT* [OE], 17 July 2008). However, the government later changed the plan for financing the endeavor and opted for a national bond, which was formally decided in July 2009 (*BP* [OE], 2 July 2009). Negotiations with

Japan continued, necessitated by the change in the terms of reference for the Dark Red line, and the start of the bidding had to be delayed. Therefore, the wish of the Thai side to increase opportunities for Thai companies to successfully bid and for construction to start soon, without waiting for the approval from Japan, seems to have resulted in a suspension of the Japanese loan.[58] Because of this, the MRTA announced the bidding in January 2010 and bids were offered from June to July (*PCT* [OE], 2 June 2010; *KT* [OE], 1 July 2010). Then, since there were complaints about unfairness in the bidding, the contracts with the contractors were delayed and a groundbreaking in 2010 could not be held (*PCK* [OE], 15 October 2010).[59]

Thus, the progress of the urban railway plan after the Thaksin government was also extremely slow. Only the start of the construction of the Purple and Light Red lines and the preparation of the construction of the Dark Red line and the Blue line were achieved by 2010. Many factors delayed the urban railway plans, such as the supply of funds and the procedures for determining contractors, in addition to political issues.

Bus Service Problems

The two plans for buses that had surfaced in the Thaksin era were the BMA's BRT plan and the BMTA's NGV bus plan. The former stopped due to confrontation with the government, just as had occurred with the BTS extension lines, and the latter suddenly surfaced to be employed as a populist policy.

The BRT plan moved forward because of the collapse of the Thaksin government. By the Surayud government's giving permission to the BMA at the cabinet meeting in January 2007, the BMA was at last able to avoid the hurdle of getting a change in the cabinet decision (*DN* [OE], 8 January 2007). The BMA immediately signed a bid contractor for the civil engineering work, and it was planned to commence operations in February 2008. The operation of buses was to be left to Krungthep Thanakhom Company, as was the case with the BTS extension line. After moving the starting point from Surawong Road to the south of Sathon Road in accord with the recommendation of a consultancy company, construction work started in May 2007 (*PCK* [OE], 22 May 2007).[60]

However, there was a problem of bus supply. Although the BMA announced the bidding for forty-five NGV buses for the BRT in November 2007, no company was interested (*KT* [OE], 12 November 2007).[61] The BMA offered another bidding in December 2007 and two companies tendered bids (*PCK* [OE], 20 December 2007). However, since Natthanon Thawisin, the former vice secretary of the BMA, reported improprieties in the bidding to the Department of Special Investigation (*Krom sopsuan khadi phiset*), the plan was delayed (*PCK* [OE], 1 April 2008).[62] Furthermore, the discovery that one person held shares in both the winning and losing companies led to a criminal investigation, and the potential for bid rigging was thus exposed; the plan suffered a complete setback (*DN* [OE], 3 November 2008).

The BMA tried to overcome this problem by contracting with a new private contractor to ensure the operation of the BRT (*PCK* [OE], 2 February 2009). Since it took time to determine whether bid rigging had occurred, the BMA decided to leave the supply and operation of buses to another contractor by maintaining the original contract without cancelation. Finally, when bidding was held in January 2010, no company tendered bids apart from the BTSC, which in the end became the contractor to take charge of the BRT's bus supply and operation (*PCK* [OE], 27 January 2010). Although the temporary commencement of operations was expected to begin on May 15, 2010, the inaugural day was postponed to May 29 because of riots on the streets of Bangkok (*PCK* [OE], 29 May 2010). The original fare was twelve to twenty baht in the sectional fare system, but free rides were provided by the end of August, and the ten-baht flat fare was adopted after that, before readopting the original fare (ibid.).

While the first BRT opened at last, its reputation was poor because of traffic congestion on the roads along which the BRT passed due to the resulting decrease in lanes (*N* [OE], 1 June 2010). Moreover, because the BRT had to share lanes with other vehicles on flyovers and the Rama III Bridge, the travel time of the BRT exceeded the original schedule; sometimes it took more than one hour during rush hour to travel a distance that had been estimated to take only thirty minutes. The number of users remained low: while the original estimate was 30,000 passengers per day, in fact, there were only 19,000 in the free period, and this dropped to 13,000 passengers after fares began to be levied (*PCK*

[OE], 27 December 2010). In reaction, students' fares were reduced by half in November 2010, and the introduction of a sectional fare system from January 2011 was postponed. Although the BRT was expected to be the new urban transport system, it did not succeed in Bangkok, where privately owned cars continued to dominate road surfaces.

The plan to introduce NGV buses became a political issue and did not progress. The plan was reexamined under the Surayud interim government and was returned to the drawing board in March 2007 (*PCK* [OE], 12 March 2007). However, when the Samak government came to power the next year, it was proposed at the cabinet meeting in June that the BMTA lease 6,000 NGV air-conditioned buses from the Ministry of Transport (*BP* [OE], 11 June 2008). This plan was proposed as a restructuring of the BMTA. The old-model buses were to be eliminated by these NGV buses, and the ordinary BMTA buses, which were the main means of travel for people, were also to be abolished. Although the estimated fare was as high as fifteen baht, which was far higher than the ordinary bus fare, the BMTA insisted that the use of thirty-baht-per-day tickets would make it cheaper for passengers who had to repeatedly transfer on ordinary buses.[63] When opposition to the abolition of ordinary buses arose, Samak announced that the plan would be removed from the cabinet meeting's agenda, and that he would examine the matter personally (*KT* [OE], 17 June 2008). He appointed a special committee to consider the plan. A downsized plan of procuring 4,000 NGV buses was approved at the cabinet meeting in September 2007, just before Samak lost his post (*PCT* [OE], 29 September 2008).[64] Although the BMTA aimed at holding the bidding by the end of December, the formation of the new Abhisit government prohibited this from happening.

Since Sophon Saram of the Bhumjaithai Party assumed the post of the minister of transport in the Abhisit government, the Ministry of Transport tried to promote this plan. However, there was a strong public reaction against it as faulty and the Democrat Party criticized it. Therefore, the Democrat Party was cautious in advancing it. While the BMTA changed the terms of reference ten times and submitted it to the cabinet meeting in May 2009, basic consent was only obtained with the condition that the daily 4,780-baht rent per car should be reviewed (*DN* [OE], 19 May 2009).[65] Although the BMTA later reduced the rent to 4,442 baht and resubmitted it to the cabinet, at its meeting in July it decided to postpone the decision after asking the NESDB to examine the merits and demerits of the lease plan (*PCT* [OE], 4 June 2009). There were those who were of the dissenting opinion that purchase was more desirable than leasing. After examination by the NESDB, it was confirmed that leasing would require a smaller fiscal burden. Therefore, the plan was finally consented to at the cabinet meeting in October 2009 (*PCT* [OE], 5 October 2009).

However, some conditions were attached to the cabinet's decision, and the lease plan was not actually furthered. The main conditions included the early retirement of 7,009 employees and the development of sheds and gas stands owned by the BMTA. These were not problems that could be solved simply or rapidly. When these problems were was taken up again at the cabinet meeting in August 2010, it was determined to install a new workgroup because only 2,200 employees had joined the early retirement plan and it was necessary to secure the funds for developing sheds and gas stands (*PCK* [OE], 10 August 2010). Although this NGV bus plan, which became a political football in the political strife between the Democrat and Bhumjaithai parties, obtained consent of the cabinet, there was no concrete progress. The introduction of the new-style air-conditioned NGV buses to replace private buses started in 2007, which resulted in the rapid increase in the private air-conditioned buses in 2009 (see table 6.3) (*PCK* [OE], 1 October 2007).[66] The minibuses, which originated from illegal *songthaeo*, were also replaced by NGV buses in February 2010, and the old green minibuses were completely eliminated (*KT* [OE], 17 February 2010).[67] Although the BMTA's NGV bus plan did not progress, increase in the use of NGV buses to economize on the soaring oil prices was continuing steadily.

Apart from the plan of introducing a cheap air-conditioned bus service with NGV buses, which was presented as part of the "dream-selling policy" in the era of Thaksin, another policy in which a populist element was still stronger appeared at this time. This was the free bus service that the Samak government introduced in August 2008. It aimed at reducing living expenses to compensate for the high prices of commodities due to the rapidly soaring oil prices that had been introduced by the Samak government. It applied to eight hundred ordinary BMTA buses (*PCK* [OE], 1 August 2008).[68] The Kukrit government had once come up with a similar policy for students and the poor, but now anyone could ride the bus for free. However, the privately operated routes, which consisted of about half of all routes, were not included, and private buses opposed the plan because it would decrease their income. This populist policy was also continued under the subsequent Abhisit government.

Thus, the bus problem was not solved by the Thaksin administration; in fact, the bus policy had strayed. The BMA's BRT plan was much delayed as a result of the BMA-government conflict and did not meet original expectations. The NGV bus plan, which surfaced as a last-minute measure to improve the BMTA's management, did not progress because of new political conflicts. Meanwhile, bus service in Bangkok leaned in the direction of populism with the introduction of free buses.

Limits on the "Dream-Selling Policy"

Construction Methods and Sources of Funds

The major reasons why the urban railway policy of the Thaksin government changed so frequently and generally did not result in anything groundbreaking were the conflicting interests presented by expanding the network rapidly and adopting a low fare level for populist motives, and the constraints of the financial situation. Although the government was expanding lines by pushing forward a plan for the expansion of support on one hand and requiring a low fare on the other, the important problem of where the money would come from was not solved. Therefore, the plan changed multiple times in terms of construction and management methods.

Table 6.1 shows the changes in the construction methods experimented with: the detailed design, turnkey, and design-and-build systems. Although the government had to bear certain expenditures with any of these methods, raising funds was the contractor's responsibility in the turnkey method; since the government would only need to repay after a long period, it could postpone the problem. On the other hand, since the private sector needed to provide all the funds for construction, the turnkey method raised concerns about rising interest rates and final construction costs. When using the two-tiered operation system, which involved joint investment, the procurement of operational equipment could be provided by private sectors. But if the government agency was operating by itself, the government would also have to come up with the necessary funds.

Since the BMTIP reported that the use of private investments became difficult when construction terms were shortened to six years and when aiming for simultaneous development of all lines, it was suggested that the mass transit development fund and the existing Wayuphak Fund[69] from the national budget should be utilized (OTP 2004, sec. 8, 2–3).[70] Therefore, the construction method was specified as the bid system based on the typical detailed design system. As for the urban railway fund, although Thaksin announced the idea of raising funds from the private sector by securing 3 percent interest in October 2003, the use of the Wayuphak Fund was opposed by the Ministry of Finance (*N* [OE], 30 October 2003; *KT* [OE], 13 October 2003). There were other proposals, such as increasing the fuel tax and automobile registration fees to put into the urban railway development fund. However, since it was impossible to supply the large amount of at least 500 billion baht by using only these measures, none of these materialized.

Therefore, the turnkey method and the barter method came to the fore. The construction of the Airport Rail Link, which became the only urban railway whose construction had started during the era of Thaksin, adopted this turnkey method. The First-Stage Urban Railway Development Plan that emerged after the plan was downsized by Phongsak changed into a turnkey method plan, and it simultaneously used the barter method to fund construction. In particular, it aimed to fund urban railway development by exchanging agricultural products. In the prime minister's radio program, "Prime Minister Thaksin Tells the People," on December 3, 2005, Thaksin explained that Thailand would be able to obtain an urban railway only by growing rubber (*PCK* [OE], 3 December 2005).[71] However, although Phongsak spoke with diplomats of several nations about the barter method, he never got a favorable reply, and it was dropped as a necessary condition in the plan "Thailand: Partnership for Development" (*PCK* [OE], 28 October 2005).

Agencies such as the National Economic and Social Advisory Board (*Sapha thi prueksa setthakit lae sangkhom haeng chat*) opposed the turnkey method, which had succeeded in the three-line construction plan of the interim government, noting that the screening process might become opaque and unjust. So, the government returned to the method of securing funds in advance (*PCK* [OE], 4 July 2006). The design-and-build system, which involved carrying out design and construction simultaneously, was adopted to hasten construction, and the barter method was left as an option. So negotiations began with the JBIC for a loan at the time of the first Blue line construction. Although Thaksin had once said that Thailand had graduated from being a recipient country, there was no more advantageous source of funds than the JBIC loan in terms of interest rate and long-term payment.

However, since the yen loan from Japan required time, and the desired hope of encouraging Thai companies to be selected in contract bidding waned, there arose in Thaksin's period the idea of covering construction costs by floating a national bond issue. Although construction costs for the Blue line were high because of the need to place some of the line underground, the government opted to use funds from the national bond sale, instead of the yen loan; the government saw from the Dark Red line plan that negotiations with Japan would be protracted in response to Thailand's request to make the terms of reference more advantageous to Thai companies. This was based on political considerations and aimed to help the Thai construction industry. As a result, except for one joint venture, the successful bidders for the five contracts of the Blue line were all Thai.[72]

Management Methods and Fare System

Along with financing, the management method and fare system also became problematic. The URMAP assumed the management by private sectors through a two-tiered operation system, and by starting construction with the section that was in maximum demand, they lengthened the construction period. However, since the BMTIP opted to construct all lines in a short period, management had to be left to government agencies; the unification of the management agencies became essential to maintain a low fare. The purchase of concessions granted to the BTSC and BMCL was included in the BMTIP for the unification of management agencies, which was estimated to cost 75 billion baht (OTP 2004, sec. 8, 1).

It was Suriya who revealed the problems in this purchasing plan; he asked the BMCL for a stock purchase and schemed to buy back the bonds from BTSC's creditors. However, the BMCL only offered three baht per share, and the BTSC pushed for negotiations of the restructuring plan with its creditors (*PCK* [OE], 1 April 2004; *N* [OE], 17 May 2004). Although a special committee was established in July 2004 and negotiations on the buying out of the concession were advancing, the purchase plan suffered a setback when Thaksin said that he would not go along with the buying of the BTSC in an election year (2005) (*PCK* [OE], 1 July 2004).[73]

Instead, the Ministry of Finance proposed setting up a holding company, which Thaksin agreed to in July 2005. The result was his asking that the BTSC and BMCL both come under the jurisdiction of that holding company (*N* [OE], 20 July 2005). This was more the unification of the businesses' operations than their buyout, and it was expected that the companies would only rebound slightly. This plan also did not progress, and it was settled in October that the Mass Transit Authority would be installed to regulate the operators (*PCK* [OE], 19 October 2005). This Mass Transit Authority would regulate all transport operators in Bangkok, such as buses and boats, and be given the authority of setting and distributing fares. Although the Urban Transit Authority Act was set to materialize in March 2006, to date it has still not been realized.

The government discovered that purchasing the BTSC or BMCL as a means of unifying the management of urban railways was indispensable because of the populist pressure to keep fares low. Although the BMTIP expected a sectional fare system with a minimum fare of ten baht, the fare system was changed to a flat fare of fifteen to twenty baht when the plan was expanded in December 2004 as part of the election campaign. Therefore, the statement that both the BTSC and BMCL needed to be purchased to reduce fares was also part of a populist ploy.

As of the end of 2010, both the BTSC and BMCL adopted a sectional fare system ranging from fifteen to forty baht.[74] Although the BMCL applied a special flat fare of ten baht for one month after the July 2004 opening, the number of users decreased from 250,000 to 150,000 persons after it changed to the sectional fare system (*DN* [OE], 13 September 2004). Moreover, if passengers transferred between the BTS sky train and subway, they would have to pay two fares, causing further problems. Therefore, the government set forth a plan for a flat rate for all lines. This was a rational policy in terms of easing traffic congestion by reducing privately owned car drivers and reducing the ever-soaring costs of importing oil; it cannot be labeled as a mere populist policy.

However, it was only a "dream" failing to take into account the realities that the low fares would discourage the participation of the private sector, that a considerable amount of funds would be required to offset the insufficiency in fare revenues, and that the SRT and BMTA, to maintain low fares, had accumulated large deficits. When the government denied the extension of the BTS, it had argued that it would require high fares. However, if Bangkokians had to choose between rapid development of railways with high BTS-type fares and stagnation of railway development with the promise of low fares, it was clear that a majority would choose the former.

Both the BTSC and BMCL set up a discount fare system in order to increase the number of users, and this had been popular. In particular, the BTSC has been attracting regular users with its thirty-trip ticket. Issued in August 2000, it had a high discount rate and was popular because it enabled users to use the train for only eighteen baht for any distance. Thus, management by the private sector did not necessarily mean that fares would be higher.[75] The "dream" of constructing many lines in a short period and allowing anyone to use them for fifteen baht regardless of the distance was being touted, on the one hand; but, on the other hand, time passed while the plan was repeatedly changed because of a deadlock in securing funds. An example of this inconsistency was the Purple line, for which bidding was suddenly halted because of profitability problems, although the notification of bids had already gone out.[76]

After the Thaksin government was ousted, the public-private partnership (PPP) system was introduced as a solution to the fare problem. The government, which had examined the Purple line train operation system, became determined to adopt the PPP gross cost system in January 2010 (*PCK* [OE], 7 January 2010).[77] This system is a form of the two-tiered operation system in which the government pays the expenses of civil engineering work, and the private company whom the government entrusts pays for the procurement of signal, electrical, and station equipment, and the rolling stock, and takes charge of the operation and maintenance of the trains. Although the fare was set up uniquely in the case of the present Blue line, in which the private operator collected and distributed a part of the income to the MRTA, the fare would be established and collected by the MRTA, which would pay an operation fee to private operators that was almost the same as that of the BTS extension lines and the BRT.[78] Since the government could determine the fare level, it was expected that the fare level would be reduced. However, if the fare level was too low, the operational fee became higher than the fare revenue that the MRTA received. Therefore, to maintain a low fare, some system that makes up the cost is required.

Products of Compromise: Airport Rail Link

In the midst of this inconsistency between a populist policy and the financial reality, urban railway development hardly progressed in the Thaksin period. A total of 7.4 kilometers of two BTS extension lines by the BMA and 28.5 kilometers of Airport Rail Links by the SRT were all that was started for construction during the period. Since the BMA constructed the two extension lines independently, the Airport Rail Link was virtually the only example of an urban railway whose construction was started by the Thaksin government.

However, in reality, the Airport Rail Link plan was only the product of compromise. Although Thaksin originally did not pay attention to the development of railway access to the new airport, the importance of an airport access railway was recognized with the approaching completion of the new airport. The Suvarnabhumi Airport, which aimed at becoming a hub airport in Asia, had to catch up with other newly constructed hub airports such as those in Hong Kong and Kuala Lumpur, where airport access railways had been included. An airport without railway access was outdated.[79] Therefore, although the decision was long overdue, if an access railway was not realized even in the near future, the Suvarnabhumi Airport would have no hope of competing against other Asian hub airports.

In fact, the Airport Rail Link was insufficient as an urban railway. The bid was performed by the quickest turnkey method because there was not enough time to perform a detailed design and secure a source of funds. The contractual coverage was advantageous to the private sector.[80] Although granting the concession for operation to a private company was initially considered, the SRT decided to operate it by itself to avoid problems such as those experienced by the BTS and subway due to a fare reduction policy (*PCK* [OE], 8 May 2006). Furthermore, to limit construction costs as much as possible, the least number of stations were built; there were only six intermediate stations on the 28.5-kilometer line from Phayathai to Suvarnabhumi, resulting in an average length of 4 kilometers between stations.[81] It seemed that, at most, only an interval of fifteen minutes would be possible since there was too low a supply of rolling stock.[82]

Furthermore, this plan only included the construction of elevated tracks for the Airport Rail Link, and not the elevated track for the existing railway. Therefore, the Eastern line trains would have to run at ground level with a single track between Phayathai and Hua Mak, precisely where the Hopewell plan had suffered a setback and where no intermediate level crossings would be removed. Although the avoidance of the increase in cost by including the construction of an elevated track for the existing railway and the rapid completion of the plan were the likely reasons for this, it was actually a regression, since the revised Hopewell plans targeted removing all level crossings at the elevated track of the existing railway.[83]

The construction of the Airport Rail Link, which aimed to open in November 2007, was also delayed, and the realization of rail access to the Suvarnabhumi Airport, which opened in September 2006, was postponed. The main reason was the SRT's delay in providing a construction site. The SRT had to remove the slums lying within the right-of-way for the contractor within 90 days. However, the work was much delayed, and the lots were not handed over until March 2007 (*DN* [OE], 28 March 2007). Therefore, the contractor asked for an extension of the construction period; it received an extension of 730 days (*PCT* [OE], 29 January 2009).[84] Thus the contractor's completion term was late by about two years, set for November 4, 2009, and the commencement-of-business schedule set at least ninety days later, in early 2010.[85]

However, since the operator had not been identified, the opening was not possible, despite the construction having been completed in November 2009 (*DN* [OE], 10 November 2009). Although the SRT planned to establish a subsidiary to operate the Airport Rail Link, the SRT's employees opposed the restructuring plan, including the establishment of a subsidiary. They went on strike, delaying the opening significantly. Thus, the SRT decided to entrust the operation to DB International GmbH, which had been employed as the consultant for the operation preparations, and signed with it in May 2010.[86] The operation of the Airport Rail Link only started in August 2010, after a delay of about three years (*RGI* [OE], 24 August 2010).

After the opening, problems occurred. Since the internal construction of the city terminal at Makkasan was unfinished, airline boarding procedures at the city terminal could not be carried out until January 2011. Although the transfer facility with the BTS at Phayathai was completed, the transfer between Makkasan and Phetchaburi stations on the Blue line was inconvenient, and there were few users of the Makkasan station. A special fare was adopted for both local and express trains, and during 2010, the daily number of users was 42,000 and 800 persons respectively. The number of express train users in particular was much less than the target of 2,200 passengers (*PCT* [OE], 3 January 2010).[87] The boarding and luggage deposit procedures at the Makkasan city terminal, which started in 2011, also have very few users, and the terminal is almost completely deserted.[88]

Thus, the function of the Airport Rail Link as an urban railway for carrying commuters and students was overwhelmingly higher than its function as an access railway to the airport, which was meant to be its main function. A complete mismatch appeared in demand and supply. In fact, the Airport Rail Link, the only railway construction started by the Thaksin government, was also only a product of compromise.

Buses in the Age of Urban Railways

The process of urban railway development, which began in Bangkok in the late 1990s, was slowed by the repeated changes in policy. As a result, buses continue to maintain the leading role in urban transport. However, a decrease in the number of passengers in the 2000s is noteworthy, and a change in roles was needed because users of urban railways have increased in number.

As shown in figure 6.5, the network of bus routes in Bangkok has expanded since 1988. There were routes established with the opening of new roads, as well as newly established bus routes on existing roads due to the extension of the city area. Moreover, access routes to the Suvarnabhumi Airport, which opened in 2006, also established a large number of routes. Furthermore, compared with 1988 (see figure 5.3), the operation of air-conditioned buses also increased significantly; air-conditioned buses are now operating on most roads. Table 6.8 contains a list of bus routes in 2008 and shows that the number of routes was 220 at that time. Among them, 98 were operated by private companies, and the number of air-conditioned bus routes became the majority at 123 routes. The expressway bus and all-night bus routes also increased, which meant that bus service has also diversified.

Table 6.8. Bus Routes in Bangkok, 2008

Route No.	Line	Service			
		Private Operation	Air-Conditioned Bus	All-Night Bus	Express-way Bus
1	Thanon Tok–Tha Tian				
2	Pakkhlong Talat–Samrong			o	o
3	Mochit 2–Khlong San		o	o	
4	Phasi Charoen Pier–Khlong Toei Port		o	o	
5	Mochit 2–Chakkrawat	o			
6	Phrapradaeng–Bang Lamphu	o			
7	Hua Lamphong–Khlong Khwang			o	
7	Hua Lamphong–Sueksanari School	o	o		
7K	Phutthamonthon 2–Phahurat				
8	Memorial Bridge–Happy Land Market	o			
9	Soi Kamnan Maen Shed–Mochit 2	o			
10	Phasi Charoen Pier–Nangloeng	o			
11	Sinakharin Shed–Mabunkhrong		o		
12	Huai Khwang–Former Ministry of Commerce		o		
13	Huai Khwang–Khlong Toei Port				
14	Siyan–Khlong Toei Port	o			
15	Bang Lamphu–Tha Phra				
16	Surawong–Sinarong Shed		o		
17	Rama II Road–Victory Monument	o			
18	Tha It Shed–Victory Monument				
19	Phutthamonthon 2–Thewet	o			
20	Tha Dindaeng–Phra Chunlachomklao Fort		o		
21	Chulalongkorn University–Thungkhru		o		o
22	Sathu Pradit Shed–Bokaeo Shed		o	o	

Route No.	Line	Service			
		Private Operation	Air-Conditioned Bus	All-Night Bus	Express-way Bus
23	Samrong–Thewet		○	○	○
24	Prachaniwet 3 Estate–Victory Monument		○		○
25	Tha Chang–Paknam		○	○	○
26	Victory Monument–Minburi		○	○	○
27	Minburi–Victory Monument	○		○	
28	Ratchayothin–New Southern Line Bus Terminal	○	○		
29	Thammasat University Rangsit Campus–Hua Lamphong	○	○		○
30	Nonthaburi–Tha Phra	○			
32	Pakkret–Wat Pho		○		
33	Pathumthani–Sanam Luang	○			
34	Rangsit–Hua Lamphong		○	○	○
35	Saochingcha–Phrapradaeng Junction	○			
36	Huai Khwang–Si Phraya		○		
36K	Bokaeo Shed–Victory Monument				
37	Wat Chaengron–Mahanak		○		
38	Chankasem Ratchaphat University–Ramkhamhaeng University Bang Na Campus	○			
39	Sanam Luang–Talat Thai	○	○	○	
40	Rama IX Road–New Southern Line Bus Terminal	○			
42	Tha Phra–Saochingcha Circle line				
43	Pinthong Market–Thewet	○			
43	Sueksanari 2 School–Khlong San Pier	○			
44	Khlong Chan Estate–Tha Tian	○	○		
45	Samrong–Si Phraya				○
46	Ramkhamhaeng University Bang Na Campus–Rong Mueang	○		○	
47	Land Department–Khlong Toei Port				
48	Ramkhamhaeng University Bang Na Campus–Wat Pho	○			
49	Mochit 2–Hua Lamphong		○		
50	Rama VII Bridge–Lumphini Park		○		○
51	Pakkret–Wat Pho	○			
52	Pakkret–Bang Sue Station	○			
53	Thewet Circle Line				
54	Huai Khwang Circle Line			○	

Route No.	Line	Service			
		Private Operation	Air-Conditioned Bus	All-Night Bus	Express-way Bus
56	Krung Thon Bridge Circle Line	○			
57	Thonburi Circle Line	○			
58	Minburi–Pratunam	○		○	
59	Rangsit–Sanam Luang		○	○	
60	Suan Sayam–Pakkhlong Talat		○	○	○
62	Sathu Pradit–Victory Monument		○		
63	Agricultural Market 3–Victory Monument		○	○	○
64	Nonthaburi–Sanam Luang	○		○	
65	Wat Paknam–National Theater				
66	Prachaniwet 2 Estate–New Southern Line Bus Terminal		○		
67	Wat Samiannari–Chong Nonsi		○		
68	Samaedam–Bang Lamphu		○		
69	Tha It–Victory Monument	○	○		○
70	Prachaniwet 3 Estate–Sanam Luang		○		○
71	Suan Sayam–Wat Thatthong			○	
72	Khlong Toei Port–Thewet		○		
73	Huai Khwang–Memorial Bridge		○		
73K	Bokaeo Shed–Memorial Bridge		○	○	
74	Huai Khwang–Khlong Toei Port	○			
75	Wat Phutthabucha–Tha Tian		○		
76	Samaedam Estate–Phloenchit		○		
77	Rama III Road–Mochit 2		○		
79	Phutthamonthon 2–Ratchaprasong		○		
80	Wat Sinuan–Sanam Luang		○	○	
80K	Wo Po O 11 Estate–Tha Phra				
81	Omnoi–Phra Pinklao Bridge	○			
82	Phrapradaeng–Bang Lamphu		○	○	
84	Omyai–Khlong San			○	
84K	Samphran–Khlong San	○			
85	Wat Chaengron–Hua Lamphong	○			
88	Wat Thungkhru–Latya	○			
89	Taling Chan Police Station–Bangkok Technical College	○			
90	Pathumthani Pier–Mochit 2	○			
91	Setthakit Estate–Sanam Luang		○	○	

Route No.	Line	Service			
		Private Operation	Air-Conditioned Bus	All-Night Bus	Express-way Bus
91K	Sanam Luang 2–Tha Phra				
92	Khlong Tan–Priest Hospital	○			
92	Lomklao Estate–Victory Monument	○	○		
93	Laem Thong Athlete Village–Si Phraya		○		
95	Rangsit–Ramkhamhaeng University		○	○	
95K	Rangsit–The Mall Bang Kapi		○	○	
96	Suan Sayam–Mochit 2				
97	Nonthaburi–Priest Hospital		○	○	
98	Huai Khwang–Onnut station	○			
99	Lamsali Junction–Siyan Pier	○			
101	Wat Mueang–Bang Mot				
102	Paknam–Rama III Road		○		○
104	Pakkret–Victory Monument	○	○		
105	Mahachai New Town–Khlong San		○		
107	Bang Khen–Khlong Toei		○		○
108	Tha Phra–Ratchayothin	○			
109	Ramkhamhaeng University–Hua Lamphong	○			
110	Rama VII Bridge–Thewet	○			
111	Talat Phlu–Bukkhalo Circle Line				
113	Minburi–Hua Lamphong	○	○		
114	Agricultural Market 3–Lam Lukka Junction		○		
115	Suan Sayam–Silom	○			
116	Wat Namdaeng–Sathon	○			
117	Nonthaburi–Second BMA Office				
120	Mahachai–Khlong San	○			
122	Huai Khwang–Mochit 2	○			
123	Omyai–Sanam Luang	○			
124	Mahidol University Salaya Campus–Arun Amarin Bridge	○			
125	Mahidol University Salaya Campus–Samsen station	○			
126	Bang Khen–Ramkhamhaeng University	○			
127	Arun Amarin Bridge–Bang Buathong	○			
129	Bang Khen–Samrong		○		○
131	Minburi–Nongchok	○			
132	Bang Chak–Bang Phli Estate	○			

Route No.	Line	Service			
		Private Operation	Air-Conditioned Bus	All-Night Bus	Express-way Bus
133	Phrakhanong–Bang Phli Estate	○			
134	Mochit 2–Bang Buathong		○	○	
134K	Khlong Chan Estate–Ministry of Commerce			○	
136	Mochit 2–Customs Department				
137	Ramkhamhaeng–Ratchadaphisek Circle Line		○		
138	Mochit 2–Phrapradaeng		○		○
139	Ramkhamhaeng University Bang Na Campus–Victory Monument	○	○		○
140	Victory Monument–Samaedam Shed		○		○
141	Samaedam Shed–Chulalongkorn University		○		○
142	Thonburi Estate–Paknam		○		○
143	Happy Land Market–Latkrabang	○			
145	Mochit 2–Paknam		○	○	
146	Bang Khae–Outer Ring Road Circle Line	○			
147	Daokhanong–Outer Ring Road Circle Line	○			
149	Phutthamonthon 2 Shed–Ekkamai	○			
150	Pakkret–Ramkhamhaeng University	○	○		○
150	Pakkret–Minburi	○	○		
151	Soi Latphrao 71–Hua Takhe	○			
152	Happy Land Market–Lomklao Estate				
154	Watcharaphon Estate–Khlong Toei	○			
156	Satriwitthaya 2 School–Raminthra		○		
157	Phutthamonthon 2–Huai Khwang	○			
157	Omyai–Mochit 2	○		○	
159	Phutthamonthon 2–Mochit 2	○			
162	Khlong Toei–Sayam	○			
163	Phutthamonthon 3–Huai Khwang	○			
164	Mahidon University Salaya Campus–Victory Monument	○			
165	Phutthamonthon 3–Bangkok Yai District Office	○			
166	Mueang Thong Thani–Victory Monument		○		○
167	Khlong San–Bang Bon	○			
168	Suan Sayam–Victory Monument		○		
169	Bang Khunthian Circle Line	○			
170	Omyai–Mochit 2	○	○		
171	Thonburi Estate–Laem Thong Athlete Village	○	○		

Route No.	Line	Service			
		Private Operation	Air-Conditioned Bus	All-Night Bus	Express-way Bus
172	Happy Land Market–Bang Khunthian	○	○		
173	Thonburi Estate–Minburi	○	○		
174	Happy Land Market–Krathum Baen	○	○		
175	Talat Phlu–Agricultural Market 3	○			
177	Bang Buathong–Victory Monument Circle Line	○	○		
178	Sukhonthasawat Circle Line				
179	Rama VII Bridge–MCOT Junction				
180	Rama III Road–Ramkhamhaeng University Bang Na Campus				○
182	Ramkhamhaeng University Bang Na Campus–Victory Monument	○			
183	Omyai–Victory Monument	○	○		
185	Rangsit–Khlong Toei		○		
187	Khlong 3–Si Phraya				○
188	Chatuchak–Khlong 6				
201	Victory Monument–Taling Chan	○			
203	Nonthaburi–Sanam Luang		○	○	
204	Second BMA Office–Ratchawong Pier		○		
205	Customs Department–Tha Phra		○		
206	Kasetsart University–Prawet		○	○	○
207	Ramkhamhaeng University–Ramkhamhaeng University Bang Na Campus	○	○		
501	Minburi–Hua Lamphong		○	○	
502	Minburi–Victory Monument		○		
503	Rangsit–Sanam Luang		○		○
504	Rangsit–Thanon Tok		○		
505	Pakkret–Lumphini Park		○		
507	Paknam–New Southern Line Bus Terminal	○	○		○
508	Paknam–Tha Rat		○		○
509	Mochit 2–Bang Khae		○		
510	Talat Thai–Victory Monument		○		○
511	Paknam–New Southern Line Bus Terminal		○	○	○
512	Mochit 2–Pakkhlong Talat		○		
513	Rangsit–Samrong		○		○
514	Minburi–Silom		○	○	○

Route No.	Line	Service			
		Private Operation	Air-Conditioned Bus	All-Night Bus	Express-way Bus
515	Salaya–Victory Monument		○		
516	Thewet–Buathong Estate		○		
517	Mochit 2–Latkrabang		○		
519	Suan Sayam–Sathu Pradit Shed		○		
520	Talat Thai–The Mall Bang Kapi		○		
522	Rangsit–Victory Monument		○		○
523	Latphrao–Khlong 6	○	○		
524	Bang Khen–Sanam Luang	○	○		
528	Sainoi–Rama IX Road		○		
529	Samaedam–Mochit 2	○	○		○
536	Paknam–Mochit 2		○		
537	Victory Monument–Bang Phli	○	○		
538	Ratchamongkhon Institute of Technology Pathumthani Campus–Si Ayutthaya Road	○	○		
539	Omyai–Si Ayutthaya Road	○	○		
542	Pinklao–Victory Monument Circle Line	○	○		
543	Agricultural Market 3–Bang Khen Shed		○		
544	Bang Khunthian–Namdaeng	○	○		
545	Nonthaburi–Samrong	○	○		
547	Mahidon University Salaya Campus–Victory Monument	○	○		
549	Suvarnabhumi Airport–Minburi Shed		○	○	
550	Suvarnabhumi Airport–Happy Land		○	○	
551	Suvarnabhumi Airport–Victory Monument		○	○	○
552	Suvarnabhumi Airport–Khlong Toei		○	○	
552A	Suvarnabhumi Airport–Paknam		○	○	
553	Suvarnabhumi Airport–Paknam		○		
554	Suvarnabhumi Airport–Rangsit		○	○	○
555	Suvarnabhumi Airport–Rangsit		○	○	○
556	Suvarnabhumi Airport–New Southern Line Bus Terminal		○	○	○
558	Suvarnabhumi Airport–Samaedam		○	○	○
559	Suvarnabhumi Airport–Rangsit		○		○
Total		98	123	45	42

SOURCE: KSMK n.d.

Fig. 6.5. Bus Network in Bangkok, 2008

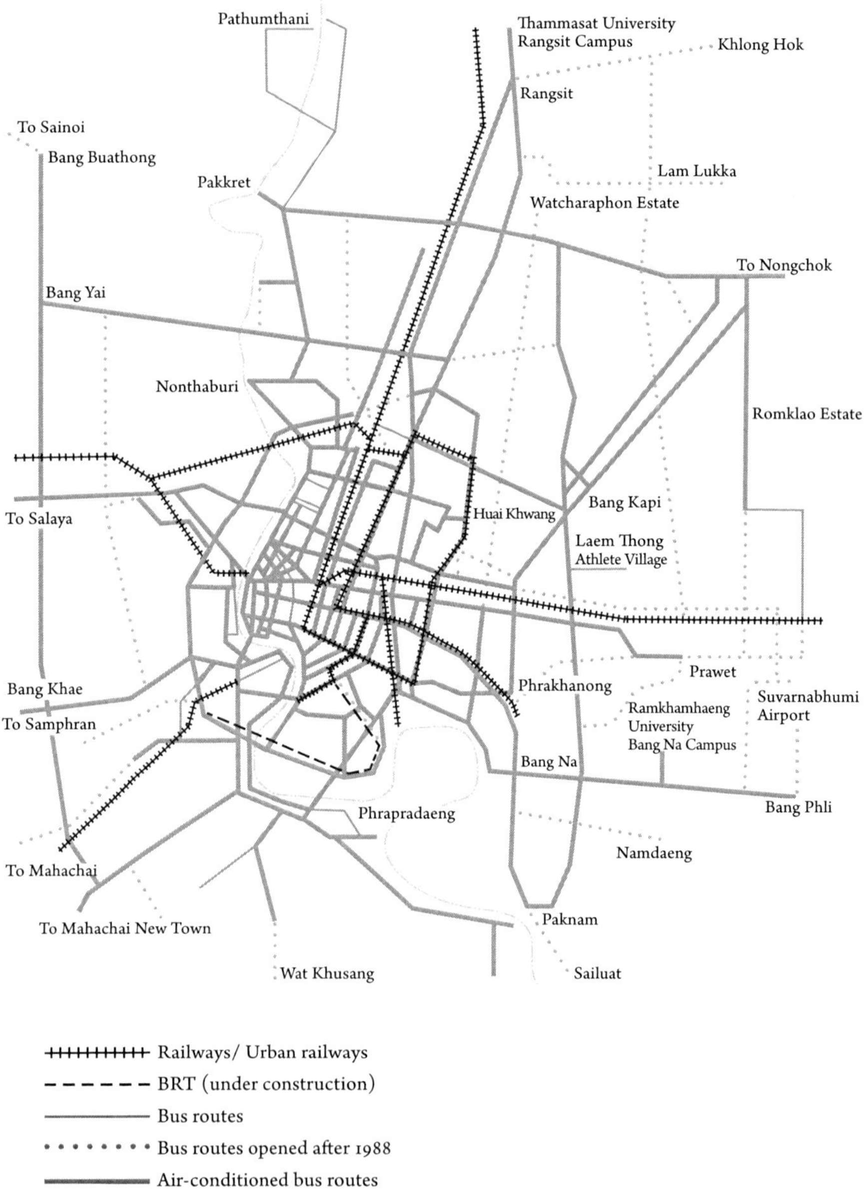

Note: Map excludes bus routes of category four (bus routes within the province).

Nevertheless, the number of bus users decreased while the number of urban railway users increased. This was due to the punctuality and speed of the urban railway. As shown in table 6.9, the number of urban railway users per day showed an increase of a little under four times from about 150,000 in 2000 to about 580,000 in 2010, and if we include the Airport Rail Link, the number in 2010 is likely to have been more than 600,000 persons. Since the total length of the urban railways mostly doubled in the meantime, except for the Airport Rail Link, this meant that the growth of the number of users was twice that of the length.

Table 6.9. Number of Daily Urban Railway Passengers, 2000–2010

Year	BTS Sky Train	MRT Subway	Total
2000	148,641		148,641
2001	161,146		161,146
2002	217,133		217,133
2003	264,360		264,360
2004	287,140	147,458	434,598
2005	324,561	163,403	487,964
2006	361,335	158,196	519,531
2007	379,610	164,507	544,117
2008	363,737	169,813	533,550
2009	372,438	174,657	547,095
2010	395,820	181,870	577,690

NOTE: BTS figures are for the fiscal year from April to March.
SOURCES: BTSG for 2009/10; BMCL for 2008, for 2010.

On the other hand, as shown in table 6.10, the number of daily bus users decreased by half from 4,840,000 in 2000 to 2,250,000 in 2010. Although the number of users of free buses is not reflected in this figure, the number of users of the free buses in 2010 can be estimated at about 480,000 persons from the fact that the numbers of free and non-free buses were almost the same. The total number thereby should be increased to 2,730,000 persons. Nevertheless, the number of decreasing bus users contrasts with the increase in the number of urban railway users. Since the margin of the decline in the number of bus users is larger than the increase in the number of urban railway users, it is clear that the reduction in the number of bus users cannot be explained only by the transition to urban railways.

Although the role of buses was destined to change to being feeders of the urban railways while the urban railway network expanded, the network of bus routes in Bangkok remained almost unchanged. While transportation routes extended into the suburbs, the original bus network in the city stayed the same. The only new feeder bus routes established were those run by the BTSC and BRT.[89] Although there have been examples of conventional bus stops being shifted closer to urban railway stations, there has been no construction of transfer stations for connecting urban railways with buses.[90] Therefore, the function of buses as feeders is low, and the users of urban railways go to and from stations by other means of transport, such as vans and motorcycle taxis.[91]

The plans to introduce NGV buses and free bus service, which were promoted under the "dream-selling policy," were insufficient to change the role of the buses as the feeders for urban railways. It was important to provide a bus service that was not only cheap, but also able to coordinate with the urban railways. Although the BMTA also planned to reorganize the bus routes into 155 routes according to the plan to introduce NGV buses, administration's success in upgrading the role of the buses as feeders has been restricted (*PCK* [OE], 13 July 2010).[92] The times had changed and urban railways now played the leading role in mass transit. The bus service inherited from former times remained fundamentally unchanged, and its renovation was not incorporated into the "dream-selling policy." This was the main factor for the considerable decrease in the number of bus users.

Table 6.10. Number of Daily Bus Passengers, 2001–2010

Fiscal Year	BMTA Buses			Private Buses			Total		
	Ordinary	Air-conditioned	Total	Ordinary	Air-conditioned	Total	Ordinary	Air-conditioned	Grand Total
2001	1480,557	1,090,099	2,570,656	1,924,812	346,725	2,271,537	3,405,369	1,436,824	4,842,193
2002	1,401,931	1,123,242	2,525,173	1,966,388	375,359	2,341,747	3,368,319	1,498,601	4,866,920
2003	1,125,213	1,261,399	2,386,612	1,632,570	566,848	2,199,417	2,757,783	1,828,247	4,586,029
2004	1,164,862	900,460	2,065,322	1,690,547	440,540	2,131,087	2,855,409	1,341,000	4,196,409
2005	1,124,346	830,793	1,955,139	1,680,474	418,667	2,099,141	2,804,820	1,249,460	4,054,280
2006	999,846	766,545	1,766,391	1,526,647	379,852	1,906,499	2,526,493	1,146,397	3,672,890
2007	932,947	747,805	1,680,752	1,426,172	374,505	1,800,677	2,359,119	1,122,310	3,481,429
2008	706,306	892,491	1,598,797	1,083,427	470,464	1,553,891	1,789,733	1,362,955	3,152,688
2009	505,639	607,784	1,113,423	813,036	434,787	1,247,823	1,318,675	1,042,571	2,361,246
2010	480,353	568,089	1,048,442	783,505	417,124	1,200,629	1,263,858	985,213	2,249,071

Note 1: Numbers of private bus users are estimated by using the ratio of public BMTA buses to private buses.
Note 2: Beginning in August 2008, figures exclude the number of free bus passengers.
Source: Data from *SC* for 2010.

7

Regulation and Politicization of Urban Transport in Bangkok

Transition in Means of Transport

Tramways and Suburban Railways

In accordance with the development of urban transport in cities in developing countries, the first modern means of urban transport introduced in Bangkok was the tramway. Compared to other Southeast Asian cities, Bangkok's 1888 opening of its first tramway was relatively late. As mentioned previously, Batavia was the first Southeast Asian city to introduce the tramway (1869), and tramways also appeared in such cities as Manila, Saigon, Rangoon (Yangon), Singapore, and Penang before the first tramway opened in Bangkok (Dick and Rimmer 2003, 68; Dick 2003, 348; Doling 2012, 3–4).[1] Subsequently, tramways were also opened in Surabaya, Hanoi, and Mandalay, and thus they appeared in all the major Southeast Asian cities.[2]

Throughout the world, transportation modes generally evolved in the order of horsepower, steam power, and electric power. Essentially, there were two types of cities in the world: those that shifted to electric power from horsepower and others that made the transformation starting from steam power. While Jakarta and Manila shifted from horsepower to electric power through steam power, in other cities, operations began at steam power and shifted to electric power.[3] Bangkok shifted directly from horsepower to electric power, without experiencing steam power. Although the electrification of tramways in Bangkok was the earliest in Asia, its advance depended on a foreign engineer, Westenholz, and was merely a private company's decision. However, the problem with Bangkok's tramways was a structural one. The structure of the track—a single track on one side of the road—remained unchanged until the abolition of tramways in the 1960s. Although I did not gather information about tracks in all cities, it seems that double-tracked sections existed in other cities. For example, in Rangoon, a 17-kilometer section of the 22-kilometer total length had double tracks at the end of the 1900s, and an entire 10-kilometer line in Mandalay, the second largest city in Burma, was also double-tracked (Wright et al. 1910, 301, 374). A section of the inner city of Penang was also double-tracked, with the tracks lying in the center of the road (Francis and Ganley 2006, 24). This structural problem of the tracks in Bangkok barred the development of tramways. Its entire 50-kilometer tramway network consisting only of a single track can be said to be exceptional. This was not due to the policy of private operators but rather of the government or municipality that permitted the construction of tramways on roads.

Although Bangkok's tramways had this structural problem, they survived unexpectedly long for Southeast Asia. Singapore was the first to abolish tramways, in 1926 (Dick and Rimmer 2003, 238), when they were substituted by trolley buses. Tramways in Penang were similarly abolished by 1936 through the introduction of trolley buses (Francis and Ganley 2006, 23). Talk of introducing trolley buses surfaced in Bangkok during the end of the 1920s, due to Singapore's experience. In Manila, tramways were also abolished after the destruction of the old city in World War II, and they were not revived after the war (Dick and Rimmer 2003, 270). Tramways in Rangoon and Mandalay were likewise not revived (Ota 1967, 216–17). Tramways that did survive the war were eventually eliminated from use: they disappeared from Jakarta and Surabaya in 1960. Therefore, the abolition of tramways in Bangkok was relatively late (ibid., 70; Dick 2003, 382).[4] Finally, all tramways disappeared from Southeast Asian cities with the abolition of the tramway line in Hanoi in 1989 (Doling 2012, 93).

Although suburban railways had appeared in advanced countries, they were scarce in developing countries.[5] In addition to Bangkok, which was exceptional in Southeast Asia, suburban railways substantially appeared in only one other Southeast Asian city, Jakarta.[6] There, state railways electrified the circular section in the inner city in 1927 and operated trains at fifteen-minute intervals (Dick and Rimmer 2003, 279). The function of this electrified railway as a means of urban transport was greater than that in Bangkok.[7] Nevertheless, the movement toward an urban railway in Bangkok started earlier. In this regard, the Paknam railway can be said to be the first suburban railway that functioned as a mode of intra-urban transport in Southeast Asia. As with the introduction of electric trams, this was another measure taken by a private foreign company as part of its economic activities.

Buses

The history of buses and their development in Bangkok is mostly in accord with the history of urban transport in other cities in developing countries. The first bus appeared in Bangkok around 1910, slightly earlier than in other Southeast Asian cities. Although little information is available about the early history of bus services, we know that Singapore and Rangoon started regular bus operations in 1920 and 1926 (Dick and Rimmer 2003, 237, 300). In Manila, the Manila Electric Railway and Light Company, which operated the tramways, started the expansion of its bus network in 1927, and by 1941 the transport volume of buses exceeded that of tramways (ibid., 266). Thus, there were many cities where bus services expanded after the 1920s, and it was from the latter half of the 1920s that the competition between tramways and buses became significant in Bangkok.

Paratransit vehicles, or jitneys, such as *songthaeo* in Bangkok, also appeared in other Southeast Asian cities. Bus service in Bangkok started with *songthaeo*-type buses, and all buses operating in Bangkok were of the paratransit type until the first box-type bus was introduced in the 1950s. However, there were two types of *songthaeo*: those operated with official permission and those operating illegally. In Singapore, these *songthaeo*-type buses were called "mosquito buses," and they substituted for the municipality's regular buses; they were abolished in 1921 after only one year of operation (ibid., 237–38). In Manila, the paratransit vehicles called jeepneys appeared after World War II, and they quickly proliferated (ibid., 270).

In several cities, these paratransit vehicles drove out or were absorbed by "traditional" buses. Regular buses disappeared in Surabaya and

Bandung owing to competition with paratransit vehicles. Manila became a world of jeepneys after the Manila Electric Railway and Light Company abolished its bus service in 1948 (ibid., 269–70). On the other hand, in Singapore, in 1935, the municipality unified the operation of mosquito buses by various Chinese entrepreneurs into eleven operators who were responsible for bus operations in the city (ibid., 239). Although "traditional" buses and paratransit vehicles continued to coexist in Bangkok, by turning some paratransit vehicles into legal, regular buses, the "traditional" buses generally predominated.

Bus unification, which was finally realized in the mid-1970s in Bangkok, had also been experienced in many cities. The bus operations by the eleven operators in Singapore referred to above were unified in 1973 into one company (Leinbach and Chia 1989, 199). In Manila, 120 bus operators were unified in 1981 (ibid.). Like Bangkok, various cities experienced the coexistence of many operators, and the unification of the operators in those cities took place around the same time as in Bangkok. Thus, the process of private operators' starting bus operations, unification of paratransit services through absorption by private companies, and finally, the unification of entrepreneurs into one company, were common in Southeast Asian cities.

However, public management after unification in Bangkok was unique for Southeast Asia. The unified operators in Manila and Singapore were private companies, and most other cities also had bus services operated by private firms. Public management caused various problems; it increased paratransit services such as illegal *songthaeo* as there was a shortage of buses immediately after nationalization and afterwards, the appearance of vans. Political motivations related to populist policies were behind this nationalization, and Bangkok saw a higher degree of politicization of urban transport than was seen in neighboring countries.

Urban Railways

The changes in urban transport, beginning with the introduction of tramways and suburban railways, continuing through to the establishment of urban railways and ending in the age of buses, are common in the history of developing countries. However, probably the most prominent feature in Bangkok's history was the thirty-year period that it took to realize urban railways following the emergence of the plans. For example, in Singapore, the first urban railway plan surfaced in 1976, and the decision to proceed with construction was made in the same year. Actual construction started in 1983, and the first section was opened in 1987 (Dick and Rimmer 2003, 247). The first urban railway plan surfaced in Bangkok in the early 1970s, and the decision on construction was made in 1979. But subsequent follow-up on that decision was extremely slow. The first groundbreaking of the Hopewell plan took place in 1993, and the first rail service started at the end of 1999, by the Bangkok Mass Transit System Company (BTSC).[8]

One feature of Bangkok's railway history is that several agencies were simultaneously developing urban railway plans. Agencies with jurisdiction over urban railways and transport operators differed: the BTS was under the jurisdiction of the Bangkok Metropolitan Administration (BMA); the subway (Blue line) was under the Mass Rapid Transit Authority of Thailand (MRTA), and the Airport Rail Link under the State Railways of Thailand (SRT). Singapore adopted a two-tiered operation system: the Land Transport Authority performed civil engineering work and the Singapore Mass Rapid Transit Company, a public corporation, operated the trains. Private operators also participated in train operation for the lines opened since 2003 (Yeung 2008, 48). In Hong Kong, the Mass Transit Railway Company and the Kowloon-Canton Railway Company, both public corporations, operated MRT lines constructed after the 1970s and the existing railways until 2007, when the two were merged (ibid., 3).

However, Bangkok's railway history is not necessarily unique; there are several cases in other cities in which train operators differ for every line. Even in Singapore, a private company has entered into the business, and thus there are two operators. The situation in Kuala Lumpur was the same as in Bangkok, and there were five different operators: KTM Komuter, the suburban service on existing railways; two LRTs called STAR and Putra; the access railway to Kuala Lumpur International Airport; and a monorail.[9] The existence of several operators often causes problems in transferring between lines, such as long walking distances between transfer stations and double-levying of fares when transferring. To address this and to realize a flat fare system in Bangkok, the idea of public purchase of BTSC surfaced during the time of the Thaksin administration.

In the case of Bangkok, the methods of construction and management differed for all three plans. It is likely that the BTS was the first example in the world of a railway built with the BOT method of using 100 percent private investment. However, since the BTSC had no capacity to construct extension lines due to the necessary civil engineering work, the BMA constructed the structure and entrusted the operations to the BTSC. The MRTA adopted the same two-tiered operation method as Singapore, and the BMCL is set to take charge of the operation. Although the Airport Rail Link was constructed with a turnkey method and initially the SRT was to manage it itself, it established a subsidiary and eventually abandoned operation. Like Bangkok, Kuala Lumpur has also used various construction methods.

From a technical viewpoint, each urban railway in Bangkok was newly built. There are two options for introducing urban railways: converting existing railways into urban railways and constructing new urban railways on new routes. In Bangkok, the latter was adopted. Therefore, each urban railway line was electrified and had a standard gauge of 1,435 millimeters, while the existing railway lines were non-electrified ones with a narrow gauge of 1,000 millimeters.[10] Although the SRT has jurisdiction over the Airport Rail Link and most sections run parallel with the existing railway, both the gauge and the operating systems differ completely. In developing countries, new urban railways are built separately from existing railways in most cases, but there are some cases of utilizing existing railways as urban railways, such as the cases of the KTM Komuter in Kuala Lumpur and electric commuter trains in Jakarta. Although it was possible in Thailand to utilize existing railways, the country's inter-urban railways are not really participating in urban transport due to the failure of the Hopewell plan.[11]

Thus, although various systems are intermingled in Bangkok's urban railways, based on the number of users, it can be said that the railways have been formally established. Comparing the numbers of users in other Southeast Asian cities, almost 2 million passengers traveled per day in 2010 on the 109-kilometer network in Singapore, and about a million passengers per day in 2009 on the 46-kilometer network in Manila (Kakizaki 2012, 177). Bangkok's railways do not reach the extent of those in Singapore and Manila: the number of daily users in 2010 was 580,000 on the 46-kilometer network, excluding the Airport Rail Link.

The daily number of passengers in Kuala Lumpur in 2010 was about 370,000 persons on a 121-kilometer network, excluding suburban service on the KTM Komuter (ibid., 177–79), and hence the number of users in Bangkok is clearly higher than in Kuala Lumpur.[12] Bangkok is larger than Kuala Lumpur, and consequently its transport density is higher. The number of users of urban railways in Bangkok is by no means small.

Viability of Paratransit Services and BRT

Although the viability of paratransit services and bus rapid transit (BRT) in urban transport in developing countries has been pointed out in previous studies, the attitudes in Bangkok towards these two means of transport are ambiguous.

Paratransit services existed from the beginning, namely as *songthaeo* converted from trucks. Although the type of bus changed from the *songthaeo*-type to "traditional" box-type bus, illegal *songthaeo* also always coexisted with the latter. Since the shortage of buses was severe in the confusion accompanying the unification of buses in the middle of the 1970s, the number of *songthaeo* increased rapidly. The Bangkok Mass Transit Authority (BMTA) legalized *songthaeo,* and they were finally converted into box-type minibuses. In addition, vans appeared as a new type of paratransit vehicle in the latter half of the 1990s, and the BMTA also decided to legalize them and place them under its jurisdiction. Paratransit services, thus, appeared naturally to meet the increasing demand in Bangkok, and they were finally legalized under the jurisdiction of a public agency after it became impossible to ignore their existence. Although not mentioned in this study, the policy on motorbike taxis, another form of paratransit vehicle, was the same.

Apart from motorbike taxis, there are three types of paratransit vehicles in Bangkok: vans, minibuses, and *songthaeo*. Although there are some illegal *songthaeo*, called *si lo*, and some unregistered vans, all other paratransit vehicles are under the jurisdiction of the BMTA.[13] These paratransit services emerged because of a demand for them, and they can continue their business given guaranteed users and certain profits. Therefore, it is possible to operate these paratransit services more effectively.

However, the problem is whether public agencies are sufficiently able to regulate them. Complaints regarding safety and service on both minibuses and vans are frequently heard. Even though the BMTA's jurisdiction over vans started in 2000, illegal vans still exist and their number is not inconsiderable. According to the BMTA's annual report, competition by illegal *songthaeo* and vans was one reason why the agency's original target income for public transportation has not been achieved, year after year (KSMK for 2009, 60). After the December 2010 accident in which a van was hit on the expressway by a sedan from behind and nine passengers in the van were killed, the safety of the vans has become an issue (*BP* [OE], 22 January 2011). Moreover, even when the vans were placed under the jurisdiction of the BMTA, brokers still maneuvered secretly in many cases and no strict measures were taken to curtail them. It is a fact that paratransit vehicles appeared because the "traditional" bus service was insufficient, and they exist because of user support. However, the regulation of paratransit services in Bangkok seems to be insufficient under the present circumstances, and regulations such as those implemented in Kuala Lumpur or Hong Kong, which are deemed successful, seem impossible to implement in Bangkok.[14]

Meanwhile, it is difficult to say that BRTs are fully functioning in Bangkok. Although they started initial operations in 2010, the number of users remains low and is much less than the target of 30,000 persons per day. The greatest factor responsible for these low numbers is the low reliability of buses compared to that of urban railways. The travel time on buses is prolonged by waiting for signals or due to traffic congestion. Although bus priority signals were originally planned to be used, the police fear that such signals may lead to the aggravation of road congestion. Therefore, BRTs, like common vehicles, are forced to wait for signals. Furthermore, privately owned car users have strongly resisted the reduction of lanes. In February 2011, the police allowed general vehicles to operate on certain sections of BRT-dedicated lanes during rush hours (*PCK* [OE], 14 January 2011). Thus, since user support is not forthcoming and the negative reaction from car users is strong, full exploitation of the BRT in Bangkok is still a challenge.

Although Banister (2005) asserted that there have been improvements in urban transport service due to using the BRT and warned against over-reliance on urban railways in developing countries, in Bangkok, the preexistence of the urban railway before the expansion of the BRT appears to have led to a lack of support for the latter. If the BRT had been introduced prior to urban railways, perhaps it would have been seen as more reliable and a means of shortening travel times when compared with conventional buses.[15] In Jakarta, with commuter trains using only existing railways, the BRT is supported as a modern urban transport system, and there is also talk of substituting the BRT for a suspended urban railway plan there (*NKS,* 26 September 2011).[16] In Bangkok, however, the BRT was not supported by either the users of private cars or other public transport.

Furthermore, if the scale of Bangkok city is considered, it can be said that the city is beyond the stage where it can be serviced by the BRT. Although theirs is a somewhat old argument, Thompson et al. (1990, 36–37) say that for urban railways to be financially successful, a city must have a minimum population of 5 million and must service 15,000 persons per hour in one direction.[17] The population of Bangkok already reached 5 million in 1980, and if the urban railways had been built as planned at that time, they should have been profitable. Although the BRT could potentially function effectively in cities such as Chiang Mai where the population is small, Bangkok may have grown beyond the stage in which the BRT can be utilized effectively.[18]

Thus, in a city such as Bangkok, where public agencies are not fully regulated, the viability of paratransit services may become negligible. For a city of Bangkok's size, the BRT no longer functions as a substitute for urban railways and cannot be expected to be used as a basic means of transport.

Strengthening of Regulation

From Private to Public Management

As the paratransit services in Bangkok are not fully regulated, regulation of urban transport in Bangkok remains insufficient. Nevertheless, regulation of tramways, suburban railways, buses, and urban railways has been gradually strengthened. The common vector for this success was the transition from private to public management.

Private companies established by foreign capitalists began operating tramways and suburban railways as economic activities. Although Thai capitalists opposed these foreign companies and established a new company to operate the tramways, these systems were finally unified by a foreign company. Even if the conditions of concession were observed, those for the first Paknam Railway Company (PRC) and Bangkok Tramway were the most relaxed, and they became more severe for the lines constructed later. In the case of tramways, the government began collecting a commission as "track rent," and a share of the profits, too. Although both privately operated tramways and suburban railways tried to expand their networks and make the transition to electrification, they could not escape the constraints of their concessions, and they were eventually nationalized between the 1930s and 1940s.

Private operators, both Thai and Chinese, started bus operations in Bangkok. Public operators appeared later, after the Bangkok Municipality and the Transport Company entered the business in the 1930s and the Express Transportation Organization (ETO) in the 1950s. Government regulation of buses was institutionalized gradually. The Department of Public and Municipal Affairs initially issued special permissions for the bus operators, and then, after the enforcement of the 1954 Transport Act, the Ministry of Communications began to supervise their operations and five-year concessions were granted. The Transport Regulation Committee performed the actual regulation, and decided on the abolition of bus routes and cancelation of concessions at certain times. A plan to integrate bus operations also surfaced repeatedly from the 1930s on, and it was reconsidered in the 1970s as a measure for avoiding a fare hike. Finally, the unification and nationalization occurred in the form of the establishment of a public corporation in 1975, which was succeeded by a public authority the following year.

Urban railways, on the other hand, had a more complicated privatization process. The urban railway plan surfaced in the 1970s but could not materialize as a purely private business because of the immense amount of investment that was required. Although at the beginning, the government planned construction using funds from the national budget, it changed its mind owing to a budget shortage and decided to adopt the BOT method of having 100 percent private investment. However, this plan failed, and hence it was decided that the ETA would contribute a maximum of 25 percent, which resulted in the concession grant to Lavalin. As this process shows, management went from public to private and then returned to public.

Then, during the economic boom the Hopewell and BTS plans, which adopted the BOT method of using 100 percent private investment, appeared, and the possibility of the urban railway business as a private enterprise increased. Urban railways under private management materialized because the BTS was successful, but the Hopewell plan failed. However, the MRTA, which aimed to use the same BOT method of having 100 percent private funding, abandoned this plan after it was required to put lines underground and it adopted construction with a two-tiered operation. The BTSC also gave up on the BTS extension with self-financing and took charge of operations only on the extension lines that the BMA itself had built. Since the populist policies of the Thaksin government required fares to be low, the government tried to buy out the BTSC and BMCL to that end. So, after the 1990s, management of urban railways also turned from private to public.

Comparing these processes with the public transport supply cycle mentioned in the introduction, both common features and differences can be seen. The public transport supply cycle delineated by Gomez-Ibanez and Meyer is the cycle in which the transport business started by private companies is nationalized owing to the aggravation of low profitability by government regulation, and finally returns to private management after the service and efficiency degrade and the costs rise (Vasconcellos 2001, 133–34). Since tramways, suburban railways, and buses shifted from private to public management, the first half of this cycle—the process of transferring the management from private to public—applies in the case of Bangkok. In the case of buses, the increase in the number of buses and the restraint on a fare hike by the government decreased operator profitability, resulting in the degradation of the service. In the case of urban railways, although nationalization has not yet occurred, if low profitability owing to government regulation is viewed to be the same as the emphasis on low fare levels that surfaced in the Thaksin government period, then the changes in them are in accord with the first half of this cycle.

As for tramways and suburban railways, because they were operated by foreign companies the processes leading to nationalization differed somewhat. The government's regulation increased, and the profitability subsequently suffered.[19] Nevertheless, it did not immediately result in a degradation in service. Instead, they still expanded their business, examples of which include electrification of the entire PRC line and expansion of the Siam Electric Company's (SEC) tramway network. However, because the government refused to extend the period of the concessions, they had to accept their final fate of nationalization, which restricted new investments in the final stage. In the case of tramways and suburban railways, nationalization snatched away the rights of foreign companies. This was fundamentally different from the case of bus businesses.

Problems of Public Management

Although all means of public transport except urban railways were finally nationalized, this failed to solve all problems. For tramways and suburban railways, attitudes toward positively utilizing the property after nationalization were lacking, and finally both were abolished. The reason for the elimination of tramways and suburban railways was that the businesses in charge of them were not sufficiently focused on making them work, because they were not the organization's main business. Although their viability was reduced by competition with buses, it was nationalization that finally led to the elimination of trams and suburban trains. Because tramways were set to be abolished in other cities, their abolition in Bangkok due to structural failure now seems to have been unavoidable. However, it is regrettable that the suburban railways should have been put to use as urban railways.

Nationalization caused new problems for buses. Although the inflow of illegal *songthaeo*, caused by the shortage of transport capacity, was one problem, the biggest issue was the loss-making operations that accompanied nationalization. The government did not need to cover deficits in bus operations when private companies were operating the buses. But after nationalization it was forced to bear a large part of the burden. A fall in efficiency and an increase in costs accompanied BMTA's takeover of management, such as outlays for personnel expenses and for purchase of broken-down private buses. The new business was restricted by the loss-making operations, which resulted in the decline in quality of service. Although the BMTA introduced private microbuses again, it could not keep up with demand with only its own buses, so illegal vans began to appear.

To avoid the problems caused by nationalization, bus operations in Bangkok were privatized once again. This corresponds to the latter half of the public transport supply cycle and is mostly in accord with Vasconcellos's "corporate" public transport supply cycle.[20] In the case of

Bangkok, though, it did not reach the stage of complete privatization. Rather, the number of operations directly managed by the BMTA were reduced through the expansion of privately operated buses. Since the BMTA took over jurisdiction for all illegal vehicles including *songthaeo*, minibuses that succeeded the illegal *songthaeo*, and newly emerging illegal vans, the ratio of BMTA buses fell to 20 percent of the total number of buses. The BMTA did better as a jurisdictional agency than as a bus operator, and there was a plan to transform the agency into a permanent jurisdictional agency to improve its business.

Although the BMTA strengthened its jurisdiction, it could not satisfactorily regulate the quality of services. When the Transport Company monopolized regional bus concessions at the end of the 1950s, it was criticized as "a tiger lying down and eating." The same situation was feared if the BMTA were transformed into a jurisdictional agency. Since there was much user dissatisfaction with private buses and paratransit services at that time, unless the situation was improved, the BMTA's transformation into a jurisdictional agency would not gain support from the public.

Recent politicization of urban transport is another factor constraining the BMTA's transformation into a jurisdictional agency. First, the bus operations in Bangkok were nationalized in order to realize the Kukrit government's free bus plan. Next, the NGV bus plan, which appeared during the period of the Thaksin government, aimed at providing air-conditioned bus service at low cost to Bangkok passengers in order to revive the previously downsized BMTA. The Samak government started a free bus service in 2008 using BMTA buses, which would be impossible for private buses.[21] Since there is a tendency for the BMTA to increasingly play the role of the implementer of populist policies, the bus business in Bangkok is once again heading in the direction of nationalization.

Government and Municipal Management

While bus operations in Bangkok were finally unified under a government public agency, a unification plan under the municipality had also surfaced in the process. Thus, there were two options for public management: government management or municipal management. Diplomacy was required to determine the choice.

The first unification proposal, which surfaced in the 1930s, was a municipalization plan. It appeared simultaneously with the establishment of the Bangkok Municipality and was based on the idea that transport services within each city should be left to the municipal government. Although the plan aimed for gradual municipalization by making the new routes available only to the municipalities and reducing the share of private operators, it ended in failure owing to the collapse of municipalities' bus services during the Second World War. Unification under national government management was sought in the 1950s, when gradual integration under the ETO was the target. However, this was stopped by Prime Minister Phibun's relief policy. Then, in the postwar "development" era, municipalization of bus operations resurfaced. This, too, ended in failure, though, and the plan changed to unification under private operators. Finally, the unification under government management emerged in the mid-1970s.

Even after the BMTA was organized, there was still a movement for municipalization (i.e., management under the BMA). While the chronic deficit of the BMTA continued in the 1980s, a plan to transfer jurisdiction to the BMA had surfaced. Although the plan languished for a while after its introduction, it reappeared in the latter half of the 1990s. This occurred simultaneously with the BMTA downsizing plan. In the 2000s, when Samak became the BMA governor, the transfer plan resurfaced. Samak asked only for the transfer of ordinary buses, but the government was lukewarm in its reaction. In the end, this plan failed, too. However, the BRT plan, which arose under the subsequent BMA governor Aphirak, was finally accepted, and the BMA entered the bus operation business in 2010.

The problem regarding nationalization or municipalization revolves around the question whether the government or the city (the BMA in this case) has jurisdiction over a city's urban transport. While one side argues that urban transport should be managed by the city because it is a service for the residents of that specific area, another, deep-rooted opinion holds that the government should control it because cities lack the capacity to manage the service. When the BTS extension plan was not supported by the government and construction was left to the MRTA after the cabinet meeting, the BMA showed its opposition to the government by insisting that urban transport should be brought under the jurisdiction of the municipal government. The government aimed to unify the jurisdiction of urban railways and would eventually deprive the BMA of jurisdiction over the BTS.

Having a unified jurisdictional agency for urban transport certainly improves user convenience. But giving the jurisdiction to a national government agency goes against the mainstream thinking in developed countries. In those countries, it is common practice for the local government in each city to take charge of the city's urban transport, and the government agency does not manage urban transport directly, even though it may provide subsidies. To increase the local government's capability, it is important to strengthen the city's rights of tax collection to increase its annual revenues (Rimmer and Dick 2009, 272–73). Although many citizens were dubious about the municipality's capability when the plan for bus unification surfaced in the 1960s, the present BMA is constructing the extension lines of the BTS and BRT by itself and therefore should be able to take charge of the city's urban transport.[22] The fact that the national government persists in retaining its jurisdiction indicates that it has certain interests in urban transport.

Politicization of Urban Transport

Confrontation between Jurisdictional Agencies

When we review the history of urban transport in Bangkok, we inevitably see the politicization of urban transport whenever regulation is strengthened. Urban transport increasingly holds an important meaning for politicians, who utilize it for their own interests. As a result, urban transport policy can be distorted and exposed to various evils. While in Hong Kong institutional arrangements were put in place to prevent the MRT from being used as a "political toy," Bangkok was not so lucky. Urban transport in Bangkok became a "political toy."

The first sign of the politicization of urban transport was the conflict between the Ministries of Interior and Communications involving jurisdiction over bus operations. The Ministry of Interior, which had jurisdiction over the Department of Public and Municipal Affairs, supervised bus operations since the department issued special permissions for regular bus operations. Then, the jurisdiction over buses was shifted to the Ministry of Communications by the 1954 Transport Act. The Ministry of Interior now promoted municipalization, because municipalities were under the ministry. However, the Ministry of Communications naturally opposed these moves and promoted the unification of bus operators under its public agencies or through a private sector–led integration. Finally, the Ministry of Communications came out victorious.

Discord between agencies was also seen regarding the jurisdiction over urban railways. The ETA was established in 1972 to take charge of Bangkok's expressways and urban railways and was placed under the Ministry of Interior. Thus, the Ministry of Interior newly secured jurisdiction over urban railways. However, the ETA's urban railway development plan failed, and the plan was transferred to the newly established MRTA in 1992. Because the MRTA was placed under the Prime Minister's Office, the number of ministries with jurisdiction over transport-related agencies increased further. Finally, both the ETA and MRTA were transferred to the Ministry of Transport through the restructuring of government ministries and agencies in 2002, which placed all transport-related agencies under the Ministry of Transport. Thus, the discord between the agencies over urban transport finally ended.

However, the conflict between the government and BMA became intense. This began during the Thaksin administration, and the first confrontation was related to the problem of the BTS extension lines ordered under Samak, the BMA governor. This conflict intensified further during the time of Aphirak, the subsequent governor, when the government objected to the BTS extension plan and the BMA-promoted BRT plan. Finally, the BMA took into its own hands the construction of the BTS extension lines, and the BRT plan also gained government approval after the collapse of the Thaksin government. Although the conflict seemed to have ended after the fall of the Thaksin government, it actually continued. The discord between the Ministry of Transport and BMA was visible when the cabinet decided that the construction of the Dark Green and Light Green lines would be carried out not by the BMA but by the MRTA under the pro-Thaksin government. The conflict continued under the subsequent anti-Thaksin group's Abhisit government. As mentioned previously, these political conflicts delayed the BTS extension line plan and BRT plan.

The conflict can be explained from the viewpoint of political strife and the struggle over rights. The conflict between the national government and the BMA during the Thaksin era was related to the larger strife in national politics. Thaksin feared that with the success of the BMA's urban railway plan and BRT plan, Bangkokians would shift their support to the Democrat Party from which the BMA governor came. Therefore, he exploited the right of government approval to block the BMA's plans. Although the BMA decided to implement the BTS extension plan without obtaining government permission, the BRT plan was kept waiting until after the coup that ousted Thaksin's government. This political strife was one of the factors for the delay in the development of Bangkok's urban transport.

Expansion of Vested Interests

The involvement of vested interests seems to have been another factor in the growing conflict between jurisdictional agencies. Two types of profits can be gained by having jurisdiction over private enterprises: formal profit and informal profit. The fees that the Transport Company gained from the unification of regional buses are examples of the former. Asking a jurisdictional agency to have a violation overlooked is an example of the latter. What is referred to as "rent-seeking" also serves as a source of informal profit, as is the expansion of interests that the government came to demand in the form of profit allocation from the tramway business, which was initially placed under a non-interference policy. The confrontation between the Ministries of Interior and Communications involving the jurisdiction of bus operation can also be recognized as a conflict involving vested interests acquired from bus operators. When the bus fares were temporarily increased in 1967, a report was published exposing the fact that high officials in the Ministry of Communications held bus company stock. Thus, the existence of a connection between the jurisdictional agency and operators under them resulted in conflict between government agencies.

After the 1970s, the interests acquired from urban transport were greatly expanded in accordance with the emergence of the urban railway plans. Here infrastructure building in urban transport played a significant role. Although entrepreneurs had to build their own infrastructures such as tracks for tramways and suburban railways, the buses that came later ran on roads, which were developed by the public sector, and so bus operators only had to procure buses. This is the same as the two-tiered operation method: the infrastructural development was carried out separately from the framework of urban transport.

However, new urban railways required the construction of elevated lines or underground tunnels, which in turn required an immense amount of investment compared with bus operations. The infrastructure-building features required for the development of urban railways are extensive, similar to those needed for dam construction or road building, and the construction had to be assigned to large-scale general contractors. The dangers of rent-seeking in the construction of urban railways arose, which in turn raised the question of the expansion of rights involving urban transport. Thus the Ministry of Interior secured its interests in the construction of both highways and urban railways. These were the large-scale infrastructural developments that the ETA established in 1972 and were placed under the ministry's jurisdiction. Although the Ministry of Interior had lost its interests in the jurisdiction of buses, it secured far larger interests. It also seems that the MRTA, which was newly installed in 1992 and placed under the Prime Minister's Office, was designed to snatch away the interests of the Ministry of Interior.

Furthermore, the conflict between the Ministry of Transport and the BMA under the anti-Thaksin group's Abhisit government included competition over interests in urban railways. Both Abhisit and Sukhumphan, the next BMA governor, were members of the then ruling Democrat Party, so there should have been no need for the BMA and the government to confront each other to gain interests. However, the Bhumjaithai Party, which acquired power in the Ministry of Transport, was opposed to returning its once-gained interests to the BMA. Therefore, even though the anti-Thaksin group held political power, conflict over the BTS extension between the government and the BMA inherited from the Thaksin period continued. This is another example of how urban railways involve great competition between vested interests.

There were also vested interests involving buses. The plan to introduce NGV buses proposed during the Thaksin administration continued even after the fall of that government; the public regarded it as a source of corruption and the opposition Democrat Party was also against it.

However, after the formation of the Abhisit Democrat government, the Bhumjaithai Party, which controlled the Ministry of Transport, sought its continuation, thus deepening its conflict with the Democrat Party. Although the basic plan was approved at the cabinet meeting, Abhisit repeatedly asked the Ministry of Transport for a reexamination, and the plan failed to make any headway during his tenure.[23] This was analogous to the conflict over the BTS extension line in that it was the result of the Bhumjaithai Party's resistance to losing its interests in the NGV bus introduction plan.

Thus, the politicization of urban railways continued and the conflict over interests became more severe because urban railways involved large-scale infrastructure development. Although these interests never came out onto the table, their existence was widely reported by the mass media.[24] As long as urban transport is regarded as a hotbed of competing vested interests, conflict over them will continue and delay development. The expansion of the vested interests involving urban transport was thus another factor that delayed the development of urban transport in Bangkok.

Emergence of Populist Policies

Because urban transport is indispensable to many people's daily lives and is an important means of travel particularly for the low-income group, politicians use it as a "political toy." So urban transport became a target of populist policies, and politicians' pressure on urban transport policy increased.

A low fare was the most important factor when urban transport was targeted for populist policies. Politicians aimed to gain support from the low-income group by maintaining a fare level that this group could afford, ignoring the issue of profitability of the business. The Thanom government, in the latter half of the 1960s, first engaged in such behavior. The withdrawal of the bus fare hike in 1968 was a concrete measure: it withdrew the already-approved 50 percent fare hike and returned the fare to its original amount. The large-scale resistance by passengers to the fare hike served as the backdrop for this event as many politicians believed that controversy needed to be eliminated before the upcoming general election. Subsequently, the Kukrit government's free bus policy for the poor in 1975 also contained aspects of populism and resulted finally in the integration of buses under government management. Thus, the trial of maintaining low bus fares or introducing free bus services due to political motives was the beginning of applying populist policies in urban transport in Bangkok.

While the problem of the bus fare persisted into the 1980s, it was the Thaksin government that set urban transport as simply an object of populist vote-getting. Here, the development of urban railways became the main object, and the "dream" was sold to Bangkokians by displaying two pillars: a low fare level and swift development of the plans.[25] The movement toward a populist policy for urban railways became particularly remarkable during the campaign for the 2005 general election. At that time, the master plan was reorganized to complete an urban railway network of no fewer than 354 kilometers in six years with a flat-fare system of fifteen to twenty baht. However, despite efforts to shorten the required construction period to three years and to adopt the turnkey method for rapid development, none of the "dreams" which Thaksin promised were ever realized.

The expansion of the city of Bangkok and the increase in the number of users of urban transport led to urban transport's becoming a target of populist policies. Until the 1950s, the size of the population in Bangkok was not so large and the problems of urban transport were not political. However, after entering the "age of development," the city expanded quickly and the number of urban transport users also increased. Under such circumstances, the issue of bus fares surfaced as part of populist policies for Bangkokians, and it was increasingly used politically. The Thaksin government also followed this practice. Although before the 2005 election Thaksin had been lukewarm about the development of urban transport, he used it as an issue and part of the "dream" offered up to Bangkok voters during the election.

Populist policies in urban transport may be valuable for city residents in the short term. Maintenance of low bus fare may reduce residents' living expenses and increase their disposable income. Considering the relatively high fare levels of the BTS and subway, it is very attractive if urban railways can be ridden for only a fifteen to twenty baht charge, regardless of the distance or number of transfers. And nothing would be better than the rapid development of urban railways for people who have to struggle through congested traffic day in, day out. Therefore, using urban transport as part of a populist policy was an important step to enhancing the quality of the city residents' lives.

However, the problem was the feasibility of these policies. It became a problem when the expense of realizing the development of urban railways could only be achieved by either maintaining a low fare or by proceeding with rapid development. The burden of the withdrawal of the fare hike in the age of the Thanom government directly affected the private bus operators, while the government incurred only an indirect burden for the expense. However, after the free bus policy of the Kukrit government was implemented, the expense for the operation of free buses and the maintenance of a low fare weighed heavily on the government, which had to deal with the BMTA's cumulative deficit. The free bus service started in 2008 continues in the form of the government's paying the BMTA's operational expenses.

Although no concrete measures were executed for urban railways, the procurement of expenses for the realization of the "dream" that was promised during the electoral campaign became a problem. This becomes clear through an analysis of the frequent changes in the policy after the 2005 general election. The bid for the Purple line was suddenly halted, although preparations had been fully made, because it became clear that there was a problem regarding the profits. If gaining a profit is problematic, financing the construction will generally be difficult. The Thaksin government tried to overcome this construction problem by using the turnkey method, mainly to postpone dealing with the profit problem. The fact that the conventional detailed design system was changed into the turnkey method since the first-stage urban railway development plan was proposed in October 2005 also supports the notion that urban transport was a target of populist policies. Then, while the turnkey method was maintained, the barter method with rubber was also introduced in the "Thailand: Partnership for Development" plan, announced in December 2005. Probably, these changes derived from the deadlock of financing the development of urban railways.

It is not impossible to maintain a low transport fare,[26] and losses can be covered by subsidies. Some argue that developing countries should manage urban transport services as public transport by providing government subsidies.[27] However, a series of populist urban transport policies implemented in Thailand arose for mostly political motives, without careful consideration. Therefore, at the stage of actual execution, problems arose, and the plans did not progress. That it was regarded as part of a politically motivated populist policy was another factor that delayed the development of urban transport in Bangkok.

Conclusion

Summary

The history of urban transport in Bangkok started with the introduction of tramways in the 1880s; suburban railways, buses, and urban railways came later. Urban transport reached a level comparable with other megacities in developing countries. But the process was extremely slow and has experienced various problems. This study aimed to reveal the historical organization of urban transport in Bangkok and to analyze how it developed, especially looking at its regulation and politicization.

Tramways and suburban railways appeared in the era of King Rama V. The development of tramways, which began with the granting of concessions for seven tramlines in 1887, started as an economic activity of foreign companies. In 1893, electric trams were introduced for the first time in Asia. Later, Thais also entered the tramway business and competed with the SEC, the foreign company led by Westenholz, to acquire new tramway concessions. Although Prince Narathip's Siamese Tramway Company received a concession, the burden of sharing profits with the government, which soared as a result of competition, was too heavy, and eventually it was purchased under pressure from the SEC.

Suburban railways developed by private enterprises emerged in the mid-1880s, and the railway to Paknam opened in 1893 as the first railway in Thailand. The earlier Burapha Railway plan, however, made no progress. Although the construction of future private railways was restricted under the government's state-oriented railway policy, the Maeklong Railway from Bangkok to Maeklong via Thachin opened in 1907. Initially, both Paknam and Maeklong lines functioned only as inter-urban railways. They later aimed to service intra-urban transport after absorbing the demands of inter-urban transport.

Competition between rail transport and buses began during the reign of King Rama VI and continued through World War II. The tramway business, which had been temporarily stagnant, grew again beginning in the mid-1910s, and Siamese Tramway became profitable for the first time since its founding. New lines to the suburbs were constructed in the 1920s to counterbalance the competing buses, and the Siamese Tramway was finally merged with the SEC in 1927. However, since there was also competitive response from bus operators by the duplication of bus routes, the tramway network was not expanded any further. The movement toward urban railways started with the PRC's introduction of a frequent electric tram service in the inner city in 1912. Although the electrification of the entire line was planned in the 1920s, after the extension of the electrified section, the plan was abandoned owing to problems with the concession period. Electrification was realized at last by SEC investment. The MRC also started the operation of electric trams through partial electrification of its line in the inner city, but it did not continue with further electrification because of the Great Depression. Both the PRC and the MRC refrained from new investments when their concessions were about to expire, and they were finally nationalized in 1936 and 1945 respectively.

The operation of buses started around 1910 by private operators, and the network was extended soon after. Although initially the focus was on the routes to the suburbs where the tramways had not yet arrived, competition with the tramways soon became evident, and the SEC asked the government not to approve new bus routes that would compete with its trams. For their part, private bus operators requested permission to expand the bus business in order to provide more jobs to Thais. The government, however, adopted a policy of municipalization, leaving bus operations to be managed by the newly established municipalities and allowing them to approve the opening of any new bus routes. While the competition with buses intensified, the SEC canceled its agreement with the government, and the competition between tramways and buses intensified after the Bangkok Municipality established a new bus route that ran parallel with the SEC's Bang Kholaem line.

The stagnation of rail transport and the expansion of bus services are noteworthy from the wartime period through the postwar years of recovery. Rail transport, which maintained the leading role of urban transport in Bangkok until then, raised its status temporarily as the competitive power of buses diminished during the war. However, when the tramways were nationalized after the war, both suburban railways and tramways failed to raise significant investments, and the status quo continued. As a result, rail transport could not develop further, and its status fell to a relatively low level.

On the other hand, municipalization of bus operations suffered a setback because of the war, and new private operators entered the fray after it. Therefore, while the Ministry of Interior planned to integrate bus operations through nationalization, the Ministry of Communications, which was in charge, sought unification under the ETO. The ETO had newly entered the bus business in Bangkok, but since Phibun followed a relief policy aimed at helping private operators out of political motives, the ETO unification policy was suspended, and another policy was adopted that was advantageous to private operators. Although Phibun thought that it would help him in the electoral campaign, the result was the reverse: the further deterioration in the quality of bus services only increased user dissatisfaction.

Then, between the period of "development" and the age of "democratization," there was a turning point when rail transport disappeared and buses became the only means of urban transport and were unified. This occurred when Sarit decided that rail transport was spoiling Bangkok's "beauty" and both the suburban railways and the tramways were abandoned and most were abolished. The entire Paknam line and a section of the Maeklong line were eliminated, and all tramways with a total length of about fifty kilometers were also abolished by 1968. Thus, rail transport almost disappeared from Bangkok, and buses became the only means of mass transport in the city.

However, buses, which now assumed the leading role in urban transport, once again faced the problem of unification. Initially the problem surfaced in the form of compensating for the privatization that had occurred during the Phibun era. Although the Bangkok Municipality's unification plan attracted attention for some time, an independent unification plan by private operators supported by the Ministry of Communications was finally adopted. Later, with the problem of the bus fare hike, the necessity for bus unification intensified, and the government decided to unify the services through the renewal of concessions expiring in 1975. But a concrete modality of unification had not been arrived at until the last moment, and unification under a public corporation, which was decided hurriedly, was finally accomplished in 1975. Later management of this public corporation was transferred to the newly established BMTA, and bus operations were unifed through a policy of nationalization.

The mid-1970s until the end of the 1990s was the age of emerging urban railway plans, but considerable time went by before these plans were realized. They had surfaced as the solution to Bangkok's transport problem. But due to the huge costs of construction, the government wavered, and construction using the BOT modality of involving the private sector was aimed for. Because private enterprises' reaction was lukewarm, bidding had to be reannounced after the government agreed to accept 25 percent of the financial burden. Finally, Lavalin of Canada was awarded the concession. However, this plan foundered in the wake of the 1992 Black May incident. In the economic boom of the 1990s, the SRT's Hopewell plan and the BMA's BTS plan emerged as new urban railway plans using the BOT method. The MRTA, which inherited the urban railway plan of the ETA, also adopted the BOT method, and it accepted bids after the proposed routes were changed. Although the Hopewell plan suffered a setback, the MRTA plan was finally implemented as a subway with a two-tiered operation method of vertical separation. The BTS plan finally materialized at the end of 1999, although it was negatively affected by the economic crisis.

The BMTA's bus operations, after the unification and reorganization of the bus services, required urgent attention. Most buses purchased from private operators were in bad condition, and the BMTA increased the number of buses either by purchasing or leasing them. Moreover, many illegal *songtaeo* began operating owing to the shortage of buses after the unification. The BMTA authorized them by placing them under its jurisdiction and finally made them convert to minibuses. However, the BMTA had been operating at a loss since the time of its establishment, and its cumulative deficit expanded continually as a result of its low fare level. To eliminate these loss-making operations, a plan was formulated to downsize the BMTA by increasing the number of private buses. This then resulted in a reversion to the situation before the bus unification.

Stagnation of urban transport development in Bangkok during the 2000s was caused by the politicization of urban transport as part of a populist trend and by bitter political conflicts during the time of the Thaksin government. Although Thaksin announced a plan for the rapid development of the urban railway network with a low fare level as a populist policy to appeal to city residents and voters, the "dream" he promised was not realized because of the immense construction costs that the plan implied. Meanwhile, the BMA, which was hampered in extending its BTS urban railway network by government stonewalling, decided to act on its own while the government dithered. The BRT plan, which had not progressed, again because of the Thaksin government's negative reaction, began to take off after Thaksin fell from power in a military coup. However, the BTS and BRT waited a long time because of the various obstacles and constraints.

As for bus operations, the BMTA downsized in the late 1990s, and a plan to transfer to the BMA was also considered. But bus policy was, like urban railway policy, used toward populist political ends, so the plan of operating air-conditioned buses with a low fare by purchasing a large number of NGV buses was hatched. Although the plan continued after the Thaksin government, it did not progress because of political conflicts within the anti-Thaksin government led by the Democrat Party and strong public criticism that the government was a hotbed of corruption. Implementation was delayed although the plan was approved by the cabinet. On the other hand, free bus service for some ordinary buses was implemented as a populist policy, and the profile of the BMTA rose again.

When summarizing the transition in the means of urban transport in Bangkok, the sequence was tramways, suburban railways, buses, and urban railways; this was analogous to the process in many cities in developing countries. Nevertheless, there are some unique characteristics in the Bangkok case, such as the emergence of suburban railways and the attempts to have them function as urban railways, the unification of bus operation under public management, and the long period of time that it took to realize urban railways. And paratransit vehicles and BRT, which are considered important in urban transport theory in developing countries, could not become key players in solving contemporary Bangkok's urban transport problem.

When we look at the regulation of urban transport, we note that there was the tendency for something that started as a private sector business to eventually come under public management through the strengthening of regulations. In the case of urban railways, the BTS eventually came under private management, but the tendency toward nationalization later resurfaced. When analyzing the significance of strengthening public regulation of urban transport, we need to take into account the political uses to which urban transport policy are put. Inter-agency conflict for jurisdiction has existed since the 1950s and relates to political and economic competition between vested interests. Because urban railways in particular require large-scale, expensive infrastructure building, competition for a share of the take by vested interests was great and accelerated the conflicts between the jurisdictional agencies. Politicians also used urban transport policy as a vehicle for their populist vote-getting: for instance, Thaksin's promising to maintain low fares and simultaneously rapidly develop the transport network. However, since there was no concrete financial backing, these promised "dreams" could never be realized. The plans made no progress and only resulted in a series of repetitive changes in policy direction.

Thus, strengthening the regulation of urban transport in Bangkok originated from its politicization; politicization, in turn, was enhanced by the scramble of interests involved in urban transport and the populist uses for the announced policy. This became the main factor that delayed the development of urban transport in Bangkok.

Suggested Further Research and Measures

This study has attempted to trace the historical organization of urban transport in Bangkok and to analyze the influence of politicization on this history. Below I wish to suggest some subjects for further research and measures on urban transport policy in Bangkok.

Among the subjects deserving further research is the role of water transport, which should be mentioned first. Bangkok, the so-called "Venice of the East," is a city dependent upon water transport, and a regular boat service for urban transport has existed here for many years.[1] I mentioned in chapter 1 the construction of facilities to connect tramways with the river ferries; there was, for instance, the Paklat Tramway, which was connected to Bangkok by water transport. The traffic on both banks of the Chaophraya River depended on ferries until the bus service crossing the Memorial Bridge opened in 1932. Although regular boat service linking up with tramways was abandoned after the expansion of the road network in Bangkok, the operation of an express boat service on the Chaophraya River started at the end of the 1960s and continues to the present day. Sources about water transport are scarce in the National Archives. But if other sources, such as newspapers, are examined, the history of water transport in Bangkok as urban transport may be traced to some extent.[2]

An important topic that I did not cover at all in this study is vehicles for lease, such as taxis. I only included here means of transport that operate on fixed routes, but leasable vehicles should also be included in the definition of public transport. The history of these vehicles is also long, and their origins go back to the rickshaws that appeared at the end of the nineteenth century. There were *samlo* that used pedal-driven and motorized tricycles, and later motorized tricycles converted from Daihatsu Midgets, called *tuktuk,* appeared. These have come to be famous as a symbol of the city, in fact. Sedan-type taxis also proliferated, and many taxis painted in various colors can now be seen in Bangkok. Motorbike taxis appeared in the 1980s and have become the most common means of public transport for many Bangkokians. Except for the taxi, each of these belongs to the category of paratransit, and research on these vehicles would be helpful to fill out the picture.[3]

Furthermore, it is necessary to investigate the transitions in urban transport policy, which this study revealed mainly through official archival sources, more of which will become available in the future. The sources currently available at the National Archives of Thailand date to the 1960s and 1970s; I also consulted other sources, such as annual reports. Newspapers were crucial to study the historical organization of urban transport. Although the larger frame of historical facts examined in this study will stay the same, the background to particular policies and the government's examination process might eventually become clearer from archival sources.[4] Therefore, I expect that understanding about these matters will deepen further if new archival sources can be used.

The measures suggested for Bangkok's urban transport policy can be reduced to two major areas: the rapid development of urban railways and the strengthening of coordination between the various means of transport. It will be necessary to promote construction of the urban railway network, and to widen the network on the basis of the master plan. As seen in chapter 6, the construction of new routes finally started in the late 2000s. As of the end of 2013, construction was underway on the Purple line, the Blue line, the Dark Green line (a BTS extension line) between Bearing and Paknam, and the Dark Red line.[5] This is to be followed by the construction of the Dark Green line between Mochit and Khukhot, the Pink line, and the Yellow line. Although these routes cannot be opened according to the time schedule of the master plan, it is indispensable to advance their development without further significant delay.

To that end, it will be necessary to lessen political intervention as much as possible. Although urban transport in Bangkok has already become a "political toy" and it is a difficult task to keep it from being so exploited, it will be necessary to take certain measures, following Hong Kong's example. The Yingluck Shinawatra government, which came into power in 2011, announced a populist policy of a flat fare of twenty baht as a campaign pledge, following in the footsteps of the Thaksin Shinawatra government. If this campaign pledge is fulfilled, the extension plan of the urban railways would be hampered again (*PCC* [OE], 23 July 2011).[6] Considering previous circumstances, the prospective unification of operators and the realization of a low fare level using a subsidy may be appropriate; however, emphasis should be placed at present on the expansion of the network.[7]

The frequent changes of plans as in the past should be avoided. In a country such as Thailand, where political power changes frequently, realization of a plan is unnecessarily delayed, particularly if the transport development plan changes with each change of government. The reexamination of the once-fixed master plan should be avoided and the plan should be maintained. For example, an October 2011 report stated that the Yingluck government was planning to change the standard of the Pink line from the original monorail to a heavy rail. This would require remaking the documents for the bid already created, and would delay its opening for a few years from the original target of 2015 (*DN* [OE] 7 October 2011).[8] It is advisable to avoid such sudden policy changes because they are both an obstacle to the rapid development of the urban railways and also a waste of funds.

To strengthen the coordination between various means of transport, it is important to improve the connection facilities between urban railways and buses so that urban railways become the main and buses the supporting means of transportation. Although the length of the urban railway network in Bangkok totals eighty-five kilometers as of the end of 2013, few measures have been taken to coordinate BMTA bus routes with the urban railways. Therefore, connections between the two are quite inconvenient. Very few stations—mainly, the Mochit and the Victory Monument stations of the BTS—function as transfer points between urban railways and buses.[9] While there are bus stops at these stations, there is no example of a bus terminal being newly constructed in front of a station. Although the newly constructed BRT has the transfer facilities that enable it to function as a feeder for the urban railways, a radical reorganization of the bus network is needed to strengthen the coordination with the urban railways.

Paratransit services should be considered as feeders for urban railways. However, under the present circumstances, the regulation of paratransit services is insufficient. Numerous users transfer between the urban railways and vans at the Mochit and Victory Monument stations. Motorbike taxi stands have appeared in front of many stations, and the users of urban railways use motorbike taxis for transport between their houses, workplaces, and stations. If a network of legal paratransit services originating at urban railway stations was constructed, quality service provision would be possible, including in *soi,* where large-sized buses cannot operate. Paratransits also need to improve their quality of service to attract middle-class private car owners, and the regulation power to achieve this standard should be vested in jurisdictional agencies such as the BMTA.

As is clear from the above, various defects persist in Bangkok's urban transport policy. It cannot be overemphasized that conquering these problems and providing better urban transport services are essential to the solution of the city's transport problem. The future of urban transport in Bangkok will be determined by whether it can learn from the lessons of the past.

Notes

Introduction

1. Although many means of transport available in a city are included in the phrase "urban transport," private transport, such as privately owned cars, is excluded in this study.

2. The term "megacity" usually refers to a large-sized city with a population of more than ten million. Although the population of Bangkok (Bangkok Metropolitan Administration) is about six and a half million, the Bangkok metropolitan area's population, including the neighboring provinces, is about ten million.

3. Although BTS is the name of the operation company, generally it is also used as a common name for the elevated railway itself. For details, see chapter 5.

4. The details of the lines are as follows: the 23.5-kilometer original BTS lines, the 20-kilometer subway, the 2.2-kilometer BTS extension (Taksin Bridge–Wongwian Yai), and the 28.5-kilometer Airport Rail Link. As of the end of 2013, the 5.3-kilometer BTS extension between On Nut and Bearing and the 5.3-kilometer BTS extension between Wongwian Yai and Bang Wa had been added to the network, with the total, therefore, of 84.8 kilometers of urban railways.

5. The average number of daily users during weekdays in 2010 was about 450,000 persons for the BTS and about 210,000 persons for the subway. In addition, about 40,000 persons per day used the Airport Rail Link.

6. *Songthaeo* are buses that are converted from trucks, with two parallel benches on their carriages, attached roofs, and steps on the rear for getting on and off. As will be mentioned in chapter 2, the first buses to appear in Thailand were these *songthaeo*.

7. The Hopewell plan is named after the company to which the concession was given by the SRT. For details, see chapter 5.

8. The phrase "dream-selling policy" came to appear here and there in the newspapers after 2006, sarcastically referring to the Mega Project. It referred to the large-scale populist policy for the infrastructure development plan, which was meant to provide "dreams" to the people but never materialized.

9. Since transport economics (and occasionally transport geography) deals with transport from the viewpoint of quantitative analysis, and transport engineering focuses mainly on the technical points, the studies of these disciplines are excluded here. In addition, for the details of the changes in urban transport studies in Japan, see Miki (2010).

10. Countries such as Malaysia and Thailand now have fairly well-developed economies, but they are still included here as developing countries.

11. Few examples of suburban railways have appeared in developing countries other than in Jakarta in Southeast Asia. At this point, Bangkok is a somewhat exceptional case.

12. The "traditional" public traffic referred to here includes the public transport modes generally seen in developed countries, such as regular buses using large-sized vehicles, sedan-type taxis, and electric trains.

13. In this study, the term "public management" means management by a public organization such as the government and municipalities, and is used as the antonym of private management. Therefore, government management, metropolitan management, and municipal management exist as subclassifications of public management.

14. Curitiba, Brazil, was known as the first city in the world to introduce bus rapid transit (BRT), and it improved the convenience of public traffic by constructing a bus network that combined BRT and existing buses (Banister 2005, 198–99). As for the BRT, see following note.

15. The BRT is a bus system that aims to improve speed and stable operation by constructing dedicated bus lanes in the middle of roads, similar to tramways. The installment of ticket gates at the station and the entrainment by the purchase of a ticket similar to urban railways is common, along with a high platform at the station to assist smooth boarding and departure. The BRT was also introduced in cities in developed countries, such as Ottawa.

16. The public transport supply cycle in Gómez-Ibáñez and Meyer refers to a transport business started by private enterprise and then nationalized with reduced profitability because of the regulation of the government. It finally returns to private management by the deterioration of service stemming from a decrease in efficiency and the increase in costs. On the other hand, Vasconcellos's "savage" public transport supply cycle also starts from private operation, but collectivization and exclusion of new entry then occur to avoid the issues of profitability. Then, the interests are divided by a mafia by monopoly, and finally regulation is strengthened or public management is set up. The "corporate" public transport supply cycle starts with the establishment of a public corporation, but it incurs losses due to increase in political pressure, and finally it is privatized. Lastly, the "irresponsible" public transport supply cycle starts with private operation under the conditions provided by a public

authority, and then illegal entrepreneurs such as paratransits appear because of the deterioration of service once the private operator pursues higher profits.

17. The fact that the Siam Electric Company (later "Corporation") changed its name to the Thai Electric Corporation at the end of the 1930s is only mentioned after describing the situation of tramway operation during the 1900s.

18. Two books about the railways in Thailand by railway enthusiasts outline the situation of suburban railways after nationalization, although they are not academic studies (Ramaer 2009, Whyte 2010). Moreover, a general interest book I wrote on the railway history of Thailand also introduces an outline of the movement toward suburban railways (Kakizaki 2012).

19. The official name of this agency is recognized as the agency that has jurisdiction over the urban railways rather than as the operator of buses. However, it should not be confused with the jurisdiction over other means of urban transport since the agency that had the jurisdiction over the expressways and urban transport, the ETA, had already been established.

20. Anek Laothammathat (2006, 83–102) posits that the beginning of populism (*prachaniyom*) in Thailand starts with the Thaksin government organized in 2001, and that political leaders up to that point were not populists. On the other hand, according to Tamada (2009b, 79–87), Thaksin is not a populist; he explains that the anti-Thaksin group use the term to criticize Thaksin. Although measures such as the free bus policy can be regarded as populist, they do not fulfill all conditions of populism, according to Tamada; these consist of a "leader whose face is visible, the appeal to the people who complain of their peripheral situations, the challenge to the existing elites, and the gain of support by the simple and clear confrontation diagram" (ibid., 79).

21. In 2009, the average number of daily users of the regular ferries and boats in Bangkok was about 250,000: 159,000 on the ferries across the Chaophraya, 34,000 on the express boats in the Chaophraya, and 55,000 on the express boats in the Saen Saep Canal (SC for 2009, 112–16). The operation of these express boats was started in order to compensate for the deteriorating bus service owing to traffic congestion. The ferries started in 1969 and the express boats in 1990 (*SN*, 17 May 1969; *SRSW*, 14 April 1990). Although the ETO started the operation of the express boats on the Chaophraya in response to a governmental request, the service was privatized after two years of operation because of its poor financial condition.

22. Furthermore, the Department of Royal Secretariat records are used frequently, similar to those of the Secretariat of the Cabinet among the National Archives of Thailand, but very few studies use other archives.

23. On the reorganization of the government ministries and agencies by 1993, see Tamada (1996).

24. Since these two records have been recognized as the most important sources in the historical studies of Thailand, other records tend to be rarely used.

25. Although the Ministry of Interior records (Mo.) also exist, archives on the tramways are not included.

26. Several volumes of annual reports on the public authorities are available, but the study on urban transport that used them cannot be found.

27. The original MRTA (Metropolitan Rapid Transit Authority) became the Mass Rapid Transit Authority of Thailand in 2002.

28. For example, the oldest extant annual report of the BMTA is from 1986, and only those after 1990 are available for every year. The annual reports of the public agencies in Thailand were not maintained reliably.

29. Although the financial indicators are published, most other statistics are not published in the annual reports of the private enterprises who managed the tramways and the suburban railways.

30. The number of users of the public BMTA buses is based on the number of tickets sold; no statistics are available on the number of users of the private buses.

Chapter 1. Introduction of Rail Transport, 1880s–1900s

1. As Britain and France planned railway programs passing through Thai territory in the 1880s, the government had to respond to these challenges. For details, see Kakizaki (2005, 80–84).

2. NA Ko To. 5/1, "*Phra darunrak krap thun krommamuen thewawong*, 26 March 1886."

3. NA Ro. 5 No. 21/1 "Tramway Concession, Bangkok, 5 May 1887."

4. Charoen Krung Road, opened in 1864, starts from the south of the palace heading east and then south toward Bang Kholaem along the Chaophraya River; it was then the longest road in Bangkok at nine kilometers. Foreigners called this road New Road.

5. Kueakun (1977, 173) explains that the business was transferred to the Bangkok Tramway in 1892 after the opening of the tramway; Sa-nguan (1986, 81) says that it was transferred due to the poor state of business, though the year of transfer is not mentioned. However, the fact is that the concession was transferred to the company one month after the grant. The year 1892 referred to by Kueakun is the year when the company reregistered as a Danish company.

6. Though earlier studies say the whole line was opened on this day, it was only half of the line that was opened at that time [*BT*, 2 December 1891].

7. According to *BT* (12 December 1891), the section between the Bangkok Dock and Bang Kholaem was still in the red as only one year had passed since its opening. Therefore, it can be surmised that this section had opened in late 1890.

8. This was the Sprague-type electric tram that was introduced by Frank Sprague, an American, at Richmond in 1887 (Noda et al. 1986, 90–91). There were about 350 tram lines in use in America, Europe, and Australia in 1891 (*BT*, 9 December 1891).

9. Earlier studies say that electric tram operation started on the whole line. However, the first electrified section was the newly opened section in 1890.

10. In Japan, though a trial run of a Sprague-type electric tram was held in 1890, the first electric tramway for general transport was the Kyoto Electric Railway, which opened in 1895 (Noda et al. 1986, 90–91). Following Bangkok, electric tramways were introduced in Batavia in 1899, Mandalay in 1904, and Singapore and Penang in 1905, among Southeast Asian cities.

11. According to *BT* (18 August 1894), electric tram operation expanded to the whole line in the early half of 1894.

12. There are several documents regarding the transfer of nationality in NA Ro. 5 No. 21/3, which suggest that the transfer to Thai registry had been decided. However, its nationality was transferred to Danish registry as the majority of shares were held by Danish investors.

13. NA Ro. 5 No. 21/8, "*Phraya chonlayutyothin thawai krommamuen naret,* 11 December 1893."

14. NA Ro. 5 No. 21/11, "*Krommamuen phitthayalap bangkhom thun phrabatsomdet phrachaoyuhua,* 12 July 1895."

15. Ibid., The announcement of the construction of Yaowarat Road was issued in February 1892 by the Department of Public Works (Kanokwali 2001, 255–59).

16. NA Ro. 5 No. 21/11, "*Phrabatsomdet phrachaoyuhua thung krommaluang naret.*"

17. Ibid. "*Phraratchakrasae,* 20 January 1900."

18. The construction of Yaowarat Road was delayed due to the difficulty of acquiring land, and it was only in 1899 that the last section was opened (Kanokwali 2001, 255–59; NA Ro. 5 No. 5. 5/4, "*Raingan sukhaphiban thang puang pracham pi rattanakosin sok 118*"). This seems to have been the main reason that the plans for tramway construction on this road were delayed.

19. The rate of track rent was 2.5 percent in the first ten years, and then rose 2.5 percent for every ten years until reaching 4 percent in the final ten years.

20. NA Ro. 5 No. 21/11, "*Phraratchakrasae,* 20 January 1900."

21. The Bangkok–Phetchaburi railway was the third private railway to be granted a concession. However, Westenholz failed to procure enough capital and finally sold the concession to Prince Narathip. After it was transferred again several times, the government bought it back and decided to construct it by itself. For details, see Kakizaki (2005, 95–97). The power-distributing business was started by the old Siam Electricity Company established by royals and nobles in 1888, but it was transferred to foreigners in 1897 due to the poor profits, and the SEC, a Danish company, inherited it in 1898. For details, see Wipharat (1992, 30–76).

22. NA Ro. 5. 21/11, "*Raingan prachum senabodi sapha,* 24 September 1901. As electric railways or tramways were large consumers of power, it was common

in Japan that power distribution companies amalgamated with railways or tramways to electrify them in order to stabilize their businesses.

23. On the malfeasance of Prince Narathip when he was deputy minister of finance, see Tasaka and Nishizawa (2003, 51–58).

24. NA Ro. 5 Yo Tho. 5. 5/11, "*Krommamuen phitthayalap krap bangkhom thun phrabatsomdet phrachaoyuhua*, 26 September 1896." Though the prince applied for a change of route, it was rejected, and he finally transferred the concession in the following year. The Phrabat Tramway started operation in February 1903, but demand was quite low, since it was a local branch line from the government Northern line, except during the festival season at Phrabat every February.

25. NA Ro. 5 No. 21/36, "*Krommaluang sanphasat lae uenuen krap bangkhom thun phrabatsomdet phrachaoyuhua*, 2 April 1903." Prince Narathip was another example of an aristocrat engaged in business activities.

26. Ibid. "*Krommaluang naret krap bangkhom thun phrabatsomdet phrachaoyuhua*, 12 January 1903." In 1900, Westenholz applied for the construction of the tramway between Phraya Si and Bang Lamphu via Tha Tian, a part of the City Wall line, the Hua Lamphong line to Sao Chingcha, and the Chakkrawat line (NA Ro. 5 No. 21/26, "Aage Westenholz to Krom Luang Nares Vorariddhi, 9 October 1900").

27. The king decided to select more a favorable application at the ministers' meeting on April 23, 1903 (Ro 5 No. 21/36, "*Raingan senabodi sapha*, 23 April 1903").

28. Ibid, "*Krommaluang naret krap bangkhom thun phrabatsomdet phrachaoyuhua*, 17 June 1903."

29. Prince Damrong later insisted that for the sake of passengers the tramway business should not be monopolized by one company (NA Ro. 5 No. 21/36 "*Khwam nai raingan prachum senabodi sapha*, 7 March 1904").

30. NA Ro. 5 No. 21/52, "Agreement between the Siamese Tramway Co., Ltd. and the Siam Electric Co., Ltd."

31. NA Ro. 5 No. 21/38, "*Phraya nonthaburi lae phraya ruetthiwong krap bangkhom thun phrabatsomdet phrachaoyuhua*, 28 November 1902." It would be further extended from Talat Phlu westward to the Thachin River along the Phasi Charoen Canal.

32. Ibid., "*Raingan prachum senabodi*, 24 May 1904."

33. Ibid. Later the section between Wat Kanlayanmit and Taphan Hok seems to have been removed.

34. NA Ro. 5 No. 21/38, "*Chaophraya surasakmontri krap bangkhom thun somdet phraboromma orasathirat*, 5 June 1907."

35. Ibid, "*Raingan prachum senabodi sapha*, 6 June 1907."

36. NA Ro. 5 No. 21/52, "*Krommamuen narathip krap bangkhom thun phrabatsomdet phrachaoyuhua*, 3 May 1904."

37. Ibid.

38. Ibid., "Memorandum on the Question Whether an Extension on the Siamese Tramway Line, as Prayed for by Prince Nara Would Conflict with the Concession of the SEC Co., Ltd., 6 December 1905."

39. NA Ro. 5 No. 21/78, "*Chotmai khokhwam rueang phrachaonongyathoe krommamuen narathip praphanphong kho phraratchathan phraboromrachanuyat sang rot rang pakkret*, 26 June 1906."

40. Ibid. This part of the Dusit Extension line was the section between Duang Duean (Sukhothai) Road and the mouth of the Samsen Canal.

41. It was the Mueang Non Tramway Company that would construct this tramway, whose northern terminus would be the mouth of the Rangsit Canal, opposite Pathumthani.

42. NA Ro. 5 No. 21/100, "*Krommaluang naret thun krommakhun sommot amonphan*, 12 October 1906."

43. At that time the road network in Bangkok was completely isolated, and it was only after the overthrow of the absolute monarchy in 1932 that the construction of roads to the provinces began.

44. For example Sa-nguan (1986, 129) notes that the company suspended the construction program for several years due to a shortage of capital, and it was the king's loan that enabled the construction. Holm (1977, 55) says that the king invested a half of its total capital of 400,000 baht because he intended to let his people know how to construct and manage railways, as well as to supervise them.

45. NA Ro. 7 Pho. 1/19, "*Krommaluang thewawong krap bangkhom thun phrabatsomdet phrachaoyuhua*, 2 August 1886."

46. According to NA Ro. 5 Yo Tho. 5. 4/2, "*Kampani rotfai burapha limitet*," the concession for the Bangkok–Ban Mai railway was also granted in September 13, 1886.

47. *Burapha* means east.

48. NA Ro. 5 Yo Tho. 5. 4/2, "*Krommakhun narit krap bangkhom thun phrabatsomdet phrachaoyuhua*, 2 November 1889."

49. It was only between Hua Lamphong and Khlong Toei that carriages were passable; beyond that, the road was merely an embankment built for the use of telegram line construction.

50. They planned a new railway from Phrakhanong on the Paknam Railway to Chachoengsao and reapplied for the concession, as the original one had already expired. However, as there were other applicants for the railway between Bangkok and Chachoengsao, at the ministers' meeting in 1899 it was decided to ask all applicants to submit information on how they planned to procure their capital (Kakizaki 2005, 94–100).

51. The official name is Samut Sakhon, and it is also called Mahachai nowadays.

52. NA Ro. 5 Yo Tho. 5. 2/13, "*Phrabatsomdet phrachaoyuhua thueng krommamuen phitthayalap*, 15 March 1897."

53. NA Ro. 5 Yo Tho. 5. 8/4, "*Nangsue sanya anuyat tham thang rotfai tae krungthep mahanakhon pai ban mahachai*."

54. According to NA Ro. 5 Yo Tho. 5. 8/6, "Prospectus Tachin Railway Company Limited," the original capital was one million baht.

55. NA Ro. 5 Yo Tho. 5. 8/7, "*Krommakhun narit krap bangkhom thun phrabatsomdet phrachaoyuhua*, 19 September 1904."

56. Ibid., "*Raingan prachum senabodi sapha*, 24 April 1905."

57. NA Ro. 5 Yo Tho. 5. 8/2, "*Nangsue sanya anuyat tham thang rotfai tae thachin pai maeklong*."

58. NA Ro. 5 Yo Tho. 5. 8/9, "*Phraya sisahathep krap bangkhom thun phrabatsomdet phrachaoyuhua*, 5 October 1908."

59. NA Ko To. 5. 3/3, "*Borisat rotfai paknam prakat riak hun lae chichaeng ngoppraman kha kosang*." This was the same number of passengers traveling between Bangkok and Paknam by boat.

60. According to NA Ko To. 5. 3/3, "*Borisat rotfai paknam prakat riak hun lae chichaeng ngoppraman kha kosang*," the prospectus supposed the third-class fare between Bangkok and Paknam as 0.5 baht, which was maintained during the 1920s. Though fares for the second and first class were fixed as double and three times the third-class fare. The numbers of passengers of these classes were not included in the revenue estimates.

61. Ibid., "*Borisat rotfai paknam prakat riak hun lae chichaeng ngoppraman kha kosang*."

62. NA Ko To. 5. 15/12, "Paknam Railway Company, Ltd. Directors' Report for the Half-year Ended 30 June 1923."

63. NA Ro. 5 Yo Tho. 5. 8/8, "Report of the Board of Directors for Presentation to the Shareholders of the Tachin Railway Company, Limited."

64. NA Ro. 5 Yo Tho. 5. 8/6, "Prospectus Tachin Railway Company Limited."

65. NA Ko To. 5. 15/10, "Meklong Railway Company, Limited. Report of the Board of Directors for Presentation to the Shareholders at the 15th Ordinary General Meeting."

66. At the general meetings of MRC shareholders, the reduction in freight revenues was always explained as the result of a decrease in the fishery catch.

67. NA Ro. 5 No. 21/088, "Aage Westenholz to Krom Luang Nares Vorariddhi, 17 March 1906."

68. The track rent for the Samsen line in 1907 was 8,075 baht, which was 2.5 percent of annual gross receipts, but the Siamese Tramway had to pay 47,600 as fixed rent in that year (NA Ro. 5 No. 21/90, "James S. Smyth to Phra Norasart, 9 August 1906").

69. NA Ro. 5 No. 21/109, "*Krommamuen narathip praphanphong krap bangkhom thun somdet phraborom orasathirat makutrachakuman*, 17 August 1907."

70. Ibid., "*Khat chak raingan prachum senabodi sapha*, 8 August 1907."

71. In the end, the number of shares acquired by the SEC was 3,126 shares, one share more than half (*BTWM*, 2 September 1907).

72. NA Ro. 5 No. 21/36, "*Khwam nai raingan prachum senabodi sapha*, 7 March 1904."

73. Since the government asked that the Dusit Extension line be removed as it would be in the way of the construction of a new wall to expand the Dusit Garden, that 1.6-kilometer section of the line was taken out in 1910. The government instead approved the connection of the Dusit Extension line with the Samsen line via Baiphon (Uthong Nai) Road. The company seems to have eliminated the direct route along Khosua (Phitsanulok) Road to the power plant by extending the track from Baiphon Road to the power plant via Samsen Road. As the remaining section of the Dusit Extension line between Samsen Road and the mouth of the Samsen Canal became an isolated section, it should have been later transferred to Siam Electric. However, as NA Ro. 6 No, 13/3, "Prince Narathip to His Most Gracious Majesty the King, 9 April 1913" shows, it was still operated by the Siamese Tramway as of April 1913.

74. NA Ro. 5 No. 21/97, "A. Westenholz to Krom Luang Damrong, 18 January 1909." The SEC would change its nationality to Belgian registry, and then become a Thai company in 1927, accomplishing the merger with the Siamese Tramway.

75. NA Ro. 5 No. 5. 10/26, "*Krommaluang naret krap bangkhom thun phrabatsomdet phrachaoyuhua*, 9 April 1906."

76. Ibid. These two lines were the extension lines to piers at Tha Tian and Ban Mo.

77. NA Ro. 5 No. 21/82, "Aage Westenholz to Krom Luang Nares Vorariddhi, 15 November 1905." The SEC planned the same extension to construct a new shed in 1902, but postponed it, since it could not procure enough land (NA Ro. 5 No. 21/35, "Aage Westenholz to Krom Luang Nares Vorariddhi, 17 February 1902").

78. By 1912, the Pakkret-bound ship had ten trips a day, and the Paklat-bound ship offered a twenty-five-minute interval service between 6:20 am to 7:20 pm (Siam Directory 2005, 48) .

79. The Transport Company "Motor", Ltd. was a foreign company established in 1906. It made an agreement with Menam Motor Boat to prevent competition and gained the right to operate on the Bangkok Yai Canal exclusively (*BTWM*, 2 May 1906; *BTWM*, 26 November 1907). However, it sold the rights in 1909 to Menam Motor Boat for 20,000 baht due to low profits.

80. NA Ro. 5 No. 21/106, "Aage Westenholz to Krom Luang Nares Vorariddhi, 18 August 1906."

81. The Paklat Canal was the shortcut on a crook of the Chaophraya River. Originally it was constructed in 1722 in the Ayutthaya era, but later the land

was reclaimed in 1784 since seawater was flowing into the upstream areas. The present canal was then dug at the west of the original one in 1815.

82. NA Ro. 5 No. 21/106, "Raingan senabodi sapha, 28 March 1907."

83. Ibid., "*Phraya sukhumnaiwinit krap rian krommakhun sommot*, 20 May 1908."

84. The first motor railcar was the motor trolley introduced by the Thachin Railway in 1906, but it was probably not used for general transport due to its small size (*BTWM*, 18 April 1906). In 1908, the PRC also introduced a larger railcar between Hua Lamphong and Khlong Toei (*BTWM*, 27 February 1909).

85. NA Ro. 5 No. 21/49, "L. R. de la Mahotière to His Excellency Chow Phya Devesrwongsevivat, 1 February 1906."

86. NA Ro. 5 No. 21/56, "*Krommaluang naret krap bangkhom thun phrabatsomdet phrachaoyuhua*, 22 February 1906."

87. Ibid., "*Raingan senabodi sapha*, 22 February 1906."

88. NA Ro. 5 No. 21/95, "*Krommaluang naret thung* Monsieur F. Didier, 9 July 1906."

89. This was the transport of meat from the slaughterhouse in Bang Kholaem which since September 1903 replaced the transport by rickshaw (*BTWM*, 13 August 1903).

90. NA Ro. 5 No. 21/111, "*Phraya sukhumnaiwinit krap bangkhom thun phrabatsomdet phrachaoyuhua*, 21 February 1908."

91. NA Ro. 5 No. 21/95, "Aage Westenholz to L. R. de la Mahotière, 24 January 1907."

92. Ibid., "Aage Westenholz to Krom Luang Damrong, 25 February 1808."

93. NA Ro. 5 No. 21/90, "James S. Smyth to H. R. H. Prince Naret, 19 October 1906."

94. NA Ro. 5 No. 21/1, "Tramway Concession, Bangkok, 5 May 1887."

95. NA Ro. 5 No. 10/37, "Aage Westenholz to Chao Phya Yomaraj, 15 February 1909." Carriages were classified into four types, among which the first category was the largest with a capacity of more than four persons and hauled by two horses.

96. NA Ro. 5 No. 21/97, "*Chaophraya yommarat krap bangkhom thun phrabatsomdet phrachaoyuhua*, 29 September 1909."

97. For the railway policy at that time, see chapter 4 in Kakizaki (2005).

98. For the unofficial imperialism through railways see Davis and Wilburn (1991).

99. As Prince Damrong insisted at the ministers' meeting in May 1906 that private railways should not be permitted any more, it became impossible to develop private railways in Thailand from then on (Kakizaki 2005, 101).

100. At first the government rejected all railway plans including the right of land acquisition or exploitation, since it deemed that the acquisition of rights along the railway lines would threaten the kingdom's sovereignty. It took note

of the example of China. It came to doubt the guarantee of interest rates even if such conditions were not included. For details, see Kakizaki (2007). The guarantee of interest rates was an encouragement adopted in many countries where the construction of private railways were encouraged. It was a system in which the government would compensate for shortages if the dividend rate was lower than the guaranteed rate due to low profits.

Chapter 2. Emergence of Competition, 1910s–1930s

1. The government started the construction of a new power plant in 1911, which started operation from 1914. For details, see Wipharat (1992, 134–91).

2. As the Siamese Tramway had earlier only issued preferred share dividends, the dividend rate for ordinary share was not yet available.

3. NA Ro. 6 No. 13/3, "Prince Narathip et al. to His Most Gracious Majesty the King, 9 April 1913."

4. Ibid.

5. This was calculated from the track rent in 1919 mentioned in *BTWM*, 17 February 1920.

6. The districts within three canals were the area surrounded by the Chaophraya and the Phadung Krung Kasem Canal, which was the outermost canal among three canals surrounding the palace. Old Bangkok's urban area was limited to this area until Charoen Krung Road and Trong (Rama IV) Road were constructed beyond it in the latter half of the nineteenth century.

7. Phrakhanong district used to belong to Phrapradaeng province and was transferred to Phra Nakhon province after the elimination of Phrapradaeng province in 1931.

8. NA Ro. 6 No. 13/6, "*Chaophraya yommarat krap bangkhom thun phrabatsomdet phrachaoyuhua*, 5 June 1925."

9. Ibid., "*Chaophraya yommarat krap bangkhom thun phrabatsomdet phrachaoyuhua*, 14 September 1925."

10. NA Ro. 6 No. 8. 4/11, "*Banchi rotyon rapchang banthuek khon doisan pracham thanon nai changwat phra nakhon.*"

11. The concessions of both companies would terminate at the end of 1949; this also applied to the new lines. The track rents were also the same: 3,000 baht per mile for the SEC and 7.5 percent of gross receipts for the Siamese Tramway. As the track rent of the Siamese Tramway became higher, the government asked the SEC to apply the same rent, which was rejected by the company (NA Ro. 6 No. 13/6, "*Chaophraya yommarat rian chaophraya mahithon*, 3 July 1925.").

12. NA Ro. 5 No. 21/96, "Aage Westenholz to Krom Luang Naret, 15 August 1906." The company then reapplied for another line from Bang Rak, running along Silom Road, then turning right to Convent Road and crossing Sathon Road to Khlong Toei, whose route lay about five hundred meters south of the Paknam Railway.

13. NA Ro. 7 Pho. 12/2, "*Raingan prachum senabodi sapha*, 5 January 1927."

14. Ibid. See also "*Raingan prachum senabodi sapha*, 7 March 1927."

15. The original color of the SEC's tram is unknown, but the company should have changed the color to yellow around 1909 as *BTWM* (5 August 1909), mentioned that the company would decide the color by hearing from opinions of passengers after introducing new bright colors as a trial.

16. NA Ro. 7 Pho. 12. 1/7, "*Krom phraya nakhon sawan krap bangkhom thun phrabatsomdet phrachaoyuhua*, 8 May 1930."

17. Ibid. "W. L. Grut to the Prince of Nagara Svarga, 27 March 1930."

18. The Rama VI Bridge, upstream from the Memorial Bridge, opened in 1927 and was the first bridge across the Chaophraya River. However, there was only a railway across the bridge and no road had yet been constructed, since there was no urban area around the bridge. Space for the road on the bridge had been prepared, however.

19. NA Ro. 7. Pho. 12. 1/7, "*Krom phraya nakhon sawan krap bangkhom thun phrabatsomdet phrachaoyuhua*, 8 May 1930."

20. NA Ro. 7 Pho. 12. 1/5, "*Krommaluang lop buri chaeng ma yang chaophraya mahithon*, 28 December 1927," *BTWM* (15 January 1929). The Dusit Extension line was ordered to be removed to Phitsanulok Road from Uthong Nai Road to prevent scenic damage around the Dusit Palace. The Ratchawong line was reported to be abolished by a donation from merchants along the road. The first case of abolishment of tramways was that of part of the Dusit Extension line in 1910 due to the extension of the Dusit Palace.

21. According to *BTWM* (28 March 1907), the motor railcar ordered by the PRC would arrive in four months. The railcar collided with an automobile on the night of September 1 (*BTWM*, 2 September 1908).

22. According to *BTWM* (28 March 1907), the railcar would run every twenty minutes between Hua Lamphong and Khlong Toei, but it may have been an interval of forty minutes, since there was only one railcar.

23. NA Ro. 7 Pho. 1/19, "*Maioe rian chao krom rotfai*, 19 February 1909." The reason for the danger was that the length between two axles was less than half of the total car length and the center of gravity was inadequate since the engine was above the floor.

24. NA Ro. 7 Pho. 1/19, "T. Heyward Hays to His Most Gracious Majesty the King, 29 July 1921."

25. Ibid. "*Krommamuen kamphaengphet krap bangkhom thun phrabatsomdet phrachaoyuhua*, 23 May 1922."

26. Ibid. "*Krommamuen kamphaengphet krap bangkhom thun phrabatsomdet phrachaoyuhua*, 10 August 1925."

27. Ibid.

28. The sixty-minute interval of the Paknam-bound train should have

started to cope with the bus competition after the opening of the road between Bangkok and Paknam.

29. Another object of the SEC was the opening of power distribution in Paknam via the Paknam Railway.

30. The Railway Commission rejected the application as there was an opinion that the SEC would aim to succeed the PRC in case of the termination of concession (NA Ro. 7 Pho. 1/19, "*Krommamuen kamphaengphet krap bangkhom thun phrabatsomdet phrachaoyuhua*, 22 January 1926.").

31. NA Ko To. 5. 15/10, "T. Heyward Hays to His Royal Highness Prince Purachatra."

32. NA Ro. 5 Yo Tho. 5. 8/6, "Prospectus Tachin Railway Company Limited."

33. According to the prospectus, it expected one fourth of the average gross receipt of 50,000 baht per mile on the Bangkok side. The population of two districts (Buppharam and Ratchakharuha) where the electric tram would run was 27,000 persons, which was more than the population of the two districts (Pathumwan and Bang Rak) where the electric tram of the Paknam Railway ran (NA Ro. 6 No. 27/3, "*Banchi chamnuan phonlamueang nai khet 25 tambon*").

34. NA Ro. 7. Pho. 1/1, "W. B. Grut to H. R. H. the Prince of Kambaeng Bajra, 28 February 1925."

35. NA Ro. 7 Pho. 1/1, "*Krommaluang kamphaengphet krap bangkhom thun phrabatsomdet phrachaoyuhua*, 3 June 1927."

36. Ibid. "*Krommaluang kamphaengphet krap bangkhom thun phrabatsomdet phrachaoyuhua*, 17 April 1931." The electric tram operation between Wat Sing and Bang Bon was suspended before the termination of the concession because of the frequent stealing of electric wiring.

37. NA [3] So Ro. 0201. 39. 1. 1/5, "*Ratthamontri wa kan krasuang setthakan thueng nayok ratthamontri*, 15 October 1935."

38. Ibid. "*Ratthamontri wa kan krasuang setthakan thueng nayok ratthamontri*, 20 January 1936." The construction of the road between Bangkok and Paknam (Sukhumvit Road) started in 1927 but did not proceed due to the difficulty of land acquisition. After the issue of the land condemnation act in 1933 and the military importance of the road was made clear in the rebellion of Prince Boworadet, the construction proceeded smoothly.

39. Ibid. "*Raingan prachum khana ratthamontri*, 29 January 1936."

40. Ibid. "*Raingan kan prachum khana kammakan phicharana rueang sampathan borisat rotfai paknam chamkat khrang thi 4*, 25 February 1936."

41. Ibid. "*Raingan prachum khana ratthamontri*, 11 March 1936."

42. NA [3] So Ro. 0201. 39. 1. 1/5, "*Raingan prachum khana ratthamontri*, 19 August 1936."

43. NA [2] So Ro. 0201. 68. 2. 1/5, "*Ratthamontri wa kan krasuang setthakan thueng nayok ratthamontri*, 30 May 1938." The details concerning the Aerial Transport will be described later.

44. NA [2] So Ro. 0201. 66. 2/1, "*Ratthamontri wa kan krasuang setthakan thueng nayok ratthamontri*, 16 August 1940."

45. Ibid. "*Ratthamontri wa kan krasuang setthakan thueng nayok ratthamontri*, 14 January 1941."

46. Ibid. "*Prathan kammakan kan phicharana damnoenkan cheracha sue rotfai sai maeklong thueng lekhathikan khana ratthamontri*, 25 February 1941." Since the concession stipulated the names of such components as buildings and machineries, the components of track such as rails, sleepers, and bridges were not referred to. Therefore, the committee judged that they were the "railways" that the government could take over free of charge.

47. Ibid. "*Ratthamontri wa kan krasuang setthakan thueng lekhathikan khana ratthamontri*, 5 May 1941."

48. Ibid. "*Ratthamontri wa kan krasuang khamanakhom thueng lekhathikan khana ratthamontri*, 29 October 1942."

49. Ibid. "*Ratthamontri wa kan krasuang khamanakhom thueng lekhathikan khana ratthamontri*, 7 December 1942."

50. NA [2] So Ro. 0201. 66. 2/4, "*Ratthamontri wa kan krasuang khamanakhom thueng lekhathikan khana ratthamontri*, 13 August 1945."

51. Ibid. "*Lekhathikan khana ratthamontri thueng ratthamontri wa kan krasuang khamanakhom*, 13 November 1945."

52. As the management of the Phrabat Tramway was so loose, its concession was rescinded and the operation was succeeded by the Tha Ruea Railway in 1930. The abolition of both railways was approved in July 1942 and they likely ceased their operations soon after. They probably aimed to gain profit from the disposal of their railway materials, whose values rapidly rose due to the war.

53. Phra Phakdinoraset started in business by importing sewing machines in 1893, and then succeed in ice manufacture after trying several other businesses. For more details on his career, see Suehiro (1989, 359–60).

54. NA Ro. 5 No. 21/56, "*Krommaluang naret krap bangkhom thun phrabatsomdet phrachaoyuhua*, 6 April 1906." These were electric buses.

55. N A Ro. 5 No. 21/81, "C. L. Groundwater to H. R. H. Prince Naret, 24 November 1905."

56. Ibid. "Draft Reply to Mr. Groundwater."

57. NA [2] So Ro. 0201. 68. 2. 2/4, "*Ratthamontri wa kan krasuang mahatthai thueng lekhathikan khana ratthamontri*, 31 October 1941."

58. NA [2] So Ro. 0201. 66. 3/5, "*Samnao raingan prachum khana ratthamontri*, 25 November 1938."

59. As far as I could find, there was only one minute of the meeting remaining; the committee discussed the application for new bus routes or change of routes all together (NA [2] So Ro. 0201. 63. 2/8, "*Raingan kan prachum kammakan phicharana rueangrao lae kham kho doen rotyon satharana pracham thang khrang thi 1/2478*, 8 May 1935").

60. According to *BTWM* in August 1936, it was reported that the company's proposal to operate buses to Don Mueang and Paknam had been rejected.

61. The level of train service to Paknam after the electrification of the whole line was only four trips, just as in the era of steam-powered trains, but later increased to sixty-minute interval service in the latter half of the 1930s.

62. The road to Don Mueang was opened on August 1, 1936, by extending Phayathai Road to the north (*PCC*, 1 August 1936).

63. NA [2] So Ro. 0201. 66/11, "*Ratthamontri wa kan krasuang setthakan thueng nayok ratthamontri*, 13 October 1938."

64. NA Ro. 7 Mo. 17/11, "*Senabodi krasuang mahatthai krap bangkhom thun phrabatsomdet phrachaoyuhua*, 7 February 1930."

65. The first five-year program was the first subprogram of the eighteen-year program for highway construction planned in 1936. For details, see Kakizaki (2009, 28–33).

66. The plan for the construction of the King Taksin statue emerged in 1934, but it was only completed in 1954 under Phibun after the war (Phaibun 1997, 702).

67. According to NA [2] So Ro. 0201. 63. 2/8, "*Raingan kan prachum kammakan phicharana rueang rao lae kham kho doen rotyon satharana pracham thang khrang thi 1/2478*, 8 May 1935," there had already been bus service between Bang Lamphu and Wongwian Yai in May 1935. At the meeting, the application of route extension to the Maeklong Railway's station at Wongwian Yai was approved. As the applicant was Chulin Lamsam, the Nakhon Thon Company was one of the businesses of the Lamsam family, who would later go on to form the Thai Farmers Bank group.

68. This was the second-class fare between Samyaek and Witthayu.

69. NA Ro. 7 Pho. 12/6, "*Krommaphra nakhon sawan chaeng khwam ma yang chaophraya mahithon*, 2 July 1931."

70. NA Ro. 6 No. 13/6, "*Chaophraya yommarat krap bangkhom thun phrabatsomdet phrachaoyuhua*, 5 June 1925."

71. NA [2] So Ro. 0201. 63. 2/8, "*Sanoe kammakan phicharana rueang rao doen rot*."

72. NA [2] So Ro. 0201. 66. 3/1, "*Phraya thepphahatsadin kap phuak rian phraya manopakon*, 15 July 1932."

73. Ibid. "*Raingan prachum khana ratthamontri*, 12 March 1937."

74. Ibid. "*Ratthamontri wa kan krasuang mahatthai thueng lekhathikan khana ratthamontri*, 17 May 1937."

75. It was reported that ten to twenty buses started operation along the Bang Kholaem line. They were probably illegal buses. The name "mosquito bus" was also used in Singapore, where it referred to a small bus with seven seats operated by individuals or small enterprises (Dick and Rimmer 2003, 238).

76. NA Ro. 7 Pho. 12. 1/7, "W. L. Grut to the Prince of Nagara Svarga, 27 March 1930."

77. NA [2] So Ro. 0201. 63. 2/10, "J. Knudtzon to Phra Boribhandh Yuddhakich, 7 May 1937."

78. According to *BTWM* (11 May 1939), a Thai newspaper article reported that the SEC had decided to introduce trolley buses in the near future.

79. For example, in *BTWM* (15 September 1938), a correspondent opined that the municipality should substitute trolley buses for tramways by removing tramway tracks instead of introducing buses.

80. On the strike of rickshaw laborers, see Phanni (1999, 102–6).

81. According to NA Ro. 6 No. 13/4, "*Phraya sithammathirat rian phraya chakkrapani*, 16 February 1921," the number of employees gathered was sixty-four persons, and the police persuaded them to go back to work, although the company reported to the police that they had plotted an uprising.

82. NA Ro. 6 No. 13/4, "*Chaophraya yommarat rian chaophraya mahithon*, January 17, 1923."

83. Ibid.

84. Though Thompson (1967, 615) says that the union was established in 1897 and registered officially in October 1932 by the request of the government, it is unknown to what extent it was organized in 1897.

85. On the private railway plans that emerged at that time, see Kakizaki (2005, 93–97).

86. For details, see ibid, 127–32.

87. NA [2] So Ro. 0201. 66. 2/4, "*Lekhathikan khana kammakan kritsadika thueng palat krasuang khamanakhom*, 17 May 1945."

88. The People's Party, which overthrew the absolute monarchy in the revolution of 1932, announced six revolutionary principles, among which the principles of economic independence and the guarantee of economic activities justified economic nationalism. For details, see Suehiro (1989) and Nambara (1998).

89. Since the operation of buses, mostly by Thais, emerged in the 1920s and caused the competition with the SEC's tramways, opposition toward the SEC also emerged, since it was seen as depriving Thais of work opportunities. (For an example, see *BTWM*, 23 May 1928.) A "foreign company," under the general understanding of that time, was a company that had a high level of foreign capital and most of whose board members were foreigners, whether the company was technically registered abroad or not.

90. Though it was not caused by the termination of concessions, the new Navigation Act, stipulating a level of Thai capital at more than 65 percent, forced two foreign companies (the Thai Steam Navigation and the Siam Steam Packet) to close in 1940; their businesses were taken over by the government.

91. The construction cost virtually determined the capital of companies as

the construction costs of the Paknam Railway, the Thachin Railway, and the old Maeklong Railway were 400,000 baht, 1 million baht, and 1 million baht respectively. Therefore, even if the gross revenues of the MRC exceeded the PRC's, the gap of net profit would be reduced due to differences in depreciation costs. Also, the dividend rate of the PRC would be better than the MRC's even if the net profits of both companies were the same, because the former's capital or the number of its shares was less. From the table of dividend rates for chartered companies at that time in Suehiro (1989, 95), we can see that the PRC achieved quite a high rate.

92. The dividend rate of the SEC, which subleased the PRC, had also dropped precipitously after the Great Depression.

93. NA [2] So Ro. 0201. 63. 2/10, "J. Knudtzon to Phra Boribhandh Yuddhakich, 7 May 1937."

94. NA [2] So Ro. 0201. 63. 2/11, "*Banthuek rueang borisat faifa sayam khoporechan chamkat lot thun laeo mai khuen thun*."

95. NA [2] So Ro. 0201. 63. 2/10, "*Raingan prachum khana ratthamontri*, 22 September 1939." After the final capital reduction at the end of 1939, the total value of capital became 11,280,000 baht, which was half of the original sum (*BTWM*, 15 March 1940).

96. *Songthaeo* seem to have been the general type of bus at that time. The first bus operated by Loet Setthabut was also a kind of *songthaeo*, with two parallel benches on both sides of the carriage on a Ford truck; it could carry ten passengers (Sa-nguan 1986, 67). Even though the types were similar, the officially permitted scheduled buses (*rot pracham thang*) and *songthaeo* were completely separate, and *songthaeo* probably meant "unpermitted, illegal private bus." These *songthaeo* still legally operate in small lanes (*soi*) in Bangkok and rural areas.

97. NA [2] So Ro. 0201. 66. 3/5, "*Ratthamontri wa kan krasuang mahatthai thueng nayok ratthamontri*, 23 September 1938." The application was finally rejected.

Chapter 3. Expansion of Bus Networks, 1940s–1950s

1. It seems that the revival of this section was carried out after the business was inherited by Bangkok Electricity in 1950.

2. At the shareholders meeting in 1942, the capital of the Ratchawong, Atsadang, and part of Silom lines was refunded, so the Atsadang branch line had probably been abolished by that time (*BT*, 7 March 1942).

3. NA [2] So Ro. 0201. 63. 2/5, "*Phu chatkan thuapai borisat faifa thai khoporechan chamkat thueng phana ratthamontri wa kan krasuang mahatthai*, 30 May 1945."

4. Although the trial run of tramcars on the Bang Kholaem line was started at the beginning of May 1945, satisfactory operation was impossible due to the

shortage of electricity (*SK*, 4 May 1945). The plant was back in operation on June 18, 1945 (FN 1988, 22).

5. NA [2] So Ro. 0201. 63. 2/15, "*Phu chatkan thuapai borisat faifa thai khoporechan chamkat thueng phana ratthamontri wa kan krasuang mahatthai*, 19 April 1945."

6. NA [3] So Ro. 0201. 39. 1. 1/7, "*Rotfai sai paknam banchi sadaeng ngoen rairap raichai lae kamrai nai kan doen rot.*"

7. According to *BTWM* (3 February 1941), there were *songthaeo* (mosquito buses) available between Bangkok and Paknam in addition to the buses of the Aerial Transport Company.

8. NA Bo Ko. Sungsut 1. 7/2, "*Huana kong chat kan doen rot khet 1 (khram chittalan) rian o tho ro*, 7 February 1942."

9. The Aerial Transport Company changed its name to the Transport Company in 1939 since its business had diversified and its bus business had also become important (*BTWM*, 30 May 1939).

10. As of November 1941, the Singburi (Lopburi) line had ten buses and the Prachinburi line had seven buses daily, and each bus likely made one round trip per day (NA [2] So Ro. 0201. 68. 2. 2/5, "*Kan doen rotyon borisat khonsong chamkat*").

11. NA [2] So Ro. 0201. 68. 2. 2/5, "*Kan doen rotyon borisat khonsong chamkat*."

12. Ibid., "*Ratthamontri wa kan krasuang khamanakhom thueng lekhathikan khana ratthamontri*, 5 March 1942."

13. NA [2] So Ro. 0201. 66. 3/7, "*Banchi rot pracham thang nai phranakhon lae thonburi.*"

14. Ibid., "*Ratthamontri wa kan krasuang mahatthai thueng lekhathikan khana ratthamontri*, 29 June 1943."

15. Ibid., "*Lekhathikan nayok ratthamontri thueng ratthamontri wa kan krasuang mahatthai*, 11 August 1943."

16. Ibid., "*Ratthamontri wa kan krasuang mahatthai thueng lekhathikan nayok ratthamontri*, 13 August 1943." The four routes were as follows: between the Ratchawong pier and Nang Loeng, between Wat Kaeofa (Kiakkai) pier and Ratchaprasong, between Ratchathewi and the Victory Monument, and between the Samsen market and Saochingcha.

17. Ibid., "*Lekhathikan thi prachum palat krasuang thueng palat krasuang mahatthai*, 6 September 1943."

18. Ibid., "*Palat krasuang mahatthai thueng lekhanukan thi prachum palat krasuang*, 4 January 1944."

19. Ibid., "*Lekhanukan thi prachum palat krasuang thueng palat krasuang kalahom lae khamanakhom*, 12 January 1944."

20. Ibid., "*Palat krasuang khamanakhom thueng lekhanukan thi prachum palat krasuang*, 24 January 1944."

21. Ibid.

22. NA [2] So Ro. 0201. 68. 2. 2/5, "*Ratthamontri wa kan krasuang khamanakhom thueng nayok ratthamontri*, 1 May 1945."

23. The Department of Transport was asking to return the trucks that the Ministry of Defense offered, since the former received many used Japanese military trucks from the Allied Forces after the end of the war (NA [2] So Ro. 0201. 68. 2. 2/5, "*Ratthamontri wa kan krasuang kalahom thueng lekhathikan khana ratthamontri*, 18 October 1945").

24. According to NA [2] So Ro. 0201. 63. 2/17, "*Phu chatkan thuapai kan faifa krungthep rian lekhathikan khana ratthamontri*, 1 August 1950," the budget of Bangkok Electricity in fiscal year 1950 was about 18 million baht, among which 11,281,600 baht was for the cost of purchasing the TEC's business.

25. NA [2] So Ro. 0201. 63. 2/20, "*Ratthamontri wa kan krasuang mahatthai rian lekhathikan khana ratthamontri*, 13 August 1951." The eight lines were as follows; the 3.3-kilometer Ratchadamnoen line, the 3.8-kilometer Phanfa–Pratunam line, the 6.6-kilometer Yommarat–Bang Sue station line, the 4.3-kilometer Odian–Thewet line, the 8.7-kilometer Si Phraya–Saphan Khwai line, the 6.6-kilometer Pratunam–Samsen power station line, the 8.2-kilometer Daokhanong–Bang Lamphu line, and the 7.1 kilometer Talat Phlu–Odian line.

26. Ibid.

27. Although there had already been two bus routes on Sukhumvit Road, the extension of the tramway to Phrakhanong was approved at the cabinet meeting on December 19, 1951, due to the shortage of buses (NA [2] So Ro. 0201. 63. 2/19, "*Lekhathikan khana ratthamontri rian ratthamontri wa kan krasuang mahatthai*, 21 December 1951").

28. NA [2] So Ro, 0201. 63, 2/20, "*Ratthamontri wa kan krasuang mahatthai rian lekhathikan khana ratthamontri*, 13 August 1951."

29. Ibid., "*Lekhathikan khana ratthamontri rian ratthamontri wa kan krasuang mahatthai*, 24 December 1951."

30. The plan of introducing trolley buses was again reported in the newspapers in 1955, but there was no concrete progress on this in the end (*SN*, 10 April 1955).

31. According to NA Kho Kho. 0202. 2. 13/3, "Thailand, and General & Scientific Aspects. Communications," the Phloenchit line was supposed to have been opened for traffic in 1951, but there was little evidence of its actual operation. As far as I know, the only material showing the operation of this line is the document mentioning that the operation of tramcars on this line should be suspended after 6:00 pm for the relief of traffic congestion when the ceremony to commemorate the Constitution was to be held at Lumphini Park (NA Kho Kho. 0202. 3. 5/062, "*Banthuek*, 1956"). Since it is not contained in the map of the annual report of MEA for 1958, it seems that this line had already been abolished by 1958.

32. There were level crossings for the two railway lines at two places: the crossings between the Paknam and Maenam branch lines and between the Bang Buathong Railway and the Southern line. In both cases the state railways had been constructed late. A reverse example did not exist. However, the tramway of Lopburi, which was opened in 1955, crossed the Northern line of SRT at the same level.

33. NA Kho Kho. 0202. 2. 13/3, "Thailand, General & Scientific Aspects: Communications."

34. NA [2] So Ro. 0201. 63. 2/19, "*Lekhathikan khana ratthamontri rian ratthamontri wa kan krasuang mahatthai*, 21 December 1951."

35. NA Kho Kho. 0202. 9. 5/4, "*Banthuek raingan kan prachum khrang thi 1 khong khana kammakan sakha setthakit kan khamanakhom*, 12 November 1954."

36. NA Kho Kho. 0202. 2/39, "*Banthuek raingan kan prachum khrang thi 1/2498 khong khana kammakan sakha setthakit kan khamanakhom*, 30 January 1955."

37. NA Kho Kho. 0202. 9. 5. 7/66, "*Banthuek raingan kan prachum khana kammakan rotfai haeng prathet thai khrang thi 18/2502*, 9 July 1959." However, since the abolition of the Paknam line was decided in the discussion stage of the plan, the plan of introducing diesel cars was also eliminated.

38. NA [3] So Ro. 0201. 39. 1. 1/13, "*Ratthamontri wa kan krasuang khamanakhom rian lekhathikan khana ratthamontri*, 31 May 1942."

39. NA Kho Kho. 0202. 9. 5. 7/6, "*Banthuek raingan kan prachum khana kammakan rotfai haeng prathet thai khrang thi 23/95*, 21 June 1952."

40. This road (Setthakit Road) went north from Samut Sakhon to the Bangkok–Nakhon Pathom road (Phetkasem Road); the distance to Bangkok was about forty kilometers.

41. NA [2] So Ro. 0201. 66. 2/4, "*Palat krasuang khamanakhom rian palat krasuang kan khlang*, 12 May 1950." The original plan was to increase the power supply to substitute for steam-hauled trains between Khlong San and Mahachai by two electric trains using the power generated at a waterfall at Kanchanaburi, or through reinforcement of the power station at Bangkok Electricity's Wat Liap. However, the plan was changed due to the low level of feasibility.

42. NA Kho Kho. 0202. 9. 2/2, "*Prakat rotfai lem thi 13 chabap thi 52*, 28 December 1959."

43. Although details are not known about these internal combustion railcars, it is surmised that they resembled the motorcars that were used to carry Japanese troops. According to NA Ko Kho. 0301. 8. 2/273, "The Maeklong Railway Improvement Project 1956," they were called Japanese diesel rail trucks, and hauled two trailers each. In addition, three cars like motorcars (*rot disen*) are listed on the Maeklong line from 1952, but the details are also unknown.

44. NA Kho Kho. 0202. 9. 7/19, "*Khrongkan prapprung thang rotfai sai mae klong*, 8 November 1963."

45. In October 1945, the Ministry of Defense asked the Department of Transport for the return of its trucks, since the latter had purchased many ex-Japanese military trucks (NA [2] So Ro. 0201. 68. 2. 2/5, "*Ratthamontri wa kan krasuang kalahom thueng lekhathikan khana ratthamontri*, 18 October 1945").

46. NA [2] So Ro. 0201. 66. 3/10, "*Banthuek rueang kan chat tang ongkan borikan doen rotyon doisan*."

47. Ibid.

48. NA Kho Kho. 0202. 3. 5/10, "*Bamrung tothong krap rian than phu banchakan thi khaorop*, November 1954."

49. NA [2] So Ro. 0201. 66. 3/10, "*Ratthamontri wa kan krasuang mahatthai rian lekhathikan khana ratthamontri*, 15 March 1952."

50. Ibid., "*Ratthamontri chuai wa kan krasuang khamanakhom rian lekhathikan khana ratthamontri*, 26 August 1952."

51. NA Kho Kho. 0202. 11. 4/1, "*Raingan pracham pi tae roemtang thueng 31 thanwakhom 2495*." The original purpose of establishing the ETO was for Thais to take back the shipping-and-discharging business for freight at railway stations, which hitherto had been monopolized by Chinese operators.

52. NA [2] So Ro. 0201. 68. 2. 1/12, "*Ratthamontri wa kan krasuang khamanakhom rian lekhathikan khana ratthamontri*, 21 June 1948." The management over air transport was transferred to Siamese Airways Company (*Borisat doen akat chamkat*), first established in March 1947. Thai Navigation was the old Siam Steam Packet Company, which had been established by a foreign national; it was purchased by the government in 1940.

53. NA [2] So Ro. 0201. 66. 3/11, "*Lekhathikan khana ratthamontri rian ratthamontri khamanakhom khlang phu amnuaikan ro so pho phu chatkan borisat khonsong chamkat*, 12 January 1953."

54. NA Kho Kho. 0202. 13. 1/11, "*Panha an phueng tong chichaeng to phu thue hun nai khrao prachum yai saman pracham pi khong borisat khonsong chamkat*, 10 May 1948."

55. The gross profit in fiscal year 1950 was 950,000 baht, but the net balance was in the red by about 60,000 baht; only in fiscal year 1951 could it make a net profit of 400,000 baht.

56. [2] So Ro. 0201. 66/28, "*Ratthamontri wa kan krasuang khamanakhom rian lekhathikan khana ratthamontri*, 8 June 1953."

57. NA Kho Kho. 0202. 11. 1/4, "*Banthuek kan prachum khana kammakan ongkan rapsong sinkha lae phatsaduphan khrang thi 2/2496*, 3 February 1953."

58. Ibid., "*Banthuek kan prachum khana kammakan ongkan rapsong sinkha lae phatsaduphan khrang thi 7/2496*, 26 June 1953."

59. Ibid., "*Banthuek kan prachum khana kammakan ongkan rapsong sinkha lae phatsaduphan khrang thi 8/2496*, 24 July 1953."

60. NA Kho Kho. 0202. 11. 1/5, "*Banthuek kan prachum khana kammakan ongkan rapsong sinkha lae phatsaduphan khrang thi 5/2497*, 28 May 1954."

61. The Talat Phlu–Khlong Toei route was divided into two separate routes at the intermediate stop of Wat Traimit.

62. NA Kho Kho. 0202. 11. 4/2, "*Raingan pracham pi tangtae 1 mesayon 2497 thueng 31 minakhom 2498*."

63. NA Kho Kho. 0202. 11. 4/4, "*Raingan pracham pi tangtae 1 mesayon 2498 thueng 31 minakhom 2499*."

64. NA Kho Kho. 0202. 3. 5/45, "*Phon kan phicharana klaiklia hai borisat phranakhon thonburi khonsong chamkat kap borisat ro so pho nakhon thon chamkat ruam khao pen borisat diao kan*." Although the Phranakhon Thonburi Company was founded in 1953, it is said that it had been a collection of bus owners and was internally divided from the beginning.

65. Ibid.

66. NA Kho Kho. 0202. 3. 5/74, "*Sathit prichasin krap rian phana than palat krasuang khamanakhom*, 24 May 1956."

67. Ibid., "*Sathit prichasin krap rian phana phon ruea ek luang chamnan atthayut*, 19 June 1956."

68. NA Kho Kho. 0202. 3. 5/72, "*Palat krasuang khamanakhom rian lekhathikan khana ratthamontri*, 27 July 1956."

69. NA Kho Kho. 0202. 11. 1/6, "*Banthuek kan prachum khana kammakan ongkan rapsong sinkha lae phatsaduphan khrang thi 7/2498*, 26 August 1958."

70. The board of ETO interpreted this cabinet decision to only prohibit the expansion of its direct bus business in Bangkok, and neither joint companies nor regional bus businesses were included in the prohibition (NA Kho Kho. 0202. 11. 1/6, "*Banthuek kan prachum khana kammakan ongkan rapsong sinkha lae phatsaduphan khrang thi 7/2498*, 26 August 1955").

71. The Committee for Examining the Applications of Bus Operations then changed its name to the Bus Operations Examining Committee.

72. NA Kho Kho. 0202. 3. 5/4, "*Prathan khana kammakan phicharana kan doen rot pracham thang sanoe than o to ro lae ro mo cho mo*, 9 July 1954."

73. Ibid.

74. The standard here meant the bus with box-type body that was commonly used in Western countries, not the traditional *songthaeo*-type bus that was converted from a small truck.

75. NA Kho Kho. 0202. 3. 5/4, "*Prathan khana kammakan phicharana kan doen rot pracham thang sanoe than o to ro lae ro mo cho mo*, 9 July 1954."

76. NA [2] So Ro. 0201. 66/28, "*Ratthamontri wa kan krasuang khamanakhom rian lekhathikan khana ratthamontri*, 8 June 1953."

77. NA Kho Kho. 0202. 3/42, "*Athibodi krom kan khonsong kho prathan sanoe than ratthamontri chuai wa kan krasuang khamanakhom*, 9 July 1954."

78. The minister of the interior was to be inaugurated as a vice chairman.

79. NA Kho Kho. 0202. 3. 5/10, "*Banthuek kan prachum phu chatkan rot pracham thang nai changwat phranakhon lae thonburi*, 28 May 1954."

80. NA Kho Kho. 0202. 3. 5/5, "*Huana kong khonsong thang bok kho prathan sanoe than ratthamontri chuai wa kan krasuang khamanakhom*, 21 October 1954."

81. NA Kho Kho. 0202. 3. 5/60, "*Wichai wanitchathat kho prathan krap rian than prathan khana kammakan khuapkhum kan khonsong*, 15 November 1956."

82. NA Kho Kho. 0202. 3. 5/10, "*Banthuek kan prachum phu chatkan rot pracham thang nai changwat phranakhon lae thonburi*, 28 May 1954."

83. NA Kho Kho. 0202. 3. 5/37, "*Ratthamontri chuai wa kan krasuang khamanakhom rian lekhathikan khana ratthamontri fai kan mueang*, 21 February 1955."

84. Since the rearrangement of bus routes according to the Transport Act had to be announced in the Royal Gazette, these new routes were published in the Gazette in March 1955 as the "Notice of the Transport Regulation Committee (*Prakat khana kammakan khuapkhum kan khonsong*)." Henceforth, announcements were published in the Royal Gazette for any revision to or elimination of a particular route, or the establishment of a new route.

85. NA Kho Kho. 0202. 3. 4. 1/7, "*Raingan kan prachum khana kammakan khuapkhum kan khonsong khrang thi 7/2498*, 21 July 1955."

86. NA Kho Kho. 0202. 11. 1/5, "*Banthuek kan prachum khana kammakan ongkan rapsong sinkha lae phatsaduphan khrang thi 10/2497*, 22 October 1954."

87. According to *SN* (3 April 1955), a route number was specified on each bus and bus stop for the passenger's convenience.

88. NA Kho Kho. 0202. 3. 5/12, "*Thoem khamkhachon krap rian than ratthamontri chuai wa kan krasuang khamanakhom*, 29 June 1955."

89. NA Kho Kho. 0202. 3. 5/57, "*Athibodi krom kan khonsong kho prathan sanoe than ratthamontri chuai wa kan krasuang khamanakhom*, 7 October 1955."

90. NA Kho Kho. 0202. 3. 5/39, "*Krongthip sunthonket krap rian khana kammakan khuapkhum kan khonsong*, 14 July 1955."

91. NA Kho Kho. 0202. 3. 5/46, "*Sanoe thawisuk krap rian phana ratthamontri chuai wa kan krasuang khamanakhom*, 19 July 1955."

92. NA Kho Kho. 0202. 3. 4. 1/9, "*Raingan kan prachum khana kammakan khuapkhum kan khonsong khrang thi 9/2498*, 5 September 1955."

93. Although the Rama VI Bridge was the first bridge across the Chaophraya River and opened for traffic in 1927, at the beginning it was only for railway use, with space set aside for future use as a roadway. When it was rebuilt after destruction during the war, a roadway was constructed on it for the first time, and it became the second bridge connecting Thonburi to Bangkok.

94. NA Kho Kho. 0202. 3. 5/21, "*Athibodi krom kan khonsong kho prathan sanoe than ratthamontri chuai wa kan krasuang khamanakhom*, 12 November 1955."

95. NA Kho Kho. 0202. 3. 4. 1/9, "*Raingan kan prachum khana kammakan khuapkhum kan khonsong khrang thi 9/2498*, 5 September 1955."

96. NA Kho Kho. 0202. 3. 4. 1/23, "*Raingan kan prachum khana kammakan khuapkhum kan khonsong khrang thi 2/2500*, 14 March 1957."

97. NA Kho Kho. 0202. 3. 4. 1/24, "*Raingan kan prachum khana kammakan khuapkhum kan khonsong khrang thi 3/2500*, 7 June 1957." Three routes (Routes 50–52) were newly established routes among these twenty routes.

98. NA Kho Kho. 0202. 3/134, "A. Sunanonta to Andre J. Jacobs, 17 November 1960."

99. Although the figure in 1960 was reported in November, the abolition of tramways started from the end of 1960, as will be mentioned later. Therefore, the total length of fifty kilometers probably did not change during this period.

100. NA Kho Kho. 0202 .3. 5/39, "*Lekhathikan nayok ratthamontri rian palat krasuang khamanakhom*, 30 September 1955."

101. NA Kho Kho. 0202. 3. 5/57, "*Ratthamontri chuai wa kan krasuang khamanakhom rian lekhathikan nayok ratthamontri*, 16 July 1956."

102. NA Kho Kho. 0202. 3. 5/116, "*Athibodi krom kan khonsong kho prathan sanoe than ratthamontri wa kan krasuang khamanakhom*, 21 June 1957."

103. NA Kho Kho. 0202. 3. 5/81, "*Huana kong theknik sanoe than palat krasuang khamanakhom*, 14 September 1956."

104. NA Kho Kho. 0202. 3. 4. 1/20, "*Banthuek raingan kan prachum anukammakan phicharana senthang doen khrang thi 3/2499*, 21 December 1956."

105. NA Kho Kho. 0202. 3. 5/30, "*Kha ratchakan krom sapphasamit kho prathan krap rian than athibodi krom truat ratchakan phaendin*, 29 June 1955."

106. NA Kho Kho. 0202. 3/81, "*Palat krasuang khamanakhom rian athibodi krom truat ratchakan phaendin*, 7 February 1956."

107. The Si Lueang Company (*Borisat si lueang chamkat*), which applied for Route 44 and was not selected, had complained to the prime minister about the Makkasan Company's acquisition of Route 37 (NA Kho Kho. 0202. 3. 5/77, "*Salai siphirom krap kho prathan krap rian phana than nayok ratthamontri*, 22 March 1956").

108. In addition, although the fare level before is not clear, since the trucks on Charoen Krung Road at the end of the war collected fifty satang to one baht, it is surmised that the fare level fell after the war to at least the level of twenty satang.

Chapter 4. Unification of Buses, 1960s–1970s

1. Sarit called for the "cleaning of the country" and set forth various policies for the recovery of "fine sight." In Bangkok, the abolition of pedicabs (tricycle rickshaws) is mentioned as among the first of these policies.

2. NA Kho Kho. 0202. 9. 5/4, "*Banthuek raingan kan prachum khrang thi 1 khong khana kammakan sakha setthakit kan khamanakhom*, 12 November 1954."

3. NA Kho Kho. 0202. 9. 5. 7/56, "*Banthuek raingan kan prachum khana kammakan rotfai haeng prathet thai khrang thi 10/2502*, 31 March 1959."

4. According to Higgins (1959, 75), there were ten trips on the 1959 timetable of the Paknam line, among which two were eliminated.

5. NA Kho Kho. 0202. 9. 5. 7/56, "*Banthuek raingan kan prachum khana kammakan rotfai haeng prathet thai khrang thi 10/2502*, 31 March 1959."

6. NA Kho Kho. 0202. 9. 5. 3/1, "*Banthuek raingan kan prachum dao doen rot lae khonsong khrang thi 14/2502*, 16 June 1959."

7. The plan to eliminate railways in Bangkok under Sarit's "fine sight" policy affected not only the Paknam and Maeklong lines, but also the main line between Hua Lamphong and Bang Sue. For details, see Kakizaki 2009, 129–31.

8. NA Kho Kho. 0202. 9. 5. 3/24, "*Banthuek raingan kan prachum dao doen rot lae khonsong khrang thi 39/2502*, 11 December 1959."

9. NA Kho Kho. 0202. 9. 5. 7/169, "*Banthuek raingan kan prachum khana kammakan rotfai haeng prathet thai khrang thi 11/2505*, 21 March 1962." Although it was planned to transfer them to the Maeklong line, this was canceled when the termination plan surfaced. Finally they were scrapped, since the height of the couplers differed. In addition, the SRT asked the MEA whether they would be used in tramways in Bangkok. However, the MEA refused since the specifications for the rolling stock differed.

10. For example, the revival of the Paknam line was considered in 1966 when the construction of a new iron mill was planned at Samrong (NA Kho Kho. 0202. 9. 5. 7/281, "*Banthuek raingan kan prachum khana kammakan rotfai haeng prathet thai khrang thi 19/2509*, 29 June 1966").

11. This new line would connect Wat Sing, the terminus of local trains from Khlong San, with Taling Chan on the Southern line.

12. The right-of-way between Khlong San and Wongwian Yai was converted to Charoen Rat Road, and the tracks were left in the middle of the three-lane road that was used for the transport of rolling stock to enter the workshop.

13. NA Kho Kho. 0202. 9. 7/19, "*Khrongkan prapprung thang rotfai sai maeklong*, 8 November 1963."

14. NA Kho Kho. 0202. 9. 5/54, "*Banthuek raingan prachum rueang khrongkan prapprung rotfai sai maeklong*, 18 February 1965."

15. NA O Ko. 0201. 2. 2. 6/1, "*Phu wa kan rotfai haeng prathet thai rian palat krasuang khamanakhom*, 7 May 1968."

16. Although the new line between Hua Lamphong and Khlong San was planned as a single track at the beginning, it was changed to a double track in view of its future function as urban transport. The overhead railway from Hua Lamphong was to run as far as Wongwian Yai, and to reach the Talat Phlu station of the conventional Maeklong line at ground level, so there would be no level crossing to cause traffic congestion between Hua Lamphong and Wongwian Yai.

17. NA [1] Ko Kho. 1. 3. 3. 2. 1/50, "S. C. Hardy to Mr. Chaleo Vajrabukka, 16 April 1970."

18. TIC 21678, "Thonburi-Paktho Highway, April 1973."

19. On the effects of the Friendship Highway on freight transport on the Northeastern line, see Kakizaki (2009, 311–16).

20. The number of daily trips between Khlong Saen and Mahachai is based on RFT for 1974 (57) because the number before the opening of the road between Wongwian Yai and Mahachai is not available. The number for 1974 may be correct, since there was no mention of the train trips being reduced once the road opened in the previous year. Although there is a mention that the number of daily trips between Ban Laem and Maeklong was reduced in 1973, since the number of trips before was unknown, the number of trips after the revision in October 1966 is used here (NA Kho Kho. 0202. 9. 1/103, "*Prakat kan rotfai haeng prathet thai*, 20 September 1966."). The number of local trains to Wat Sing is based on the figure in 1971 (RFT for 1971, 55). The express trains were operated on both of the sections, but by 1977 they were eliminated.

21. It was surmised that the cause of this fire was the negligence of a guard (*SN*, 2 September 1958).

22. Unlike the former plan, this was the conversion of existing tramways into trolley bus routes.

23. The abolishment of both sections was requested, as the former section would hinder the construction of a parking lot by covering the Lot Canal, and the latter section would raise the possibility of accidents after the introduction of an automatic signaling system.

24. This was further reduced to nine cars in 1965: three cars between Tha Chang and Samyot and six cars between the Enlistee Statue and Maensi.

25. There was a long article commemorating the abolition of all tramways in *Sayam Nikon* on October 2, 1966, just after the abolition, but there were no other articles before and after the abolition (*SN*, 2 October 1968).

26. For example, there was an editorial about the abolition of the Silom line that agreed with the removal of tramways in order to utilize the limited number of roads (*SN*, 25 August 1960).

27. It was pointed out that mandating the "preservation" of tramways by law would become problematic if they became obstructive and had to be removed in the future.

28. NA Kho Kho. 0202. 3. 4. 1/26, "*Raingan kan prachum khana kammakan khuapkhum kan khonsong khrang thi 5/2500*, 22 October 1957."

29. Ibid.

30. NA Kho Kho. 0202. 3. 4. 1/27, "*Raingan kan prachum khana kammakan khuapkhum kan khonsong khrang thi 5/2500*, 7 December 1957." Although two other companies operated on Route 28 in addition to the Sinthumit Company

as shown in table 3.5, routes were distributed later by company, and Route 28 was taken over by Sinthumit alone.

31. NA Kho Kho. 0202. 3. 4. 1/28, "*Raingan kan prachum khana kammakan khuapkhum kan khonsong khrang thi 1/2501*, 30 January 1958." Since the Thai Thawon Company objected to this decision, it might have established another company and regained a concession for the same routes under a new name. The old operators in the Si Borikan Company organized the separate company similarly and obtained the concession, although the name of the company had changed.

32. NA Kho Kho. 0202. 3. 4. 1/30, "*Raingan kan prachum khana kammakan khuapkhum kan khonsong khrang thi 3/2501*, 16 May 1958."

33. Among them, the elimination of Routes 22 and 49 was called for by the concession holders—the ETO and the Transport Company respectively.

34. NA Ko Tho Mo. 1. 4. 5/6 "*Phon waiwingrop krap rian phana phon ek praphat charusathian*, 16 January 1962."

35. According to the operators, the Department of Transport asked to improve three conditions within ninety days: all buses would be unified by the company, it would acquire its own land for a garage, and it would improve the welfare of its employees.

36. NA Kho Kho. 0202. 13. 1/91, "*Athibodi krom kan khonsong kho prathan sanoe than palat krasuang khamanakhom*, 14 May 1958."

37. *SRWR* (21 April 1960) reported that the Transport Regulation Committee had submitted a report to the Ministry of Communications suggesting that the bus businesses in Bangkok should be unified by the Transport Company.

38. In fact, the Transport Company abolished Route 49 and took charge of two routes newly inherited from the previous private operators.

39. As will be discussed below, since the Transport Company gained the concession of bus operation within twenty-five provinces around Bangkok, it was ordered to install three bus terminals in Bangkok. Ekkamai is the location of the Eastern line bus terminal, and special routes 2 to 4 are the inter-bus-terminal routes.

40. Unauthorized *songthaeo* continued operation on those roads where bus routes were abolished. In the case of regular buses, they had to provide the agreed-upon number of buses, and if they reduced trips due to low demand, they might face cancelation of their concessions. But *songthaeo* were able to operate freely, and they could delay their departures until they had enough passengers. Therefore, the break-even level for *songthaeo* was lower than for buses. Even where regular bus routes had not yet been established, if there were roads where automobiles could run and a minimum demand, *songthaeo* could start operating there.

41. NA Kho Kho. 0202. 3/116, "*Lak kan lae withi kan khuapkhum kan khonsong duai rot pracham thang nai khet 25 changwat*, 17 August 1959." The

range of each line was as follows: the Northern line from Bangkok to Nakhon Sawan; the Northeastern and Central lines to Khorat and Ang Thong; the Eastern line to Prachinburi; the Southeastern line to Trat; and the Southern line to Chumphon, Kanchanaburi, and Suphanburi. In addition, included in the total number of routes were the routes that did not terminate at Bangkok.

42. Although there were buses from Bangkok to beyond Khorat that started operating after the opening of the Friendship Highway, the main target area was for the time being up to Khorat since the roads beyond Khorat had not yet been improved.

43. NA Kho Kho. 0202. 3/116, "*Lak kan lae withi kan khuapkhum kan khonsong duai rot pracham thang nai khet 25 changwat*, 17 August 1959."

44. NA Kho Kho. 0202. 3. 4. 1/47, "*Charun chaloemtian rian prathan kammakan khana kammakan khuapkhum kan khonsong*, 24 September 1959."

45. Ibid. "*Banthuek kan prachum khana kammakan khuapkhum kan khonsong khrang thi 9/2502*, 28 September 1959."

46. NA Kho Kho. 0202. 2/6, "*Sathanakan setthakit khong prathet thai kan khamanakhom lae kan khonsong*, 1960." Since the revenues from the water transport business deteriorated due to competition with the private sector, it was abolished in August 1958.

47. NA Kho Kho. 0202.13. 1/106, "*Raingan kan prachum kammakan khrang thi 205*."

48. The bus routes that the Transport Company obtained concessions for included not only highways connecting Bangkok with the regions, but all feeder roads branching off from the trunk roads, such as rural roads where regular buses had already operated. Routes to villages where local *songthaeo* operated also came under the umbrella of the Transport Company

49. NA Kho Kho. 0202. 3. 6/8, "*Chao khong rot doisan tang changwat phu dairap khwam dueatron 70 khon rian than ratthamontri wa kan krasuang mahatthai*, 1961."

50. NA Kho Kho. 0202. 3. 6/4, "*Kitti Bunprasit Rian Phana Than Chom Phon Sarit Thanarat*, 1 August 1963."

51. The fare system of the Transport Company was as follows; ten satang per kilometer up to 100 kilometers, six satang per kilometer between 101 and 400 kilometers, and four satang per kilometer beyond 401 kilometers (KS 1960, 81).

52. The phrase "a tiger lying down and eating" would ever after be the press's ironic metaphor for the Transport Company.

53. NA Ko Tho Mo. 1. 4. 5/2, "*Banthuek rueang kan doen rot pracham thang nai khet thetsaban nakhon krungthep*."

54. Ibid. "*Chamnan yuwabun kho prathan sanoe phana ratthamontri wa kan krasuang mahatthai*, 10 February 1961."

55. Ibid. "*Banthuek rueang kan doen rot pracham thang nai khet thetsaban nakhon krungthep*."

56. Ibid.

57. NA Ko Tho Mo. 1. 4. 5/7, "*Mati khana ratthamontri kiaokap rueang doen rot pracham thang.*"

58. NA [2] Ko Kho. 1. 3. 16/2, "A Technical Assistance and Equipment Program for a Unified Municipal Bus System Bangkok, Thailand, 12 October 1961."

59. NA Ko Tho Mo. 1. 4. 5/2, "*Chamnan yuwabun kho prathan sanoe phana ratthamontri wa kan krasuang mahatthai,* 19 March 1962."

60. Many newspaper articles, mostly critical of the municipality's bus plan, can be found in NA Ko Tho Mo. 1. 4. 5/5.

61. NA Ko Tho Mo. 1. 4. 5/7, "*Mati khana ratthamontri kiaokap rueang doen rot pracham thang.*"

62. NA Ko Tho Mo. 1. 4. 5/2, "*Sathon honglatdarom krap rian phana nayok ratthamontri,* 25 June 1962." The interest of the supplier's credit was 7.5 to 7.75 percent per year, which was much higher than the interest of Export-Import Bank of 1.75 to 2 percent. Moreover, even if the loan from the Export-Import Bank was to be used, the expense would be higher because American buses had to be purchased.

63. Ibid. "*Chamnan yuwabun rian huana kong setthakit samnakngan palat krasuang kan khlang,* 16 May 1962."

64. Ibid. "*Raingan kan prachum kammakan phicharana panha kiaokap kan prapprung kan satharanupaphok lae kan charachon ruam thang kan ruam rot pracham thang nai changwat phranakhon lae thonburi khrang thi 1,* 3 August 1962."

65. NA Ko Tho Mo. 1. 4. 5/7, "*Khrongkan rueang kan ruam kitchakan rotyon doisan pracham thang nai nakhon luang krungthep thonburi,* 1 January 1963."

66. NA Ko Tho Mo. 1. 4. 5/5, "*Phuchatkan borisat rotme thai thawon mai ruam kap borisat nakhon luang khonsong,* 17 June 1962," *SN*, 7 July 1962.

67. NA Ko Tho Mo. 1. 4. 5/7 "*Khrongkan rueang kan ruam kitchakan rotyon doisan pracham thang nai nakhon luang krungthep thonburi,* 1 January 1963."

68. NA Kho Kho. 0202. 3. 4. 1/55, "*Banthuek kan prachum khana kammakan khuapkhum kan khonsong khrang thi 1/2506,* 12 July 1963."

69. NA Kho Kho. 0202. 2. 10/21, "*Ratthamontri wa kan krasuang khamanakhom krap rian phana than nayok ratthamontri,* 13 January 1964."

70. NA Kho Kho. 0202. 11. 1/12, "*Banthuek kan prachum khana kammakan ongkan rap song sinkha lae phatsaduphan khrang thi 5/06,* 28 June 1963."

71. NA Kho Kho. 0202. 13. 1/12, "*Banthuek raingan kan prachum khana kammakan borisat khonsong chamkat khrang thi 1/2507,* 10 January 1964."

72. NA Kho Kho. 0202. 3. 4. 1/56, "*Banthuek kan prachum khana kammakan khuapkhum kan khonsong khrang thi 1/2507,* 30 April 1964."

73. NA Kho Kho. 0202. 2. 10/21, "*Ratthamontri wa kan krasuang khamanakhom krap rian phana than nayok ratthamontri,* 13 January 1964."

74. The Department of Transport hived off its air transportation section in 1963 and its name was changed to the Department of Land Transport (KTB 1991, 24).

75. NA Kho Kho. 0202. 3. 4. 1/61, "*Banthuek kan prachum khana kammakan khuapkhum kan khonsong khrang thi 3/2508*, 23 August 1963." For example, since there was a partial operation of buses terminating at Phrapradaeng, the intermediate bus stop, on Route 20 between Tha Dindaeng and the Phra Chunlachomklao Fort, the partial operation was independent as Route 82.

76. It is clear that the bus routes announced in the Gazette were "the city bus routes (Phranakhon, Thonburi, Nonthaburi, Pathumthani, and Samut Prakan)," which were different from the previous "bus routes in Phranakhon Thonburi" (*RKB*, vol. 82, no. 83, 9–55).

77. NA Kho Kho. 0202. 3. 4. 1/61, "*Banthuek kan prachum khana kammakan khuapkhum kan khonsong khrang thi 1/2509*, 17 February 1966."

78. With this change, nine routes changed from the earlier sectional system to a flat fare of fifty satang (NA Kho Kho. 0202. 3. 6/7, "*Banthuek kan prachum khana kammakan khuapkhum kan khonsong khrang thi 12/2502*, 30 December 1959.")

79. There were allowances and rewards other than the salary for employees, in fact, so the total monthly net income was about 1,000 baht. The Ministry of Interior was asking not only for a raise of the whole income but a raise in the salary by at least 60 percent.

80. It increased by twenty-five satang because that was the smallest denomination then in circulation.

81. Although this committee had been established before the fare hike, it was revived due to the amount of criticism. The chairperson was the vice director of NEDB, and there was an attempt to show fairness by including committee members from outside the Ministry of Communications, such as the Revenue Department and the National Statistics Office.

82. The supply of pork in Bangkok had been quasi-monopolized by the Samakkhi Livestock Trading Company, so only the pigs slaughtered within Bangkok could be sold as pork, and the company monopolized the slaughter of an agreed-upon number at that time. However, due to the rise of the price of pork and ensuing criticism of the policy, the government liberalized the policy. See Kakizaki (2009, 194–96).

83. NA [2] Ko Kho. 1. 4/67, "*Thaloeng thamrongnawasawat kho prathan sanoe phana nayok ratthamontri*, 17 September 1968." The committee consented to the following requests: reduction of fuel tax; reduction of the renewal fee for bus registration to one hundred baht; a low-interest-loan fund for bus operators; extension of the concession term to ten years; easing of route changes; conversion of opening hours of governmental agencies and schools; reduction of casualty insurance to third parties; application of an Investment

Promotion Act; transfer of part of the Transport Company's concessions to the Sirimit Company; stricter regulation of the illegal *songthaeo* by the Police Department; conversion of the fare system to a sectional system on two long-distance routes; and the formulation of a long-term bus operation plan by the Department of Land Transport.

84. Ibid.

85. The Department of Land Transport divided all bus routes throughout the country into four categories: 1: intra-city bus, 2: inter-province bus terminating at Bangkok, 3: other inter-province bus, 4: intra-province bus. The department had been establishing bus routes and selecting concession operators since 1964. The bus routes in Bangkok were classified as category one, and those routes that were removed under the rearrangement were newly established as bus routes in categories 3 or 4.

86. NA [2] Ko Kho. 1. 4/67 "*Ratthamontri chuai wa kan krasuang khamanakhom rian phana ratthamontri wa kan krasuang khamanakhom*, March 1970."

87. Ibid.

88. Confrontations among students who were the leading players of the political change in 1973 occurred after the incident, and vocational school students later become involved. Many buses were attacked in July 1974, with some buses destroyed and drivers and conductors physically assaulted.

89. Since the intra-province bus routes of category four within Bangkok and its neighboring provinces had been established one by one since 1968, and operators were selected for each route, the number of operators taking charge of these branch routes increased by seventeen operators, though the operators of bus routes of category one decreased by three.

90. The operation of student buses was started in 1953 and continued intermittently.

91. The Bus Operator Association was joined by those operators, mainly small operators, who were concerned with the establishment of the Nakhon Luang Transport Company when unification under it was promoted.

92. The plan of the Bus Operator Association also assumed the transfer to a public company in the long term.

93. When establishing a stock company in those days, it was ruled that a private sector entity had to contribute 70 percent of the total capital.

94. NA Kho Kho. 0202. 9. 5. 3/24, "*Banthuek raingan kan prachum dan doen rot lae khonsong khlang thi 38, 39/02*, 11 December 1959."

95. Although Sarit also planned the elimination of the section between Hua Lamphong and Bang Sue on the Northern line, the main line, the American consultants who were helping the country design a national highway system at the time argued that the railway should be maintained, noting that it would be

necessary to construct twenty-four road lanes as a substitute if it were eliminated (Kakizaki 2009, 131). Incidentally, at this time there were about 10,000 persons per day using the Hua Lamphong station.

96. Nevertheless, it still acquired seventy-six seats in the whole country, and as the party with the most votes it could lead a coalition government (Kato 1996, 162–63).

97. The Democrat Party came in first in the January 1975 general election, and Seni, the party leader, formed a cabinet. However, since the party's policy speech was rejected in parliament due to the failure of coalition negotiations, the Social Action Party (*Phak kit sangkhom*) of Kukrit established the coalition government (Kato 1996, 178–80). The free buses for the poor were abolished by the end of May 1976, after the change of government (Samrit n.d., vol. 1, 65).

98. NA Kho Kho. 0202. 13/26, "*Rueang thi prathan chaeng hai thi prachum phuea sap lae phuea phicharana*, 11 January 1965."

99. NA [2] Ko Kho. 1. 3. 16/2, "A Technical Assistance and Equipment Program for a Unified Municipal Bus System Bangkok, Thailand, 12 October 1961"; NA [2] Ko Kho. 1. 1. 27/1, "*Thang khong thetsaban nakhon luang pi 2516*." The figure in 1973 is only for the area of the old Bangkok Municipality.

Chapter 5. Revival of Rail Transport, 1970s–1990s

1. The three lines were as follows: the Mochit–Phadung Krungkasem Canal line, the Phrakhanong–Hua Lamphong line, and the Samyan–Khlong Toei line. Among them, the first two were to be constructed first.

2. The termini of the original three lines are slightly different from those at the time of figure 5.1.

3. NA [2] Ko Kho. 1. 1. 27. 1/16, "*Kan thang phiset haeng prathet thai*." The estimated construction costs of railway and bus systems were 7,600 million and 3,900 million baht respectively. In addition, the six-hundred-meter section crossing under Ratchadamnoen Road on the Phrakhanong–Bang Sue line was to be an underground structure.

4. The first stage line of the MRTA (the Blue line) between Hua Lamphong and Bang Sue opened in 2004 and was part of the Phrakhanong and the Sathon lines; the original Orange line was proposed to run on almost the same route as that of the Memorial Bridge line.

5. The Department of Highways was placed under the Ministry of National Development from 1963 to 1972. The BMA was established in 1972 by upgrading the former Bangkok Municipality.

6. NA [2] Ko Kho 1. 1. 27. 3/2, "*Rueang kan phicharana borisat wisawakon thi prueksa thang dan rabop kan khonsong muanchon*."

7. NA [2] Ko Kho. 1. 1. 27. 1/6, "*Ratthamontri wa kan krasuang mahatthai rian lekhathikan khana ratthamontri*, 28 January 1980."

8. Ibid.

9. Bunchu was a politician who came from business circles. He entered politics after serving as president of Bangkok Bank and he exerted political and business influence from the 1980s to the first half of the 1990s. The ETA had also already begun prior registration of qualification for the bid, even before the cabinet decision. (NA [2] Ko Kho. 1. 1. 27. 3. 1/6, "*Raingan kan prachum khana anukammakan khatlueak khuen thabian borisat phu rapmao thi mi khunnasombat mosom phuea khao ruam pramun nai khrongkan kosang rabop rotfaifa khonsong muanchon khrang thi 1/2523*, 30 June 1980").

10. NA [2] Ko Kho. 1. 1. 27. 3/6, "*Rueang kan damnoen kan rabop khonsong muanchon*."

11. Although both had been neglected for a long time, the Taksin Bridge was later utilized for the extension of the BTS. The new bridge was built and used from 2009. On the other hand, there was no chance that the Phra Pokklao Bridge would be used because this section would be constructed as an underground structure.

12. Besides the BOT method, there are other types as well, such as the BTO (Build-Transfer-Operate) type and the BOOT (Build-Own-Operate-Transfer) type. The term "BOT" is used here as a general term to denote the development of social capital by utilizing the private sector.

13. The total expense was 12,780 million baht, since the expense of 547 million baht for land condemnation was contained within this figure; minus this amount, the expense would be 12,233 million baht.

14. The UTDC system, the unmanned automatic LRT by the linear motor drive developed by UTDC of Canada, was put in practical use from 1985 in Detroit and Vancouver.

15. The Lavalin Corporation is a Canadian construction firm that has carried out infrastructure development programs all over the world. In Thailand it also participated with Thai companies in the construction of the track and power systems of the MRTA's first line.

16. Bombardier Inc. is a Canadian transport vehicle maker manufacturing railway rolling stock and aircraft. It purchased the UTDC system in Canada in February 1992, which has been adopted in LRT plans around the world, such as in Kuala Lumpur.

17. This agency was the upgraded version of the former Land Transport Management Committee (*Khana kammakan chat rabop kan charachon thang bok*) in 1992. The committee, established in 1978, consisted of the heads of relevant ministries and agencies and was headed by the minister of interior.

18. Although the operation of the air-conditioned buses was accepted by the Transport Regulation Committee in 1970, it did not result in their actually being put into operation (*SRSW*, 1 February 1970).

19. Routes A9 and A10, which were circle routes in the inner city, were changed into these suburb-inner city routes.

20. Because the behavior of drivers and conductors was often poor, the BMTA wished to abolish minibuses by substituting two minibuses with one large-sized bus.

21. For example, the fare from the inner city to Minburi in the suburbs fell to 2 baht from 4.5 baht (*SRSW*, 3 March 1985).

22. Although this subsidy was given in the form of loans from the government's Savings Bank (*thanakhan omsin*), the payment was the burden of the Ministry of Finance.

23. In addition, the initial annual concession fee was 300 million baht, which was to be subsequently raised by 50 million baht every year for fifteen years. Since the income was to be allocated to the SRT from the ninth year, the total amount that the SRT would obtain would be as much as 54,110 million baht (*KT*, 1 October 1997).

24. Since the Thanayong Company had substantially gained management rights over the BTSC, the BTS plan was also called the "Thanayong plan."

25. Chotchoi is a rich and famous woman and a daughter of Chin Sophonphanit, the founder of Bangkok Bank (Bello et al. 1998, 114). She won a seat in the Senate in March 2000.

26. In the plan, about 13 percent of the 300-*rai* (480,000-square-meter) park was due to be used (*BP* [OE], 15 November 1999).

27. In addition, the corruption involved in selecting Sun Estate Company came to light. Furthermore, because of economic stagnation, the construction had not started. Therefore, the Ministry of Finance decided to cancel the contract with Sun Estate in May 2000 (*BP* [OE], 3 May 2000).

28. On the activities of Chotchoi from October 1993 to September 1995, see Chotchoi et al. (1995, 6–13).

29. The name "Skytrain" came to be used for the BTS plan after the construction proceeded using elevated structures.

30. The suit was withdrawn in July since the BMA had already released the information about the BTS plan.

31. Both were solved by changing part of the design.

32. For details, see the following chapter. Although it was decided to use some bridge pillars between Bang Sue and Rangsit for the construction of the Red line, all pillars between Yommarat and Hua Mak were removed for the construction of the Airport Rail Link.

33. In this master plan, the urban railway routes were identified by colors, as will be described in the following chapter. The routes of Hopewell and the BTS were assigned as Red and Green lines respectively. Apart from them, there

was a Purple line under the jurisdiction of an as yet undetermined agency. In addition, the Blue line and the Green line were later named officially as the Chaloem Ratchamongkhon line and the Chaloem Phrakiat Phrachonmaphansa 6 Rop line respectively, but both were seldom used.

34. Due to the delay in train procurement as will be mentioned later, the whole line was opened in July 2004.

35. Although the feeder bus service was due to be introduced with the opening of the BTS, the operation was only started on seven routes in a tentative way from August 1, 2000 (*KT* [OE], 2 August 2000). By showing a BTS ticket it could be used for free. A park-and-ride facility using the shopping center at Onnut on the Sukhumvit line was developed, and the BMA also started a park-and-ride point near the Mochit station in May 2000. In addition, since at the beginning of 2000 the number of passengers decreased gradually from about 200,000 to about 160,000, the company set the acquisition of 300,000 riders per day as the temporary target by discounted coupons and the abovementioned feeder bus (*DN* [OE], 8 August 2000).

36. This was the privatization of the First Operation District, which operated a total of 300 buses on eleven routes in those days; it had racked up a deficit of 5 million baht per month.

37. The special air-conditioned bus routes for the microbuses were announced for the first time in the Royal Gazette on September 2, 1992 (*RKB*, vol. 119, no. 110, 9668–9675).

38. Although the vans are non-stop in principle, they do stop on many routes to allow users to get on and off.

39. A total of 117 routes for the vans were announced in the Royal Gazette from April 1999 to December 2000 (*RKB*, vol. 116, no. 17].

40. The BTSC started operating feeder buses on six routes in August 2000, and the operation was entrusted to the Bangkok Microbus Company.

41. As for the unpaid fuel cost, the original amount of about 3 billion baht was reduced to 2,763 million by reducing the interest rate, and the Savings Bank loaned the same amount with a payment by the Ministry of Finance.

42. The total amount of fuel cost assistance (provided from January 1991 to June 1992), including the interest, was 9,384 million baht (KSMK 2005, 12).

43. The loan was to come from the government's Krungthai Bank. The government did not provide direct subsidy to the BMTA. It had procured the funds in the form of loans from the government's bank with the guarantee of the Ministry of Finance.

44. Although the western section of the Phrakhanong line between Hua Lamphong and Bang Sue was removed from the master plan that the OCMLT decided on, the greater part of the route was bequeathed to the Purple line between the National Library and Bang Phut.

45. The Don Mueang Tollway is the expressway constructed by the BOT method above the national highway Route 31 (Wiphawadi Rangsit Road) under the Department of Highways. The plan emerged around 1986, and the concession was granted in 1989. It was opened for traffic in 1994. The West German survey was the basis for the second-stage expressway plan. The concession was granted in 1988 with the BOT method, and the first section was opened for traffic in 1993.

46. The plan was further reduced to the sharing of the existing railways with the urban railways in the Thaksin government period.

47. According to Suehiro, Thailand faced serious economic depression after the 1960s: low-growth between 1979 and 1982, and the world economic recession and structural adjustment between 1982 and 1984 (Suehiro and Higashi 1999, 3–5).

48. Although the total length was almost the same, the construction cost of the BTS was about 55 billion baht including the cost of rolling stock, while the first-stage line of the MRTA cost about 110 billion baht.

49. However, if distance is compared, the expressways spanned a total of 27 kilometers, while the urban railways spanned a total of 59 kilometers. Therefore, the construction costs per kilometer were about 300 million baht for the expressways and about 200 million baht for the urban railways. It seems that the costs of the urban railways were underestimated. In addition, the reason for the high cost of the first-stage expressway plan was the expense of building the Rama IX Bridge across the Chaophraya River.

50. The cost of the civil engineering was 670 million dollars, and the cost of the train operation was 650 million dollars.

51. In February 2000, the BTSC earned about 5 million baht per day, while its expenditure including the interest payment was 8 million baht (*KT* [OE], 3 February 2000).

52. The BMA was planning for the extension of the BTS lines with 100 percent private investment as well as the construction of the BTS, which was approved at the cabinet meeting in February 2000 (*KT* [OE], 1 March 2000). Although the BTSC was also receptive to the construction of the extension lines at the beginning, it later realized that independent construction would be difficult.

53. Chotchoi had once insisted that the air pollution below a BTS station would become a problem because of the accumulation of exhaust gas from cars passing under it. Air pollution did rise in fact at some stations, and the Office of Environmental Policy and Planning had to ask the BTSC for the installation of exhaust equipment (*BP* [OE], 9 February 2000). Therefore, although the downsizing of the station to reduce air pollution was considered for the BTS extension lines, only minor changes were made after all.

54. The MRTA applied to the government committee overseeing mega

transport projects in May 2000 for the construction of the section between Hua Lamphong and Tha Phra, one of the extension lines of the Blue line, but it requested reexamination since the construction costs of 40 billion baht were too high (*BP* [OE], 22 May 2000). The 4.9-kilometer section was to be an underground structure for this extension, and high construction costs were estimated for the crossing under the Chaophraya River.

55. The BMTA purchased its buses from major automobile companies in Japan, Europe, and the United States, such as Hino, Isuzu, Volvo, and Mercedes Benz, and their conditions were better than those run by private operators, who purchased only the chassis and assembled the bodies by themselves.

56. The figures in 2003 were the total length and total area of roads under the jurisdiction of the BMA, which may differ from the figures in 1973 in terms of the classification or type of road.

57. The fare hike in 1997 was based on the elimination of the old blue buses, which normally collected a fare of 2.5 baht, and the minibuses, which collected the same fare as the blue , maintained the 2.5-baht fare after that hike for a while.

Chapter 6. A Confused Urban Transport Policy, 2000s

1. Although the MRTA was renamed in 2000, the abbreviated name in English and Thai was not changed.

2. Since the grant of the concession to the BMCL in August 2000 was about a half year behind schedule because of the government's conflicting wishes, and the BMCL's contract for purchasing rolling stock was also overdue by December 2001, the original schedule to open a partial section at the end of 2002, and to open the whole line in mid-2003 became unfeasible.

3. Since the agencies relating to communication that had been put under the jurisdiction of the Ministry of Communications were transferred to the newly established Ministry of Information and Communication Technology, the name of the ministry in English changed to the Ministry of Transport. However, the name in Thai did not change.

4. The bid for the operator was due to be held in December 1997 and the concession was to be granted by November 1998 (RFM for 1998, 14). Although the BMCL's contract for the rolling stock was due to be made with the Alstom-Mitsubishi consortium, which initially tendered the lowest price, the MRTA was in a hurry to make a contract and since the negotiation was protracted, finally the BMCL decided to contract with Siemens [*PCT* [OE], 7 January 2002].

5. It was reported that Suriya ordered the SRT to conduct the feasibility study, considering that the plan would be financially profitable by developing the real estate at the Makkasan workshop, although he did not consent to it initially.

6. In a turnkey system the contractor has to design and construct the project using its own funds and receives payment from the owner after completion.

Although there are some merits to this system in that the owner does not have to have a detailed design or a source of funds in advance, there are also several disadvantages, including that the interest burden becomes high because a private contractor raises a construction fund, which results in a rise of construction costs, and the process of selecting a contractor can be obscure since there are no clear standards of selection..

7. Thaksin described the previous four years as the "four years of problem-solving," and the next four years as the "four years of investment for the future," and stated that large-scale investment, such as infrastructure development, would be pushed forward. The other four components were the development of the national highway network, the development of the national water supply system, educational system development, and economic structural reform. In addition, although the urban railway development plan was a six-year plan, as a campaign pledge it was claimed to be completed in four years.

8. Although Khamroplak, the director of the OTP, supposed that the extension between Hua Lamphong and Tha Phra should be carried out first as of January 2004, she changed her mind and decided that priority would be given to the section between Bang Sue and Bang Yai in March (KT [OE], 9 January 2004; PCT [OE], 15 March 2004). She explained that this was because the construction of the latter was easier with the whole elevated line, and the time necessary for completion would also be less.

9. The reduction of the existing railways of the Red line involved reducing the construction costs by relocating the terminal for long-distance trains in the suburbs and constructing only tracks for the urban railway. However, it was not really a "savings" plan since a new railway would have to be constructed independently in order not to divide the existing railway network. The reduction of stations meant saving on construction costs for station-building by putting stations every two kilometers at the beginning instead of the original plan of one-kilometer intervals. Since the public was no longer satisfied with the government's policy for urban railway development without reduction of construction costs, stop-gap measures, such as reducing the number of tracks or stations, were the result.

10. According to Nara (2004, 70), the route would total 263.5 kilometers. For the routes contained in the plans, see figure 5.4. The new airport access line of the Green line is not shown in that figure, however.

11. The BMTIP explained that the original C-shaped lines were altered to become more suitable straight routes passing through the city (OTP 2004).

12. Although it predicted total completion by 2009, the operation of some sections would be started in 2010 as shown in table 6.2.

13. Aphirak wanted to extend the BTS, a plan he had inherited from the previous governor, Samak, and stated that the BRT plan, as a campaign pledge, had to be promoted.

14. The Don Mueang Tollway was the expressway constructed above national highway Route 31 (Wiphawadi Rangsit Road) by the Department of Highways using the BOT method. Suriya negotiated with the company to reduce the toll to twenty baht from the original fifteen to fifty-three baht.

15. This was according to the estimate of the MFC Asset Management Company, Ltd., which was advising on the establishment of a holding company for urban railway management.

16. The Taksin Transport Center plan was to be a terminal for long-distance trains and buses to the south near the intersection of the Dark Green line and the Dark Red line (the present Maeklong line). When it was explained at the briefing session that the residents of 1,700 households would be forced to move, they rose in opposition to it. In the end, this plan was downsized to construct only the station of the Dark Green line (Wuthakat station) and the Dark Red line.

17. The route change to Bang Khen was explained as strengthening its function as a feeder line of the Red line.

18. Although the first two lines were an extension of the existing lines, the last section was a branch line from the existing line.

19. Although the original plan aimed at the construction of an elevated road from the Taksin Bridge to the Outer Ring Road (*Thanon wongwaen rop nok*) via the Phasi Charoen Canal, since there was criticism that this would spoil the environment around a historical canal, the construction only went as far as the point where the road reached the canal. In addition, the line between Chong Nonsi and the Rama III road, which was approved by cabinet consent in 2000, was also a route along the canal and was a part of the tramway plans along the canals.

20. The BTSC had been taking pains over raising funds from the beginning and was saddled with a large amount of debt.

21. As seen in the previous chapter, since the foundation of the pillars of the Taksin Bridge was already built simultaneously with the road bridge, the bridge construction of the Chaophraya ended at an early stage.

22. It seems that the BMA decided to open the bidding since it became impossible to further extend the terms of the letter of credit.

23. The alternative routes were the 18-kilometer line from the Queen Sirikit Center station on the Blue line to Samrong via the Rama IV Road and the Old Paknam Line Road to substitute for the Samrong line, and the 10-kilometer line between Phayathai and Phrannok to substitute for the Light Green line between the National Stadium and Phrannok.

24. Although the government asserted that it was uneconomical to purchase rolling stock and construct a depot on a few kilometers of railway, the BMA replied that it would use the existing depot of the BTSC and that operations would also be entrusted to it.

25. Since the bid in 2003 was performed separately between this section and the Bearing–Samrong section, the negotiation with a successful bid contractor was also easy.

26. The fare of 3.5 baht was the minimum fare for the ordinary bus (red bus) at that time.

27. The SRT, which also continued to operate at a loss, had also claimed that ordinary train service was PSO, and had gained a subsidy from the government.

28. The advance tickets consisted of a one-day ticket, a one-week ticket, and a one-month ticket, both for the ordinary buses and the air-conditioned buses. However, they could only be used on the BMTA buses.

29. Although the income of the BMTA in fiscal year 2002 was about 69,800 million baht, it decreased to about 64,600 million baht the next year.

30. The change of the route numbers of the tens and the ones was also made in some routes.

31. On Latphrao Road, one lane of the outbound lanes was used as the inbound bus lane from 1995 (KSMK for 1995, 8–9). From the beginning, the lanes for the LRT were secured in the center of the road on Narathiwat Road, and opened for traffic in 1997; they were used as bus lanes from 1998 (*N* [OE], 1 December 1997). However, since the former had no bus stop on the way, and the latter had few users, both were abolished in 2001 (*DN* [OE], 25 January 2001). These buses were called traffic-island buses (*rotme ko klang*).

32. Since the BTS extension line is to pass through Ratchaphruek Road, this route will be connected to the BTS line at two places: the starting point and the terminal point.

33. In addition, the terminal point of this route was extended from the original Nawamin Road to the 8-km point (Ko Mo 8) on Ram Inthara Road.

34. The fare of the air-conditioned buses at that time was based on a sectional fare system, and the minimum fare was eleven to twelve baht.

35. The retail price of natural gas at that time was fixed at 8.5 baht per kilogram (http://www.pttplc.com/th/news-energy-fact-oil-price-bangkok.aspx?). Natural gas became relatively cheap compared to the rapid jump of petroleum prices.

36. It was proposed that the BMTA would buy natural gas at 20.5 baht per kilogram against the original price of 8.5 baht and the balance of 12 baht would be collected for the cost of buses.

37. With a detailed design system, a consultancy firm is commissioned to come up with the design, and bids are invited based on that. In a design-and-build system a bid is invited based only on a basic design with details to be determined by the bidder/contractor. Generally, this design-and-build system was used in the case of the underground sections; the Blue line was the first subway to adopt it. However, since this system contains more room for uncertainty than in a detailed design system, there are concerns that the process of selecting a winning bidder is less clear and fair.

38. Democrat Party stalwart Aphirak was accused of being involved in a dubious deal to supply fire trucks and fire boats, and resigned only two months after being reelected.

39. The Bhumjaithai Party is a political party led by Newin Chidchob that broke off from the Thaksin group's People's Power Party (*Phak phalang prachachon*). It played a big role in helping the Democrat Party led by Abhisit come to power (Tamada 2009a, 46–47).

40. In this plan, the sections of the Dark Green line and the Light Green line were changed: the Dark Green line became the Sukhumvit line and its extension, and the Light Green line became the Silom line and its extension.

41. The OTP claimed the reasons for changing the Light Green line were that the alignment of the route became hook-like, since both starting and terminal points of were on the Thonburi side, and that two lanes of Rama I Road would be reduced if the elevated track were to go underground on this road.

42. The monorails that the BMA planned are the 18-kilometer Bang Na–Suvarnabhumi Airport line, the 15-kilometer second BMA office–Yommarat line, and the 5-kilometer Siam circle line, all of which were different from the routes on the master plan (*DN* [OE], 9 November 2009).

43. CBTC is also called a radio-type train control. A conventional track circuit signaling system relies on the short-circuits of the rail and wheels to detect the presence of a train; CBTC systems use telecommunications. Although initially the BTSC had used a track circuit system from Siemens, it decided to renovate the signal system to increase train frequency, since the Siemens signal system did not have the flexibility of other manufacturers'.

44. The BTSC tried to arrange its debts by submitting a management revitalization scheme to the bankruptcy court in February 2006; it needed the permission of the bankruptcy court for a new investment program. The BTSC's debt adjustment was finalized in October 2008 (*DN* [OE], 30 October 2008).

45. During the period before the formal opening, passengers could ride for free on the extended section; fare collection started after the formal opening.

46. Krungthep Thanakhom Company is a subsidiary of the BMA and had its origins in the Saha Samakkhi Livestock Sales Company (*Borisat saha samakkhi kha sat chamkat*), a livestock slaughter business established in Bangkok in 1955.

47. The Taksin Bridge station was a temporary station that used half of the elevated double track as a platform, which was to be removed when the line was extended to Thonburi. However, since it was the only transfer point with water transport on the Chaophraya River, many passengers used this station. Thus, its removal was problematic. Therefore, only one section of this station became single track and the operation interval of the Silom line was also extended by a minimum of four minutes. In order to ease the shortage of transport capacity caused by this, the newly introduced trains were four-car, not three-car, as before. Moreover, since the change to CBTC of the BTSC was delayed, a change

of the signal system was also needed at the Surasak station, one station before the Taksin Bridge station, and the stoppage time at this station increased.

48. The "Strong Thailand Plan" was an investment plan of 1,560 billion baht from 2010 to 2012 intended to stimulate business, job creation, infrastructure development, etc. (http://www.tkk2555.com/online/index.php?page_id=4).

49. Later, further delays became unavoidable due to the great flood in 2011 and to the construction of the Blue line, which affected construction of the Bang Wa station, the terminus. The partial section between Wongwian Yai and Talat Phlu was finally opened for traffic in February 2013, and the remainder in December of the same year (*KT* [OE], 4 December 2013).

50. However, due to heavy flooding in 2011, the construction was forced to slow down; as of the end of 2013, the estimated opening year is 2016.

51. Although the total cost of construction had been estimated in 2006 as 31.2 billion baht, when the bid was tendered in 2008, it had gone up to 36.1 billion baht (*DN* [OE], 13 August 2008). Since oil prices rose suddenly in 2008, a further reexamination was necessary, and the final figure was 41 billion baht (*PCT* [OE], 18 August 2008).

52. The operation of diesel railway cars started in December 2012, with only six round-trip trains per day (*PCT* [OE], 10 December 2012). This Red line plan calls for the construction of an elevated track of the existing SRT with electrification, and it is more like a suburban railway than an urban railway since the tracks will be shared with the SRT's long-distance passenger trains and freight trains. Since the double-tracking was already performed in the 1990s and there are only a few level crossings on the section between Bang Sue and Taling Chan, the construction of the overhead bridges for roads across the railway is lower than the construction of the elevated tracks. The operation of diesel railway cars is possible even in the present condition.

53. At that time, the government accepted the extension of ten kilometers northward from Rangsit to Thammasat University's Rangsit campus.

54. It was reported that the reason for increasing the number of contracts was to increase the possibility of Thai companies' winning the bid since it was difficult for them to compete with the many Chinese companies joining the international bidding.

55. Since the bidder's submitted price was higher than the maximum price approved by the cabinet, the negotiation with the bidder took a long time before contracting in the beginning of 2013 (*PCK* [OE], 18 January 2013). The construction finally started in April 2013.

56. According to the plan, 22 percent of the Hopewell pillars would be reused (*PCT* [OE], 15 October 2007).

57. In fact, since the one-kilometer section between Bang Sue and Taopun was included in the earlier construction plan for the Purple line, the actual section to be constructed would be between Taopun and Tha Phra.

58. Since the consent of the Japanese side was needed for a yen loan when making a term of reference or selecting a successful bidder, the procedure had taken more time than expected.

59. The parliament's Anti-Corruption Committee (*Kammathikan pongkan lae prappram kan thutcharit lae praphruet mi chop*) pointed out that the rise of the base price just before the MRTA's bid was questionable. In the end, the contracts were signed in February 2011, and the construction started in April (KK for 2011, 127–28).

60. Since it would be necessary to cross heavily trafficked Silom and Sathon Roads if the starting point were located at Surawong Road, the route will be shortened by having buses U-turn at the south of the Sathon Road, and the Chong Nonsi station of the BTS will be connected with a 300-meter access way.

61. The low level of the basic price, the short period of delivery, and the high fine to be levied for breach of contract were considered as the reasons for the lack of commercial interest.

62. She complained that the price of buses was too high at about 7,500,000 baht per bus.

63. With the jump in oil prices, the ordinary bus fare at that time rose to 7.5 baht for the red BMTA buses and 8.5 baht for private white buses.

64. In addition, such expenses as installing IC apparatuses in private buses were reduced, and the original budget of 111.7 billion baht was reduced to 62.6 billion baht.

65. The price included repair costs.

66. Apart from introducing new air-conditioned buses, the old buses were renovated as NGV buses.

67. As for the NGV minibuses, the reconstruction of the old minibuses was not accepted. In addition, the colors of the private NGV buses were changed when the NGV buses were introduced: pink was for the ordinary buses, yellow for the air-conditioned buses, and orange for the minibuses.

68. In addition to the free bus in Bangkok, the free third-class train ride on the SRT's ordinary trains included the use of a certain amount of water and electricity at no charge.

69. The Wayuphak Fund was established to purchase the stocks of government corporations held by the Ministry of Finance by raising funds from the private sector with high interest rate, but the amount was far less than the target of 100 billion baht (Pasuk and Baker 2004, 112–13).

70. Three choices were suggested: (1) 100 percent from the Wayuphak Fund; (2) 71.4 percent from the Wayuphak Fund, 14.3 percent from the national budget, and 14.3 percent from the urban railway fund; and (3) 50 percent from the Wayuphak Fund and 50 percent from the national budget. However, it noted that it is uncertain whether these funds could be supplied, and concluded that some sort of appropriation from the national budget was necessary.

71. He explained as follows: "For example, if there is a country that wants rubber, rubber trees will be planted simultaneously with the railway construction. Tapping rubber will become possible when the railways are completed. Then, rubber will be productive for twenty years without spending a baht of money. Twenty years later the old trees will be used to make furniture, and the railways will remain for us."

72. The joint venture consortium consisted of a Chinese company and a Thai company.

73. MFC Asset Management Company pointed out that it was a waste of money to expend at least 75 billion baht for buying back two companies, and advised that it be used for new line development. This was another factor in suspending the purchasing plan.

74. The fare of the BTS is not a mileage system but a sectional system. Although it was initially 10 to 40 baht, the fare was raised to 15 to 40 baht from March 2007. Although the fare of the subway was initially 12 to 31 baht, it was changed to 16 to 41 baht after several revisions. From July 3, 2010, the fare was to be reduced by 1 baht over the following two years. As of the end of 2013, BTS fares range from 15 to 42 baht and the subway's from 16 to 40 baht.

75. The BTSC started the sale of the thirty-trips pass in August 2000, and it contributed to the increase of users since regular users could use the train for as low as 18 baht for general passengers and 12 baht for students. The price of this pass rose a little in September 2006 to 20 baht and 15 baht per trip respectively. Then the number of trips was changed in May 2010, which resulted in a 20 baht and 15 baht price for a fifty-trip pass. Although at the beginning the BMCL had offered a 15 percent discount for IC card users (30 percent discount for students), it started selling an 800-baht, one-month pass which enabled the passenger to have unlimited rides within a one-month period. The price was subsequently raised to 1,200 baht.

76. Furthermore, the estimation of profit that caused the suspension was calculated by using the mileage fare system that the BMTIP was expecting. If a fifteen-baht flat fare were used, the result would have been even worse.

77. In Thailand, it is called the PPP Gross Cost system instead of simply PPP.

78. In the case of the conventional two-tiered operation method, the operator needs to recoup the investment from fares and advertising revenue, but in the case of the PPP system, it will collect it from the operational fees paid to it.

79. For example, the new Hong Kong airport, which opened in 1998, had an airport access subway opening in the same year, and the new Kuala Lumpur airport, which opened in 1998, completed the railway access to the city in 2002 (Nihon Chikatetsu Kyokai 2000, 75; Dick and Rimmer 2003, 336).

80. This project is under suspicion because the SRT has taken over the guaranteed commission of 1,600 million baht of the private loan, which is

regarded as one of the unjust projects of the Thaksin government in "The Coup-d'état White Paper" released after the coup d'état. [*PCK* [OE], 22 November 2006].

81. Constructing fifteen intermediate stations in the URMAP and ten or eleven stations in the BMTIP was also considered.

82. Since the rolling stock for the plan was four four-car trains for the express line and five three-car trains for the city line (the local train) (Cho Bang Toei 2006, 4–5), the maximum interval on the city line would be fifteen minutes if the local train could run between Phayathai and the airport in thirty minutes. In fact, after the opening in August 2010, the actual interval of the city line trains during the rush-hour was fifteen minutes, and a few additional trains are running between Phayathai and Hua Mak by using spare trains.

83. In the end, the Airport Rail Link was separated from the Light Red line of the master plan. In the master plan of 2010, it was decided to construct a new Light Red line between Phayathai and Hua Mak separately by constructing elevated tracks for the existing railway.

84. The extension was accepted in three steps: 180 days for the flood damage, 370 days for the delay in providing a construction site, and 180 days for the skyrocketing prices of oil and construction materials.

85. The contract regulated that the operation would start after a ninety-day test run, and the original completion term was August 7, 2007.

86. Http://www.db-international.de/site/db_international/en/news news_100517.html. The DBI originated in a transport consultancy firm founded in Germany in 1966, and it has now become the international division of the Deutsche Bahn group.

87. As for the city line, the original sectional fare of 15 to 45 baht was reduced to the 15-baht flat fare, and the original 150-baht fare for the express line was reduced to 100 baht, which is valid for a round trip.

88. Although two companies, Thai Airways International and Bangkok Airways, installed airline check-in counters at the Makkasan terminal, since the express line had to be used for check-in, the counter would be closed three hours before the departure time. And since access to the terminal was extremely inconvenient, the average number of passengers was only fifteen persons for Thai Airways International and one to two persons for Bangkok Airways, leading the latter to close the service (*PCK* [OE], 29 June 2011). Therefore, State Railway of Thailand Electrified Train Company (*Borisat rotfaifa ro fo tho chamkat*), the subsidiary of the SRT that was eventually founded in 2011, reduced the frequency of the express train between Makkasan and the airport from fifteen- to forty-minute intervals; instead, it started an express train service between Phayathai and the airport every thirty minutes. It also reduced the fare of the express train to 90 baht for a single trip and 150 baht for a round trip.

89. On the BTS feeder buses, see chapter 5, note 35.

90. Although the parking lot for park-and-ride was built on the occasion of the Blue line construction, there was no example of constructing a bus terminal at the station for a transfer with buses. Although the Victory Monument station and the Mochit station of the BTS are functioning to some extent as nodal points with buses, neither was developed as a new bus terminal simultaneously with the urban railway development.

91. The number of the vans under the jurisdiction of the BMTA is about 6,650 as of 2009, and if we assume one hundred persons per van per day, the total number of users becomes a little less than 1.7 million persons per day. Although not all routes start from urban railway stations, there are quite a few routes that start from stations, such as the Victory Monument station and the Mochit station.

92. Although in July 2010, the new route numbers were displayed together with the old numbers, the practice was suspended soon after due to passengers' confusion. Some bus routes were to be shortened by starting or terminating at urban railway stations in order to function as rail feeder routes. However, most bus routes remain the same with only their route numbers changed.

Chapter 7. Regulation and Politicization of Urban Transport in Bangkok

1. The first tramways were opened in Saigon in 1881, in Rangoon in 1884, and in Singapore in 1885. In addition, although Dick and Rimmer claim that the first tramway in Penang opened in 1893, it was actually opened for traffic in the first half of the 1880s (Francis and Ganley 2006, 10).

2. The introduction of tramways in these cities was as follows: Surabaya in 1889, Hanoi in 1901, and Mandalay in 1904 (Dick and Rimmer 2003, 68, 300; Wright et al. 1910, 374; Doling 2012, 85).

3. In Mandalay, the first tramway was electric (Wright et al. 1910, 374).

4. The exact dates when trams were eliminated from Rangoon and Mandalay are unknown.

5. For example, in the United States, the development process of urban transport was sequenced as follows: horse-powered tramways, electric tramways, and inter-urban and suburban railways. The age of the inter-urban and suburban railway was from 1900 to 1930 (Taaffe et al. 1996, 175).

6. Although the Manila Suburban Railways Company built the twelve-kilometer railway from Manila to suburban Pasig in 1908 (Dick and Rimmer 2003, 265), it is unclear whether this was a suburban railway or an extension line of a tramway.

7. The electric trains that operated in Jakarta were akin to large-size rolling stock, unlike in Bangkok, where rolling stock similar to tramcars was used.

8. The Kriangsak government decided in 1979 to construct a heavy rail system as mass rapid transit.

9. For an outline of the development process of urban railways in Kuala Lumpur, see Kakizaki (2012, 177–79).

10. As for the electric power supply system, the direct current 750V with a third rail was adopted for the BTS and MRTA, and the exchange 25,000V with an overhead cable for the Airport Rail Link.

11. However, the Light Red line and the Dark Red line, currently under construction, will share elevated tracks with long-distance trains; they will be the first urban railways that use existing railways.

12. The daily users of KTM Komuter number about 100,000 persons. In addition, since the airport access railway occupies about half of the 121-kilometer network, the transport density there rises further if limited only to the LRTs and monorail.

13. *Si lo* are light trucks with two parallel benches on their carriages. Although they had been operating on lease as taxies or *samlos*, they have entered into a regular service by fixing their routes as regular buses. Therefore, private bus operators have repeatedly complained to the government that their users are being taken away by *si lo*.

14. In Hong Kong, the system of registering minibuses started in 1969 and shifted to a licensing system in 1972, which defined routes and fares (Wang 1993, 22).

15. When the introduction of mass rapid transit in Bangkok was planned in the 1970s, there was a suggestion to build an elevated structure between Hua Lamphong and Khlong Toei in order to operate buses. It would have been the first BRT if it had been realized.

16. Commuter trains in Jakarta are not a good example of sophisticated urban railways; congestion is so severe that many passengers even ride on the roofs. However, many used trains have been sent from Japan in recent years, and since they have a higher fare than ordinary trains and are air-conditioned, congestion has somewhat decreased on these trains.

17. Apart from these, such conditions as an average per capita income of USD 1,800 or more and a fair system similar to buses are also mentioned.

18. However, in the suburbs with wide roads, the possibility of introducing the BRT as a feeder for urban railways still exists.

19. For example, the fall of profitability forced tramway companies to increase the level of profit allocation to the government due to the battle to acquire concessions during the era of King Rama V.

20. The "corporate" public transport supply cycle is the cycle from the establishment of a public company to its privatization through the fall into loss-making operations caused by the reduction of efficiency.

21. The Yingluck Shinawatra government (decidedly pro-Thaksin, as Yingluck is Thaksin's sister), which came into power in 2011, suggested a review of the free bus and train policies, but it was never carried out (*KT* [OE]*)*, 15 August 2011).

22. However, since the present Bangkok metropolitan area is much larger than the range of the BMA, it seems more effective to establish a new agency that covers

the metropolitan area, including neighboring provinces, and allow this agency to comprehensively regulate urban transport in the greater metropolitan area.

23. Although the Yingluck government that came to power in July 2011 is considering the revival of the NGV bus plan, a concrete proposal has not yet emerged as of December 2011.

24. For example, regarding the bid for the Purple line construction, *PCC* (*OE*, 24 July 2008) reported that the successful bid contractors had already been decided for the three contracts ahead of time and that 15 percent of the contract amount would flow back to the politicians.

25. Suehiro states that the Mega Project should be regarded as the result of priority given to the national projects advantageous to large-scale business or foreign investors rather than to grassroots economic stimulus (Suehiro 2009, 175). However, in the development of urban railways, Thaksin aimed not only at the development of infrastructure, such as urban railways, but also at qualitative aspects such as low flat fares and rapid development. Therefore, I consider this to be an expression of a populist policy aimed at city residents.

26. Subsidies were provided from the early 1890s in Europe, and most urban railways nationalized by the 1920s depended on subsidies. Subsidies were also granted after the 1970s in the United States, where private companies had been managing urban transport for a long time (Pucher 2004, 220–21). Therefore, it is recognized in Europe and the United States that the management of public transport only by fare receipts is basically impossible, and the shortage of operational expenses needs to be covered by subsidy (Nihon Chikatetsu Kyokai 2000, 6–7).

27. For example, Vasconcellos (2001, 298) insists that public transport service should be maintained even if government subsidy is required, and Thompson et al. (1990, 37) note that one condition for the success of urban railway development in developing countries is that the fare should be set at a level where it can compete with buses and that a certain amount of financial support is required to achieve that. On the other hand, even if the government does not outlay direct aid, there is the example of Hong Kong where the urban railway business operates on a commercial basis; the government permits an entrepreneur to earn profits from land development (Yeung 2007, 51–56).

Conclusion

1. As far as I know, the oldest source indicating the existence of a regular boat service in Bangkok is an advertisement of the Meinam Steam Flotilla Company in the 1 September 1888 edition of *BT*. According to the ad, a boat operated every two hours from 6:00 am to 6:00 pm between Bang Kholaem and Samsen.

2. There are many newspaper reports regarding the general meeting of shareholders of water transport companies such as the Menam Motor Boat Company, as well as the SEC and the PRC in the prewar period, but nothing exists after the war.

3. Although there is no study on paratransit vehicles, there are several studies regarding the people involved in paratransit services. Phanni Bualek (1999) studied rickshaw coolies, and motorbike taxis are described in the studies on informal economy by Fujimaki (2001) and Endo (2014).

4. For example, the Ministry of Communication's available records, which played an important role in this study, only cover the period up to the end of the 1960s. Later archives will become available some day, although the release of new archives is slow and it is unknown just when newer material will be released.

5. The construction of the Dark Green line between Bearing and Paknam started in March 2012 under the jurisdiction of the MRTA (*PCK* [OE], 5 March 2012).

6. The Ministry of Transport considered the adoption of a flat fare of twenty baht for the MRTA and the Airport Rail Link, and it claimed to show how the reduction in fare revenues would be compensated by government subsidies after adopting a low fare for the BTS.

7. In September 2011, the transport minister Sukamphon Suwannathat of the Yingluck government claimed that the Pheu Thai Party pledged in its election campaign that a flat fare of twenty baht would be adopted after the completion of ten urban railways, and that it would not breach this pledge even if it was necessary to wait for its realization to be feasible (*KT* [OE], 15 September 2011).

8. Although the reason given for this is to reinforce transport capacity, it will mean not only a delay in completion, but also that construction costs may soar. The result of reinvestigation was finally submitted in February 2012, suggesting that the original plan of adopting a monorail system will be suitable (*PCT* [OE], 19 April 2012).

9. There are other examples of bus stops being incidentally located close to urban railway stations, but they are usually served by the existing buses operating in parallel with urban railways and few routes play the role of feeders.

Bibliography

Primary Sources

National Archives of Thailand (NA) (in historical sequence)

Bangkok Metropolitan Administration Records (*Ekkasan krungthep mahanakhon*: Ko Tho Mo.).

Department of Royal Secretary Records, the Rama V Reign (*Ekkasan krom ratcha- lekhathikan, ratchakan thi 5*: Ro. 5).

Ministry of Local Government files (*Krasuang nakhonban*: Ro. 5 No.).

Ministry of Public Works files (*Krasuang yothathikan*: Ro. 5 Yo Tho.).

Department of Royal Secretary Records, the Rama VI Reign (*Ekkasan krom ratcha-lekhathikan, ratchakan thi 6*: Ro. 6).

Ministry of Local Government files (*Krasuang nakhonban*: Ro. 6 No.).

Department of Royal Secretary Records, the Rama VII Reign (*Ekkasan krom ratcha-lekhathikan, ratchakan thi 7*: Ro. 7).

Ministry of Commerce and Communications files (*Krasuang phanit lae khamanakhom*: Ro. 7 Pho.).

Ministry of Interior files (*Krasuang mahatthai*: Ro. 7 Mo.).

Ministry of Communications Records (*Ekkasan krasuang khamanakhom*: Kho Kho.)

Ministry of Finance Records (*Ekkasan krasuang kan khlang*: [1] Ko Kho., [2] Ko Kho.).

Ministry of Foreign Affairs Records (*Ekkasan krasuang kan tangprathet*: Ko To.).

Ministry of Industry Records (*Ekkasan krasuang utsahakam*: O Ko.).

Secretariat of the Cabinet Records (*Ekkasan samnak lekhathikan khana ratthamontri*: [2] So Ro., [3] So Ro.).

Supreme Commander Headquarters Records (*Ekkasan kong banchakan thahan sungsut*: Bo Ko. Sungsut).

British Parliamentary Papers

Diplomatic and Consular Reports on Trade and Finance, Siam. Trade and Commerce of the Consular District of Bangkok (DRC).

Annual Reports, Statistics, Periodicals

Bangkok Metro Public Company Limited (BMCL). *Annual Report.*

BTS Group Holdings Public Company Limited (BTSG). *Raingan pracham pi* [Annual Report, BTS Public Company Limited].

Faifa Nakhon Luang, Kan (FN). *Raingan pracham pi kan faifa nakhon luang* [Annual Report, Metropolitan Electricity Authority].

Khamanakhom, Krasuang (KK). *Raingan pracham pi krasuang khamanakhom* [Annual Report, Ministry of Communications].

Khonsong Muanchon Krungthep, Ongkan (KSMK). *Raingan pracham pi ongkan khonsong muanchon krungthep* [Annual Report, Bangkok Mass Transit Authority].

Ratchakitchanubeksa (RKB). [National Gazette].

Rotfai Haeng Prathet Thai, Kan (RFT). *Raingan pracham pi kan rotfai haeng prathet thai* [Annual Report, the State Railways of Thailand].

Rotfaifa Mahanakhon, Ongkan (RFM). *Raingan pracham pi ongkan rot faifa mahanakhon* [Annual Report, the Metropolitan Rapid Transit Authority].

Rotfaifa Khonsong Muanchon Haeng Prathet Thai, Kan (RFMT). *Raingan pracham pi kan rot faifa khonsong muanchon haeng prathet thai* [Annual Report, the Mass Rapid Transit Authority of Thailand].

Royal State Railways of Siam (RSRS). *Annual Report on the Administration of the Royal State Railways.*

Sathiti Charachon (*SC*) [Traffic Statistics].

Statistical Yearbook of Thailand (*SYB*).

Thang Phiset Haeng Prathet Thai, Kan (TPT). *Raingan pracham pi kan thang phiset haeng prathet thai* [Annual Report, the Expressway and Rapid Transit Authority of Thailand].

Transport Statistics (*TS*).

Thai Information Center, Chulalongkorn University (TIC)

TIC 21678 "Thonburi-Paktho Highway. 1973/04."

Newspapers and Journals

Asahi Shimbun (AS)

Bangkok Post (BP)

Bangkok Post Weekly Review (BPWR)

Bangkok Post Year-End Economic Review (BPYEER)

Bangkok Times (BT)

Bangkok Times Weekly Mail (BTWM)

Deli Nius (DN)

Ikhon Nius (IN)

Krungthep Thurakit (KT)

The Nation (N)

Nihon Keizai Shimbun (NKS)

Phu Chatkan (PCK)
Prachachat (PCC)
Prachachat Thurakit (PCT)
Railway Gazette International (RGI)
Sayam Nikon (SN)
Sayam Rat (SR)
Sayam Rat Sapda Wichan (SRSW)
Si Krung (SK)
Siam Rath Weekly Review (SRWR)
Thai Mai (TM)
Than Setthakit (TSK)

Secondary Sources

In Thai

Anek Laothammathat. 2006. *Thaksina-prachaniyom* [Thaksin's Populist Policies]. Bangkok, Matichon.

Bangkok Guide, ed. 1988. *Krungthep doenthang* [Bus Guide]. Bangkok, Bangkok Guide.

Castrol (Thailand). 1994. *Ratchayan luang boran haeng sayam* [Royal Automobile Stables of Siam]. Bangkok, Carl Haartman & Sons.

Chali Iamkrasin. 1981. *Loet Samantao: Racha rot me khon raek haeng krung sayam* [Loet Samantao]. Bangkok, Ruangsin.

Charuni Khongkun. 2006. "Kan chat rabop khonsong muanchon khong ongkan khonsong muanchon krungthep (pho so 2519–2542)" [Mass Transportation Management of Bangkok Mass Transit Authority, 1976–1999]. Unpublished M.A. Thesis, Sinakharinwirot University.

Chittima Khuptanon et al. 1992. *Rattha wisahakit nai yuk ratthaban nai anan panyarachun: Rattha wisahakit dan kan khonsong lae khamanakhom* [Public Organizations during the Anan Government: Public Organizations in Transport Sector]. Bangkok, Khrongkan Samnak Wichai lae Wikhro Ngoppraman Fai Nitibanyat.

Cho. Bang Toei. 2006. "Rotfaifa sai duan tha akatsayan Suwannaphum" [Express Train to Suwannaphum Airport]. In *Rotfai samphan*, vol. Mokkarakhom–Kumphaphan 2549: 4–5.

Chotchoi Sophonphanit et al. 1995. *Samut pok khiao: Khomun chak khadi prawattisat khrongkan rabop khonsong muanchon krungthep mahanakhon (Thanayong)* [Green Book: Data from the Historical Suit about Bangkok Mass Rapid Transit Program (Thanayong)]. Bangkok.

Faifa Nakhon Luang, Kan (FN). 1988. *30 pi kan faifa nakhon luang* [30th Anniversary of Metropolitan Electricity Authority]. Bangkok, FN.

Ikhon Nius (IN). 1993. *Ikhon Nius chabap phiset: 65 ratthawisahakit thai* [65 Thai Public Enterprises]. Bangkok, IN.

Kan Khonsong Thang Bok, Krom (KTB). 1991. *50 pi krom kan khonsong thang bok* [50th Anniversary of Department of Land Transportation]. Bangkok, KTB.

Kanokwali Chuchaiya. 2001. *Photchananukrom wisamanayam thai: Wat wang thanon saphan pom* [Encyclopedia of Proper Noun: Temples, Palaces, Roads, Bridges and Forts]. Bangkok, Ratchabandittayasathan.

Khamroplak Suratsawadi. 2000. *Kan sueksa lae kan wichai phuea chi nam lae kamnot krop nayobai kan phatthana mueang: Krungthep mahanakhon lae parimonthon kap kan kae panha charachon* [Study for Making Urban Development Policy: Greater Bangkok and Traffic Problems]. Bangkok, Bangkok Metropolitan Administration.

Khonsong Chamkat, Borisat (KS). 1960. *Sathapana khrop rop 30 pi 13 karakdakhom 2503 borisat khonsong chamkat* [30th Anniversary of the Transport Co., Ltd.]. Bangkok, KS.

Khonsong Muanchon Krungthep, Ongkan (KSMK). 1985. *9 pi ongkan khonsong muanchon krungthep* [9th Anniversary of Bangkok Mass Transit Authority]. Bangkok, KSMK.

______. 1998a. *Phaen kan prapprung lae prap lot khanat khong ongkan khonsong muanchon krungthep* [Improvement and Downsizing Plan of Bangkok Mass Transit Authority]. Bangkok, KSMK.

______. 1998b. *Phaen patibat kan phoem botbat phak ekkachon khong ongkan khonsong muanchon krungthep* [Plan for Increasing Private Sector's Role of Bangkok Mass Transit Authority]. Bangkok, KSMK.

______. 2001. *25 pi ko tang ongkan khonsong muanchon krungthep* [25th Anniversary of Bangkok Mass Transit Authority]. Bangkok, KSMK.

______. 2005. *Ongkan khonsong muanchon krungthep* [Bangkok Mass Transit Authority]. Bangkok, KSMK.

______. n.d. *Senthang doen rot doisan pracham thang nai khet krungthep lae changwat klaokhiang* [Bus Route Map in Bangkok and Its Vicinity]. Bangkok, KSMK.

Kriangsak Charoenwongsak. 2007. *Ti phae meka prochek: Rueang yai klaiklai tua* [Describing Mega Project]. Bangkok, Success Media.

Krungthep Mahanakhon (KTM). 2009. *2.2 ko mo mueang aphiwat: Senthang rot faifa sai prawattisat kham maenam Chaophraya* [2.2 km Rail Extension in Great City: Historical Railway across the Chaophraya]. Bangkok, KTM.

Krungthep Thurakit (KT). 1997. *Thotsawat setthakit fong sabu* [The Decade of the Bubble Economy]. Bangkok, The Nation.

Kueakun Yuenyong-anan. 1977. "Kan phatthanakan khamanakhom thang bok nai ratchasamai phrabatsomdet phrachunlachomklao chaoyuhua" [The Development of Inland Communication during the Reign of King Chulalongkorn]. Unpublished M.A. Thesis, Sinakharinwirot University.

Nara Khamnamuen. 2004. *Theknoloyi kan khonsong satharana nai mueang: Rabop khonsong satharana nai ko tho mo* [Technology of Urban Public Transport: Public Transport System in Bangkok]. Bangkok, TISTR.

Phaibun Kanchanaphibun, ed. 1997. *Anuson khroprop 100 pi phana chomphon po Phibunsongkhram 14 karakkadakhom 2540* [100th Anniversary of Marshal Phibun Songkhram]. Lopburi, Sun Kan Thahan Puen Yai.

Phanni Bualek. 1999. *Kuli lak rot kap prawattisat raengngan thai* [Rickshaw Coolie and History of Labor in Thailand]. Bangkok, Mueang Boran.

Phongphan Channgoen. 1999. "Rotfai phuea hai borikan tha akatsayan sakon krungthep haeng thi 2" [Rail Service Serving Second Bangkok International Airport]. Unpublished M.A. Thesis, Chulalongkorn University.

Praman Adireksan. 1997. *Chiwit muea phan pai 84 pi* [84th Anniversary of Praman Adireksan]. Bangkok.

Rangsan Thanaphonphan and Kanlaya Udomwithit, eds. 1993. *Mati samkhan khong khana ratthamontri wa duai setthakit yuk ratthaban phon ek Chatchai Chunhawan singhakhom 2531–kumphaphan 2534* [Important Cabinet Approvals on Economy under Chatchai Government]. Bangkok, Samakhom Sangkhommasat haeng Prathet Thai.

Rabop Khonsong Muanchon Krungthep Chamkat, Borisat (RKMK). 2008. *Rang wiwat phatthana mueang: Kan khonsong rabop rang phuea khunnaphap chiwit khong chao krungthep mahanakhon* [Evolution of the Rail: Development of the City]. Bangkok, RKMK.

Rapsong Sinkha Lae Phatsaduphan, Ongkan (RSP). 1987. *Chalong khrop rop 60 pi ro so pho* [60th Anniversary of the Express Transportation Organization]. Bangkok, RSP.

Rotfaifa Mahanakhon, Ongkan (RFM). 1993. *Khrongkan rot faifa mahanakhon raya thi 2* [The Second Stage Metropolitan Rapid Transit Program]. Bangkok, RFM.

______. 1998. *Sara samkhan khrongkan rot faifa mahanakhon* [The Brief of the Metropolitan Rapid Transit Program]. Bangkok, RFM.

Rotfaifa Khonsong Muanchon Haeng Prathet Thai, Kan (RFMT). 2004. *Khrongkan rotfaifa mahanakhon sai chaloem ratchamongkhon* [The M.R.T. Chaloem Ratchamongkhon Line]. Bangkok, RFMT.

Rotfai haeng Prathet Thai, Kan (RFT). 1970. *Thi raluek nai wan khlai sathapana kitchakan rotfai khrop rop 72 pi* [72th Anniversary of State Railways of Thailand]. Bangkok, RFT.

Samat Ratchaphalasit. 2007. *Poet pom rotfaifa thi khon krungthep tong ru* [Revealing Mass Transit Problem that Bangkokian Must Know]. Bangkok, Amarin Printing.

Samnak Nayok Ratthamontri (SNR). 1992. *Ngan khong ratthaban Anan Panyarachun* [The Results of Anan Panyarachun Government]. Vol. 1. Bangkok, SNR.

Samnakngan Nayobai Lae Phaen Kan Khonsong Lae Charachon (SNK). 2005. *3 pi so no kho* [3 Years of Office of Transport and Policy and Planning]. Bangkok, SNK.

______. 2010. *Khrongkan sueksa prap phaen maebot rabop khonsong muanchon thang rang nai khet krungthep mahanakhon lae parimonthon* [Mass Rapid Transit Master Plan in Bangkok Metropolitan Region: M-MAP]. Bangkok, SNK.

Samrit Miwong-ukhot, ed. n.d. *Patithin khao lae hetkan nai prathet rop 10 pi: Pho so 2519 thueng pho so 2528.* [News and Incidents during decade: 1976–1985]. 3 vols. Bangkok, Sayamban.

Sa-nguan Ankhong. 1986. *Sing raek nai mueang thai lem 2* [First Things in Thailand, Vol. 2]. Bangkok, Phraephitthaya.

Sathaban Wichai Phuea Kan Phatthana Prathet Thai (SWPT). 1994. *Samut pok khao TDRI: Panha charachon nai krungthep: Mi thang kae khai ru mai?* [Traffic Problems in Bangkok]. Bangkok, SWPT.

Sayam Rat (SR). 1992. *Sayam Rat chabap kiat yot: Phlik faem khrongkan muen lan* [Reveal the Mega Projects]. Bangkok, SR.

Somchai Phairotthirarat. 1974. "Botbat khong prathet maha amnat tawantok nai kan sang thang rotfai khong prathet thai nai ratchasamai phrabatsomdet phrachunlachomklao chaoyuhua lae phrabatsomdet phramongkutklao chaoyuhua" [The Role of the Western Imperial Countries on Railway Construction of Thailand in the Reign of King Rama V and VI]. Unpublished M.A. Thesis, Chulalongkorn University.

Somsi Chatsakunwilai. 1992. "Ongkan Khonsong Muanchon Krungthep" [Bangkok Mass Transit Authority]. In Chittima et al., *Rattha wisahakit nai yuk ratthaban nai Anan Panyarachun: Rattha wisahakit dan kan khonsong lae khamanakhom*, 1–24.

Thang Phiset Haeng Prathet Thai, Kan (TPT). n.d. *Khrongkan rabop rotfaifa Khonsong muanchon suan thi 1 khan thi 1 nai krungthep mahanakhon* [Mass Transit System Part I Stage I Program in Bangkok]. Bangkok, TPT.

______. 1982. *Nangsue thi raluek nueang nai phithi poet thang duan sai Dindaeng–Tharuea 4 Mokkarakhom 2525* [Anniversary Book of the Opening Ceremony for Dindaeng–Tharuea Expressway]. Bangkok, TPT.

Thawisin Supwatthana. 1982. "Kan long thun thang setthakit khong chaonai thai" [Economic Invest of Royalties and Nobles in Thailand]. In *Ruam botkhwam prawattisat* 5: 54–93.

Tho Phuthao. 1989. *Khong kao rao luem: Rotfai-ruea me-thale-rotrang* [Old Things that We have Forgotten]. Bangkok, Phi Wathin.

Uthai Hiranto. 1980. *Kan pokkhrong thongthin* [Local Administration].

Bangkok, Odien Store.
Wipharat Diong. 1991. "Phatthanakan khong kitchakan faifa nai prathet thai rawang pi pho so 2427–2488" [Development of Electricity Industry in Thailand, 1884–1941]. Unpublished M.A. Thesis, Thammasat University.
Witthaya Aphinyanon. 2001. "Kan sueksa khrongkan rabop kan khonsong thang rotfai chanmueang doi chai khrongsang thanon yok radap nai krungthep mahanakhon (Hopewell)" [The Analysis of Railways Transportation System Using the Structure of Hopewell Project]. Unpublished M.A. Thesis, Kasetsart University.

In Other Languages

Armstrong-Wright, Alan. 1993. *Public Transport in Third World Cities.* London, HMSO.
Banister, David. 2005. *Unsustainable Transport: City Transport in the New Country.* London, Routledge.
Barat, Josef. 1990 "Institutional Frameworks for Planning Transport in Third World Cities." In Dimitriou, ed. *Transport Planning for Third World Cities,* 216–65.
Bello, Walden, Shea Cunningham, and Li Kheng Poh. 1998. *A Siamese Tragedy: Development and Disintegration in Modern Thailand.* London, Zed Books.
Davis, Clarence B., and Kenneth E. Wilburn, Jr. eds. 1991. *Railway Imperialism.* New York, Greenwood Press.
Dick, Howard. 2003. *Surabaya, City of Work: A Socioeconomic History, 1900–2000.* Singapore, Singapore University Press.
Dick, Howard, and Peter J. Rimmer. 2003. *Cities, Transport, and Communications: The Integration of Southeast Asia since 1850.* Basingstoke, Palgrave MacMillan.
Dimitriou, Harry T. ed. 1990. *Transport Planning for Third World Cities.* London, Routledge.
Doling, Tim. 2012. *The Railways and Tramways of Viet Nam.* Bangkok, White Lotus.
Endo Tamaki. 2014. *Living with Risk: Precarity and Bangkok's Urban Poor.* Kyoto, Kyoto University Press.
Francis, Ric, and Colin Ganley. 2006. *Penang Trams, Trollybuses, and Railways: Municipal Transport History 1880s–1963.* Penang, Areca Books.
Hujimaki Shun. 2001. *Roji no keizai shakaigaku: Tai no Informal Sector ni tsuite* [Socio-economics of the Street: Informal Sector in Bangkok]. Tokyo: Mekong.
Hanson, Susan, and Genevieve Giuliano, eds. 2004. *The Geography of Urban Transportation, Third Edition.* New York, The Guilford Press.
Higgins, J. Wally. 2006. *Hakkutsu color shashin: 1950–1960 nendai tetsudo genfukei kaigai hen* [1950–1960's Historic Railway Scene: Overseas

Volume]. Tokyo, JTB Publishing.
Hilling, David .1996. *Transport and Developing Countries*. London, Routledge.
Holm, David Frederich. 1977. *The Role of the State Railways in Thai History, 1892–1932*. Unpublished Ph.D. Dissertation, Yale University.
Institution of Civil Engineers, ed. 1990. *Rail Mass Transit for Developing Countries: Proceedings of the Conference Organized by the Institution of Civil Engineers, and Held in London on 9–10 October 1989*. London, Thomas Telford.
Kakizaki Ichiro. 2000. *Tai keizai to tetsudo 1885–1935 nen* [Thai Economy and Its Railways, 1885–1935]. Tokyo, Nihon Keizai Hyoronsha.
______. 2005. *Laying the Tracks: The Thai Economy and Its Railways 1885–1935*. Kyoto, Kyoto University Press.
______. 2007a. "Tai ni okeru tetsudo kan no keisei 1885–1910 nen: Dare ga dono yoni ninshiki shitanoka" [Forming the Recognition towards Railways in Thailand, 1885–1910]. In *Sicho (The Journal of History)*, 62:2–26.
______. 2007b. *Monogatari tai no rekishi*. Tokyo, Chuo Koron Shinsha. [The History of Thailand].
______. 2009. *Tetsudo to doro no seiji keizaigaku: Thai no kotsu seisaku to shohin ryutsu* 1935–1975 nen [Political Economy of Railways and Highways: Transport Policy and Commodity Flow in Thailand, 1935–1975]. Kyoto, Kyoto University Press.
______. 2012. *Rails of the Kingdom: The History of Thai Railways*. Bangkok, White Lotus.
Kato Kazuhide. 1996. *Tai gendai seiji shi: Kokuo o genshu tosuru minshushugi* [History of Modern Politics in Thailand]. Tokyo, Kobundo.
King, Ross. 2008. *Kuala Lumpur and Putrajaya: Negotiating Urban Space in Malaysia*. Singapore, NUS Press.
Kitagawa Daijiro. 2010. *Kindai toshi Pari no tanjo: Tetsudo, metro jidai no nekkyo* [The Birth of Modern City, Paris]. Tokyo, Kawaide Shobo Shinsha.
Leinbach, Thomas R., and Chia Lin Sien. 1989. *South-East Asian Transport: Issues in Development*. Singapore, Oxford University Press.
Leung, C. K. 1993. "The Process of Transport Policy Making." In Wang and Yeh, *Keep a City Moving*, 31–41.
McCargo, Duncan. 1997. *Chamlong Srimuang and the New Thai Politics*. London, Hurst & Co.
Miki Masafumi. 2010. *Toshi kotsu no seiritsu* [The Formation of Urban Transport]. Tokyo, Nihon Keizai Hyoronsha.
Morisugi Hisayoshi, and Atsushi Fukuda. 1998. "Kotsu mondai" [Transport Problems]. In Tasaka, ed. *Ajia no daitoshi 1: Bangkok*, 213–33.
Nagai Fumio. 2003. "Tai no chiho jichi seido kaikaku: Chiho bunken iinkai o chushinni" [Reform of Local Administration in Thailand]. In Sakumoto and Imaizumi, eds. *Ajia no minshuka katei to ho*, 273–310.

Nambara Makoto. 1998. *Economic Plan and the Evolution of Economic Nationalism in Siam in the 1930s*. Unpublished Ph.D. Dissertation, SOAS, University of London.

Nihon Chikatetsu Kyokai. 2000. *Sekai no chikatetsu: 115 toshi no saishin joho.* [Subways of the World]. Tokyo, Sankai Do.

Noda Masaho et al. 1986. *Nihon no tetsudo: Seiritsu to tenkai* [Railways in Japan]. Tokyo, Nihon Keizai Hyoronsha.

Office of the Commission for the Management of Land Traffic (OCMLT). 2001. *URMAP: Urban Rail Transportation Master Plan (BMA and Surrounding Areas).* Bangkok, OCMLT.

Office of Transport and Policy and Planning (OTP). 2004. *Bangkok Mass Transit Implementation Plan*. Bangkok, OTP.

Ota Tsunezo. 1967. *Biruma ni okeru nihon gunseishi no kenkyu* [A Study of Japanese Military Administration in Burma]. Tokyo, Yoshikawa Kobundo.

Pasuk Phongphaichit and Chris Baker. 2004. *Thaksin: The Business of Politics in Thailand.* Chiang Mai, Silkworm Books.

Pendakur, V. Setty. 1984. *Urban Transport in ASEAN*. Singapore, Institute of Southeast Asian Studies.

Porphant Ouyyanont. 1994. *Bangkok and Thai Economic Development: Aspects of Change, 1820–1970*. Unpublished Ph.D. Dissertation, University of New England.

Pucher, John. 2004. "Public Transport." In Hanson and Giuliano, eds. *The Geography of Urban Transportation, Third Edition,* 199–236

Ramaer, R. 2009. *The Railways of Thailand.* Bangkok, White Lotus.

Rimmer, Peter J., and Howard Dick. 2009. *The City in Southeast Asia: Patterns, Processes and Policy*. Singapore, NUS Press.

Sakumoto Naoyuki, and Imaizumi Shinya, ed. 2003. *Ajia no minshuka katei to ho*. Chiba, Institute of Developing Economies. [Process of Democratization and Laws in Asia].

Shimada Yukinori, and Kimura Kan, eds. 2009. *Populism, minshushugi, seiji shido: Seidoteki henkakuki no hikaku seijigaku* [Populism, Democracy, and Political Guidance]. Kyoto, Minerva Shobo.

Siam Directory 1912, The. 2005 [1912]. Bangkok, White Lotus (reprint).

Simon, David. 1996. *Transport and Development in the Third World.* London, Routledge.

Suehiro, Akira. 1989. *Capital Accumulation in Thailand 1855–1985*. Tokyo, Center for East Asian Cultural Studies.

______, ed. 1998. *Tai no toukei seido to shuyo keizai seiji data*. Tokyo, Institute of Developing Economies. [Statistical System and Major Economic and Political Data of Thailand].

______. 2009. *Tai: Chushin koku no mosaku*. Tokyo, Iwanami Shoten. [Thailand].

Suehiro Akira, and Higashi Shigeki, eds. 1999. *Tai no keizai seisaku: Seido, soshiki, actor* [Economic Policy in Thailand]. Tokyo, Institute of Developing Economies.

Taaffe, Edward J., Howard L. Gautheir, and Morton E. O'Kelly. 1996. *Geography of Transportation, Second Edition*. Upper Saddle River, Prentice-Hall.

Takada Takao. 1952a. "Tai koku no tetsudo tsuioku sono 1: Maeklong tetsudo" [Reminiscence of Railways in Thailand 1]. In *Tetsudo pictorial* 2 (5) :6–8.

______. 1952b. "Tai koku no tetsudo tsuioku sono 4: Paknam densha" [Reminiscence of Railways in Thailand 4]. In *Tetsudo pictorial* 2 (10) :6–8.

Tasaka Toshio, ed. 1998. *Ajia no daitoshi 1: Bangkok* [Megacities in Asia 1: Bangkok]. Tokyo, Nihon Hyoronsha.

Tasaka Toshio, and Nishizawa Kikuo. 2003. *Bangkok tochi shoyu shi josetsu.* [The Introductory History of Land Possession in Bangkok]. Tokyo, Nihon Hyoronsha.

Tamada Yoshifumi. 1996. *Tai gyosei soshiki shi 1892–1993 nen: Kyokuijou no soshiki no hensen* [The History of Public Administration in Thailand, 1892–1993]. Kyoto, Center of South Easi Asian Studies, Kyoto University.

______. 2009a. "Tai no seijika retsuden 5: Abhisit seiken no tateyakusha nado" [Politicians in Thailand]. In *Tai koku joho* 43 (1): 46–49.

______. 2009b. *Tai no populism to minshuka: Thaksin seiken no shubo to omei* [Populism and Democratization in Thailand]. In Shimada and Kimura, eds. *Populism, Democracy, and Political Guidance*, 75–96.

Thomson, J. M., R. J. Allport, and P. R. Fouracre. 1990. "Rail Mass Transit in Developing Cities: The Transport and Road Research Laboratory Study." In Institution of Civil Engineers ed. *Rail Mass Transit for Developing Countries*, 21–39.

Thompson, Virginia. 1967 [1941]. *Thailand: The New Siam*. New York, Paragon Book Reprint (reprint).

Unger, Danny. 1998. *Building Social Capital in Thailand: Fibers, Finance and Infrastructure*. Oxford, Cambridge University Press.

Vasconcellos, Eduardo A. 2001. *Urban Transport, Environment and Equity: The Case for Developing Countries*. London, Earthscan Publications.

Wang, Liang Huew, and Anthony Gar-on Yeh. 1993. *Keep a City Moving: Urban Transport Management in Hong Kong*. Tokyo, Asian Productivity Organization.

Whyte, B. R. 2010. *The Railway Atlas of Thailand. Laos and Cambodia.* Bangkok, White Lotus.

Wilson, Constance M. 1983. *Thailand: A Handbook of Historical Statistics.* Boston, G. K. Hall.

Wright, Arnold, H. A. Cartwright, H. A., and O. Breakspear. 1910. *Twentieth Century Impressions of Burma: Its History, People, Commerce, Industries, and Resources*. London, Lloyd's Greater Britain Publishing.

Wright, Arnold, and Oliver T. Breakspear, eds. 1994 [1903]. *Twentieth Century Impressions of Siam: Its History, People, Commerce, Industries, and Resources*. Bangkok, White Lotus (reprint).

Yeung, Rikkie. 2008. Moving Millions: *The Commercial Success and Political Controversies of Hong Kong's Railways.* Hong Kong, Hong Kong University Press.

Websites

DB International GmbH (DBI) (http://www.db-international.de/)

PTT Public Company Limited (PTT) (http://www.pttplc.com/)

Thai Khem Khaeng (http://www.tkk2555.com/)

Index

Abhisit Vejjajiva, 297–98, 306, 309, 311, 346, 348–49
Aerial Transport Company, 69, 76, 79, 94–95, 100, 102
age of democratization, 200
age of development, 198, 200, 205, 350
Airport Rail Link, 1, 266–67, 300, 312, 316–18, 327, 335–36
Alcatel Company, 302–3
Allegri, C., 48
Amnuai Wirawan, 235
Amon Sirikaya, 226
Anan Panyarachun, 215, 227, 249
Aphirak Kosayothin, 276–77, 281–82, 284, 286–87, 297, 302, 344, 346
Asia-Euro Consortium, 214
Asian Games, Thirteenth, 239
Atsadang Road, 43
Ayutthaya, 3

Baiphong Road (Uthong Nai Road), 53
Bamrung Mueang Road, 28
Ban Kluai, 151
Ban Laem, 37, 70–71, 114–15, 152–55
Ban Mai. *See* Chachoengsao
Ban Thawai, 55–56
Bandung, 5, 334
Bang Bon, 68, 102
Bang Buathong, 227
Bang Buathong Railway, 71, 76
Bang Chak, 67
Bang Kapi, 130, 132–33, 178, 277
Bang Khae, 117, 216, 267, 295, 306
Bang Khen, 278
Bang Kholaem (Thanon Tok), 19, 21, 43–45, 54–55, 84, 105, 132
Bang Khunthian, 163
Bang Khwang, 76
Bang Krabue, 26, 33, 44, 57, 110, 135, 156
Bang Krabue pier, 110
Bang Lamphu, 77
Bang Lamphu Canal, 42
Bang Na, 65, 208, 227
Bang Phli, 178, 227
Bang Pu, 113, 147, 178, 296
Bang Rak, 50, 55–57, 73
Bang Sue, 57, 108, 149, 207–8, 235, 253, 263–64, 267, 269, 271, 278, 295–96, 304–6
Bang Wa, 304
Bang Yai, 267, 271, 304
Bang Yiruea, 56
Bangkok Bridge, 163, 287, 289
Bangkok Dock, 21
Bangkok Electricity, 106–8, 110–11, 136–37, 147, 153–54
Bangkok Land Company, 235
Bangkok Mass Transit Authority (BMTA), 9, 13–14, 194–95, 215–16, 220–27, 242–48, 257–61, 289, 294, 307, 309–11, 328, 337–38, 342–44, 351, 361
  downsizing plan, 249–51, 284, 356

Bangkok Mass Transit Authority (*continued*)
plan for increasing private sector's role, 250–51, 290, 356–57
transfer plan to BMTA, 250, 284–85
Bangkok Mass Transit Implementation Plan (BMTIP), 267, 270–71, 276, 279, 281, 298, 312–14
Bangkok Mass Transit System (BTS), 1–2, 9, 263–64, 271, 280–81, 284, 287, 289, 297, 300, 302, 314–15, 317–18, 335–36, 345, 350, 356–58, 361
construction, 235–38, 240–42, 248, 252, 255–57
extension, 269, 277, 279–81, 283–85, 287, 289, 296–99, 302, 304, 307, 316, 341, 344, 346–49, 360
Bangkok Mass Transit System Company (BTSC), 233, 236, 238, 241–42, 248, 255, 280, 283, 296, 302–3, 308, 328, 336, 341
purchase plan by the government, 281, 297, 313–14, 335
Bangkok Metro Company (BMCL), 263, 265–66, 315, 336, 341
purchase plan by the government, 313–14
Bangkok Metropolitan Administration (BMA), 9, 13–14, 211, 227, 233, 236–38, 241, 247, 249–53, 264–65, 269, 276–77, 283–85, 302–4, 307–8, 335–36, 341, 344–48, 356–57
Bangkok Mass Transit plan. *See* Bangkok Mass Transit System (BTS)
bus rapid transit (BRT) plan. *See* bus rapid transit (BRT)
conflict with the Ministry of Transport, 297–99
conflict with the Samak government, 296–97
conflict with the Thaksin government, 279–83, 286–87, 289
Bangkok Municipality, 3, 76, 92–94, 97, 105, 116–17, 119, 123, 132, 147, 155, 199, 204, 207, 340, 344, 354–55
bus unification plan, 168–71
start of bus operation, 80, 83–85
Bangkok Microbus Company, 246
Bangkok–Paknam Road. *See* Sukhumvit Road
Bangkok Rattanakosin Automobile Company, 222
Bangkok Tramway Company, 20, 25–27, 47, 340
dividends, 22
electrification, 22, 24–25
gross receipts, 22, 25
Bangkok Transport Company, 243
Bangkok Yai Canal, 29
Banharn Silapa-acha, 250
Banthat Thong Road, 133
barter method, 9, 312–13, 351
Battambang, 35
Bearing, 282, 295, 297, 303–4, 360
Belgium, 60–61
Bhumjaithai Party, 297–98, 309–10, 348–49
Black May incident, 215, 356
Board of Railway Commissioners, 66, 68, 70
Bombardier, Inc., 215, 303
Boworadet, Prince, 76
Brazil, 3, 5–6
Budget Department, 250
Build-Operate-Transfer (BOT), 213, 215, 231, 233, 235, 238, 336, 340–41, 356
Bunchu Rotchanasathian, 212
Bunphong Company, 117
Burapha Railway Company, 34, 51
Burma, 34, 332
buses
air-conditioned buses, 1, 216–18, 220–21, 227, 246–48, 251, 258, 284–86, 290, 292, 294, 309–10, 319, 357

all-night buses, 227, 258, 319
BMTA buses (directly operated), 220–22, 244–46, 249–51, 261, 290, 294, 309–10, 343, 361
bus concessions, 74, 95, 124, 127, 130, 132–35, 139–40, 144–45, 160–63, 166–74, 180, 182–83, 188–90, 192–93, 200–201, 222, 248, 343, 355
expressway buses, 227, 258, 319
fare hikes, 135, 144–46, 168, 178–82, 188–89, 200, 223–26, 244, 249, 260, 285, 292, 340–41, 349, 351, 355
feeder buses, 242, 248, 328
free buses, 190, 192, 200, 226, 260, 310–11, 327–28, 343, 349–51, 357
microbuses, 246–48, 342
minibuses, 2, 4, 222, 243–44, 251, 258, 310, 337, 343, 356
"mosquito buses," 83, 94, 333–34
NGV buses, 290, 294–95, 307–11, 328, 343, 348–49, 357
ordinary (non air-conditioned) buses, 216, 218, 220, 226–27, 251, 260, 284–86, 292, 294, 309, 344, 357
private buses (before unification), 94, 124, 130, 132, 135, 166–67, 171, 201
private buses (under BMTA), 220–21, 223, 243–46, 249–51, 290, 292, 294, 310–11, 340, 342–43, 351, 354, 356
special permission buses 74, 79–80, 82, 94–95, 100, 105, 117, 122, 126–27, 130, 340, 345
student buses, 190, 192
See also *songthaeo*; vans
Bus Operators Association, 190–91
bus rapid transit (BRT), 6–7, 269, 278, 284, 286–88, 289, 307–9, 316, 328, 337–39, 344–47, 357, 361
bus unification
by Bangkok Municipality, 168–71
by ETO, 119, 121–25
by Nakhon Luang Transport Company, 171–73
by Transport Company, 166–68
formation of BMTA, 192–95
formation of Mahanakhon Transport Company, 188–92

Canada, 214, 356
carriage, 43, 45, 48, 50, 72
Chachoengsao (Ban Mai), 33–34
Chaeng Watthana Road, 178
Chamlong Srimuang, 233, 236
Chamnan Yuabun, 169
Chanthaburi, 113
Chaophraya River, 26, 29, 32–33, 38, 44, 55, 61, 67, 76–77, 110, 115, 150–51, 163, 196, 208, 212–13, 296, 304, 306, 358–59
Chaowarat Sutlapha, 249
Charansanitwong Road, 133, 163
Charoen Krung Road, 3, 19, 50, 56, 62, 72, 79–80, 84–85, 92, 94–95, 97, 116–17, 121, 123–24, 138, 146, 150
Chatchai Choonhavan, 214
Chavalit Yongchaiyut, 250
Chiang Mai, 110, 339
Chitlom, 238
Chonburi, 113, 147
Chong Nonsi, 279, 287, 289
Chongrak Norasin, Phraya, 73
Chotchoi Sophonphanit, 236–38
Chuan Leekpai, 235, 279
Chulalongkorn University, 285
Chumphon, 166
Chunlachomklao Fort, 163
communication-based train control (CBTC), 303
conductors, 247, 292
Constitutional Revolution, 15, 87
coup d'état, 123, 160, 181, 270, 295, 347, 357
Credit Suisse–First Boston Company (CSFB), 242

Damrong, Prince, 28, 31, 34, 42, 45, 87
Daokhanong, 77, 208
Darunrak, Phra, 19
DB International GmbH, 318
DC Transit Company, 169–71
De Richelieu, Commodore, 19–20, 25, 35
Democrat Party, 200, 276–77, 281, 297, 309–10, 347–49, 357
Denmark, 27, 42, 60
Department of Land Transport. *See* Department of Transport
Department of Local Government, 61
Department of Public and Municipal Affairs, 74, 84, 94, 107, 122, 125, 153, 340, 345
Department of Public Works, 212
Department of Special Investigation, 308
Department of Transport, 12, 106, 124, 126–27, 134, 138, 140–41, 162, 166–67, 174, 216, 221
design-and-build method, 231, 233, 311, 313
detailed design system, 212, 231, 277, 295, 304–5, 311–12, 316, 351
Dindaeng, 208
Don Mueang, 76–77, 102–3, 108, 216, 264
Don Mueang Tollway, 253, 276
dream-selling policy, 2, 310–11, 328
Dusit, 28–29, 42, 53, 55–57
Dusit Thani Hotel, 238, 240

Eastern ETO Automobile Operation Company, 123
economic boom, 340, 356
economic crisis, 238, 240–41, 271, 356
Enlistee Statue, 156
Europe, 21, 54, 72, 92
ETO Automobile Operation Company, 123
ETO Nakhon Thon Company, 124
Export-Import Bank, United States, 169–71
express boats, 359
Express Transportation Organization (ETO), 12–13, 144–46, 161–62, 172, 199, 201, 344, 355
  expansion of bus business, 121–25, 130, 135, 138–39
expressway, 199, 208, 210–11, 215, 231, 233, 251, 253, 256, 260, 287, 338
Expressway and Rapid Transit Authority of Thailand (ETA), 13, 210–15, 227, 233, 235, 252–55, 257, 260, 340, 346, 348, 356

ferry, 11, 37, 153, 196
fire protection, 43, 45, 47
Four-Year Investment for the Future, 267, 276, 281
France, 72, 154, 302
Franco-Japanese Consortium, 214
freight transport, 38–39, 126, 153
Friendship Highway, 153, 166
fuel, 15, 97, 103, 105–6, 138, 179, 188–89, 191, 227, 249–50, 290, 292, 294

gauges
  meter gauge, 34, 336
  standard gauge, 34–35, 336
Germany, 188, 207–8, 213–14, 239,
Groundwater, C. L., 72–73

Hanoi, 331–32
Hat Amara, 178
Hong Kong, 6–7, 231, 242, 316, 335, 338, 345, 360
Hopewell Company, 231, 235, 237, 253, 255, 264
Hopewell plan, 2, 8, 227, 233, 235, 239, 252–53, 255, 264–65, 269, 271, 306, 317, 335–36, 340–41, 356
Hua Lamphong, 25–6, 28, 37, 43, 54, 60–63, 66–67, 100–101, 106–8, 111, 123, 127, 130, 147–49, 151, 198,

207–8, 211, 235, 239, 253, 263–64, 267, 271, 295, 306
Hua Lamphong Canal, 149
Huai Khwang, 163
Huamak, 231, 239

imperialism, 49, 88
International Finance Corporation (IFC), 241
International Monetary Fund (IMF) 239
Italian-Thai Development Company, 282, 303, 305

Jacobsen, W. T., 41
Jakarta, 21, 331–32. 336, 339
Japan, 23, 34, 80, 154, 305–7, 313
Japan Bank for International Cooperation (JBIC), 270, 277, 305–6, 313
Japan International Cooperation Agency (JICA), 238, 270
Johnson, Axel, 19

Kamphaengphet, Prince, 60
Kasatsuek Bridge, 57, 72, 106, 155
Kasetsart University, 133, 282, 287
Khaelai, 278
Khamroplak Suratsawadi, 8–9, 278
Khlong Bangphai, 304
Khlong San, 39, 67–68, 70–71, 101, 114–16, 149–51, 153, 196
Khlong Tan, 208
Khorat, 35, 110, 166,
Kriangsak Chamanan, 212
Kriangsak Charoensak, 9–10
Krung Kasem Road, 61
Krung Thon Bridge, 163
Krungthep Thanakhom Company, 303–4, 307
Kueakun Yuenyong-anan, 7–8
Kukrit Pramoj, 190–91, 193, 200, 226, 310, 343, 349, 351

La Mahotière, L. R. de, 45–46, 48–49
labor movement, 85–87
Laem Thong Athlete Village, 221
Lak Mueang, 21, 106
Lam Lukka, 279, 296
Lampang, 110
Latphrao, 132–33, 208, 214, 276
Latphrao Road, 287
Lavalin International Company, 214–15, 233, 235, 254, 340, 356
loans, 152, 169–71, 199, 210, 212, 214, 238, 240–42, 250, 304–7, 313
Local Sanitary Department, 45, 49, 51
locomotives
  diesel locomotives, 114
  steam locomotives, 22, 114
Loesak Sombatsiri, 189
Loet Setthabut. *See* Phakdinoraset
Loftus, Alfred John, 19, 33, 35
Lopburi, 110–11, 156
Lumphini Park, 172, 236–37

Maeklong. *See* Samut Songkhram
Maeklong Railway Company (MRC), 37, 49, 88–89, 91, 101, 106–7, 353–54.
  dividends, 39, 89
  electrification, 67–68
  gross receipts, 39, 68
  nationalization, 70–71
  See also Thachin Railway; suburban railway lines (Maeklong line)
Maeklong River, 152
Maenam (freight station), 149,
Maensi, 156
Magic Eye, 236
Maha Phruettharam Road, 61, 156
Mahachai. *See* Samut Sakhon
Mahanak Canal, 42
Mahanakhon Transport Company, 192–95, 200, 215–16, 220, 223, 258
Makkasan, 110, 318
Makkasan Automobile Company, 132, 135, 139

Makkasan workshop, 113, 149
Manankhasila Party, 145
Mandalay, 331–32
Manila, 3, 5, 21, 331–34, 336
Manopakon, Phraya, 83
Mass Rapid Transit Authority of Thailand (MRTA), 13, 267, 270–71, 297–98, 300, 304, 306, 316, 335–36, 341, 344, 346, 348, 356
  construction of subway, 233, 235–40, 252–57, 263–65
Mass Rapid Transit Master Plan (2010), 298–99
Mass Transit Master Plan (1994), 239–40, 270
Mass Transit System (MTS) Plan
  First Stage MTS Plan, 208–13, 252, 254
  First Stage Part 1 MTS Plan, 214, 227, 235, 252, 255
Mater Dei School, 238
Mega Project, 9, 267, 269–70, 276, 278, 282
Memorial Bridge, 61, 77, 150
Menam Motor Boat Company (Paklat tramway), 44, 358
Metropolitan Electricity Authority (MEA), 13–14, 153–56
Metropolitan Rapid Transit Authority (MRTA). *See* Mass Rapid Transit Authority of Thailand (MRTA)
microbuses, 246–48, 342
middle class, 205, 247–48, 258–59, 361
Minburi, 130, 276–77
minibuses, 2, 4, 222, 243–44, 251, 258, 310, 337, 343, 356
Ministry of Commerce and Communications, 12
Ministry of Communications (Transport), 11–12, 106, 113, 125–26, 132, 145, 162, 173–74, 179–81, 188, 210–11, 222, 225, 253, 263, 265, 276, 285, 287, 309, 340, 346, 355
  conflict with BMA, 297–99
  conflict with Ministry of Interior, 121–22, 125, 138–39, 170, 173, 198–99, 347–49
Ministry of Defense, 105–6
Ministry of Economic Affairs, 70, 100
Ministry of Finance, 13, 108, 111, 121, 171, 249, 264, 285, 305, 312, 314
Ministry of Interior, 12–13, 69, 80, 83, 86–87, 95, 105, 107, 147–48, 156, 168, 180, 210–11, 233, 235, 253, 289, 355
  conflict with Ministry of Communications, 121–22, 125–27, 138, 168, 198–99, 345–46
Ministry of Local Government, 12, 48–49, 86
Ministry of Public Works, 12
Ministry of Transport. *See* Ministry of Communications
Mit Songsoem Trading Company, 127, 161
Mochit, 236, 282, 287, 289, 295, 297, 360–61
Montri Hongphanit, 231
"mosquito buses," 83, 94, 333–34. See also *songthaeo*
motor railcars, 62–63, 67–68
motor tricycles. See *sam lo*
Motor Vehicle Act, 94–95
motorcycle taxis, 328
Muang Thong Mass Transit Company, 235, 237–38, 254–55
Mueang Nonthaburi Automobile Company, 132–33, 135

Nai Loet Company, 72, 133, 140, 189–93
Nakhon Luang Transport Company, 171–74, 188, 191, 199, 201
Nakhon Sawan, 166
Nakhon Thon Company, 77, 94
Nara Khamanamun, 8–9
Narathip, Prince, 27–29, 31–33, 40–41, 43, 47, 50, 54

Narathiwat Road, 287
Naret, Prince, 25–26, 28, 32–33, 44–45, 48, 73
National Archives of Thailand, 11, 14, 72, 359
National Economic and Social Development Board (NESDB), 212, 240, 243, 250, 255, 310
National Economic Development Board (NEDB), 151, 182
National Stadium, 298
Natthanon Thawisin, 308
New Phetchaburi Road. *See* Phetchaburi Road
newspapers, 2, 11, 13–14, 29, 33, 48, 51, 63, 84, 134, 138, 145, 160, 168, 180, 236, 359
Ngamwongwan Road, 133, 163, 178
Nikon Chamnong, 287
Nongchok, 162
Nonthaburi, 76–77, 105, 117, 174, 304
Nonthaburi Bridge, 163
Nonthaburi Municipality, 77, 79–80, 130, 138, 172, 178
Nonthaburi, Phraya, 29

Office of the Commission for the Management of Land Traffic (OCMLT), 215, 237, 239, 252–53, 264, 270–71
Office of Transport and Traffic Policy and Planning (OTP), 265, 278, 281, 287, 297–98
oil crisis, 212, 255
oil prices, 189, 292, 305, 310
Onnut, 221, 279, 282, 303–4
Overseas Economic Cooperation Fund, Japan (OECF), 238

Padung Krung Kasem Canal, 61
Pak Khlong Talat, 132
Pakkret, 32–33, 44, 117, 130, 178, 216, 276
Pakkret Tramway Company, 31–33
Paklat. *See* Phrapradaeng
Paklat Canal, 44
Paklat Tramway. *See* Menam Motor Boat Company
Paknam. *See* Samut Prakan
Paknam Railway Company (PRC), 2, 20, 26, 22–29, 35–36, 43, 49, 55, 57, 59–60, 76, 88, 93, 100–102, 333, 340–41, 353–54.
  dividends, 37–38, 89, 91
  electrification, 62–67
  gross receipts, 39, 63, 65
  nationalization, 68–70
  See also suburban railway lines (Paknam line)
Paktho, 151–3
Paratransit, 4–7, 333–34, 337–39, 343, 357, 358, 361
park-and-ride facility, 242
passenger transport, 39, 63, 68, 116, 121, 239
Pathumthani, 130, 163
Pathumwan, 55–57
Penang, 331–32
People's Party, 15, 83, 125
Petroleum Authority of Thailand, 249
Phahonyothin, 297
Phahonyothin Road (Don Mueang Road), 76–77, 287
Phakdinoraset, Phra (Loet Setthabut), 72–73, 79, 91, 94
Phasi Charoen Canal, 279
Phayathai, 1, 317
Phetchaburi (city), 26, 28, 167
Phetchaburi (station), 318
Phetchaburi Road (New Phetchaburi Road), 178, 204
Phetkasem Road, 117
Phibun Songkhram, Plaek, 105, 113, 123, 125, 138, 145, 160, 198–200, 355
Phichai Rattakun, 240
Phichit Rattakun, 250
Phira Bus Company, 117
Phitthayalap, Prince, 25

Phloenchit Road, 108, 238
Phong Punnakan, 161, 179–80
Phongsak Raktaphongpaisan, 263, 269, 276, 294, 312
Phonimit, 231
Phra Nangklao Bridge, 240, 271
Phra Pokklao Bridge, 212
Phrabat Tramway Company, 28, 71
Phrakhanong, 57, 101, 105–6, 108, 110, 132, 134, 178, 208, 233, 253,
Phranakhon Thonburi Transport Company, 124
Phrannok, 298
Phrapradaeng (Paklat), 44,
population, 55–57, 67, 74, 101, 138, 197–98, 204, 259, 339, 350
populist policy, 11, 190, 200–201, 205, 226, 260, 276–79, 283–84, 290, 294–95, 297, 307, 310–11, 314–16, 334, 341, 343, 349–52, 357–58, 360
power distribution, 27, 42–43, 45, 51, 107, 137, 153–54
power plant, 22, 26, 29, 42–43, 51–52, 60, 153
Prachaniwet, 221
Prachathipok Road, 61
Prachinburi, 102
Praman Adireksan, 123–24, 126
Praphat Charusathian, 156, 211
Pratunam, 57, 72, 110, 133
Prem Tinsulanonda, 212, 214, 243, 249
public service obligation (PSO), 285–86
Public Works Department, 48
public-private partnership (PPP), 315

rail transport, 3, 5, 9, 15–16, 46, 116, 135–37, 160, 195, 197, 207, 354–55
railway
  airport access railway, 265–66, 316
  light railway, 29, 31, 37, 71
  private railway, 33, 50, 70, 87–88
  state railway, 35–37, 49
railway lines
  Eastern line, 252, 265, 317
  Maenam branch line, 55, 74, 108, 110, 252
  Northeastern line, 153
  Northern line, 32, 55
  Southern line, 149, 151
Railway Department, 12, 35–36, 49, 63, 70–71, 87, 100, 107, 111
Rama I Road, 57, 298
Rama III Bridge, 289, 308
Rama III Road, 279, 287
Rama VI Bridge, 133
Rama IV Road, 59–60, 66, 100–101, 147, 149, 196, 204, 237–38
Rama V, King, 8, 12, 15, 27, 49, 72, 353
Rama V Road, 57
Rama VI, King, 12, 15, 51, 54, 354
Rama VII, King, 12, 15, 236
Rangsit, 106, 127, 130, 231, 295, 305–6
Rangsit Canal, 26,
Ratchaburi, Prince, 60, 72
Ratchadaphisek Road, 227
Ratchawithi, 140
Ratchawong Road, 43
Ratchayothin, 280
Residence of Chaophraya Rattanabodin, 29, 31
rickshaws, 4, 50, 85–86
Royal Gazette, 130, 133, 160, 216
Ruetthiwong, Phraya, 29, 31

Saha Watthanakit Company, 144, 162
Saigon, 331
Sainoi, 296
Sala Daeng, 57, 62–63, 97, 108
Samakkhitham Company, 132
sam lo, 4, 83, 85, 359
Sam Yaek, 156
Samak Sundaravej, 243, 249, 279–82, 284–85, 296, 306, 309–10, 343–44, 346
Samat Ratchaphalasit, 9–10
Samrong, 132, 148–49, 178, 240, 280
Samsen, 25, 60, 107, 153–54

Samsen Canal, 55, 110
Samsen Road, 32, 57,
Samut Prakan (Paknam), 33–35, 37–39, 63, 66–67, 69–70, 76–77, 95, 100–101, 103, 108, 113, 118, 121, 174, 178, 216, 295, 297, 360
Samut Sakhon (Thachin, Mahachai), 35–36, 39, 70–71, 102, 114–16, 152–53, 279, 353
Samut Songkhram (Maeklong), 36–37, 39, 70–71, 151–53, 353
Samyot, 156
Sanam Luang, 21, 144
Sanambin Nam, 134
Sa-nguan Ankhong, 8–9, 72, 77
Sanphasat, Prince, 28
Santi Phromphat, 306
Sanya Thammasak, 189–90, 211
Saphan Daeng, 108
Saphan Khwai, 107
Saphan Lueang, 54, 57, 59, 154
Saphan Mai, 295, 297
Sarit Thanarat, 16, 147, 149, 167, 173, 195–96, 198, 355
Sathon Bridge. *See* Taksin Bridge
Sathon Road, 55, 307
Seni Pramoj, 193, 200
Si Borikan Company, 161
si lo, 337, 409
Si Lueang Company, 172
Si Nakhon Company, 79, 134, 140, 144, 193
Si Phraya, 123, 140
Siam (station), 1, 233
Siam Automobile Company, 76
Siam Cement Company, 57
Siam Commercial Bank, 242
Siam Electric Railway Company, 26–27
Siam Electricity Company (Siam Electric Corporation, SEC), 8, 27, 32–33, 37, 42–46, 51–53, 57, 59–61, 63, 66–69, 71–72, 78, 80, 83–84, 88, 91–95, 97, 341, 353–54.
  dividends, 47, 83
  gross receipts, 26, 28, 40–41, 82, 85–86
  See also Thai Electric Corporation
Siamese Tramway Company, 26–29, 31–33, 40–43, 46, 50–55, 57, 60–61, 85–86, 110, 155–56, 353–54
  dividends, 41, 47, 53–54
  gross receipts, 41, 54
Siemens AG, 266, 302
Siemreap, 35
Sigg, Henry, 20
Silom, 238
Silom Road, 1, 57, 154, 155, 204
Singburi, 102
Singapore, 3, 22, 331–36
Sino-Thai Engineering and Company, 266
Sinthumit Company, 161
Skytrain, 213, 238
Somchai Wongsawat, 297
songthaeo
  before unification, 83, 94–95, 100, 105–6, 116–17, 119, 121, 123, 130, 133, 138, 167, 183, 194, 333–34, 337–38, 342
  under BMTA, 2, 220–22, 244, 247, 251, 258, 343
  See also "mosquito buses"
Sophon Saram, 298, 309
Southeast Asia, 3, 21–23, 332–34
State Railways of Thailand (SRT), 2, 12–13, 110–11, 113–15, 136–37, 147–49, 151, 207, 210, 223, 227, 231, 252–53, 257, 264–66, 270, 305–6, 315–18, 335–36
strikes, 85–86, 130, 193–94, 317
Strobel, Edward H., 32
Strong Thailand Plan, 304
suburban railway
  concession, 20, 33–37, 59–60, 65–71, 88–91, 339, 354
  electric tram, 60, 62–68, 101–2, 113, 115, 197, 333, 354
  electrification, 8, 60, 63–68, 89, 93, 101, 114–15, 197, 305, 341, 354

suburban railway lines
  Maeklong line, 113–16, 136–37, 147, 149–53, 160, 195–97, 207–8, 353, 355
  Paknam line, 100, 108, 111–15, 136–37, 147–49, 195–98, 211, 355
Sukhothai Palace, 110
Sukhumphan Boriphat, 297–98, 304, 348
Sukhumvit Road (Bangkok–Paknam Road), 1, 3, 100–101, 108, 149, 253,
Sun Estate Company, Ltd., 236
Surabaya, 5, 22, 331–33
Surasak, 233
Surasakmontri, Chaophraya, 31, 72
Surawong Road, 307
Surayud Chulanont, 295–96, 304, 307, 309
Suriya Chungrungruangkit, 263, 265–67, 269, 313
Suvarnabhumi Airport, 1, 264, 266, 269, 316–18

Taksin Bridge (Sathon Bridge), 212
Taksin Bridge (station), 279–80, 300, 302–13
Taksin Transport Center, 278
Taksin Road, 149, 279, 281
Talat Phlu, 29, 44, 55–56, 61, 67, 107, 117, 149–50
Talat Phlu Tramway Company, 29, 31–32, 67
Taling Chan, 151, 231, 295
Tao Pun, 304
taxis, 4, 11, 126, 359
Tha Chang, 84, 134, 156
Tha Phra, 295, 306
Tha Tian, 19, 105, 132,
Tha Wasukri, 123
Thachin. *See* Samut Sakhon
Thachin Railway Company, 29, 36–7, 67, 70, 88. *See also* Maeklong Railway; suburban railway lines (Maeklong line)
Thachin River, 35, 37, 151–53
Thai Automobile Company, 79
Thai Bamrung Transport Company, 133–34, 139–41, 161
Thai Electric Corporation (TEC), 97, 99, 106–7, 111. *See also* Siam Electricity Company
Thai Rak Thai Party, 267, 276–77, 282, 297
Thai Thawon Company, 140–41, 161, 172
Thailand: Partnership for Development, 9, 269, 276, 278, 351
Thaksin Shinawatra, 2, 9–10, 16, 252, 263–67, 269–71, 276–83, 289, 292, 294–9, 302–4, 307, 310–16, 318, 335, 341, 343, 346–48, 350–51, 357–58, 360
Thammasat University, 284
Thanayong Company, Ltd., 233, 241–42
Thanon Tok. *See* Bang Kholaem
Thawi Chunlasap, 183
Thawit Klinprathum, 193
Thepharak, 279
Thepphahatsadin, Phraya, 83
Thewawong, Prince, 19, 28, 34
Thewet, 61, 106, 156
Thonburi, 29, 31, 56, 61, 67, 74, 77, 107, 133, 151–53, 197, 278, 289, 298, 303, 306
Thonburi Municipality, 80, 117, 119, 130
trains. *See* rail transport; railway; suburban railway; urban railway
tramways
  concession, 19–20, 25–29, 32–33, 43–51, 59, 61–62, 71, 74, 76, 84, 93, 99–100, 106, 339, 353
  double-car traffic, 44–46
  double tracks, 52, 92, 137, 197, 332
  electric tramcar, 22, 24–25, 353
  fare hike, 99

- horse-drawn tramway, 21–22, 24, 331
- single track, 19, 44, 46, 52, 92, 197, 332
- steam tramway, 22, 31–32, 331

track rent, 26, 28–29, 41, 43–44, 46–48, 50–51, 53–54, 82–84, 340

tramway lines
- Atsadang line, 43–46, 97
- Bang Kholaem line, 19, 25–27, 41, 43–44, 46, 48–49, 54–56, 61, 73–74, 82, 84–86, 154, 156, 196
- Bang Sue line, 57, 108, 110, 154, 156
- Circle line, 155–56, 160
- City Wall line, 25–26, 28–29, 43
- Dusit line, 29, 42, 85, 154, 156
- Dusit Extension line, 29, 31–33, 42, 53, 62, 110
- Hua Lamphong line, 28–29, 82, 85, 208, 110, 156
- Lopburi line, 110–11, 156
- Pathumwan line, 57, 108, 155
- Phloenchit line, 108, 110
- Ratchaprarop line, 110
- Ratchawong line, 43–46, 62
- Samsen line, 25–29, 32, 40–44, 46–47, 53–54, 57, 59–60, 67, 82, 85–86, 110, 147, 154, 156, 196
- Silom line, 57, 97–98, 108, 110, 154–55
- Worachak line, 28

Transport Act, 136–37, 129, 166, 340, 346

Transport Company, 12–13, 102–3, 121–24, 144–45, 161–62, 170–73, 188, 191, 199, 201, 220, 340, 343, 347, 355
- unification of regional bus, 166–68

Transport Regulation Committee, 127, 129–30, 133, 135, 138–40, 160–61, 166, 172, 175, 180, 340

Trat, 95, 166

Treasury Department, 236

tricycles. See *sam lo*

trolley buses, 61–62, 84, 92–93, 107–8, 110, 137, 154–55, 332

trucks, 116, 121, 123, 222

tuktuk. See *sam lo*

turnkey method, 266, 269, 295. 311–12, 316, 336, 350–51

two-tiered system, 238, 254–57, 263, 280, 283, 311, 313, 315, 335–36, 341, 348

Ubon, 35

Unger, Danny, 8, 10, 253

United States, 21–22, 169–70, 199

United Thai People's Party, 200

urban railway
- concession, 212–15, 231, 233, 235, 237–39, 241, 246, 253–55, 264–65, 280, 297, 313–14, 316, 340, 356
- fare hike, 241
- heavy rail, 208, 211, 213, 360
- light rapid transit (LRT), 5, 208, 213, 233, 335
- monorail, 2, 207, 299, 335, 360
- subway, 1–4, 7, 263, 265–66, 314, 317, 335, 350, 356

urban railway lines
- Blue line, 239–40, 252–53, 263–64, 267, 271, 295–97, 300, 304, 306–313, 316, 318, 335, 360
- Brown line, 277
- Gray line, 299
- Green line (Dark Green line, Light Green line), 271, 279, 295–8, 300, 346, 360
- Memorial Bridge line (MTS), 208, 212, 252
- Orange line, 240, 252, 270, 279, 298
- Pink line, 276, 360
- Phrakhanong line (MTS), 208, 211, 214, 235, 252–3
- Purple line, 267, 269, 271, 277–78, 295–96, 304–6, 315, 351, 360
- Red line (Dark Red line, Light Red line), 269, 271, 278, 295, 298, 304–7, 313, 360

urban railway lines (*continued*)
Samrong line (BTS extension), 279–80, 282
Sathon line (MTS), 208, 212, 214, 235, 252–53
Silom line (BTS), 253, 303
Sky Blue line, 299
Sukhumvit line (BTS), 233
Taksin line (BTS extension), 279–83
Yellow line, 271, 276, 296–97, 360
Urban Rail Transportation Master Plan (URMAP), 271, 313
Urban Transportation Development Corporation (UTDC), 213–15
Uthong Nai Road. *See* Baiphong Road

vans, 4, 246–48, 290, 328, 334, 337–38, 342–43, 361
Vasconcellos, Eduardo A., 5–6, 10, 342
Victory Monument, 107, 233, 236, 361

Washington, DC, 169
Watchanakun Company, 144
Wat Kanlayanamit, 29, 31
Wat Sai, 68
Wat Saket, 85
Wat Sing, 67, 102, 115–16, 151, 153
Wat Thewarat Kunchon, 29
Wat Yannawa, 21
water transport, 1, 14, 26, 110, 121–22, 167, 358–59
Watthana, 108, 133–34,
Westenholz, Aage, 22, 25–26, 28, 32–33, 40–42, 44–48, 52, 72, 332, 353
Wiphawadi Rangsit Road, 130
Wira Muksikkaphong, 213
Witthayu, 57, 59–60, 66–67, 101, 111, 134–35, 214
Wongwian July 22, 133–34
Wongwian Yai, 77, 149–52, 196, 208, 280, 300, 302–4
Xavier, L. M., 35–36

Yaowarat Road, 25–26
Yatmit Company, 141, 161
Yingluck Shinawatra, 360
Yommarat, 231, 239
Yommarat, Chaophraya, 82
Yotse, 57, 61, 72, 107–8, 155, 298